Con

Essentia

Time Out Guides Limited
Universal House
251 Tottenham Court Road
London W1T 7AB
Tel   + 44 (0)20 7813 3000
Fax   + 44 (0)20 7813 6001
Email guides@timeout.com
www.timeout.com

Editorial
Editor Dominic Earle

Managing Director Peter Fiennes
Editorial Director Ruth Jarvis
Business Manager Dan Allen
Editorial Manager Holly Pick
Assistant Management Accountant Ija Krasnikova

Design
Art Director Scott Moore
Art Editor Pinelope Kourmouzoglou
Senior Designer Kei Ishimaru
Guides Commercial Designer Jodi Sher

Picture desk
Picture Editor Jael Marschner
Acting Deputy Picture Editor Liz Leahy
Picture Desk Assistant/Researcher Ben Rowe

Advertising
New Business & Commercial Director Mark Phillips
International Advertising Manager Kasimir Berger
Head of French Advertising Sales Charlie Sokol

Marketing
Sales & Marketing Director, North America
  & Latin America Lisa Levinson
Group Commercial Art Director Anthony Huggins
Circulation & Distribution Manager Dan Collins
Marketing Co-ordinator Alana Benton

Production
Group Production Manager Brendan McKeown
Production Controller Katie Mulhern

Time Out Group
Chairman & Founder Tony Elliott
Chief Executive Officer David King
Group Financial Director Paul Rakkar
Group General Manager/Director Nichola Coulthard
Time Out Communications Ltd MD David Pepper
Time Out International Ltd MD Cathy Runciman
Time Out Magazine Ltd Publisher/
  Managing Director Mark Elliott
Group Commercial Director Graeme Tottle
Group IT Director Simon Chappell

Contributors
Sections in this guide were written by:
Anna Brooke, Alison Culliford, Dominic Earle,
Natasha Edwards and Katie Walker.

The editor would like to thank all contributors to
the *Time Out Paris* guide, whose work forms the
basis for parts of this guide.

Cover photography Rob Greig, Corbis.

Retouching They did it (020 7928 9008).

Luggage Heys X Case suitcases at John Lewis
(www.johnlewis.com).

Airport seating OMK Associates Ltd
(www.omkassociates.com).
Photograph Gregory Mild (www.gregorymild.com).

Model Keira Ball.

Printed and bound by St Ives (Peterborough) Ltd,
Storeys Bar Road, Eastern Industry, Peterborough,
Cambs, PE1 5YS.

ISBN 978-1-84670-281-5
Distribution by Comag Specialist (01895 433 800)
Distributed in USA by Comag (+44 1895 433 600)

See p17.

See p6.

See p92.

See p115.

Paris in Focus

Celebrating Cocteau

The Maison de Jean Cocteau is a fitting tribute to one of France's finest artists.

As a revered poet, painter, playwright and film-maker, Jean Cocteau's artistic legacy pervades many aspects of French culture. Yet the man himself has always been something of an elusive figure. But now, thanks to the hefty financial input of Pierre Bergé (partner of the late Yves Saint Laurent and a close friend of Cocteau's) and five years of refurbishment, his old country house in Milly-la-Forêt, less than an hour from Paris, has been transformed into a fascinating museum, the Maison de Jean Cocteau.

Cocteau moved to Milly-la-Forêt in 1947 to escape the glitz of the capital. Following his death from a heart attack at the age of 74, in 1963, his long-term partner Edouard Dhermite (who starred in Jean-Pierre Melville's 1950 film adaptation of *Les Enfants Terribles*) locked up the study, bedroom and living room, leaving more than 500 oil paintings, drawings, sculptures and photographs untouched for decades.

The three rooms have all been faithfully restored, leaving one with the impression that Cocteau only left a few minutes before. The living room is wonderfully flamboyant, with antique furniture and gold palm trees framing a Bérard painting of Oedipus. The bedroom, meanwhile, with its four-poster bed and a mural of a castle, boasts a fairytale quality reminiscent of Cocteau's masterful romantic fantasy *La Belle et la Bête*. Finally the study, with its leopard print walls and erotic memorabilia, offers the most intimate glimpse into the artist's creative process, by turns both inspiring and provocative.

The rest of the house has been converted into exhibition space with two galleries: one a collection of portraits of Cocteau by artists such as Picasso, Warhol and Modigliani; the other dedicated to temporary collections. A projection room showing documentaries and Cocteau's films concludes the visit, but the adventure continues outside in the gardens surrounding the house, dotted with strange sculptures, where he used to enjoy strolling and writing.

Cocteau's body rests nearby, in the Chapelle Saint-Blaise-des-Simples (rue de l'Amiral de Graville, Milly-la-Forêt, 01.64.98.84.94, open 10am-12.30pm, 2-6pm Wed-Sun). The interior, like a scaled-down Sistine Chapel, is covered in murals painted by Cocteau in 1960. His epitaph, 'Je reste avec vous' (I stay with you), seems to have as much resonance today as ever.

Maison de Jean Cocteau
15 rue du Lau, 91490 Milly-la-Forêt (01.64.98.11.50, www.jeancocteau. net). Open Mar-Oct 10am-7pm Wed-Sun. Early Jan, Nov-Dec 2-6pm Wed-Sun. Closed mid Jan-Feb. Admission €7; €4.50 reductions; free under-10s.

Electric avenue

Delanoë's eco-friendly car hire scheme gets the green light.

Emboldened by the runaway success of his Vélib bike hire initiative, Mayor Bertrand Delanoë is launching another green transport innovation: an eco-friendly car hire system. Dubbed 'Autolib', the new project will allow subscribers to pick up and drop off a car at any one of 1,000 designated stations, 700 of which will be located in Paris and the rest in the neighbouring suburbs.

Legal and financial stumbling blocks have slimmed down the project from its original conception, and delayed the original launch date, but the scheme is now set to begin at the end of 2011 with a fleet of 3,000 green cars – Delanoë was adamant that the vehicles should be 100 per cent electric, with 4,000 recharging points across the 700 Paris stations. The Bluecars, made by Bolloré, will seat four passengers and should be able to cover 250km between charges, allowing drivers to use the Péripherique and motorways just outside the city centre. Unlike the Vélib initiative, Autolib will require an obligatory subscription fee, ranging from €12 per month for an annual pass to €10 per day for a one-off daily pass, as well as a valid driving licence. The half-hourly rate, meanwhile, ranges from €5 to €8. Each vehicle will be tracked in real time, and when drivers have finished their hire period, they will be guided to the nearest available parking spot.

Public reaction to the scheme seems to be generally positive, perhaps encouraged by a survey showing that 16 per cent of Parisians currently use their cars less than once a month. For a city that always seemed to put the car above all else, Paris is certainly cleaning up its act.

Gypsy kings

The show must go on for Romanès Cirque Tsigane.

Since it first brought its caravans and candlelit big top to Paris 18 years ago, Romanès Cirque Tsigane has touched the hearts of Parisians. But last year the emotion of the songs that Délia Romanès performs as her daughters twirl in aerial hoops took on a new meaning. The circus, which only wants to be left alone to do what it does best, went political after the Romanian musicians who have worked for it for several years were refused a renewal of their work permits, and Alexandre Romanès was fined €19,000 for employing people illegally, a claim he stridently denies.

The irony is staggering. This year Romanès published his second book of poetry with Gallimard and received fan letters from Mayor Bertrand Delanoë and the Pope. In June 2010, the circus was flown to China to represent French culture at the Shanghai World Expo.

The ex-lion tamer and his fiery wife, who fled the Ceausescu regime to come to France, have fought back in spectacular form. On 4 October 2010, the atmosphere was electric as 1,500 people crowded into the small village of caravans on the edge of the 17th arrondissement for a free benefit show. Jane Birkin was there, along with Sandrine Bonnaire, the deputy mayor and innumerable musicians, actors, journalists and families who had seen and loved the circus before. Four shows ran one after another, and deafening roars of appreciation went up as money poured into the hat. As we write, a petition in support of the circus has gathered more than 20,000 signatures.

Despite all their hassles, the Romanès have started a new season that runs until at least the end of April 2011. Then they will take to the road, probably returning in the autumn.

'We are not asking for anything,' says Délia, 'just to allow people to discover our culture. The gypsies are the true Europeans.'

Romanès Cirque Tsigane
42 bd de Reims/rue de Courcelles, 17th (01.40.09.24.20, www. cirqueromanes.com). Tickets €20; €10-€15 reductions.

The Belleville bunch

Art is on the up in the city's north-east.

Up amid the tenements, Chinese restaurants and old industrial spaces straddling the 19th and 20th arrondissements either side of rue de Belleville, a handful of galleries are injecting a much-needed burst of energy into the Paris art scene. New Yorker Larry Gagosian may have opened a much-publicised offshoot in the *beaux quartiers* off avenue Matignon, but these galleries put on serious shows, appear at the right international art fairs and have stealthily been luring collectors and artists up to offbeat north-east Paris to see what's going on.

Galerie Jocelyn Wolff (78 rue Julien-Lacroix, 20th, 01.42.03.05.65, www.galeriewolff.com) was the first in the area in 2003. Located at the bottom of a brick apartment building, it's hard to tell what is storage and office space and what is exhibition space in interesting shows that include morbid drawings by Valérie Favre, early conceptual artists and sculptures by Guillaume Leblon.

Bugada & Cargnel.

In the next street along, **Galerie Crèvecoeur** (4 rue Jouye-Rouve, 09.54.57.31.26, www.galeriecreve coeur.com), opened by Axel Dibie, and **Galerie Marcelle Alix** (09.50.04 16 80, www.marcellealix. com), alias Cécilia Becanovic and Isabelle Alfonsi, occupy two small shopfront spaces, conveniently opposite cult wine bistro Le Baratin (*see p56*). Dibie is typical of the Belleville spirit, cramming in an energetic programme of exhibitions, readings and performances into a tiny gallery space.

At **Bugada & Cargnel** (7-9 rue de l'Equerre, 19th, 01.42.71.72.73, www.bugadacargnel.com), Italo-French couple Claudia Cargnel and Frédéric Bugada swapped the chic Marais premises of the Cosmic Galerie for a glass-roofed 1930s garage, with their own flat above. Artists range from Matt Collishaw, one of the original Frieze generation YBAs, to rising French star Cyprien Gaillard, winner of the Prix Marcel Duchamp 2010 (with a solo exhibition at the Centre Pompidou in September 2011). Should you be in any doubt that a gallery might itself be an artwork, last autumn Pierre Bismuth duplicated the entire entrance booth and office in a full-scale identikit reproduction.

Other recent arrivals include **Balice Hertling** (47 rue Ramponeau, 20th, 01.40.33.47.26, www.balicehertling. com) and Suzanne Tarasieve's 13th arrondissement émigré **Loft 19** (Passage de l'Atlas, 5 villa Marcel Lods, 19th, 01.45.86.02.02, www.suzanne-tarasieve.com). Indeed, while the 13th's rue Louise Weiss had a whiff of local subsidies in the late 1990s, there's a more genuine grass roots feel in Belleville, although some of the Louise Weiss communal spirit seems to have transferred here – autumn 2010 saw the first Belleville Art Biennale (www.labiennaledebelleville.fr).

Raffles at the Royal

After two years in the dark, the Royal Monceau is back to full five-star health.

Paris is preparing for a deluge of five-star arrivals in the next few years, with Asian chains Shangri-La, Mandarin Oriental and Peninsula all opening up in the French capital. But Raffles is first in the queue, opening up the legendary Royal Monceau on avenue Hoche after two years' renovation. The result is a supremely classy retreat set far enough away from the brash lights of the Champs-Elysées, but near enough to enjoy the boutiques of rue du Faubourg-St-Honoré. The entrance lobby is refreshingly low-key for a five-star, with a contemporary art bookstore, La Librairie des Arts, off to one side. This is a hotel that takes its art appreciation seriously, with its own art agenda blog, a special art concierge and a 100-seat screening room replete with raspberry-flavoured popcorn courtesy of Pierre Hermé.

Philippe Starck was in charge of the hotel refit, and his cheeky touches are everywhere, such as in the sinfully red fumoir, Fumée Rouge, with its individual cigar safety deposit boxes. The heart of the hotel is the Grand Salon, a long room divided by flowing drapes, and off this lies La Cuisine, a multi-tasking restaurant–bar so beloved of hip hotels with a handsome lit-up bar on the back wall.

Upstairs, the bedrooms are a studied jumble, with beds in the middle of the room, pictures leaned up against the wall, a guitar waiting to be strummed and a lampshade decked with scribbled notes. But beyond all this designer frippery lie some gorgeous treats, including a vast walk-in wardrobe with bevelled mirror surround, spacious bathroom with twin sinks and walk-in shower, and a huge mirror that magically transforms into a TV. Breakfast is a lavish affair, with all sorts of organic goodies, along with a chef to cook up whatever takes your fancy.

In hotel-speak, this is something of a soft opening and work is still continuing, but in 2011 the Royal Monceau will be operating at full strength and will boast a kids' club and palatial spa with the largest indoor hotel swimming pool in the city, along with a concept store run by L'Eclaireur.

Royal Monceau
37 av Hoche, 8th (01.42.99.88.00, www.leroyalmonceau.com). Rates €730-€930 double.

Paris in Focus cont.

Computer culture

Digital design comes to the Gaîté Lyrique.

After a ten-year revamp, the belle époque **Gaîté Lyrique** theatre (3 bis rue Papin, 3rd, www.gaite-lyrique.net), built in 1862, has been turned into Paris's first digital cultural centre; a seven-floor, multidisciplinary concert hall-cum-gallery that thrusts visitors deep into the realms of digital art, music, graphics, film, fashion, design, video games and even sushi-shaped memory sticks, on sale in the Gaîté's quirky boutique.

It's not the first time the building has undergone a transformation. After being an *haut-lieu* of operetta and Russian ballet, it was pillaged by the Nazis, only to become a circus school in the 1970s and a mini-theme park in the 1980s. But this time its multi-million euro interior, which combines the original belle époque foyer with starkly modern spaces by architect Manuelle Gautrand, is set to become a permanent fixture on the city's cultural scene.

The opening schedule features events and installations at the forefront of technology and creation. There will be no less than three electronic music concerts each week and around 120 live multimedia performances a year, along with guest appearances by artists, musicians and DJs (including Gilles Petersen three weekends a year) and film projections. You can even just pop into the funky space for a decent cup of coffee and a flick through the magazines.

Exhibition-wise, expect interactivity and the best of Europe's cutting-edge art scene. First up, Berlin next! (29 March-3 April 2011) looks at how Berlin's underground scene has surfaced to become an international reference for alternative urban culture. Next, the Mike Pyke & Friends exhibition (21 April-29 May 2011) takes over with wacky films, sound creations and installations imagined by Mike Pyke, the creator of London's avant-garde Universal Everything design studio. Finally, Summer Skate (18 June-14 August) wraps up the first half of the year with an analysis of skating culture in society, from the Beastie Boys and hip hop to Spike Jonze's films, fashion and video games.

Not a lot of bottle

Paris's new sparkling water fountain carries a serious message.

The French capital is littered with no less than 820 drinking water fountains; from bog-standard taps on the sides of *sanisettes* (Paris's self-cleaning public loos) to arty-looking modern street units fitted in the year 2000. The city even lies on top of a deep-seated natural water source called the Albien, from which spurt three fountains whose soft water is favoured by purist tea drinkers (place Paul Verlaine, 13th; 125 square Lamartine, 16th; square de la Madone, 18th). It's an impressive offering, especially when you learn that for centuries Parisians drank water straight from the Seine, and now Paris's water provider, Eau de Paris, has gone one step further by installing the country's first chilled sparkling water fountain – La Pétillante – in the Jardin de Reuilly in the 12th.

It may sound like a gimmick, but the message behind the installation is wholly serious. Parisians all have access to clean, mineral-rich tap water. but prefer to drink bottled stuff – especially fizzy, seen as the champagne of the water world.

According to the Earth Policy Institute, France is the world's eighth biggest consumer of bottled water, with each person drinking around 28 gallons of still or sparkling water in 2009, which equates to an estimated 262,000 tonnes of plastic waste.

Eau de Paris hopes that by enticing Parisians to drink sparkling public water (otherwise known as Champagne Sarkozy; under Chirac, water was nicknamed Château Chirac), they will rekindle the public's confidence in standard tap water and thus reduce plastic waste.

The concept has already been tested in Italy, where 215 sparkling water fountains are making a real difference: each one provides 3,500 litres of water a day, which saves the equivalent of 2,300 1.5-litre bottles. That's 50 tonnes less CO_2 and 400kg less carbon monoxide in the atmosphere, which is definitely worth raising a glass to.

FURNISHED RENTALS IN PARIS

QUALITY APARTMENTS IN EXCELLENT CENTRAL LOCATIONS IN THE HEART OF PARIS
MINIMUM 4 NIGHTS STAY

MY PARIS VISIT APARTMENTS ARE CAREFULLY SELECTED FOR THEIR MIX OF PARISIAN CHARM,
CONTEMPORARY COMFORT AND STYLE AND GOOD VALUE FOR MONEY

MANAGED APARTMENTS WITH PROFESSIONAL BILINGUAL WELCOME SERVICE :

SAVINGS UP TO 25%

Email: direct@parisvisitservices.com

PARIS VISIT SERVICES:
13, RUE DU ROULE 75001 PARIS

Tel: +33 (0)1 42 96 17 84

Chambre de commerce
et d'industrie de Paris

MEMBER 2011

PARIS
Convention
and Visitors Bureau

francobritish
chamber of commerce & industry

www.myparisvisit.com

Cooking up a storm

Le Chateaubriand is the star of Paris's bistronomy scene. **Katie Walker** samples its delights.

While the rest of the world tightens its purse strings, restaurants continue to thrive in Paris. Despite the gloomy economic forecast, Parisians seem reluctant to deprive themselves of this particular pleasure. Wander through the streets of St-Germain-des-Prés, the Marais, Canal St-Martin or Pigalle any night of the week and you'll be hard-pressed to find a table, while the most popular restaurants continue to fill up several weeks to several months ahead.

Many are classic old favourites, but the last few years have also seen the rise of the neo-bistro scene, updated for a new generation. At the very centre is Le Chateaubriand (*see p56*), the *coeur d'artichaut* of this new dining trend which the compulsive categorisers call 'bistronomy' (not a word necessarily embraced by the chefs themselves – marketing speak is truly not their thing).

So, what are the magic ingredients of the bistronomy boom? First, take the same flair long associated with Parisian gastronomy but use a little less finesse and significantly more innovation; next, add world-beating raw ingredients of thoroughly researched provenance and chefs who are generally young

Inaki Aizpitarte.

autodidacts enjoying success with their first business (Inaki Aizpitarte, Le Chateaubriand's Basque chef-owner, was previously a *paysagiste*, his sommelier an actor, his olive oil supplier a tight-rope walker). Finally, liberally sprinkle with reasonable prices, and an atmosphere which is informal, relaxed and intentionally unbourgeois.

Such culinary wizardry is a rare find, and it's about as easy to reserve a table at Le Chateaubriand as it is to order a Spam fritter. But don't be deterred. If no one answers the phone, try turning up at 9pm and waiting for the second sitting. Enjoy a glass of biodynamic wine at the bar, happy in the knowledge that, according to S.Pellegrino's *World's 50 Best Restaurants 2010*, you're about to eat at the 11th best restaurant in the world.

The food

The food is the thing at Le Chateaubriand, which serves a get-what-you're-given *menu unique*, each course a minimal and inventive combination of scrupulously sourced produce. Meat, fish, fruit and vegetables are respected, but not the recipe rule book. The no-frills A4 piece of white paper on 27 January 2011 offered the following:

Amuse bouche (ceviche)
****
Morue d'Alcorta pil-pil, pommes de terre
****
Saint-Jacques, carottes, moelle
****
Agneau, legumes 'oubliés', agrumes
****
Pommes, butternut, rose chocolat, celeri ou fromages du jour

The kitchen buys many of its delectable treats locally. Le Chateaubriand's olive oil comes from La Tête dans les Olives (2 rue Ste-Marthe, 10th, 09.51.31.334, www.latete danslesolives.com), a tiny shop in the pretty, Mediterranean-looking rue Ste-Marthe. Owner Cedric Casanova goes to Sicily every six weeks, where he organises and advises 26 farmers on how to make the fruit of their 20,000 olive trees attractive to the Paris market. Should you wish to sample more of his Sicilian products, including pasta made by his fishing buddy, Cedric has opened a restaurant with one table next door. It seats five, but if you're only a party of two it costs the same – €150. Booking is by email and currently there's a three-month waiting list to enjoy his tomatoes, figs and extraordinarily heady oregano.

The chef

Inaki Aizpitarte has a light touch. In the kitchen he refrains from beating ingredients into submission, instead relishing the natural

Le Chateaubriand.

flavour of things. In person, he's pretty undemonstrative and certainly doesn't feel the need to convince you of a carefully considered personal manifesto. Truth is, he'd rather solicit an opinion about the lemons tenderised in a vacuum pack for five hours, which arrive on the bar with two spoons.

This is all rather refreshing in light of the control freakery we've come to expect from some chefs at the top of this game. So, too, are his career plans. With no supermarket endorsements or TV shows in his sights ('absolutely non!'), Aizpitarte is focusing solely on Le Chateaubriand and the recently opened Rem Koolhaus-designed Le Dauphin, a tapas-style restaurant a few doors down at 131 avenue Parmentier, where sub-€10 dishes include *magret séché*, *tempura de gambas* and *tarte au citron meringuée*.

As at Le Chateaubriand, sourcing is all-important at Le Dauphin. Bread comes from Du Pain et des Idées (*see p77*). Voted best baker in Paris in 2008 by Gault Millau, the charismatic Christophe Vasseur is proud to supply his *pain des amis* – a flat bread with a thick crust and nutty flavour – to Le Dauphin, but he corrects the assumption that it gets delivered: 'The waiters come by and pick it up, and pay on the spot.' Meanwhile, local bobos and discerning old ladies with wicker baskets queue for his colourful puff pastry *escargots* with rum and raisin, chocolate and pistachio, or praline.

The staff

Almost exclusively male, as hirsute as Eric Cantona or Sebastian Chabal, friendly and just a little flirtatious, the staff at Le Chateaubriand attract nearly as much attention as the food they serve. A job here must be a great gig to get, not just because the waiters seem to be treated more like band members than hired hands, but also because it can lead to a shiny future. Last year, former sommelier David Loyola opened the hugely successful Aux Deux Amis (45 rue Oberkampf, 11th, 01.58.30.38.13). Winner of the Fooding du Meilleur Petit Luxe 2010 prize, this tiny bar is permanently packed, but it's a wholly different vibe from the rammed student hangouts around the Oberkampf metro nearby. Vodka caramel is strictly *interdit* – instead, customers enjoy organic wines and deliciously simple dishes such as tortilla de Jeannine for just €3.50.

The area

When Aizpitarte opened his restaurant on decidedly unglamorous avenue Parmentier in the 11th, he was hailed as a pioneer in the kitchen and the arrondissement. Such is the hoopla he's created, there is inevitably talk of a new Goncourt scene. Property prices are on the up and the proprietors of the *branché* Chez Jeanette and Chez Justine have chosen a site opposite Le Chateaubriand and Le Dauphin for their new venture, Le Floréal (73 rue du Fbg-du-Temple, 11th, 01.42.08.81.03) – an American-style diner serving hamburgers and cupcakes (and favourite of Matthieu Almeric, Daniel Craig's good-looking nemesis in *Quantum of Solace*). Goncourt locals are quick to point out that the area is no Haut Marais, but the bobos seem to be headed this way all the same, crossing the Canal Saint-Martin to eat at Le Chateaubriand, drink at supremely shabby-chic Le Carillon (18 rue Alibert, 10th, 01.42.39.81.88), and create a whole new corner of Paris that they can call their own.

Inaki's address book

Cave

Le Verre Volé
38 rue Oberkampf, 10th (01.43.14.99.46, www.leverrevole.fr).

Pâtisserie

Pierre Hermé
72 rue Bonaparte, 6th (01.43.54.47.77, www.pierreherme.com).

Restaurants

Le Baratin
3 rue Jouye-Rouve, 20th (01.43.49.39.70).

La Bigarrade
106 rue Nollet, 17th (01.42.26.01.02, www.bigarrade.fr).

Le Verre Volé
67 rue de Lancry, 10th (01.48.03.17.34, www.leverrevole.fr).

Le Verre Volé.

Class of 2011

Alison Culliford charts the rise of the capital's new social tribes, from JCD to *néo-bobo*.

Once upon a time, Parisians were either BCBG (*bon chic bon genre* – the French equivalent of Sloane Rangers) – or cool. Belonging to either one of these groups – or appearing to – was as easy as buying the right accessory. A Lacoste V-neck slung casually around the shoulders for the BCBG; a Palestinian *keffiyeh* worn as a scarf for the hipster. But all this has changed. While Britain's chavs were appropriating the crocodile logo, Paris was undergoing a very different social metamorphosis: boboisation.

A diminutive for bourgeois-bohemian, the term 'bobo' was invented by the American David Brooks in his sociological study *Bobos in Paradise* (Simon & Schuster, 2000). The

enlightened elite of the information age, bobos were a bundle of paradoxes: anti-establishment but consumerist, economically conservative left-wingers, 'green' owners of 4x4s.

Somehow it was all lost in translation and Parisians embraced boboism as their own creation: after all, they could lay claim to both *bourgeois* and *bohème* as distinctly Parisian social denominations. Bringing them together meant you no longer had to be ashamed of being *bourgeois*. Paris added a gloss of style and it became chic to be a bobo. Living in a 'loft' (which just involved knocking out a few walls in your Haussmannian apartment), buying organic, espousing a freelance lifestyle – it was the natural successor to the gauche caviar of the 1970s. But then, as escalating rents gentrified virtually all of inner Paris, sealing it off from the *banlieue*, suddenly no one wanted to be bobo any more.

Nouvel Observateur's eating and drinking trend bible *400 Lieux Branchés* declared the word taboo in its 2010 edition because of its perjorative connotations, though *Nouvel Observateur* clearly struggles to find a replacement, resorting to *trentenaires* (thirtysomethings). Classic bobos can still be seen – for instance at the 20th-century design fair Puces du Design they were out in force, wheeling their designer pushchairs while buying the type of furniture their parents threw out for inflated prices. But Paris now has a new fauna, desperately trying to be different while still remaining the same.

Bécébranché

Jean-Philippe is 'Versaillais and proud', as his Facebook group proclaims. BCBG version 2.0, he is a sleeker, more connected version of his father, who uses his iPhone to organise the perpetual round of *apéros*, *soirées en boîte* and *pique-niques*. Jean-Phil has never been so happy to be pigeonholed, seing Jean Sarkozy and Kate Middleton as the media-hyped role models of his tribe – after all, blue blood doesn't count for everything these days. Raised in Versailles, like most of his pals he now has a small pad with a good postcode (the 16th or, at a push, the 17th) with which his parents indulged him so he could sow his wild oats before the inevitable big Catholic marriage. The style he and his chums sport is a more relaxed version of the BCBG look, incorporating Converse, figure-skimming jackets, shirts and jeans for the boys, Repetto *ballerines* and Gérard Darel handbags for the girls. But the main difference between Jean-Phil and the BCBG of the past is that his girlfriend Marie-Christine wears a thong under her jeans, and his mobile contains not only the number of his priest but of his dealer.
Natural habitat L'Arc (12 rue de Presbourg, 16th) and Longchamp (*see p102*) for the Prix de l'Arc de Triomphe.
Career Banking (BNP) or, if female, in an art gallery.
Reads *Paris Match*, *Le Figaro*.
Politics Sarkozy forever.

Dandy-décadent

An example of Paris's most colourful fauna, Ayméric spends a great deal of time preening his facial hair. Handlebar moustache, Victorian sideburns and floppy coiffure are the current look of this more virile version of the belle époque dandy. He flies in the face of traditional Paris uniformity, and his extensive wardrobe runs from vintage Paco Rabanne to 1970s gold lamé shirts. Ayméric is on everyone's party list and his life is a constant round of private views, magazine launches, artistic happenings and record label parties. Despite appearances, Ayméric is heterosexual, rampantly so, and is constantly surrounded by an adoring female fan club who dress in vintage fur and Isabel Marant.
Natural habitat Experimental Cocktail Club (37 Rue Saint-Sauveur, 2nd), Hôtel du Nord (102 Quai de Jemmapes, 10th), Le Baron (*see p101*).
Career Art publishing, multimedia and DJs at private parties.
Reads Frédéric Beigbeder, *The Sartorialist*.
Politics May the best-dressed win.

Experimental Cocktail Club.

Intello-précaire

These days it just isn't easy being an intellectual in Paris. Since leaving the Sorbonne, Noémie has done a succession of internships with book publishers but it never seems to lead to a job. She tries to keep her spirits up by teaching French to foreigners, attending *café-philo* meetings, book signings and Nouvelle Vague director's cut screenings, and enjoys earnest debate over Lebanese food at her friends' supper parties, where she never seems to meet the right man (could her brains be scaring them off?). She dreams of playing De Beauvoir to a better-looking Sartre, and thinks she should look for an older man – maybe becoming a mistress would be liberating. Daddy rents a flat for her in the 5th, and she keeps saying she must get rid of the old Doisneau posters but they remind her of her halcyon student days.
Natural habitat Bar Basile (34 rue de Grenelle, 7th) opposite Sciences-Po or the literary café Les Editeurs (*see p68*), where she hopes to run into an editor looking for

an assistant while whiling away a *crème* for several hours.
Career Hopefully publishing, one day.
Reads Anything published by Gallimard, *Le Monde*.
Politics Parti Socialiste, but would rather Ségolène Royal was the leader.

JCD (jeune cadre dynamique)

After his prestigious Grande Ecole d'Ingénieurs where he didn't meet any girls until the final year ball, André rapidly rose through the ranks of a prominent telecoms company to his present position, where he manages an aggressive programme deploying phone masts across Africa. He lives in a Quai de Grenelle condominium with a view of the Eiffel Tower, which is ideal as it has secure parking for his BMW, ensuring he need never be late for work on strike days. His apartment is bare except for his Bang & Olufsen stereo and his iMac, though his fridge is always

> **'Victorian sideburns are the current look of this more virile version of the belle époque dandy.'**

stocked with champagne and beers, for when his *potes* come round to watch the rugby. These days, André finds his powers of seduction much enhanced by his Paul Smith suits and his car, but he's not into settling down until he's got his MBA and moved to London, where he dreams of living in 'Nottinge 'ill' and dating a sexually liberated British girl like Kelly Reilly, his pin-up since Klapisch's *Russian Dolls*.
Natural habitat Bar of the Plaza Athénée (*see p110*), shopping for late-night foie gras and champagne at Monop' (www.monoprix.fr) or picking up fresh pasta at Fuxia (www.fuxia.fr).
Career Telecoms exec.
Reads *Le Figaro*, *L'Express*.
Politics Ultra-capitalist.

Jemenfoutiste

It's official: a Gallup poll has revealed that the French are the most pessimistic nation on earth, but Lionel *s'en fout de tout ça. Il s'en fout du gouvernement, il s'en fout de la crise économique, il s'en fout du foot, putain!* In other words, he doesn't give a flying f*** for anything at all. The only thing that gets him worked up is when people use *Jemenfoutiste* as an insult – for him it is a badge of honour (incidentally, Jemenfoutisme began as a genuine philosophy at the end of the 19th century, but Lionel *s'en fout de ça aussi*).
Natural habitat The Jemenfoutiste prefers bars where you can still get a *demi* for €2.50, preferably with free couscous. Le Chope du

Château Rouge (40 rue de Clignancourt, 18th) suits him fine, though *il s'en fout des bobos de merde* who have invaded his favourite café.
Career Nothing, he's a professional *chômeur*.
Reads *Canard Enchaîné*, comic books.
Politics *Il s'en fout.*

Néo-bobo

Florence is committed – to organic food, natural childbirth, the preservation of the rainforests and independent journalism. This baby bobo is a product of the noughties, where she saw her elder siblings only pretend to care about what matters. Not for her the titanium kitchen, the iPad and the 4x4. Our *néo-bobo* still ekes out an existence in a rented flat (albeit now €800 a month) on the Canal St-Martin and takes part in a community vegetable purveying scheme, whereby she mans a stall once a month to sell Ile-de-France-produced broccoli only to those who've ordered it in advance. But let's not be too harsh: the *néo-bobo* is our future. Paris might not have a working class any more, but it has held out, in its own way, against globalisation.
Natural habitat Nanashi (31 rue de Paradis, 10th), a bobo organic canteen, or picking up her veg box from outside Epicerie de la Cour (cour des Petites Ecuries, 10th).
Career Works for an NGO.
Reads *Le Monde Diplomatique*, *Courrier International*, www.mediapart.fr.
Politics Green.

Nanashi.

www.parisaddress.com

Short term apartment rentals in Paris

Live in Paris like a true Parisian!
You wish to live Paris from "within", like a true Parisian?
Saint-Germain-des-Prés, the Latin Quarter, the Marais...

Paris Address invites you to discover picturesque and lively central apartments.

Prices all included, instant availability and easy-booking on the website.

Calendar

The city through the year.

Paris is positively bursting with culture, from film festivals to world music. During summer, classical music moves outdoors, with many urban parks turning into alfresco concert venues. Among them is the lovely Parc Floral de Paris, which holds weekend concerts throughout the warmer months.

However, there are also plenty of less highbrow diversions in the city, especially at Paris-Plages, the beach on the Seine. Elsewhere, Solidays, Rock en Seine, Festival des Inrockuptibles and the Techno Parade all attract top acts. And if sports fans don't manage to get tickets for the French Open or the Six Nations, there's always the Marathon de Paris and the finale of the Tour de France – crowd-pulling events for which tickets aren't required.

Mar-June

Fashion Week
Various venues (www.modeaparis.com). **Date** Mar, July, Oct & Jan.
Paris presents its haute couture and prêt-à-porter collections at a variety of venues across town, but to invited guests only. See the website for accreditation details. Fall-Winter Haute Couture takes place 4-7 July 2011.

Le Printemps des Poètes
Various venues (01.53.80.08.00, www.printempsdespoetes.com). **Date** 7-21 Mar 2011.
The 2011 edition of this popular national poetry festival – entitled 'D'Infinis Paysages' – explores the strong links between poetry and the natural world, and focuses on the work of Michel Butor, René Depestre, André Velter and Kenneth White.

French Tennis Open.

Printemps du Cinéma
Various venues (www.printempsducinema.com). **Date** end Mar.
Film tickets at a variety of cinemas all across the city are cut to a bargain €3.50 for this popular three-day film bonanza, now in its 12th year.

Banlieues Bleues
Various venues in Seine-St-Denis (01.49.22.10.10, www.banlieuesbleues.org). **Admission** €14-€20. **Date** 11 Mar-8 Apr 2011.
An annual five-week festival of French and international jazz, blues, R&B, soul, funk, flamenco and world music.

Le Chemin de la Croix
Square Willette, 18th. Mº Abbesses or Anvers. **Date** Good Friday.
A crowd of pilgrims follows the Archbishop of Paris from the bottom of Montmartre up to Sacré-Coeur as he performs the Stations of the Cross.

Foire du Trône
Pelouse de Reuilly, 12th (www.foiredutrone.com). Mº Porte Dorée. **Admission** free; rides €2-€5. **Date** Apr-June.
France's biggest funfair runs for two months, with a mix of stomach-churning rides, bungee jumping and candyfloss. It's well worth buying a pass (around €30) in advance. See the website for details. At the weekends the Mairie runs a free shuttle bus service from Bercy and Nation (every 10-15mins).

Marathon de Paris
Av des Champs-Elysées, 8th, to av Foch, 16th (01.41.33.15.68, www.parismarathon.com). **Date** 10 Apr 2011.
One of the world's most picturesque marathons, with up to 40,000 runners heading from the Champs-Elysées along the Right Bank to the Bois de Vincennes, and back along the Left Bank to the Bois de Boulogne. The 2010 men's winner was Ethiopian Tadesse Tola in 2hrs 6mins 41secs.

Paris Bike Days
Parc Floral de Paris, Bois de Vincennes, 12th (www.parisbikedays.com). Mº Porte Dorée. **Date** mid Apr.
Paris Bike Days is all about getting people on bikes – of every type. This spring festival, based in the Bois de Vincennes, allows visitors to try out racers on closed roads and mountain bikes on specially designed forest trails, as well as on a bump-filled 'pump track'. There's also a range of BMX, trial and electric bikes available for test spins. Once you've found the right bike, you can buy it onsite, sign up for a club or splash out on a cycling holiday. There are also shows by leading BMX and trial riders.

Foire de Paris
Paris-Expo, pl de la Porte de Versailles (01.49.09.60.00, www.foiredeparis.fr). Mº Porte de Versailles. **Admission** €12; €7 reductions; free under-7s. **Date** 28 Apr-8 May 2011.
This enormous lifestyle fair includes world crafts and foods, the latest health gizmos, plus everything you need to know about buying a swimming pool or doing up your home.

Fête du Travail
Date 1 May.
May Day is strictly observed. Key sights (the Eiffel Tower aside) close, and unions march in eastern Paris via Bastille. Sweet-smelling posies of lily of the valley (*muguet*) are sold on every street corner.

Le Printemps des Rues
Various venues (01.47.97.36.06, www.leprintempsdesrues.com). **Admission** free. **Date** early May.
This annual two-day street-theatre festival has an experimental vibe.

La Fête des Enfants du Monde
Various venues (www.koinobori.org). **Date** May.
A Franco-Japanese festival with shows, exhibitions and concerts.

La Nuit des Musées
All over France (www.nuitdesmusees.culture.fr). **Admission** free. **Date** mid May.
During this pan-European one-night culture fest, museums open their doors late for special events and entertainment, including concerts, dance, lectures, unique access and special exhibitions.

Art St-Germain-des-Prés
Various venues (www.artsaintgermaindespres.com). **Admission** free. **Date** end May. *See p12* **Arty parties**.

Gay Pride March. *See p12.*

Quinzaine des Réalisateurs
Forum des Images, Porte St-Eustache, Forum des Halles, 1st (01.44.76.63.00, www.quinzaine-realisateurs.com). Mº Les Halles. **Admission** €5.50. **Date** 12-22 May 2011.
The Cannes Directors' Fortnight sidebar comes to Paris; 2010 was the 31st anniversary of this festival of screenings and events.

Festival Jazz à Saint-Germain-des-Prés
Various venues, St-Germain-des-Prés (www.espritjazz.com). **Date** mid May.
This two-week celebration of jazz and blues on the Left Bank celebrated its tenth anniversary in 2010.

French Tennis Open
Stade Roland-Garros, 2 av Gordon-Bennett, 16th (01.47.43.48.00, www.frenchopen.org). Mº Porte d'Auteuil. **Admission** €21-€75. **Date** 17 May-5 June 2011.
The glitzy Grand Slam tournament, whose clay courts have been the downfall of many a champion, always attracts a selection of showbiz stars.

Foire St-Germain
Pl St-Sulpice & venues in St-Germain-des-Prés, 6th (01.43.29.61.04, www.foiresaintgermain.org). Mº St-Sulpice. **Admission** free. **Date** late May-July.
St-Germain-des-Prés lets its hair down for six weeks of concerts, theatre and workshops.

Unmissable events

Histoire Idéale de la Mode Contemporaine Vol.2: 1990-2000
Exhibition
Until 8 May 2011. Musée des Arts Décoratifs (see p21).
The second part of this fashion retrospective features landmark pieces such as Vivienne Westwood's prêt-à-porter autumn-winter 1995-1996 collection and Alexander McQueen's flower skirts.

A Streetcar Named Desire
Theatre
Until 2 June 2011. Comédie Française (see p104).
Lee Breuer directs this classic postwar drama charting the emotional disintegration of Blanche Dubois.

Réinstallations
Exhibition
Until 4 July 2011. Centre Pompidou (see p32).

Kylie Minogue
Concert
15 March 2011. Palais Omnisports de Paris-Bercy (see p102).

One of a series of retrospectives the Centre Pompidou is dedicating to major figures in contemporary art, *Réinstallations* takes a new look at the work of François Morellet through some 25 works of varying scale that retrace the key inflections in his development from 1963 to the present.

The diminutive Aussie songstress and her Aphrodite Les Folies tour roll into the French capital for one night only. Tickets are, of course, like gold dust.

Manet, Inventeur du Moderne
Exhibition
5 April-3 July 2011. Musée d'Orsay (see p45).
Paris's first major Manet exhibition for nearly 30 years focuses on his later,

Arty parties

Timing your trip to Paris to coincide with a night of *vernissages* (private views) gives a taste not only of the art on offer but also of the personalities who frequent the art scene, a real entrée into Paris life. Providing you look the part – obvious freeloading is ill-advised – you can turn up to most private views without an invitation.

The journal *L'Officiel Galeries & Musées*, which you can pick up free in most galleries, has a diary of *vernissages*. The second and last Thursdays of the month are the most popular dates, with ten to 15 galleries opening a new exhibition. But the big rendezvous of the year – unmissable if you are

serious about this sort of thing – is **Art St-Germain-des-Prés** (*see p11*) in May. Nicknamed the 'block party', it sees more than 50 galleries get together to showcase their top artists, with red carpets spread outside each gallery.

The galleries involved are mostly concentrated on rue de Seine, rue des Beaux-Arts, rue Visconti, rue Guénégaud and rue Mazarine, and a whole cross-section of boho locals turn out for a drop of wine and conversation: artists, dealers, ageing musicians, film directors, eccentrics, fur-clad ladies, rich kids and celebrities – this is definitely one weekend when *flânerie* will get you everywhere.

Festival de St-Denis
Various venues in St-Denis (01.48.13.12.10, www.festival-saint-denis.com). M° St-Denis Basilique. **Admission** €9-€55. **Date** June-July.
The Gothic St-Denis basilica and other historic buildings in the neighbourhood host four weeks of top quality classical concerts.

Fête du Vélo
Across Paris (www.feteduvelo.fr). **Date** early June.
The Fête du Vélo is a celebration of urban riding with cyclists invited to meet up at various points in the suburbs and pedal to Paris en masse. The result is what the organisation calls '*la convergence*', with a procession of two-wheelers meeting up for a huge picnic in the city centre. Visitors can also try in-line skating, as well as bicycles designed for children and people of reduced mobility.

Prix de Diane
Hippodrome de Chantilly, 16 av du Général-Leclerc, 90209 Chantilly (03.44.62.41.00, www.prix-de-diane.com). **Admission** €8; €4 reductions; free under-18s. **Date** 12 June 2011.
The French Derby draws the crème de la crème of high society to Chantilly, sporting silly hats and keen to have a flutter at this handsome racecourse next to the famous château and stables.

Fête de la Musique
All over France (01.40.03.94.70, www.fetede lamusique.fr). **Admission** free. **Date** 21 June.
Free gigs (encompassing all musical genres) take place across the country as part of this festival on the summer solstice.

Gay Pride March
Information: Centre Gai et Lesbien (01.43.57.21.47, www.centrelgbtparis.org). **Date** 25 June 2011.
Outrageous floats and flamboyant costumes parade towards Bastille; then there's an official fête and various club and nightlife events.

Festival Chopin à Paris
Orangerie de Bagatelle, Parc de Bagatelle, Bois de Boulogne, 16th (01.45.00.22.19, www.frederic-chopin.com). M° Porte Maillot, then bus 244. **Admission** €16-€37. **Date** June, July.
Candlelit evening recitals of Chopin's works are held in the Bagatelle gardens.

Paris Jazz Festival
Parc Floral de Paris, Bois de Vincennes, 12th (www.parisjazzfestival.fr). M° Château de Vincennes. **Admission** Park €5; €2.50 reductions; free under-7s. **Date** June, July.

Two months of free jazz weekends in the delightful surroundings of the Parc Floral.

Solidays
Longchamp Hippodrome (01.53.10.22.22, www.solidays.org). M° Porte Maillot. **Admission** Day €32. Weekend €49. **Date** end June.
A three-day music festival, for the benefit of AIDS charities. The 2010 event saw performances from the likes of Rodrigo y Gabriela.

July-Sept

Paris Cinéma
Various venues (01.55.25.55.25, www.pariscinema.org). **Admission** varies. **Date** early July.
Premieres, tributes and restored films make up the diverse programme at the city's excellent summer film-going initiative.

Le Quatorze Juillet (Bastille Day)
All over France. **Date** 14 July.
France's national holiday commemorates the storming of the Bastille in 1789. The evening before the holiday, Parisians dance at place de la Bastille. At 10am on the 14th, crowds line up along the Champs-Elysées as the President reviews a full military parade. By night, the Champ de Mars fills for the fireworks display.

Le Tour de France
Av des Champs-Elysées, 8th (01.41.33.14.00, www.letour.fr). **Date** 24 July 2011.
The ultimate spectacle in cycling is reserved for the end of July when the world's biggest bike race arrives in Paris. After three weeks of racing, the battle for the leader's famed yellow jersey is all but over, and the final stage usually climaxes in a mass sprint with everyone finishing together. It's an incredible spectacle as the riders propel themselves at speeds of up to 65 km/h (40mph) around nine laps of a four-mile finishing circuit that takes in the Champs-Elysées and Tuileries area. Turn up early for a front-row spot.

Etés de la Danse
Théâtre du Châtelet, 1st (01.40.28.28.40, www.lesetesdeladanse.com). M° Châtelet. **Tickets** €13-€100. **Date** early-late July.
A three-week festival featuring an impressive line-up of both classical and contemporary dance. The 2010 edition saw performances from the likes of Ana Laguna and Mikhail Baryshnikov.

Paris, Quartier d'Eté
Various venues (01.44.94.98.00, www.quartierdete.com). **Admission** free-€22. **Date** mid July-mid Aug.
A series of classical and jazz concerts, dance and theatre performances in outdoor venues.

Paris-Plages
Various venues (08.20.00.75.75, www.paris.fr). **Admission** free. **Date** mid July-mid Aug.
Palm trees, huts, hammocks and around 2,000 tonnes of fine sand bring a seaside vibe to the city. The project began in 2002 and there are now three venues – two on opposite banks of the Seine and one around the Bassin de la Villette in the 19th. As well as urban sunbathing, there's a floating pool, concerts, boules, art classes and a lending library too. Plans are afoot to make the *plage* permanent. Under the scheme, a stretch of the Left Bank from the Musée d'Orsay to just before the Eiffel Tower would become a park, footpath and cycle track. There might even be small off-shore islands.

Le Cinéma en Plein Air
Parc de la Villette, 19th (01.40.03.75.75, www.villette.com). M° Porte de Pantin. **Admission** free. **Date** mid July-end Aug.
A themed season of films screened under the stars on Europe's largest inflatable screen.

Festival Classique au Vert
Parc Floral de Paris, Bois de Vincennes, 12th (01.45.43.81.18, www.classiqueauvert.fr). M° Château de Vincennes. **Admission** Park €5; €2.50 reductions; free under-7s. **Date** Aug, Sept.
Free classical recitals in a park setting every weekend throughout August and September.

Fête de l'Assomption
Cathédrale Notre-Dame de Paris, pl du Parvis Notre-Dame, 4th (01.42.34.56.10, www.cathedraledeparis.com). M° Cité/RER St-Michel Notre-Dame. **Admission** free. **Date** 15 Aug.
A national holiday. Notre-Dame becomes a place of religious pilgrimage for Assumption Day.

Rock en Seine
Domaine National de St-Cloud (www.rock enseine.com). **Admission** Day €45. 3 days €99. **Date** 26-28 Aug 2011.
Three days, three stages, and one world-class line-up of rock and indie groups. Big names such as Massive Attack, Paolo Nutini and Arcade Fire all made an appearance in 2010.

Le Tour de France.

HELOISE BERGMAN

Unmissable events (cont)

less well-known works and explores the historical context behind the founder of modernism.

Sweeney Todd
Theatre
22 April-21 May. Théâtre du Châtelet (see p104).
Stephen Sondheim's Fleet Street barber brings his murderous ways to the stage at the Théâtre du Châtelet more than 30 years after its Broadway debut.

Fin de Partie
Theatre
10-22 May 2011. Théâtre de la Madeleine (see p104).
Beckett's classic was originally written in French and later traslated as *Endgame* by the playwright himself.

French Tennis Open
Sport
17 May-5 June 2011. Stade Roland-Garros (www.frenchopen.org).

The second event in the Grand Slam calendar and the most prestigious clay court competition in the world. Rafael Nadal and Francesca Schiavone will be the defending champions in 2011.

Rain
Dance
25 May-7 June 2011. Opéra Garnier (see p97).
Flemish choreographer Anne Teresa De Keersmaeker's mesmerising

2001 piece *Rain* comes to the Palais Garnier.

Out of Time
Dance
1-10 June 2011. Théâtre National de Chaillot (see p104).
Irish dance phenomenon Colin Dunne's acclaimed one-man show playfully explores his relationship with an art form that has shaped his life, integrating text, film and sound design.

Jazz à la Villette
Cité de la Musique & various venues (01.44.84.44.84, www.jazzalavillette.com). **Admission** €12-€35. **Date** early Sept.
The first fortnight in September brings one of Paris's best jazz festivals, including the new series of Jazz for Kids concerts.

Festival Paris Ile-de-France
Various venues (01.58.71.01.10, www.festival-ile-de-france.com). **Tickets** varies. **Date** early Sept-mid Oct.
Classical, contemporary and world music festival set in various venues around Paris.

Techno Parade
www.technoparade.fr. **Date** mid Sept.
The Saturday parade (finishing up at Bastille) marks the start of electro music festival Rendezvous Electroniques.

Journées du Patrimoine
All over France (www.journeesdupatrimoine. culture.fr). **Date** mid Sept.
Embassies, ministries, scientific establishments and corporate headquarters open their doors to the public, allowing for some fascinating glimpses of their interiors. The festive Soirée du Patrimoine takes place on the first Journée. Get *Le Monde* or *Le Parisien* for a full programme.

Festival d'Automne
Various venues. Information: 156 rue de Rivoli, 1st (01.53.45.17.00, www.festival-automne.com). **Admission** €7-€45. **Date** mid Sept-late Dec.
This major arts festival focuses on bringing challenging contemporary theatre, dance and modern opera to Paris. It is also intent on bringing non-Western culture into the French consciousness.

Oct-Dec

Nuit Blanche
Various venues (39.75, www.paris.fr). **Admission** free. **Date** early Oct.
One of the city's most distinctive festivals offers culture by moonlight as galleries and museums host special installations, and swimming pools, bars and clubs stay open into the night.

Prix de l'Arc de Triomphe
Hippodrome de Longchamp, Bois de Boulogne, 16th (01.44.30.75.00, www.prixarcdetriomphe. com). M° Porte d'Auteuil, then free shuttle bus. **Admission** €8; €4 reductions; free under-18s. **Date** early Oct.
France's richest flat race attracts the elite of horse racing for a weekend of pomp and ceremony.

Mondial de l'Automobile
Paris-Expo, pl de la Porte de Versailles (01.56.88.22.40, www.mondial-automobile. com). M° Porte de Versailles. **Admission** €12; €6 reductions; free under-10s. **Date** Oct 2012.
Started in 1898, the biennial Paris Motor Show features cutting-edge design from all over the world.

FIAC
Various venues (01.47.56.64.20, www.fiacparis.com). **Admission** €28; €15 reductions; under-12s free. **Date** mid Oct.
The Louvre and the Grand Palais are the two main venues for this week-long international contemporary art fair, along with a series of outdoor installations in the Jardins des Tuileries.

Fête des Vendanges de Montmartre
Rue des Saules, 18th (www.fetedesvendanges demontmartre.com). M° Lamarck Caulaincourt. **Date** mid Oct.

This is perhaps the most quintessentially Gallic of the capital's annual festivals. The event takes place in Montmartre in the vicinity of the Clos Montmartre vineyard, which sits on the northern side of the Butte. Although the vines cover a mere 1,560sq m and produce an average of just 1,000 bottles a year, the modest harvest is the pretext for a long weekend of Bacchanalian street parties.

Les Puces du Design
Quai de la Loire, 19th (01.53.40.78.77, www.pucesdudesign.com). M° Jaurès. **Admission** free. **Date** Oct & May.
Having moved to the up-and-coming end of the canal, this biannual weekend-long fair specialises in modern and vintage furniture, and design classics.

Festival des Inrockuptibles
Various venues (01.42.44.16.16, www.lesinrocks.com). **Admission** varies. **Date** early Nov.
This festival, which is curated by popular music mag *Les Inrockuptibles*, boasts a decent selection of top international indie, rock, techno and trip hop acts. Bill-toppers in 2010 included Scissor Sisters and LCD Soundsystem.

Armistice Day
Arc de Triomphe, 8th. M° Charles de Gaulle Étoile. **Date** 11 Nov.
To commemorate French combatants who served in the World Wars, the President lays wreaths at the Tomb of the Unknown Soldier under the Arc de Triomphe. The *bleuet* (a cornflower) is worn.

Fête du Beaujolais Nouveau
Various venues (www.beaujolaisgourmand. com). **Date** late Nov.
The third Thursday in November sees cafés and wine bars buzzing in the capital as patrons assess the new vintage.

Africolor
Various venues in suburbs, including Montreuil, St-Denis & St-Ouen (01.47.97.69.99, www.africolor.com). **Admission** €5-€15. **Date** late Nov-late Dec.
This month-long music and dance festival has been running for more than 20 years, featuring artists from all across Africa.

Paris sur Glace
Pl de l'Hôtel de Ville, 4th; M° Hôtel de Ville. *Pl Raoul Dautry, 15th;* M° Montparnasse Bienvenüe. *Information: 39.75, www. paris.fr.* **Admission** free (skate hire €6). **Date** Dec-Mar.
These locations are turned into outdoor ice rinks for the winter season.

Noël (Christmas)
Date 24, 25 Dec.
Christmas is a family affair in France, with a dinner on Christmas Eve (*le Réveillon*), normally after mass. Usually the only bars and restaurants open are the ones in the city's main hotels.

New Year's Eve/New Year's Day
Date 31 Dec, 1 Jan.
Jubilant crowds swarm along the Champs-Elysées. Nightclubs and restaurants hold expensive New Year's Eve soirées, and on New Year's Day the Grande Parade de Paris brings floats, bands and dancers.

Jan-Feb 2012

Fête des Rois (Epiphany)
Date 6 Jan.
Pâtisseries sell *galettes des rois*, cakes with a frangipane filling in which a *fève*, or tiny charm, is hidden.

Mass for Louis XVI
Chapelle Expiatoire, 29 rue Pasquier, 8th (01.42.65.35.80). M° St-Augustin. **Date** Jan.
On the Sunday closest to 21 January – the anniversary of the beheading of Louis XVI in 1793 – right-wing crackpots mourn the end of the monarchy.

Nouvel An Chinois
Around av d'Ivry & av de Choisy, 13th. M° Porte de Choisy or Porte d'Ivry. *Also av des Champs Elysées, 8th.* **Date** 23 Jan 2012.
Lion and dragon dances, and lively martial arts demonstrations to celebrate the Chinese New Year.

Six Nations
Stade de France, 93210 St-Denis (www.rbs6nations.com). RER B La Plaine Stade de France or RER D Stade de France St-Denis. **Admission** varies. **Date** Feb-Mar.
Brits and Celts invade the French capital for three big rugby weekends in spring. Make sure that you log on to the website at least three months in advance to be in with any chance of getting tickets.

Le Cinéma en Plein Air.

WILLIAM BEAUCARDET

Così Fan Tutte
Opera
16 June-16 July 2011. Opéra Garnier (see p97).
Swiss-born conductor Philippe Jordan leads Ezio Toffolutti's graceful production of Mozart's opera in the ornate surroundings of the Palais Garnier.

Les Brigands
Opera
24 June-2 July 2011. Théâtre National de l'Opéra Comique (see p98).
François-Xavier Roth conducts Jacques Offenbach's wonderfully inventive three-act operetta, first perfromed at Paris's Théâtre des Variétés in 1869.

Le Tour de France
Sport
2-24 July 2011. www.letour.fr.
This year's race is the 98th edition and involves nearly 3,500km of pedalling between the start in the Vendée and the finish line on the Champs-Elysées. In between there are climbs aplenty, including twice up the famous 2,645m Col du Galibier to celebrate the 100th anniversary of the Tour's first ascent up the col, and a stage in Italy.

Charles Aznavour
Concert
7 September-6 October 2011. Olympia (see p98).
At the age of 87, singer Charles Aznavour returns for a month-long residency at the venue that launched his career more than 50 years ago.

Brian Wilson
Concert
20 September 2011. Casino de Paris (www.casinodeparis.fr).
The former Beach Boys front man drops into Paris on his world tour to promote his new album, *Brian Wilson Reimagines Gershwin*.

Sightseeing

Museums, galleries and great days out

Photograph **Zoran Karapancer**

Sightseeing

Cathédrale Notre-Dame de Paris.

Neatly contained within the Périphérique and divided by the Seine into left and right banks, Paris is a compact city. The city's 20 arrondissements (districts) spiral out, clockwise and in ascending order, from the Louvre. Each piece of this jigsaw has its own character.

The Paris métro is reliable, and local buses are frequent and cheap. However, the city is best seen from ground level, whether on foot or, courtesy of the Vélib' bike hire scheme, on two wheels.

SEEING THE SIGHTS

To skip the queues, try to avoid visiting major attractions at the weekend. Major museums are less busy during the week, especially if you take advantage of the late-night opening offered by many of

Critics' choice

1 **Musée d'Orsay**
Post-revamp, the Musée d'Orsay will be gleaming in 2011. See p45.

2 **Grande Galerie de l'Evolution**
A majestic natural history display. See p39.

3 **The Louvre**
Extravagant architecture and extraordinary art. See p28.

4 **Musée Gustave Moreau**
Wonderful museum dedicated to Symbolist painter Moreau. See p32.

5 **Cimetière du Père-Lachaise**
Illustrious corpses galore in the city's most famous cemetery. See p35.

the big museums. Note that most national museums are closed on Tuesdays, but all are free on the first Sunday of the month. Many municipal museums close on Mondays.

PACKAGE DEALS

The most economical way to visit a large number of museums is with a **Paris Museum Pass** (www.parismuseum pass.fr), which offers access to more than 60 museums and attractions. Participating attractions, which include the Louvre and the Musée d'Orsay, are denoted in our listings with PMP. Covering two days (€32), four days (€48) or six days (€64), passes are available from participating locations and tourist offices.

The Galeries Nationales du Grand Palais also operate an annual pass. The **Sesame** (www.rmn.fr) grants free entry (with queue-jumping rights), shop discounts and various other privileges. The card costs €47 for an individual, €79 for a couple and €22 for 13-25s.

The Seine & Islands

Along the Seine

Like some mythical deity, Paris emerged from the waters of its river. The Seine was the transport route that brought settlers here in the first place, many millennia ago, and it gave them the economic wherewithal to stay put: it's no accident that the city's coat of arms consists of waves and a boat. As the city grew, so did the river's cultural importance, until it became what it still is today – the symbolic boundary between intellectual Left Bank Paris and the mercantile activities of the Right Bank.

In between the two sides, like a double bullseye, are the islands: the western Ile de la Cité, with its heavy payload of history, state machinery and religious grandeur; and the adjacent Ile St-Louis, once a mess of marshland and islets, and now one of the most exclusive residential districts in the city. Paris rippled out from the former, and splashes out in the upmarket boutiques of the latter.

It's at its best in summer. Port de Javel and Jardin Tino-Rossi become open-air dancehalls; and there's the summer jamboree of Paris-Plages, Mayor Delanoë's inspired city beaches that bring sand, palm trees, loungers and free entertainment to both sides of the Seine. After a few teething problems, the **Piscine Joséphine-Baker** (see p103) has revived the floating swimming pool concept that was so popular in the 19th and early 20th centuries. Come on Sundays, and stretches of riverside roads will be closed for the benefit of cyclists and rollerskaters. And, of course, there's a wealth of boat tours (see p119). By 2012, Delanoë hopes to take the experiment one step further by redesigning the Left Bank and banning cars completely. His ambitious plans for a stretch of road between the Musée d'Orsay and Pont de l'Alma involve a long promenade dotted with riverside parks, cafés, sports facilities and possibly a floating cinema.

The bridges

From the honeyed arches of the oldest, the **Pont Neuf**, to the handsome, swooping lines of the newest, the **Passerelle Simone-de-Beauvoir**, the city's 37 bridges are among the best-known landmarks in the city, and enjoy some of its best views.

There was already a bridge on the site of the **Petit Pont** in the first century BC,

when the Parisii Celts ran their river trade and toll-bridge operations. The Romans put up a cross-island thoroughfare in the form of a reinforced bridge to the south of Ile de la Cité, and another one north of it (where the **Pont Notre-Dame** now stands), thus creating a straight route all the way from Orléans through to Belgium.

Since then, the city's *ponts* have been bombed, bashed by buses and boats, weather-beaten and even trampled to destruction: in 1634, the Pont St-Louis collapsed under the weight of a religious procession. In the Middle Ages, the handful of bridges linking the islands to the riverbanks were lined with shops and houses, but the flimsy wooden constructions regularly caught fire or got washed away. The Petit Pont sank 11 times before councillors decided to ban building on top of bridges.

The Pont Neuf was inaugurated in 1607 and has been standing sturdy ever since. This was the first bridge to be built with no houses to obstruct the view of the river. It had a raised stretch of road at the edge to protect walkers from traffic and horse dung (the new-fangled 'pavement' soon caught on); the alcoves that now make pit stops for lovers were once filled with tooth-pullers, peddlers and *bouquinistes*.

The 19th century was boom time for bridge-building: 21 were built in all, including the city's first steel, iron and suspension bridges. The **Pont de la Concorde** used up what was left of the Bastille after the storming of 1789; the romantic **Pont des Arts** was the capital's first solely pedestrian crossing (built in 1803 and rebuilt in the 1980s). The most glitteringly exuberant bridge is the **Pont Alexandre III**, with its bronze and glass, garlanding and gilded embellishments. More practical is the **Pont de l'Alma**, with its Zouave statue that has long been a flood monitor: when the statue's toes get wet, the state raises the flood alert and starts to close the quayside roads; when he's up to his ankles in Seine, it's no longer possible to navigate the river by boat. This offers some indication of how devastating the great 1910 flood was, when the plucky Zouave disappeared up to his neck.

The 20th century brought some spectacular additions. **Pont Charles-de-Gaulle**, for example, stretches resplendent like the wing of a huge aeroplane, and iron **Viaduc d'Austerlitz** (1905) is striking yet elegant as it cradles métro line 5. The city's newest crossing, the Passerelle Simone-de-Beauvoir, is a walkway linking the Bibliothèque Nationale to the Parc de Bercy.

Ile de la Cité

In the 1st & 4th arrondissements.
The Ile de la Cité is where Paris was born around 250 BC, when the Parisii, a tribe of Celtic Gauls, founded a settlement on this convenient bridging point of the Seine. Romans, Merovingians and Capetians followed, in what became a centre of political and religious power right into the Middle Ages:

HELOISE BERGMAN

royal authority at one end, around the Capetian palace; the Church at the other, by Notre-Dame.

When Victor Hugo wrote *Notre-Dame de Paris* in 1831, the Ile de la Cité was still a bustling quarter of narrow medieval streets and tall houses: 'the head, heart and very marrow of Paris'. Baron Haussmann performed a marrow extraction when he supervised the expulsion of 25,000 people from the island, razing tenements and some 20 churches, and leaving behind large, official buildings – the law courts, the **Conciergerie**, Hôtel-Dieu hospital, the police headquarters and the cathedral. The lines of the old streets are traced into the parvis in front of **Notre-Dame**.

Perhaps the most charming spot on the island is the western tip, where Pont Neuf spans the Seine. Despite its name, it is in fact the oldest bridge in Paris, begun under the reign of Henri III and Catherine de Médicis in 1578 and taking 30 years to complete. In 1991, the bridge (or, rather, a full-size facsimile of it) starred in Leos Carax's budget-busting film *Les Amants du Pont Neuf*.

Down the steps is a leafy triangular garden, square du Vert-Galant. You can take to the water here on the Vedettes du Pont Neuf. In the centre of the bridge is an equestrian statue of Henri IV; the original went up in 1635, was melted down to make cannons during the Revolution, and replaced in 1818. On the bridge's eastern side, place Dauphine, home to restaurants, wine bars and the ramshackle Hôtel Henri IV, was built in 1607, on what was then a sandy bar that flooded every winter. It was commissioned by Henri IV, who named it in honour of his son, the future King Louis XIII. The brick and stone houses, similar to those in place des Vosges (though subsequently much altered to accommodate sun terraces), look out over the quays and square. The third, eastern side was demolished in the 1860s, when the new Préfecture de Police was built. Known by its address, quai des Orfèvres, it was immortalised by Clouzot's film and Simenon's Maigret novels.

The towers of the Conciergerie dominate the island's north bank. Along with the Palais de Justice, it was originally part of the Palais de la Cité, residential and administration complex of the Capetian kings. It occupies the site of an earlier Merovingian fortress and, before that, the Roman governor's house. Etienne Marcel's uprising prompted Charles V to move the royal retinue to the Louvre in 1358, and the Conciergerie was assigned a more sinister role as a prison for people awaiting execution. The interior is worth a visit for its prison cells and the vaulted Gothic halls. On the corner of boulevard du Palais, the Tour de l'Horloge, built in 1370, was the first public clock in Paris.

Sainte-Chapelle, Pierre de Montreuil's masterpiece of stained glass and slender Gothic columns, stands among the nearby law courts. Enveloping the chapel, the Palais de Justice was built alongside the Conciergerie. Behind elaborate wrought-iron railings, most of the present buildings around the fine neo-classical entrance courtyard date from the 1780s reconstruction by Desmaisons and Antoine. After passing through security, you can visit the **Salle des Pas Perdus**, busy with plaintiffs and barristers, and sit in on cases in the civil and criminal courts. The Palais is still the centre of the French legal system.

Across boulevard du Palais, behind the Tribunal du Commerce, place Louis-Lépine is occupied by the Marché aux Fleurs, where horticultural suppliers sell flowers, cacti and exotic trees. On Sundays, they are joined by caged birds and small animals in the Marché aux Oiseaux. The Hôtel-Dieu, east of the market place, was founded in the seventh century. During the Middle Ages, your chances of survival here were, at best, slim; today, the odds are much improved. The hospital originally stood on the other side of the island facing the Latin Quarter, but after a series of fires in the 18th century it was rebuilt here in the 1860s.

Notre-Dame cathedral dominates the eastern half of the island. On the parvis in front of the cathedral is the bronze 'Kilomètre Zéro' marker, the point from which distances between Paris and the rest of France are measured. The **Crypte Archéologique** hidden under the parvis gives a sense of the island's multi-layered past, when it was a tangle of alleys, houses, churches and cabarets. Notre-Dame is still a place of worship, and holds its Assumption Day procession, Christmas Mass and Nativity scene on the parvis.

Walk through the garden by the cathedral to appreciate its flying buttresses. To the north-east, a medieval feel persists in the few streets untouched by Haussmann, such as rue Chanoinesse, rue de la Colombe and rue des Ursins,

though the crenellated medieval remnant on the corner of rue des Ursins and rue des Chantres was redone in the 1950s for the Aga Khan. The capital's oldest love story unfolded in the 12th century at 9 quai aux Fleurs, where Héloïse lived with her uncle Canon Fulbert, who had her tutor and lover, the scholar Abélard, castrated. Héloïse was sent to a nunnery. Behind the cathedral, in a garden at the eastern end of the island, is the **Mémorial des Martyrs de la Déportation**, remembering people sent to Nazi concentration camps.

Cathédrale Notre-Dame de Paris

Pl du Parvis-Notre-Dame, 4th (01.42.34.56.10, www.cathedraledeparis.com). M° Cité/RER St-Michel. **Open** 8am-6.45pm Mon-Fri; 8am-7.15pm Sat, Sun. *Towers* Apr-Sept 10am-6.30pm daily (*June, Aug* until 11pm Sat, Sun). Oct-Mar 10am-5.30pm daily. **Admission** free. *Towers* €8; €5 reductions; free under-18s. PMP. **Credit** MC, V. Notre-Dame was constructed between 1163 and 1334, and the amount of time and money spent on it reflected the city's growing prestige. The west front remains a high point of Gothic art for the balanced proportions of its twin towers and rose window, and the three doorways with their rows of saints and sculpted tympanums: the *Last Judgement* (centre), *Life of the Virgin* (left) and *Life of St Anne* (right). Inside, take a moment to admire the long nave with its solid foliate capitals and high altar with a marble Pietà by Coustou. To truly appreciate the masonry, climb up the towers. The route runs up the north tower and down the south. Between the two you get a close-up view of the gallery of chimeras – the fantastic birds and hybrid beasts designed by Viollet-le-Duc along the balustrade. After a detour to see the Bourdon (the massive bell), a staircase leads to the top of the south tower.

La Conciergerie

2 bd du Palais, 1st (01.53.40.60.80). M° Cité/RER St-Michel Notre-Dame. **Open** *Mar-Oct* 9.30am-6pm daily. *Nov-Feb* 9am-5pm daily. **Admission** €6.50; €4.50 reductions; free under-18s (accompanied by an adult). *With Sainte-Chapelle* €11; €7.50 reductions. PMP. **Credit** MC, V. The Conciergerie looks every inch the forbidding medieval fortress. However, much of the façade was added in the 1850s, long after Marie-Antoinette, Danton and Robespierre had been imprisoned here. The 13th-century Bonbec tower, built during the reign of St Louis, the 14th-century twin towers, César and Argent, and the Tour de l'Horloge all survive from the Capetian palace. The visit takes you through the Salle des Gardes, the medieval kitchens with their four huge chimneys, and the Salle des Gens d'Armes, an impressive vaulted Gothic hall built between 1301 and 1315 for Philippe 'le Bel'. After the royals moved to the Louvre, the fortress became a prison under the watch of the Concierge. The wealthy had private cells with their own furniture, which they paid for; others crowded on beds of straw. A list of Revolutionary prisoners, including a hair-dresser, shows that not all victims were nobles. In Marie-Antoinette's cell, the Chapelle des Girondins, are her crucifix, some portraits and a guillotine blade.

La Crypte Archéologique

Pl Jean-Paul II, 4th (01.55.42.50.10). M° Cité/RER St-Michel Notre-Dame. **Open** 10am-6pm Tue-Sun. **Admission** €4; €2-€3 reductions; free under-14s. PMP. **Credit** (€15 minimum) MC, V. Hidden under the forecourt in front of the cathedral is a large void that contains bits and pieces of Roman quaysides, ramparts and hypocausts, medieval cellars, shops and pavements, the foundations of the Eglise Ste-Geneviève-des-Ardens (the church where Geneviève's remains were stored during the Norman invasions), an 18th-

In the neighbourhood

The Seine & Islands
Ile de la Cité is the bullseye of the capital, where its history begins – home to the law courts, Notre-Dame and a dinky flower market. East from here, Ile St-Louis is one of the smartest addresses in the capital.

The Louvre
The world's largest museum, the Louvre is home to some 35,000 works of art, from ancient Egypt to the 19th century. Crowds can be oppressive, especially around the *Mona Lisa*, but there's also plenty of space for contemplation.

Opéra to Les Halles
At the western end of this stretch, it's all large-scale consumerism and high-end culture; to the east are sleaze, buzz and Les Halles, home to the grim Forum des Halles mall. Heading south, the Tuileries gardens provide respite.

Champs-Elysées & Western Paris
The city's most famous thoroughfare, the Champs-Elysées has been transformed of late. At its western end, the Arc de Triomphe is also gleaming after a refurb. Western Paris is a civilised mix of important museums and grand residences.

Montmartre & Pigalle
Montmartre has one of the city's densest concentrations of tourists. After the views and the Sacré-Coeur, explore the romantic sidestreets. The popular image of Pigalle covers sex shops and neon, but the area is cleaning up its act.

Beaubourg & the Marais
Beaubourg is home to the Centre Pompidou, which holds Europe's largest collection of modern art. The Marais, with ancient buildings and a street plan largely unmolested by Haussmann, is the heartland of Jewish and gay Paris.

Bastille & Eastern Paris
Bastille is not so much revolutionary as creative these days; now the area around the iconic place de la Bastille is well stocked with record shops, music venues and lively bars.

North-east Paris
The drab Gare du Nord is many visitors' first taste of Paris. But east are Belleville and Ménilmontant, two of the city's most multicultural areas and now a real nightlife hub.

The Latin Quarter & the 13th
Academic tradition persists in the Latin Quarter, home to the Panthéon and the Sorbonne. Further east, the vast ZAC Rive Gauche development project means the 13th is on the up.

St-Germain-des-Prés & Odéon
Intellectual heritage and some of the most expensive coffee in the city are to be found in St-Germain-des-Prés & Odéon, now best known for fashion houses and luxury brands.

Montparnasse & Beyond
There's just enough of a good-time feel in Montparnasse at night to recall the area's artistic heyday in the '20s and '30s. South, Parc Montsouris offers relief from the urban sprawl.

The 7th & Western Paris
The 7th arrondissement is home to many of Paris's finest museums and the Eiffel Tower, its most celebrated monument. Elsewhere, this is a rarefied area of smart shops and posh homes.

HELOISE BERGMAN

LeisureDirection
Your Self-Drive Holiday Specialist

GREAT HOLIDAYS IN AND AROUND
PARIS

- ○ **Fantastic Disneyland® Paris breaks for all the Family**

- ○ **Camping Holidays across France from only £5 per person per night**

- ○ **Paris city breaks via Eurostar or by ferry**

- ○ **Cottages and Villas around Paris and Ile de France**

century foundling hospital and a 19th-century sewer, all excavated since the 1960s. It's not always easy to work out exactly which wall, column or staircase is which – but you do get a vivid sense of the layers of history piled one atop another during 16 centuries.

Mémorial des Martyrs de la Déportation

Sq de l'Ile de France, 4th (01.46.33.87.56). M° Cité/RER St-Michel Notre-Dame. **Open** Oct-Mar 10am-noon, 2-5pm daily. Apr-Sept 10am-noon, 2-7pm daily. **Admission** free. This tribute to the 200,000 Jews, Communists, homosexuals and résistants deported to concentration camps from France in World War II stands on the eastern tip of the island. A blind staircase descends to river level, where simple chambers are lined with tiny lights and the walls are inscribed with verse. A barred window looks out at the Seine.

Sainte-Chapelle

6 bd du Palais, 1st (01.53.40.60.80). M° Cité/RER St-Michel Notre-Dame. **Open** Mar-Oct 9.30am-6pm daily. Nov-Feb 9am-5pm daily. **Admission** €8; €5 reductions; free under-18s (accompanied by adult). PMP. With Conciergerie €11; €7.50 reductions. **Credit** MC, V. Devout King Louis IX (St Louis, 1226-70) had a hobby of accumulating holy relics. In the 1240s, he bought what was advertised as the Crown of Thorns, and ordered Pierre de Montreuil to design a shrine. The result was Sainte-Chapelle. With 15m (49ft) windows, the upper level appears to consist almost entirely of stained glass. The windows depict hundreds of scenes from the Old and New Testaments, culminating with the Apocalypse in the rose window.

Ile St-Louis

In the 4th arrondissement.
The Ile St-Louis is one of the most exclusive residential addresses in the city. Delightfully unspoiled, it has fine architecture, narrow streets and pretty views from the tree-lined quays, and still retains the air of a tranquil backwater, curiously removed from city life.

For hundreds of years, the island was a swampy pasture belonging to Notre-Dame, known as Ile Notre-Dame and used as a retreat for fishermen, swimmers and courting couples. In the 14th century, Charles V built a fortified canal through the middle, thus creating the Ile aux Vaches ('Island of Cows'). Its real-estate potential wasn't realised until 1614, though,when speculator Christophe Marie persuaded Louis XIII to fill in the canal (present-day rue Poulletier) and plan streets, bridges and houses. The island was renamed in honour of the king's pious predecessor, and the venture proved a huge success, thanks to architect Louis Le Vau, who from the 1630s built fashionable new residences along the quai d'Anjou, quai de Bourbon and quai de Béthune, as well as the Eglise St-Louis-en-l'Ile. By the 1660s the island was full; its smart reception rooms were set at the front of courtyards to give residents riverside views.

Rue St-Louis-en-l'Ile – lined with fine historic buildings that now house quirky gift shops and gourmet food stores (many open on Sunday), quaint tearooms, stone-walled bars, restaurants and hotels – runs the length of the island. The grandiose **Hôtel Lambert** at no.2 was built by Le Vau in 1641 for Louis XIII's secretary, and has sumptuous interiors by Le Sueur, Perrier and Le Brun. At no.51 – **Hôtel Chenizot** – look out for the bearded faun adorning the rocaille doorway, flanked by stern dragons. There's more sculpture on the courtyard façade, while a second courtyard hides craft workshops and an art gallery. Across the street, the **Hôtel du Jeu de Paume** at no.54 was once a tennis court; at no.31, famous ice-cream maker **Berthillon** still draws a crowd. At the western end there are great views of the flying buttresses of Notre-Dame from the terraces of the **Brasserie de l'Ile**

St-Louis and the **Flore en l'Ile** café. At 6 quai d'Orléans, the **Adam Mickiewicz library-museum** (01.55.42.83.83, open 2-5pm Wed, 9am-noon Sat, hourly guided tours €5, free-€2 reductions) is dedicated to the Romantic poet, journalist and campaigner for Polish freedom.

Eglise St-Louis-en-l'Ile

19bis rue St-Louis-en-l'Ile, 4th (01.46.34.11.60, www.saintlouisenlile.com). M° Pont Marie. **Open** 9am-noon, 3-7pm Tue-Sun. **Admission** free. The island's church was built between 1664 and 1765, following plans by Louis Le Vau and later completed by Gabriel Le Duc. The Baroque interior boasts Corinthian columns and a sunburst over the altar, and hosts classical music concerts.

Opéra to Les Halles

In centuries gone by, these two adjoining central districts – bounded by the Grands Boulevards to the north and the river to the south – were the city's commercial and provisioning powerhouses, home to most of the newspapers, banks and major mercantile institutions. Nowadays, although there is still a strong financial slant thanks to the presence of the two stock exchanges and the Banque de France, the focus is on shopping: mass-market stuff in and around Les Halles, shading progressively into more exclusive and expensive brands the further one moves west, in particular on and just off rue St-Honoré.

Les Halles itself was, famously, the city's wholesale food market until 1969, when the Second Empire iron-framed buildings that housed it were ripped out, and a thousand commentators gnashed their teeth in print. The soulless shopping centre that filled the gap in the 1970s has been one of the city's least liked features, and is itself set to be overhauled during the next few years. The centrepiece of the project will be an undulating transparent roof called the Canopée that will hover like a clamshell over a new open-air plaza and landscaped gardens.

Tuileries & Palais-Royal

In the 1st arrondissement.
Once the monarchs had moved from the Ile de la Cité to spacious new quarters on the Right Bank, the Louvre and, later, the palaces of the **Tuileries** and **Palais-Royal** became the centres of royal power. **The Louvre** (see pp28-30) still exerts considerable influence today: first as a grandiose architectural ensemble, a palace within the city; and, second, as a symbol of the capital's cultural pre-eminence. What had been simply a fortress along Philippe-Auguste's city wall in 1190 was transformed into a royal residence with all the latest Gothic comforts by Charles V; François I turned it into a sumptuous Renaissance palace. For centuries, it was a work in progress: everyone wanted to make their mark – including the most monarchical of presidents, François Mitterrand, who added IM Pei's glass pyramid, doubled the exhibition space and added the Carrousel du Louvre shopping mall, auditorium and food halls.

The palace has always attracted crowds: first courtiers and ministers; then artists; and, since 1793, when it was first turned into a museum, art-lovers – though the last department of the Finance Ministry moved out as late as 1991. Around the Louvre, other subsidiary palaces grew up: Catherine de Médicis commissioned Philibert Delorme

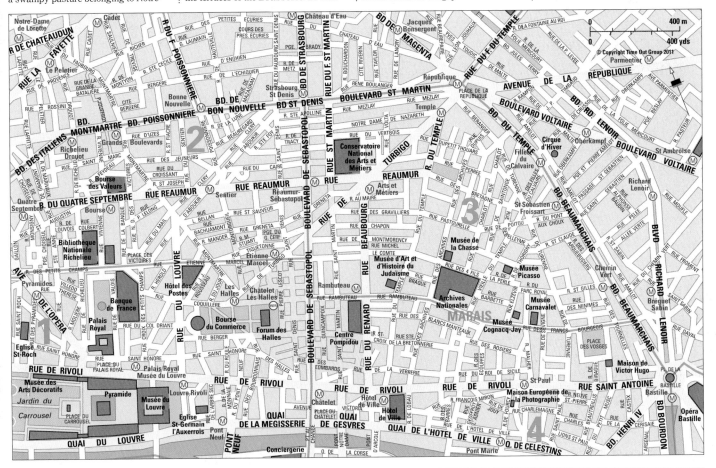

to begin work on one in the Tuileries; and Richelieu built the Palais Cardinal, which later became the Palais-Royal.

On place du Louvre, opposite Claude Perrault's grandiose western façade of the Louvre, is **Eglise St-Germain-l'Auxerrois**, once the French kings' parish church and home to the only original Flamboyant Gothic porch in Paris, built in 1435. Mirroring it to the left of the belfry is the 19th-century first arrondissement *mairie*, with its fanciful rose window and classical porch. Next door is the stylish **Le Fumoir** (*see p62*), with a Mona Lisa of its own: amaretto, orange juice and champagne.

Across rue de Rivoli from the Louvre, past the **Louvre des Antiquaires** antiques emporium (*see p81*), stands the understatedly elegant **Palais-Royal**, once Cardinal Richelieu's private mansion and now the Conseil d'Etat and ministry of culture. After a stroll in its quiet gardens, it's hard to believe that this was once the most debauched corner of Paris and the seedbed of the French Revolution.

In the 1780s, the Palais was a boisterous centre of Paris life, where aristocrats and the financially challenged inhabitants of the *faubourgs* rubbed shoulders. The coffee-houses in its arcades generated radical debate: here Camille Desmoulins called the city to arms on the eve of the storming of the Bastille; and after the Napoleonic Wars, Wellington and Field Marshal von Blücher lost so much money in the gambling dens that Parisians claimed they had won back their entire dues for war reparations. Only haute cuisine restaurant **Le Grand Véfour** (*see p48*), founded as Café de Chartres in the 1780s, survives from this era, albeit with decoration dating from a little later.

The **Comédie Française** theatre ('La Maison de Molière'; *see p104*) stands on the south-west corner. The company, created by Louis XIV in 1680, moved here in 1799. Molière himself is honoured with a fountain on the corner of rue Molière and rue de Richelieu. Brass-fronted **Café Nemours** on place Colette – Colette used to buy cigars from old-fashioned **A la Civette** nearby (157 rue St-Honoré, 1st, 01.42.96.04.99) – is another thespian favourite. In front of it, the métro entrance by artist Jean-Michel Othoniel, all glass baubles and aluminium struts, is a kitsch take on Guimard's celebrated art nouveau métro entrances.

Today, the stately arcades of the Palais-Royal house an eclectic succession of antiques dealers, philatelists, specialists in tin soldiers and musical boxes – and fashion showcases. Here you'll find the recently opened European flagship of renowned New York designer **Marc Jacobs** (*see p71*), chic vintage clothes specialist **Didier Ludot** (*see p75*), and the elegant perfumery **Salons du Palais-Royal Shiseido** (*see p80*). Passing through the arcades to rue de Montpensier, the neo-rococo Théâtre du Palais-Royal and the centuries-old café **Entr'acte** (*see p62*), you'll find narrow, stepped passages that run between here and rue de Richelieu. On the other side of the palace towards Les Halles is galerie Véro-Dodat. Built by rich *charcutiers* during the Restoration period, it features wonderfully preserved neo-classical wooden shopfronts.

At the western end of the Louvre, by rue de Rivoli, are the **Musée des Arts Décoratifs**, the **Musée de la Mode et du Textile** and the **Musée de la**

Publicité. All of these are administered independently of the Musée du Louvre, but were refreshed as part of the Grand Louvre scheme. Across place du Carrousel from the Louvre pyramid, the **Arc du Carrousel**, a mini-Arc de Triomphe, was built in polychrome marble for Napoleon from 1806 to 1809. The chariot on the top was originally drawn by the antique horses from San Marco in Venice, snapped up by Napoleon but returned in 1815. From the arch, the extraordinary axis along the **Jardin des Tuileries**, the Champs-Elysées up to the Arc de Triomphe and on to the Grande Arche de la Défense is plain to see.

The Jardin des Tuileries stretched as far as the Tuileries palace, until that was destroyed in the 1871 Paris Commune. The garden was laid out in the 17th century by André Le Nôtre and remains a pleasure area, with a funfair in summer; it also serves as an open-air gallery for modern art sculptures. Overlooking focal **place de la Concorde** is the **Musée de l'Orangerie** and the **Jeu de Paume**,

built as a court for real tennis and now a centre for photographic exhibitions.

The stretch of rue de Rivoli running beside the Louvre towards Concorde was laid out by Napoleon's architects Percier and Fontaine from 1802 to 1811, and is notable for its arcaded façades. It runs in a straight line between place de la Concorde and rue St-Antoine, in the Marais; at the western end it's filled with tacky souvenir shops – though old-fashioned hotels remain, and there are also gentlemen's outfitters, bookshop **WH Smith** (*see p70*) and tearoom **Angelina** (*see p62*). The area was inhabited by English aristocrats, writers and artists in the 1830s and '40s after the Napoleonic Wars, sleeping at **Le Meurice** (*see p108*) and dining in the fancy restaurants of the Palais-Royal.

Place des Pyramides, at the junction of rue de Rivoli and rue des Pyramides, contains a gleaming gilt equestrian statue of Joan of Arc. It is one of four statues of her in the city, and it's fêted as a proud symbol of French nationalism every May Day by supporters of the Front National.

Ancient rue St-Honoré, running parallel to rue de Rivoli, is one of those streets that changes style as it goes along: smart shops line it near place Vendôme, small cafés and inexpensive bistros predominate towards Les Halles. The Baroque **Eglise St-Roch** is still pitted with bullet holes made by Napoleon's troops when they crushed a royalist revolt in 1795. With its old houses, adjoining rue St-Roch still feels wonderfully authentic; a couple of shops are built into the side of the church. Further up stands **Chapelle Notre-Dame de l'Assomption** (1670-76), now used by the city's Polish community, its dome so disproportionately large that locals have dubbed it *sot dôme* ('stupid dome', a pun on 'Sodom').

Concept store **Colette** (*see p73*) brought some glamour to a once-staid shopping area, drawing a swarm of similar stores along in its wake. All are ideally placed for the fashionistas and film stars who touch down at **Hôtel Costes** (*see p108*). Opposite Colette is rue du Marché-St-Honoré, which once led to the covered Marché St-Honoré, since replaced by offices, in a square lined with trendy restaurants; to the north, rue Danielle-Casanova boasts 18th-century houses.

Further west along rue St-Honoré lies the wonderful, eight-sided **place Vendôme** and a perspective stretching from rue de Rivoli up to Opéra. At the end of the Tuileries, place de la Concorde, originally laid out for the glorification of Louis XV, is a masterclass in the use of open space, and spectacular when lit up at night. The winged Marly horses (only copies, the originals are in the Louvre) frame the entrance to the Champs-Elysées.

Smart rue Royale has tearoom **Ladurée** (*see p63*) and the famed restaurant **Maxim's** (3 rue Royale, 8th, 01.42.65.27.94), with a fabulous art nouveau interior. Rue Boissy d'Anglas proffers stylish shops and the trendy **Buddha Bar** (no.8, 8th, 01.53.05.90.00); and sporting luxuries at **Hermès** (*see p71*) on rue du Fbg-St-Honoré (a westward extension of rue St-Honoré), and high-end designs at **Yves Saint Laurent** (*see p73*) and others set the plush tone.

La Collection 1900

Maxim's, 3 rue Royale, 8th (01.42.65.30.47, www.maxims-musee-artnouveau.com). M° Madeleine. **Open** *Guided tours (reservations essential)* 2pm Wed-Sun (English); 3.15pm, 4.30pm (French). **Admission** €15. **No credit cards.**

Couturier Pierre Cardin has owned belle époque restaurant Maxim's since 1981, and now he has added a museum of art nouveau, which he has been collecting since the age of 18. There are rooms and rooms of exhibits, arranged so as to evoke a 19th-century courtesan's boudoir. Read Zola's *Nana* before your visit to grasp the full effect of the dreamy lake maidens sculpted in glistening faience, pewter vanity sets in the shape of reclining nudes, and beds inlaid with opium flowers to promote sleep. Dinner settings on display include Gustav Eiffel's own chunky tureens, just crying out for turtle soup.

Eglise St-Germain-l'Auxerrois

2 pl du Louvre, 1st (01.42.60.13.96, www.saint germainauxerrois.cef.fr). M° Louvre Rivoli or Pont Neuf. **Open** 8am-7pm Mon-Sat; 9am-8pm Sun. **Admission** free.

The architecture of this former royal church spans several eras: the elaborate Flamboyant Gothic porch is the most striking feature. Inside, there's the 13th-century Lady Chapel and a carved bench by Le Brun made for the royal family in 1682. The church achieved notoriety on 24 August 1572, when its bell signalled the St Bartholomew's Day massacre.

Eglise St-Roch

296 rue St-Honoré, 1st (01.42.44.13.20). M° Pyramides or Tuileries. **Open** 8am-7pm daily. **Admission** free.

Living history

A gaggle of tourists waiting at the entrance to the Passage des Princes in Paris's theatre district are hailed from afar by a man running in a bowler hat. Jean-Jacques de la Tour, as he introduces himself, is a 19th-century historian investigating the mystery of Nathaniel de Cantaussel, who was murdered in Passage Jouffroy in 1870 but whose body was never found. Thus begins a thoroughly original tour by **Visites-Spectacles** (01.48.59.92.97, www.visites-spectacles.com) of Paris's covered passages that plunges you into a world of *élégantes*, courtesans, pickpockets and greedy industrialists – the Second Empire brought to life.

As he leads us though the Passage des Panoramas, Passage des Variétés, Passage Verdeau and Passage Jouffroy, where the mystery is delightfully solved, Jean-Jacques packs his narrative with delicious trivia about the life of the *boulevardiers*: a dish of small birds that was eaten with a napkin over your head, Masonic symbolism in the Eiffel Tower, the construction of

unforgeable visiting cards and silk umbrellas, and a popular romantic walk that involved looking at the cadavers in a morgue. He teases people, poses enigmas and drops in a few modern references for laughs. But there's more: surprises pop out from doorways in the form of other actors in character – a dandy court reporter, a courtesan who knew Cantaussel's lover, a prostitute who makes people's black thoughts disappear in flames, and the vivacious Fée Verte (absinthe personified) who dances down a boulevard then disappears behind a newspaper stand. And clues materialise too in the windows of some of the historic shops that line the passages.

A huge amount of information is packed into 90 minutes, knitted into an engaging theatrical performance with convincing actors and great costumes. As a historical tour and interactive theatre performance rolled into one, it's great value for money and a brilliant way to discover things even the history books don't tell you.

ROBIN CAMBIANICA

Musée de l'Orangerie.

OLIVER KNIGHT

Begun in the 1650s in what was then the heart of Paris, this long church was designed chiefly by Jacques Lemercier; work took so long, the church was consecrated only in 1740. Famed parishioners and patrons are remembered in funerary monuments: Le Nôtre, Mignard, Corneille and Diderot are all here, as are busts by Coysevox and Coustou, Falconet's statue *Christ on the Mount of Olives* and Anguier's superb *Nativity*. Bullet marks from a 1795 shoot-out between royalists and conventionists still pit the façade.

Jardin des Tuileries

Rue de Rivoli, 1st. M° Concorde or Tuileries. **Open** *Apr, May* 7am-9pm daily; *June-Aug* 7am-11pm daily; *Sept-Mar* 7.30am-7.30pm daily. **Admission** free.

Between the Louvre and place de la Concorde, the gravelled alleyways of these gardens have been a chic promenade ever since they opened to the public in the 16th century; and the popular mood persists with the funfair that sets up along the rue de Rivoli side in summer. André Le Nôtre created the prototypical French garden with terraces and central vista running down the *Grand Axe* through circular and hexagonal ponds. When the Tuileries palace was burned down during the Paris Commune in 1871, the park was expanded. As part of Mitterrand's Grand Louvre project, fragile sculptures such as Coysevox's winged horses were transferred to the Louvre and replaced by copies, and the Maillol sculptures were returned to the Jardins du Carrousel; a handful of modern sculptures has been added, including bronzes by Laurens, Moore, Ernst, Giacometti, and Dubuffet's *Le Bel Costumé*. Replanting has restored parts of Le Nôtre's design and replaced damaged trees.

Jeu de Paume

1 pl de la Concorde, 8th (01.47.03.12.50, www. jeudepaume.org). M° Concorde. **Open** noon-9pm Tue; noon-7pm Wed-Fri; 10am-7pm Sat, Sun (last entry 30mins before closing). **Admission** €7; €5 reductions. **Credit** MC, V.

The Centre National de la Photographie moved into this site in 2005. The building, which once served as a tennis court, has been divided into two white, almost hangar-like galleries. It is not an intimate space, but it works well for showcase retrospectives. A video art and cinema suite in the basement shows new digital installation work, as well as feature-length films made by artists. There's also a sleek café and a decent bookshop.

Musée des Arts Décoratifs

107 rue de Rivoli, 1st (01.44.55.57.50, www.lesartsdecoratifs.fr). M° Palais Royal Musée du Louvre or Pyramides. **Open** 11am-6pm Tue, Wed, Fri-Sun; 11am-9pm Thur. **Admission** (with Musée de la Mode & Musée de la Publicité) €9; €7.50 reductions; free under-18s. PMP. **Credit** MC, V.

Taken as a whole with the Musée de la Mode et du Textile and Musée de la Publicité (for both, *see right*), this is one of the world's major collections of design and the decorative arts. Located in the west wing of the Louvre, the venue reopened a few years ago after a decade-long, €35-million restoration of the building and of 6,000 of the 150,000 items donated mainly by private collectors.

The major focus here is French furniture and tableware. From extravagant carpets to delicate crystal and porcelain, there is much to admire. Clever spotlighting and black settings show the exquisite treasures – including *châtelaines* made for medieval royalty and Maison Falize enamel work – to their best advantage. Other galleries are categorised by theme: glass, wallpaper, drawings and toys. There are cases devoted to Chinese head jewellery and the Japanese art of seduction with combs. Of most immediate attraction to the layman are the reconstructed period rooms, ten in all, showing how the other (French) half lived from the late 1400s to the early 20th century.

Musée de la Mode et du Textile

107 rue de Rivoli, 1st (01.44.55.57.50, www.lesartsdecoratifs.fr). M° Palais Royal Musée du Louvre or Pyramides. **Open** 11am-6pm Tue, Wed, Fri-Sun; 11am-9pm Thur. **Admission** (with Musée des Arts Décoratif & Musée de la Publicité) €9; €7.50 reductions; free under-18s. PMP. **Credit** MC, V.

This municipal fashion museum, home to some 16,000 costumes and 35,000 fashion accessories, holds Elsa Schiaparelli's entire archive and hosts exciting themed exhibitions. Dramatic black-walled rooms make a fine background to the clothes, and video screens and a small cinema space show how the clothes move, as well as interviews with the creators.

Musée de l'Orangerie

Jardin des Tuileries, 1st (01.44.77.80.07, www.musee-orangerie.fr). M° Concorde. **Open** 9am-6pm Wed-Sun. **Admission** €7.50; €5 reductions; free under-18s, all 1st Sun of mth. PMP. **Credit** MC, V.

The reopening of this Monet showcase a few years ago means the Orangerie is now firmly back on the tourist radar: expect long queues. The look is utilitarian and fuss-free, with the museum's eight, tapestry-sized *Nymphéas* (water lilies) paintings housed in two plain oval rooms. They provide a simple backdrop for the astonishing, ethereal romanticism of Monet's works, painted late in his life. Depicting Monet's 'jardin d'eau' at his house in Giverny, the *tableaux* have an intense, dreamy quality – partly reflecting the artist's absorption in the private world of his garden. Downstairs, the Jean Walter and Paul Guillaume collection of Impressionism and the Ecole de Paris is a mixed bag of sweet-toothed Cézanne and Renoir portraits, along with works by Modigliani, Rousseau, Matisse, Picasso and Derain.

Musée de la Publicité

107 rue de Rivoli, 1st (01.44.55.57.50, www.lesartsdecoratifs.fr). M° Palais Royal Musée du Louvre or Pyramides. **Open** 11am-6pm Tue, Wed, Fri-Sun; 11am-9pm Thur. **Admission** (with Musée des Arts Décoratifs & Musée de la Mode) €9; €7.50 reductions; free under-18s. PMP. **Credit** MC, V.

The upstairs element of the trio of museums in the Louvre west wing, the advertising museum has a distressed interior by Jean Nouvel. Only a fraction of the vast collection of posters, promotional objects and packaging can be seen at one time; vintage posters are accessed in the multimedia space.

Palais-Royal

Pl du Palais-Royal, 1st. M° Palais Royal Musée du Louvre. **Open** Gardens 7.30am-8.30pm daily. **Admission** free.

Built for Cardinal Richelieu by Jacques Lemercier, this building was once known as the Palais Cardinal. Richelieu left it to Louis XIII, whose widow Anne d'Autriche preferred it to the chilly Louvre and rechristened it when she moved in with her son, the young Louis XIV. In the 1780s, the Duc d'Orléans, Louis XVI's fun-loving brother, enclosed the gardens in a three-storey peristyle and filled it with cafés, shops, theatres, sideshows and accommodation to raise money for rebuilding the burned-down opera. In stark contrast to Versailles, the Palais-Royal was a place where people of all classes could mingle, and its arcades became a trysting venue. Today, Daniel Buren's installation of black-and-white striped columns graces the main courtyard.

Place de la Concorde

1st/8th. M° Concorde.

This is the city's largest square, its grand east–west perspectives stretching from the Louvre to the Arc de Triomphe, and north–south from the Madeleine to the Assemblée Nationale across the Seine. Royal architect Gabriel designed it in the 1750s, along with the two colonnaded mansions astride rue Royale; the west one houses the chic Hôtel de Crillon (*see p108*) and the Automobile Club de France, the other is the Naval Ministry. In 1792, the centre statue of Louis XV was replaced with the guillotine that would be used on Louis XVI, Marie-Antoinette and many more. The square was embellished in the 19th century with sturdy lampposts, the Luxor obelisk (from the Viceroy of Egypt), and ornate tiered fountains that represent navigation by water.

Place Vendôme

1st. M° Opéra or Tuileries.

Elegant place Vendôme got its name from a *hôtel particulier* built by the Duc de Vendôme that stood on the site. Opened in 1699, the eight-sided square was conceived by Hardouin-Mansart to show off an equestrian statue of the Sun King, torn down in 1792 and replaced in 1806 by the Colonne de la Grande Armée. Modelled on Trajan's Column in Rome and featuring a spiral comic strip illustrating Napoleon's military exploits, it was made from 1,250 Russian and Austrian cannons captured at the Battle of Austerlitz. During the 1871 Commune this symbol of 'brute force and false glory' was pulled down; the present column is a replica. Hardouin-Mansart only designed the façades, with their ground-floor arcade and giant Corinthian pilasters; the buildings behind were put up by nobles and speculators. Today, the square houses sparkling jewellers, top fashion houses and the justice ministry. At no.12, you can visit the Grand Salon where Chopin died in 1849; its fabulous allegorical decoration dates from 1777 and has been restored as part of a museum above the jewellers Chaumet (01.44.77.26.26).

The Bourse

In the 1st & 2nd arrondissements.

Far less frenzied than Wall Street, the city's traditional business district is squeezed between the elegant calm of the Palais-Royal and shopping hub the Grands Boulevards. Along rue du Quatre-Septembre, **La Bourse** (the stock exchange) is where financiers and stockbrokers beaver away in grandiose buildings. The Banque de France, France's national central bank, has occupied the 17th-century **Hôtel de Toulouse** since 1811, its long gallery still hung with Old Masters. Nearby, fashion and finance meet at stylish **place des Victoires**, designed by Hardouin-Mansart, forming an intimate circle of buildings today dedicated to fashion.

West of the square is shop-lined galerie Vivienne, the smartest of the covered passages in Paris, adjoining galerie Colbert. Also look out for temporary exhibitions at the **Bibliothèque Nationale de France – Richelieu**. You can linger at the luxury food and wine merchant **Legrand** (*see p79*), or head along passage des Petits-Pères to admire the 17th- to 18th-century **Eglise Notre-Dame-des-Victoires**, the remains of an Augustine convent with a cycle of paintings around the choir by Carle van Loo.

Rue de la Banque leads to the Bourse, behind a commanding neo-classical colonnade. The area has a relaxed feel – it's dead at weekends – but animated pockets exist at places such as **Le Vaudeville** (29 rue Vivienne, 2nd, 01.40.20. 04.62) and **Gallopin** (40 rue Notre-Dame-des-Victoires, 2nd, 01.42.36.45.38), busy brasseries frequented by stockbrokers and journalists. Rue des Colonnes is a quiet street lined with graceful porticoes and acanthus motifs dating from the 1790s; its design nemesis, the 1970s concrete-and-glass HQ of Agence France-Presse, the nation's biggest news agency, stands on the other side of busy rue du Quatre-Septembre.

Bibliothèque Nationale de France – Richelieu & Musée du Cabinet des Médailles

58 rue de Richelieu, 2nd (01.53.79.59.59, www.bnf.fr). M° Bourse. **Open** Phone for details. **Credit** AmEx, MC, V.

The history of the French National Library began in the 1660s, when Louis XIV moved manuscripts that couldn't be housed in the Louvre to this lavish Louis XIII townhouse. The library was first opened to the public in 1692, and by 1724 it had received so many new acquisitions that the adjoining Hôtel de Nevers had to be added.

Some of the original painted decoration by Romanelli and Grimaldi can still be seen in Galeries Mansart and Mazarine. The highlights, however, are the two circular reading rooms: the Salle Ovale, which is full of researchers, note-takers and readers, and the magnificent Salle de Travail, a temple to learning, with its arrangement of nine domes supported on slender columns. On the first floor is the Musée du Cabinet des Médailles, a modest two-room collection of coins and medals, including Greek, Roman and medieval examples. There is also a miscellany of other items, including Merovingian king

Dagobert's throne, Charlemagne's chess set and small artefacts from the Classical world and ancient Egypt. The whole site is undergoing renovation until 2017, and while much of the library's stock will remain on site, some of the collection has been moved to the Bibliothèque National de France François Mitterrand (see p40). During the first phase of works, entry to the site will be at 5 rue Vivienne.

La Bourse

Palais Brongniart, pl de la Bourse, 2nd (01.49.27.14.70, http://palaisbourse.euronext. com). M° Bourse. **Open** Guided tours only; call 1 wk in advance. **Admission** €8.50; €5.50 reductions. **No credit cards.**
After a century at the Louvre, the Palais-Royal and rue Vivienne, in 1826 the Stock Exchange was transferred to the Bourse, a dignified testament to First Empire classicism designed at Napoleon's behest by Alexandre Brongniart. It was enlarged in 1906 to create a cruciform interior, where brokers buzzed around a central enclosure known as the *corbeille* ('basket' or 'trading floor'). Computers have made the design obsolete, but the pace remains frenetic.

Place des Victoires

1st, 2nd. M° Bourse.
This circular square, the first of its kind, was designed by Hardouin-Mansart in 1685 to show off a statue of Louis XIV that marked victories against Holland. The original statue was destroyed after the Revolution (although the massive slaves from its base are now in the Louvre), and replaced in 1822 with an equestrian statue by Bosio. Among the occupants of the grand buildings that encircle the 'square' are fashion boutiques Kenzo and Victoire.

Opéra & Madeleine

Charles Garnier's wedding-cake **Palais Garnier** is all gilt and grandeur, as an opera house should be. Garnier was also responsible for the ritzy **Café de la Paix** (see p62) and the **InterContinental Paris Le Grand** (see p109) overlooking place de l'Opéra. Behind, in the basement of what is now the Hôtel Scribe, the Lumière brothers held the world's first public cinema screening in 1895. Outfitter **Old England** (no.12, 9th, 01.47.42.81.99), just opposite on boulevard des Capucines, with its wooden counters, Jacobean-style ceilings and old-style goods and service, could have served as their costume consultants. The **Olympia** concert hall (see p98), the celebrated host of the Beatles, Piaf and anyone in *chanson*, was knocked down, but rose again nearby. Over the road at no.35, pioneering portrait photographer Nadar opened a studio in the 1860s, frequented by the likes of Dumas père, Offenbach and Doré. In 1874, it hosted the first Impressionists' exhibition. Pedestrianised rue Edouard VII, laid out in 1911, leads to the octagonal square of the same name with Landowski's equestrian statue of the English monarch. Through an arch, another square contains the belle époque **Théâtre de l'Athénée-Louis Jouvet**.

The **Madeleine**, a monument to Napoleon's army, guards the end of the boulevard. At the head of rue Royale, its classical portico mirrors the Assemblée Nationale on the other side of place de la Concorde over the river, and the interior is a riot of marble and altars. Well worth a browse is extravagant delicatessen **Fauchon** (see p80) and other luxury food shops; here, too, is haute cuisine restaurant **Senderens** (see p52).

Landmark department stores **Printemps** (see p69) and the **Galeries Lafayette** (see p69), which opened just behind the Palais Garnier in the late 19th century, also merit investigation. Behind the latter stands the Lycée Caumartin, designed as a convent in the 1780s by Bourse architect Brongniart, and later one of

the city's most prestigious schools. West along boulevard Haussmann is a small square containing the **Chapelle Expiatoire** dedicated to Louis XVI and Marie-Antoinette.

Chapelle Expiatoire

29 rue Pasquier, 8th (01.44.32.18.00). M° St-Augustin. **Open** 1-5pm Thur-Sat. **Admission** €5; €3.50 reductions; free under-18s. PMP.
The chapel was commissioned by Louis XVIII in memory of his executed predecessors, his brother Louis XVI and Marie-Antoinette. Their remains, along with those of 3,000 victims of the Revolution, including Camille Desmoulins, Danton, Malesherbes and Lavoisier, were found in 1814 on the spot where the altar stands. The year after, the bodies of Louis XVI and Marie-Antoinette were transferred to the Basilique St-Denis; the pair are now represented by marble statues, kneeling at the feet of Religion. Every January, ardent (albeit unfulfilled) royalists gather here for a memorial service.

Eglise de la Madeleine

Pl de la Madeleine, 8th (01.44.51.69.00, www.eglise-lamadeleine.com). M° Concorde or Madeleine. **Open** 9.30am-7pm daily. **Admission** free.
The building of a church on this site began in 1764, and in 1806 Napoleon sent instructions from Poland for Barthélémy Vignon to design a 'Temple of Glory' dedicated to his Grand Army. After the emperor's fall, construction slowed and the building, by now a church again, was finally consecrated in 1845. The exterior is ringed by huge, fluted Corinthian columns, with a double row at the front, and a frieze of the Last Judgement just above the portico. Inside are giant domes, an organ and pseudo-Grecian side altars in a sea of multicoloured marble. It's a favourite venue for society weddings.

Eglise St-Augustin

46 bd Malesherbes, 8th (01.45.22.23.12). M° St-Augustin. **Open** Sept-June 8.30am-7pm Mon-Fri; 8.30am-noon, 2.30-7.30pm Sat; 8.30am-12.30pm, 4-7.30pm Sun. *July, Aug* 10am-1pm, 4-7pm Tue-Fri; 10am-noon, 4-7.30pm Sat; 10am-12.30pm, 4-7.30pm Sun. **Admission** free.
St-Augustin, designed between 1860 and 1871 by Victor Baltard, architect of the defunct Les Halles pavilions, is not what it seems. The domed, neo-Renaissance stone exterior is merely a shell: inside is an iron vault structure; even the decorative angels are cast in metal. Impressive paintings by Adolphe William Bouguereau hang in the transept.

Musée de la Franc-Maçonnerie

16 rue Cadet, 9th (01.45.23.43.97, www.godf. org). M° Cadet. **Open** 2-6pm Tue-Sat. Closed 2wks July, Aug, 1wk Sept. **Admission** €6; €4 reductions; free under-18s. **No credit cards.**

Tucked away at the back of the French Masonic Great Lodge, the Musée de la Franc-Maçonnerie first opened in 1973. It traces the history of French freemasonry, ranging from information on stonemasons' guilds to prints of masons General Lafayette and the 1848 revolutionary leaders Blanc and Barbès. The museum reopened in February 2010 after a hefty makeover.

Musée de l'Opéra

Palais Garnier, 1 pl de l'Opéra, 9th (01.53.79.37.47, www.bnf.fr). M° Opéra. **Open** 10am-5pm daily. **Admission** €7; €5 reductions; free under-18s. **No credit cards.**
The Palais Garnier houses temporary exhibitions relating to current opera or ballet productions, along with a permanent collection of paintings, scores and bijou opera sets housed in period cases. The entrance fee includes a visit to the auditorium, if rehearsals permit.

Musées des Parfumeries-Fragonard

9 rue Scribe, 9th (01.47.42.04.56) & 39 bd des Capucines, 2nd (01.42.60.37.14). M° Opéra. **Open** 9am-6pm Mon-Sat; 9am-5pm Sun. **Admission** free.
The rue Scribe museum showcases the collection of perfume house Fragonard: five rooms range from Ancient Egyptian ointment flasks to Meissen porcelain scent bottles; the boulevard des Capucines museum (closed Sun) has bottles by Lalique and Schiaparelli.

Palais Garnier

1 pl de l'Opéra, 9th (08.92.89.90.90, www.operadeparis.fr). M° Opéra. **Open** 16 July-5 Sept 10am-6pm daily. 6 Sept-15 July 10am-5pm daily. *Guided tours in English* (08.25.05.44.05) July, Aug 11.30am, 2.30pm daily. Sept-June 11.30am, 2.30pm Wed, Sat & Sun. **Admission** €9; €5 reductions. Guided tours €12; €6-€10 reductions. **Credit** AmEx, MC, V.
The Palais Garnier is a monument to Second Empire high society. The comfortably upholstered auditorium seats more than 2,000 people – and the exterior is just as opulent, with sculptures of music and dance on the façade, Apollo topping the copper dome, and nymphs bearing torches. Carpeaux's sculpture *La Danse* shocked Parisians with its frank sensuality: in 1869, someone threw a bottle of ink over its marble thighs. The original is now safe in the Musée d'Orsay, where there's also a massive scale model of the building. The Grand Foyer, with its mirrors and parquet, coloured marble, moulded stucco, sculptures and paintings by Baudry, have all been magnificently restored. You can also visit the Grand Escalier, the auditorium with a false ceiling painted by Chagall in 1964, red satin and velvet boxes, and the library and museum – it was once the emperor's private salons, where he could

Palais Garnier.

arrive directly by carriage on the ramp at the rear of the building. The Opéra Garnier is now also home to a wonderful new boutique (see p80).

Quartier de l'Europe

Its streets named after European cities, the area from Gare St-Lazare towards place de Clichy was the Impressionists' quarter. In those days, it epitomised modernity, with the station, which opened in 1837, serving the line from Paris to St-Germain-en-Laye (it was rebuilt in the 1880s). The long shabby commuter hub has had a revamp; a glass dome now disgorges travellers from the métro interchange. The adjoining **Hôtel Concorde Opéra Paris** (see p109) was the city's first great station hotel, with a grandiose hallway built by Eiffel in 1889 for visitors to the Exposition Universelle as he was putting up his Tower. Monet, who lived nearby in rue d'Edimbourg, depicted the steam age in *La Gare St-Lazare* and *Pont de l'Europe*; Pissarro and Caillebotte painted views of the new boulevards, and Manet had a studio on rue de St-Petersbourg. Rue de Budapest remains a red-light district; rue de Rome has long been home to stringed-instrument makers. East of St-Lazare stands the **Eglise de la Trinité**.

Eglise de la Trinité

Pl Estienne-d'Orves, 9th (01.48.74.12.77, www.latriniteparis.com). M° Trinité. **Open** 7.15am-8pm Mon-Fri; 9am-8.30pm Sat; 8.30am-8.30pm Sun. **Admission** free.
Noted for its tiered bell tower, this neo-Renaissance church was constructed between 1861 and 1867. Composer Olivier Messiaen (1908-92) was organist at the church for over 30 years.

The Grands Boulevards

Contrary to popular belief, the string of Grands Boulevards between Madeleine and République (des Italiens, Montmartre, Poissonnière, Bonne-Nouvelle, St-Denis, St-Martin) was not built by Baron Haussmann, but by Louis XIV in 1670, replacing the fortifications of King Philippe-Auguste's city wall. Their ramparts have left their traces in the strange changes of levels, with stairways climbing up to side streets at the eastern end. The boulevards burgeoned after the French Revolution, as residences, theatres and covered passages were put up on land taken from aristocrats and monasteries. To this day, they offer a glimpse of the city's divergent personalities – a stroll from Opéra to République runs from luxury shops via St-Denis prostitutes – and the phrase *théâtre des boulevards* is still used for lowbrow theatre. Between boulevard des Italiens and rue de Richelieu is place Boïeldieu and the **Opéra Comique** (*see p98*), where Bizet's *Carmen* had its première in 1875.

The 18th-century Hôtel d'Angny, now the town hall of the ninth arrondissement, was once home to the infamous *bals des victimes*, where every guest had to have a relative who had lost his or her head to the guillotine. The **Hôtel Drouot** auction house is ringed by antiques shops, coin- and stamp-dealers and wine bar Les Caves Drouot, where auctiongoers and valuers congregate.

There are several grand *hôtels particuliers* on rue de la Grange-Batelière, which leads on one side down the curious passage Verdeau, occupied by antiques dealers, and on the other back to the boulevards via passage Jouffroy. With its grand, barrel-vaulted glass-and-iron roof, this is home to the lovely **Hôtel Chopin** (*see p109*), shop windows of doll's houses, walking sticks, art books and film posters, and the colourful entrance of the **Grévin** waxworks (*see p86*).

Over the boulevard, passage des Panoramas is the oldest remaining covered arcade in Paris. When it opened in 1800, panoramas – vast illuminated circular paintings – of Rome, Jerusalem, London and other cities drew large crowds. Today, it contains tearoom **L'Arbre à Cannelle** (no.57, 2nd, 01.45.08.55.87), coin- and stamp-sellers, furniture-makers and old-fashioned printer **Stern** (no.47), established in 1840. The passage leads into a tangle of other little passages and the stage door of the **Théâtre des Variétés** (7 bd Montmartre, 2nd, 01.42.33.09.92), a pretty neo-classical theatre.

Rue du Fbg-Montmartre is home to celebrated belle époque *bouillon* **Chartier** (no.7, 9th, 01.47.70.86.29), which serves up hundreds of meals a day to the budget-minded. The street is also part of a significant Jewish quarter, less well known than the Marais, that grew up in the 19th century. There are several kosher bakers, restaurants and France's largest synagogue at 44 rue de la Victoire, an opulent Second Empire affair completed in 1876. Cobbled Cité Bergère, constructed in 1825 with desirable residences, now houses budget hotels, though the pretty iron-and-glass *portes-cochères* remain. On rue Richer stands the art deco **Folies-Bergère** (no.32, 9th, 08.92.68.16.50), only sporadically used for cabaret revues. To the south of boulevard Bonne-Nouvelle lies **Sentier**, and to the north rue du Fbg-Poissonnière is a mixture of rag-trade outlets and *hôtels particuliers*.

Back on the boulevard is evidence of a move north of the Marais by trendsetting hubs, including **Rex** and chic **De la Ville Café** (*see p62*). East of here are Louis XIV's twin triumphal arches, the **Porte St-Martin** and **Porte St-Denis**, which were erected to commemorate his military victories.

Le Grand Rex

1 bd Poissonnière, 2nd (08.92.68.05.96, www.legrandrex.com). M° Bonne Nouvelle. **Tour** *Les Etoiles du Rex* every 5mins 10am-7pm Wed-Sun; daily during school hols. **Admission** €9.80; €8 reductions. *Tour & film* €14.80; €13 reductions. **Credit** AmEx, MC, V.

Opened in 1932, this huge art deco cinema was designed by Auguste Bluysen with fantasy Hispanic interiors by US designer John Eberson. Go behind the scenes in the crazy 50-minute guided tour (*see p86*), which includes a presentation about the construction of the auditorium and a visit to the production room, complete with nerve-jolting Sensurround effects.

Hôtel Drouot

9 rue Drouot, 9th (01.48.00.20.20, www.drouot.fr). M° Richelieu Drouot. **Open** 11am-6pm Mon-Sat. **Auctions** 2pm Mon-Sat.

A spiky aluminium-and-marble concoction is the unlikely location for France's second largest art market – though it is now rivalled by Sotheby's and Christie's. Inside, escalators take you up to a number of small salerooms, where everything from medieval manuscripts and antique furniture to oriental arts, modern paintings, posters, jewellery and fine wines might be up for sale. Details of forthcoming auctions are published in the weekly *Gazette de l'Hôtel Drouot*.

Other locations Drouot-Montaigne, 15 av Montaigne, 8th (01.48.00.20.80); Drouot-Montmartre, 64 rue Doudeauville, 18th (01.48.00.20.99).

Porte St-Denis & Porte St-Martin

Rue St-Denis/bd St-Denis, 2nd/10th; 33 bd St-Martin, 3rd/10th. M° Strasbourg St-Denis.

These twin triumphal gates were erected in 1672 and 1674 at important entry points to the city as part of Colbert's strategy to glorify Paris and celebrate Louis XIV's victories on the Rhine. They are modelled on the triumphal arches of Ancient Rome. The Porte St-Denis is based on a perfect square with a single arch, bearing Latin inscriptions and decorated with military trophies and battle scenes. Porte St-Martin bears allegorical reliefs of Louis XIV's campaigns.

Les Halles & Sentier

In the 1st & 2nd arrondissements.

Les Halles is an ugly nexus of commerce and entertainment, with a massive RER-métro interchange as its centrepiece. The area is undergoing a huge makeover during the next few years, however.

For centuries, Les Halles was the city's wholesale food market. Covered markets were set up here in 1181 by King Philippe-Auguste; in the 1850s Baltard's spectacular cast-iron and glass pavilions were erected. In 1969, the market was relocated to the southern suburb of Rungis. Baltard's ten pavilions were knocked down (one was saved and now stands at Nogent-sur-Marne), leaving a giant hole. After a long political dispute, it was filled in the early 1980s by the miserably designed **Forum des Halles** underground shopping and transport hub, and the unloved Jardin des Halles.

East of the Forum, in the middle of place Joachim-du-Bellay, stands the Renaissance **Fontaine des Innocents**. The canopied fountain has swirling stone reliefs of water nymphs and titans by Jean Goujon (the ones you see today are copies; the originals are in the Louvre). It was inaugurated for Henri II's arrival in Paris in 1549 on the traditional royal route along rue St-Denis. It was moved and reconstructed here when the nearby Cimetière des Innocents, the city's main burial ground, was demolished in 1786, after flesh-eating rats started gnawing into people's living rooms; the bones were transferred to the catacombs.

Pedestrianised rue des Lombards is a beacon of live jazz, with **Sunset/ Sunside** (*see p99*), **Baiser Salé** (*see p99*) and **Au Duc des Lombards** (*see p99*). In 1610, King Henri IV was assassinated by a Catholic fanatic named François Ravaillac on nearby rue de la Ferronnerie. Today, the street has become an extension of the Marais gay circuit.

The ancient, easternmost stretch of rue St-Honoré runs into the southern edge of Les Halles. The Fontaine du Trahoir stands at the corner with rue de l'Arbre-Sec. Opposite, the **Hôtel de Truden** (52 rue de l'Arbre-Sec) was built in 1717 for a rich wine merchant; in the courtyard on rue des Prouvaires, the market-traders' favourite **La Tour de Montlhéry** (*see p51*) serves up meaty fare through the night. Fashion chains line the commercial stretch of the rue de Rivoli south of Les Halles. Running towards the Seine, ancient little streets such as rue des Lavandiers-Ste-Opportune and rue Jean-Lantier show a different side of Les Halles. Between rue de Rivoli and the Pont Neuf is the once celebrated but now defunct department store La Samaritaine. Closed since 2005, it is now being converted into a luxury hotel that is due to open in 2013. From here, quai de la Mégisserie leads towards Châtelet.

Looming over the northern edge of the Jardin des Halles is the massive **Eglise St-Eustache**, with Renaissance motifs inside and chunky flying buttresses outside. At the western end of the gardens is the circular, domed **Bourse de Commerce**. In front of it, an astrological column is all that remains from a grand palace belonging to Marie de Médicis that stood here.

The empire of French designer **Agnès b** (*see p74*) stretches along most of rue du Jour, with outlets such as **Kiliwatch** (*see p75*) clustered along rue Tiquetonne. On rue Etienne-Marcel, the restored **Tour Jean Sans Peur** is a weird Gothic relic of the fortified medieval townhouse of Jean Sans Peur, duke of Burgundy.

Busy, pedestrianised rue Montorgueil is lined with grocers, delicatessens and cafés. Some historic façades remain from when this was an area in which the well-heeled and the working class mingled: **Pâtisserie Stohrer** (no.51, 2nd, 01.42.33.38.20), founded in 1730 and credited with the invention of the sugary *puits d'amour*; and the golden snail sign hanging in front of **L'Escargot Montorgueil** (no.38, 01.42.36.83.51), a restaurant established in 1832.

Stretching north, bordered by boulevard de Bonne-Nouvelle to the north and boulevard Sébastopol to the east, lies Sentier, the historic garment district, and cocky rue St-Denis, which has long relied on strumpets and strip joints. The grime is unremitting along its northern continuation, rue du Fbg-St-Denis.

Rue Réaumur is lined with striking art nouveau buildings. Between rue des Petits-Carreaux and rue St-Denis is the site of the medieval Cour des Miracles – a refuge where paupers would 'miraculously' regain use of their eyes or limbs. A disused aristocratic estate, it was a sanctuary for the underworld until it was cleared out in 1667.

Sentier's streets buzz with porters shouldering linen bundles, as sweatshops churn out copies of catwalk creations. Streets such as rue du Caire, rue d'Aboukir and rue du Nil reflect the craze that followed Napoleon's Egyptian campaign in 1798 and 1799 – look out too for sphinx heads and mock hieroglyphics at 2 place du Caire.

Bourse de Commerce

2 rue de Viarmes, 1st (01.55.65.55.65). M° Louvre Rivoli. **Open** *tour groups* 9am-6pm Mon-Fri. **Admission** free.

Housing the Paris chamber of commerce, this trade centre for coffee and sugar was built as a grain market in 1767. The circular building was then covered by a wooden dome, replaced by an avant-garde iron structure in 1809. In his novel *Notre-Dame de Paris*, Victor Hugo summed up the building thus: *'Le dôme de la Halle-au-Blé est une casquette de jockey anglais sur une grande échelle.'*

Eglise St-Eustache

Rue du Jour, 1st (01.42.36.31.05, www.saint-eustache.org). M° Les Halles. **Open** 9.30am-7pm Mon-Fri; 10am-7pm Sat; 9am-7pm Sun. **Admission** free.

This massive, barn-like church, built between 1532 and 1640, has a Gothic structure but Renaissance decoration in its façade and Corinthian capitals. Among the paintings in the side chapels are a *Descent from the Cross* by Luca Giordano; pieces by John Armleder were added in 2000. Murals by Thomas Couture adorn the 19th-century Lady chapel. There is a magnificent 8,000-pipe organ, and free recitals are held at 5.30pm on Sundays.

Forum des Halles

1st. M° Les Halles/RER Châtelet Les Halles. **Admission** free.

The labyrinthine mall and transport interchange extends three levels underground and includes the Ciné Cité multiplex cinema and the Forum des Images, as well as shops and the Forum des Créateurs, a section for young designers. Despite an open central courtyard, a sense of gloom prevails. All should change by 2012, with a new landscaping of the whole area.

Pavillon des Arts

Les Halles, 101 rue Rambuteau, 1st (01.42.33. 82.50). M° Châtelet. **Open** 11.30am-6.30pm Tue- Sun. **Admission** €5.50; €2.50-€4 reductions; free under-14s. **No credit cards**.

This gallery in Les Halles hosts exhibitions on anything from photography to local history.

Tour Jean Sans Peur

20 rue Etienne-Marcel, 2nd (01.40.26.20.28, www.tourjeansanspeur.com). M° Etienne Marcel. **Open** *Mid Nov-Mar* 1.30-6pm Wed, Sat, Sun. *Apr-mid Nov* 1.30-6pm Wed-Sun. Tour 3pm. **Admission** €5; €3 reductions; free under-7s. *Tour* €8. **No credit cards**.

This Gothic turret (1409-11) is the remnant of the townhouse of Jean Sans Peur, duke of Burgundy. He was responsible for the assassination of his rival Louis d'Orléans, which sparked the Hundred Years' War and saw Burgundy become allied to the English crown. You can climb the tower, which has rooms leading off the stairway.

Champs-Elysées & Western Paris

There seems to be an unwritten law in France that no mention of the capital's most famous thoroughfare can be made in print or broadcast media without immediately calling it *'la plus belle avenue du monde'*. In truth, it's not especially beautiful and it heaves with cars and crowds – especially the section west of the Rond-Point – at pretty much any time of the day. The hordes aren't here for beauty, though. They're here for the shops, which the avenue, after years in the retail doldrums, now supplies in upmarket abundance.

The posh shopping going on along and around the Champs is entirely in keeping with the prevailing wealth and grandeur in the eighth arrondissement, and in the adjoining 16th and 17th. But fortunately, in the midst of all this rampant consumerism and airy affluence are a good number of museums covering such cerebral topics as architecture, human evolution and life on the ocean waves.

Champs-Elysées

In the 8th & 16th arrondissements.

The Champs-Elysées is, and has long been, a symbolic gathering place. Sports victories, New Year's Eve, displays of military might on 14 July – all are celebrated here. Over the past decade, the avenue has undergone a renaissance, thanks initially to a facelift instigated by Jacques Chirac.

Chi-chi shops and chic hotels have set up in the 'golden triangle' (avenues George V, Montaigne and the Champs): **Louis Vuitton** (*see p71*), **Chanel** (*see p71*) and **Jean-Paul Gaultier** (*see p71*), the **Marriott** (70 av des Champs-Elysées, 8th, 01.53.93.55.00) and **Pershing Hall** (12 rue de Marignan, 8th, 01.40.76.34.44). The **Four Seasons George V** (*see p109*) has undergone a revamp, and fashionable restaurants such as **Spoon, Food & Wine** (*see p110*) draw affluent and screamingly fashionable crowds. Crowds line up for the glitzy **Le Lido** cabaret (*see p84*), the now commercialised **Queen** nightclub (*see p101*) and numerous cinemas, or stroll down the avenue to floodlit place de la Concorde. The famous **Drugstore Publicis** (*see p69*) is where locals head to stock up on late-night wines and groceries.

This great spine of western Paris started life as an extension to the Tuileries, laid out by Le Nôtre in the 17th century. By the Revolution, the avenue had reached its full extent, but it was during the Second Empire that it became a focus for fashionable society, military parades and royal processions. Bismarck was so impressed when he arrived with the conquering Prussian army in 1871 that he had a replica, the Ku'damm, built in Berlin, and Hitler's troops made a point of marching down it in 1940, as did their Allied counterparts four years later.

The lower, landscaped reach of the avenue hides two theatres and elegant restaurants **Laurent** (41 av Gabriel, 8th, 01.42.25.00.39) and **Ledoyen** (1 av Dutuit, 8th, 01.53.05.10.01), housed in fancy Napoleon III pavilions. At the Rond-Point des Champs-Elysées, no.7 (now the Artcurial gallery bookshop and auction house) and no.9 give visitors some idea of the magnificent mansions that once lined the avenue. From here on, it's platinum cards and lanky women aplenty, as avenue Montaigne rolls out a full deck of fashion houses.

Models and magnates nibble on the terrace at fashionable restaurant **L'Avenue** (no.41, 8th, 01.40.70.14.91). You can admire the lavish **Hôtel Plaza Athénée** (*see p110*) and Auguste Perret's innovative 1911-13 **Théâtre des Champs-Elysées** concert hall (*see p98*), with an auditorium painted by Maurice Denis and lights by Lalique.

South of the avenue, the glass-domed **Grand Palais** and Petit Palais, both built for the 1900 Exposition Universelle and still used for major art exhibitions, create a magnificent vista across the elaborate Pont Alexandre III to Les Invalides. The rear wing of the Grand Palais, opening on to avenue Franklin-D-Roosevelt, contains the **Palais de la Découverte** science museum.

To the north lie more smart shops, antiques dealers and bastions of officialdom; on circular place Beauvau, wrought-iron gates herald the Ministry of the Interior. The 18th-century Palais de l'Elysée, the official presidential residence, is at 55-57 rue du Fbg-St-Honoré. Nearby, with gardens extending to avenue Gabriel, are the palatial **British Embassy** and the ambassadorial residence, which was once the Hôtel Borghèse.

The western end of the Champs-Elysées is dominated by the **Arc de Triomphe** towering above place Charles-de-Gaulle, also known as L'Etoile. Built by Napoleon, the arch was modified to celebrate the Revolutionary

armies. From the top, visitors can gaze over the square (commissioned later by Haussmann), with 12 avenues radiating out in all directions.

South of the arch, avenue Kléber leads to the monumental buildings and terraced gardens of the panoramic Trocadéro, which now houses the aquarium and cinema, **Cinéaqua**. The vast 1930s **Palais de Chaillot** dominates the hill and houses four museums, plus the **Théâtre National de Chaillot** (*see p104*).

To the west of Chaillot, on avenue du Président-Wilson, are two major museums: the **Musée d'Art Moderne de la Ville de Paris** and the **Palais de Tokyo Site de Création Contemporaine** are both inside the **Palais de Tokyo** building. Opposite is the **Musée Galliera**, used for fashion exhibitions, and up the hill at place d'Iéna are the Asian and oriental art collections of the **Musée National des Arts Asiatiques – Guimet**.

Towards the Champs-Elysées, the former townhouse of avant-garde patron Marie-Laure de Noailles has been given a rather cheeky revamp. It now houses the **Galerie-Musée Baccarat**.

Arc de Triomphe
Pl Charles-de-Gaulle (access via underpass), 8th (01.55.37.73.77). M° Charles de Gaulle Etoile. **Open** *Oct-Mar* 10am-10.30pm daily. *Apr-Sept* 10am-11pm daily. **Admission** €9; €5.50 reductions; free under-18s. PMP. **Credit** AmEx, MC, V.
See below **Triumphal arch**.

Cimetière de Passy
2 rue du Commandant-Schloesing, 16th (01.53.70.40.80). M° Trocadéro. **Open** *16 Mar- 5 Nov* 8am-5.30pm Mon-Fri; 8.30am-5.30pm Sat; 9am-5.30pm Sun. *6 Nov-15 Mar* 8am-6pm Mon-Fri; 8.30am-6pm Sat; 9am-6pm Sun. **Admission** free.
Since 1874, this cemetery has been one of the most desirable Paris locations in which to be laid to rest. Here you'll find Debussy and Fauré,

Manet and his sister-in-law Berthe Morisot, writer Giraudoux, along with various generals and politicians.

Cinéaqua
2 av des Nations Unies, 16th (01.40.69.23.23, www.cineaqua.com). M° Trocadéro. **Open** *Apr-Sept* 10am-7pm daily. *Oct-Mar* 10am-6pm daily. **Admission** €19.50; €12.50-€15.50 reductions; free under-3s. **Credit** MC, V.
This aquarium and three-screen cinema is a wonderful attraction and a key element in the renaissance of the once moribund Trocadéro. Many people have baulked at the admission price, but there are often discounts via the website.

Cité de l'Architecture et du Patrimoine
Palais de Chaillot, 1 pl du Trocadéro, 16th (01.58.51.52.00, www.citechaillot.fr). M° Trocadéro. **Open** 11am-7pm Mon, Wed, Fri-Sun; 11am-9pm Thur. **Admission** €8; €5 reductions; free under-18s. **Credit** MC, V.
This architecture and heritage museum impresses principally by its scale. The ground floor is filled with life-size mock-ups of cathedral façades and heritage buildings, and interactive screens place the models in context. Upstairs, darkened rooms house full-scale copies of medieval and Renaissance murals and stained-glass windows. The highlight of the modern architecture section is the walk-in replica of an apartment from Le Corbusier's Cité Radieuse in Marseille. Temporary exhibitions are hosted in the large basement area.

Fondation d'Enterprise Paul Ricard
12 rue Boissy d'Anglas, 8th (01.53.30.88.00, www.fondation-entreprise-ricard.com). M° Concorde. **Open** 10am-7pm Mon-Fri. **Admission** free.
The Pastis firm promotes modern art with the Prix Paul Ricard, where young French artists are shortlisted by an independent curator for an annual prize. This coincides with FIAC (*see p13*) each autumn.

Fondation Mona Bismarck
34 av de New-York, 16th (01.47.23.38.88, www.monabismarck.org). M° Alma Marceau. **Open** 10.30am-6.30pm Tue-Sat. Closed Aug. **Admission** free.
The Fondation provides a chic setting for eclectic exhibitions, from Etruscan antiquities to folk art.

Fondation Pierre Bergé Yves Saint Laurent
3 rue Léonce-Reynaud, 16th (01.44.31.64.00, www.fondation-pb-ysl.net). M° Alma Marceau. **Open** 9.30am-1pm, 2.30-6pm Mon-Fri. Closed Aug. **Admission** €5; €3 reductions; free under-10s. **Credit** AmEx, MC, V.
When Yves Saint Laurent bowed out of designing in 2002, he reopened his fashion house as this foundation, exhibiting Picasso and Warhol paintings with the dresses they closely inspired. Every sketch and every *toile* has been carefully catalogued, and many of Saint Laurent's friends and clients have presented the designer with the dresses he created for them, stored in the upper floors at precisely 18 degrees centigrade and a hygrometric level of 50 per cent.

Galerie-Musée Baccarat
11 pl des Etats-Unis, 16th (01.40.22.11.00, www.baccarat.fr). M° Boissière or Iéna. **Open** 10am-6pm Mon, Wed-Sat. **Admission** €5; €3.50 reductions; free under-18s. **Credit** *Shop* AmEx, DC, MC, V.
Philippe Starck has created a neo-rococo wonderland in the former mansion of the Vicomtesse de Noailles. From the red carpet entrance with a chandelier in a fish tank to the Alchemy room, decorated by Gérard Garouste, there's a play of light and movement that makes Baccarat's work sing. See items by designers Georges Chevalier and Ettore Sottsass, services made for princes and maharajahs, and monumental items made for the great exhibitions of the 1800s.

Galeries Nationales du Grand Palais
3 av du Général-Eisenhower, 8th (01.44.13.17.17, www.grandpalais.fr). M° Champs-Elysées Clemenceau. **Open** times vary. **Admission** €11-€12; €8 reductions; free under-13s. **Admission** *Before 1pm with reservation* €12. *After 1pm without reservation* €9 reductions; free under-13s. **Credit** MC, V.
Built for the 1900 Exposition Universelle, the Grand Palais was the work of three different architects, each of whom designed a façade. During World War II it accommodated Nazi tanks. In 1994, the magnificent glass-roofed central hall was closed when bits of metal started falling off. After major restoration, the Palais reopened in 2005.

Triumphal arch

The **Arc de Triomphe** (*see above*) is the city's second most iconic monument after the Eiffel Tower – older, shorter, but far more symbolically important: indeed, the island on which it stands, in the centre of the vast traffic junction of l'Etoile, is the nearest thing to sacred ground in all of secular France, indelibly associated as it is with two of French history's greatest men. The first was the man who had it built. Napoleon ordered the Arc de Triomphe's construction in 1809 as a monument to the achievements of his armies, but he never lived to see it finished: the arch was only completed in 1836 (although the emperor did view a full-size wood and canvas mock-up when he entered the city with his new wife Marie-Louise of Austria in 1810). Nonetheless, it bears the names of Napoleon's victories and key military subordinates, and is decorated on its flanks with a frieze of battle scenes and sculptures, including Rude's famous *Le Départ des Volontaires* (aka La Marseillaise).

The Arc has had martial associations ever since: victorious French troops paraded through it at the end of World War I, and the tomb of the Unknown Soldier lies under its centre, below an eternal flame that is relit in a solemn

ceremony every evening. The man who relit it on 26 August 1944 is the Arc's other great figure, Charles de Gaulle, who followed the reignition ceremony with an iconic march through Paris; the text of his famous 1940 radio broadcast from London is immortalised in a bronze plaque in the ground.

Despite such grand associations, until recently the interior of the Arc was far less impressive, having changed little since the 1930s. As Jean-Paul Ciret, director of cultural development for France's national monuments, put it: 'The way we were showing the Arc to visitors was not worthy of an important landmark. There was no light inside, and the ceiling was dirty.'

But now, after a revamp by architect Christophe Girault and artist Maurice Benayouna, there is an impressive new museum with interactive screens and multimedia displays allowing visitors to look at other famous arches throughout Europe and the world, as well as screens exploring the Arc's tumultuous 200-year history, before heading up to the roof and taking in one of the finest views in the city. And last June saw the finishing touches when the four largest bas-reliefs were once again revealed to the public in all their splendour.

Musée d'Art Moderne de la Ville de Paris

11 av du Président-Wilson, 16th (01.53.67.40.00, www.mam.paris.fr). M° Alma Marceau or Iéna. **Open** 10am-6pm Tue-Sun. **Admission** free. *Temporary exhibitions* €4.50-€9; €3/€4.50 reductions; free under-13s. **No credit cards.**

This monumental 1930s building, housing the city's modern art collection, is strong on the Cubists, Fauves, the Delaunays, Rouault and Ecole de Paris artists Soutine and van Dongen. The museum was briefly closed in May 2010 after the theft of five masterpieces. The €100-million haul netted paintings by Picasso, Matisse, Braque, Modigliani and Léger.

Musée de la Contrefaçon

16 rue de la Faisanderie, 16th (01.56.26.14.00). M° Porte Dauphine. **Open** 9am-12.30pm, 2-5.30pm Tue-Sun. **Admission** €4; €3 reductions; free under-12s. **No credit cards.**

This museum was set up by the French anti-counterfeiting association with the aim of deterring forgers, but playing spot-the-fake with brands such as Reebok, Lacoste and Vuitton is fun for visitors.

Musée Dapper

35bis rue Paul-Valéry, 16th (01.45.00.91.75, www.dapper.com.fr). M° Victor Hugo. **Open** 11am-7pm Mon, Wed-Sun. **Admission** €6; €4 reductions; free under-26s, all last Wed of mth. **Credit** MC, V.

Named after 17th-century Dutch humanist Olfert Dapper, the Fondation Dapper began as an organisation dedicated to preserving sub-Saharan art. Reopened in 2000, the venue houses a performance space, bookshop and café. Each year it stages two African-themed exhibitions.

Musée National des Arts Asiatiques – Guimet

6 pl d'Iéna, 16th (01.56.52.53.00, www.musee guimet.fr). M° Iéna. **Open** 10am-5.45pm Mon, Wed-Sun (last entry 5.15pm). **Admission** €7.50; €5.50 reductions; free under-18s. PMP. **Credit** *Shop* AmEx, DC, MC, V.

Founded by industrialist Emile Guimet in 1889 to house his collection of Chinese and Japanese religious art, and later incorporating oriental collections from the Louvre, the museum has 45,000 objects from neolithic times onwards. Lower galleries focus on India and South-east Asia, centred on stunning Hindu and Buddhist Khmer sculpture

from Cambodia. Don't miss the Giant's Way, part of the entrance to a temple complex at Angkor Wat. Upstairs, Chinese antiquities include mysterious jade discs. Afghan glassware and Moghul jewellery also feature.

Musée National de la Marine

Palais de Chaillot, 17 pl du Trocadéro, 16th (01.53.65.69.69, www.musee-marine.fr). M° Trocadéro. **Open** 10am-6pm Mon, Wed-Sun. **Admission** *Main collection & temporary exhibitions* €9; €3-€7 reductions; free under-6s. *Main collection* €7; €5 reductions; free under-18s. PMP. **Credit** *Shop* MC, V.

French naval history is outlined in detailed models of battleships and Vernet's series of paintings of French ports (1754-65). There's also an imperial barge, built when Napoleon's delusions of grandeur were reaching their zenith in 1810.

Palais de Chaillot

Pl du Trocadéro, 16th. M° Trocadéro. **Admission** free.

This immense pseudo-classical building was constructed by Azéma, Boileau and Carlu for the 1937 international exhibition, with giant sculptures of Apollo by Henri Bouchard, and inscriptions by Paul Valéry. The Palais houses the Musée National de la Marine and the Musée de l'Homme (closed for renovation until 2012). In the east wing are the Théâtre National de Chaillot (*see p104*) and the Cité de l'Architecture et du Patrimoine (*see p24*).

Palais de la Découverte

Av Franklin-D-Roosevelt, 8th (01.56.43.20.21, www.palais-decouverte.fr). M° Champs-Elysées Clemenceau or Franklin D. Roosevelt. **Open** 9.30am-6pm Tue-Sat; 10am-7pm Sun (last entry 30mins before closing). **Admission** €7; €4.50 reductions; free under-5s. *Planetarium* €3.50. **Credit** AmEx, MC, V.

This science museum houses designs dating from Leonardo da Vinci's time to the present. Models, real apparatus and audiovisual material bring displays to life, and permanent exhibits cover astrophysics, astronomy, biology, chemistry, physics and earth sciences. The Planète Terre section highlights meteorology, and one room is dedicated to the sun. There are shows at the Planetarium too.

Palais de Tokyo: Site de Création Contemporaine

13 av du Président-Wilson, 16th (01.47.23.54.01, www.palaisdetokyo.com).

M° Alma Marceau or Iéna. **Open** noon-midnight Tue-Sun. **Admission** €9; €4.50-€6 reductions; free under-18s, art students. When it opened in 2002, many thought the Palais' stripped-back interior was a design statement. In fact, it was a response to tight finances. The 1937 building has now come into its own with a skylit central hall hosting exhibitions and performances. Extended hours and a funky café have drawn a younger audience, and the roll-call of artists is impressive (Pierre Joseph, Wang Du and others). The name dates to the 1937 Exposition Internationale, but is also a reminder of links with a new generation of artists from the Far East.

Monceau & Batignolles

In the 8th & 17th arrondissements. Parc Monceau, with its neo-antique follies and large lily pond, lies at the far end of avenue Hoche (the main entrance is on boulevard de Courcelles, the circular pavilion by Ledoux). Three museums capture the extravagance of the area when it was newly fashionable in the 19th century: the **Musée Jacquemart-André**, with its Old Masters, the **Musée Nissim de Camondo** (superb 18th-century decorative arts), and the **Musée Cernuschi** (Chinese art). There are some nice exotic touches too, such as the unlikely red lacquer **Galerie Ching Tsai Too** (48 rue de Courcelles, 8th), built in 1926 for a dealer in oriental art near the wrought-iron gates of Parc Monceau, and the onion domes of the Russian Orthodox **Alexander Nevsky Cathedral** on rue Daru. Built in the mid 19th century, when a stay in Paris was essential to the education of every Russian aristocrat, it is still at the heart of an émigré little Russia.

Famed for its stand during the 1871 Paris Commune, the Quartier des Batignolles to the north-east towards place de Clichy is more working class, housing the rue de Lévis market,

tenements lining the deep railway canyon and square des Batignolles park, with the pretty **Eglise Ste-Marie-de-Batignolles** looking on to a semi-circular square. It's fast becoming trendy, with a restaurant scene to match.

Alexander Nevsky Cathedral

12 rue Daru, 17th (01.42.27.37.34, www.cathedrale-orthodoxe.com). M° Courcelles. **Open** times vary. **Admission** free.

All onion domes, icons and incense, this Russian Orthodox church was completed in 1861 in the neo-Byzantine Novgorod-style of the 1600s, by the tsar's architect Kouzmin, responsible for the Fine Arts Academy in St Petersburg.

Cimetière des Batignolles

8 rue St-Just, 17th (01.53.06.38.68). M° Porte de Clichy. **Open** 16 Mar-6 Nov 8am-5.45pm Mon-Fri; 8.30am-5.45pm Sat; 9am-5.45pm Sun & public hols. 7 Nov-15 Mar 8am-5.15pm Mon-Fri; 8.30am-5.15pm Sat; 9am-5.15pm Sun & public hols. **Admission** free.

Squeezed inside the Périphérique are the graves of poet Paul Verlaine, Surrealist André Breton, and Léon Bakst, costume designer of the Ballets Russes.

Musée Cernuschi

7 av Velasquez, 8th (01.53.96.21.50, www.cernuschi.paris.fr). M° Monceau or Villiers. **Open** 10am-6pm Tue-Sun. **Admission** free. *Temporary exhibitions* €7.50-€9; €3.80-€6 reductions; free under-18s.

Since the banker Henri Cernuschi built a *hôtel particulier* by the Parc Monceau for the treasures he found in the Far East in 1871, this collection of Chinese art has grown steadily. The fabulous displays range from legions of Han and Wei dynasty funeral statues to refined Tang celadon wares and Sung porcelain.

Musée Jacquemart-André

158 bd Haussmann, 8th (01.45.62.11.59, www.musee-jacquemart-andre.com). M° Miromesnil or St-Philippe-du-Roule. **Open** 10am-6pm daily. **Admission** €11; €8.50 reductions; free under-7s. **Credit** AmEx, MC, V.

Long terrace steps and a pair of stone lions usher visitors into this grand 19th-century mansion, home to a collection of *objets d'art* and fine paintings. The collection was assembled by Edouard André and his artist wife Nélie Jacquemart, using money inherited from his rich banking family.

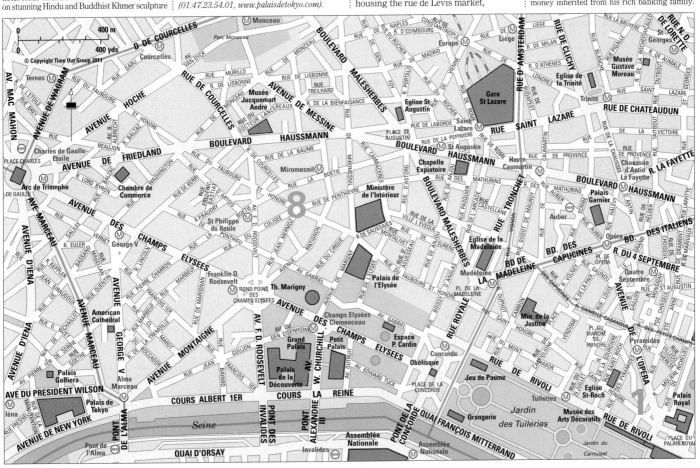

The mansion was built to order to house their art hoard, which includes Rembrandts, Tiepolo frescoes and various paintings by Italian masters Uccello, Mantegna and Carpaccio. The adjacent tearoom, with its fabulous tottering cakes, is a favourite with the smart lunch set.

Musée National Jean-Jacques Henner

43 av de Villiers, 17th (01.47.63.42.73, www.musee-henner.fr). M° Malesherbes. **Open** 11am-6pm Mon, Wed-Sun. **Admission** €5; free-€3 reductions.

Reopened in 2009 after four years of renovation, the Musée National Jean-Jacques Henner traces the life of one of France's most respected artists, from his humble beginnings in Alsace in 1829 to his rise as one of the most sought-after painters in Paris. On the first floor, Alsatian landscapes and family portraits are a reminder of the artist's lifelong attachment to his native region. What brought the artist most acclaim (and criticism), however, was his trademark nymph paintings.

Musée Nissim de Camondo

63 rue de Monceau, 8th (01.53.89.06.50, www.lesartsdecoratifs.fr). M° Monceau or Villiers. **Open** 10am-5.30pm Wed-Sun. **Admission** €7; €5 reductions; free under-18s. PMP. **Credit** AmEx, MC, V.

Put together by Count Moïse de Camondo, this collection is named after his son Nissim, who was killed in World War I. Moïse replaced the family's two houses near Parc Monceau with this palatial residence and lived here in a style in keeping with his love of the 18th century. Grand first-floor reception rooms are filled with furniture by craftsmen of the Louis XV and XVI eras, silver services, Sèvres and Meissen porcelain, Savonnerie carpets and Aubusson tapestries.

Parc Monceau

Bd de Courcelles, av Hoche, rue Monceau, 8th. M° Monceau. **Open** *Nov-Mar* 7am-8pm daily. *Apr-Oct* 7am-10pm daily. **Admission** free.

Surrounded by grand *hôtels particuliers* and elegant Haussmannian apartments, Monceau is a favourite with well-dressed children and their nannies. It was laid out in the 18th century for the Duc de Chartres in the English style, with a lake, lawns and a variety of follies: an Egyptian pyramid, a Corinthian colonnade, Venetian bridge and sarcophagi.

Passy & Auteuil

In the 16th arrondissement.

West of l'Etoile, the extensive 16th arrondissement is the epitome of bourgeois respectability, with grandiose apartments and exclusive residences lining the private roads. It's also home to some seminal examples of modernist architecture, plus several of the city's most important museums.

When Balzac lived at no.47 rue Raynouard in the 1840s, Passy was a country village (it was absorbed into the city in 1860) where the rich came to take cures at its mineral springs – a history alluded to by rue des Eaux. The novelist's former abode, **Maison de Balzac**, is open to the public. The **Musée du Vin** is of interest if only for its setting in the cellars of the wine-producing Abbaye de Minimes, destroyed in the Revolution. Rue de Passy, formerly the village high street, and parallel rue de l'Assomption, are the focus of local life, with fashion shops and *traiteurs*, the department store **Franck et Fils** (80 rue de Passy, 16th, 01.44.14.38.00) and a covered market.

West of the former high society pleasure gardens of the Jardin du Ranelagh you'll find the **Musée Marmottan**, with its superb collection of Monet's late water-lily canvases, other Impressionists and Empire furniture.

FEATURED ESTABLISHMENT

Next to the Pont de Grenelle stands the circular **Maison de Radio France**, the giant home of state broadcasting. You can attend concerts (*see p97*) or take a tour around its endless corridors. From here, in more upmarket Auteuil, you can head up rue Fontaine, the best place to find art nouveau architecture by Hector Guimard, of métro entrance fame. He also designed the less ambitious nos.19 and 21. At no.96 pay homage to Proust, who was born here.

Nearby, the **Fondation Le Corbusier** occupies two of the architect's avant-garde houses in square du Dr-Blanche. A little further up rue du Dr-Blanche sculptor Henri Bouchard himself commissioned the studio and house that is now the dusty **Atelier-Musée Henri Bouchard**. Much of the rest of Auteuil is private territory, with exclusive streets of residences off rue Chardon-Lagache; the studio of 19th-century sculptor Jean-Baptiste Carpeaux remains, looking rather lost, at no.39 boulevard Exelmans. The top storey was added by Guimard.

West of the 16th, across the Périphérique, sprawls the parkland of **Bois de Boulogne**. At porte d'Auteuil are the romantic **Serres d'Auteuil** and sports venues the **Parc des Princes**, home of football club Paris St-Germain (for both, *see p102*), and **Roland Garros** (*see p102*), host of the French Tennis Open. Another attraction will open in 2012: the **Fondation Louis-Vuitton**, to be housed in a new Frank Gehry glass construction.

Bois de Boulogne

16th. M° Les Sablons or Porte Dauphine. **Admission** free.

Covering 865 hectares, the Bois was once the Forêt de Rouvray hunting grounds. It was landscaped in the 1860s, when artificial grottoes and waterfalls were created around the Lac Inférieur. The Jardin de Bagatelle (route de Sèvres à Neuilly, 16th, 01.40.67.97.00) is famous for its roses, daffodils and water lilies, and contains an orangery that rings to the sound of Chopin in summer. The Jardin d'Acclimatation (*see p88*) is a children's amusement park, with a miniature train, farm, rollercoaster and boat rides. The Bois also boasts two racecourses (Longchamp and Auteuil), sports clubs and stables.

Castel Béranger

14 rue La Fontaine, 16th. M° Jasmin.

Guimard's masterpiece of 1895-98 epitomises art nouveau in Paris. From outside you can see his love of brick and wrought iron, asymmetry and renunciation of harsh angles not found in nature. Green seahorses climb the façade, and the faces on the balconies are thought to be self-portraits, inspired by Japanese figures, to ward off evil spirits.

Fondation Le Corbusier

Villa La Roche, 8-10 square du Dr-Blanche, 16th (01.42.88.41.53, www.fondation lecorbusier.fr). M° Jasmin. **Open** 1.30-6pm Mon; 10am-6pm Tue-Thur; 10am-5pm Fri, Sat. Closed Aug. **Admission** €2-€4; free under-14s. **No credit cards.**

Designed by Le Corbusier in 1923 for a Swiss art collector, this house shows the architect's ideas in practice, with its stilts, strip windows, roof terraces and balconies, built-in furniture and an unsuspected use of colour inside: sludge green, blue and pinky beige. A sculptural cylindrical staircase and split volumes create a variety of geometrical vistas; inside, Le Corbusier's own neo-Cubist paintings and furniture sit alongside pieces by Perriand. Adjoining Villa Jeanneret houses the foundation's library.

Le Jardin des Serres d'Auteuil

3 av de la Porte d'Auteuil, 16th (01.40.71.75.23). M° Porte d'Auteuil. **Open** *Winter* 10am-5pm daily. *Summer* 10am-6pm daily. **Admission** free.

These romantic glasshouses were opened in 1895 to cultivate plants for Paris parks and public spaces. Today, there are seasonal displays of orchids and begonias. Look out for the steamy tropical pavilion, which is home to palms, birds and Japanese ornamental carp.

Maison de Balzac

47 rue Raynouard, 16th (01.55.74.41.80). M° Passy. **Open** 10am-6pm Tue-Sun. **Admission** €4; €2-€3 reductions; free under-13s. **Credit** MC, V.

Honoré de Balzac rented this apartment in 1840 to escape his creditors. Converted into a museum, it has memorabilia spread over several floors. Mementos include first editions and letters, plus portraits of friends and the novelist's mistress Mme Hanska, with whom he corresponded for years before they married. Along with a 'family tree' of his characters that extends across several walls, you can see Balzac's desk and the monogrammed coffee pot that fuelled all-night work on *Comédie Humaine*.

Musée Marmottan – Claude Monet

2 rue Louis-Boilly, 16th (01.44.96.50.33, www.marmottan.com). M° La Muette. **Open** 11am-9pm Tue (last entry 8.30pm); 11am-6pm Wed-Sun (last entry 5.30pm). **Admission** €9; €5 reductions; free under-8s. **Credit** MC, V.

Originally a museum of the Empire period left to the state by collector Paul Marmottan, this old hunting pavilion has become a famed holder of Impressionist art thanks to two bequests: the first by the daughter of the doctor of Manet, Monet, Pissarro, Sisley and Renoir; the second by Monet's son Michel. Its Monet collection, the largest in the world, numbers 165 works, plus sketchbooks, palette and photos. A special circular room was created for the breathtaking late water lily canvases; upstairs are works by Renoir, Manet, Gauguin, Caillebotte and Berthe Morisot, 15th-century primitives, a Sèvres clock and a collection of First Empire furniture.

Musée du Vin

Rue des Eaux, 16th (01.45.25.63.26, www.museeduvinparis.com). M° Passy. **Open** 10am-6pm Tue-Sun. **Admission** (with guidebook and glass of wine) €11.90; €9.90 reductions; free under-14s, diners in the restaurant. **Credit** *Shop, restaurant* AmEx, DC, MC, V.

Here the Confrères Bacchiques defend French wines from imports and advertising laws. In the cellars of an old wine-producing monastery are displays on the history of viticulture, with waxwork peasants, old tools, bottles and corkscrews. Visits finish up with a wine tasting and, a paid extra, a meal.

Montmartre & Pigalle

Back in the 1930s, literary geographers such as the celebrated *flâneur* Léon-Paul Fargue could still describe Montmartre as 'a pocket of provincial France lodged in Paris', but these days it's one of the most conspicuously tourist-heavy parts of the city. That's not to say it has entirely lost its soul, however: the district that was only made an official part of the city in 1860 is riddled with romantic narrow streets and the famous steep staircases of countless black-and-white photos, and it's easier than one might think to lose sight of the package holiday hordes. And although Montmartre's artistic star has faded, its appetite for after-dark revelry hasn't: there's a wealth of hip bars and cafés here, and at the bottom of the hill, in once-notorious Pigalle, the seediness of yesteryear is steadily being replaced by hot music venues and nightspots.

Montmartre

In the 18th arrondissement.

Perched on a hill (or *butte*), Montmartre is the highest point in Paris, its tightly

Belmondo rediscovered

For most people in France, the name Belmondo has always been associated with Nouvelle Vague actor Jean-Paul; that sexy, thick-lipped heartthrob, with a distinguished boxer's nose, who shot to stardom in 1960s films such as Jean-Luc Godard's *A Bout de Souffle* (Breathless). What most of us don't know is that the actor's father, Paul (1898-1982), was one of France's most important 20th-century sculptors, and one of the last to use neoclassical, academic techniques.

Many of his works (characterised by harmonious forms, unfussy lines and smooth surfaces) epitomise the 1930s style, particularly the gracious proportions of *La Danse*, in the Théatre de Chaillot, which was commissioned for Paris's Universal Exposition in 1937; and two statues in the Jardin de Tuileries (a well-hung *Apollo* and an elegant *Jeanette*). Since the war, Paul Belmondo's talents have mysteriously remained unknown to most, but the spanking new **Musée Belmondo** (14 rue de

L'Abreuvoir, 92100 Boulogne-Billancourt, 01.55.18.69.01, www.museepaulbelmondo.fr, open 2-6pm Tue-Fri, 11am-6pm Sat, Sun), set inside in the 18th-century, neoclassical Château Buchillot in Boulogne-Billancourt, looks set to thrust his works back into the limelight. The space, entirely revamped by architects Chartier-Corbasson, is an interior designer's dream – the mix of stark white, black and timber materials lend a different mood to each section. Several rooms harbour niches and alcoves in which Belmondo's sculpture's sit enticingly, as if in a workshop; and numerous artificial backdrops, along with raised floors and frames, create multiple sightlines. Clever use of natural and artificial lighting highlights the detail on each sculpture, and a special 'replica' room on the first floor encourages visitors to feel the works' grooves and textures.

The visit ends in the château gardens, where works created by Belmondo's contemporaries – Raoul Lamourdedieu, Pierre Traverse, Léon Séverac, Karl-Jean Longuet, Henri Le Pecq, Marcel Chauvenet-Delclos and Marguerite Cossaceanu-Lavrillier – pepper the lawns in 1930s glory. A real treat for lovers of art deco and a godsend on a sunny day.

The Louvre

The world's largest museum is also its most visited, with an incredible 8.5 million visitors in 2009. It is a city within the city, a vast, multi-level maze of galleries, passageways, staircases and escalators. It's famous for the artistic glories it contains within, but the very fabric of the museum is a masterpiece in itself – or rather, a collection of masterpieces modified and added to from one century to another. And because nothing in Paris ever stands still, the additions and modifications continue into the present day, with a major new Islamic Arts department set to open in 2012, and the franchising of the Louvre 'brand' via new outposts in Lens (www.louvre lens.fr) and Abu Dhabi. If any place demonstrates the central importance of culture in French life, this is it.

Much like the building itself, the Louvre's collections were built up over the centuries. They encompass a rich visual history of the western world, from Ancient Egypt and Mesopotamia to the 19th century. Indeed, one of the most impressive things about the Louvre is the way it juxtaposes architecture and content. Look up from a case of Greek or Roman antiquities and you might see an 18th-century painted ceiling, or two doves by Braque. In the Egyptian section you'll find Louis XIV's bedchamber, complete with gilded bed, while Renaissance art is housed in the Grande Galerie, where the Sun King performed the 'scrofula ceremony', blessing the sick. In between exhibits, the Louvre's long windows afford stunning views of the building's façades, gardens and lovely interior courtyards.

Some 35,000 works of art and artefacts are on show, split into eight departments and housed in three wings: Denon, Sully and Richelieu. Under the atrium of the glass pyramid, each wing has its own entrance, though you can pass from one to another. Treasures from the Egyptians, Etruscans, Greeks and Romans each have their own galleries in the Denon and Sully wings, as do Middle Eastern and Islamic art. The first floor of Richelieu is taken up with European decorative arts from the Middle Ages up to the 19th century, including room after room of Napoleon III's lavish apartments.

The main draw, though, is the painting and sculpture. Two glass-roofed sculpture courts contain the famous Marly horses on the ground floor of Richelieu, with French sculpture below and Italian Renaissance pieces in the Denon wing. The Grand Galerie and Salle de la Joconde (home to the *Mona Lisa*), like a mini Uffizi, run the length of Denon's first floor with French Romantic painting alongside. Dutch and French painting occupies the second floor of Richelieu and Sully. Jean-Pierre Wilmotte's minimalist galleries in the Denon wing were designed as a taster for the Musée du Quai Branly, with art from Africa, the Americas and Oceania.

Mitterrand's Grand Louvre project expanded the museum two-fold. But the organisation and restoration of the Louvre are still a work in progress: check the website or lists in the Carrousel du Louvre to see which galleries are closed on certain days to avoid missing out on what you want to see.

The museum is also trying to strike a balance between highbrow culture and accessibility. Photography was banned in 2005 at the request of mainly French visitors, who complained that it interfered with their enjoyment; meanwhile, laminated panels found throughout provide a surprisingly lively commentary and the superb website is a technological feat unsurpassed by that of any of the world's major museums.

ADVANCE TICKETS AND ENTRANCE

IM Pei's glass pyramid is a wonderful piece of architecture, but it's not the only entrance to the museum – there are three others. Buying a ticket in advance means you can go in directly via the passage Richelieu off rue de Rivoli, or via the Carrousel du Louvre shopping mall (there are steps down either side of the Arc de Triomphe du Carrousel, at 99 rue de Rivoli or from the métro).

Advance tickets are valid for any day, and are available from the Louvre website or branches of Fnac

and Virgin Megastore (for both, *see p82*). You can buy one from the Virgin in the Carrousel du Louvre and use it immediately. Another option is to buy a ticket at the Cour des Lions entrance (closed Fridays) in the south-west corner of the complex, convenient for the Italian collections. The Louvre is also accessible with the all-in Paris Museum Pass. Finally, don't forget that the Louvre is closed on Tuesdays.

OTHER TIPS

● The Louvre's website, much of which is in English, is an unbeatable resource. Every work on display is photographed, and you can search the Atlas database by room, artist or theme.
● Laminated cards in each room provide useful background information. Audioguides (€6, €2-€4 reductions; ID must be left) are available at the main entrances in the Carrousel du Louvre.
● Don't attempt to see more than two collections in one day. Your ticket is valid all day and you can leave and re-enter the museum as you wish.
● On Fridays after 6pm entry is free for the under-26s, but if you plan to make several visits, the Carte Louvre Jeunes (€15 per year under-26s, €30 per year under-30s) is worth getting.
● Some rooms are closed on a weekly basis – check on 01.40.20.53.17 or at www.louvre.fr.

The Louvre

Rue de Rivoli, 1st (01.40.20.50.50, recorded information 01.40.20.53.17, disabled access 01.40.20.59.90, www.louvre.fr). M° Palais Royal Musée du Louvre. **Open** 9am-6pm Mon, Thur, Sat, Sun; 9am-10pm Wed, Fri. **Admission** *Permanent collections* €9.50 (incl entry to the Musée Delacroix but not shows at the Salle Napoléon); €6 6-9.45pm Wed, Fri; free under-18s, all 1st Sun of mth. PMP. *Exhibitions* €11. *Combined ticket* €14; €12 6-9.45pm Wed, Fri. **Credit** AmEx, MC, V.

The collections

History of the Louvre

Sully: lower ground floor. Shown as dark brown on Louvre maps.
Here you can explore the medieval foundations of the Louvre, dating back to Philippe-Auguste's reign. Uncovered in 1985 during excavations for the Grand Louvre project, they include the remains of the moat that once surrounded the fort and the pillars of two drawbridges; the La Taillerie tower, with heart symbols cut into the stone by masons; and the outside of the dungeons. A well and a portion of ground have been left undisturbed, showing artefacts just as they were found, and a scale model shows the fortress at the time of Charles V. An exhibition in the Saint-Louis room – a guard room from the era of Philippe-Auguste, discovered in 1882 – recounts the history of the Louvre through rare archaeological finds.

Ancient Egypt

Denon: lower ground floor; Sully: lower ground, ground & 1st floors. Green on Louvre maps.
Announced by the pink granite Giant Sphinx (1898-1866 BC), the Egyptian department divides into two routes. The Thematic Circuit on the ground floor presents Nile culture (fishing, agriculture, hunting, daily and cultural life, religion and death). One of the big draws is the Mastaba of Akhethetep, a decorated burial chamber from Sakkara dating back to 2400 BC. Six small sphinxes, apes from Luxor and the lion-headed goddess Sekhmet recreate elements of temple complexes, while stone sarcophagi, mummies, amulets, jewellery and entrails form a vivid display on funeral rites. A display of Egyptian furniture (room 8, ground floor) dating from 1550 to 1069 BC contains pieces that look almost contemporary in design.

On the first floor the Pharoah Circuit is laid out chronologically, from the Seated Scribe and other stone figures of the Ancient Empire, via the painted figures of the Middle Empire, to the New Empire, with its animal-headed statues of gods and goddesses, hieroglyphic tablets and papyrus scrolls. Look for the statue of the god Amun protecting Tutankhamun, and the black diorite 'cube statues' of priests and

attendants. The collection, one of the largest hoards of Egyptian antiquities in the world, has its origins in Napoleon's Egyptian campaign of 1798 and 1799, and the work of Egyptologist Jean-François Champollion, who deciphered hieroglyphics in 1824. The Coptic gallery, on the lower ground floor, houses textiles and manuscripts.

Oriental antiquities

Richelieu: lower ground & ground floors; Sully: ground floor. Yellow on Louvre maps.
This section deals with Mesopotamia, Persia and the Levant from the fifth millennium BC to the first century AD. The huge Mesopotamian rooms contain glistening diorite sculptures from the Akkad dynasty and Gudea from the third millennium BC; in some cases, only the feet have survived intact. Make sure you don't miss the serene alabaster sculpture of Ebih-II, the superintendant of Mari (room 1b), and the earliest evidence of writing, in the form of fourth-century BC Sumerian tablets (room 1a). The Hammurabi Code, an essential document of Babylonian civilisation, is a black basalt stele recording 282 laws beneath reliefs of the king and the sun god; it's one of the oldest collections of laws in the history of mankind (room 3).

Next come two breathtaking palace reconstructions: the great court, c713 BC, from the palace of Sargon II at Khorsabad (in present-day Iraq), with its giant bearded and winged bulls and friezes of warriors and servants (room 4); and the palace of Darius I at Susa (now Iran), c510 BC, with its glazed-brick reliefs of archers, lions and griffins (room 12). The double-bull-headed column was one of 36 such gigantic supports at the palace. Entering the Iranian section, you find 5,000-year-old statues from Susa housed in the circular room 8, and a fine view of the Cour Napoleon. The Levantine section includes Cypriot animalistic vases and carved reliefs from Byblos.

Islamic arts

Richelieu: lower ground floor. Turquoise on Louvre maps.
The Louvre's Islamic decorative arts include early glassware, tenth- to 12th-century dishes decorated with birds and calligraphy, traditional Iranian blue-and-white wares, Iznik ceramics, intricate inlaid metalwork from Syria, tiles, screens, weapons and funerary steles. The highlight is three magnificent 16th-century kelims. In 2005, a Saudi prince, Prince Walid bin Talal, gave over €17 million – one of the largest donations in French cultural history – for a new Islamic wing to be built as an extension to the southern wing. The Department of Islamic Arts is currently closed, but is scheduled to reopen in a new gallery in the Cour Visconti in 2012.

Greek, Roman & Etruscan antiquities

Denon: lower ground & ground floors; Sully: ground & 1st floors. Blue on Louvre maps.
The Winged Victory of Samothrace, a headless Greek statue dating from the second century BC, stands sentinel at the top of the grand staircase, giving an idea of its original dramatic impact on a promontory overlooking the Aegean sea. This huge department is made up of pieces amassed by François I and Cardinal Richelieu, plus the Borghese collection (acquired in 1808), and the Campana collection of thousands of painted Greek vases and small terracottas. Endless dark rooms on the first floor harbour small bronze, silver and terracotta objects, but the really exciting stuff is on the ground floor. The grandiose, vaulted marble rooms are a fitting location for masterpieces such as the 2.3m (7.5ft) *Athena Peacemaker* and the *Venus de Milo* (room 12), and overflow with gods and goddesses, swords and monsters. Also on the ground floor are artefacts from the Etruscan civilisation of south-central Italy, spanning the seventh century

BC until submission to the Romans in the first century AD. The highlight is the painted terracotta Sarcophagus of the Cenestien Couple (c530-510 BC), which illustrates a smiling couple reclining at a banquet. Key Roman antiquities include a vivid relief of sacrificial animals, intricately carved sarcophagi, mosaic floors and the Boscoreale Treasure: magnificent silverwork excavated at a villa near Pompeii. Pre-classical Greek art on the lower ground floor includes a large Cycladic head and Mycenean triad.

French painting

Denon: 1st floor; Richelieu: 2nd floor; Sully: 2nd floor. Red on Louvre maps.
There are around 6,000 of the most famous paintings in the world on show here, the most impressive being the huge 18th- to 19th-century canvases hanging in the Daru and Mollien rooms in the Denon wing, serving Classicism and Romanticism respectively. Here, art meets politics with David's enormous *Sacre de Napoléon*, Gros's propagandising *Napoléon Visitant le Champ de Bataille d'Eylau* and Delacroix's flag-flying *La Liberté Guidant le Peuple*. Géricault's beautiful but disturbing *Le Radeau de la Méduse* illustrates the grisly true story of the abandoned men who resorted to cannibalism and murder after a famous shipwreck in 1816, while his generals on flame-eyed horses fuel the myth of the dashing French officer. Biblical and historical scenes rub shoulders with aristocracy and grand depictions of great moments in mythology. Ingres' *Grande Odalisque* is also found here, along with a new Ingres acquisition, a portrait of the Duc d'Orléans.

In the Richelieu wing you can find the earliest known non-religious French portrait, an anonymous depiction of French king Jean Le Bon (c1350); the *Pietà de Villeneuve-les-Avignon*, later attributed to Enguerrand Quarton; Jean Clouet's Portrait of François I (marking the influence of the Italian Renaissance on portraiture); and various works from the Ecole de Fontainebleau,

including the anonymous *Diana the Huntress*, an elegant nude who strangely resembles Diane de Poitiers, the mistress of Henri II. Poussin's religious and mythological subjects epitomise 17th-century French classicism, and are full of erudite references for an audience of cognoscenti. His works spill over into the Sully wing, where you'll also find Charles Le Brun's wonderfully pompous *Chancellier Séguier* and his four grandiose battle scenes, in which Alexander the Great is a suitable stand-in for Louis XIV.

The 18th century begins with Watteau's *Gilles* and the *Embarkation for Cythera*. Works by Chardin include sober still lifes, but also fine figure paintings. If you're used to the sugary images of Fragonard, don't miss the *Fantaisies*, which forgo sentimentality for fluent, broadly painted fantasy portraits, intended to capture moods rather than likenesses. Also in the Sully wing are sublime neo-classical portraits by David, Ingres' *La Baigneuse* and *Le Bain Turc*, portraits and Orientalist scenes by Chassériau, and landscapes by Corot.

French sculpture

Richelieu: lower ground & ground floors. Light brown on Louvre maps.
French sculpture is displayed in and around the two covered courts created by the Grand Louvre scheme. A tour of the medieval regional schools takes in the *Virgins* from Alsace, 14th-century figures of Charles V and Jeanne de Bourbon that once adorned the exterior of the Louvre, and the late 15th-century tomb of Philippe Pot, an effigy of a Burgundian knight carried by eight mourners. Fine Renaissance memorials, fountains and portals include Jean Goujon's friezes from the Fontaine des Innocents.

In the Cour Marly, pride of place goes to Coustou's *Chevaux de Marly*, rearing horses being restrained by their grooms, plus two earlier equestrian pieces by Coysevox. Hewn from single blocks of marble, they were sculpted for the royal château at Marly-le-Roi before being moved to the Tuileries gardens, where copies

The Louvre (continued)

now stand. In Cour Puget are the four bronze captives by Martin Desjardins, Clodion's rococo frieze and Pierre Puget's twisting, Baroque *Milo of Croton*. Amid the 18th-century heroes and allegorical subjects, look out for Pigalle's *Mercury* and *Voltaire*.

Italian & Spanish painting

Denon: 1st floor. Red on Louvre maps.
Starting from the Sully end of the Denon wing, three rooms of fragile frescoes by Botticelli, Fra Angelico and Luini, and 13th- to 15th-century Florentine paintings on wood by Cimabue, Giotto, Fra Angelico and Lippi, open the Italian department, before you move into the long, skylit Grande Galerie. To the right, the Salle des Sept Mètres has highlights of the Sienese school, including Simone Martini's Christ Carrying the Cross and Piero della Francesca's Portrait of Sigismondo Malatesta. Now that the Mona Lisa has moved, there is no need to bowl along the Grande Galerie at speed in your haste to see her, missing the wonders on either side.

Most notably, about a quarter of the way along on the left are Leonardo's *Virgin of the Rocks*, *Virgin and Child with Saint Anne* and *Saint-Jean Baptiste*, which form part of the Northern Italian section, along with Bellini's *Calvary* and *Portrait of a Man* and Raphael's *Portrait of Dona Isabel de Requesens*. The first turning on the right after the da Vincis leads into the Salle de La Joconde, whose toffee-coloured brushed concrete walls provide a suitably golden setting for Veronese's lavish *Wedding at Cana*, his *Crucifixion* and *Sainte Famille* and other Venetian masterpieces such as Lotto's *Adulterous Woman* and red-robed *Christ Carrying the Cross*, Tintoretto's *Suzanne Bathing* and Bassano's earthy canvases. Don't miss the exquisite Titians hidden behind the *Mona Lisa* on her stand-alone wall.

A trip back down the Passage de Mollien, containing 16th-century cartoons, frames Giorgio Vasari's *Annunciation*, revealing how much better it is to stand back and look at these paintings. In between the two in the Grande Galerie are Arcimboldo's famous *Four Seasons*, various Bronzinos and Caravaggios, plus works by Albani, Carracci and Reni. A small Spanish section takes in *Christ on the Cross Adored by Two Donors* by El Greco and his contemporary Jusepe de Ribera's *Club Foot*.

Graphic arts

Denon: 1st floor; Sully: 2nd floor. Pink on Louvre maps.
The Louvre's huge collection of drawings includes works by Raphael, Michelangelo, Dürer, Holbein and Rembrandt. However, owing to their fragility, drawings are not shown as permanent exhibits. Four galleries (French and Northern schools on the 2nd floor; Italian and the latest acquisitions on the 1st) feature changing exhibitions. Other works can be viewed in the Salle de

Consultation only upon written application to the management (01.40.20.52.51, cabinet-des-dessins@louvre.fr).

Italian, Spanish & Northern sculpture

Denon: lower ground & ground floors. Light brown on Louvre maps.
Michelangelo's *Dying Slave* and *Captive Slave* are the showstoppers here, but other Renaissance treasures include a painted marble relief by Donatello, Adrien de Vriesse's bronze *Mercury and Psyche*, Giambologna's *Mercury* and the ethereal *Psyche Revived by Cupid's Kiss* by Antonio Canova. Benvenuto Cellini's *Nymph of Fontainebleau* relief is on the Mollien staircase.

Napoleon III's former stables were reopened in 2004 to house princely collections of statuary acquired by Richelieu and the Borghese and Albani families in the 17th and 18th centuries. The statues, either copies of classical works or restored originals, demonstrate the relationship between antique and modern sculpture. The height of the room also allows oversized works such as *Jupiter* and *Albani Alexander* to be displayed. Northern sculpture, on the lower ground floor, ranges from Erhart's Gothic *Mary Magdalene* to the neo-classical work of Thorvaldsen; pre-Renaissance Italian pieces include Donatello's clay relief *Virgin and Child*.

Northern schools

Richelieu: 2nd floor; Sully: 1st floor. Red on Louvre maps.
Northern Renaissance works include Flemish altarpieces by Memling and van der Weyden, Bosch's fantastical, proto-surrealist *Ship of Fools*, Metsys' *The Moneylender and his Wife*, and the northern mannerism of Cornelius van Haarlem. The Galerie Médicis houses Rubens' Médicis cycle; Marie de Médicis, the widow of Henri IV, commissioned the 24 canvases for the Palais de Luxembourg in the 1620s. They blend historic events and classical mythology for the glorification of the queen, never afraid to put her best features on public display. Look out for Rubens' more personal portrait of his second wife, *Hélène Fourment and her Children*, plus van Dyck's *Charles I and his Groom* and David Teniers the Younger's townscapes.

Dutch paintings in this wing include early and late self-portraits by Rembrandt, his *Flayed Ox* and the glowing nude *Bathsheba at her Bath*. There are Vermeer's *Astronomer and Lacemaker* amid interiors by De Hooch and Metsu, and the meticulously finished portraits and framing devices of Dou, plus works from the Haarlem school. German paintings in side galleries include portraits by Cranach, Dürer's *Self-Portrait* and Holbein's *Anne of Cleves*.

The rooms of Northern European and Scandinavian paintings include Caspar David Friedrich's *Trees with Crows*, the sober, classical portraits of Christian Købke, and pared-back

views by Peder Balke. A fairly modest but high-quality British collection located on the first floor of the Sully includes landscapes by Wright of Derby, Constable and Turner, and portraits by Gainsborough, Reynolds and Lawrence.

Decorative arts

Richelieu: 1st floor; Sully: 1st floor. Magenta on Louvre maps.
The decorative arts collection runs from the Middle Ages to the mid 19th century, and includes entire rooms decorated in the fashion of the day. Many of the finest medieval items came from the treasury of St-Denis, amassed by the powerful Abbot Suger, counsellor to Louis VI and VII, among them Suger's 'Eagle' (a porphyry vase), a serpentine plate surrounded by precious stones, and the sacred sword of the kings of France, dubbed 'Charlemagne's Sword' by the Capetian monarchs.

The Renaissance galleries display the *Hunts of Maximilien*, a dozen 16th-century tapestries depicting the months, zodiac and hunting scenes. Seventeenth- and 18th-century French decorative arts are shown in superb panelled rooms, and include characteristic brass and tortoiseshell pieces by Boulle. Displays then move on to French porcelain, silverware, watches and scientific instruments. Napoleon III's opulent apartments, used until the 1980s by the Ministry

of Finance, have been preserved, with chandeliers and upholstery intact.

Next to the Denon wing is the Galerie d'Apollon. It was built for Louis XIV and is a showcase of talents from this golden age: architecture by Louis Le Vau, painted ceilings by Charles Le Brun and sculpture by François Girardon, the Marsy brothers and Thomas Regnaudin. Napoleon III then commissioned Delacroix to paint the central medallion, *Apollo Vanquishing the Python*, and now it houses the crown jewels and Louis XIV vases. Merry-Joseph Blondel's *Chute d'Icare* graces the ceiling of an anteroom of the adjacent Rotonde d'Apollon.

African, Asian, Oceanic & American arts

Denon: ground floor. White on Louvre maps.
A new approach to 'arts premiers' is seen in these eight rooms in the Pavillon des Sessions. The spare, modern design allows each of the 100 key works to stand alone. The pure aesthetics of such objects as a svelte Zulu spoon with the breasts and buttocks of a woman, a sixth-century BC Sokoto terracotta head, and a recycled iron sculpture of the god Gou that anticipates Picasso can be appreciated in their own right. Computer terminals with mahogany benches offer visitors multimedia resources.

packed houses spiralling round the mound below the dome of **Sacré-Coeur**. Despite the many tourists, it's surprisingly easy to fall under the spell of this unabashedly romantic district. Climb quiet stairways, peer down narrow alleys and into ivy-covered houses and quiet squares, and explore streets such as rue des Abbesses, rue des Trois-Frères and rue des Martyrs, with their cafés, boutiques and bohemian residents.

For centuries, Montmartre was a tranquil village. When Haussmann sliced through the city centre in the mid 19th century, working-class families started to move out, and migrants poured into an industrialising Paris from across France. The population of Montmartre swelled. The *butte* was absorbed into the city of Paris in 1860, but remained proudly independent. Its key role in the Commune in 1871, fending off government troops, is marked by a plaque on rue du Chevalier-de-la-Barre.

Artists moved into the area from the 1880s. Renoir found subject matter in the cafés and *guinguettes*, and Toulouse-Lautrec patronised the local bars and immortalised its cabarets in his famous posters. Later, it was frequented by Picasso and artists of the Ecole de Paris.

You can start a wander from Abbesses métro station, one of only two in Paris (along with Porte Dauphine) to retain its original art nouveau metal-and-glass awning designed by Hector Guimard. Across place des Abbesses is art nouveau **St-Jean-de-Montmartre** church, a pioneering reinforced concrete structure with turquoise mosaics around the door. Along rue des Abbesses and adjoining rue Lepic, which winds its way up the hill, are food shops, boutiques, wine merchants and cafés, including the ever-popular **Le Sancerre** (*see p65*).

In the other direction from Abbesses, at 11 rue Yvonne-Le-Tac, is the Chapelle du Martyr. According to legend, St Denis picked up his head here after his execution in the third century. Rue Orsel, with a cluster of retro design, ethnic and second-hand clothes shops, leads to place Charles-Dullin, where a few cafés overlook the respected Théâtre de l'Atelier (1 pl Charles-Dullin, 18th, 01.46.06.49.24, www.theatre-atelier.com).

Up the hill, the cafés of rue des Trois-Frères are a popular spot for an evening drink. The street leads into sloping place Emile-Goudeau, whose staircases, streetlights and houses are particularly evocative of days gone by. The Bâteau Lavoir, a piano factory that stood at no.13, witnessed the birth of Cubism. Divided in the 1890s into a warren of studios for impoverished artists of the day, it was here that Picasso painted *Les Demoiselles d'Avignon* in 1906 and 1907, when he, Braque and Juan Gris were all residents. The building burned down in 1970, but has since been reconstructed.

On rue Lepic, which winds up the hill from rue des Abbesses, are the village's two remaining windmills: the **Moulin du Radet**, which was moved here in the 17th century from its hillock in rue des Moulins near the Palais-Royal; and the **Moulin de la Galette**, site of the celebrated dancehall depicted by Renoir (now in the Musée d'Orsay) and today a smart restaurant. Vincent van Gogh and his beloved brother Theo lived at no.54 from 1886 to 1888.

On tourist-swamped place du Tertre at the top of the hill, painters flog lurid sunset views of Paris or offer (sometimes aggressively) to draw your portrait; nearby **Espace Dalí** (11 rue Poulbot,

18th, 01.42.64.40.10, www.daliparis.com) has rather more illustrious art. Round here, so legend has it, the bistro concept was born in the early 1800s, when Russian soldiers shouted '*Bistro!*' ('Quickly!') to be served. Just off the square is **St-Pierre-de-Montmartre**, the oldest church in the district, with columns that have bent with age. Founded by Louis VI in 1133, it's an example of early Gothic, in contrast to its neighbour, the Sacré-Coeur basilica.

For all its kitsch and swarms of tourists, **Sacré-Coeur** is well worth the visit for its 19th-century excess. Rather than the main steps, take the staircase down rue Maurice-Utrillo to pause on a café terrace on the small square at the top of rue Muller, or wander down through the adjoining park to the Halle St-Pierre. The old covered market is now used for shows of naïve art, but the surrounding square and streets, known as the **Marché St-Pierre**, are packed with fabric shops.

On the north side of place du Tertre in rue Cortot is the quiet 17th-century manor that houses the **Musée de Montmartre**, dedicated to the neighbourhood and its former famous inhabitants. Dufy, Renoir and Utrillo all used to have studios in the entrance pavilion. Nearby in rue des Saules is the Montmartre vineyard, planted by local artist Poulbot in 1933 in commemoration of the vines that once covered the area. The grape harvest here every autumn is a local highlight, celebrated with great pomp. Further down the hill, among rustic, shuttered houses, is the cabaret **Au Lapin Agile** (*see p84*). This old artists' meeting point got its name from André Gill, who painted the inn sign of a rabbit (the 'lapin à Gill').

A series of squares leads to rue Caulaincourt, crossing the **Cimetière de Montmartre** (enter on avenue Rachel, reached by stairs from rue Caulaincourt or place de Clichy). A stone's throw south of here is the pocket-sized *chanson* venue **Les Trois Baudets** (*see p99*), which saw the Paris debuts of Brel, Brassens, Vian, Gainsbourg, Gréco and others. Winding down the back of the hill, avenue Junot is lined with exclusive residences, such as the avant-garde house built by Adolf Loos for poet Tristan Tzara at no.15, exemplifying his Modernist maxim: 'Ornament is crime.'

Cimetière de Montmartre
20 av Rachel, access by staircase from rue Caulaincourt, 18th (01.53.42.36.30). M° Blanche or Place de Clichy. **Open** *6 Nov-15 Mar* 8am-5.30pm Mon-Fri; 8.30am-5.30pm Sat; 9am-5.30pm Sun & public hols. *16 Mar-5 Nov* 8am-6pm Mon-Fri; 8.30am-6pm Sat; 9am-6pm Sun & public hols. **Admission** free.
Truffaut, Nijinsky, Berlioz, Degas, Offenbach and German poet Heine are all buried here. So, too, are La Goulue, the first great cancan star and model for Toulouse-Lautrec, celebrated local beauty Mme Récamier, and the consumptive heroine Alphonsine Plessis, inspiration for Dumas's *La Dame aux Camélias* and Verdi's *La Traviata*. Flowers are still left on the grave of pop diva and gay icon Dalida, who used to live on nearby rue d'Orchampt.

Musée d'Art Halle St-Pierre
2 rue Ronsard, 18th (01.42.58.72.89, www.halle saintpierre.org). M° Anvers. **Open** *Jan-July, Sept-Dec* 10am-6pm daily; *Aug* noon-6pm Mon-Fri. **Admission** €7.50; €6 reductions; free under-4s. **Credit** *Shop* MC, V.
The former covered market in the shadow of Sacré-Coeur specialises in *art brut, art outsider* and *art singulier* from its own and other collections.

Musée de Montmartre
12 rue Cortot, 18th (01.49.25.89.37, www.museedemontmartre.fr). M° Anvers or Lamarck-Caulaincourt. **Open** 11am-6pm Tue-

Cimetière de Montmartre.

Sun. **Admission** €8; €4-€6 reductions; free under-12s. **Credit** *Shop* MC, V.
At the back of a garden, this 17th-century manor displays the history of the hilltop, with rooms devoted to composer Gustave Charpentier and a tribute to the Lapin Agile cabaret, with original Toulouse-Lautrec posters. There are paintings by Suzanne Valadon, who had a studio above the entrance pavilion, as did Renoir, Raoul Dufy and Valadon's son Maurice Utrillo.

Sacré-Coeur
35 rue du Chevalier-de-la-Barre, 18th (01.53.41.89.00, www.sacre-coeur-montmartre.com). M° Abbesses or Anvers. **Open** *Basilica* 6am-10.30pm daily. *Crypt & dome* Winter 10am-5.45pm daily. Summer 9am-6.45pm daily. **Admission** free. *Crypt & dome* €5. **Credit** MC, V.
Work on this enormous mock Romano-Byzantine edifice began in 1877. It was commissioned after the nation's defeat by Prussia in 1870, voted for by the Assemblée Nationale and built from public subscription. Finally completed in 1914, it was consecrated in 1919 – by which time a jumble of architects had succeeded Paul Abadie, winner of the original competition. The interior boasts lavish mosaics.

La Goutte d'Or

The area north of Barbès Rochechouart métro station was the backdrop for Zola's *L'Assommoir*, his novel set among the district's laundries and absinthe cafés. Today, heroin has replaced absinthe as the means of escape.

La Goutte d'Or is primarily an African and Arab neighbourhood, and can seem like a slice of the Middle East or a state under perpetual siege due to the frequent police raids. Down rue Doudeauville, you'll find lively ethnic music shops; rue Polonceau contains African grocers and Senegalese restaurants. Mayor Delanöe has tried to attract young designers to the area by designating rue des Gardes 'rue de la mode', and square Léon is the

focus for La Goutte d'Or en Fête in June, which brings together local musicians. Some of them, such as Africando and the Orchestre National de Barbès, have become well known across Paris. A market sets up under the métro tracks along boulevard de la Chapelle on Monday, Wednesday and Saturday mornings, with stalls of exotic vegetables and rolls of African fabrics.

Further north, at porte de Clignancourt, is the city's largest flea market, the Marché aux Puces de St-Ouen.

Pigalle

In the 9th arrondissement.
In the 1890s, Toulouse-Lautrec's posters of Jane Avril at the Divan Japonais, Chat Noir and Moulin Rouge, and of *chanson* star Aristide Bruant, immortalised Pigalle's cabarets and were landmarks of art and advertising. At the end of the 19th century, 25 of the 58 buildings on rue des Martyrs were cabarets (a few, such as the drag shows Michou and Madame Arthur, remain today); others were *maisons closes*. But it's still a happening street: Le Divan Japonais is now **Le Divan du Monde** (*see p100*), a club and music venue; a hip crowd packs into **La Fourmi** (*see p100*) opposite; and up the hill, there's a cluster of *atelier*-boutiques where designers have set up their sewing machines at the back of the shop.

Along the boulevard, behind its bright red windmill, the **Moulin Rouge** (*see p84*), once the image of naughty 1890s Paris, is now a cheesy tourist draw. Its befeathered dancers still cancan and cavort across the stage, but are no substitute for La Goulue and Joseph Pujol – *le pétomane* who could pass wind melodically. In stark contrast is the **Cité Véron** next door, a cobbled alley with a small theatre and cottagey buildings. The famous **Elysée Montmartre** music hall (*see p100*) today has an array of concerts and club nights, but the **Folie's Pigalle** (*see p100*) nightspot retains its undeniable Pigalle flavour with its after-parties and drag queens.

Musée de l'Erotisme
72 bd de Clichy, 18th (01.42.58.28.73, www.musee-erotisme.com). M° Blanche. **Open** 10am-2am daily. **Admission** €9; €6 reductions. **Credit** MC, V.
Seven floors of erotic art and artefacts amassed by collectors Alain Plumey and Joseph Khalif. The first three run from first-century Peruvian phallic pottery through Etruscan fertility symbols to Yoni sculptures from Nepal; the fourth gives a history of Paris brothels; and the recently refurbished top floors host exhibitions of modern erotic art.

La Nouvelle Athènes

Just south of Pigalle and east of rue Blanche lies this often overlooked quarter, dubbed the New Athens when it was colonised by a wave of artists, writers and composers in the early 19th century. Long-forgotten actresses and *demi-mondaines* had mansions built here; some are set in tiny rue de la Tour-des-Dames, which refers to one of the many windmills owned by Couvent des Abbesses. To glimpse more of these miniature palaces, wander through the adjoining streets and passageways.

Just off rue Taitbout is square d'Orléans, a remarkable housing estate built in 1829 by the English architect Edward Cresy. These flats and studios attracted the glitterati of the day, including George Sand and her lover Chopin. In the house built for Dutch painter Ary Scheffer in nearby rue Chaptal, the **Musée de la Vie Romantique** displays Sand's mementos.

The **Musée Gustave Moreau** on rue de La Rochefoucauld is reason alone to visit, featuring the artist's apartment and studio. Fragments of bohemia can still be gleaned in the area, although the Café La Roche, where Moreau met Degas for drinks and rows, has been downsized to **Café Matisse** (57 rue Notre-Dame-de-Lorette, 9th, 01.53.16.44.58). Degas painted most of his ballet scenes in rue Frochot, and Renoir hired his first proper studio at 35 rue St-Georges. A few streets away in Cité Pigalle, a collection of studios, is van Gogh's last Paris house (no.5), from where he moved to Auvers-sur-Oise. There is a plaque here, but nothing marks the building in rue Pigalle where Toulouse-Lautrec slowly drank himself to an early grave.

The area around the neo-classical **Eglise Notre-Dame-de-Lorette** was built up in Louis-Philippe's reign and was famous for its courtesans or *lorettes*, elegant ladies named after their haunt of rue Notre-Dame-de-Lorette. In 1848, Gauguin was born at no.56; from 1844 to 1857, Delacroix had a studio at no.58. The latter then moved to place de Furstemberg in the sixth (now the Musée Delacroix).

The lower stretch of rue des Martyrs is packed with tempting food shops, and a little further up the hill you should look out for the prosperous residences of the Cité Malesherbes and avenue Trudaine. Circular place St-Georges was home to the true Empress of Napoleon III's Paris: the Russian-born Madame Païva. She lived in the neo-Renaissance no.28, thought to be outrageous at the time of its construction. La Païva shot herself after a passionate affair with the millionaire cousin of Chancellor Bismarck.

Musée National Gustave Moreau
14 rue de La Rochefoucauld, 9th (01.48.74.38.50, www.musee-moreau.fr). M° Trinité. **Open** 10am-12.45pm, 2-5.15pm Mon, Wed-Sun. **Admission** €5; €3 reductions, all Sun; free under-18s. PMP. **Credit** MC, V.
Downstairs shows the Symbolist painter's obsessive collector's nature with family portraits, Grand Tour souvenirs and a boudoir devoted to the object of his unrequited love, Alexandrine Durem. Upstairs is Moreau's fantasy realm, which plunders Greek mythology and biblical scenes for canvases filled with writhing maidens, trance-like visages, mystical beasts and strange plants. Don't miss the trippy masterpiece *Jupiter et Sémélé* on the second floor. Printed on boards that you can carry around the museum are the artist's lengthy, rhetorical and mad commentaries.

Musée de la Vie Romantique
Hôtel Scheffer-Renan, 16 rue Chaptal, 9th (01.55.31.95.67, www.vie-romantique.paris.fr). M° Blanche or St-Georges. **Open** 10am-6pm Tue-Sun. *Tearoom mid May-mid Oct 11.30am-5.30pm Tue-Sun.* **Admission** free. *Exhibitions* €9; €3.30 reductions; free under-14s. **Credit** AmEx, DC, MC, V.
When Dutch artist Ary Scheffer lived in this small villa, the area teemed with composers, writers and artists. Aurore Dupin, Baronne Dudevant (George Sand) was a guest at Scheffer's soirées, along with great names such as Chopin and Liszt. The museum is devoted to Sand, although the watercolours, lockets, jewels and plastercast of her right arm that she left behind reveal little of her ideas or affairs.

Beaubourg & the Marais

Whereas historic *quartiers* like Montmartre and St-Germain-des-Prés are well past their heyday, the Marais has been luckier, and for the last two decades has been one of the hippest parts of the city, stuffed with modish hotels, boutiques and restaurants – in no small part due to its popularity with the gay crowd. It's also prime territory for arts lovers, thanks to its generous quotient of museums, and its tightly knit street plan – largely untouched by Haussmann – makes it a charming place in which to get lost. The Marais' neighbour to the west is Beaubourg, whose focal point is the iconic Centre Pompidou, with the city's all-important Hôtel de Ville a stone's throw to the south.

Beaubourg & Hôtel de Ville

In the 4th arrondissement.
Modern architecture in Paris took off with the **Centre Pompidou**, a benchmark of inside-out high-tech designed by Richard Rogers and Renzo Piano that's as much an attraction as the **Musée National de l'Art Moderne** within. The piazza outside attracts all manner of street performers and artists; the reconstructed **Atelier Brancusi**, which was left by the sculptor to the state, was moved here from the 15th.

On the other side of the piazza, rue Quincampoix houses galleries, bars and cobbled passage Molière, with its old shopfronts and the **Théâtre Molière** (01.44.54.53.00). Beside the Centre Pompidou is place Igor-Stravinsky and the Fontaine Stravinsky – full of spraying kinetic fountains, and a colourful snake by the late artists Niki de Saint Phalle and Jean Tinguely – as well as the red-brick **IRCAM** music institute (*see p97*), also designed by Renzo Piano.

Place des Vosges.

South of here stands the spiky Gothic **Tour St-Jacques**. Towards the river, on the site of the Grand Châtelet (a fortress put up in the 12th century to defend Pont au Change), place du Châtelet's Egyptian-themed fountain is framed by twin theatres designed by Davioud as part of Haussmann's urban improvements in the 1860s. They're now two of the city's main arts venues: the **Théâtre de la Ville** (*see p98*) and the **Théâtre du Châtelet** (*see p104*), an opera and concert hall.

Beyond Châtelet, the **Hôtel de Ville** (city hall) has been the symbol of municipal power since 1260. The equestrian statue out front is of 14th-century merchant leader and rebel Etienne Marcel. Revolutionaries made the Hôtel de Ville their base in the 1871 Commune, but it was set on fire by the Communards themselves and wrecked during savage fighting. It was rebuilt according to the original model, on a larger scale, in fanciful neo-Renaissance style, with knights in armour along the roof and statues of French luminaries dotted all over the walls. The square outside was formerly called place de Grève, after the nearby riverside wharf where goods were unloaded for market. During the 16th-century Wars of Religion, Protestant heretics were burned in the square, and the guillotine stood here during the Terror, when Danton, Marat and Robespierre made the Hôtel de Ville their own seat of government. Today, the square hosts an ice rink every December, and screenings of major sports events. Across the road stands the Bazar de l'Hôtel de Ville department store, or BHV (*see p69*).

Atelier Brancusi
Piazza Beaubourg, 4th (01.44.78.12.33, www.centrepompidou.fr). M° Hôtel de Ville or Rambuteau. **Open** 2-6pm Mon, Wed-Sun. **Admission** free. **Credit** AmEx, V.
When Constantin Brancusi died in 1957, he left his studio and its contents to the state, and it was later moved and rebuilt by the Centre Pompidou. His fragile works in wood and plaster, the endless columns and streamlined bird forms show how Brancusi revolutionised sculpture.

Centre Pompidou (Musée National d'Art Moderne)
Rue St-Martin, 4th (01.44.78.12.33, www.centre pompidou.fr). M° Hôtel de Ville or Rambuteau. **Open** 11am-9pm (last entry 8pm) Mon, Wed-Sun (until 11pm some exhibitions). **Admission** *Museum & exhibitions* €10-€12; €8-€9 reductions; free under-18s, 1st Sun of mth (museum only). PMP. **Credit** AmEx, DC, MC, V.
The primary colours, exposed pipes and air ducts make this one of the best-known sights in Paris. The Centre Pompidou (or 'Beaubourg') holds the largest collection of modern art in Europe, rivalled only in its breadth and quality by MoMA in New York. Sample the contents of its vaults (50,000 works of art by 5,000 artists) on the website, as only a fraction – about 600 works – can be seen for real at any one time. Or take the TGV to Metz, where the Centre Pompidou Metz opened in 2010.

For the main collection, buy tickets on the ground floor and take the escalators to level four for post-1960s art. Level five spans 1905 to 1960. There are four temporary exhibition spaces on each of these two levels (included in the ticket). Main temporary exhibitions take place on the ground floor, in gallery two on level six, in the south gallery, level one and in the new Espace 315, which is devoted to artists aged under 40.

On level five, the historic section takes a chronological sweep through the history of modern art, via Primitivism, Fauvism, Cubism, Dadaism and Surrealism up to American Color-Field painting and Abstract Expressionism. Masterful ensembles let you see the span of Matisse's career on canvas and in bronze, the variety of Picasso's invention, and the development of cubic orphism by Sonia and Robert Delaunay. Others on the hits list include Braque, Duchamp, Mondrian, Malevich, Kandinsky, Dali, Giacometti, Ernst, Miró, Calder, Magritte, Rothko and Pollock. Don't miss the reconstruction of a wall of André Breton's studio,

OLIVER KNIGHT

combining the tribal art, folk art, flea-market finds and drawings by fellow artists that the Surrealist artist and theorist had amassed.

The photography collection also has an impressive roll call, including Brassaï, Kertész, Man Ray, Cartier-Bresson and Doisneau.

Level four houses post-'60s art. Its thematic rooms concentrate on the career of one artist or focus on movements such as Anti-form or *arte povera*. Recent acquisitions line the central corridor, and at the far end you can find architecture and design. Video art and installations by the likes of Mathieu Mercier and Dominique Gonzalez-Foerster are in a room devoted to *nouvelle création*.

Hôtel de Ville
29 rue de Rivoli, 4th (01.42.76.40.40, www.paris.fr). M° Hôtel de Ville. **Open** 10am-7pm Mon-Sat.
Rebuilt by Ballu after the Commune, the palatial, multi-purpose Hôtel de Ville is the very heart of the city administration, and a place in which to entertain visiting dignitaries. Free exhibitions are held in the Salon d'Accueil (open 10am-6pm Mon-Fri). The rest of the building, which is accessible by weekly guided tours (you need to book in advance), has parquet floors, marble statues, crystal chandeliers and painted ceilings.

Tour St-Jacques
Square de La-Tour-St-Jacques, 4th. M° Châtelet.
Loved by the Surrealists, this solitary Flamboyant Gothic belltower with its leering gargoyles is all that remains of St-Jacques-La-Boucherie church, built for the powerful Butchers' Guild in 1508-22. The statue of Blaise Pascal at the base commemorates his experiments on atmospheric pressure, carried out here in the 17th century. A weather station now crowns the 52m (171ft) tower.

The Marais

In the 3rd & 4th arrondissements.
The narrow streets of the Marais contain aristocratic *hôtels particuliers*, art galleries, boutiques and stylish cafés, with beautiful carved doorways and early street signs carved into the stone. The Marais, or 'marsh', started life as a piece of swampy ground inhabited by a few monasteries, sheep and market gardens. This was one of the last parts of central Paris to be built up. In the 16th century, the elegant Hôtel Carnavalet and Hôtel Lamoignon sparked the area's phenomenal rise as an aristocratic residential district; Henri IV began building **place des Vosges** in 1605. Nobles and royal officials followed, building smart townhouses where literary ladies such as Mme de Sévigné held court. The area fell from fashion a century later; many of the narrow streets remained unchanged as mansions were transformed into workshops, crafts studios, schools, tenements, and even, on rue de Sévigné, a fire station.

Rue des Francs-Bourgeois, crammed with impressive mansions and original boutiques, runs like a backbone right through the Marais, becoming more aristocratic as it leaves the food shops of rue Rambuteau behind. Two of the most refined early 18th-century residences are **Hôtel d'Albret** (no.31), a venue for jazz concerts during the Paris, Quartier d'Eté festival (*see p12*), and the palatial **Hôtel de Soubise** (no.60), the national archives. Begun in 1704 for the Prince and Princesse de Soubise, it has interiors by Boucher and Lemoine and currently hosts the **Musée de l'Histoire de France**, along with the neighbouring Hôtel de Rohan. There's also a surprising series of rose gardens.

Facing the Archives Nationales, the **Crédit Municipal** (no.55) acts as a sort of municipal pawnshop: people exchange goods for cash, and items never reclaimed are sold at auction. On the corner of rue Pavée is the Renaissance Hôtel Lamoignon, with a magisterial courtyard adorned with

Corinthian pilasters. Built in 1585, it now contains the **Bibliothèque Historique de la Ville de Paris** (no.24, 01.44.59.29.40). Further up, the **Musée Carnavalet** runs across the Hôtel Carnavalet and the Hôtel le Peletier de St-Fargeau.

At its eastern end, rue des Francs-Bourgeois leads into the beautiful brick-and-stone place des Vosges. At one corner is the **Maison de Victor Hugo**, where the writer lived from 1833 to 1848. An archway in the south-west corner leads to the **Hôtel de Sully**, accommodating the Patrimoine Photographique. Designed in 1624, the building belonged to Henri IV's minister, the Duc de Sully.

Several other important museums are also found in sumptuous *hôtels*. The Hôtel Salé on rue de Thorigny, built in 1656, was nicknamed ('salty') after its owner, Fontenay, who collected the salt tax. Home to the **Musée National Picasso**, it is currently under restoration until 2012. Nearby, the pretty Hôtel Donon, built in 1598, contains the **Musée Cognacq-Jay** and has remarkable 18th-century panelled interiors, and the Hôtel Guénégaud contains the **Musée de la Chasse et de la Nature**.

The Marais has also long been a focus for the Jewish community. Today, Jewish businesses are clustered along rue des Rosiers, rue des Ecouffes and rue Pavée, where there's a synagogue designed by Guimard. Originally made up mainly of Ashkenazi Jews, who fled the pogroms in eastern Europe at the end of the 19th century (many were later deported during World War II), the community expanded in the 1950s and '60s with a wave of Sephardic Jewish immigration after French withdrawal from North Africa.

The lower ends of rue des Archives and rue Vieille-du-Temple are the centre of café life and the hub of the gay scene. Bars such as the **Open Café** (*see p95*) draw gay crowds in the early evening. In their midst, the 15th-century **Cloître des Billettes** at 22-26 rue des Archives is the only surviving Gothic cloister in Paris.

Workaday rue du Temple is full of surprises. Near rue de Rivoli, **Le Noveau Latina** (*see p91*) specialises in Latin American films and holds tango balls in the room above. At no.41, an archway leads into the former Aigle d'Or coaching inn, now the **Café de la Gare** *café-théâtre* (*see p84*). Further north, at no.71, the grandiose Hôtel de St-Aignan, built in 1650, contains the **Musée d'Art et d'Histoire du Judaïsme**. The top end of rue du Temple and adjoining streets such as rue des Gravilliers are packed with costume jewellery, handbag and rag-trade wholesalers in what is the city's oldest Chinatown.

The north-west corner of the Marais hinges on the **Musée des Arts et Métiers**, a science museum with early flying machines displayed in the 12th-century chapel of the former priory of St-Martin-des-Champs, and the adjoining Conservatoire des Arts et Métiers. Across rue St-Martin on square Emile-Chautemps, the **Théâtre de la Gaîté Lyrique** is set to reopen in March 2011 as a centre for contemporary music and the 'digital arts'.

Despite the Marais' rise to fashion, the less gentrified streets around the northern stretch of rue Vieille-du-Temple towards place de la République are awash with designers on the rise and old craft workshops. Rue Charlot, housing an occasional contemporary art gallery at the passage de Retz at no.9, is typical of the trend. At the top, the **Marché des Enfants-Rouges** (once an orphanage

whose inhabitants were attired in red uniforms) is one of the city's oldest markets, founded in 1615.

Hôtel de Sully
62 rue St-Antoine, 4th (01.42.74.47.75, www.jeudepaume.org). M° St-Paul. **Open** noon-7pm Tue-Fri; 10am-7pm Sat, Sun. **Admission** €5; €2.50 reductions. **Credit** MC, V.
Along with the Jeu de Paume, the former Patrimoine Photographique forms part of the two-site home for the Centre National de la Photographie.

Maison de Victor Hugo
Hôtel de Rohan-Guéménée, 6 pl des Vosges, 4th (01.42.72.10.16, www.musee-hugo.paris.fr). M° Bastille or St-Paul. **Open** 10am-6pm Tue-Sun. **Admission** free. *Exhibitions* prices vary. **Credit** MC, V.
Victor Hugo lived here from 1833 to 1848, and today the house is a museum devoted to the life and work of the great man. On display are his first editions, nearly 500 drawings and, more bizarrely, Hugo's home-made furniture.

Musée d'Art et d'Histoire du Judaïsme
Hôtel de St-Aignan, 71 rue du Temple, 3rd (01.53.01.86.53, www.mahj.org). M° Rambuteau. **Open** 11am-6pm Mon-Fri; 10am-6pm Sun. Closed Jewish hols. **Admission** €6.80; €4.50 reductions; free under-18s. **Credit** *Shop* MC, V.
It's fitting that a museum of Judaism should be lodged in one of the grandest mansions of the Marais, for centuries the epicentre of local Jewish life. It sprang from the collection of a private association formed in 1948 to safeguard Jewish heritage after the Holocaust. Pick up a free audio-guide in English to help you navigate through displays illustrating ceremonies, rites and learning, and showing how styles were adapted across the globe through examples of Jewish decorative arts. Photographic portraits of modern French Jews, each of whom tells his or her own story on the audio soundtrack, bring a contemporary edge. There are documents and paintings relating to the emancipation of French Jewry after the Revolution and the infamous Dreyfus case, from Zola's *J'Accuse!* to anti-Semitic cartoons. Paintings by the early 20th-century avant-garde include works by El Lissitsky and Chagall. The Holocaust is marked by Boris Taslitzky's stark sketches from Buchenwald and Christian Boltanski's courtyard memorial to the Jews who lived in the building in 1939, 13 of whom died in the camps.

Musée des Arts et Métiers
60 rue Réaumur, 3rd (01.53.01.82.00, www.arts-et-metiers.net). M° Arts et Métiers. **Open** 10am-6pm Tue, Wed, Fri-Sun; 10am-9.30pm Thur. **Admission** €6.50; €4.50 reductions; free under-26s, 6-9.30pm Thur & 1st Sun of mth. PMP. **Credit** V.
The 'arts and trades' museum is, in fact, Europe's oldest science museum, founded in 1794 by the constitutional bishop Henri Grégoire, initially as a way to educate France's manufacturing industry in useful scientific techniques. Housed in the former Benedictine priory of St-Martin-des-Champs, it became a museum proper in 1819; it's a fascinating, attractively laid out and vast collection of treasures. Here are beautiful astrolabes, celestial spheres, barometers, clocks, weighing devices, some of Pascal's calculating devices, amazing scale models of buildings and machines that must have demanded at least as much engineering skill as the originals, the Lumière brothers' cinematograph, an enormous 1938 TV set, and still larger exhibits like Cugnot's 1770 'Fardier' (the first ever powered vehicle) and Clément Ader's bat-like, steam-powered Avion 3. The visit concludes in the chapel, which now contains old cars, a scale model of the Statue of Liberty, the monoplane in which Blériot crossed the Channel in 1909, and a Foucault pendulum. Try to time your visit to coincide with one of the spellbinding demonstrations of the museum's old music boxes in the Théâtre des Automates.

Musée Carnavalet
23 rue de Sévigné, 3rd (01.44.59.58.58, www.carnavalet.paris.fr). M° St-Paul. **Open** 10am-6pm Tue-Sun. **Admission** free. *Exhibitions* €7; €3.50-€5.50 reductions; free under-13s. **Credit** *Shop* AmEx, MC, V.
Here, 140 chronological rooms depict the history of Paris, from pre-Roman Gaul to the 20th century. Built in 1548 and transformed by Mansart in 1660, this fine house became a museum in 1866, when Haussmann persuaded the city to preserve its beautiful interiors. Original 16th-century rooms house Renaissance collections, with portraits by Clouet and furniture and pictures relating to the Wars of Religion. The first floor covers the period up to 1789, with furniture and paintings displayed in restored,

period interiors; neighbouring Hôtel Le Peletier de St-Fargeau covers the period from 1789 onwards. Displays relating to 1789 detail that year's convoluted politics and bloodshed, with prints and memorabilia, including a chunk of the Bastille. There are items belonging to Napoleon, a cradle given by the city to Napoleon III, and a reconstruction of Proust's cork-lined bedroom.

Musée de la Chasse et de la Nature
Hôtel Guénégaud, 62 rue des Archives, 3rd (01.53.01.92.40, www.chassenature.org). M° Rambuteau. **Open** 11am-6pm Tue-Sun. **Admission** €6; €4.50 reductions; free under-18s & 1st Sun of mth.
A two-year overhaul turned the three-floor hunting museum from a musty old-timer into something really rather special. When it reopened in 2007, it had kept the basic layout and proportions of the two adjoining 17th-century mansions it occupies, but many of its new exhibits and settings seem more suited to an art gallery than a museum. The history of hunting and man's larger relationship with the natural world are examined in things like a quirky series of wooden cabinets devoted to the owl, wolf, boar and stag, each equipped with a bleached skull, small drawers you can open to reveal droppings and footprint casts, and a binocular eyepiece you can peer into for footage of the animal in the wild. A cleverly simple mirrored box contains a stuffed hen that is replicated into infinity on every side; and a stuffed fox is set curled up on a Louis XVI chair as though it were a domestic pet. Thought-provoking stuff.

Musée Cognacq-Jay
Hôtel Donon, 8 rue Elzévir, 3rd (01.40.27.07.21, www.paris.fr/musees). M° St-Paul. **Open** 10am-6pm Tue-Sun. **Admission** free.
This museum houses a collection put together in the early 1900s by La Samaritaine founder Ernest Cognacq and his wife Marie-Louise Jay. They stuck mainly to 18th-century French works, focusing on rococo artists such as Watteau, Fragonard, Boucher, Greuze and pastellist Quentin de la Tour, though some English artists (Reynolds, Romney, Lawrence) and Dutch and Flemish names (an early Rembrandt, Ruysdael, Rubens), plus Canalettos and Guardis, have managed to slip in. Pictures are displayed in panelled rooms with furniture, porcelain, tapestries and sculpture of the same period.

Musée de l'Histoire de France
Hôtel de Soubise, 60 rue des Francs-Bourgeois, 3rd (01.40.27.60.96, www.archivesnationales. culture.gouv.fr/chan/chan/musee). M° Hôtel de Ville or Rambuteau. **Open** 10am-12.30pm, 2-5.30pm Mon, Wed-Fri; 2-5.30pm Sat, Sun. **Admission** €3; €2.30 reductions; free under-18s. **Credit** V.
Documents and artefacts covering everything from the founding of the Sorbonne to an ordinance about umbrellas are displayed in the recently renovated Hôtel de Soubise. Its rococo interiors feature paintings by François Boucher and Carle van Loo.

Place des Vosges
4th. M° St-Paul.
Paris's first planned square was commissioned in 1605 by Henri IV and inaugurated by his son Louis XIII in 1612. With harmonious red-brick and stone arcaded façades and steeply pitched slate roofs, it differs from the later pomp of the Bourbons. Laid out symmetrically with carriageways through Pavillon de la Reine on the north side and Pavillon du Roi on the south, the other lots were sold off as concessions to officials and nobles (some façades are imitation brick). It was called place Royale prior to the Napoleonic Wars, when the Vosges was the first region to pay its war taxes. Mme de Sévigné, salon hostess and letter-writer, was born at no.1bis in 1626. At that time the garden hosted duels and trysts; now it attracts children from the nearby nursery school.

The St-Paul district

In 1559, Henri II was fatally wounded jousting on today's rue St-Antoine, marked by Pilon's marble *La Vierge de Douleur* in the **Eglise St-Paul-St-Louis**. South of rue St-Antoine is the sedate residential area of St-Paul, lined with dignified 17th- and 18th-century façades. The linked courtyards of Village St-Paul house antiques sellers. On rue des Jardins-St-Paul is the largest surviving section of the fortified wall of Philippe-Auguste (www.philippe-auguste.com), complete with towers.

Mitigate your flight with

Trees for Cities

and make your trip mean something for years to come.

http://carboncalculator.treesforcities.org/

Charity registration number 1032154

By St-Paul métro station on the corner of rue François-Miron and rue de Fourcy is the Hôtel Hénault de Cantorbe, renovated and given a minimalist modern extension as the **Maison Européenne de la Photographie**. Down rue de Fourcy towards the river, across a medieval formal garden, you can see the rear façade of the Hôtel de Sens, a rare medieval mansion built as the Paris residence of the Archbishops of Sens in the 15th century, with an array of turrets. It is home to the **Bibliothèque Forney** (1 rue du Figuier, 01.42.78.14.60, closed Mon & Sun), which as exhibitions of applied arts and graphic design.

Near Pont Sully are square Henri-Galli, with a rebuilt piece of the Bastille, and the **Pavillon de l'Arsenal**, built by a rich timber merchant to put on art shows, and home to displays relating to Paris architecture.

Winding rue François-Miron leads you back towards the Hôtel de Ville. At 17 rue Geoffroy-l'Asnier, the Mémorial du Martyr Juif Inconnu is being extended as part of the **Mémorial de la Shoah**, a museum, memorial and study centre devoted to the Holocaust that opened in 2005. As you pass no.26, note the Cité des Arts complex of artists' studios, and the ornate lion's head and giant shell motif on the doorway of the 17th-century Hôtel de Châlon-Luxembourg. Rue du Pont-Louis-Philippe contains jewellers, designer furniture and gift shops, and stepped rue des Barres boasts tearooms overlooking the chevet of the **Eglise St-Gervais-St-Protais**.

Eglise St-Gervais-St-Protais

Pl St-Gervais, 4th (01.48.87.32.02). M° Hôtel de Ville. **Open** times vary. **Admission** free.
Gothic at the rear and classical at the front, this church also has an impressive Flamboyant Gothic interior, most of which dates from the 16th century. The nave gives an impression of enormous height, with tall columns that soar up to the vault. There are plenty of fine funerary monuments, especially the baroque statue of Chancellor Le Tellier.

Eglise St-Paul-St-Louis

99 rue St-Antoine, 4th (01.42.72.30.32). M° St-Paul. **Open** 8am-8pm Mon-Fri; 8am-7.30pm Sat; 9am-8pm Sun. **Admission** free.
This domed Baroque Counter-Reformation church is modelled, like all Jesuit churches, on the Chiesa del Gesù in Rome. Completed in 1641, it features a single nave, side chapels and a three-storey façade featuring statues of Saints Louis, Anne and Catherine – all replacements. The provider of confessors to the kings of France, the Eglise St-Paul-St-Louis was richly endowed until Revolutionary iconoclasts pinched its treasures, including the hearts of Louis XIII and XIV. Afterwards, in 1802, it was converted back into a church, and today it houses Delacroix's *Christ in the Garden of Olives*.

Maison Européenne de la Photographie

5-7 rue de Fourcy, 4th (01.44.78.75.00, www.mep-fr.org). M° St-Paul. **Open** 11am-8pm Wed-Sun. **Admission** €6.50; €3.50 reductions; free under-8s, all 5-8pm Wed. **Credit** MC, V.
Probably the capital's best photography exhibition space, hosting retrospectives by Larry Clark and Martine Barrat, along with work by emerging photographers. The building, an airy mansion with a modern extension, contains a huge permanent collection. The venue organises the biennial Mois de la Photo and the Art Outsiders festival of new media web art in September.

Le Mémorial de la Shoah

17 rue Geoffroy-l'Asnier, 4th (01.42.77.44.72, www.memorialdelashoah.org). M° Pont Marie or St-Paul. **Open** 10am-6pm Mon-Wed, Fri, Sun; 10am-10pm Thur. *Research centre* 10am-5.30pm Mon-Wed, Fri, Sun; 10am-7.30pm Thur. **Admission** free.
Airport-style security checks mean queues, but don't let that put you off: the Mémorial du Martyr Juif Inconnu is an impressively presented and moving memorial to the Holocaust. Enter via the Wall of Names, where limestone slabs are engraved with the first and last names of each of the 76,000 Jews deported from France from 1942 to 1944 with, as an inscription reminds the visitor, the say-so of the Vichy government. The basement-level permanent exhibition documents the plight of French and European Jews through photographs, texts, films and individual stories: 'The French,' reads one label (captioning is also given in English), 'were not particularly interested in the fate of French Jews at this point.'

Pavillon de l'Arsenal

21 bd Morland, 4th (01.42.76.33.97, www.pavillon-arsenal.com). M° Sully Morland. **Open** 10.30am-6.30pm Tue-Sat; 11am-7pm Sun. **Admission** free. **Credit** *Shop* MC, V.
The setting is a fantastic 1880s gallery with an iron frame and glass roof; the subject is the built history of Paris; the result is disappointing. The ground floor houses a permanent exhibition on the city's development, but space and funds are lacking to the extent that exhibits are limited to a few storyboards, maps and photos, and three city models set into the floor (done more impressively at the Musée d'Orsay).

Bastille & Eastern Paris

French history's biggest event took place in this part of town: the storming of the grim fortress-prison that kicked off the Revolution in 1789. The spot is now a large roundabout (you can see a chunk of the foundations in the métro station underneath) that is usually choked with traffic – except when it's choked with mass demonstrations: Bastille is a political hotspot to this day. The streets immediately north and east are particularly strong on good yet affordable restaurants, and the Bercy district has seen its star rise with the arrival a few years ago of the Cinémathèque Française, and the shops and cafés at Bercy Village.

Bastille

In the 11th, 12th and 20th arrondissements.

Place de la Bastille has been a potent symbol of popular rebellion ever since 1789. The area was transformed in the 1980s with the arrival of the **Opéra Bastille** (*see p97*), along with fashionable cafés, restaurants and bars. The present-day square occupies the site of the long-vanished prison ramparts, and is dominated by Opéra's curved façade. Opened in 1989 on the bicentenary of Bastille Day, the venue remains controversial, criticised for its poor acoustics and design. South of the square is the Port de l'Arsenal marina, where the Canal St-Martin meets the Seine. The canal continues underground north of the square, running beneath boulevard Richard-Lenoir, site of a lively outdoor market on Sunday mornings.

Rue du Fbg-St-Antoine has been the heart of the furniture-makers' district for centuries. Furniture showrooms still line the street, though they've been joined by clothes shops and bars. Cobbled rue de Lappe typifies the shift, as the last remaining furniture workshops hold out against theme bars overrun at weekends by suburban youths. Pockets of bohemian resistance remain on rue de Charonne, however, with the **Pause Café** (*see p66*) and its busy terrace, bistro **Chez Paul** (no.13, 11th, 01.47.00.34.57) and dealers in colourful 1960s furniture. Rue des Taillandiers and rue Keller are a focus for record stores, streetwear shops and fashion designers.

Narrow street frontages hide cobbled alleys, lined with craftsmen's workshops or quirky bistros dating from the 18th century. Note the cours de l'Ours, du Cheval Blanc, du Bel Air (and hidden garden) and de la Maison Brûlée, the passage du Chantier on rue du Fbg-St-Antoine, the rustic-looking passage de l'Etoile d'Or and the passage de l'Homme, with wooden shopfronts on rue de Charonne. This area was originally located outside the city walls on the lands of the Convent of St-Antoine (parts of which survive as the Hôpital St-Antoine). In the Middle Ages, skilled furnituremakers not belonging to the city's restrictive guilds earned the area a reputation for free thinking that was cemented a few hundred years later during the Revolution.

Further down rue du Fbg-St-Antoine is place d'Aligre, home to a rowdy, cheap produce market, a more sedate covered food hall and the only flea market within the city walls. The road ends in the major intersection of place de la Nation, another grand square. It was originally called place du Trône, after a throne that was positioned here when Louis XIV and his bride Marie-Thérèse entered the city in 1660. After the Revolution, between 13 June and 28 July 1799, thousands were guillotined on the site, their bodies carted to the nearby Cimetière de Picpus. The square still has two of Ledoux's toll houses and tall Doric columns from the 1787 Mur des Fermiers-Généraux. In the centre stands Jules Dalou's sculpture *Le Triomphe de la République*, erected for the centenary of the Revolution in 1889. East of place de la Nation, broad cours de Vincennes has a market on Wednesday and Saturday mornings.

North of place de la Bastille, boulevard Beaumarchais divides Bastille from the Marais. East of place Voltaire, on rue de la Roquette, which heads east towards the Ménilmontant area and **Père-Lachaise** cemetery, a small park and playground marks the site of the prison de la Roquette, where a plaque remembers the 4,000 Resistance members imprisoned here in World War II.

Cimetière du Père-Lachaise

Bd de Ménilmontant, 20th (01.55.25.82.10). M° Père-Lachaise. **Open** *6 Nov-15 Mar* 8am-5.30pm Mon-Fri; 8.30am-5.30pm Sat; 9am-5.30pm Sun. *16 Mar-5 Nov* 8am-6pm Mon-Fri; 8.30am-6pm Sat; 9am-6pm Sun & hols. **Admission** free.
Père-Lachaise is the celebrity cemetery – it has almost anyone French, talented and dead that you care to mention. Finding a particular grave can be tricky, so buy a map from the hawkers at the Père-Lachaise métro or from shops nearby. Highlights include Chopin's medallion portrait and the muse of Music, plus famous neighbours La Fontaine and Molière, who knew each other in real life and now share the same fenced-off plot.

La Maison Rouge – Fondation Antoine de Galbert

10 bd de la Bastille, 12th (01.40.01.08.81, www.lamaisonrouge.org). M° Quai de la Rapée. **Open** 11am-7pm Wed, Fri-Sun; 11am-9pm Thur. **Admission** €7; €5 reductions; free under-13s. **Credit** MC, V.
Set in a former printworks, the Red House is an independently run space that alternates monographic shows of contemporary artists' work with pieces from different private art collections.

Bercy & Daumesnil

The **Viaduc des Arts** is a former railway viaduct along avenue Daumesnil; its row of glass-fronted arches enclose craft boutiques and workshops. Above sprout the blooms and bamboo of the **Promenade Plantée**, which continues through the Jardin de Reuilly and east to the **Bois de Vincennes**.

Eglise du Saint-Esprit is a copy of Istanbul's Hagia Sofia; the nearby **Cimetière de Picpus** contains the graves of many of the victims of the Terror, as well as American War of Independence hero General La Fayette.

Just before the Périphérique, the **Palais de la Porte Dorée** was built in 1931 for the Exposition Coloniale. It features striking, albeit politically incorrect, reliefs on the façade and two beautiful art deco offices. Originally the Musée des Colonies, then the Musée des Arts d'Afrique et d'Océanie (its collections now absorbed by the **Musée du Quai Branly**; *see p46*), it's home to the **Cité Nationale de l'Histoire de l'Immigration**. There's also an aquarium in the basement.

As recently as the 1980s, wine was unloaded from barges at Bercy, but after redevelopment this stretch of the Seine is now home to the vast Ministère de l'Economie et du Budget and, to the west, the **Palais Omnisports de Paris-Bercy** (*see p102*). To the east is the Bercy Expo exhibition and trade centre. In between lie the modern **Parc de Bercy** and the former American Center, built in the 1990s by Frank Gehry. It has now reopened as the Cinémathèque Française. At the eastern edge of the park is **Bercy Village**, where warehouses have been restored and opened as shops and cafés. Another conversion is the Pavillons de Bercy, with the **Musée des Arts Forains**, a collection of fairground rides and carnival salons.

Bois de Vincennes

12th. M° Château de Vincennes or Porte Dorée.
This is Paris's biggest park, created when the former royal hunting forest was landscaped by Alphand for Baron Haussmann. There are boating lakes, a Buddhist temple, a racetrack, restaurants, a baseball field and a small farm. The park also contains the Cartoucherie theatre complex (*see p104*). The Parc Floral is a cross between a botanical garden and an amusement park, including Paris-themed crazy golf, with water drawn from the Seine, and an adventure playground. Next to the park stands the imposing Château de Vincennes, where England's Henry V died in 1422. Jazz concerts take place in the Parc Floral on summer weekends; *see p12*.

Cimetière de Picpus

35 rue de Picpus, 12th (01.43.44.18.54). M° Daumesnil, Nation or Picpus. **Open** *15 Apr-14 Oct* 2-6pm Tue-Sun. *15 Oct-14 Apr* 2-4pm Tue-Sun. **Admission** €3. **No credit cards.**
Redolent with revolutionary associations, French and American, this cemetery in a working convent is the resting place for the thousands of victims of the Revolution's aftermath, guillotined at place du Trône (now place de la Nation) between 14 June and 27 July 1794. At the end of a walled garden is a graveyard of aristocratic French families. In one corner is the tomb of General La Fayette, who fought in the American War of Independence and was married to the aristocratic Marie Adrienne Françoise de Noailles. Clearly marked are the sites of two communal graves, and you can see the doorway where the carts arrived. It was thanks to a maid who had seen the carts that the site was rediscovered, including the cemetery and adjoining convent, founded by descendants of the Noailles family. In the chapel, two tablets list the names and occupations of the executed: 'domestic servant' and 'farmer' figure alongside 'lawyer' and 'prince and priest'.

Cité Nationale de l'Histoire de l'Immigration

293 av Daumesnil, 12th (01.58.51.52.00, www.histoire-immigration.fr). M° Porte Dorée. **Open** 10am-5.30pm Tue-Fri; 10am-7pm Sat, Sun. **Admission** €3-€5; €2-€3.50 reductions; free under-26s. *Aquarium* €4.50-€5.70; €3-€4.20 reductions. PMP. **No credit cards.**
Set in the stunning, colonial-themed Palais de la Porte Dorée (built in 1931 for the World Colonial Fair), the permanent collections here trace over 200 years of immigration history. There are thought-provoking images (film and photography), everyday objects (suitcases, accordions, sewing machines and so on) and artworks that symbolise the struggles immigrants had to face when integrating into French society. Don't miss the permanent exhibition area, Repères (bearings), that looks at why many immigrants chose France, the problems they faced upon arrival, and the way sport, work, language, religion and culture can ease integration. One of the most moving areas is the Galerie des Dons – a collection of personal memorabilia donated by individuals whose families came from foreign countries.

Eglise du Saint-Esprit

186 av Daumesnil, 12th (01.44.75.77.50, www.st-esprit.org). M° Daumesnil. **Open** 9.30am-noon, 3-7pm Mon-Fri; 9.30am-noon, 3-6pm Sat; from 9am Sun. **Admission** free.

Behind a red-brick exterior cladding, this unusual 1920s concrete church follows a square plan around a central dome, lit by a scalloped ring of windows. Architect Paul Tournon was directly inspired by the Hagia Sofia cathedral in Istanbul, though rather than mosaics, the inside is decorated with frescoes.

Musée des Arts Forains

53 av des Terroirs-de-France, 12th (01.43.40.16.22, www.pavillons-de-bercy.com). M° Cour St-Emilion. **Open** groups only, min 15 people, by appointment. **Admission** €12.50; €4 reductions. **No credit cards.**

Housed in a collection of Eiffel-era wine warehouses is a fantastical collection of 19th- and early 20th-century fairground attractions. The venue is hired out for functions on most evenings, and staff may well be setting the tables when you visit. Of the three halls, the most wonderful is the Salon de la Musique, where a musical sculpture by Jacques Rémus chimes and flashes in time with the 1934 Mortier organ and a modern-day digital grand piano playing *Murder on the Orient Express*. In the Salon de Venise you are twirled round on a gondola carousel; in the Salon des Arts Forains you can play a ball-throwing game that sets off a race of moustachioed waiters. The venue is open only to groups of 15 or more, but individuals can visit on the occasional guided tours. Call ahead.

Parc de Bercy

Rue de Bercy, 12th. M° Bercy or Cour St-Emilion. **Open** *Winter* 8am-5.30pm Mon-Fri; 9am-5.30pm Sat, Sun. *Summer* 8am-9pm Mon-Fri; 9am-9pm Sat, Sun.

Created in the 1990s, the Bercy park features a large lawn, a grid with square rose, herb and vegetable plots, an orchard, and gardens laid out to represent the four seasons.

Le Viaduc des Arts

15-121 av Daumesnil, 12th (www.viaduc-des-arts.fr). M° Gare de Lyon or Ledru-Rollin.

Glass-fronted workshops in the arches beneath the Promenade Plantée provide showrooms for furniture and fashion designers, picture-frame gilders, tapestry restorers, porcelain decorators, and chandelier, violin and flute makers.

North-east Paris

In the city's folklore, north-east Paris is working-class Paris – and although patches of it are gentrifying and little actual industry remains, the area still has a distinctive rough and ready vibe. Many of the streets here are somewhat on the tatty side, but others are artsy and fashionable, especially those close to the Canal St-Martin; and large swaths of the north-east – for example rue du Fbg-St-Denis and the thoroughfares leading off it – are excitingly multi-ethnic, with thriving North African, Turkish and Caribbean enclaves. In the top right corner is La Villette (through which the German occupiers entered the city in 1940), with its science museums, wacky landscaped gardens and arts space in the former city undertaker's.

Fbg-St-Denis to Gare du Nord

In the 10th arrondissement.

North of Porte St-Denis and Porte St-Martin, two of the oldest thoroughfares leading out of the city, rue du Fbg-St-Denis and rue du Fbg-St-Martin, traverse an area that was transformed in the 19th century by the railways, when it became the site of the Gare du Nord and Gare de l'Est. The grubby rue du Fbg-St-Denis is almost souk-like with its food shops, narrow passages and sinister courtyards. Garishly lit passage Brady is a surprising piece of India in Paris, full of restaurants, hairdressers and costume shops, whereas the art deco passage du Prado is more a continuation of the Sentier rag trade. The rue du Fbg-St-Martin follows the trace of the Roman road out of the city, and is full of children's clothes wholesalers, atmospheric courtyards and the ornate Mairie for the tenth. Rue des Petites-Ecuries ('Little Stables Street') was once known for saddlers, but now has shops, cafés and jazz venue **New Morning** (*see p99*), and is home to Turkish and Afro-Caribbean communities.

Rue de Paradis is known for its porcelain and glass outlets, and rue d'Hauteville shows traces of the area's grander days (notably the **Petit Hôtel Bourrienne**, at no.58, a Consulaire-style apartment open to the public). Opposite, the Cité Paradis is an alley of early industrial buildings. At the top of the street are the twin towers and terraced gardens of the **Eglise St-Vincent-de-Paul**. Behind, on rue de Belzunce, is Chez Casimir at no.6 (10th, 01.48.78.28.80). On boulevard Magenta, **Marché St-Quentin**, built in the 1860s, is one of the city's last few remaining cast-iron, covered market halls.

Boulevard de Strasbourg was cut through in the 19th century to create a vista up to the Gare de l'Est. At no.2, a neo-Renaissance creation houses the last fan-maker in Paris and the **Musée de l'Eventail**. Towards the station, Eglise St-Laurent (69 bd de Magenta, 119 rue du Fbg-St-Martin, 10th) is one of the city's oldest churches, an eclectic composition with a 12th-century tower, Gothic nave, Baroque lady chapel, 19th-century façade and 1930s stained glass. Between the Gare de l'Est and **Canal St-Martin** are the restored **Couvent des Récollets** and Square Villemin park.

Couvent des Récollets

148 rue du Fbg-St-Martin, 10th. M° Gare de l'Est. **Admission** free.

Founded as a monastery in the 17th century when still outside the city walls, this barracks, spinning factory and hospice was a military hospital from 1860 to 1968. Left empty, the convent was squatted by artists, Les Anges des Récollets, in the early 1990s. The buildings were renovated and reopened in 2004. One half, the Maison des Architectes, hosts a garden café and architectural debates. The other is the Centre International d'Accueil et d'Echanges des Récollets: 85 studios and duplexes for foreign 'creators' – artists and researchers (from painters to neurobiologists) – invited to stay here for extended periods. In rehabilitating the building, architect Frédéric Vincendon left traces of its history: the ghostly 17th-century stonework, 20th-century reinforced concrete columns and squatters' graffiti.

Eglise St-Vincent-de-Paul

5 rue Belzunce, 10th (01.48.78.47.47, www.paroissesvp.fr). M° Gare du Nord. **Open** 2-7pm Mon; 8am-noon, 2-7pm Tue-Fri; 8am-noon, 2-7.30pm Sat; 9.30am-noon, 4.30-7.30pm Sun. **Admission** free.

Set at the top of terraced gardens, this church was begun in 1824 by Lepère and completed in 1844 by Hittorff. The twin towers, pedimented Greek temple portico and sculptures of the four evangelists along the parapet are in high classical mode. The interior has a splendid double-storey arcade of columns, murals by Flandrin and church furniture by Rude.

Gare du Nord

Rue de Dunkerque, 10th (08.91.36.20.20). M° Gare du Nord.

The grandest of the great 19th-century train stations (and Eurostar terminal since 1994) was designed by Hittorff between 1861 and 1864. A conventional stone façade, with Ionic capitals and statues representing towns served by the station, hides a vast iron-and-glass vault.

Musée de l'Eventail

2 bd de Strasbourg, 10th (01.42.08.90.20, www.annehoguet.fr). M° Strasbourg St-Denis. **Open** 2-6pm Mon-Wed (Mon-Fri during school hols). *Children's activities* Wed afternoons. Closed Aug. **Admission** €6; €3-€4 reductions; free under-8s. **No credit cards.**

Anne Hoguet keeps the tradition of her ancestors alive in this arcane museum inside a 19th-century apartment, which has been a fan-maker's *atelier* since 1805. One room houses the tools of the trade; beside it is Hoguet's studio, where she works on fans for fashion and the stage. The former *salle d'exposition*, lined in blue silk, is where the collection of almost 1,000 historic fans is shown in glass cases and stored in cabinets.

Petit Hôtel Bourrienne

58 rue d'Hauteville, 10th (01.47.70.51.14). M° Bonne Nouvelle or Poissonnière. **Open** *Guided visits 1-15 July, Sept* noon-6pm daily. Rest of year by appointment Sat. **Admission** €7. **No credit cards.**

A rare example of the Consulaire style, this small *hôtel particulier* was built in 1789-98. It was occupied by Fortunée Hamelin, born (like her friend the Empress Josephine) in Martinique, and notorious for parading topless down the Champs-Elysées. A bedroom boudoir painted with tropical birds was her only decoration before the site was taken over by Louis Fauvelet de Bourrienne, Napoleon's private secretary. He had it decorated according to the latest fashion, making sure to keep his political options open (the dining room ceiling is painted with motifs favourable to monarchy and empire).

Canal St-Martin to La Villette

In the 10th & 19th arrondissements

Canal St-Martin, built between 1805 and 1825, begins at the Seine at Pont Morland, disappears underground at Bastille, hides under boulevard Richard-Lenoir, then emerges after crossing rue du Fbg-du-Temple, east of place de la République. Rue du Fbg-du-Temple itself is scruffy and cosmopolitan, lined with cheap grocers and discount stores, hidden courtyards and stalwarts of Paris nightlife: **Le Gibus** (*see p100*), bar-restaurant **Favela Chic** (*see p101*) and vintage dancehall **La Java** (*see p101*), as well as the **Palais des Glaces** (no.37, 10th, 01.42.02.27.17, www.palaisdesglaces.com), which programmes seasons of French comics.

The first stretch of the canal, lined with shady trees and crossed by iron footbridges and locks, has the most appeal. The quays are traffic-free on Sundays. Many canalside warehouses have been snapped up by artists and designers or turned into loft apartments.

East of here, the Hôpital St-Louis was commissioned in 1607 by Henri IV to house plague victims, and was built as a series of isolated pavilions in the same brick-and-stone style as place des Vosges, far enough from the town to prevent risk of infection. Behind the hospital, the rue de la Grange-aux-Belles housed the Montfaucon gibbet, put up in 1233, where victims were hanged and left to the elements. East of the hospital, the lovely cobbled rue Ste-Marthe and place Ste-Marthe have a provincial air, busy at night with multi-ethnic eateries.

North, on place du Colonel-Fabien, is the headquarters of the **Parti Communiste Français**, a modernist masterpiece built between 1968 and 1971 by Brazilian architect Oscar Niemeyer with Paul Chemetov and Jean Deroche. The canal disappears briefly again under place de Stalingrad, a locale best avoided after dark. The square was landscaped in 1989 to showcase the Rotonde de la Villette, one of Ledoux's grandiose 1780s toll houses that once marked the boundary of Paris; it now displays exhibitions and archaeological finds.

Here the canal widens into the Bassin de la Villette, and the new developments along the quai de Loire and further quai de la Marne, as well as some of the worst 1960s and '70s housing in the colossal blocks that stretch along rue de Flandres. At 104 rue d'Aubervilliers, the old municipal undertaker's is now a multimedia art space, **104**.

At the eastern end of the basin is an unusual 1885 hydraulic lifting bridge, Pont de Crimée. Thursday and Sunday mornings add vitality with a market at place de Joinville. East of here, the Canal de l'Ourcq (created in 1813 to provide drinking water, as well as for freight haulage) divides: Canal St-Denis runs north towards the Seine, and Canal de l'Ourcq continues east through La Villette and the suburbs. Long the city's main abattoir district, still reflected in the Grande Halle de la Villette and in some of the old meaty brasseries along boulevard de la Villette, the neighbourhood has been revitalised since the late 1980s by the postmodern **Parc de la Villette** complex, with the **Cité des Sciences et de l'Industrie** science museum and the **Cité de la Musique** concert hall.

104

104 rue d'Aubervilliers, 19th (01.53.35.50.00, www.104.fr). M° Riquet. **Open** 11am-9pm Tue-Sat; 11am-8pm Sun. **Admission** free. *Exhibitions* €5; €3 reductions; free under-6s. **Credit** AmEx, MC, V.

It's more than a century since Montmartre was the centre of artistic activity in Paris. But now the north of Paris is again where the action is – albeit a couple of kilometres east of place du Tertre, in a previously neglected area of bleak railway goods yards and dilapidated social housing. 104, described as a 'space for artistic creation', occupies a vast 19th-century building on the rue d'Aubervilliers that used to house Paris's municipal undertakers. The site was saved from developers by Roger Madec, the mayor of the 19th, who's made its renovation the centrepiece of a massive project of cultural and urban renewal. There aren't any constraints on the kind of work the resident artists do – 104 is open to 'all the arts' – but they're expected to show finished pieces in one of four annual 'festivals'. And they're also required to get involved in projects with the public. The complex also houses a bookshop and a restaurant.

La Cité des Sciences et de l'Industrie

La Villette, 30 av Corentin-Cariou, 19th (01.40.05.70.00, www.cite-sciences.fr). M° Porte de la Villette. **Open** 9.30am-6pm Tue-Sat; 9.30am-7pm Sun. **Admission** €8; €6 reductions; free under-7s. PMP. **Credit** MC, V.

This ultra-modern science museum pulls in five million visitors a year. Explora, the permanent show, occupies the upper two floors, whisking visitors through 30,000sq m (320,000sq ft) of space, life, matter and communication: scale models of satellites including the Ariane space shuttle, planes and robots, plus the chance to experience weightlessness, make for an exciting journey. In the Espace Images, try the delayed camera and other optical illusions, draw 3D images on a computer or lend your voice to the *Mona Lisa*. The hothouse garden investigates developments in agriculture and bio-technology. The Cité des Enfants runs workshops for younger children. See the website for details.

Musée de la Musique

Cité de la Musique, 221 av Jean-Jaurès, 19th (01.44.84.44.84, www.cite-musique.fr). M° Porte de Pantin. **Open** noon-6pm Tue-Sat; 10am-6pm Sun. **Admission** €8; €6.40 reductions; free under-18s. PMP. **Credit** AmEx, MC, V.

Alongside the concert hall, this innovative music museum houses a gleamingly restored collection of instruments from the old Conservatoire, interactive computers and scale models of opera houses and concert halls. Visitors are supplied with an audio guide in a choice of languages, and the musical commentary is a joy, playing the appropriate instrument as you approach each exhibit. Alongside the trumpeting brass, curly woodwind instruments and precious strings are more unusual items, such as the Indonesian gamelan orchestra, whose sounds influenced the work of Debussy and Ravel. Concerts in the amphitheatre use instruments from the collection.

Parc de la Villette

Av Corentin-Cariou, 19th (01.40.03.75.75, www.villette.com). M° Porte de la Villette. Av Jean-Jaurès, 19th. M° Porte de Pantin.

Dotted with red pavilions, or *folies*, the park was designed by Swiss architect Bernard Tschumi and is a postmodern feast. The *folies* serve as glorious giant climbing frames, as well as a first-aid post, burger bar and children's art centre. Kids shoot down a Chinese dragon slide, and an undulating suspended path follows the Canal de l'Ourcq. As well as the lawns, which are used for an open-air film festival in summer, there are ten themed gardens bearing evocative names such as the Garden of Mirrors, of Mists, of Acrobatics and of Childhood Frights. South of the canal are the Zénith (*see p98*), and the Grande Halle de la Villette – now used for trade fairs, exhibitions and September's jazz festival (*see p13*). It is flanked by the Conservatoire de la Musique and the Cité de la Musique, with rehearsal rooms, concert halls and the Musée de la Musique.

Belleville, Ménilmontant & Charonne

In the 11th, 19th & 20th arrondissements.
When the city boundaries were expanded in 1860, Ménilmontant, Belleville and Charonne, once villages that provided Paris with fruit, wine and weekend escapes, were all absorbed. They were built up with housing for migrants, first from rural France and later from former colonies in North Africa and South-east Asia. The area encompasses one of the city's most beautiful parks, the romantic **Buttes-Chaumont**. Despite attempts to dissipate workers' agitation by splitting the village between the 11th, 19th and 20th administrative districts, Belleville became the centre of opposition to the Second Empire. Cabarets, artisans and workers typified 1890s Belleville; colonised by artists in the 1990s, today Belleville is a trendy hangout.

On boulevard de Belleville, Chinese and Vietnamese shops rub shoulders with Muslim and kosher groceries, and couscous and falafel eateries; a street market takes place here on Tuesday and Friday mornings.

North of here, along avenue Simon-Bolivar, is Parc des Buttes-Chaumont. This is the most desirable part of north-east Paris, with Haussmannian apartments overlooking the park: to the east, near place de Rhin-et-Danube, is a small area of tiny, hilly streets lined with small houses and gardens, known by locals as the Quartier Mouzaïa.

Up on the slopes of the Hauts de Belleville, there are views over the city from rue Piat and rue des Envierges, which lead to the modern but charming **Parc de Belleville** with its Maison des Vents devoted to birds and kites. Below the park, rue Ramponneau mixes new housing and relics of old Belleville. At no.23 an old smithy has changed into La Forge, an artists' squat.

'Mesnil-Montant' used to be a few houses on a hill with vines and fruit trees – then came the bistros, bordellos and workers' housing. It became part of Paris in 1860 along with Belleville, and has a similar history. These days it's a thriving centre of alternative Paris, as artists and young professionals have moved in. Although side streets still have male-only North African cafés, rue Oberkampf is home to some of the city's most humming bars, many following the runaway success of the pivotal **Café Charbon** (*see p67*).

The area mixes 1960s and '70s housing projects with older dwellings, some gentrified, some derelict. Just below rue des Pyrénées, which cuts through the 20th, you can rummage around the rustic Cité Leroy or Villa l'Ermitage, cobbled cul-de-sacs of little houses and gardens, and old craft workshops. Rue de l'Ermitage has a curious neo-Gothic house at no.19 – and a bird's-eye view from the junction with rue de Ménilmontant, right down the hill to the Centre Pompidou. On rue Boyer,

Party in the park

There are plenty of handsomely ordered opportunities to indulge in a bit of park life in Paris, from the pathways of the Jardin des Tuileries to the ponds of the Jardin du Luxembourg. But if you're looking for something a little less formal, one patch of greenery definitely worth a stroll is **Parc des Buttes-Chaumont** (*see below*). Set high up in Belleville and often missed by weekenders keen not to stray too far from the tourist loop, this 19th arrondissement gem is one of the city's most magical spots.

When the city's boundaries were expanded in 1860, Belleville – once a village that provided Paris with fruit, wine and weekend escapes – was absorbed and the Buttes-Chaumont was created on the site of a former gypsum and limestone quarry. The park, with its meandering paths, waterfalls, temples and vertical cliffs, was designed by Adolphe Alphand for Haussmann, and was opened as part of the celebrations for the Universal Exhibition in 1867.

After lounging with the locals for a few hours, head for the park's hugely hip hangout, the wonderfully jolly Rosa Bonheur *guinguette* (www.rosabonheur.fr). Open till midnight, it makes the perfect place to sip an *apéro* and take in the stunning views of the city below.

La Maroquinerie (*see p67*) puts on an eclectic mix of literary events, political debate and live music, and at 88 rue de Ménilmontant, art squat **La Miroiterie** opens house for art shows and the *magasin gratuit*, a free swap shop.

East of Père-Lachaise on rue de Bagnolet, **La Flèche d'Or** (*see p98*), a converted station on the defunct Petite Ceinture railway line, is a landmark music venue. Beyond, the medieval Eglise St-Germain-de-Charonne is at the heart of what is left of the village of Charonne. Set at the top of steps next to its presbytery, below a hill once covered with vines, it is the only church in Paris, except St-Pierre-de-Montmartre, still to have its own graveyard. Below here, centred on the old village high street of rue St-Blaise, is a prettified backwater of quiet tearooms and bistros, where old shops have been taken over by art classes.

Towards porte de Bagnolet, where rue de Bagnolet and rue des Balkans meet on the edge of a small park, the **Pavillon de l'Hermitage** is a small aristocratic relic built in the 1720s for Françoise-Marie de Bourbon, the daughter of Louis XIV, when it was in the grounds of the Château de Bagnolet. A little further south at porte de Montreuil, cross the Périphérique for the Puces de Montreuil market (Mon, Sat, Sun).

Eglise St-Germain-de-Charonne
Pl St-Blaise, 20th (01.43.71.42.04). M° Porte de Bagnolet. **Admission** free. **Open** 9am-7pm.
The old village church of Charonne dates mainly from the 15th century, though one massive column and the bell tower remain from an earlier structure. The interior is almost square, with a triple nave and a simple organ loft. Two side altars have striking modern paintings (a crucifixion and a pietà) by Paul Rambié; a niche contains a wood statue of St Blaise.

Musée Edith Piaf
5 rue Crespin-du-Gast, 11th (01.43.55.52.72). M° Ménilmontant. **Open** *By appointment only* 1-6pm Mon-Wed. **Admission** free.
Set in an apartment where Piaf lived at the age of 18, when she sang on the streets of Ménilmontant, this tiny museum consists of two red-painted rooms crammed with letters, pictures, framed discs and objects belonging to the singer. Curator Bernard Marchois doesn't speak English. It helps, therefore, to have seen the Marion Cotillard film before you go, to allow you to piece together the scrapbook of Piaf's highly mythologised life. The museum's real treasures are two letters, one a chatty number written on her 28th birthday, and another more passionate pen to actor Robert Dalban. These – and the well-worn, human-sized teddy bear cuddling a tiny monkey soft toy – are the only clues to the real Piaf, the greatest singer the nation has ever known.

Parc des Buttes-Chaumont
Rue Botzaris, rue Manin, rue de Crimée, 19th. M° Buttes Chaumont. **Open** *Oct-Apr* 7am-8pm daily. *May-Aug* 7am-10pm daily. *Sept* 7am-9pm daily.
See above **Party in the park**.

The Latin Quarter & the 13th

The Latin Quarter holds a considerable mystique for many foreign visitors, thanks to the historical presence of Hemingway, Orwell and Miller and to it being the seedbed of the 1968 revolt. Granted, many of the narrow, crooked streets (like the Marais, the Latin Quarter was another part of Paris largely untouched by Haussmann) are charming, and there are some real architectural glories, especially ecclesiastical ones; but the crowds can make the experience of seeing them rather dispiriting. The 'Latin' in the area's name probably derives from the fact that it has been the

university quarter since medieval times, when Latin was the language of instruction. To the east of the Latin Quarter, the part of the 13th arrondissement known as the ZAC Rive Gauche, anchored by the four book-like towers of the Bibliothèque Nationale, is one of the city's fastest rising quarters.

St-Séverin & St-Julien-le-Pauvre

In the 5th arrondissement.
Boulevard St-Michel used to be synonymous with student rebellion; now it's a largely unprepossessing ribbon of fast-food joints and clothing shops, though **Gibert Joseph** (*see p70*) continues to furnish books and stationery to students. East of here, the semi-pedestrianised patch by the Seine has retained much of its medieval street plan. Rue de la Huchette and rue de la Harpe are now best known for their kebabs and pizzas, though there are 18th-century wrought-iron balconies and carved masks in the latter street. At the tiny **Théâtre de la Huchette** (*see p104*), Ionesco's absurdist drama *La Cantatrice Chauve* (*The Bald Soprano*) has been playing constantly since 1957. Also of interest are rue du Chat-qui-Pêche, supposedly the city's narrowest street, and rue de la Parcheminerie, named after the parchment sellers and copyists who once lived here. Among the tourist shops stands the city's most charming medieval church, the **Eglise St-Séverin**, with leering gargoyles, gabled side chapels and an exuberantly vaulted Flamboyant Gothic interior.

Across ancient rue St-Jacques is the **Eglise St-Julien-le-Pauvre**, built as a resting place for 12th-century pilgrims. Nearby rue Galande has old houses and the Trois Mailletz cabaret at no.56 (5th, 01.43.54.42.94). The medieval cellars of the **Caveau des Oubliettes** jazz club (*see p99*) were used as a prison after the French Revolution (*oubliette* is the French word for a pit into which prisoners were thrown, then forgotten). At no.42, arts cinema **Studio Galande** (*see p91*) draws goths for late-night screenings of *The Rocky Horror Picture Show* every Friday and Saturday. Just outside the church, in place Viviani, stands what is perhaps the city's oldest tree, a false acacia that was planted in 1602; it's now half-swamped by ivy and propped up by concrete buttresses.

The little streets between here and the eastern stretch of boulevard St-Germain are among the city's oldest: streets such as rue de Bièvre, which follows the course of the Bièvre river that flowed into the Seine in the Middle Ages, rue du Maître-Albert, and rue des Grands-Degrès, with traces of old shop signs painted on its buildings' façades. Remnants of the Collège des Bernardins, built for the Cistercian order, can be seen in rue de Poissy, where the 13th- to 14th-century gothic monks' refectory is being restored after service as firemen's barracks. Nearby are the **Eglise St-Nicolas du Chardonnet** (23 rue Bernardins, 5th, 01.44.27.07.90), associated with the schismatic Society of St Pius X and one of a small number of churches where you can hear the Tridentine Mass in Paris, and the art deco **Maison de la Mutualité** (24 rue St-Victor, 5th, 01.40.46.12.00), where you'll find everything from trade unions meetings to rock concerts.

At 47 quai de la Tournelle, the 17th-century Hôtel de Miramion now contains the **Musée de l'Assistance Publique**, devoted to the history of Paris hospitals. You'll find food for all budgets along quai de la Tournelle, starting with Michelin-starred **La Tour d'Argent** (*see p59*), said to have been founded as an inn in 1582. After 60 years at the helm, owner Claude Terrail died in 2006, passing the restaurant to his son André. Place Maubert, now a breezy morning marketplace (Tue, Thur, Sat), witnessed the hanging of Protestants during the 16th-century Wars of Religion. Just behind the square, the modern police station is home to an array of grisly criminal evidence in the **Musée de la Préfecture de Police.**

On the corner of boulevard St-Germain and boulevard St-Michel stand the striking ruins of the late second-century **Thermes de Cluny**, the Romans' main baths complex; the adjoining Gothic Hôtel de Cluny provides a suitable setting for the **Musée National du Moyen Age**, the national collection of medieval art. Adjoining boulevard St-Germain, its garden has been replanted with species portrayed in medieval tapestries, paintings and treatises.

Eglise St-Julien-le-Pauvre

Rue St-Julien-le-Pauvre, 5th (01.43.54.52.16, www.sjlpmelkites.fr). M° Cluny La Sorbonne. **Open** 9.30am-1pm, 3-6.30pm daily. **Admission** free.

A former sanctuary for pilgrims en route to Compostela, this much-mauled church dates from the late 12th century, on the cusp of Romanesque and Gothic, and has capitals richly decorated with vines, acanthus leaves and winged harpies. Once part of a priory, it became the university church when colleges migrated to the Left Bank, and was the site of riotous university assemblies. Since 1889, it has been used by the Greek Orthodox Church.

Eglise St-Séverin

3 rue des Prêtres-St-Séverin, 5th (01.42.34.93.50, www.saint-severin.com). M° Cluny La Sorbonne or St-Michel. **Open** 11am-7.30pm daily. **Admission** free.

Built on the site of the chapel of the hermit Séverin, itself set on a much earlier Merovingian burial ground, this lovely Flamboyant Gothic edifice was long the parish church of the Left Bank. It was rebuilt on various occasions to repair damage after ransacking by Normans and to meet the needs of the growing population. The church dates from the 15th century, though the doorway, carved with foliage, was added in 1837 from the demolished Eglise St-Pierre-aux-Boeufs on Ile de la Cité. The double ambulatory is famed for its forest of 'palm tree' vaulting, which meets at the end in a unique spiral column that inspired a series of paintings by Robert Delaunay. The bell tower, a survivor from one of the earlier churches on the site, has the oldest bell in Paris (1412). Around the nave are stained-glass windows dating from the 14th and 15th centuries (most of those in the side chapels are by 19th-century Chartres master Emile Hersh), and the choir apse has striking stained glass designed by artist Jean René Bazaine in the 1960s. Next door, around the former cemetery, is the only remaining charnel house in Paris.

Musée de l'Assistance Publique

Hôtel de Miramion, 47 quai de la Tournelle, 5th (01.40.27.50.05, www.aphp.fr). M° Maubert Mutualité. **Open** 10am-6pm Tue-Sun. Closed Aug. **Admission** €4; €2 reductions; free under-13s. PMP. **No credit cards.**

The history of Paris hospitals, from the days when they were receptacles for abandoned babies to the dawn of modern medicine, is shown through paintings, prints, and a mock ward and pharmacy.

Musée National du Moyen Age – Thermes de Cluny

6 pl Paul-Painlevé, 5th (01.53.73.78.00, www.musee-moyenage.fr). M° Cluny La Sorbonne. **Open** 9.15am-5.45pm Mon, Wed-Sun. **Admission** €8; €6 reductions; free under-18, all 1st Sun of mth. PMP. **Credit** *Shop* MC, V.

The national museum of medieval art is best known for the beautiful, allegorical *Lady and the Unicorn* tapestry cycle, but it also has important collections of medieval sculpture and enamels. The building itself, commonly known as Cluny, is also a rare example of 15th-century secular Gothic architecture, with its foliate Gothic doorways, hexagonal staircase jutting out of the façade and vaulted chapel. It was built from 1485 to 1498 – on top of a Gallo-Roman baths complex. The baths, built in characteristic Roman bands of stone and brick masonry, are the finest Roman remains in Paris. The vaulted *frigidarium* (cold bath), *tepidarium* (warm bath), *caldarium* (hot bath) and part of the hypocaust heating system are all still visible. A themed garden fronts the whole complex. Recent acquisitions include the illuminated manuscript *L'Ascension du Christ* from the Abbey of Cluny, dating back to the 12th century, and the 16th-century triptych *Assomption de la Vierge* by Adrien Isenbrant of Bruges.

Musée de la Préfecture de Police

4 rue de la Montagne-Ste-Geneviève, 5th (01.44.41.52.50, www.prefecturedepolice.interieur.gouv.fr). M° Maubert Mutualité. **Open** 9am-5pm Mon-Fri; 10am-5pm Sat. **Admission** free. **No credit cards.**

The police museum is housed in a working *commisariat*, which makes for a slightly intimidating entry procedure. You need to walk boldly past the police officer standing guard outside and up the steps to the lobby, where you have to ask at the reception booth to be let in – queuing, if necessary, with locals there on other, usually police-related, errands. The museum is on the second floor; start from the *Accueil* and work your way clockwise.

None of the displays is labelled in English (though there is a bilingual booklet), and a handful are not labelled at all; but if you have basic French and any sort of interest in criminology, this extensive collection is well worth seeing. It starts in the early 17th century and runs to the Occupation, via the founding of the Préfecture de Police by Napoleon in 1800. Exhibits include a prison register open at the entry for Ravaillac, assassin of Henri IV; a section on the Anarchist bombings of the 1890s; the automatic pistol used to assassinate President Doumer in 1932; a blood-chilling collection of murder weapons – hammers, ice picks and knives; sections on serial killers Landru and Petiot; and less dangerous items, such as a gadget used to snag banknotes from the apron pockets of market sellers.

The Sorbonne, Montagne Ste-Geneviève & Mouffetard

In the 5th arrondissement.

An influx of well-heeled residents in the 1980s put paid to the days of horn-rims, pipes and turtlenecks: accommodation here is now well beyond the reach of most students. The intellectual tradition persists, however, in the concentration of academic institutions around Montagne Ste-Geneviève, and students throng the specialist bookstores and art cinemas on rue Champollion and rue des Ecoles.

The district's long association with learning began in about 1100, when a number of renowned scholars, including Pierre Abélard, began to live and teach on the Montagne, independent of the established cathedral school of Notre-Dame. This loose association of scholars came to be referred to as a 'university'. The Paris schools attracted students from all over Europe, and the 'colleges' – in reality student residences dotted round the area (some still survive) – multiplied, until the University of Paris was given official recognition with a charter from Pope Innocent III in 1215.

By the 16th century, the university – named the **Sorbonne**, after the most famous of its colleges – had been co-opted by the Catholic Church. A century later, Cardinal Richelieu rebuilt it. Following the Revolution, when it was forced to close, Napoleon revived the Sorbonne as the cornerstone of his new, centralised education system. The university participated enthusiastically in the uprisings of the 19th century; it was also a seedbed of the 1968 revolt, when it was occupied by protesting students. These days, it's decidedly less turbulent. Also on rue des Ecoles, the independent **Collège de France** was founded in 1530 by a group of humanists led by Guillaume Budé under the patronage of François I. The neighbouring **Brasserie Balzar** (no.49, 5th, 01.43.54.13.67) has been fuelling amateur philosophy for years.

From here, climb rue St-Jacques to rue Soufflot for the most impressive introduction to place du Panthéon. Otherwise, follow rue des Carmes – with its Baroque chapel, now used by the Syrian Church – and continue on rue Valette past the brick and stone entrance of the **Collège Ste-Barbe**, where Ignatius Loyola, Montgolfier and Eiffel studied. Alternatively, follow the serpentine rue de la Montagne-Ste-Geneviève; at the junction of rue Descartes, cafés and eccentric wine bistros overlook the sculpted 19th-century entrance to what was once the elite Ecole Polytechnique (since moved to the suburbs) and is now the research ministry. There's a small park here, and popular bistro **L'Ecurie** (2 rue Laplace, 5th, 01.46.33.68.49) – an old stable burrowed into medieval cellars.

Louis XV commissioned the huge, domed **Panthéon** to honour Geneviève, the city's patron saint, but it was converted during the Revolution into a secular temple for France's *grands hommes*. The surrounding place du Panthéon, also conceived by Panthéon architect Jacques-Germain Soufflot, is one of the city's great set pieces: looking on to it are the elegant fifth arrondissement town hall and, opposite, the law faculty. On the north side, the Ste-Geneviève university library, built by Labrouste with an iron-framed reading room, contains medieval manuscripts. On the other side you'll find the historic **Hôtel des Grands Hommes** (no.17, 5th, 01.46.34.19.60, www.hoteldesgrandshommes.com), where Surrealist mandarin André Breton invented 'automatic writing' in the 1920s.

Pascal, Racine and the remains of Sainte Geneviève are all interred within **Eglise St-Etienne-du-Mont**, on the north-east corner of the square. Just behind it, within the illustrious and elitist Lycée Henri IV, is the Gothic-Romanesque **Tour de Clovis**, part of the former Abbaye Ste-Geneviève. Take a look through the entrance (open during termtime) and you'll also catch glimpses of the cloister and other structures.

Further from place du Panthéon, along rue Clovis, is a chunk of Philippe-Auguste's 12th-century city wall. The exiled monarch James II once resided at 65 rue du Cardinal-Lemoine, in the severe buildings of the former Collège des Ecossais (now a school), founded in 1372 to house Scottish students; the king's brain was preserved here until carried off and lost during the French Revolution. Other well known ex-residents include Hemingway, who lived at 79 rue du Cardinal-Lemoine (note the plaque) and 39 rue Descartes in the 1920s, and James Joyce; the latter completed *Ulysses* while staying at 71 rue du Cardinal-Lemoine. Rimbaud lived in rue Descartes, and Descartes lived on nearby rue Rollin.

This area is still a mix of tourist picturesque and gentle village, where some of the buildings hide surprising courtyards and gardens. Pretty place de la Contrescarpe has been a famous rendezvous since the 1530s, when writers as renowned as Rabelais, Ronsard and Du Bellay frequented the Cabaret de la Pomme de Pin at no.1; it still has some lively cafés. When George Orwell stayed at 6 rue du Pot-de-Fer in 1928 and 1929 (he described his time here and his work as a dishwasher in *Down and Out in Paris and London*), it was a place of astounding poverty; today, the street is lined with bargain bars and restaurants, and the restored houses along rue Tournefort bear little relation to the garrets of Balzac's *Le Père Goriot*.

Rue Mouffetard, originally the road to Rome and one of the oldest streets in the city, winds south as a suite of cheap bistros, Greek and Lebanese tavernas and knick-knack shops thronged with tourists; the vibe described by Hemingway – 'that wonderful narrow crowded market street, beloved of bohemians' – has faded. The street market (Tue-Sat, Sun morning) on the lower half seethes on weekends, when it spills on to the square and around the cafés in front of the **Eglise St-Médard**. There's another busy market, more frequented by locals, at place Monge (Wed, Fri, Sun morning).

Back to the west of the Panthéon, head south beyond rue Soufflot and you'll notice that rue St-Jacques becomes prettier. Here you'll find several ancient buildings, including the elegant *hôtel* at no.151, good food shops, vintage bistro **Perraudin** (no.157, 5th, 01.46.33.15.75) and the **Institut Océanographique** (no.195, 5th, 01.44.32.10.70, www.oceano.org), which has well-stocked aquariums much loved by children. Rue d'Ulm contains the elite **Ecole Normale Supérieure** (no.45, 5th, 01.44.32.30.00, www.ens.fr), occupied in protest by the unemployed in January 1998; in an echo of 1968, students also joined in.

Turn off up hilly rue des Fossés-St-Jacques to discover place de l'Estrapade; in the 17th century the *estrapade* was a tall wooden tower from which deserters were dropped repeatedly until they died. Nearby, in rue des Irlandais, the Centre Culturel Irlandais hosts concerts, exhibitions, films, plays and spoken-word events promoting Irish culture. Back to the west of rue St-Jacques, rue Soufflot and broad rue Gay-Lussac (a hotspot of the May 1968 revolt), with their Haussmannian apartment buildings, lead to boulevard St-Michel and the Jardin du Luxembourg.

Further south along rue St-Jacques, in the potters' quarter of Roman Lutetia, is the least altered and most ornate of the city's Baroque churches, the landmark **Eglise du Val-de-Grâce**. Round the corner, at 6 rue du Val-de-Grâce, is the former home of Alfons Maria Mucha, the influential Moravian art nouveau artist, who was best known for his posters of Sarah Bernhardt.

Collège de France

11 pl Marcelin-Berthelot, 5th (01.44.27.12.11, 01.44.27.11.47, www.college-de-france.fr). M° Cluny La Sorbonne or Maubert Mutualité/RER Luxembourg. **Open** 9am-5pm Mon-Fri. **Admission** free.

Founded in 1530 with the patronage of François I, the college is a place of learning and a research institute. The present building dates from the 16th and 17th centuries; there's also a later annexe. All lectures are free and open to the public; some have been given by such eminent figures as anthropologist Claude Lévi-Strauss, philosopher Maurice Merleau-Ponty and mathematician Jacques Tits.

Eglise St-Etienne-du-Mont

Pl Ste-Geneviève, 5th (01.43.54.11.79, www.saintetiennedumont.fr). M° Cardinal Lemoine/RER Luxembourg. **Open** *Sept-May* 8.45am-7.30pm Tue-Fri; 8.45am-noon, 2-7.45pm Sat; 8.45am-12.15pm, 2.30-7.45pm Sun. *July, Aug* 10am-noon, 4-7.15pm Tue-Sun. **Admission** free.

Geneviève, patron saint of Paris, is credited with having miraculously saved the city from the ravages of Attila the Hun in 451, and her shrine has been a site of pilgrimage ever since. The present church was built in an amalgam of Gothic and Renaissance styles between 1492 and 1626, and once adjoined the abbey church of Ste-Geneviève. The façade mixes Gothic rose windows with rusticated roman columns and reliefs of classically draped figures. The interior is wonderfully tall and light, with soaring columns and a classical balustrade. The stunning Renaissance rood screen, with its double spiral staircase and ornate stone strapwork, is the only surviving one in Paris, and was possibly designed by Philibert Delorme. The decorative canopied wooden pulpit by Germaine Pillon dates from 1651, and is adorned with figures of the Graces and supported by a muscular Samson sitting on the defeated lion. Sainte Geneviève's elaborate neo-Gothic brass-and-glass shrine (shielding the ancient tombstone) is located to the right of the choir, surrounded by an assorted collection of reliquaries and dozens of marble plaques bearing messages of thanks. At the back of the church (reached through the sacristy), the catechism chapel constructed by Baltard in the 1860s has a cycle of paintings relating the saint's life story.

Eglise St-Médard
141 rue Mouffetard, 5th (01.44.08.87.00, www.saintmedard.org). Mº Censier Daubenton.
Open 8am-12.30pm, 2.30-7.30pm Tue-Sat; 8.30am-12.30pm, 4-8.30pm Sun. **Admission** free.
The original chapel here was a dependency of the Abbaye Ste-Geneviève. The rebuilding towards the end of the 15th century created a somewhat larger, late Gothic structure best known for its elaborate vaulted ambulatory.

Eglise du Val-de-Grâce
Pl Alphonse-Laveran, 5th (01.40.51.51.92). RER Luxembourg or Port-Royal. **Open** noon-6pm Tue, Wed, Sat, Sun. **Admission** €5; €2.50 reductions; free under-6s. **No credit cards.**
Anne of Austria, the wife of Louis XIII, vowed to erect 'a magnificent temple' if God blessed her with a son. She got two. The resulting church and surrounding Benedictine monastery – these days a military hospital and the Musée du Service de Santé des Armées – were built by François Mansart and Jacques Lemercier. This is the most luxuriously Baroque of the city's 17th-century domed churches, its ornate altar decorated with twisted barley-sugar columns. The swirling colours of the dome frescoes painted by Pierre Mignard in 1669 (which Molière himself once eulogised) are designed to give a foretaste of heaven. In contrast, the surrounding monastery offers the perfect example of François Mansart's classical restraint.

Musée du Service de Santé des Armées
Val de Grâce, pl Alphonse-Laveran, 5th (01.40.51.51.92). RER Luxembourg or Port

Royal. **Open** noon-6pm Tue, Wed, Sat, Sun. **Admission** €5; €2.50 reductions; free under-6s. **No credit cards.**
Housed in the royal convent designed by Mansart, next door to a military hospital, this museum traces the history of military medicine via replicas of field hospitals and ambulance trains, and displays of antique medical instruments. The section on World War I demonstrates how the conflict propelled medical progress.

Le Panthéon
Pl du Panthéon, 5th (01.44.32.18.00). Mº Cardinal Lemoine/RER Luxembourg. **Open** 10am-6pm (until 6.30pm summer) daily. **Admission** €8; €5 reductions; free under-18s (if accompanied by an adult). PMP. **Credit** MC, V.
Soufflot's neo-classical megastructure was the architectural *grand projet* of its day, commissioned by a grateful Louis XV to thank Sainte Geneviève for his recovery from illness. But by the time it was ready in 1790, a lot had changed; during the Revolution, the Panthéon was rededicated as a 'temple of reason' and the resting place of the nation's great men. The austere barrel-vaulted crypt now houses Voltaire, Rousseau, Hugo and Zola. New heroes are installed but rarely: Pierre and Marie Curie's remains were transferred here in 1995; Alexandre Dumas in 2002. Inside are Greek columns and domes, and 19th-century murals of Geneviève's life by Symbolist painter Puvis de Chavannes, a formative influence on Picasso during the latter's blue period.
Mount the steep spiral stairs to the colonnade encircling the dome for superb views. A replica of Foucault's Pendulum hangs here; the original proved that the earth does indeed spin on its axis, via a universal joint that lets the direction of the pendulum's swing rotate as the earth revolves.

La Sorbonne
17 rue de la Sorbonne, 5th (01.40.46.22.11, www.sorbonne.fr). Mº Cluny La Sorbonne. **Open** *Tours* by appointment. Closed July & Aug.
Founded in 1253, the University of the Sorbonne was at the centre of the Latin Quarter's intellectual activity from the Middle Ages until 1968, when it was occupied by students and stormed by the riot police. The authorities then split the University of Paris into safer outposts, but the Sorbonne still houses the Faculté des Lettres. Rebuilt by Richelieu and reorganised by Napoleon, the present buildings date from the late 1800s, and have a labyrinth of classrooms and lecture theatres, as well as an observatory tower. The elegant dome of the 17th-century chapel dominates place de la Sorbonne; Cardinal Richelieu is buried inside. It's only open to the public for exhibitions or concerts.

Around the Jardin des Plantes

In the 5th arrondissement.
The quiet, easternmost part of the fifth arrondissement is home to yet more academic institutions, the Paris mosque and another Roman relic. Old-fashioned bistros on rue des Fossés-St-Bernard contrast with the forbidding 1960s architecture of the massive university campus of Paris VI and VII, the science faculty (known as Jussieu) built on what had been the site of the important Abbaye St-Victor. Between the Seine and Jussieu is the strikingly modern, glass-faced **Institut du Monde Arabe**, which has a programme of concerts and exhibitions and a restaurant with a great view. The **Jardin Tino Rossi**, by the river, contains the slightly dilapidated **Musée de la Sculpture en Plein Air**; in summer this is a spot for dancing and picnicking.
Hidden among the hotels of rue Monge is the entrance to the **Arènes de Lutèce**, a Roman amphitheatre. The remains of a circular arena and its tiers of stone seating were discovered in 1869. Excavation started in 1883, thanks to lobbying by Victor Hugo. Nearby rise the white minaret and green pan-tiled roof of the **Mosquée de Paris**, built in 1922. Its beautiful Moorish tearoom is a student haunt.
The mosque looks over the **Jardin des Plantes** botanical garden. Opened in 1626 as a garden for medicinal plants, it features an 18th-century maze and a winter garden bristling with rare species. It also houses the Muséum National d'Histoire Naturelle, with its brilliantly renovated **Grande Galerie de l'Evolution**, and a zoo, La Ménagerie, an unlikely by-product of the Revolution, when royal and noble collections of wild animals were impounded. Street names and the lovely animal-themed fountain on the corner of rue Cuvier pay homage to the many naturalists and other

scientists who worked here. A short way away, at 11-13bis rue Geoffroy-St-Hilaire, the words 'Chevaux', 'Poneys' and 'Anes' are still visible on the façade of the old horse market.

Arènes de Lutèce
Rue Monge, rue de Navarre or rue des Arènes, 5th. Mº Cardinal Lemoine or Place Monge. **Open** *Summer* 9am-9.30pm daily. *Winter* 8am-5.30pm daily. **Admission** free.
This Roman arena, where wild beasts and gladiators fought, could seat 10,000 people. It was still visible during the reign of Philippe-Auguste in the 12th century, then disappeared under rubble. The site was rediscovered in 1869 and now incorporates a romantically planted garden. These days, it attracts skaters, footballers and boules players.

Grande Galerie de l'Evolution
36 rue Geoffroy-St-Hilaire, 2 rue Bouffon or pl Valhubert, 5th (01.40.79.56.01, www.mnhn.fr). Mº Gare d'Austerlitz or Jussieu. **Open** *Grande Galerie* 10am-6pm Mon, Wed-Sun. *Other galleries* 10am-5pm Mon, Wed-Fri; 10am-6pm Sat, Sun. **Admission** *Grande Galerie* €7; €5 reductions; free under-26s. *Other galleries* (each) €7; €5 reductions; free under-26s. **No credit cards.**
Located within the Jardin des Plantes (*see below*), this beauty of a 19th-century iron-framed, glass-roofed structure has been modernised with lifts, galleries and false floors, and filled with life-size models of tentacle-waving squids, open-mawed sharks, tigers hanging off elephants and monkeys swarming down from the ceiling. The centrepiece is a procession of African wildlife across the first floor that resembles the procession into Noah's Ark. Glass-sided lifts take you up through suspended birds to the second floor, which deals with man's impact on nature and rewiring of evolution (crocodile into handbag). The third floor focuses on endangered and extinct species. The separate Galerie d'Anatomie Comparée et de Paléontologie contains over a million skeletons and a world-class fossil collection.

Institut du Monde Arabe
1 rue des Fossés-St-Bernard, 5th (01.40.51.38.38, www.imarabe.org). Mº Jussieu. **Open** *Museum* closed for renovation. *Library* 1-8pm Tue-Sat. *Café* 11am-7pm Tue-Sun. *Tours* 3pm Tue-Fri; 3pm & 4.30pm Sat, Sun. **Admission** *Roof terrace, library* free. PMP. *Exhibitions* varies. *Tours* €8. **Credit** MC, V.
A clever blend of high-tech and Arab influences, this Seine-side *grand projet* was constructed between 1980 and 1987 to a design by Jean Nouvel. Shuttered windows, inspired by the screens of Moorish palaces, act as camera apertures, contracting or expanding according to the amount of sunlight. A museum covering the history and archaeology of the Islamic Arab world, which usually occupies the upper floors, is closed for renovations until mid 2011. In the meantime, there's an excellent Middle East bookshop on the ground floor and the views from the roof terrace (to which access is free) are fabulous.

Jardin des Plantes
36 rue Geoffroy-St-Hilaire, 2 rue Buffon, pl Valhubert or 57 rue Cuvier, 5th. Mº Gare d'Austerlitz, Jussieu or Place Monge. **Open** *Main garden* Winter 8am-5.30pm daily. Summer 7.30am-7.45pm daily. *Alpine garden* Apr-Oct 8am-4.40pm Mon-Fri; 1.30-6pm Sat; 1.30-6.30pm Sun. Closed Nov-Mar. *Ménagerie* 9am-6pm Mon-Sat; 9am-6.30pm Sun. **Admission** *Alpine Garden* free Mon-Fri; €1 Sat, Sun. *Jardin des Plantes* free. *Ménagerie* €8; €6 reductions; free under-4s. **Credit** AmEx, MC, V.
The Paris botanical garden – which contains more than 10,000 species and includes tropical greenhouses and rose, winter and Alpine gardens – is an enchanting place. Begun by Louis XIII's doctor as the royal medicinal plant garden in 1626, it opened to the public in 1640. The formal garden, which runs between two dead-straight avenues of trees parallel to rue Buffon, is like something out of *Alice in Wonderland*. There's also the Ménagerie (a small zoo) and the terrific Grande Galerie de l'Evolution (*see above*). Ancient trees on view include a false acacia planted in 1636 and a cedar from 1734. A plaque on the old laboratory declares that this is where Henri Becquerel discovered radioactivity in 1896.

Jardin Tino Rossi (Musée de la Sculpture en Plein Air)
Quai St-Bernard, 5th. Mº Gare d'Austerlitz. **Open** 8am-dusk Mon-Fri; 9am-dusk Sat, Sun. **Admission** free.
This open-air sculpture museum by the Seine fights a constant battle against graffiti. Still, it's a pleasant enough, if traffic-loud, place for a stroll.

Musée National du Moyen Age – Thermes de Cluny.

OLIVIA RUTHERFORD

Jardin Tino Rossi. *See p39.*

Most of the works are second-rate, aside from Etienne Martin's bronze *Demeure I* and the Carrara marble *Fenêtre* by Cuban artist Careras. From May to September, the gardens turn into an open-air dance studio.

La Mosquée de Paris

2 pl du Puits-de-l'Ermite, 5th (01.45.35.97.33, tearoom 01.43.31.38.20, baths 01.43.31.18.14, www.mosquee-de-paris.net). M° Monge. **Open** *Tours* 9am-noon, 2-6pm Mon-Thur, Sat, Sun (closed Muslim hols). *Tearoom* 10am-11.30pm daily. *Restaurant* noon-2.30pm, 7.30-10.30pm daily. *Baths* (women) 10am-9pm Mon, Wed, Sat; 2-9pm Fri; (men) 2-9pm Tue, Sun. **Admission** €3; €2 reductions; free under-7s. *Tearoom free. Baths* €15-€35. **Credit** MC, V.
Some distance removed from the Arabic-speaking inner-city enclaves of Barbès and Belleville, this vast Hispano-Moorish construct is nevertheless the spiritual heart of France's Algerian-dominated Muslim population. Built from 1922 to 1926 with elements inspired by the Alhambra and the Bou Inania Medersa in Fès, the Paris mosque is dominated by a stunning green-and-white tiled square minaret. In plan and function it divides into three sections: religious (grand patio, prayer room and minaret, all for worshippers and not curious tourists); scholarly (Islamic school and library); and, via rue Geoffroy-St-Hilaire, commercial (café and domed hammam). La Mosquée café (open 9am-midnight daily) is delightful – a modest courtyard with blue-and-white mosaic-topped tables shaded beneath green foliage and scented with the sweet smell of sheesha smoke (€6). Charming waiters distribute *thé à la menthe* (€2), along with syrupy, nutty North African pastries, sorbets and fruit salads.

Les Gobelins & La Salpêtrière

In the 13th arrondissement.
Its defining features might be 1960s tower blocks, but the 13th arrondissement is also historic, especially in the area bordering the fifth. The **Manufacture Nationale des Gobelins**, home to the state weaving companies, continues a tradition founded in the 15th century, when tanneries, dyers and weaving workshops lined the Bièvre river. This putrid waterway became notorious, and the slums that grew up around it were depicted in Victor Hugo's *Les Misérables*.
The area was tidied up in the 1930s, when a small park, square René-Le-Gall, was laid out on the allotments used by

tapestry workers. The river was built over, but local enthusiasts have since opened up a small stretch in the park. Nearby, through a gateway at 17 rue des Gobelins, you can spot the turret and first floor of a medieval house, recently renovated as apartments. The so-called Château de la Reine Blanche on rue Gustave-Geffroy is named after Queen Blanche of Provence, who had a château here; it was probably rebuilt in the 1520s for the Gobelin family. Blanche was also associated with a nearby Franciscan monastery, of which a fragmentary couple of arches survive on the corner of rue Pascal and rue de Julienne.
In the northern corner of the 13th, next to Gare d'Austerlitz, sprawls the huge Hôpital de la Pitié-Salpêtrière founded in 1656, with its striking **Chapelle St-Louis**.
The busy intersection of place d'Italie has seen a number of developments in recent years. Opposite the 19th-century town hall stands the Centre Commercial Italie 2, a bizarre high-tech confection. It houses a shopping centre but, sadly, no longer the Gaumont Grand Ecran Italie cinema. You'll also find a food market on boulevard Auguste-Blanqui (Tue, Fri, Sun).

Chapelle St-Louis-de-la-Salpêtrière

47 bd de l'Hôpital, 13th (01.42.16.04.24). M° Gare d'Austerlitz. **Open** 8.30am-6pm Mon-Fri, Sun; 11am-6pm Sat. **Admission** free.
This austerely beautiful chapel, designed by Libéral Bruand and completed in 1677, features an octagonal dome in the centre and eight naves in which the sick were separated from the insane, the destitute from the debauched. Around the chapel sprawls the vast Hôpital de la Pitié-Salpêtrière, founded on the site of a gunpowder factory (hence the name, derived from saltpetre) by Louis XIV to house rounded-up vagrant women. It became a centre for research into insanity in the 1790s, when renowned doctor Philippe Pinel began to treat some of the inmates as sick rather than criminal; Charcot later pioneered neuropsychology here, famously receiving a visit from Freud. Salpêtrière is today one of the city's main teaching hospitals, but the chapel is also used for contemporary art installations, notably during the Festival d'Automne (*see p13*), when its striking architecture provides a backdrop for artists such as Bill Viola, Anish Kapoor and Nan Goldin.

Manufacture Nationale des Gobelins

42 av des Gobelins, 13th (tours 01.44.08.53.59). M° Les Gobelins. **Open** *Tours* 4pm Thur; 2.30pm, 4pm Sat. **Admission** €10; €6 reductions; free under-7s. **No credit cards.**
The royal tapestry factory was founded by Colbert when he set up the Manufacture Royale des Meubles de la Couronne in 1662; it's named after Jean Gobelin, a dyer who owned the site. It reached the summit of its renown during the *ancien régime*, when Gobelins tapestries were produced for royal residences under artists such as Le Brun. Tapestries are still made here and visitors can watch weavers at work. The tour (in French) through the 1912 factory takes in the 18th-century chapel and the Beauvais workshops.

Chinatown & the Butte-aux-Cailles

South of rue de Tolbiac, the shop signs suddenly turn Chinese or Vietnamese, and even McDonald's is decked out *à la chinoise*. The city's main Chinatown runs along avenue d'Ivry, avenue de Choisy and into the 1960s tower blocks between. Whereas much of the public housing in and around Paris is pretty bleak, here a distinctly eastern vibe reigns, with restaurants, Vietnamese *pho* noodle bars and Chinese pâtisseries, hairdressers and purveyors of exotic groceries; not to mention the expansive **Tang Frères** supermarket (48 av d'Ivry, 13th, 01.45.70.80.00). There's even a Buddhist temple hidden in a car park beneath the tallest tower (av d'Ivry, opposite rue Frères d'Astier-de-la-Vigerie, 13th). Lion and dragon dances, and martial arts demonstrations, take place on the streets at **Chinese New Year** (*see p13*).
In contrast to Chinatown, the villagey Butte-aux-Cailles, occupying the wedge between boulevard Auguste-Blanqui and rue Bobillot, is a neighbourhood of old houses, winding streets, funky bars and restaurants. This area, which was home in the 19th century to many small factories, was one of the first to fight during the 1848 Revolution and the Paris Commune.
The Butte has preserved its rebellious character, with residents standing up to urban planners and commercial

developers. This predominantly *soixante-huitard* resistance is concentrated in the cobbled rue de la Butte-aux-Cailles and rue des Cinq-Diamants. Here you'll find relaxed, inexpensive bistros such as **Le Temps des Cerises** (18 rue Butte-aux-Cailles, 13th, 01.45.89.69.48), run as a co-operative, and **Chez Gladines** (30 rue des Cinq-Diamants, 13th, 01.45.80.70.10). The cottages built in 1912 in a mock-Alsatian style around a central green at 10 rue Daviel were among the earliest public-housing schemes in Paris. Just across rue Bobillot, the **Piscine Butte-aux-Cailles** (*see p103*) is a charming Arts and Crafts-style swimming pool.
Further south, you can explore passage Vandrezanne, the little houses and gardens of square des Peupliers, rue des Peupliers and rue Dieulafoy, and the flower-named streets of the Cité Florale. By the Périphérique, the **Stade Charléty** (17 av Pierre-de-Coubertin, 13th, 01.44.16.60.60) is that unlikely thing, a superb piece of stadium architecture.

Further east

The construction in the mid-1990s of the **Bibliothèque Nationale de France** breathed life into the desolate area, now known as the **ZAC Rive Gauche**, between Gare d'Austerlitz and the Périphérique. The ambitious, long-term ZAC project includes a new university quarter, new housing projects and a tramway providing links to the suburbs. The city's newest bridge, the pedestrian-only **Passerelle Simone-de-Beauvoir**, spans the Seine between the BNF and the Cinémathèque Française; the floating Piscine Josephine-Baker (*see p103*) is now a focus for the extended Paris-Plages entertainments; and Paris's latest big cultural venue, the much-delayed **Cité de la Mode et du Design** (**Docks en Seine**), which was originally due to open in early 2009 but is still waiting to cut the ribbon. Further south-east, rue Watt is the lowest street in Paris (it runs below river level). At 12 rue Cantagrel is Le Corbusier's Cité de Réfuge de l'Armée de Salut hostel, a reinforced concrete structure built to house 1,500 homeless men.

Bibliothèque Nationale de France François Mitterrand

10 quai François-Mauriac, 13th (01.53.79.59.59, www.bnf.fr). M° Bibliothèque François Mitterrand. **Open** 2-7pm Mon; 9am-7pm Tue-Sat; 1-7pm Sun. **Admission** *1 day* €3.30. *1 year* €35; €18 reductions. **Credit** MC, V.
Opened in 1996, the new national library was the last and costliest of Mitterrand's *grands projets.* Its architect, Dominique Perrault, was criticised for his dated design, which hides readers underground and stores the books in four L-shaped glass towers. He also forgot to specify blinds to protect books from sunlight; they had to be added afterwards. In the central void is a garden (filled with 140 trees, which were transported from Fontainebleau at enormous expense). The library houses over ten million volumes and can accommodate 3,000 readers. The research section, just below the public reading rooms, opened in 1998. Much of the library is open to the public: books, newspapers and periodicals are accessible to anyone over 18, and you can browse through photographic, film and sound archives in the audio-visual section.

Cité de la Mode et du Design (Docks en Seine)

28-36 quai d'Austerlitz, 13th. M° Chevaleret or Gare d'Austerlitz.
The striking bright green Cité de la Mode et du Design was due to open in 2009, containing restaurants and cafés, a concert and club venue, shops, the Institut Français de la Mode fashion and management school, and a riverside promenade. The fashion school is up and running, but the rest is a long way behind schedule.

St-Germain-des-Prés & Odéon

Like the Latin Quarter, St-Germain-des-Prés is another area that no longer quite lives up to its legend: these days, it's more sartorial than Sartrian. In the middle third of the 20th century, the area was prime arts and intello territory, a place known as much for its high jinks as its lofty thinking: the haunt of Picasso, Giacometti, Camus, Prévert and, *bien sûr*, the Bonnie and Clyde of French philosophy, Jean-Paul Sartre and Simone de Beauvoir; the hotspot of the Paris jazz boom after World War II; and the heart of the Paris book trade. This is where the cliché of café terrace intellectualising was coined, but nowadays most of the local patrons of the Flore and the Deux Magots are in the fashion business, and couturiers have largely replaced publishers. Never mind: it's a smart and attractive part of the city to wander around in, and also has some very good restaurants.

From the boulevard to the Seine

In the 6th arrondissement.
Hit by shortages of coal during World War II, Sartre shunned his cold apartment on rue Bonaparte. 'The principal interest of the Café de Flore,' he noted at the time, 'was that it had a stove, a nearby métro and no Germans.' Although you can spend more on a few coffees than on a week's heating these days, the **Café de Flore** (see p68) remains an arty favourite, and hosts *café-philo* evenings in English. Its rival, **Les Deux Magots** (see p68), facing historic **Eglise St-Germain-des-Prés**,

is frequented largely by tourists. Nearby is the celebrity favourite **Brasserie Lipp** (151 bd St-Germain, 6th, 01.45.48.53.91); art nouveau fans tend to prefer **Brasserie Vagenende** (142 bd St-Germain, 6th, 01.43.26.68.18). The swish bookshop **La Hune** (see p70) provides sustenance of a more intellectual kind.

St-Germain-des-Prés grew up around the medieval abbey, the oldest church in Paris and site of an annual fair that drew merchants from across Europe. There are traces of its cloister and part of the abbot's palace behind the church on rue de l'Abbaye. Constructed in 1586 in red brick with stone facing, the palace prefigured the architecture of **place des Vosges**. Charming place de Furstemberg (once the palace stables) is home to the house and studio where the elderly Delacroix lived when painting the murals in St-Sulpice; it now houses the **Musée National Delacroix**. Wagner, Ingres and Colette lived on nearby rue Jacob; its elegant 17th-century *hôtels particuliers* now contain specialist book, design and antiques shops and a few pleasant hotels.

Further east, rue de Buci hosts a street market and upmarket food shops, and is home to cafés **Les Etages** (no.5, 6th, 01.46.34.26.26) and **Bar du Marché** (no.16, 6th, 01.43.26.55.15). **Hôtel La Louisiane** (60 rue de Seine, 6th, 01.44.32.17.17, www.hotellalouisiane.com) has hosted jazz stars Chet Baker and Miles Davis, and Existentialist lovers Sartre and de Beauvoir. Rue de Seine, rue des Beaux-Arts and rue Bonaparte (Manet was born in the latter, at no.5, in 1832) are still packed with art galleries. It was in rue des Beaux-Arts, at the Hôtel d'Alsace, that Oscar Wilde complained about the wallpaper and then checked out for good. Now fashionably renovated, it has

rechristened itself **L'Hôtel** (see p114). **La Palette** (see p68) and **Bistrot Mazarin** (42 rue Mazarine, 6th, 01.43.29.99.01, www.bistrotmazarin.com) are good pit stops with enviable terraces; rue Mazarine, with shops selling lighting, vintage toys and jewellery, also has Terence Conran's brasserie **L'Alcazar** (no.62, 6th, 01.53.10.19.99, www.alcazar.fr) and hip club **Wagg** (see p101).

On quai de Conti stands the neo-classical Hôtel des Monnaies, built at the demand of Louis XV by architect Jacques-Denis Antoine; formerly the mint (1777-1973), it's now the **Musée de la Monnaie**, a coin museum. Next door stands the domed **Institut de France**, cleaned to within an inch of its crisp, classical life. Opposite, the iron Pont des Arts footbridge leads directly to the Louvre. Further along, the city's main fine arts school, the **Ecole Nationale Supérieure des Beaux-Arts**, occupies an old monastery.

Ecole Nationale Supérieure des Beaux-Arts (Ensb-a)
14 rue Bonaparte, 6th (01.47.03.50.00, www.ensba.fr). M° St-Germain-des-Prés. Open 1-7pm Tue-Sun. Admission €4; €2 reductions. Exhibitions prices vary. Credit V.
The city's most prestigious fine arts school resides in what remains of the 17th-century Couvent des Petits-Augustins, the 18th-century Hôtel de Chimay, some 19th-century additions and some chunks of assorted French châteaux that were moved here after the Revolution (when the buildings briefly served as a museum of French monuments, before becoming the art school in 1816). The entrance is on quai Malaquais.

Eglise St-Germain-des-Prés
3 pl St-Germain-des-Prés, 6th (01.55.42.81.33, www.eglise-sgp.org). M° St-Germain-des-Prés. Open 8am-7.45pm Mon-Sat; 9am-8pm Sun. Admission free.
The oldest church in Paris. On the advice of Germain (later Bishop of Paris), Childebert, son of Clovis, had a basilica and monastery built here around 543. It was first dedicated to St Vincent,

and came to be known as St-Germain-le-Doré ('the gilded') because of its copper roof, then later as St-Germain-des-Prés ('of the fields'). During the Revolution the abbey was burned and a saltpetre refinery installed; the spire was added in a clumsy 19th-century restoration. Still, most of the present structure is 12th century, and ornate carved capitals and the tower remain from the 11th. Tombs include those of Jean-Casimir, the deposed King of Poland who became Abbot of St-Germain in 1669, and of Scots nobleman William Douglas. Under the window in the second chapel is the funeral stone of philosopher-mathematician René Descartes.

Institut de France
23 quai de Conti, 6th (01.44.41.44.41, www.institut-de-france.fr). M° Louvre Rivoli or Pont Neuf. Open Tours Sat, Sun (01.44.41.43.32, www.monum.fr; call for times). Admission €8; €6 reductions. No credit cards.
This elegant domed building with two sweeping curved wings was designed as a school by Louis Le Vau and opened in 1684. The five academies of the Institut (Académie Française, Académie des Inscriptions et Belles-Lettres, Académie des Beaux-Arts, Académie des Sciences, Académie des Sciences Morales et Politiques) moved here in 1805. Inside is Mazarin's ornate tomb by Hardouin-Mansart, and the Bibliothèque Mazarine (open to over-18s with ID and two photos; €15/year). The Académie Française was founded by Cardinal Richelieu in 1635 with the aim of preserving the purity of French from corrupting outside influences.

Musée de la Monnaie de Paris
11 quai de Conti, 6th (01.40.46.56.66, www.monnaiedeparis.fr). M° Odéon or Pont Neuf. Open 11am-5.30pm Tue-Fri; noon-5.30pm Sat, Sun. Closed Aug. Admission free. Credit Shop AmEx, MC, V.
Housed in the handsome neo-classical mint built in the 1770s, this high-tech museum tells the tale of global and local coinage from its pre-Roman origins, using sophisticated displays and audio-visual presentations. The history of the franc, from its wartime debut in 1360, is outlined in detail.

Musée National Delacroix
6 rue de Furstemberg, 6th (01.44.41.86.50, www.musee-delacroix.fr). M° St-Germain-des-Prés. Open Sept-May 9.30am-5pm Mon, Wed-Sun. June-Aug 9.30am-5.30pm Mon, Wed-Fri; 9.30am-5.30pm Sat, Sun. Admission €5; free under-18s; all on 1st Sun of mth. PMP. Credit MC, V.

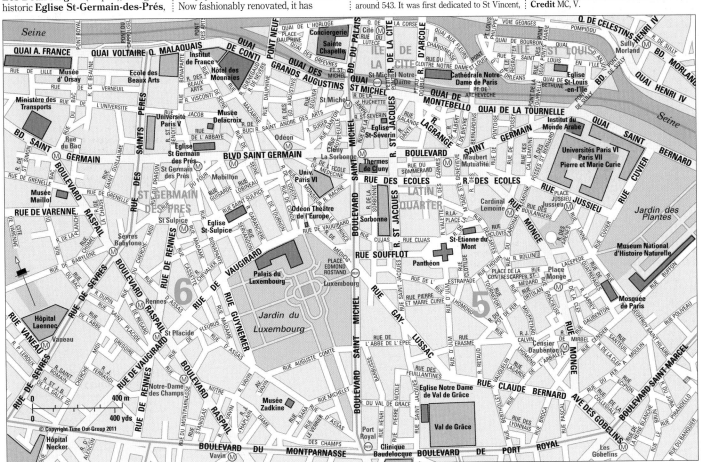

Eugène Delacroix moved to this apartment and studio in 1857 in order to be near the Eglise St-Sulpice, where he was painting murals. This collection includes small oil paintings, free pastel studies of skies, sketches and lithographs, as well as his palette.

St-Sulpice & the Luxembourg

In the 6th arrondissement.

Crammed with historic buildings and inviting shops, the quarter south of boulevard St-Germain between Odéon and Luxembourg epitomises civilised Paris. Just off the boulevard lies the covered market of St-Germain, now the site of a shopping arcade, auditorium, food hall and underground swimming pool. There are bars and bistros along rue Guisarde, nicknamed rue de la Soif ('thirst street') thanks to its carousers; it contains the late-night **Birdland** bar (no.8, 6th, 01.43.26.97.59) and a couple of notable bistros: **Mâchon d'Henri** (no.8, 6th, 01.43.29.08.70) and **Brasserie Fernand** (no.13, 6th, 01.43.54.61.47). Rue Princesse and rue des Canettes are a mix of budget restaurants and bars.

Pass the fashion boutiques, pâtisseries and antiquarian book and print shops and you come to **Eglise St-Sulpice**, a surprising 18th-century exercise in classical form with two unmatching turrets and a colonnaded façade. The square in front was designed in the 19th century by Visconti; it contains his imposing, lion-flanked Fontaine des Quatre Points Cardinaux (a pun on cardinal points and the statues of Bishops Bossuet, Fénelon, Massilon and Flechier, none of whom was actually a cardinal). It's now the centrepiece for the **Foire St-Germain**, a summer arts fair.

Among shops of religious artefacts, the chic boutiques on place and rue St-Sulpice include **Yves Saint Laurent** (*see p73*), **Vanessa Bruno** (*see p74*) and milliner **Marie Mercié** (*see p76*). Prime shopping continues further west: clothes on rue Bonaparte and rue du Four, and accessory and fashion shops on rue du Dragon, rue de Grenelle and rue du Cherche-Midi. If you spot a queue in the latter, it's most likely for the bread at **Poilâne** (*see p77*). Across the street, at the junction of rue de Sèvres and rue du Cherche-Midi, César's bronze *Centaur* is the sculptor's tribute to Picasso.

The early 17th-century chapel of St-Joseph-des-Carmes – once a Carmelite convent, now hidden within the **Institut Catholique** (21 rue d'Assas, 6th, 01.44.39.52.00, www.icp.fr) – was the scene of the murder of 115 priests during the Terror in 1792. To the east lies wide rue de Tournon, lined by such grand 18th-century residences as the Hôtel de Brancas (no.6), with figures of Justice and Prudence over the door. This street leads to the **Palais du Luxembourg**, which now serves as the Senate, and the adjoining **Jardin du Luxembourg**.

Towards boulevard St-Germain is the neo-classical **Odéon, Théâtre de l'Europe** (*see p104*), built in 1779 and recently renovated. A house in the square in front was home to Revolutionary hero Camille Desmoulins, who incited the mob to attack the Bastille in 1789. It's now occupied by **La Méditerranée** (2 pl de l'Odéon, 6th, 01.43.26.02.30, www.la-mediterranee.com); the restaurant's menus and plates were designed by Jean Cocteau. Joyce's *Ulysses* was first published in 1922 by Sylvia Beach at the celebrated **Shakespeare & Co** (*see p70*) at 12 rue de l'Odéon.

Further along the street, at 12 rue de l'Ecole-de-Médecine, is the neo-classical Université René Descartes (Paris V) medical school, and the **Musée d'Histoire de la Médecine**. The Club des Cordeliers, set up by Danton in 1790, devised revolutionary plots across the street at the **Couvent des Cordeliers** (no.15); the 14th-century refectory, all that remains of the monastery founded by St Louis, houses modern art exhibitions. Marat, one of the club's leading lights, was stabbed to death in the bathtub at his home in the same street; David depicted the moment after the crime in his iconic painting, the *Death of Marat*. This was the surgeons' district: observe the building at no.5, once the barbers' and surgeons' guild. Climb rue André-Dubois to rue Monsieur-le-Prince to budget restaurant **Polidor** (no.41, 6th, 01.43.26.95.34, www.polidor.com), open since 1845.

Eglise St-Sulpice

Pl St-Sulpice, 6th (01.42.34.59.98, www.paroisse-saint-sulpice-paris.org). M° St-Sulpice. **Open** 7.30am-7.30pm daily. **Admission** free.

It took 120 years and six architects to finish St-Sulpice. The grandiose façade, with its two-tier colonnade, was designed by Jean-Baptiste Servandoni. He died in 1766 before the second tower was finished, leaving one tower a good five metres shorter than the other. The trio of murals by Delacroix in the first chapel – *Jacob's Fight with the Angel, Heliodorus Chased from the Temple* and *St Michael Killing the Dragon* – create a suitably sombre atmosphere.

Jardin & Palais du Luxembourg

Pl André Honnorat, pl Edmond-Rostand or rue de Vaugirard, 6th (01.44.54.19.49, www.senat.fr/visite). M° Odéon/RER Luxembourg. **Open** *Jardin* summer 7.30am-dusk daily; winter 8am-dusk daily.

The palace itself was built in the 1620s for Marie de Médicis, widow of Henri IV, by Salomon de Brosse on the site of the former mansion of the Duke of Luxembourg. Its Italianate style was intended to remind her of the Pitti Palace in her native Florence. The palace now houses the French parliament's upper house, the Sénat (open only by guided visits).

The mansion next door (Le Petit Luxembourg) is the residence of the Sénat's president. The gardens, though, are the real draw: part formal (terraces and gravel paths), part 'English garden' (lawns and mature trees), they are the quintessential Paris park. The garden is crowded with sculptures: a looming Cyclops (on the 1624 Fontaine de Médicis), queens of France, a miniature Statue of Liberty, wild animals, busts of Flaubert and Baudelaire, and a monument to Delacroix. There are orchards and an apiary. After closing for more than a year, the Musée National du Luxembourg (19 rue de Vaugirard, 01.40.13.62.00, www.museeduluxembourg.fr) is due to reopen in February 2011. Most interesting, though, are the people: a mixture of *flâneurs* and *dragueurs*, chess players and martial-arts practitioners, as well as children on ponies, in sandpits, on roundabouts and playing with the sailing boats on the pond.

Musée d'Histoire de la Médecine

Université Paris-Descartes, 12 rue de l'Ecole-de-Médecine, 6th (01.40.46.16.93, www.bium.univ-paris5.fr/musee). M° Odéon or St-Michel. **Open** *Mid July-Sept* 2-5.30pm Mon-Fri. *Oct-mid July* 2-5.30pm Mon-Wed, Fri, Sat. **Admission** €3.50; €2.50 reductions; free under-8s. **No credit cards.**

The history of medicine is the subject of the medical faculty collection. There are ancient Egyptian embalming tools, a 1960s electrocardiograph and a gruesome array of saws used for amputations. You'll also find the instruments of Dr Antommarchi, who performed the autopsy on Napoleon, and the scalpel of Dr Félix, who operated on Louis XIV.

Musée des Lettres et Manuscrits

222 Blvd St-Germain, 6th (01.42.22.48.48, www.museedeslettres.fr). M° Rue du Bac. **Open** 10am-6pm Tue, Wed, Fri-Sun; 10am-8pm Thur. **Admission** €7; €5 reductions; free under-12s. **Credit** (€16 minimum) MC, V.

More than 2,000 documents and letters give an insight into the lives of the great and the good, from Magritte to Mozart. Einstein arrives at the theory of relativity on notes scattered in authentic disorder, Baudelaire complains about money problems in a letter, and HMS *Northumberland*'s log-book records the day Napoleon boarded the ship to be taken to St Helena.

Montparnasse & Beyond

Yet another artists' quarter that has long since lost the character – and the characters – that made its name, Montparnasse is now conspicuously lacking in charm. Between the two world wars, it was the emblematic 'gay Paree' district of after-dark merriment and fruitful artistic exchange – and it was also remarkably cosmopolitan. A great number of its most prominent figures were expats (including its best chronicler, the Hungarian photographer Brassaï), and the late-night bars and artists' studios formed a bubble of cordial international relations that was irreparably popped in 1939. The local atmosphere soured further with the completion of the much-loathed Tour Montparnasse in the early 1970s, a dark monolith that casts an ominous spell on the whole quarter. Granted, this is rich territory for art museums – but with the exception of the Fondation Cartier, they're all about past glories.

Montparnasse

In the 6th & 14th arrondissements.

Artists Picasso, Léger and Soutine fled to 'Mount Parnassus' in the early 1900s to escape the rising rents of Montmartre. They were soon joined by Chagall, Zadkine and other refugees from the Russian Revolution, along with Americans such as Man Ray, Henry Miller, Ezra Pound and Gertrude Stein. Between the wars the neighbourhood was the epitome of modernity: studios with large windows were built by avant-garde architects; artists, writers and intellectuals drank and debated in the quarter's showy bars; and naughty pastimes – including the then risqué tango – flourished.

Sadly, the Montparnasse of today has lost much of its former soul, dominated as it is by the lofty **Tour Montparnasse** – the first skyscraper to be built in central Paris. The dismay with which its construction was greeted prompted a change in building regulations in the city. At its foot are a shopping centre, the **Red Light** (*see p100*) and **Mix Club** (*see p101*) nightclubs, and, in winter, an open-air ice rink. There are fabulous panoramic views from the café on the 56th floor.

The old Montparnasse station witnessed two events of historical significance. In 1898, a runaway train burst through its façade; and on 25 August 1944, the German forces surrendered Paris here. The station was rebuilt in the 1970s, a grey affair above which can be found the surprising Jardin Atlantique, the **Mémorial du Maréchal Leclerc** and the **Musée Jean Moulin**.

Rue du Montparnasse, appropriately for a street near the station that sends trains to Brittany, is dotted with crêperies. Nearby, strip joints have replaced most of the theatres on ever-saucy rue de la Gaîté, but boulevard Edgar-Quinet has pleasant cafés and a street market (Wed, Sat), plus the entrance to the **Cimetière du Montparnasse**. Boulevard du Montparnasse still buzzes at night, thanks to its many cinemas and dining spots: giant art deco brasserie **La Coupole** (*see p60*); opposite, classic café **Le Select** (*see p68*); **Le Dôme** (no.108, 14th, 01.43.35.25.81), now a top-notch fish restaurant and bar; and restaurant **La Rotonde** (no.105, 6th, 01.43.26.48.26, www.rotonde montparnasse.com). All were popularised by the literati between the wars, and now use this heritage to their advantage; Le Select seems the most authentic of the bunch. Nearby, on boulevard Raspail, stands Rodin's statue of Balzac, whose rugged rather than flattering appearance caused such a scandal that it was put in place only after the sculptor's death.

For a whiff of Montparnasse's artistic history, wander down rue de la Grande-Chaumière. Bourdelle and Friesz taught at the venerable **Académie de la Grande-Chaumière** (no.14, 01.43.26.13.72, www.grande-chaumiere.fr), frequented by Calder, Giacometti and Pompon among others (it still offers drawing lessons); Modigliani died at no.8 in 1920, ruined by tuberculosis, drugs and alcohol; nearby **Musée Zadkine** occupies the sculptor's old house and studio. Rue Vavin and rue Bréa, leading to the Jardin du Luxembourg, have become an enclave of children's shops. Look out for no.6, the 1912 white-tiled apartment building where art nouveau architect Henri Sauvage lived.

Further east on boulevard du Montparnasse, literary café **La Closerie des Lilas** (no.171, 6th, 01.40.51.34.50, www.closeriedeslilas.fr) was a pre-war favourite with everyone from Lenin and Trotsky to Picasso and Hemingway; brass plaques on the tables indicate where each historic figure used to sit. Next to it is the lovely **Fontaine de l'Observatoire**, featuring bronze turtles and thrashing sea horses by Frémiet, and figures of the four continents by Carpeaux.

From here, the Jardins de l'Observatoire form part of the green axis between the Palais du Luxembourg and the royal observatory, the **Observatoire de Paris**. A curiosity next door is the Maison des Fontainiers, built over an expansive (now dry-ish) underground reservoir that was originally commissioned by Marie de Médicis to supply water to fountains around the city.

A relatively recent addition to boulevard Raspail is the glass and steel **Fondation Cartier pour l'Art Contemporain**. Designed by architect Jean Nouvel, it houses the jewellers' head offices and an exhibition space dedicated to contemporary art and photography.

West of the train station, the redevelopment of Montparnasse is also evident in the circular place de Catalogne, a piece of 1980s postmodern neo-classicism designed by Mitterrand's favourite architect, Ricardo Bofill, and the housing estates of rue Vercingétorix.

There are still traces of the old, arty Montparnasse for those willing to look for it: in impasse Lebouis, an avant-garde studio building has recently been converted into the **Fondation Henri Cartier-Bresson**; at 21 avenue du Maine, an ivy-clad alleyway of old studios contains the artist-run exhibition space Immanence, as well as the **Musée du Montparnasse**, housed in the former academy and canteen of Russian painter Marie Vassilieff; on rue Antoine-Bourdelle, the **Musée Bourdelle** includes another old cluster of studios, where sculptor Antoine Bourdelle, Symbolist painter Eugène Carrière and, briefly, Marc Chagall all worked.

Towards Les Invalides, on rue Mayet, craft and restoration workshops are still tucked away in the old courtyards.

Cimetière du Montparnasse

*3 bd Edgar-Quinet, 14th (01.44.10.86.50).
M° Edgar Quinet or Raspail.* **Open** *16 Mar-5 Nov* 8am-6pm Mon-Fri; 8.30am-6pm Sat; 9am-6pm Sun. *6 Nov-15 Mar* 8am-5.30pm Mon-Fri; 8.30am-5.30pm Sat; 9am-5.30pm Sun. **Admission** free.
Formed by commandeering three farms (you can still see the ruins of a windmill by rue Froidevaux), the Montparnasse boneyard has literary clout: Beckett, Baudelaire, Sartre, de Beauvoir, Maupassant, Ionesco and Tristan Tzara all rest here. There are also artists, including Brancusi, Henri Laurens, Frédéric Bartholdi (sculptor of the Statue of Liberty) and Man Ray. The celebrity roll-call continues with Serge Gainsbourg, André Citroën and actress Jean Seberg.

Fondation Cartier pour l'Art Contemporain

261 bd Raspail, 14th (01.42.18.56.50, www.fondation.cartier.fr). M° Denfert-Rochereau or Raspail. **Open** 11am-10pm Tue; 11am-8pm Wed-Sun. **Admission** €7.50; €5 reductions; free under-10s & under-18s 2-6pm Wed. **Credit** AmEx, MC, V.
Jean Nouvel's glass and steel building, an exhibition centre with Cartier's offices above, is as much a work of art as the installations inside. Shows by artists and photographers have wide-ranging themes, such as 'Birds' or 'Desert'. Live events around the shows are called Nuits Nomades.

Fondation Dubuffet

137 rue de Sèvres, 6th (01.47.34.12.63, www.dubuffetfondation.com). M° Duroc. **Open** 2-6pm Mon-Fri. Closed Aug. **Admission** €6; €4 reductions; free under-10s. **No credit cards.**
You walk up a winding garden path to get to this museum, founded by Jean Dubuffet, wine merchant and master of *art brut*. The foundation ensures that a fair body of his works is accessible to the public. There's a changing display of Dubuffet's lively drawings, paintings and sculptures, as well as models of the architectural sculptures from the *Hourloupe* cycle. The foundation also looks after the Closerie Falballa, the 3D masterpiece of the Hourloupe cycle, housed at Périgny-sur-Yerres, east of Paris.

Fondation Henri Cartier-Bresson

2 impasse Lebouis, 14th (01.56.80.27.00, www.henricartierbresson.org). M° Gaîté. **Open** 1-6.30pm Tue, Thur, Fri, Sun; 1-8.30pm Wed; 11am-6.45pm Sat. Closed Aug & between exhibitions. **Admission** €6; €3 reductions; free 6.30-8.30pm Wed. **No credit cards.**
Opened in 2003, this two-floor gallery is dedicated to the work of acclaimed photographer Henri Cartier-Bresson. It consists of a tall, narrow *atelier* in a 1913 building, with a minutely catalogued archive, open to researchers, and a lounge on the fourth floor screening films. In the spirit of Cartier-Bresson, who assisted on three Jean Renoir films and drew and painted all his life (some drawings are also found on the fourth floor), the Fondation opens its doors to other disciplines with three annual shows. The convivial feel of the Fondation – and its Le Corbusier armchairs – fosters relaxed discussion with staff and other visitors.

Mémorial du Maréchal Leclerc de Hauteclocque et de la Libération de Paris & Musée Jean Moulin

Jardin Atlantique, 23 allée de la 2e DB (above Gare Montparnasse), 15th (01.40.64.39.44, www.ml-leclerc-moulin.paris.fr). M° Montparnasse Bienvenüe. **Open** 10am-6pm Tue-Sun. **Admission** free. *Exhibitions* €4; €2-€3 reductions; free under-13s. **Credit** *Shop* MC, V.
This double museum retraces World War II and the Resistance through the Free French commander Maréchal Leclerc and left-wing hero Jean Moulin. Documentary material and film archives complement an impressive 270° slide show, complete with sound effects, which tells the story of the Liberation of Paris.

Musée-Atelier Adzak

3 rue Jonquoy, 14th (01.45.43.06.98). M° Plaisance. **Open** usually 3-7pm Sat, Sun (call in advance). **Admission** free.
The eccentric house, studio and garden built by the late Roy Adzak, a British-born painter and sculptor who died in 1987, harbour traces of the conceptual artist's plaster body columns and dehydrations. Now a registered charity, it gives mostly foreign artists a chance to exhibit in Paris.

Musée Bourdelle

16-18 rue Antoine-Bourdelle, 15th (01.49.54.73.73, www.bourdelle.paris.fr). M° Falguière or Montparnasse Bienvenüe. **Open** 10am-6pm Tue-Sun. **Admission** free. *Exhibitions* €7; €3.50-€5.50 reductions; free under-14s. **Credit** MC, V.
The sculptor Antoine Bourdelle (1861-1929), who was a pupil of Rodin, produced a number of monumental works including the modernist relief friezes at the Théâtre des Champs-Elysées, which were inspired by Isadora Duncan and Nijinsky. The museum includes the artist's apartment and studios, which were also used by Eugène Carrière, Dalou and Chagall. A 1950s extension tracks the evolution of Bourdelle's equestrian monument to General Alvear in Buenos Aires, and his masterful *Hercules the Archer*. A new wing by Christian de Portzamparc houses bronzes, including various studies of Beethoven in different guises.

Musée du Montparnasse

21 av du Maine, 15th (01.42.22.91.96, www.museedumontparnasse.net). M° Montparnasse Bienvenüe. **Open** 12.30-7pm Tue-Sun. **Admission** €6; €5 reductions; free under-12s. **No credit cards.**
Set in one of the last surviving alleys of studios, this was home to Marie Vassilieff, whose academy and cheap canteen – 'la Cantine des Artistes' – welcomed poor artists, including famous names such as Picasso, Cocteau, Matisse, Braque and Modigliani. Shows focus on present-day artists and the area's creative past.

Musée Pasteur

Institut Pasteur, 25 rue du Dr-Roux, 15th (01.45.68.82.83, www.pasteur.fr). M° Pasteur. **Open** 2-5.30pm Mon-Fri. Closed Aug. **Admission** €7; €3 reductions. **Credit** MC, V.
The flat where the famous chemist and his wife lived at the end of his life (1888-95) has not been touched; you can see their furniture and possessions, photos and instruments. An extravagant mausoleum on the ground floor houses Pasteur's tomb, decorated with mosaics depicting his scientific achievements.

Musée de la Poste

34 bd de Vaugirard, 15th (01.42.79.24.24, www.ladressemuseedelaposte.com). M° Montparnasse Bienvenüe. **Open** 10am-6pm Mon-Sat. **Admission** €5; €3.50 reductions; free under-26s. *PMP. Temporary exhibitions* €6.50; €5 reductions; free under-13s. **No credit cards.**
From among the uniforms, pistols, carriages, official decrees and fumigation tongs emerge snippets of history: during the 1871 Siege of Paris, hot-air balloons and carrier pigeons were used to get post out of the city, and balls crammed with hundreds of letters were floated down the Seine in return, mostly never to arrive. The second section covers French and international philately.

Musée Zadkine

100bis rue d'Assas, 6th (01.55.42.77.20, www.zadkine.paris.fr). M° Notre-Dame-des-Champs/RER Port-Royal. **Open** 10am-6pm Tue-Sun. **Admission** free. *Exhibitions* €4; €2-€3 reductions; free under-13s. **Credit** (€15 minimum) MC, V.
Works by the Russian-born Cubist sculptor Ossip Zadkine are displayed around this tiny house and garden near the Jardin du Luxembourg. Zadkine's works cover musical, mythological and religious subjects, and his style varies with his materials. There are drawings and poems by Zadkine and paintings by his wife, Valentine Prax.

Observatoire de Paris

61 av de l'Observatoire, 14th (01.40.51.22.21, www.obspm.fr). M° St-Jacques/RER Port-Royal. **Tours** Email visite.paris@obspm or write to Observatoire de Paris, 61 av de l'Observatoire, 75014 Paris. **Admission** free.
The Paris observatory was founded by Louis XIV's finance minister, Colbert, in 1667; it was designed by Claude Perrault (who also worked on the Louvre), with labs and an observation tower. The French meridian line drawn by François Arago in 1806 (which was used here before the Greenwich meridian was adopted as an international standard) runs north–south through the centre of the building. The dome on the observation tower was added in the 1840s. You'll need to apply for an appointment at the Observatoire by letter, but it's also worth checking the website for openings linked to astronomical happenings – or visit on the Journées du Patrimoine (*see p13*).

Tour Montparnasse

33 av du Maine, 15th (01.45.38.52.56, www.tourmontparnasse56.com). M° Montparnasse Bienvenüe. **Open** *1 Oct-31 Mar* 9.30am-10.30pm Mon-Thur, Sun; 9.30am-11pm Fri, Sat. *1 Apr-30 Sept* 9.30am-11.30pm daily. **Admission** €11; €4.70-€8 reductions; free under-7s. **Credit** MC, V.
Built in 1974 on the site of the old station, this 209m (686ft) steel-and-glass monolith is actually shorter than the Eiffel Tower, but better placed for fabulous views of the city – including, of course, the Eiffel Tower itself. A lift whisks you up in 38 seconds to the 56th floor, where you'll find a display of aerial scenes of Paris, an upgraded café-lounge, a souvenir shop – and lots and lots of sky. On a clear day you can see up to 40km (25 miles). Another lift takes you all the way up to the roof. Classical concerts are held on the terrace.

Denfert-Rochereau & Montsouris

In the 14th & 15th arrondissements.
In the run-up to the 1789 Revolution, the bones of six million Parisians were taken from the handful of overcrowded city cemeteries and wheelbarrowed to the **Catacombes**, a vast network of tunnels that stretches under much of Paris. The sections under the 13th and 14th arrondissements are open to the public; the gloomy Denfert-Rochereau entrance is next to one of the toll gates of the Mur des Fermiers-Généraux, built by Ledoux in the 1780s.

The bronze *Lion de Belfort* dominates the traffic-laden place Denfert-Rochereau, a favourite starting point for the city's countless political demonstrations. The regal beast was sculpted by Bartholdi, of Statue of Liberty fame, and is a scaled-down replica of one in Belfort that commemorates the brave defence by Colonel Denfert-Rochereau of the town in 1870. Nearby, the southern half of rue Daguerre is a sociable, pedestrianised market street (Tuesday to Saturday, Sunday mornings) brimming with cafés and food stores.

One of the big draws of the area is the **Parc Montsouris**, with lovely lakes, dramatic cascades and an unusual history. Surrounding the western edge of the park are a number of modest, quiet streets – including rue du Parc Montsouris and rue Georges-Braque – that used to be lined during the 1920s and '30s with charming villas and artists' studios by avant-garde architects Le Corbusier and André Lurçat. On the southern edge of the park sprawls the **Cité Universitaire** complex.

Les Catacombes

1 av du Colonel-Henri-Rol-Tanguy, 14th (01.43.22.47.63, www.catacombes-de-paris.fr). M°/RER Denfert Rochereau. **Open** 10am-5pm Tue-Sun. **Admission** €8; €4-€6 reductions; free under-14s. **Credit** (€15 minimum) MC, V.
This is the official entrance to the 3,000km (1,864-mile) tunnel network that runs under much of the city. With public burial pits overflowing in the era of the Revolutionary Terror, the bones of six million people were transferred to the *catacombes*. The bones of Marat, Robespierre and their cronies are packed in with wall upon wall of their fellow citizens. A damp, cramped tunnel takes you through a series of galleries before you reach the ossuary, the entrance to which is announced by a sign engraved in the stone: 'Stop! This is the empire of death.' The tour lasts approximately 45 minutes and the temperature in the tunnels is 14°C.

OLIVIA RUTHERFORD
Jardin du Luxembourg.

Cité Universitaire

*17 bd Jourdan, 14th (01.44.16.64.00,
www.ciup.fr). RER Cité Universitaire.*
The Cité Internationale Universitaire de Paris is
an odd mix. Created between the wars in a mood
of internationalism and inspired by the model of
Oxbridge colleges, its 37 halls of residence across
landscaped gardens were designed in a variety
of supposedly authentic national styles. Some
are by architects of the appropriate nationality
(Dutchman Willem Dudok, for instance, designed
the De Stijl-style Collège Néerlandais); others, such
as the Khmer sculptures and bird-beak roof of the
Asie du Sud-Est building, are merely pastiches.
The Brits get what looks like a minor public
school; the Maison Internationale is based on
Fontainebleau; the Swiss and Brazilians get Le
Corbusier. You can visit the sculptural white
Pavillon Suisse (01.44.16.10.16, www.fondation
suisse.fr), which has a Le Corbusier mural on the
ground floor. The spacious landscaped gardens
are open to the public, and the newly renovated
theatre stages drama and modern dance.

Parc Montsouris

Bd Jourdan, 14th. RER Cité Universitaire.
Open 8am-dusk Mon-Fri; 9am-dusk Sat, Sun.
The most colourful of the capital's many parks,
Montsouris was laid out for Baron Haussmann by
Jean-Charles Adolphe Alphand. It includes a series
of sweeping, gently sloping lawns, an artificial
lake and cascades. The park is also home to a rich
selection of bird life. On the opening day in 1878,
the lake inexplicably emptied, and the engineer
responsible committed suicide.

The 15th arrondissement

The expansive 15th arrondissement has
little to offer tourists, though as a largely
residential district it has plenty of good
restaurants, street markets, and some
good small shops, notably on rue du
Commerce and rue Lecourbe. It's worth
making a detour to visit **La Ruche**
('beehive'), designed by Eiffel as a
wine pavilion for the 1900 Exposition
Universelle and moved here to serve
as artists' studios. Nearby is **Parc
Georges Brassens**, opened in 1983,
and at the porte de Versailles the
sprawling **Paris-Expo** exhibition
centre was created in 1923.

Parc Georges Brassens

Rue des Morillons, 15th. **Open** 8am-dusk Mon-Fri;
9am-dusk Sat, Sun.
Built on the site of the old Abattoirs de Vaugirard,
Parc Georges Brassens prefigured the industrial
regeneration of Parc André Citroën and La Villette.
The gateways, crowned by bronze bulls, have
been kept, as have a series of iron meat-market
pavilions, which house a second-hand book market at weekends. The Jardin des Senteurs is
planted with aromatic species, and a small vineyard yields 200 bottles of Clos des Morillons every
year. The park is named in honour of the legendary French singer, who lived nearby at 42 rue
Santos-Dumont.

Paris-Expo

*1 pl de la Porte de Versailles, 15th
(01.40.68.22.22, www.viparis.com).
Mº Porte de Versailles.*
This vast exhibition centre, spread over different
halls, hosts all manner of trade and art fairs.
Many, such as the Foire de Paris (*see p11*), are
open to the public.

La Ruche

*Passage de Dantzig, 15th (www.la-ruche.fr).
Mº Convention or Porte de Versailles.*
Have a peep through the fence to see the iron-
framed former wine pavilion built by Gustave
Eiffel for the 1900 Exposition Universelle, and
later rebuilt by philanthropic sculptor Alfred
Boucher to be let as studios for struggling artists.
Chagall, Soutine, Brancusi, Modigliani, Lipchitz
and Archipenko all spent periods here, and the
140 studios are still sought after by today's artists
and designers.

The 7th & Western Paris

The seventh arrondissement is one large
workshop, dotted with the machinery of

Eiffel Tower. *See p46.*

state and diplomacy: this is the home of
France's parliament, several ministries
and a gaggle of foreign embassies, as
well as the French army's training
establishment and the headquarters of
UNESCO. Visually speaking, much of the
district is formal and aloof, albeit smart,
and there are few attractions to draw the
visitor – with the sizeable exceptions,
naturally, of the Invalides, the Rodin
museum and a certain A-shaped
assembly of 19th-century iron lattice
beside the river. The other major
attraction, the Musée d'Orsay, should
be gleaming in 2011 after a large-scale
renovation of the upper floors.

The Faubourg St-Germain

In the 7th arrondissement.
In the early 18th century, when the Marais
went out of fashion, aristocrats built
palatial new residences on the Faubourg
St-Germain, the district developing
around the site of the former city wall.
It is still a well-bred part of the city,
government ministries and foreign
embassies colouring the area with flags
and diplomatic plates. Many fine *hôtels
particuliers* survive; glimpse their elegant
entrance courtyards on rue de Grenelle,
rue St-Dominique, rue de l'Université
and rue de Varenne.

Just west of St-Germain, the 'Carré
Rive Gauche' or 'Carré des Antiquaires'
– the quadrangle enclosed by quai
Voltaire, rue des Sts-Pères, rue du Bac
and rue de l'Université – is filled with
antiques shops. On rue des Sts-Pères,
chocolatier **Debauve & Gallais** (no.30,
7th, 01.45.48.54.67), with its period
interior, has been making chocolates

since 1800. Rue du Pré-aux-Clercs, named
after a field where students used to duel,
is now a favourite with fashion insiders.
There are still students to be found on
adjoining rue St-Guillaume, home of the
prestigious **Fondation Nationale
des Sciences-Politiques** (no.27, 7th,
01.45.49.50.50), more commonly known
as 'Sciences-Po'.

Rue de Montalembert is home to two
of the Left Bank's most fashionable
hotels: the **Hôtel Montalembert**
(*see p116*) and the Hôtel du Pont-
Royal, a gastronomic magnet ever
since the addition of the trendy **Atelier
de Joël Robuchon** (www.joel-
robuchon.com). By the river, a Beaux-
Arts train station – the towns once
served still listed on the façade – houses
the unmissable art collections of the
Musée d'Orsay; outside on the
esplanade are 19th-century bronze
animal sculptures.

Next door is the lovely 1780s Hôtel de
Salm, once the Swedish embassy and now
home to the **Musée National de la
Légion d'Honneur et des Ordres
de Chevalerie** (2 rue de la Légion
d'Honneur, 7th, 01.40.62.84.25), devoted
to France's honours system since
Louis XI. The Legion of Honour was
established by Napoleon in 1802. Across
the street, a modern footbridge, the
Passerelle Solférino, crosses the Seine
to the Tuileries. The fancy Hôtel
Boucharon today houses the **Musée
Maillol**. Right beside its curved
entrance, the Fontaine des Quatre
Saisons by Edmé Bouchardon features
statues of the seasons surrounding
allegorical figures of Paris above the
rivers Seine and Marne.

You'll have to wait for the open-house
Journées du Patrimoine (*see p13*) to
see the decorative interiors and private
gardens of other *hôtels*, such as the
Hôtel de Villeroy (Ministry of
Agriculture; 78 rue de Varenne, 7th),
Hôtel Boisgelin (Italian Embassy; 51
rue de Varenne, 7th), **Hôtel d'Avaray**
(Dutch ambassador's residence; 85 rue
de Grenelle, 7th), **Hôtel d'Estrées**
(Russian ambassador's residence; 79 rue
de Grenelle, 7th) or **Hôtel de Monaco**
(Polish Embassy; 57 rue St-Dominique,
7th). Among the most beautiful is the
Hôtel Matignon (57 rue de Varenne,
7th), residence of the prime minister.
Once used by French statesman
Talleyrand for lavish receptions, it
contains the biggest private garden in
Paris. The Cité Varenne at no.51 is a lane
of exclusive houses complete with
private gardens.

Rue du Bac is home to the city's oldest
and most elegant department store,
Le Bon Marché ('the good bargain'),
and to an unlikely pilgrimage spot,
the **Chapelle de la Médaille
Miraculeuse**. On nearby rue de
Babylone, handy budget bistro **Au
Babylone** (no.13, 7th, 01.45.48.72.13)
has been serving up cheap lunches for
decades, but the Théâtre de Babylone,
where Beckett's *Waiting for Godot* was
premiered in 1953, is long gone.

At the foot of boulevard St-Germain,
facing place de la Concorde across the
Seine, is the **Assemblée Nationale**, the
lower house of the French parliament.
Behind, elegant place du Palais-Bourbon
leads into rue de Bourgogne, a rare
commercial thoroughfare amid the
official buildings, with some delectable
pâtisseries and fancy designer
furniture showrooms.

Nearby, the mid 19th-century **Eglise
Ste-Clotilde** (12 rue Martignac, 7th,
01.44.18.62.60), with its skeletal twin
spires, is an early example of Gothic
Revival. Beside the Assemblée is the
Foreign Ministry, often referred to by its
address, 'quai d'Orsay'. Beyond it, a long,
grassy esplanade leads up to golden-
domed Les Invalides. The vast military
hospital complex, with its Eglise du
Dôme and St-Louis-des-Invalides
churches, all built by Louis XIV,
epitomises the official grandeur of the
Sun King as expression of royal and
military power. It now houses the
Musée de l'Armée, as well as
Napoleon's tomb inside the Eglise du
Dôme. Stand with your back to the dome
to survey the cherubim-laden Pont
Alexandre III and the **Grand** and
Petit Palais over the river, all put up
for the 1900 Exposition Universelle.

Just beside Les Invalides is the
Musée National Rodin, occupying the
charming 18th-century Hôtel Biron and
its romantic gardens. Many of his great
sculptures, including the *Thinker*, the
Burghers of Calais and the swarming
Gates of Hell, are displayed in the
building and around the gardens – as are
those of his mistress, Camille Claudel.

Assemblée Nationale

*33 quai d'Orsay, 7th (01.40.63.60.00,
www.assemblee-nationale.fr). Mº Assemblée
Nationale.*
Like the Sénat, the Assemblée Nationale (also
known as the Palais Bourbon) is a royal building
adapted for republicanism. It was built between
1722 and 1728 for the Duchesse de Bourbon,
daughter of Louis XIV and Madame de Montespan,
who also put up the neighbouring Hôtel de Lassay
for her lover, the Marquis de Lassay. The *palais*
was modelled on the Grand Trianon at Versailles,
with a colonnaded *cour d'honneur* opening on to
rue de l'Université and gardens running down to
the Seine. The Prince de Condé extended the palace,

linked the two *hôtels* and laid out place du Palais-Bourbon. The Greek temple-style façade facing Pont de la Concorde (the rear of the building) was added in 1806 to mirror the Madeleine.

Flanking this riverside façade are statues of four great statesmen: L'Hôpital, Sully, Colbert and Aguesseau. The Napoleonic frieze on the pediment was replaced by a monarchist one after the restoration: between 1838 and 1841, Cortot sculpted the figures of France, Power and Justice. After the Revolution, the palace became the meeting place for the Conseil des Cinq-Cents. It was the forerunner of the parliament's lower house, which set up here for good in 1827. Visits are by arrangement through a serving *député* (if you're French) – or, after long queuing, during the Journées du Patrimoine (*see p13*).

Chapelle de la Médaille Miraculeuse
Couvent des Soeurs de St-Vincent-de-Paul, 140 rue du Bac, 7th (01.49.54.78.88, www.chapellenotredamedelamedaille miraculeuse.com). M° Sèvres Babylone. **Open** 7.45am-1pm, 2.30-7pm Mon, Wed-Sun; 7.45am-7pm Tue. **Admission** free.
In 1830, saintly Catherine Labouré was said to have seen a vision of the Virgin, who told her to cast a medal that copied her appearance – standing on a globe with rays of light appearing from her outstretched hands. This kitsch chapel – murals, mosaics, statues and the embalmed bodies of Catherine and her mother superior – attracts two million pilgrims every year. Reliefs in the courtyard tell the nun's story.

Espace Fondation EDF
6 rue Récamier, 7th (01.53.63.23.45, www.edf.fr). M° Sèvres Babylone. **Open** noon-7pm Tue-Sun. **Admission** free.
This former electricity substation, converted by Electricité de France for PR purposes, is now used for varied, well-presented exhibitions.

Les Invalides & Musée de l'Armée
Esplanade des Invalides, 7th (08.10.11.33.99, www.invalides.org) or Les Invalides. **Open** Apr-Sept 10am-6pm Mon, Wed-Sat; 10am-9pm Tue; 10am-6.30pm Sun. Oct-Mar 10am-5pm Mon-Sat; 10am-5.30pm Sun. Closed 1st Mon of mth. **Admission** *Courtyard* free. *Musée de l'Armée & Eglise du Dôme* €9; €7 reductions; free under-18s. PMP. **Credit** MC, V.

Topped by its gilded dome, the Hôtel des Invalides was (and in part still is) a hospital. Commissioned by Louis XIV for wounded soldiers, it once housed as many as 6,000 invalids. Designed by Libéral Bruand (the foundations were laid in 1671) and completed by Jules Hardouin-Mansart, it's a magnificent monument to Louis XIV and Napoleon. Behind lines of cannons and bullet-shaped yews, the main (northern) façade has a relief of Louis XIV (Ludovicus Magnus) and the Sun King's sunburst. Wander through the main courtyard and you'll see grandiose two-storey arcades and a statue of Napoleon glaring down from the end; the dormer windows around the courtyards are sculpted to look like suits of armour.

The complex contains two churches – or, rather, a sort of double church: the Eglise St-Louis was for the soldiers, the Eglise du Dôme for the king. An opening behind the altar connects the two. The long, barrel-vaulted nave of the church of St-Louis is hung with flags captured from enemy troops. Since 1840 the Baroque Eglise du Dôme has been dedicated to the worship of Napoleon, whose body was brought here from St Helena. On the ground floor, under a dome painted by de la Fosse, Jouvenet and Coypel, are chapels featuring monuments to Vauban, Foch and Joseph Napoleon (Napoleon's older brother and King of Naples, Sicily and Spain). Napoleon II (King of Rome) is buried in the crypt opposite his father the emperor. Two dramatic black figures holding up the entrance to the crypt, the red porphyry tomb, the ring of giant figures, and the friezes and texts eulogising the emperor's heroic deeds give the measure of the cult of Napoleon, cherished in France for ruling large swaths of Europe and for creating an administrative and educational system that endures to this day.

The Invalides complex also houses the enormous Musée de l'Armée, which is in effect several museums in one. Even if militaria are not your thing, the building is splendid, and there's some fine portraiture, such as Ingres' *Emperor Napoleon on his Throne*. The Antique Armour wing is packed full of armour and weapons that look as good as new, many displaying amazing workmanship, from the 16th-century suit made for François I to cabinets full of swords, maces, crossbows and muskets and arquebuses. The Plans-Reliefs section is a collection of gorgeous 18th- and 19th-century scale models of French cities, used for military strategy; also here is a 17th-century model of Mont-St-Michel, made by a monk from playing cards.

The World War I rooms bring the conflict into focus with uniforms, paintings, a scale model of a trench and, most sobering of all, white plastercasts of the hideously mutilated faces of two soldiers. The World War II wing covers the Resistance, the Battle of Britain and the war in the Pacific (there's a replica of Little Boy, the bomb dropped on Hiroshima), alternating artefacts with film footage. Also included in the entry price is the Historial Charles de Gaulle (closed on Monday).

Musée Maillol
59-61 rue de Grenelle, 7th (01.42.22.59.58, www.museemaillol.com). M° Rue du Bac. **Open** 10.30am-7pm (last admission 6.15pm) Mon, Wed, Thur, Sat, Sun; 10.30am-9.30pm (last admission 8.45pm) Fri. **Admission** €11; €9 reductions; free under-11s. **Credit** *Shop* AmEx, MC, V.
Dina Vierny was 15 when she met Aristide Maillol and became his principal model for the next decade, idealised in such sculptures as *Spring, Air* and *Harmony*. In 1995 she opened this delightful museum, exhibiting Maillol's drawings, engravings, pastels, tapestry panels, ceramics and early Nabis-related paintings, as well as the sculptures and terracottas that epitomise his calm, modern classicism. Vierny also set up a Maillol Museum in the Pyrenean village of Banyuls-sur-Mer. This Paris venue also has works by Picasso, Rodin, Gauguin, Degas and Cézanne, a whole room of Matisse drawings, rare Surrealist documents and works by naïve artists. Vierny has also championed Kandinsky and Ilya Kabakov, whose *Communal Kitchen* installation recreates the atmosphere of Soviet domesticity. Monographic exhibitions are devoted to modern and contemporary artists. Last year saw a fascinating exhibition of death's heads from Caravaggio to Damien Hirst.

Musée National Rodin
Hôtel Biron, 79 rue de Varenne, 7th (01.44.18.61.10, www.musee-rodin.fr). M° Varenne. **Open** 10am-5.45pm Tue-Sun (gardens until 6pm). **Admission** €6; €5 reductions; free under-18s, all 1st Sun of mth. PMP. *Exhibitions* €7; €5 reductions; free under-18s. *Gardens* €1; free under-18s. **Credit** MC, V.
The Rodin museum occupies the *hôtel particulier* where the sculptor lived in the final years of his life. *The Kiss*, the *Cathedral*, the *Walking Man*, portrait busts and early terracottas are exhibited indoors, as are many of the individual figures or small groups that also appear on the *Gates of Hell*. Rodin's works are accompanied by several pieces by his mistress and pupil, Camille Claudel. The walls are hung with paintings from Van Gogh, Monet, Renoir, Carrière and Rodin himself. Most visitors have greatest affection for the gardens: look out for the *Burghers of Calais*, the *Gates of Hell*, and the *Thinker*.

Musée d'Orsay
1 rue de la Légion-d'Honneur, 7th (01.40.49.48.14, www.musee-orsay.fr). M° Solférino/RER Musée d'Orsay. **Open** 9.30am-6pm Tue, Wed, Fri-Sun; 9.30am-9.45pm Thur. **Admission** €8; €5.50 reductions; free under-18s, all 1st Sun of mth. PMP. **Credit** *Shop* MC, V.
The Musée d'Orsay's famed upper galleries are undergoing a serious brush-up. The museum, originally a train station designed by Victor Laloux in 1900, houses a huge collection spanning the period between 1848 and 1914, and is normally home to a profusion of works by Delacroix, Corot, Manet, Renoir, Pissarro, Gauguin, Monet, Caillebotte, Cézanne, Van Gogh, Toulouse-Lautrec and others. The result of renovations in 2011 will be a better display of artworks, larger exhibition areas and greater visitor pleasure, but in the meantime space is substantially reduced – the museum's website has a helpful guide to what remains on the walls.

West & south of Les Invalides

The 7th & 15th arrondissements.
South-west of the Invalides is the huge **Ecole Militaire** (av de La Motte-Picquet, 7th), the military academy built by Louis XV to educate the children of penniless officers; it would later train Napoleon. The severe neo-classical building, designed by Jacques Ange Gabriel, is still used by the army and closed to the public.

From the north-western side of the Ecole Militaire begins the vast Champ de Mars, a market garden converted into a military drilling ground in the 18th century. It has long been home to the most celebrated Paris monument of all, the **Eiffel Tower**. At the south-eastern

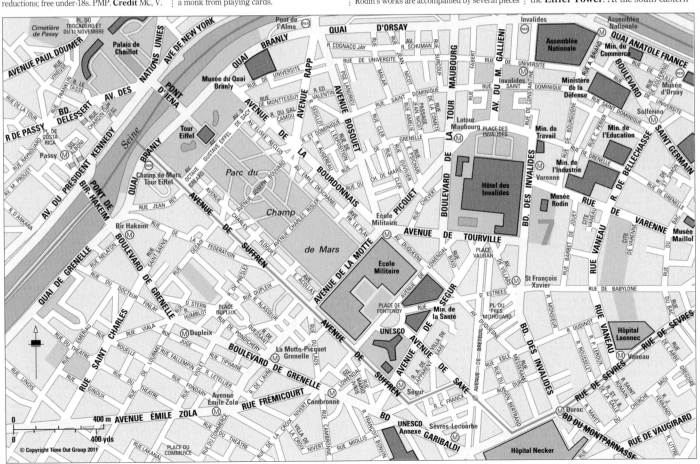

end of the Champ de Mars stands the Mur pour la Paix ('wall for peace'), erected in 2000 to articulate hopes for peace. South-east of the Ecole are the Y-shaped **UNESCO** building, built in 1958, and the modernist Ministry of Labour. Fashionable apartments line broad avenue Bosquet and avenue Suffren, though there's much architectural eclecticism in the area: look at the pseudo-Gothic and pseudo-Renaissance houses on avenue de Villars; Lavirotte's fabulous art nouveau doorway at 27 avenue Rapp; and the striking, box-shaped **Notre Dame de l'Arche de l'Alliance** church (81 rue d'Alleray, 15th, 01.56.56.62.56), which was completed in 1998.

Eiffel Tower

Champ de Mars, 7th (08.92.70.12.39, www.tour-eiffel.fr). M° Bir-Hakeim/RER Champ de Mars Tour Eiffel. **Open** *By lift* Mid June-Aug 9am-12.45am daily (last ascent 11pm). Sept-mid June 9.30am-11.45pm daily (last ascent 10.30pm). *By stairs* (1st & 2nd levels) Mid June-Aug 9am-12.45am (last ascent midnight). Sept-mid June 9.30am-6.30pm (last ascent 6pm). **Admission** *By stairs* €4.50; €3-€3.50 reductions; free under-4s. *By lift* (1st & 2nd level) €8.10; €4-€6.50 reductions; (3rd level) €13.10; €9-€11.50 reductions; free under-4s. **Credit** AmEx, MC, V.

No building better symbolises Paris than the Tour Eiffel. Maupassant claimed he left Paris because of it, William Morris visited daily to avoid having to see it from afar – and it was originally meant to be a temporary structure. The radical cast-iron tower was built for the 1889 World Fair and the centenary of the 1789 Revolution by engineer Gustave Eiffel. Eiffel made use of new technology that was already popular in iron-framed buildings. Construction took more than two years and used some 18,000 pieces of metal and 2,500,000 rivets. The 300m (984ft) tower stands on four massive concrete piers; it was the tallest structure in the world until overtaken by New York's Empire State Building in the 1930s. Vintage double-decker lifts ply their way up and down; you can walk as far as the second level. There are souvenir shops, an exhibition space, a café and even a post office on the first and second levels. The smart Jules Verne restaurant, on the second level, has its own lift in the north tower. At the top (third level), there's Eiffel's cosy salon and a viewing platform. Views can reach 65km (40 miles) on a good day, although the most fascinating perspectives are of the ironwork itself. At night, for ten minutes on the hour, 20,000 flashbulbs attached to the tower provide a beautiful effect.

Musée des Egouts

Entrance opposite 93 quai d'Orsay, by Pont de l'Alma, 7th (01.53.68.27.81). M° Alma Marceau/RER Pont de l'Alma. **Open** 11am-4pm Mon-Wed, Sat, Sun (until 5pm May-Sept). Closed 2wks Jan. **Admission** €4.30; €3.50 reductions; free under-6s. **No credit cards.**

For centuries, the main source of drinking water in Paris was the Seine, which was also the main sewer. Construction of an underground sewerage system began at the time of Napoleon. Today, the Egouts de Paris constitutes a smelly museum; each sewer in the 2,100km (1,305-mile) system is marked with a replica of the street sign above.

Musée Valentin Haüy

5 rue Duroc, 7th (01.44.49.27.27, www.avh.asso.fr). M° Duroc. **Open** times vary. **Admission** free.

This tiny museum is devoted to the history of braille. You can explore on your own with the aid of French, English or braille explanatory texts, or allow the curator, Noële Roy, to show you round. She will give a tour in English if preferred. The first exhibit is a shocking print, depicting the fairground freak show that inspired Valentin Haüy to devote his life to educating not only the blind, but also the backward public who came to laugh at the likes of this blind orchestra forced to perform in dunce's hats. Next begins the tactile tour, with a chance to touch books printed in embossed letters.

UNESCO

7 pl de Fontenoy, 7th (01.45.68.10.00, tours (book in advance) 01.45.68.03.59, www.unesco.org). M° Ecole Militaire. **Open** *Tours* 3pm Wed (in English 3pm Mon). **Admission** free.

The Y-shaped UNESCO headquarters, built in 1958, is home to a swarm of international diplomats. It's worth visiting for the sculptures and paintings – by Picasso, Arp, Giacometti, Moore, Calder and Miró – and for the Japanese garden, with its contemplation cylinder by minimalist architect Tadao Ando. Tours need to be reserved three months in advance.

Village Suisse

78 av de Suffren or 54 av de La Motte-Picquet, 15th (www.villagesuisse.com). M° La Motte Picquet Grenelle. **Open** 10.30am-7pm Mon, Thur-Sun.

The mountains and waterfalls created for the Swiss Village at the 1900 Exposition Universelle are long gone, but the village lives on. Rebuilt as blocks of flats, the street level has been colonised by some 150 boutiques offering high-quality, albeit pricey, antiques and collectibles.

Along the Seine

Downstream from the Eiffel Tower is the **Musée du Quai Branly**. A short way further on, the high-tech **Maison de la Culture du Japon** stands near Pont Bir-Hakeim on quai Branly. Beyond, the 15th arrondissement Fronts de Seine riverfront, with its tower-block developments, had some of the worst architecture of the 1970s inflicted upon it. This would-be brave new world of walkways, suspended gardens and tower blocks has no easily discoverable means of access. The adjacent Beaugrenelle shopping centre is more straightforward to get into, but remains dingy. Further west, things look up: the sophisticated former headquarters of the Canal+ TV channel (2 rue des Cévennes, 15th), designed by American architect Richard Meier, is surrounded by fine modern housing; and the pleasant **Parc André Citroën**, created in the 1990s on the site of the former Citroën car works, runs down to the Seine quayside.

Maison de la Culture du Japon

101bis quai Branly, 15th (01.44.37.95.01, www.mcjp.asso.fr). M° Bir-Hakeim/RER Champ de Mars Tour Eiffel. **Open** noon-7pm Tue, Wed, Fri, Sat; noon-8pm Thur. Closed Aug. **Admission** free.

Constructed in 1996 by the Anglo-Japanese architectural partnership of Kenneth Armstrong and Masayuki Yamanaka, this opalescent glass-fronted Japanese cultural centre screens films and puts on exhibitions and plays. It also contains a library, an authentic Japanese tea pavilion on the roof and a well-stocked book and gift shop.

Musée du Quai Branly

37 quai Branly, 7th (01.56.61.70.00, www.quaibranly.fr). RER Pont de l'Alma. **Open** 11am-7pm Tue, Wed, Sun; 11am-9pm Thur-Sat. **Admission** €8.50; €6 reductions; free under-18s, all 1st Sun of mth. *Temporary exhibitions* €7; €5 reductions; free under-18s, all 1st Sun of mth. **Credit** AmEx, DC, MC, V.

This museum, housed in an extraordinary building by Jean Nouvel, is a vast showcase for non-European cultures. Dedicated to the ethnic art of Africa, Oceania, Asia and the Americas, it joins together the collections of the Musée des Arts d'Afrique et d'Océanie and the Laboratoire d'Ethnologie du Musée de l'Homme, as well as contemporary indigenous art. Treasures include a tenth-century anthropomorphic Dogon statue from Mali, Vietnamese costumes, Gabonese masks, Aztec statues, Peruvian feather tunics, and rare frescoes from Ethiopia.

Parc André Citroën

Rue Balard, rue St-Charles or quai Citroën, 15th. M° Balard or Javel. **Open** 8am-dusk Mon-Fri; 9am-dusk Sat, Sun, public hols.

This park is a fun, postmodern version of a French formal garden,. It comprises glasshouses, computerised fountains, waterfalls, a wilderness and themed gardens featuring different coloured plants and even sounds. The tethered Eutelsat helium balloon takes visitors up for panoramic views. If the weather looks unreliable, call 01.44.26.20.00.

Great escapes

Chartres

Seen from a distance, the mismatched spires and dazzling silhouette of Chartres cathedral burst out of the Beauce cornfields and dominate the skyline of this modest town some 90 kilometres (56 miles) south-west of Paris. The cathedral is one of the finest examples of Gothic architecture in the world: its doorways bristling with sculpture, along with its stained glass, embody a complete medieval world view. The west front, or 'Royal Portal', has three sculpted doorways. Inside, there's another era of sculpture, represented in the 16th-century scenes of the life of Christ that surround the choir. The cathedral is famed, above all, for its stained-glass windows depicting biblical scenes, saints and medieval trades in brilliant 'Chartres blue', punctuated by rich reds. English-language tours by lecturer Malcolm Miller – one of the world's most knowledgeable and entertaining experts on the cathedral – take place twice daily for most of the year (noon & 2.45pm Mon-Sat, €10, €5 reductions). Audio-guides can also be hired.

Cathédrale Notre-Dame

Pl de la Cathédrale (02.37.21.75.02). **Open** *Cathedral* 8.30am-7.30pm daily. *Tower* May-Aug 9.30am-12.30pm, 2-6pm Mon-Sat; 2-6pm Sun. Sept-Apr 9.30am-12.30pm, 2-5pm Mon-Sat; 2-5pm Sun. **Admission** *Cathedral* free. *Guided tour* €7; €4.50 reductions; free under-18s.

Giverny

In 1883, Claude Monet moved his mistress and their eight children into a quaint pink-brick house he had rented in bucolic Giverny, and spent as much time cultivating a beautiful garden here as painting the water lilies in it. By 1890, he had bought his dream home and had a pond dug, bridges built and a tableau of greenery created. As Monet's eyesight began to fail, he produced endless impressions of his man-made paradise. He died here in 1926. Of the hundreds of tourists who visit here every day, not all are art lovers; there are none of his original paintings on display here. Most are simply here for the lilies. The garden (*pictured*) is as much a masterpiece as any of Monet's paintings, its famous water-lily pond, weeping willows and Japanese bridge still intact; and the charming house, the Fondation Claude Monet, is dotted with touching mementos.

Fondation Claude Monet

84 rue Claude-Monet, 27620 Giverny (02.32.51.28.21, www.fondation-monet.com). **Open** 9.30am-6pm daily. Closed Nov-Mar. **Admission** *House & garden* €6; €3.50-€4.50 reductions; free under-7s.

Versailles

Centuries of makeovers have made Versailles the most sumptuously clad château in the world – a brilliant, unmissable cocktail of extravagance. The famous Hall of Mirrors – a 73-metre (240-foot) gallery overlooking the garden hung with 357 mirrors – was commissioned in 1678 by Louis XIV and decorated by Le Brun. The gardens sprawl across eight square kilometres (three square miles) and cosist of formal parterres, ponds, elaborate statues and a spectacular series of fountains. Outside the château gates are the stables that now house the Académie du Spectacle Equestre, responsible for the elaborate shows of tightly choreographed theatrics on horseback, run by famous horse trainer Bartabas.

Château de Versailles

78000 Versailles (01.30.83.78.00, advance tickets 08.92.68.46.94, www.chateauversailles.fr). **Open** *Apr-Oct* 9am-6.30pm Tue-Sun. *Nov-Mar* 9am-5.30pm Tue-Sun. **Admission** €15; €13 reductions; free under-18s.

Consume

All the best restaurants, bars and shops

Photograph **Dave Bruel**

Restaurants

A surprising number of new restaurants are thriving in the difficult economic climate, showing that Parisians will always appreciate good food at fair prices. One notable example is **Frenchie**, a brick-walled bistro run by a young French chef who previously worked with Jamie Oliver. His limited-choice set menu, which often surprises with unexpected flavour combinations, keeps the locals coming back for two dinner sittings every night. Another is the city's first raw food restaurant, **Cru**, which has a stunning courtyard terrace. For the fashion-minded, the north-east is the place to head to new arrivals **Le Dauphin** and **Le Floréal** (for both, *see p6* **Cooking up a storm**).

Since the smoking ban came into effect, Parisians have gradually been growing more health-conscious. This shows in the popularity of cafés such as **Rose Bakery** and **Cantine Merci**, where a plate of crunchy salads topped with sprouts and served with carrot juice might replace the traditional *steak-frites* washed down with red wine. But the French continue to love classic bistro style, found in updated form at neo-bistros such as **Le Chateaubriand** and **Le Miroir**. And wine bars have become some of the best places to eat in the city, with **Racines** (where vegetables come from the garden of chef Alain Passard) and **Le Baratin** leading the way.

Except for the simplest restaurants, it's wise to book ahead. This can usually be done on the same day as your visit, although really top-notch establishments require bookings weeks or even months in advance and confirmation the day before.

All listings have been checked at the time of going to press but are liable to change. Many venues close for their annual break in August, and some close at Christmas. Restaurants are presented by area. For more reviews, refer to *Time Out Paris Eating & Drinking*, available at www.timeout.com/shop.

With our reviews, we give the average price for a main course chosen from the à la carte menu. If 'Main courses' is not listed, only prix fixe options are available. 'Prix fixe' indicates the price of the set menu at lunch and/or dinner. All bills include a service charge, but a tip of a few euros (for the whole table) is polite unless you're unhappy with the service.

The Islands

Brasserie de l'Ile St-Louis
55 quai de Bourbon, 4th (01.43.54.02.59). M° Pont Marie. **Open** noon-11.30pm Mon, Tue, Thur-Sun. Closed Aug. **Main courses** €20. **Credit** MC, V. **Brasserie**
Happily, this old-fashioned brasserie soldiers on while exotic juice bars on the Ile St-Louis come and go. The terrace has one of the best summer views in Paris and is invariably packed; the dining room exudes shabby chic. Nicotined walls make for an authentic Paris mood, though nothing here is gastronomically gripping: a well-dressed *frisée aux lardons* perhaps.

Mon Vieil Ami
69 rue St-Louis-en-l'Ile, 4th (01.40.46.01.35, www.mon-vieil-ami.com). M° Pont Marie. **Open** noon-2.30pm, 6.30-11pm Wed-Sun.
Closed 3wks Jan & 1st 3wks Aug. **Main courses** €13-€23. **Prix fixe** €41. **Credit** AmEx, DC, MC, V. **Bistro**
Antoine Westermann from the Buerehiesel in Strasbourg has created a true foodie destination here. Starters such as tartare of finely diced raw vegetables with sautéed baby squid on top impress with their deft seasoning. Typical of the mains is a cast-iron casserole of roast duck with caramelised turnips and couscous. Even the classic room has been successfully refreshed with black beams, white Perspex panels and a long *table d'hôte* down one side.

The Louvre & Palais-Royal

L'Ardoise
28 rue du Mont-Thabor, 1st (01.42.96.28.18). M° Concorde or Tuileries. **Open** noon-2.30pm, 6.30-11pm Mon-Sat; 6.30-11pm Sun. Closed 1st 3wks Aug. **Main courses** €19. **Prix fixe** €33. **Credit** MC, V. **Bistro**
One of the city's finest modern bistros, L'Ardoise attracts gourmets eager to sample Pierre Jay's reliably delicious cooking. A wise choice might be six oysters with warm chipolatas and a pungent shallot dressing; equally attractive are a gamey hare pie with an escalope of foie gras nestling in its centre. A lightly chilled, raspberry-scented Chinon is a perfect complement. Unusually, it's open on Sundays.

Chez La Vieille
37 rue de l'Arbre-Sec, 1st (01.42.60.15.78). M° Louvre Rivoli. **Open** noon-1.45pm, 7.30-9.45pm Mon-Fri. Closed Aug. **Main courses** €25. **Prix fixe** *Lunch* €26. **Credit** AmEx, MC, V. **Bistro**
The rustic ground floor of this bistro bursts with well-rounded regulars, whereas upstairs is plain and bright. A wondrous ad-lib selection of starters might include hot *chou farci* and homemade *terrine de foie gras*. Equally impressive is

foie de veau, coated in a pungent reduction of shallots and vinegar and served with potato purée. Puddings follow the same cornucopian principle as the starters. Opening hours are limited and booking essential, but the lunchtime prix fixe is a bargain.

Chez Vong
10 rue de la Grande-Truanderie, 1st (01.40.26.09.36, www.chez-vong.com). M° Etienne Marcel or Les Halles. **Open** noon-2.30pm, 7-11.30pm Mon-Sat. Closed 3wks Aug. **Main courses** €20. **Prix fixe** *Lunch* €24. **Credit** AmEx, DC, MC, V. **Chinese**
The staff at this cosy Chinese restaurant take pride in its excellent cooking. From the greeting at the door to the knowledgeable, trilingual service (Cantonese, Mandarin and French), each part of the experience is thoughtfully orchestrated. Any doubts about authenticity are extinguished with the arrival of the beautifully presented dishes. Expertly cooked spicy shrimp glistens in a smooth, characterful sauce of onions and ginger, and *ma po* tofu melts in the mouth, its spicy and peppery flavours melding with those of the fine pork mince.

Les Fines Gueules
43 rue Croix-des-Petits-Champs, 1st (01.42.61.35.41, www.lesfinesgueules.fr). M° Bourse or Sentier. **Open** 2.30-4pm, 7.30-11pm daily. **Main courses** €14-€23. **Credit** MC, V. **Bistro/wine bar**
At first glance, Les Fines Gueules might seem like an ordinary corner café, but a slightly closer look at the menu reveals unusual attention to ingredients at this mini wine bar/bistro. Even if you've never heard of Hugo (Desnoyer, star butcher and supplier to some of the city's finest restaurants) or Jean-Luc (Poujauran, a celebrity Paris baker), you can taste the difference when the pedigree steak tartare arrives with a salad of baby leaves dressed in truffle oil. There are just a few seats tucked around the bar, but upstairs is a buzzy dining room that attracts a mix of smoochy couples and business suits. A good selection of 'natural' and organic wines comes by the glass and the bottle.

Frenchie
5 rue du Nil, 2nd (01.40.39.96.19, www.frenchie-restaurant.com). M° Sentier. **Open** 8-11pm Tue; noon-2.30pm, 8-11pm Wed-Sat. **Main courses** €16. **Prix fixe** €19-€33. **Credit** MC, V. **Bistro**
Grégory Lemarchand honed his craft with Jamie Oliver in London before opening this loft-style bistro next to the market street rue Montorgueil. It has been an enormous hit thanks to the bold flavours of dishes such as gazpacho with calamari, squash blossoms and plenty of herbs; braised lamb with roasted aubergine and spinach; and coconut tapioca with strawberry sorbet. Be sure to book several days ahead for a table.

Le Grand Véfour
17 rue de Beaujolais, 1st (01.42.96.56.27, www.relaischateaux.com). M° Palais Royal Musée du Louvre. **Open** 12.30-1.30pm, 8-9.30pm Mon-Thur; 12.30-1.30pm Fri. Closed 1wk Apr, Aug, 1wk Dec. **Main courses** €74.

Brasserie de l'Ile St-Louis.

Restaurants

KARL BLACKWELL

Prix fixe *Lunch* €88. *Dinner* €268. **Credit** AmEx, DC, MC, V. **Haute cuisine**

Opened in 1784 (as the Café de Chartres), this is one of the oldest and most historic restaurants in Paris. An à la carte meal begins with a fantasia suite of delicacies: tiny frogs' legs, for example, arranged within a circle of sage sauce; a first course of creamed Breton sea urchins served in their spiny shells with a quail's egg and topped with caviar. Fish dishes may be a touch overcooked, and the adventurous desserts are not always successful, but you'll forgive all after a glass of vintage armagnac.

Kaï
18 rue du Louvre, 1st (01.40.15.01.99). M° *Louvre Rivoli.* **Open** 12.30-2.15pm, 7.30-10.30pm Tue-Sat; 7.30-10.30pm Sun. Closed 1wk Apr & 3wks Aug. **Main courses** €27. **Prix fixe** *Lunch* €38. *Dinner* €65, €110. **Credit** AmEx, MC, V. **Japanese**

This restaurant has developed a following among fashionable diners. The 'Kaï-style' sushi is a zesty take on a classic: marinated and lightly grilled yellowtail is pressed on to a roll of *shiso*-scented rice. Not to be outdone, the grilled aubergine with miso, seemingly simple, turns out to be a smoky, luscious experience. A generous main of breaded pork lacks the finesse and refinement of the starters, but is still satisfying. Thoroughly French desserts come courtesy of celebrity pastry chef Pierre Hermé.

Le Meurice
Hôtel Meurice, 228 rue de Rivoli, 1st (01.44.58.10.55, www.meuricehotel.com). M° *Tuileries.* **Open** 7-10.30am, 12.30-2pm, 7.30-10pm Mon-Fri; 7-11am Sat, Sun. Closed 2wks Feb & Aug. **Main courses** €100. **Prix fixe** *Breakfast* €36-€65. *Lunch* €78. *Dinner* €220. **Credit** AmEx, DC, MC, V. **Haute cuisine**

Yannick Alléno, chef here since 2003, has really hit his stride and is doing some glorious, if rather understated, contemporary cooking. Alléno has a light touch, teasing the flavour out of every leaf, frond, fin or fillet. Turbot is sealed in clay before cooking and then sauced with celery cream and a coulis of flat parsley. Bresse chicken stuffed with foie gras and served with truffled *sarladais* potatoes is breathtakingly good. A fine cheese tray comes from Quatrehomme; the pastry chef amazes with his millefeuille. Jacket required for men.

Restaurant du Palais-Royal
110 galerie Valois, 1st (01.40.20.00.27, www.restaurantdupalaisroyal.com). M° *Bourse, Musée du Louvre or Palais Royal.* **Open** noon-2pm, 7-10pm Mon-Sat. Closed 19 Dec-10 Jan. **Main courses** €24-€32. **Prix fixe** €60. **Credit** AmEx, DC, MC, V. **Bistro**

There can be few more magical places to dine on a summer evening than the terrace of this restaurant. Inside is memorable too: you sit in a red dining room alongside the commissars of arts and letters who work at the ministry of culture a few doors down. Risotto is a speciality and the Black, Black and Lobster is tremendous; rice simmered in rich squid ink is served al dente, topped with tender but fleshy pink lobster, sun-dried tomato and spring vegetables. Don't miss out on the *baba au rhum*.

Thaïm
46 rue de Richelieu, 1st (01.42.96.54.67). M° *Bourse or Palais Royal.* **Open** noon-3pm, 7-11.30pm Mon-Fri; 7-11pm Sat. **Main courses** €14. **Prix fixe** *Lunch* €16. *Dinner* €25-€28. **Credit** MC, V. **Thai**

Steering well away from Thai clichés, Thaïm has an elegant decor of dark wood and plum fabrics, and a brief menu that changes often, keeping the regulars coming back. Particularly good value is the three-course lunch menu, which might bring crisp fried parcels filled with spiced vegetables, an aromatic green fish curry (there is a choice of fish, meat or poultry every day), and sweet coconut-pumpkin soup. There is an extensive choice of teas, including an iced ginger-coconut version.

Zen
8 rue de l'Echelle, 1st (01.42.61.93.99, www.restaurant-zen.fr.cc). M° *Louvre Rivoli.* **Open** noon-3pm, 7-10.30pm daily. Closed Aug. **Main courses** €12. **Prix fixe** *Lunch* €10-€18. *Dinner* €25-€45. **Credit** MC, V. **Japanese**

There's no shortage of Japanese restaurants in this neighbourhood, but the recently opened Zen is refreshing in a couple of ways. First, there is no pale wood in sight; the colour scheme here is sharp white, green and yellow for a cheerful effect. Second, the menu has a lot to choose from – bowls of ramen, sushi and *chirashi*, hearty dishes such as chicken with egg on rice or *tonkatsu* – yet no detail is neglected. A perfect choice if you're spending a day at the Louvre – you can be in and out in 30 minutes.

Le Meurice.

Opéra to Les Halles

L'Autobus Impérial
14 rue Mondétour, 1st (01.42.36.00.18, www.autobus-imperial.fr). M° *Les Halles.* **Open** 10am-2am Mon-Sat. **Main courses** €18. **Prix fixe** *Lunch* €13.50, €15.50. *Dinner* €24.50, €29.50, €40. **Credit** MC, V. **Brasserie**

Tucked away in a corner of Les Halles, L'Autobus Impérial is a hidden gem. The rather unattractive entrance does little justice to the superb art nouveau dining room, built in 1910 and boasting a listed glass ceiling. Food is traditional but inventive, and remains very reasonably priced. The bar has the longest zinc counter in Paris, stretching some 12 metres, so there's plenty of room to sip on cocktails while you wait.

Bioboa
3 rue Danielle-Casanova, 1st (01.42.61.17.67). M° *Pyramides.* **Open** 10am-5pm Mon-Sat. **Main courses** €11.50. **Prix fixe** €10-€15. **Credit** V. **Organic**

The fact that this place describes itself as a 'food spa' shows how it's embracing the organic ('bio' in French) revolution. There's a high-concept air about the place: white designer chairs and tables; a beautiful bird fresco that winds through it; and a mammoth fridge overflowing with expensive mineral waters, exotic smoothies and colourful takeaway salads for the fabulously busy. A healthy feast here might consist of soft-boiled eggs with sweet roasted autumn vegetables, or a juicy tofu burger with organic ketchup – one of Bioboa's staples.

Bistrot Victoires
6 rue de la Vrillière, 1st (01.42.61.43.78). M° *Bourse.* **Open** noon-3pm, 7-11pm daily. **Main courses** €11. **Credit** MC, V. **Bistro**

Bistros with vintage decor serving no-nonsense food at generous prices are growing thin on the ground in Paris, so it's no surprise that this gem is packed to the gills with bargain-loving office workers and locals every day. The *steak-frites* are exemplary, featuring a slab of entrecôte topped with a smoking sprig of thyme, but *plats du jour* such as *blanquette de veau* (veal in cream sauce) are equally comforting. The wines by the glass can be rough, but the authentic buzz should make up for any flaws.

La Bourse ou la Vie
12 rue Vivienne, 2nd (01.42.60.08.83). M° *Bourse.* **Open** noon-10pm Mon-Fri. Closed 1wk Aug & 1wk Dec. **Main courses** €10-€20. **Credit** AmEx, MC, V. **Bistro**

After a career as an architect, the round-spectacled owner of La Bourse ou la Vie has a new mission in life: to revive the dying art of the perfect *steak-frites*. The only decision you'll need to make is which cut of beef to order with your chips, unless you pick the cod. Choose between ultra-tender *coeur de filet* or a huge *bavette*. Rich, creamy pepper sauce is the speciality here, but the real surprise is the chips, which gain a distinctly animal flavour from the suet in which they are cooked.

Chez Miki
5 rue de Louvois, 2nd (01.42.96.04.88). M° *Bourse.* **Open** noon-10pm Tue-Fri; 6-10pm Sat, Sun. **Main courses** €15. **Prix fixe** €30, €35. **Credit** MC, V. **Japanese**

There are plenty of Japanese restaurants to choose from along nearby rue Ste-Anne, but none is as original – nor as friendly – as this tiny bistro run entirely by women, next to the square Louvois. The speciality here is bento boxes, which you compose yourself from a scribbled blackboard list (in Japanese and French). For €15 you can choose two small dishes – marinated sardines and fried chicken wings are especially popular – and a larger dish, such as grilled pork with ginger. Don't miss the inventive desserts, which might include lime jelly spiked with alcohol.

DEPUR
4bis rue St-Sauveur, 2nd (01.40.26.69.66, www.droledendroit.com). M° *Etienne Marcel or Sentier.* **Open** 8am-11.30pm Mon-Sat; 8am-5pm Sun. **Main courses** €20. **Prix fixe** *Brunch* €28. **Credit** AmEx, MC, V. **Bistro**

This stylish café-bar-restaurant sits in the lobby of Le Klay, a luxurious private sports club (membership €350/month or €1,590/year). The open-brick walls give a New York vibe to the place, but it's the airy courtyard terrace that will really knock you out. Crazy cocktail names ('Lance, I'm strong!') and freshly blended protein shakes add an original note to this seriously trendy hangout. Come for breakfast (8am-noon daily, from €10) or brunch (noon-5pm Sat, Sun).

Drouant
18 pl Gaillon, 2nd (01.42.65.15.16, www.drouant.com). M° *Pyramides or Quatre Septembre.* **Open** noon-2.30pm, 7pm-midnight daily. **Main courses** €17.50-€30. **Prix fixe** *Lunch* €43-€60. *Dinner* (10.30pm-midnight) €55-€60. **Credit** AmEx, DC, MC, V. **Brasserie**

Star chef Antoine Westermann has whisked this landmark 1880 brasserie into the 21st century with bronze-coloured banquettes and butter-yellow fabrics. Westermann has dedicated this restaurant to the art of the hors d'oeuvre: they're served in themed sets of four ranging from the global (Thai beef salad with brightly coloured vegetables, coriander, and a sweet and spicy sauce) to the nostalgic (silky leeks in vinaigrette). The bite-sized surprises continue with the main course accompaniments – four of them for each dish – and the multiple mini-desserts.

Au Gourmand
17 rue Molière, 1st (01.42.96.22.19, www.augourmand.fr). M° *Palais Royal or Pyramides.* **Open** 7.30-10pm Mon, Sat; 12.30-2pm, 7.30-10pm Tue-Fri. **Main courses** €28.50. **Prix fixe** *Lunch* €30. *Dinner* €36.50. **Credit** MC, V. **Bistro**

Ochre walls and red velvet curtains give this restaurant an almost too grown-up feel, but it's worth looking beyond that to the inventive fare coming out of the kitchen. Vegetables from celebrity market gardener Joël Thiébault star alongside meat in dishes such as juicy pork cheek wrapped in caul fat under a heap of colourful spring vegetables. Vegetarians can also find contentment here, perhaps in a thick slice of grilled aubergine topped with diced cucumber, tomato and ricotta. But a disastrous rum-spiked avocado mousse for dessert shows the chef's creativity with vegetables does have its limitations.

Higuma
32bis rue Ste-Anne, 1st (01.47.03.38.59, www.higuma.fr). M° *Pyramides.* **Open** 11.30am-10pm daily. **Main courses** €8. **Prix fixe** €10.50-€12.50. **Credit** MC, V. **Japanese**

Higuma's no-nonsense food and service make it one of the area's most popular restaurants. On entering, customers are greeted by plumes of aromatic steam emanating from the open kitchen-cum-bar, where a small team of chefs ladle out giant bowls of noodle soup piled with meat, vegetables or seafood. You can slurp at the counter or sit at a plastic-topped table.

Liza
14 rue de la Banque, 2nd (01.55.35.00.66, www.restaurant-liza.com). M° *Bourse.* **Open** 12.30-2pm, 8-10.30pm Mon-Thur; 12.30-2pm, 8-11pm Fri; 8-11pm Sat; noon-4pm Sun. **Main courses** €25. **Prix fixe** *Lunch* €16, €21. **Credit** AmEx, MC, V. **Lebanese**

Liza Soughayar's restaurant showcases the style and superb food of contemporary Beirut. Lentil, fried onion and orange salad is delicious, as are

BRITTA JASCHINSKI, OLIVIA RUTHERFORD

Located in the heart of the Latin Quarter, the Bouillon Racine combines art nouveau charm and exceptionally tasty food.

Open daily noon-11pm (last order)

3 rue Racine, 6th. Mº Odéon.
Tel: 01.44.32.15.60
Email: bouillon.racine@wanadoo.fr
www.bouillonracine.com

☎ 01.44.32.15.60

Finally a real American Diner in Paris!
Featuring:
Pancakes, Bagels, REAL Burgers, Fresh Wraps, NY Style Cheesecake and much, much more!

www.breakfast-in-america.com

Now BIA is in 2 Great Locations!

BIA 1: 17, rue des Ecoles, 5th arr.
Tel: 01 43 54 50 28
(Métro: Cardinal Lenroine or Jessieu)

BIA 2: 4, rue Malher, 4th arr.
Tel: 01 42 72 40 21
(Métro: St Paul)

Open 7 days a week: 8:30-23:00. Sunday Brunch all day!

the *kebbe* (minced seasoned raw lamb) and grilled halloumi cheese with apricot preserve. Main courses such as minced lamb with coriander-spiced spinach and rice are light and well presented. Try one of the excellent Lebanese wines to accompany your meal, and finish with the halva ice-cream with carob molasses.

L'Office
3 rue Richer, 9th (01.47.70.67.31). Mº Bonne Nouvelle. **Open** 7.30-10.30pm Tue, Wed, Sat; noon-2.30pm Thur, Fri. **Prix fixe** *Lunch* €12.50. *Dinner* €25. **Credit** MC, V. **Bistro**
Brother-in-law to the chef-owner at Frenchie (*see p48*), Alsatian-born Nicolas Scheidt is making a name of his own in a neighbourhood not known for its bistros. Wallpaper-decorated pillars, big mirrors and hanging lights give the dining room a modern spirit that's reflected in the food. Not everything works perfectly but there are flashes of brilliance, as in a salad of squid, cherry tomatoes and olives, or the slow-cooked guinea hen. Good to know about in this area.

Racines
8 passage des Panoramas, 2nd (01.40.13.06.41). **Open** noon-midnight Mon-Fri. **Main courses** €15. **Credit** MC, V. **Wine bar**
The 19th-century passage des Panoramas contains an eclectic collection of shops and restaurants – among them this wildly popular wine bar opened by the former owners of La Crèmerie in St-Germain. The menu is limited to superb-quality cheese and charcuterie plates, plus a couple of hot dishes, perhaps pork cheeks stewed in red wine or braised lamb, and a few comforting desserts. Many of the intense-tasting wines are biodynamic, and despite the rather hectic atmosphere lingering over an extra glass or two is cheerfully tolerated.

La Tour de Montlhéry (Chez Denise)
5 rue des Prouvaires, 1st (01.42.36.21.82). Mº Les Halles/RER Châtelet Les Halles. **Open** noon-3pm, 7.30pm-5am Mon-Fri. Closed 15 July-15 Aug. **Main courses** €24. **Credit** MC, V. **Bistro**
At the stroke of midnight, this place is packed, jovial and hungry. Savoury traditional dishes, washed down by litres of the house Brouilly, are the order of the day. Les Halles was the city's wholesale food market, and game, beef and offal still rule here. Diners devour towering rib steaks served with marrow and a heaped platter of chips, among the best in town. Brave souls can also try *tripes au calvados*, grilled *andouillette*, or perhaps go for a stewed venison, served with celery root and home-made jam.

Champs-Elysées & western Paris

Alain Ducasse au Plaza Athénée
Hôtel Plaza Athénée, 25 av Montaigne, 8th (01.53.67.65.00, www.alain-ducasse.com). Mº Alma Marceau. **Open** 7.45-10.15pm Mon-Wed; 12.45-2.15pm, 7.45-10.15pm Thur, Fri. Closed mid July-mid Aug & 2wks Dec. **Main courses** €80-€135. **Prix fixe** €260-€360. **Credit** AmEx, DC, MC, V. **Haute cuisine**
The sheer glamour factor would be enough to recommend this restaurant, Alain Ducasse's most lofty Paris undertaking. The dining room ceiling drips with 10,000 crystals. An *amuse-bouche* of a single langoustine in a lemon cream with a touch of Iranian caviar starts the meal off brilliantly, but other dishes can be inconsistent: a part-raw/part-cooked salad of autumn fruit and vegetables in a red, Chinese-style sweet-and-sour dressing, or Breton lobster in an overwhelming sauce of apple, quince and spiced wine. Cheese is predictably delicious, as is the *rum baba comme à Monte-Carlo*.

Astrance
4 rue Beethoven, 16th (01.40.50.84.40). Mº Passy. **Open** 12.15-1.30pm, 8-9.30pm Tue-Fri. Closed 1wk Feb, 4wks Aug, 1wk Oct & 1wk Dec. **Prix fixe** *Lunch* €70. *Dinner* €190. **Credit** AmEx, DC, MC, V. **Haute cuisine**
When Pascal Barbot opened Astrance, he was praised for creating a new style of Paris restaurant – refined, yet casual and affordable. A few years later, this small, slate-grey dining room feels just like an haute cuisine restaurant. Most customers, having reserved at least a month ahead, give free rein to the chef with the 'Menu Astrance'. Barbot

has an original touch, combining foie gras with slices of white mushrooms and a lemon condiment, or sweet lobster with candied grapefruit peel, a grapefruit and rosemary sorbet, and raw baby spinach. Wines by the glass are reasonably priced.

Le Bistrot Napolitain
18 av Franklin D. Roosevelt, 8th (01.45.62.08.37). Mº St-Philippe-du-Roule. **Open** noon-2.30pm, 7.15-10.30pm Mon-Fri. Closed 1wk July, Aug & 1wk Dec. **Main courses** €25. **Credit** MC, V. **Italian**
This chic Italian bistro is as far from a tourist joint as it is possible to be. On weekday lunchtimes, it is full of suave Italianate businessmen. Generosity defines the food – not just big plates, but lashings of the ingredients that others skimp on, such as the slices of tangy parmesan piled high over rocket on the tender beef carpaccio. The pizzas are very good: the Enzo comes with milky, almost raw *mozzarella di bufala* and tasty tomatoes. For pasta you can choose between dried and fresh, with variations such as fresh saffron tagliatelle.

Granterroirs
30 rue de Miromesnil, 8th (01.47.42.18.18, www.granterroirs.com). Mº Miromesnil. **Open** 9am-8pm Mon-Fri. *Food served* noon-3pm Mon-Fri. Closed 3wks Aug. **Main courses** €21. **Prix fixe** €39, €49. **Credit** MC, V. **Bistro**
Here, the walls heave with more than 600 enticing specialities from southern France, including Périgord foie gras, charcuterie from Aubrac and a fine selection of wines. All make excellent gift ideas – but why not sample some of the goodies by enjoying the midday *table d'hôte* feast? Come in early to ensure that you can choose from the five succulent *plats du jour* on offer (such as marinated salmon with dill on a bed of warm potatoes).

Le Hide
10 rue du Général-Lanrezac, 17th (01.45.74.15.81, www.lehide.fr). Mº Charles de Gaulle Etoile. **Open** noon-3pm, 7.30-10.30pm Mon-Fri; 7.30-10.30pm Sat. **Prix fixe** €22, €29. **Credit** MC, V. **Bistro**
Ever since it opened, this snug bistro has been packed with a happy crowd of bistro-lovers who appreciate Japanese-born chef Hide Kobayashi's superb cooking and good-value prices. Expect dishes such as duck foie gras terrine with pear-and-thyme compôte to start, followed by tender *faux-filet* steak in a light foie gras sauce or skate wing with a lemon-accented *beurre noisette*. Desserts are excellent: perfect tarte tatin comes with crème fraîche from Normandy. Good, affordable wines explain the merriment, including a glass of the day for €2.

Maxan
37 rue de Miromesnil, 8th (01.42.65.78.60, www.rest-maxan.com). Mº Miromesnil. **Open** noon-2.30pm Mon; noon-2.30pm, 7.30-11.30pm Tue-Fri; 7.30-11.30pm Sat. Closed Aug. **Prix fixe** €30-€60. **Credit** MC, V. **Bistro**
This is a welcome new-wave bistro in an area where eating options tend to be fashion haunts, grand tables or tourist traps. Owner-chef Laurent Zajac uses quality seasonal ingredients, giving them a personal spin in dishes such as scallops with curry spices and artichoke hearts, classic veal sweetbreads with wild asparagus, and an exotic take on *île flottante*. Popular with ministry of interior types at lunch, quieter by night.

Pierre Gagnaire
6 rue Balzac, 8th (01.58.36.12.50, www.pierre-gagnaire.com). Mº Charles de Gaulle Etoile or George V. **Open** noon-1.30pm, 7.30-9.30pm Mon-Fri; 7.30-9pm Sun. Closed 1wk Apr & Aug. **Main courses** €105. **Prix fixe** *Lunch* €95, €245. *Dinner* €245. **Credit** AmEx, MC, V. **Haute cuisine**
At Pierre Gagnaire most starters alone cost over €90, which seems to be the price of culinary experimentation these days. The cheaper €90 lunch

menu is far from the full-blown experience of the *carte*: the former is presented in three courses, whereas the latter involves four or five plates for each course. Even the *amuse-bouches* fill the table: an egg 'raviole', ricotta with apple, fish in a cauliflower jelly, and glazed monkfish. The best thing about the lunch menu is that it includes four very indulgent desserts: clementine, raspberry and vanilla, chocolate, and passion fruit.

Rech
62 av des Ternes, 17th (01.45.72.29.47, www.rech.fr). Mº Ternes. **Open** noon-2pm, 7.30-10pm Tue-Sat. Closed 3wks Aug. **Main courses** €28. **Prix fixe** *Lunch* €30. *Dinner* €53. **Credit** AmEx, MC, V. **Bistro**
Alain Ducasse's personal touches are everywhere in this art deco seafood restaurant, which he took over in spring 2007, from the Japanese fish prints on the walls of the upstairs dining room to the blown glass candleholders on the main floor tables. The kitchen turns out the kind of precise, Mediterranean-inspired cooking you would expect from Ducasse: glistening sardine fillets marinated with preserved lemon, silky lobster ravioli and octopus carpaccio painted with pesto. As the fish dishes are light, you can justify indulging in a perfectly aged camembert and the XL éclair.

Restaurant L'Entredgeu
83 rue Laugier, 17th (01.40.54.97.24). Mº Porte de Champerret. **Open** noon-2pm, 7.30-11pm Tue-Sat. Closed 1wk Apr, 1st 3wks Aug & 1wk Dec. **Prix fixe** *Lunch* €22, €30. *Dinner* €30. **Credit** DC, MC, V. **Bistro**
Reading the menu here will make you seriously doubt your capacity for pudding. But have no fear. The heartiness of the dishes belies refined, perfectly gauged cooking, served in civilised portions. The table turnover is fast, but this is not a place to linger smoochily in any case – you'll be too busy marvelling at the sharp *gribiche* sauce cutting through the milky crisp-battered oysters,

Changing tables

Becoming a top French chef is tough work. For a start you have to be good enough to uphold the reputation of La Gastronomie Française (the world's most famous cuisine and part of UNESCO's World Heritage List since 2010). Then there's the competition – fierce and merciless, with more aspiring masterchefs than there are dream jobs to go round. Even if you do manage to become sous-chef to a legend like Alain Ducasse or Paul Bocuse, usually the only way to become head chef is by opening your own restaurant.

Fortunately for Christophe Moret, though, Michelin-starred Jean-Louis Nomicos has left the mighty **Lasserre** (17 av Franklin-Roosevelt, 8th,

01.43.59.02.13, www.restaurant-lasserre.com), where notables such as the Duke of Windsor, André Malraux and Salvador Dalí once graced the tables, to open his own restaurant, Les Tablettes de Jean-Louis Nomicos (16 av Bugeaud, 16th, 01.56.28.16.16, www.les tablettesjeanlouisnomicos.com) – a move which left a vacancy that Moret was only too happy to fill.

After seven years under Ducasse at the Plaza Athénée, 'it was time to take on a new challenge,' says Moret enthusiastically. 'I'm 44 now, and I want to prove that I can do it.' Joining him in Lasserre's kitchen is pastry chef Claire Heitzler, who left her job at the Ritz to come here.

A typical meal might start with an amuse-bouche of lettuce mousse with golden caviar, followed by scallops with caramelised Jerusalem artichokes and oodles of grated white truffles. Mains include André Malraux pigeon, a dish invented by the restaurant's founder Réné Laserre and stuffed with foie gras, or Christophe Moret's duck stuffed with truffles and turnips in lapsang souchong tea. Desserts are heavenly.

The dining room itself is a sumptuous affair, with solid silver table decorations and a retractable roof, which opens just enough for you to make out the stars – perfect for romantic summer splurges.

Granterroirs. *See p51.*

the depth and aroma of the saffron-infused fish soup, the perfect layered execution of the caramelised pork belly, and the delicate desserts. The wine list is creative and assured.

Senderens
9 pl de la Madeleine, 8th (01.42.65.22.90, www.senderens.fr). M° Madeleine. **Open** noon-2.45pm, 7.30-11.15pm daily. Closed 3wks Aug. **Main courses** €39. **Prix fixe** €110-€150 (with wine). **Credit** AmEx, DC, MC, V. **Haute cuisine**
Alain Senderens reinvented his art nouveau institution (formerly Lucas Carton) a few years ago with a *Star Trek* interior and a mind-boggling fusion menu. Now, you might find dishes such as roast duck foie gras with a warm salad of black figs and liquorice powder, or monkfish steak with Spanish mussels and green curry sauce. Each dish comes with a suggested wine, whisky, sherry or punch (to match a rum-doused *savarin* with slivers of ten-flavour pear), and although these are perfectly chosen, the mix of flavours and alcohols can prove overwhelming at times.

Stella Maris
4 rue Arsène-Houssaye, 8th (01.42.89.16.22, www.stellamaris-paris.com). M° Charles de Gaulle Etoile. **Open** noon-2.30pm, 7.30-10.30pm Mon-Fri; 7.30-10.30pm Sat. Closed 2wks Aug. **Main courses** €52. **Prix fixe** *Lunch* €49. *Dinner* €70, €99, €130. **Credit** AmEx, DC, MC, V. **Haute cuisine**

Tateru Yoshino has divided his life between Paris and Tokyo for many years. Trained by Robuchon and Troisgros, he turns out food that is resolutely French. The service is at times faltering, but charmingly so, and the space is beautiful. You might float your way through foie gras with carrots, truffles and pistachio oil, pan-fried sea bass with saffron risotto, and a perfectly lopsided Grand Marnier soufflé. The exquisite, powdery blandness of the tasting menu going-home present, *cake aux marrons glacés*, brings it all softly, dreamily, back next morning at breakfast.

La Table Lauriston
129 rue de Lauriston, 16th (01.47.27.00.07, www.restaurantlatablelauriston.com). M° Trocadéro. **Open** noon-2.30pm, 7-10.30pm Mon-Fri; 7-10.30pm Sat. Closed 3wks Aug & 1wk Dec. **Main courses** €23. **Prix fixe** *Lunch* €24. *Dinner* €40, €61. **Credit** AmEx, MC, V. **Bistro**
Serge Barbey's dining room has a refreshingly feminine touch. The emphasis here is firmly on good-quality ingredients, skilfully prepared to show off their freshness. In spring, stalks of asparagus from the Landes are expertly trimmed to avoid any trace of stringiness and served with the simplest *vinaigrette d'herbes*. More extravagant is the *foie gras cuit au torchon*, in which the duck liver is wrapped in a cloth and poached in a bouillon. Skip the crème brûlée, which you could have anywhere, and order a dessert with attitude instead: the giant *baba au rhum*.

Montmartre & Pigalle

Le Miroir
94 rue des Martyrs, 18th (01.46.06.50.73). M° Abbesses. **Open** noon-3pm, 7-11pm Tue-Sat; noon-3pm Sun. **Main courses** €15. **Prix fixe** *Lunch* €18. *Dinner* €32. **Credit** MC, V. **Bistro**
This friendly modern bistro is a welcome addition to a neighbourhood where good-value restaurants are scarce. Big mirrors, red banquettes and a glass

Taillevent
15 rue Lamennais, 8th (01.44.95.15.01, www.taillevent.com). M° George V. **Open** 12.15-1.30pm, 7.15-9.30pm Mon-Fri. Closed Aug. **Main courses** €75. **Prix fixe** *Lunch* €80-€95, €120, €190. *Dinner* €190. **Credit** AmEx, DC, MC, V. **Haute cuisine**
Prices here are not as shocking as in some restaurants at this level. *Rémoulade de coquilles St-Jacques* is a technical feat, with slices of raw, marinated scallop wrapped in a tube shape around a finely diced apple filling, encircled by a mayonnaise-like *rémoulade* sauce. An earthier and lip-smacking dish is the trademark *épeautre* – an ancient wheat – cooked 'like a risotto' with bone marrow, black truffle, whipped cream and parmesan, and topped with sautéed frog's legs. Men must wear a jacket.

ceiling at the back give it character, while the very professional food and service reflect the owners' haute cuisine training. Expect dishes such as a salad of whelks with white beans, crisp-skinned duck and chanterelle mushrooms, and a *petit pot de crème vanille* with little chocolate cakes.

Le Moulin de la Galette
83 rue Lepic, 18th (01.46.06.84.77, www.lemoulindelagalette.eu). M° Notre-Dame-de-Lorette. **Open** noon-11pm daily. Closed Aug. **Main courses** €25. **Prix fixe** *Lunch* €17, €25. *Dinner* €50. **Credit** AmEx, MC, V. **Bistro**
The Butte Montmartre was once dotted with windmills, and this survivor houses a chic modern restaurant with a few tables in the cobbled courtyard. It's hard to imagine a more picturesque setting in Montmartre, but the kitchen makes an effort nonetheless, coming up with dishes such as foie gras with melting beetroot cooked in lemon balm and juniper or suckling pig alongside potato purée. Desserts, such as figs caramelised with muscovado sugar, look like a painter's tableau. If you're on a budget, stick to the set menus and order carefully from the wine list.

Pétrelle
34 rue Pétrelle, 9th (01.42.82.11.02, www.petrelle.fr). M° Anvers. **Open** 8-10pm Tue-Sat. Closed 4wks July/Aug & 1wk Dec. **Main courses** €25. **Prix fixe** €29. **Credit** MC, V. **Bistro**
Jean-Luc André is as inspired a decorator as he is a cook, and the quirky charm of his dining room has made it popular with fashion designers and film stars. But behind the style there's some serious substance. André seeks out the best ingredients from local producers, and the quality shines through. The €29 no-choice menu is very good value for money (marinated sardines with tomato relish, rosemary-scented rabbit with roasted vegetables, deep purple poached figs) – or you can splash out with luxurious à la carte dishes such as tournedos Rossini.

Rose Bakery
46 rue des Martyrs, 9th (01.42.82.12.80). M° Notre-Dame-de-Lorette. **Open** 9am-7pm Tue-Fri (food served noon-4pm); 9am-5pm Sat, Sun. Closed 2wks Aug & 1wk Dec. **Main courses** €14. **Credit** AmEx, MC, V. **British**
This English-themed café run by a Franco-British couple stands out for the quality of its ingredients – organic or from small producers – as well as the too-good-to-be-true puddings: carrot cake, sticky toffee pudding and, in winter, a chocolate-chestnut tart. The DIY salad plate is crunchily satisfying, but the thin-crusted *pizzettes*, daily soups and occasional risottos are equally good choices. Don't expect much beyond scones in the morning except at weekends, when brunch is served to a packed-out house. The dining room is minimalist.

Beaubourg & the Marais

L'Ambassade d'Auvergne
22 rue du Grenier-St-Lazare, 3rd (01.42.72.31.22, www.ambassade-auvergne.com). M° Arts et Métiers. **Open** noon-2pm, 7.30-10pm daily. **Main courses**

Rose Bakery.

OLIVER KNIGHT, KARL BLACKWELL

Menu lexicon

Meals (repas)
petit déjeuner breakfast. **déjeuner** lunch. **dîner** dinner. **souper** late dinner, supper.

Preparation (la préparation)
en croûte in a pastry case. **farci** stuffed. **au four** baked. **flambé** flamed in alcohol. **forestière** with mushrooms. **fricassé** fried and simmered in stock, usually with creamy sauce. **fumé** smoked. **garni** garnished. **glacé** frozen or iced. **gratiné** topped with breadcrumbs or cheese and grilled. **à la grècque** vegetables served cold in the cooking liquid with oil and lemon juice. **grillé** grilled. **haché** minced. **julienne** (vegetables) cut into matchsticks. **lamelle** very thin slice. **mariné** marinated. **pané** breaded. **en papillote** cooked in a packet. **parmentier** with potato. **pressé** squeezed. **râpé** grated. **salé** salted.

Cooking type (la cuisson)
cru raw. **bleu** practically raw. **saignant** rare. **rosé** (of lamb, duck, liver, kidneys) pink. **à point** medium rare. **bien cuit** well done.

Basics (essentiels)
ballotine stuffed, rolled-up piece of meat or fish. **crème fraîche** thick, slightly soured cream. **épices** spices. **feuilleté** 'leaves' of (puff) pastry. **fromage** cheese. **fruits de mer** shellfish. **galette** round flat cake of flaky pastry, potato pancake or buckwheat savoury crêpe. **gelée** aspic. **gibier** game. **gras** fat. **légume** vegetable. **maison** of the house. **marmite** small cooking pot. **miel** honey. **noisette** hazelnut; small, round portion of meat. **noix** walnut. **noix de coco** coconut. **nouilles** noodles. **oeuf** egg; – **en cocotte** baked egg; – **en meurette** egg poached in red wine; – **à la neige** see île flottante. **parfait** sweet or savoury mousse-like mixture. **paupiette** slice of meat or fish, stuffed and rolled. **timbale** dome-shaped mould, or food cooked in one. **tisane** herbal tea. **tourte** covered pie or tart, usually savoury.

Meat (viande)
agneau lamb. **aloyau** beef loin. **andouillette** sausage made from pig's offal. **bavette** beef flank steak. **biche** venison. **bifteck** steak. **boudin noir/blanc** black (blood)/white pudding. **boeuf** beef; – **bourguignon** beef cooked Burgundy style, with red wine, onions and mushrooms; – **gros sel** boiled beef with vegetables. **carbonnade** beef stew with onions and stout or beer. **carré d'agneau** rack of lamb. **cassoulet** stew of white haricot beans, sausage and preserved duck. **cervelle** brains. **châteaubriand** thick fillet steak. **chevreuil** young roe deer. **civet** game stew. **cochon de lait** suckling pig. **contre-filet** sirloin steak. **côte** chop; – **de boeuf** beef rib. **croque-madame** sandwich of toasted cheese and ham topped with an egg. **croque-monsieur** sandwich of toasted cheese and ham. **cuisses de grenouille** frogs' legs. **daube** meat braised in red wine. **entrecôte** beef rib steak. **escargot** snail. **estouffade** meat that's been marinated, fried and braised. **faux-filet** sirloin steak. **filet mignon** tenderloin. **foie** liver; – **de veau** calf's liver. **gigot d'agneau** leg of lamb. **hachis parmentier** shepherd's pie. **jambon** ham; – **cru** cured raw ham. **jarret** ham shin or knuckle. **langue** tongue. **lapin** rabbit. **lard** bacon. **lardon** small cube of bacon. **lièvre** hare. **marcassin** wild boar. **merguez** spicy lamb/beef sausage. **mignon** small meat fillet. **moelle** bone marrow; **os à la** – marrowbone. **navarin** lamb and vegetable stew. **onglet** cut of beef, similar to *bavette*. **pavé** thick steak. **petit salé** salt pork.

pied foot (trotter). **porc** pork. **porcelet** suckling pig. **pot-au-feu** boiled beef with vegetables. **queue de boeuf** oxtail. **ragoût** meat stew. **rillettes** potted pork or tuna. **ris de veau** veal sweetbreads. **rognons** kidneys. **rôti** roast. **sang** blood. **sanglier** wild boar. **saucisse** sausage. **saucisson sec** small dried sausage. **selle** (*d'agneau*) saddle (of lamb). **souris d'agneau** lamb knuckle. **tagine** slow-cooked North African stew. **tartare** raw minced steak (also tuna or salmon). **tournedos** small slices of beef fillet, sautéed or grilled. **travers de porc** pork spare ribs. **veau** veal.

Poultry (volaille)
aiguillettes (*de canard*) thin slices (of duck breast). **blanc** breast. **caille** quail. **canard** duck; **confit de** – preserved duck. **coquelet** baby rooster. **dinde** turkey. **faisan** pheasant. **foie gras** fattened goose or duck liver. **gésiers** gizzards. **magret** duck breast. **oie** goose. **perdrix** partridge. **poulet** chicken. **suprême** (*de poulet*) fillets (of chicken) in a cream sauce.

Fish & seafood (poissons & fruits de mer)
anguille eel. **bar** sea bass. **belon** smooth, flat oyster. **bisque** shellfish soup. **bouillabaisse** Mediterranean fish soup. **brochet** pike. **bulot** whelk. **cabillaud** fresh cod. **carrelet** plaice. **colin** hake. **coquille** shell. **coquilles St-Jacques** scallops. **crevettes** prawns (UK), shrimp (US). **crustacé** shellfish. **daurade** sea bream. **eglefin** haddock. **escabèche** sautéed and marinated fish, served cold. **espadon** swordfish. **fines de claire** crinkle-shelled oysters. **flétan** halibut. **hareng** herring. **homard** lobster. **huître** oyster. **langoustine** Dublin Bay prawns, scampi. **limande** lemon sole. **lotte** monkfish. **maquereau** mackerel. **merlan** whiting. **merlu** hake. **meunière** fish floured and sautéed in butter. **moules** mussels; – **à la marinière** cooked with white wine and shallots. **morue** dried, salted cod; **brandade de** – cod puréed with potato. **oursin** sea urchin. **palourde** type of clam. **poulpe** octopus. **raie** skate. **rascasse** scorpion fish. **rouget** red mullet. **St-Pierre** John Dory. **sandre** pike-perch. **saumon** salmon. **seiche** squid. **truite** trout.

Vegetables (légumes)
aligot mashed potatoes with melted cheese and garlic. **asperge** asparagus. **céleri** celery. **céleri rave** celeriac. **cèpe** cep mushroom. **champignon** mushroom; – **de Paris** button mushroom. **chanterelle** small, trumpet-like mushroom. **choucroute** sauerkraut; – **garnie** with cured ham and sausages. **ciboulette** chive. **citronelle** lemongrass. **coco** large white bean. **cresson** watercress. **échalote** shallot. **endive** chicory (UK), Belgian endive (US). **épinards** spinach. **frisée** curly endive. **frites** chips (UK), fries (US). **gingembre** ginger. **girolle** small, trumpet-like mushroom. **gratin dauphinois** sliced potatoes baked with milk, cheese and garlic. **haricot** bean; – **vert** green bean. **mâche** lamb's lettuce. **morille** morel mushroom. **navet** turnip. **oignon** onion. **oseille** sorrel. **persil** parsley. **pignon** pine nut. **poivre** pepper. **poivron** red or green (bell) pepper. **pomme de terre** potato. **pommes lyonnaises** potatoes fried with onions. **riz** rice. **truffes** truffles.

Fruit (fruits)
ananas pineapple. **cassis** blackcurrants; blackcurrant liqueur. **citron** lemon; – **vert** lime. **fraise** strawberry. **framboise** raspberry. **groseille** redcurrant; – **à maquereau** goose-berry. **myrtille** blueberry. **pamplemousse** grapefruit. **pomme** apple. **prune** plum. **pruneau** prune. **quetsche** damson.

Desserts & cheese (desserts & fromage)
bavarois moulded cream dessert. **beignet** fritter or doughnut. **chèvre** goat; goat's cheese. **clafoutis** batter filled with fruit. **crème brûlée** creamy custard dessert with caramel glaze. **fromage blanc** smooth cream cheese. **glace** ice-cream. **île flottante** whipped egg white floating in vanilla custard. **réglisse** liquorice. **tarte aux pommes** apple tart. **tarte tatin** caramelised apple tart cooked upside down.

Soups & sauces (soupes & sauces)
aïoli garlic mayonnaise. **anchoïade** spicy anchovy and olive paste. **béarnaise** sauce of butter and egg yolk. **blanquette** 'white' stew made with eggs and cream. **potage** soup. **velouté** stock-based white sauce; creamy soup. **vichyssoise** cold leek and potato soup.

Drinks
bière beer. **eau** water; – **de robinet** tap water; – **gazeuse/pétillante** sparkling mineral water; – **plate** still mineral water. **eau de vie** fruit spirit or liqueur. **vin** wine; – **blanc** white wine; – **rouge** red wine.

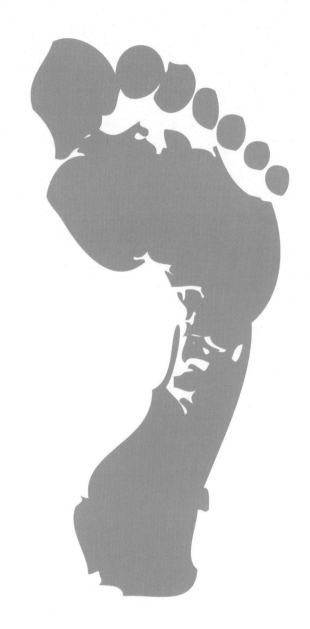

Whatever your carbon footprint, we can reduce it

For over a decade we've been leading the way in carbon offsetting and carbon management.

In that time we've purchased carbon credits from over 200 projects spread across 6 continents. We work with over 300 major commercial clients and thousands of small and medium sized businesses, which rely upon our market-leading quality assurance programme, our experience and absolute commitment to deliver the right solution for each client.

Why not give us a call?

Jane McAllister
T: London (020) 7833 6000

€18. **Prix fixe** *Lunch* €20, €28. *Dinner* (min 12 people) €38, €55, €65. **Credit** AmEx, MC, V. **Bistro**
This rustic-style *auberge* is a fitting embassy for the hearty fare of central France. An order of cured ham comes as two hefty, plate-filling slices, and the salad bowl is chock-full of green lentils cooked in goose fat, studded with bacon and shallots. The *rôti d'agneau* arrives as a pot of melting chunks of lamb in a rich, meaty sauce with a helping of tender white beans. Dishes arrive with the flagship *aligot*, the creamy, elastic mash-and-cheese concoction. Among the regional wines (Chanturgue, Boudes, Madargues), the fruity AOC Marcillac makes a worthy partner.

Breizh Café
109 rue Vieille-du-Temple, 3rd (01.42.72.13.77, www.breizhcafe.com). M° Filles du Calvaire. **Open** noon-11pm Wed-Sun. Closed 3wks Aug. **Main courses** €10. **Credit** MC, V. **Crêperie**
With its modern interior of pale wood and its choice of 15 artisanal ciders, this outpost of a restaurant in Cancale, Brittany, is a world away from the average crêperie. For the complete faux-seaside experience, you might start with a plate of creuse oysters from Cancale before indulging in an inventive buckwheat *galette* such as the Cancalaise, made with potato, smoked herring from Brittany and herring roe. The choice of fillings is fairly limited, but the ingredients are of high quality – including the use of Valrhona chocolate with 70% cocoa solids in the dessert crêpes.

Cantine Merci
111 bd Beaumarchais, 3rd (01.42.77.78.92). M° St-Sébastien Froissart. **Open** noon-3pm Mon-Sat. **Main courses** €8-€18. **Credit** MC, V. **Café**
The new fairtrade concept store Merci is all about feeling virtuous even as you indulge, and its basement canteen is a perfect example. Fresh and colourful salads, soup and risotto of the day, an organic salmon plate, and the *assiette merci* (perhaps chicken kefta with two salads) make up the brief, Rose Bakery-esque menu, complete with invigorating teas and juices. Rustic desserts add just the right handmade touch.

Chez Hanna
54 rue des Rosiers, 4th (01.42.74.74.99). M° St-Paul. **Open** noon-midnight Tue-Sun. **Main courses** €10. **Credit** MC, V. **Jewish**
By noon on a Sunday, there is a queue outside every falafel shop along rue des Rosiers. The long-established L'As du Fallafel, a little further up the street, still reigns supreme, whereas Hanna remains something of a locals' secret, quietly serving up falafel and shawarma sandwiches to rival any in the world. A pitta sandwich bursting with crunchy chickpea-and-herb balls, tahini sauce and vegetables costs €4 if you order from the takeaway window, €8 if you sit at one of the tables in the buzzy dining room overlooking the street. Either way, you really can't lose.

Chez Julien
1 rue du Pont Louis-Philippe, 4th (01.42.78.31.64). M° Pont Marie. **Open** noon-3pm, 7-11pm Mon-Sat. **Main courses** €25. **Credit** MC, V. **Bistro**
Thierry Costes discreetly took over this vintage bistro overlooking the Seine in spring 2007. The zebra banquette near the loo upstairs is most reminiscent of the Costes style, but the 1920s dining room is also unmistakably chic with plum walls, a big chandelier and red banquettes, and the terrace outside now stretches across the cobbled pedestrian street. The food is predictable and pricey – crab salad, steak with shoestring fries, roast Bresse chicken with mini-potatoes – but it's hard not to enjoy this slice of Paris life.

Chez Omar
47 rue de Bretagne, 3rd (01.42.72.36.26). M° Arts et Métiers or Temple. **Open** noon-2.30pm, 7-10.30pm Mon-Sat; 7-10.30pm Sun. **Main courses** €16. **No credit cards. North African**
The once-fashionable Omar doesn't take reservations, and the queue can stretch the length of the zinc bar and through the door. Everyone is waiting for the same thing: couscous. Prices range from €11 (vegetarian) to €24 (*royale*); there are no tagines or other traditional Maghreb mains, only a handful of French classics (duck, fish, steak). Overstretched waiters slip through the crowds with mounds of semolina, vats of vegetable-laden broth and steel platters heaving with meat, including the stellar *merguez*. Even on packed nights, there's an offer of seconds – gratis – to encourage you to stay a little while longer.

Cru
7 rue Charlemagne, 4th (01.40.27.81.84, www.restaurantcru.fr). M° St-Paul. **Open** 12.30-2.30pm, 7.30-11pm Tue-Sat; 12.30-2.30pm Sun. **Main courses** €14-€27. **Prix fixe** *Lunch* €14 (Tue-Fri), 19. **Credit** MC, V. **Bistro**
Opening a raw-food restaurant is a gamble, so the owners of Cru cheat here and there, offering root vegetable 'chips' and a few *plancha* dishes. Still, the extensive menu has plenty for the crudivore, such as some unusual carpaccios (the veal with preserved lemon is particularly good) and intriguing 'red' and 'green' plates, variations on the tomato and cucumber. The food is perfectly good, but the real reason to come here is the gorgeous terrace lurking behind this quiet Marais street.

Derrière
69 rue des Gravilliers, 3rd (01.44.61.91.95, www.derriere-resto.com). M° Arts et Métiers. **Open** 8-11pm Mon, Sun; noon-2.30pm, 8-11pm Tue, Wed; noon-2.30pm, 8pm-midnight Thur, Fri; 8pm-midnight Sat. **Main courses** €15-€20. **Prix fixe** *Lunch* €25. **Credit** MC, V. **Bistro**
Mourad Mazouz, the man behind Momo and Sketch in London, has hit on another winning formula with this apartment-restaurant in the same street as his North African restaurant 404 and bar Andy Wahloo. The cluttered-chic look by decorator Bambi Sloan mixes contemporary fixtures and antique furniture, such as the beat-up armchairs in the smoking room hidden behind a wardrobe door upstairs. It attracts a young, hip crowd that appreciates the high-calorie comfort food: roast chicken with buttery mashed potatoes, macaroni gratin with taramasalata, and chocolate mousse.

Le Gaigne
12 rue Pecquay, 4th (01.44.59.86.72, www.restaurantlegaigne.fr). M° Rambuteau. **Open** 12.15-2pm, 7.30-10.30pm Tue-Thur; 12.15-2pm, 7.30-11pm Fri, Sat. **Main courses** €24. **Prix fixe** *Lunch* €17, €23, €31. *Dinner* €42, €59. **Credit** AmEx, MC, V. **Bistro**
It's a familiar story: young chef with haute cuisine credentials opens a small bistro in an out-of-the-way street. Here, the restaurant is even tinier than usual with only 20 seats and the cooking is unusually inventive. Chef Mickaël Gaignon has worked with Pierre Gagnaire, and it shows in dishes such as *l'oeuf bio* – three open eggshells filled with creamed spinach, carrot and celeriac – or roast monkfish with broccoli purée and a redcurrant emulsion. The dining room is pleasantly modern and staff are eager to please.

Le Hangar
12 impasse Berthaud, 3rd (01.42.74.55.44). M° Rambuteau. **Open** noon-2.30pm, 7.30-11pm Tue-Sat. Closed Aug. **Main courses** €17. **No credit cards. Bistro**
It's worth making the effort to find this bistro by the Centre Pompidou, with its terrace tucked away in a hidden alley and excellent cooking. A bowl of tapenade and toast is supplied to keep you going while choosing from the comprehensive *carte*. It yields, for starters, tasty and grease-free *rillettes de lapereau* (rabbit) alongside perfectly balanced pumpkin and chestnut soup. Main courses include pan-fried foie gras on a smooth potato purée made with olive oil.

Le Petit Marché
9 rue de Béarn, 3rd (01.42.72.06.67). M° Chemin Vert. **Open** noon-4pm, 7.45pm-midnight daily. **Main courses** €17. **Prix fixe** *Lunch* €12.50. **Credit** AmEx, MC, V. **Bistro**
Petit Marché's menu is short and modern with Asian touches. Raw tuna is flash-fried in sesame seeds and served with a Thai sauce, making for a refreshing starter; crispy-coated deep-fried king prawns have a similar lightness. The main vegetarian risotto is rich in basil, coriander, cream and al dente green beans. Pan-fried scallops with lime are precision-cooked and accompanied by a good purée and more beans.

Bofinger.

OLIVER KNIGHT

Bastille & eastern Paris

A la Biche au Bois
45 av Ledru-Rollin, 12th (01.43.43.34.38). M° Gare de Lyon. **Open** noon-2pm, 7-11pm Mon-Fri. Closed 4wks July-Aug & Christmas wk. **Main courses** €15. **Prix fixe** €25. **Credit** AmEx, DC, MC, V. **Bistro**
However crowded it gets here, it doesn't matter because everyone always seems so happy with the food and the convivial atmosphere. It's impossible not to be enthusiastic about the more than generous portions offered with the €25 prix fixe menu. Mains might include tasty portions of wild duck in blackcurrant sauce, partridge with cabbage or wild venison stew. If you can still do dessert, go for one of the home-made tarts laden with seasonal fruits. The wine list has a reputation as one of the best-value selections in town. Book in advance, but expect to wait anyway.

Le Bistrot Paul Bert
18 rue Paul-Bert, 11th (01.43.72.24.01). M° Charonne or Faidherbe Chaligny. **Open** noon-2pm, 7.30-11pm Tue-Sat. Closed Aug. **Main courses** €21. **Prix fixe** *Lunch* €16.50. *Dinner* €34. **Credit** MC, V. **Bistro**
This heart-warming bistro gets it right almost down to the last crumb. A starter salad of *ris de veau* illustrates the point, with lightly browned veal sweetbreads perched on a bed of green beans and baby carrots with a sauce of sherry vinegar and deglazed cooking juices. A roast shoulder of suckling pig and a thick steak with a raft of golden, thick-cut *frites* look inviting indeed. Desserts are superb too, including what may well be the best *île flottante* in Paris. If you're in the area at lunchtime, bear in mind that the prix fixe menu is remarkable value.

Bofinger
5-7 rue de la Bastille, 4th (01.42.72.87.82, www.bofingerparis.com). M° Bastille. **Open** noon-3pm, 6pm-1am Mon-Fri; noon-1am Sat, Sun. **Main courses** €22. **Prix fixe** *Lunch* €23.50. **Credit** AmEx, DC, MC, V. **Brasserie**
Bofinger draws big crowds for its authentic art nouveau setting and its brasserie atmosphere. Downstairs is the prettiest place in which to eat, but the upstairs room is air-conditioned. An à la carte selection might start with plump, garlicky escargots or a well-made langoustine terrine, followed by an intensely seasoned salmon tartare, a generous (if unremarkable) cod steak, or calf's liver accompanied by cooked melon. Alternatively, you could have the foolproof brasserie meal of oysters and fillet steak, followed by a pungent plate of munster cheese and bowl of cumin, all washed down with the fine Gigondas at €35.50 a bottle.

L'Encrier
55 rue Traversière, 12th (01.44.68.08.16). M° Gare de Lyon or Ledru-Rollin. **Open** noon-2.30pm, 7.30-11pm Mon-Fri; 7.30-11pm Sat. Closed Aug & Christmas wk. **Main courses** €14. **Prix fixe** *Lunch* €14. *Dinner* €19, €23. **Credit** MC, V. **Bistro**
Through the door and past the velvet curtain, you find yourself face to face with the kitchen – and a crowd of locals, many of whom seem to know the charming boss personally. Start with fried rabbit kidneys on a bed of salad dressed with raspberry vinegar, perhaps, an original and wholly successful combination, and follow with goose *magret* with honey – a welcome change from the usual duck version and served with crunchy, thinly sliced sautéed potatoes. To end, share a chocolate cake, or try the popular profiteroles. The fruity Chinon is a classy red.

La Gazzetta
29 rue de Cotte, 12th (01.43.47.47.05, www.lagazzetta.fr). M° Ledru-Rollin. **Open** noon-2.30pm, 8-11pm Tue-Sat. Closed Aug. **Main courses** €25. **Prix fixe** *Lunch* €16, €20. *Dinner* €39, €52. **Credit** AmEx, DC, MC, V. **Bistro**
Opened by the team behind bar Le Fumoir (*see p62*), La Gazzetta has a similarly moody feel, with dim lighting, a long zinc bar and retro decor. Chef Petter Nilssen is Swedish, but he made his name in the south of France, and his food shows a strong Scandinavian influence in dishes such as bonito in a sweet-salty marinade with caraway, borage leaves, radish and pomelo, or new potatoes from the island of Noirmoutier off the Atlantic coast

Unico.

with seaweed butter and dill. The €38 menu is a pretty good bet, with five courses and not too many decisions to make.

Le Souk
1 rue Keller, 11th (01.49.29.05.08). M° Bastille or Ledru-Rollin. **Open** 7.30-11.30pm Tue-Fri; 11.30am-2.30pm, 7.30pm-12.30am Sat; 11.30am-2.30pm, 7.30pm-11.30am Sun. **Main courses** €18. **Prix fixe** €30, €45. **Credit** DC, MC, V. **North African**
Potted olive trees mark the entrance to this lively den of Moroccan cuisine. Start with savoury *b'stilla*, a pasty stuffed with duck, raisins and nuts, flavoured with orange-blossom water and sprinkled with cinnamon and powdered sugar. Don't fill up, though, as the first-rate tagines and couscous are enormous. The *tagine canette* (duckling stewed with honey, onions, apricots, figs and cinnamon, then showered with toasted almonds) is terrific. For dessert, try the excellent millefeuille with fresh figs, while sweet mint tea is poured in a long stream by a *djellaba*-clad waiter.

La Table de Claire
30 rue Emile-Lepeu, 11th (01.43.70.59.84, www.letabledeclaire.fr). M° Charonne. **Open** noon-2pm, 8-10.30pm Wed-Sat. **Main courses** €10. **Prix fixe** *Lunch* €13, €16. *Dinner* €31. **Credit** MC, V. **Bistro**
With black-and-white tiled floors, a Formica bar and modern light fixtures and paintings, La Table de Claire has the look of a vintage bistro but the atmosphere of a living room, animated by the genial, curly-haired Serge. Claire's food is equally homely, though with a sophisticated touch: think foie gras with baby potatoes and pearl onion jam. The monthly *chef d'un soir* nights, when the owners' talented friends prepare their own recipes, have become a popular event.

Le Train Bleu
Gare de Lyon, pl Louis-Armand, 12th (01.43.43.09.06, www.le-train-bleu.com). M° Gare de Lyon. **Open** 11.30am-3pm, 7-11pm daily. **Main courses** €30. **Prix fixe** *Lunch* €49. *Dinner* €62, €96. **Credit** AmEx, DC, MC, V. **Brasserie**
This listed dining room – with vintage frescoes and big oak benches – exudes a pleasant air of expectation. Don't expect cutting-edge cooking, but rather fine renderings of French classics. Lobster served on walnut oil-dressed salad leaves is a generous, beautifully prepared starter, as is the pistachio-studded *saucisson de Lyon* with a warm salad of small *ratte* potatoes. Mains such as veal chop topped with a cap of cheese, and *sandre* (pike-perch) with a 'risotto' of *crozettes* are also pleasant.

Unico
15 rue Paul-Bert, 11th (01.43.67.68.08, www.resto-unico.com). M° Faidherbe-Chaligny. **Open** 12.30-2.30pm, 8-11pm Tue-Sat. **Main courses** €20. **Credit** MC, V. **Argentinian**
Architect Marcelo Joulia and photographer Enrique Zanoni were wise enough to retain the vintage 1970s decor of this former butcher's shop when they opened their temple to Argentinian beef. Orange tiles and matching light fixtures provide the backdrop for the fashionable, black-dressed crowd that comes here for thick slabs of meat grilled over charcoal and served with a selection of sauces. If you find yourself hesitating, opt for the *lomo* (fillet) with *chimichurri*, a mild salsa – and don't forget to wash it down with Argentinian wine, a rarity in Paris.

Au Vieux Chêne
7 rue du Dahomey, 11th (01.43.71.67.69, www.vieuxchene.fr). M° Faidherbe-Chaligny. **Open** noon-2pm, 8-10.30pm Mon-Fri. Closed 1wk July & 2wks Aug. **Main courses** €20. **Prix fixe** *Lunch* €13.50, €17. *Dinner* €28, €33. **Credit** MC, V. **Bistro**
Although everyone loves the the zinc-capped bar by the entrance, and the tiled floor, what makes this bistro so special is its intense desire to please. A starter of langoustines encased in fine crunchy angel hair and garnished with slices of fresh mango is delicious and refreshing, and chilled tomato soup is garnished with mint, a ball of tomato sorbet and a drizzle of olive oil. Stéphane Chevassus is a gifted game cook too, as proved by the tender roast pigeon sautéed with Chinese cabbage.

North-east Paris

Le Baratin
3 rue Jouye-Rouve, 20th (01.43.49.39.70). M° Pyrénées. **Open** 12.15-3pm, 8-11pm Tue-Fri; 8-11pm Sat. **Main courses** €20. **Prix fixe** *Lunch* €15. **Credit** MC, V. **Bistro**

Star pastry chef Pierre Hermé visits this cheerful little bistro and wine bar high up in Belleville at least every two weeks to fill up on Raquel Carena's homely cooking with the occasional exotic twist. Typical of her style, which draws on her native Argentina, are tuna carpaccio with cherries, roast Basque lamb with new potatoes and spinach, and hazelnut pudding. If the food weren't so fantastic, it would still be worth coming for the mostly organic wines. Le Baratin attracts gourmands from all over Paris – so be sure to book well ahead.

A la Bière
104 av Simon-Bolivar, 19th (01.42.39.83.25). M° Colonel Fabien. **Open** noon-3pm, 7pm-1.30am daily. **Main courses** €11. **Prix fixe** €14.50. **Credit** AmEx, V. **Brasserie**
A la Bière looks like one of those nondescript corner brasseries, but what makes it stand out is an amazingly good-value €14.50 prix fixe full of fine bistro favourites. White tablecloths and fine kirs set the tone; starters of thinly sliced pig's cheek with a nice French dressing on the salad, and a home-made rabbit terrine exceed expectations. The mains live up to what's served before: charcoal-grilled entrecôte with hand-cut chips, and juicy Lyonnais sausages with potatoes drenched in olive oil, garlic and parsley.

Le Cambodge
10 av Richerand, 10th (01.44.84.37.70, www.lecambodge.fr). M° Goncourt or République. **Open** noon-2.30pm, 8-11.30pm Mon-Sat. Closed 1 Aug-15 Sept, 24 Dec-1 Jan. **Main courses** €13. **Credit** MC, V. **Cambodian**
The system at Le Cambodge is simple: you write your order on a piece of paper, including any preferences such as 'no coriander', 'no peanuts' or 'extra rice', and after a short wait the dishes appear. Two favourites are the *bobun spécial*, a hot and cold mix of sautéed beef, noodles, salad, bean sprouts and imperial rolls, and *banhoy*, a selection of the same ingredients to be wrapped in lettuce and mint leaves and dipped in a sauce. They also serve soups, salads and curries, including stewed pork in a fragrant coconut sauce.

Le Chateaubriand
129 av Parmentier, 11th (01.43.57.45.95). M° Goncourt. **Open** noon-2pm, 8-11pm Tue-Fri; 8-11pm Sat. Closed 3wks Aug, 2wks Dec. **Prix fixe** *Lunch* €20. *Dinner* €40. **Credit** AmEx, MC, V. **Bistro**
Self-taught Basque chef Inaki Aizpitarte runs this stylish bistro. Come at dinner to try the cooking at its most adventurous, as a much simpler (albeit cheaper) menu is served at lunch. Dishes have been deconstructed down to their very essence and put back together again. You'll understand if you try starters like chunky steak tartare with a quail's egg, or asparagus with tahini foam and little splinters of sesame-seed brittle. The cooking's not always so cerebral – Aizpitarte's Spanish goat's cheese with stewed apple jam is brilliant. Book well ahead. *See also p6* **Cooking up a storm**.

Dong Huong
14 rue Louis-Bonnet, 11th (01.43.57.18.88). M° Belleville. **Open** noon-10.30pm Mon, Wed-Sun. Closed 2wks Jan & 3wks Aug. **Main courses** €7. **Credit** MC, V. **Vietnamese**
The excellent food at this Vietnamese noodle joint attracts a buzzy crowd. The delicious *bánh cuôn*, steamed Vietnamese ravioli stuffed with minced meat, mushrooms, bean sprouts, spring onions and deep-fried onion, are served piping hot. *Com ga lui*, chicken kebabs with tasty lemongrass, though not as delicate, come with tasty rice. *Bò bùn chả giò* (noodles with beef and small *nem* topped with onion strips, spring onion and crushed peanuts) makes a meal in itself. For dessert, the mandarin, lychee and mango sorbets are tasty and authentic.

La Fidélité
12 rue de la Fidélité, 10th (01.47.70.19.34, www.lafidelite.com). M° Gare de L'Est. **Open** 8pm-2am Mon-Sat. **Main courses** €17. **Prix fixe** *Lunch* €15. **Credit** AmEx, MC, V. **Brasserie**
There was a huge buzz when La Clique took this place over, and so far the brasserie is setting a high standard with its elegant styling. The neighbourhood is arguably one of the least attractive in the capital, but La Fidélité has become a place of pilgrimage not only for A-listers, but also for lovers of good, well-priced food – the lunchtime prix fixe is a bargain and the *joue de boeuf* is sublime. On Thursdays and Fridays, the basement morphs into the Cave de la Fidélité, a jukebox bar.

La Madonnina
10 rue Marie-et-Louise, 10th (01.42.01.25.26). M° Goncourt or Jacques Bonsergent. **Open** noon-2.30pm, 8-11pm Mon-Thur; noon-2.30pm,

8-11.30pm Fri, Sat. Closed Aug. **Main courses** €14. **Prix fixe** *Lunch* €10.50, €15. *Dinner* €25, €35. **Credit** MC, V. **Italian**

La Madonnina flirts with kitsch so skilfully that it ends up coming off as cool. With its candles, mustard yellow walls and red-checked tablecloths, it's the perfect place for a romantic night out. La Madonnina describes itself as a *trattoria napoletana*, but most of the dishes are pan-southern Italian. The short menu changes monthly; don't miss the home-made pastas, such as artichoke and ricotta ravioli. The *cassata*, an extremely sweet Sicilian version of cheesecake, is authentic and unusual to see on menus outside Italy.

The Latin Quarter & the 13th

Atelier Maître Albert
1 rue Maître-Albert, 5th (01.56.81.30.01, www.ateliermaitrealbert.com). M° Maubert Mutualité or St-Michel. **Open** noon-2.30pm, 6.30-11pm Mon-Wed; noon-2.30pm, 6.30pm-1am Thur, Fri; 6.30pm-1am Sat; 6.30-11.30pm Sun. **Main courses** €25. **Prix fixe** *Lunch* €23, €29. *Dinner* €36. **Credit** AmEx, DC, MC, V. **Bistro**
This Guy Savoy outpost in the fifth arrondissement has slick decor designed by Jean-Michel Wilmotte. The indigo-painted, grey marble-floored dining room with open kitchen and rôtisseries on view is attractive, but it does mean that the place is very noisy at night. The short menu lets you have a Savoy classic or two to start with, including oysters in seawater *gelée*, perhaps, or more inventive dishes such as the ballotine of chicken, foie gras and celeriac in a chicken-liver sauce. Next up could be tuna served with tiny iron casseroles of dauphinois potatoes, accompanied by cauliflower in béchamel sauce.

L'Avant-Goût
26 rue Bobillot, 13th (01.53.80.24.00, www.lavantgout.com). M° Place d'Italie. **Open** noon-2pm, 7.45-10.45pm Tue-Sat. Closed 3wks Aug. **Main courses** €18.50. **Prix fixe** *Lunch* €14. *Dinner* €31. **Credit** MC, V. **Bistro**
Self-taught chef Christophe Beaufront has turned this nondescript street on the edge of the villagey Butte-aux-Cailles into one of the city's foodie destinations. Typical of Beaufront's cooking is his *pot-au-feu de cochon aux épices*, a much-written-about dish that has been on his menu for years. He now presents the pork, sweet potato and fennel garnished with deep-fried ginger on a plate with a glass of bouillon to drink on the side. It's good, if not earth-shaking; however, a starter of piquillo pepper stuffed with smoked haddock rillettes does illustrate his talent. Beaufront's food is available to take away at the *épicerie* across the street, complete with cast-iron cooking pots (to be returned).

Le Bambou
70 rue Baudricourt, 13th (01.45.70.91.75). M° Olympiades or Tolbiac. **Open** noon-3.30pm, 7-10.30pm Tue-Sun. **Main courses** €10. **Prix fixe** €15, €26. **Credit** MC, V. **Vietnamese**
The Vietnamese fare here is a notch above what is normally served in Paris. Seating is elbow to elbow and, should you come on your own, the waiter will draw a line down the middle of the paper tablecloth and seat a stranger on the other side. That stranger might offer pointers on how to eat certain dishes, such as the no.42: grilled marinated pork to be wrapped in lettuce with beansprouts and herbs and eaten by hand, dipped into the accompanying sauce (no.43 is the same thing, but with pre-soaked rice paper wrappers).

Le Buisson Ardent
25 rue Jussieu, 5th (01.43.54.93.02, www.lebuissonardent.fr). M° Jussieu. **Open** noon-2pm, 7.45-10pm Mon-Fri; 7.45-10pm Sat. Closed Aug. **Main courses** €17. **Prix fixe** *Lunch* €14.60, €18.50. *Dinner* €25, €31. **Credit** MC, V. **Bistro**
This bistro's square front dining room with its red banquettes and painted glass panels dating from 1923 has a quintessentially Paris charm, especially when compared to the surrounding kebab shops. There is plenty for adventurous eaters on chef Stéphane Maubuit's menu, such as pan-fried squid with chorizo and quinoa or white bean and pig's ear salad with pan-fried foie gras, but he also does conventional dishes (chestnut velouté with spice bread croûtons) very well. Desserts are less remarkable, but this is one of the area's best finds for the price.

Itinéraires
5 rue de Pontoise, 5th (01.46.33.60.11). M° Maubert Mutualité. **Open** noon-2pm, 8-10.30pm Tue-Thur; 8-11pm Fri, Sat. **Main

Bread & Roses. *See p59.*

courses** €22. **Prix fixe** *Lunch* €25, €34. *Dinner* €34. **Credit** AmEx, MC, V. **Bistro**
Chef Sylvain Sendra played to a full house every night at his little bistro Le Temps au Temps near the Bastille before moving to this larger space near Notre Dame. The sleek space brings together all the elements that make for a successful bistro today: a long *table d'hôtes*, a bar for solo meals or quick bites, and a reasonably priced, market-inspired menu. Not everything is a wild success, but it's hard to fault a chef who so often hits the mark, in dishes such as squid-ink risotto with clams, *botargo* (dried mullet roe) and tomato.

L'Ourcine
92 rue Broca, 13th (01.47.07.13.65). M° Les Gobelins. **Open** noon-2pm, 7-10.30pm Tue-Thur; noon-2.30pm, 7-11pm Fri, Sat. Closed Aug. **Prix fixe** *Lunch* (Tue-Fri) €24. *Dinner* €32. **Credit** MC, V. **Bistro**
This restaurant near Gobelins is a wonderful destination for anyone who really loves Basque and Béarnais cooking. Start with *pipérade*, succulent chorizo or a spread of sliced beef tongue with piquillo peppers; then try the sautéed baby squid with parsley, garlic and Espelette peppers, or the *piquillos* stuffed with puréed cod and potato. Service is friendly, and an appealing atmosphere is generated by a growing band of regulars. The wine list is short but offers several pleasant southwestern bottles. The desserts include an excellent *gâteau basque*.

Le Pré Verre
8 rue Thénard, 5th (01.43.54.59.47, www.lepreverre.com). M° Maubert Mutualité. **Open** noon-2pm, 7.30-10.30pm Tue-Sat. Closed 3wks Aug & 2wks Dec. **Main courses** €18. **Prix fixe** *Lunch* €13.50. *Dinner* €28.50. **Credit** MC, V. **Bistro**
Philippe Delacourcelle knows how to handle spices like few other French chefs. He also trained with the late Bernard Loiseau, and learned the art of French pastry at Fauchon. Salt cod with cassia bark and smoked potato purée is a classic: what the fish lacks in size it makes up for in rich, cinnamon-like flavour and crunchy texture, and smooth potato cooked in a smoker makes a startling accompaniment. Spices have a way of making desserts seem esoteric rather than decadent, but the roast figs with olives are an exception to the rule.

Ribouldingue
10 rue St-Julien-le-Pauvre, 5th (01.46.33.98.80). M° St-Michel. **Open** noon-2pm, 7-11pm Mon-Sat. **Prix fixe** €29. **Credit** MC, V. **Bistro**
This bistro facing St-Julien-le-Pauvre church is the creation of Nadège Varigny, who spent ten years working with Yves Camdeborde before opening a restaurant inspired by the cuisine of her childhood in Grenoble. It's usually full of people, including critics and chefs, who love simple, honest bistro fare, such as *daube de boeuf* or seared tuna on a bed of melting aubergine. And if you have an appetite for offal, go for the gently sautéed brains with new potatoes or veal kidneys with a perfectly prepared potato gratin. For dessert, don't miss the fresh ewe's cheese with bitter honey.

Rouammit & Huong Lan
103 av d'Ivry, 13th (01.45.85.19.23). M° Corvisart. **Open** noon-3pm, 7-11pm Tue-Fri; noon-4pm Sat, Sun. Closed 1wk Aug. **Main courses** €8. **Credit** MC, V. **Prix fixe** (Tue-Fri) €8.90, €10.80, €11.90. **Laotian**

OLIVIA RUTHERFORD, OLIVER KNIGHT

Get the local experience

Over 50 of the world's top destinations available.

Fans of South-east Asian food eventually learn to seek out Laotian holes-in-the-wall in Paris rather than splurge on flashier Thai restaurants. A perfect example is this Chinatown joint, easy to spot thanks to the queue outside the door. The food is cheap and delicious, and the service friendly. Among the highlights are *lap neua*, a tongue-tickling, chilli-spiked salad made with slivers of beef and tripe; *khao nom kroc*, Laotian ravioli filled with shrimp; and sweet, juicy prawns stir-fried with Thai basil. Even the sticky rice is exceptional.

La Tour d'Argent
15 quai de la Tournelle, 5th (01.43.54.23.31, www.latourdargent.com). M° Pont Marie or Cardinal Lemoine. **Open** 7.30-10.30pm Mon; 12.30-2.30pm, 7.30-10.30pm Tue-Sat. Closed 3wks Aug. **Main courses** €65-€130. **Prix fixe** *Lunch* €65. *Dinner* €160. **Credit** AmEx, DC, MC, V. **Haute cuisine**
This Paris institution is regaining its lustre following the death of aged owner Claude Terrail in 2006. In the kitchen, Breton-born Stéphane Haissant has brought a welcome creative touch to the menu, bringing in creative dishes such as a giant langoustine dabbed with kumquat purée and surrounded by lightly scented coffee foam. But he also shows restraint, as in duck (the house speciality) with cherry sauce and a broad bean flan. Following in his father's footsteps, Terrail's soft-spoken son André now does the rounds, making sure that the diners are happy.

St-Germain-des-Prés & Odéon

Le 21
21 rue Mazarine, 6th (01.46.33.76.90). M° Odéon. **Open** 12.30-2pm, 8-11pm Tue-Sat. **Main courses** €30. **Credit** MC, V. **Bistro**
This clubby restaurant in St-Germain-des-Prés is a big hit with a *beau monde* crowd of antiques dealers, book editors and politicians. Chef Paul Minchelli's original minimalist style has evolved towards more homely preparations, as seen in a delicious sauté of flaked cod, potatoes, onions and green peppers, or squid in a squid ink sauce with black rice. To keep the waistline-watching regulars happy, a few of his old classics are also still offered, including grilled red mullet. Don't miss the chocolate fondant cake for dessert, and don't be shy about asking for help with the pricey wine list.

Bread & Roses
7 rue de Fleurus, 6th (01.42.22.06.06, www.breadandroses.fr). M° St-Placide. **Open** 8am-8pm Mon-Sat. Closed Aug & 1wk Dec. **Main courses** €18. **Credit** AmEx, MC, V. **Bakery/café**
Come for a morning croissant and you might find yourself staying on for lunch, so tempting are the wares at this Anglo-influenced *boulangerie/épicerie*/café. Giant wedges of cheesecake sit alongside French pastries, and huge savoury puff-pastry tarts are perched on the counter. Attention to detail shows even in the authentically pale tara-masalata, which is matched with buckwheat-and-seaweed bread. Prices reflect the quality of the often organic ingredients, but that doesn't seem to deter any of the moneyed locals, who order towering birthday cakes here for their snappily dressed offspring.

Les Cinoches
1 rue de Condé, 6th (01.43.54.18.21, www.lescinoches.com). M° Odéon. **Open** 9am-2am daily. **Main courses** €16-€26. **Prix fixe** *Lunch* €18. **Credit** MC, V. **Bistro**
This small cinema-themed bistro with portraits of film stars on the walls is far from being an original concept, but gets extra points for authenticity (it used to be an arthouse cinema), a slick interior and retractable bay windows that extend the terrace to the entire restaurant on sunny days. Homesick Brits can have fish and chips, but the weekend brunch (€25) and Sunday night film screenings are a more tempting option.

Le Comptoir
Hôtel Le Relais Saint-Germain, 9 carrefour de l'Odéon, 6th (01.43.29.12.05). M° Odéon. **Open** noon-6pm, 8.30pm-11pm (last orders 9pm) Mon-Fri; noon-11pm Sat, Sun. Closed 3wks Aug. **Main courses** €15. **Prix fixe** *Dinner* (Mon-Fri) €50. **Credit** AmEx, DC, MC, V. **Brasserie**
Yves Camdeborde runs the bijou Hôtel Le Relais Saint-Germain, whose art deco dining room, modestly dubbed Le Comptoir, serves brasserie fare from noon to 6pm and on weekend nights, and a five-course prix fixe feast on weekday evenings. The single dinner sitting lets the chef take real pleasure in his work. On the daily menu, you might find dishes like rolled saddle of lamb with vegetable-stuffed 'Basque ravioli'. The catch? The prix fixe dinner is booked up as much as six months in advance.

L'Epigramme
9 rue de l'Eperon, 6th (01.44.41.00.09). M° Odéon. **Open** noon-2.30pm, 7-11.30pm Tue-Sat; 11.30am-3pm Sun. **Prix fixe** *Lunch* €22. *Dinner* €28. **Credit** MC, V. **Bistro**
L'Epigramme is a pleasantly bourgeois dining room with terracotta floor tiles, wood beams, a glassed-in kitchen and comfortable chairs. Like the decor, the food doesn't aim to innovate but sticks to tried and true classics with the occasional twist. Marinated mackerel in a mustardy dressing on toasted country bread gets things off to a promising start, but the chef's skill really comes through in main courses such as perfectly seared lamb with glazed root vegetables and intense jus. It's rare to find such a high standard of cooking at this price, so be sure to book.

La Ferrandaise
8 rue de Vaugirard, 6th (01.43.26.36.36, www.laferrandaise.com). M° Odéon/RER Luxembourg. **Open** 7-10.30pm Mon; noon-2.30pm, 7-10.30pm Tue-Thur; noon-2.30pm, 7pm-midnight Fri; 7pm-midnight Sat. **Main courses** €14. **Prix fixe** *Lunch* €15, €32. *Dinner* €32, €44. **Credit** MC, V. **Bistro**
This bistro has quickly established a faithful following. In the modern bistro tradition, the young, northern French chef serves solid, classic food with a twist. A platter of excellent ham, sausage and terrine arrives as you study the blackboard menu, and the bread is crisp-crusted, thickly sliced sourdough. Two specialities are the potato stuffed with escargots in a camembert sauce, and a wonderfully flavoured, slightly rosé slice of veal. Desserts might include intense chocolate with rum-soaked bananas and a layered glass of mango and meringue. Wines start at €14.

Germain
25-27 rue de Buci, 6th (01.43.26.02.93). M° Mabillon or Odéon. **Open** noon-midnight daily. **Main courses** €20. **Credit** MC, V. **Brasserie**
Quaint rue de Buci has been shaken up by the extravagance of Germain, a versatile brasserie halfway between *Alice in Wonderland* and London's Sketch. The heated terrace is great for people watching, and the main ground-floor room, which features the lower part of a vast yellow statue piercing through the ceiling above, is perfect for a quick lunch. There's also a cosy salon for cocktails, a more conservative dining room at the back, and a private room on the first floor with a snooker table and the top half of the yellow statue. The food is almost childishly classic, but always with a twist (ham and butter macaroni with truffle) and not as expensive as you might expect.

Huîtrerie Régis
3 rue de Montfaucon, 6th (01.44.41.10.07, www.huitrerieregis.com). M° Mabillon. **Open** noon-3pm, 6.30-11pm Tue-Sun. Closed mid July-Sept. **Main courses** €32. **Prix fixe** €34. **Credit** MC, V. **Oyster bar**
Paris oyster fans are often obliged to use one of the city's big brasseries to get their fix of shellfish, but what if you just want to eat a reasonably priced platter of oysters? Enter Régis and his 14-seat oyster bar. The tiny room feels pristine and the tables are properly laid. Here you can enjoy the freshest oysters from Marennes for around €25 a dozen. The bread and butter is fresh and wines are well chosen. Hungry souls can supplement their feast with a slice of home-made apple tart or the cheese of the day.

Lapérouse
51 quai des Grands-Augustins, 6th (01.56.79.24.31, www.laperouse.fr). M° St-Michel. **Open** noon-2.30pm, 7.30-11pm Mon-Fri; 7.30-11pm Sat. Closed 1wk Jan & Aug. **Main courses** €40. **Prix fixe** *Lunch* €35, €45. *Dinner* €105. **Credit** AmEx, DC, MC, V. **Brasserie**
One of the most romantic spots in Paris, Lapérouse was formerly a clandestine rendezvous for French politicians and their mistresses; the tiny private dining rooms upstairs used to lock from the inside. Chef Alain Hacquard does a modern take on classic French cooking: his beef fillet is smoked for a more complex flavour; a tender saddle of rabbit is cooked in a clay crust, flavoured with lavender and rosemary and served with ravioli of onions. The only snag is the cost, especially of the wine – a half-bottle of Pouilly-Fuissé is nearly €35.

Le Restaurant
L'Hôtel, 13 rue des Beaux-Arts, 6th (01.44.41.99.01, www.l-hotel.com). M° St-Germain-des-Prés. **Open** 12.30-2.30pm, 7.30-

Pancake perfection

If you picture the crêpe as the soggy letdown of French cuisine, then a trip down rue Montparnasse and rue Odessa on a weekend night could change your mind. According to the organisation Paris Breton there are 300,000 Bretons living in Paris, and Montparnasse, close to the railway station that brought them here, is their *quartier*, with queues down the street for the 15 or so crêperies.

In its finest manifestation, the buckwheat pancake, or *galette de sarrasin*, is a crisp, melt-in-the-mouth envelope for an imaginative selection of fillings that go far beyond the egg and ham staple. At the **Crêperie du Manoir Breton** (*see p60*), the Périgord is filled with *magret de canard*, creamed prunes and caramelised pear; the Landaise is smartly presented with a round of foie gras and caramelised pear on top; and the Roquefort is laden with the Ardèchois blue cheese, crème fraîche and walnuts. At the **Crêperie du Pont-Aven** (*see p60*), with its attractive red interior dating back to 1920, the Gwazenn comes with scallops, mushrooms and cream; and the Pont-Aven is filled with salmon, leeks and cream; there are even several eel variations if you're feeling adventurous.

But the star crêperie of the area, and the one with the longest queues, is the prettily decorated **Josselin** (*see p60; pictured*), where the speciality is the Couple – two layers of galette with the filling in the middle. The savoury galette is followed by the dessert Crêpe de Froment, which comes in three varieties: classic (honey and lemon or wonderful caramel beurre salé); flambéed with calvados; or a fantasy creation oozing with chocolate, banana, ice cream and whipped cream. Wash it all down with bowls of cider, of which the brut is far better than the sweet. You'll be surprised how full you feel at the end and the bill should come to no more than €20 a head.

La Tour d'Argent. *See p59.*

10pm Tue-Sat. **Main courses** €39. **Prix fixe** *Lunch* €42, €52. *Dinner* €95-€155. **Credit** AmEx, DC, MC, V. **Haute cuisine**
Since being taken over by Oxford-based Cowley Manor, L'Hôtel has rechristened its restaurant (formerly Le Belier) and put the talented Philippe Bélisse in charge of the kitchen. You can choose from a short seasonal menu with dishes such as pan-fried tuna, John Dory or suckling pig. But for the same price you can also enjoy the marvellous four-course *menu dégustation* or, even better, the *menu surprise*. Highlights of the autumn menu were the wild Breton crab stuffed with fennel, avocado and *huile d'Argan*, and a main course of pigeon on a bed of beetroot.

La Taverna degli Amici
16 rue du Bac, 6th (01.42.60.37.74). Mº Assemblée Nationale or Solférino. **Open** noon-2.30pm, 7.30-11.30pm Mon-Fri; 7.30-11.30pm Sat. Closed Aug & 1wk Dec. **Main courses** €16. **Prix fixe** *Lunch* €18. **Credit** MC, V. **Italian**
La Taverna degli Amici is the ideal spot for a quick business lunch or a big, rumbustious dinner with friends. Occupying two floors, the yellow-walled rooms are well lit and airy. Run by the exceptionally friendly Notaro family, who own, manage and cook, the restaurant is constantly bustling. Don't miss the mixed bruschette, which includes three vegetable toppings, such as grilled courgettes marinated in olive oil, lemon and parsley. Pastas feature fresh, tasty toppings, such as their most popular dish, penne with *caccioricotta* (made with ewe's milk) and rocket. Most of the regulars finish things off with home-made tiramisu.

Le Timbre
3 rue Ste-Beuve, 6th (01.45.49.10.40, www.restaurantletimbre.com). Mº Vavin. **Open** noon-2pm, 7.30-10.30pm Tue-Sat. Closed Aug & 1wk Dec. **Main courses** €17. **Prix fixe** *Lunch* €22, €26. *Dinner* €35, €45. **Credit** MC, V. **Bistro**
Chris Wright's restaurant, open kitchen included, might be the size of the average student garret, but this Mancunian aims high. Typical of his cooking is a plate of fresh green asparagus elegantly cut in half lengthwise and served with dabs of anise-spiked sauce and balsamic vinegar, and a little crumbled parmesan. Main courses are also pure

in presentation and flavour – a thick slab of pork, pan-fried but not the least bit dry, comes with petals of red onion that retain a light crunch.

Montparnasse

La Cerisaie
70 bd Edgar Quinet, 14th (01.43.20.98.98). Mº Edgar Quinet or Montparnasse. **Open** noon-2pm, 7-10pm Mon-Fri. Closed Aug & 1wk Dec. **Main courses** €15. **Prix fixe** *Lunch* €13, €19. *Dinner* €22, €27. **Credit** MC, V. **Bistro**
Nothing about La Cerisaie's unprepossessing red façade hints at the talent that lurks inside. With a simple starter of white asparagus served with preserved lemon and drizzled with parsley oil, chef Cyril Lalanne proves his ability to select and prepare the finest produce. On the daily changing blackboard menu you might find *bourride de maquereau*, a thrifty take on the garlicky southern French fish stew, or *cochon noir de Bigorre*, an ancient breed of pig that puts ordinary pork to shame. *Baba à l'armagnac*, a variation on the usual rum cake, comes with stunning chantilly.

La Coupole
102 bd du Montparnasse, 14th (01.43.20.14.20, www.flobrasseries.com/coupoleparis). Mº Vavin. **Open** 8.30am-1am daily. **Main courses** €36. **Prix fixe** €17, €27. **Credit** AmEx, DC, MC, V. **Brasserie**
La Coupole still glows with some of the old glamour. The people-watching remains superb, inside and out, and the long ranks of linen-covered tables, professional waiters, 32 art deco columns painted by different artists of the epoch, mosaic floor and sheer scale of the operation still make coming here an event. The set menu offers unremarkable steaks, foie gras, fish and autumn game stews, but the real treat is the shellfish, displayed along a massive counter. Take your pick from the *claires*, *spéciales* and *belons*, or go for a platter brimming with crabs, oysters, prawns, periwinkles and clams.

Crêperie du Manoir Breton
18 rue d'Odessa, 14th (01.43.35.40.73). Mº Edgar Quinet. **Open** noon-11pm daily. **Main courses** €6-€10. **Credit** MC, V. **Crêperie**
See p59 **Pancake perfection**.

Crêperie du Pont-Aven
54 rue du Montparnasse, 14th (01.43.22.23.74, www.creperie-de-pont-aven.com). Mº Edgar Quinet. **Open** noon-3pm, 6pm-midnight Mon-Fri; noon-midnight Sat, Sun. **Main courses** €3-€10. **Credit** MC, V. **Crêperie**
See p59 **Pancake perfection**.

Josselin
67 rue du Montparnasse, 14th (01.43.20.93.50). Mº Edgar Quinet. **Open** noon-11pm Tue-Sun. **Main courses** €5-€8. **No credit cards.** **Crêperie**
See p59 **Pancake perfection**.

L'Opportun
64 bd Edgar Quinet, 14th (01.43.20.26.89). Mº Edgar Quinet. **Open** noon-3pm, 7-11.30pm Mon-Sat. **Main courses** €19. **Prix fixe** (until 10pm) €21. *Dinner* €35. **Credit** AmEx, DC, MC, V. **Bistro**
Owner-chef Serge Alzérat is passionate about Beaujolais, dubbing his convivial cream and yellow restaurant a centre of 'beaujolaistherapy'. He's also an advocate for good, honest Lyonnais food. Thus his menu is littered with the likes of *sabodet* (thick pork sausage) with a purée of split peas, duck skin salad, *tête de veau* and meat – lots of it.

Le Plomb du Cantal
3 rue de la Gaîté, 14th (01.43.35.16.92). Mº Gaîté. **Open** noon-midnight Mon-Fri, Sat, Sun. **Main courses** €15. **Prix fixe** *Lunch* €19. **Credit** MC, V. **Bistro**
This homage to the Auvergne may suffer from its 1980s decor, but with food like this, who cares? *Aligot* (potato puréed with fresh tomme cheese) and *truffade* (potatoes sautéed with tomme) are scraped out of copper pots on to plates at the table, and the omelettes are made with three eggs and 300g of potatoes.

The 7th & western Paris

Le 144 Petrossian
18 bd de La Tour-Maubourg, 7th (01.44.11.32.32, www.petrossian.fr).

Mº La Tour Maubourg. **Open** 12.15-2.30pm, 7.30-10.30pm Tue-Sat. **Main courses** €35. **Prix fixe** *Lunch* €29, €90. *Dinner* €35, €90. **Credit** AmEx, DC, MC, V. **Russian**
Young chef Rougui Dia directs the kitchen of this famed caviar house. You'll find Russian specialities such as blinis, salmon and caviar (at €39 an ounce) from the Petrossian boutique downstairs, but Dia has added spices from all over the world. You might start with a divine risotto made with carnaroli rice, codfish caviar and parmesan. In similar Med-meets-Russia vein are main courses such as roast sea bream with a lemon-vodka sauce.

Afaria
15 rue Desnouettes, 15th (01.48.56.15.36). Mº Convention. **Open** noon-2pm, 7-11pm Tue-Sat. **Prix fixe** *Lunch* €19. *Dinner* €27. **Credit** MC, V. **Bistro**
Instead of the usual starter, main course and dessert categories, Basque-born chef Julien Duboué has divided his menu into sections such as 'les sudistes' for southern French-inspired cooking, and 'les petits appetits' for lighter dishes. Several dishes are for sharing, in particular a caveman-sized duck *magret* with balsamic fig vinegar, served on a terracotta roof tile with potato gratin perched on a bed of twigs. Other creations such as oysters with bulgur, houmous and preserved lemon show that Duboué is not just another Basque bistro chef, but a traveller who happily borrows ingredients from around the world.

L'Agassin
8 rue Malar, 7th (01.47.05.18.18, www.paris-restaurant-agassin.com). Mº Ecole Militaire. **Open** noon-2.30pm, 7-11pm Tue-Sat. Closed Aug. **Prix fixe** *Lunch* €26, €29. *Dinner* €34. **Credit** AmEx, DC, MC, V. **Bistro**
André Le Letty left Anacréon – a bistro in the 13th – to open this restaurant in the heart of aristocratic Paris. It's a curious mix of contemporary and classic, with occasional old-fashioned touches in the cooking (like the likes of skate in butter and caper sauce served with steamed potatoes) but a modern spirit. Several dishes come with supplements of €2 to €10, but these are often worth the extra cost – the *girolle* mushrooms in season are beautifully firm and juicy. The prune *clafoutis* is unusually light, with armagnac ice-cream making the perfect accompaniment.

L'Ami Jean

27 rue Malar, 7th (01.47.05.86.89, www.amijean.eu). M° Ecole Militaire. **Open** noon-2pm, 7pm-midnight Tue-Sat. Closed Aug. **Main courses** €20. **Prix fixe** €32. **Credit** MC, V. **Bistro**

This long-running Basque address is an ongoing hit thanks to chef Stéphane Jégo. Excellent bread from baker Jean-Luc Poujauran is a perfect nibble when slathered with a tangy, herby *fromage blanc* – as is a starter of sautéed baby squid on a bed of ratatouille. Tender veal shank comes de-boned with a lovely side of baby onions and broad beans with tiny cubes of ham, and house-salted cod is soaked, sautéed and doused with an elegant vinaigrette. There's a great wine list, and some lovely Brana *eau de vie* should you decide to linger.

L'Arpège

84 rue de Varenne, 7th (01.47.05.09.06, www.alain-passard.com). M° Varenne. **Open** noon-2.30pm, 8-10.30pm Mon-Fri. **Main courses** €70. **Prix fixe** *Lunch* €135. *Dinner* €360. **Credit** AmEx, DC, MC, V. **Haute cuisine**
Assuming you can swallow an exceptionally high bill – it's €42 for a potato starter, for example – chances are you'll have a spectacular time at chef Alain Passard's Left Bank establishment. His attempt to plane down and simplify the haute experience – the chrome-armed chairs look like something from the former DDR – seems a misstep; but then something edible comes to the table, such as tiny smoked potatoes served with a horseradish mousseline. A main course of sautéed free-range chicken with a roasted shallot, an onion, potato *mousseline* and pan juices is the apotheosis of comfort food. Desserts are elegant.

Le Bistro

17 rue Pérignon, 15th (01.45.66.84.03). M° Ségur. **Open** 8am-10pm daily. **Main courses** €11. **Credit** MC, V. **Bistro**
At first glance there is nothing to distinguish this corner bistro from hundreds of other cafés in Paris. In the front room, with its wood-panelled ceiling are a plastic-topped bar and a few bare tables with black banquettes, and in the back is a larger room with red-and-white checked tablecloths. Then you see the plates going by, each one – from the goat's cheese salad to the *pavé de rumsteak* – loaded with golden fried potato rounds or hand-cut chips. This is the kind of neighbourhood bistro you had almost given up hope of finding in Paris.

Au Bon Accueil

14 rue de Monttessuy, 7th (01.47.05.46.11, www.aubonaccueilparis.com). M° Alma Marceau. **Open** noon-2.30pm, 7-10.30pm Mon-Fri. Closed 2wks Aug. **Main courses** €20. **Prix fixe** *Lunch* €27. *Dinner* €31. **Bistro**
Jacques Lacipière runs Au Bon Accueil, and Naobuni Sasaki turns out the beautiful food. Perhaps most impressive is his elegant use of little-known fish such as grey mullet and meagre (*maigre*), rather than the usual endangered species. The €27 lunch menu might highlight such posh ingredients as *suprême de poulet noir du Cros de la Géline*, free-range chicken raised on a farm run by two former cabaret singers. But the biggest surprise comes with desserts, worthy of the finest pastry shops. In summer, book a table on the pavement terrace with its view of the Eiffel Tower.

Les Cocottes

135 rue St-Dominique, 7th (www.leviolon dingres.com). M° Ecole Militaire/RER Pont de l'Alma. **Open** noon-4pm, 7-11pm Mon-Sat. **Main courses** €15. **Credit** MC, V. **Bistro**
Christian Constant has found the perfect recipe for pleasing Parisians at his new bistro: a flexible menu of salads, soups, *verrines* (light dishes served in jars) and *cocottes* (served in cast-iron pots), all at bargain prices – for this neighbourhood. Service is swift and the food satisfying, though the *vraie salade César Ritz*, which contains hard-boiled egg, shouldn't be confused with US-style Caesar salad. Soups such as an iced pea velouté are spot-on, and *cocottes* range from sea bream with ratatouille to potatoes stuffed with pig's trotter.

D'Chez Eux

2 av de Lowendal, 7th (01.47.05.52.55, www.chezeux.com). M° Ecole Militaire. **Open** noon-2pm, 7-10.30pm Tue-Sat. Closed Aug. **Main courses** €30. **Prix fixe** *Lunch* €29, €34. **Credit** MC, V. **Bistro**
Arm yourself with stamina for a meal at this jovial south-western *auberge*, which looks touristy with its red-and-white checked tablecloths but attracts *bons vivants* from the neighbourhood, including the likes of Jacques Chirac. First come the help-yourself lyonnais-style 'salads' (cooked beetroot, lentils, celeriac rémoulade, ratatouille, etc), before hearty main dishes such as cassoulet or calf's liver

with sherry vinegar, which are tasty and generous if not exactly refined. The heaving dessert cart (think chocolate mousse and rice pudding) will ensure that you waddle out overfed but happy.

Gaya Rive Gauche

44 rue du Bac, 7th (01.45.44.73.73, www.pierre-gagnaire.com). M° Rue du Bac. **Open** noon-2.30pm, 7.30-10.45pm Mon-Sat. **Main courses** €30-€48. **Credit** AmEx, MC, V. **Seafood**
Superchef Pierre Gagnaire runs this comparatively affordable fish restaurant. The menu enumerates ingredients without much clue as to how they are put together, though the helpful waiters will explain if you don't like a surprise. But then surprises are what Gagnaire is famous for. The Fats Waller, for instance, turns out to be a soup of grilled red peppers with a bloody mary sorbet in the centre and daubs of quinoa, basmati rice and Chinese spinach. For the mains, diners are treated like sophisticated children – everything has been detached from the bone or carapace. Light desserts complete the formula.

Le Grand Pan

20 rue Rosenwald, 15th (01.42.50.02.50). M° Convention. **Open** 12.30-2.30pm, 7.30-11pm Mon-Fri; 7.30-11pm Sat. **Main courses** €40. **Prix fixe** *Lunch* €30. **Credit** MC, V. **Bistro**
Young chef Benoît Gauthier trained with Christian Etchebest, and he's come up with a clever formula that surfs the current Paris preference for great produce simply cooked. At dinner, a complimentary starter of soup is served – maybe courgette or white bean – and then you choose from the selection of grilled meats and lobster, many of which are designed for two people. Everything comes with a delicious mountain of home-made chips and green salad. Desserts run to homely choices like strawberry crumble or rice pudding with caramel sauce.

Jadis

208 rue de la Croix-Nivert, 15th (01.45.57.73.20, www.bistrot-jadis.com). M° Convention or Porte de Versailles. **Open** 12.15-2pm, 7.15-11pm Mon-Fri. **Main courses** €21. **Prix fixe** *Lunch* €25, €34. **Credit** MC, V. **Bistro**
The residential 15th arrondissement has more than its fair share of great bistros, and Jadis confirms the trend. In this grey-painted dining room, young chef Guillaume Delage serves a gently updated take on classic French cuisine (Jadis means 'in days gone by'). The pared-down presentation of dishes such as snails in puff pastry with oyster mushrooms and romaine lettuce lets each element speak for itself. Don't miss the wonderful cheese trolley.

Many restaurants are struggling somewhat during these chastened financial times, but old fave **Chartier** (7 rue du Faubourg-Montmartre, 9th, 01.47.70.86.29, www.restaurant-chartier.com) is still positively bursting at the seams. Opened since 1896 and now an official historic monument, this gigantic, high-ceilinged fin-de-siècle dining hall in the heart of the 9th arrondissement cooks up an atmospheric combination of frenetic service (your order is scribbled down illegibly on the paper tablecloth in front of you), shared tables and prices that will make you weep with joy – roast cicken and chips for €8.70, confit de canard at €9.70, and nothing on the wide-ranging menu above €14. Such economies of eating are quite an achievement in Paris, and at these prices you shouldn't expect anything more than cursory service and basic brasserie fare; the former soup kitchen (*bouillon*), which is tucked away in a courtyard set back from bustling rue du Faubourg-Montmartre, is not a place to linger. But for a quick, cheap meal in beautiful belle époque surroundings, it is still hard to beat.

Jules Verne

Pilier Sud, Eiffel Tower, 7th (01.45.55.61.44, www.lejulesverne-paris.com). M° Bir Hakeim or RER Tour Eiffel. **Open** 12.15-1.30pm, 7-9.30pm daily. **Main courses** €75. **Prix fixe** *Lunch* €85 (Mon-Fri), €165 (Sat, Sun), €200 (Sat, Sun). *Dinner* €200. **Credit** AmEx, DC, MC, V. **Haute cuisine**
You have to have courage to take on an icon like the Eiffel Tower, but Alain Ducasse has done just that in taking over the Jules Verne. He has transformed the cuisine and brought in his favourite designer, Patrick Jouin. Meanwhile, Ducasse protégé Pascal Féraud updates French classics, combining all the grand ingredients you'd expect with light, modern textures and sauces. Try dishes like lamb with artichokes, turbot with champagne zabaglione, and a fabulous ruby grapefruit soufflé. Reserve well ahead.

Les Ombres

27 quai Branly, 7th (01.47.53.68.00, www.lesombres-restaurant.com). M° Alma-Marceau. **Open** noon-2.30pm, 7-10.30pm daily. **Main courses** €35. **Prix fixe** *Lunch* €38. *Dinner* €95, €145. **Credit** AmEx, MC, V. **Bistro**

The view of the Eiffel Tower at night would be reason enough to come to this glass-and-iron restaurant on the top floor of the Musée du Quai Branly, but young chef Arnaud Busquet's food also demands that you sit up and take notice. The influence of Joël Robuchon – a mentor to Busquet's mentor – shows in dishes such as thin green asparagus curved into a nest with tiny *lardons* and topped with a breaded poached egg, ribbons of parmesan and meat *jus*. There is a reasonable prix fixe at lunch.

Il Vino

13 bd La Tour-Maubourg, 7th (01.44.11.72.00, www.ilvinobyenricobernardo. com). M° La Tour-Maubourg. **Open** noon-2pm, 7pm-midnight daily. **Prix fixe** *Lunch* €50, €75. *Dinner* €95. **Credit** AmEx, DC, MC, V. **Italian**
Enrico Bernardo, youngest winner of the World's Best Sommelier award, runs this restaurant where, for once, food plays second fiddle to wine. You are presented with nothing more than a wine list. Each of 15 wines by the glass is matched with a surprise dish, or the chef can build a meal around the bottle of your choice. Best for a first visit is one of the blind tasting menus for €75, €100 or (why not?) €1,000.

Le Restaurant. *See p59.*

Restaurants

Cafés & Bars

Just as it looked as if Paris would be totally swamped with trendy New York-style watering holes, in came the credit crunch and out popped the idea of capitalising on the funky period features present in Paris's cafés. **Chez Jeannette** in the tenth pioneered the idea a few years ago (keeping all of its 1940s gear and winning a Fooding prize for it); but zinc bars, marble floors and banquettes across the city are heaving sighs of relief as they too doggedly stay in place, while walls, lighting, sound systems and loos get spruced up around them. And of course, if it's real old-world Paris you're after, there's still a handful of landmark addresses, like **La Palette** with its original art deco tiles and frescoes, and **Le Cochon à l'Oreille**, an atmospheric remnant of Les Halles' heyday.

DRINKING IN PARIS

The traditional boundaries between bar, club, restaurant and dancehall are blurring. Hybrid spaces such as **La Bellevilloise** (a former Paris co-operative) and **La Maroquinerie** (previously a leather factory) house restaurant, bar, music venue and exhibition space all under one roof, and **L'Entrepôt** fulfils dual roles as a bastion of culture and coffee south of Montparnasse.

Urban regeneration still seems to be pulling punters northwards, beyond the Canal St-Martin in the tenth (home to fashionable boho bars and satisfying brunch spots) into the now ultra-trendy 19th, along the Canal de l'Ourcq. Those looking for a real 'neighbourhood' feel, meanwhile, should head into the 20th, where hidden gems like the St-Blaise district and the ever-gentrifying eastern edge of Nation are now home to fun, authentic addresses like **Chez Prosper**, **Les Pères Populaires** and the hip **Café Noir** on rue St-Blaise.

Other Right Bank hotspots include the Marais (and its north-west overspill around Etienne Marcel and Arts et Métiers métro stations); the village-like area in and around Abbesses in Montmartre; and Les Batignolles, west of Place de Clichy, where rue des Dames draws the boho overspill from Montmartre into its wealth of cafés and bars. Over on the Left Bank, St-Germain-des-Prés and Montparnasse continue to trade on a proud literary heritage, and the Butte-aux-Cailles, in the 13th, has some of the last cheap student haunts.

The sturdy brasserie and noble bistro provide food with formality akin to a restaurant, so if you're just there for a drink, you'll pay more for the social nicety of aproned and waistcoated service. You can usually run a tab, and tipping is optional (service is always included in the bill).

The Louvre & Palais-Royal

Angelina
226 rue de Rivoli, 1st (01.42.60.82.00).
M° Tuileries. **Open** 8am-7pm Mon-Fri;
9am-7pm Sat, Sun. **Credit** MC, V.

Café Marly.

Angelina is home to Paris's most lip-smackingly scrumptious desserts – all served in the faded grandeur of a belle époque salon just steps from the Louvre. The hot chocolate is pure decadence; try the speciality 'African', a velvety potion so thick that you need a spoon to consume it. Epicurean delights include the Mont Blanc dessert, a ball of meringue covered in whipped cream and sweet chestnut, and, for those with a waistline to watch, a sugar- and butter-free *brioche aux fruits rouges*. The place heaves at weekends, so be prepared to queue.

Le Café des Initiés
3 pl des Deux-Ecus, 1st (01.42.33.78.29,
www.lecafedesinities.com). M° Louvre Rivoli
or Les Halles. **Open** 7.30am-2am Mon-Fri;
9am-2am Sat, Sun. **Credit** AmEx, MC, V.
Friendly staff and a central location have turned this designer hangout into a top spot for a trendy tipple, especially after work – cocktails are just €5 between 5pm and 8pm. The main room is lined with aerodynamic red banquettes, a long zinc bar provides character, and sleek, black, articulated lamps peer down from the ceiling. When hunger strikes, homely favourites such as shoulder of lamb baked in honey or tartare of salmon never fail to please.

Café Marly
93 rue de Rivoli, cour Napoléon, 1st
(01.49.26.06.60). M° Palais Royal Musée
du Louvre. **Open** 8am-2am daily. **Credit**
AmEx, DC, MC, V.
In the arcaded terrace overlooking the Louvre's glass pyramid, this classy, Napoléon III-style hangout (reached through the passage Richelieu, the entrance for advance Louvre ticket holders) is

in an unrivalled location. One would expect nothing else from the ubiquitous Costes brothers – it's just a shame about the beer prices: it's €6 for a Heineken, so you might as well splash out €12 on a chocolate martini or a Shark, made of vodka, lemonade and grenadine. Most wines are under €10 a glass, and everything is impeccably served by razor-sharp staff. Brasserie fare and sandwiches are on offer too.

L'Entr'acte
47 rue de Montpensier, 1st (01.42.97.57.76).
M° Pyramides or Palais Royal Musée
du Louvre. **Open** 10am-1am daily.
No credit cards.
A little detour off avenue de l'Opéra, down an 18th-century staircase, and you find an unexpected congregation spread across the pavement: half are here for this little bar near the Comédie Française, half for the adjoining Sicilian pizzeria. There's food to be had at L'Entr'acte too – €10 plates of cheese and charcuterie, standard pastas and so on – but most come to enjoy an early evening glass of house Bourgueil. The interior is tiny, with an equally poky basement, but there's free Wi-Fi and even laptop loans.

Le Fumoir
6 rue de l'Amiral-de-Coligny, 1st
(01.42.92.00.24, www.lefumoir.com).
M° Louvre Rivoli. **Open** 11am-2am daily.
Closed 2wks Aug. **Credit** AmEx, MC, V.
There aren't many places around the Louvre that can compete with this elegant local institution: neo-colonial fans whirr lazily and oil paintings adorn the walls. A sleek crowd sips martinis or reads papers at the long mahogany bar (originally from a Chicago speakeasy), giving way to young

professionals in the restaurant and pretty things in the library. It feels a wee bit try-hard and resolutely well behaved, but the cocktails get tongues wagging soon enough, and the food is consistently top notch.

La Garde Robe
41 rue de l'Arbre-Sec, 1st (01.49.26.90.60). M°
Louvre Rivoli. **Open** noon-3pm, 6pm-midnight
Mon-Fri; 6pm-midnight Sat. **Credit** MC, V.
This tiny wine bar (its name means wardrobe), where bottles line the walls like books in a library, is perfect for an end-of-the-day snifter, preferably accompanied by one of the platters of delicious parma ham, cheese or oysters. Organic and bio-dynamic wines stand their ground next to vintages from around the world.

Opéra to Les Halles

Le Brébant
32 bd Poissonnière, 9th (01.47.70.01.02).
M° Grands Boulevards. **Open** 7.30am-6am
daily. **Credit** MC, V.
The change that continues to sweep the Grands Boulevards is embodied in this prominent, round-the-clock bar-bistro. There's a permanently busy terrace below a colourful, stripy awning, and the cavernous, split-level interior has a cool neo-industrial feel. Prices are steep, so push the boat out and opt for an expertly made fruit daiquiri, or a Bonne Nouvelle of Bombay Sapphire gin and Pisang Ambon. There are rarer bottled beers too – Monaco, Picon and sundry brews from Brabant. A board advertises a decent range of proper eats: *burger-frites* (€15) and so on.

Café de la Paix
12 bd des Capucines, 9th (01.40.07.36.36,
www.cafedelapaix.fr). M° Opéra. **Open** 7am-
midnight daily. **Credit** AmEx, DC, MC, V.
Lap up every detail – this is once-in-a-holiday stuff. Whether you're out on the historic terrace or looking up at the ornate stucco ceiling, you'll be sipping in the footsteps of the likes of Oscar Wilde, Josephine Baker, Emile Zola, and Bartholdi and the Franco-American Union (as they sketched out the Statue of Liberty).

Le Cochon à l'Oreille
15 rue Montmartre, 1st (01.42.36.07.56).
M° Les Halles. **Open** 11am-2am Mon-Sat.
Credit MC, V.
Some old bistros have the setting, others get the food. This little piggy (*cochon*) does a good job with both: the antique public telephone, the imposing zinc counter and the cosy wooden booths are charming reminders of Les Halles' heyday as the city's celebrated food market – note the tiles that depict scenes of the market in all its chaotic splendour. Food-wise, expect hearty, meaty dishes like stuffed pork on a bed of lentils and *confit de canard*, best accompanied by one of the 50 wines on the list. Enjoyed your meal? Write about it in the notebooks tucked away in little nooks.

La Conserverie
37bis rue du Sentier, 3rd (01.40.26.14.94).
M° Bonne-Nouvelle. **Open** 6pm-2am Mon-Sat.
Credit AmEx, MC, V.
The gorgeous *nuit bleu* interior will win you over as soon as you step inside, and by the time you sit on the velvet sofas and taste the cocktails you'll want to make this your favourite hangout. The staff are incredibly friendly by Parisian standards. There's a quirky selection of nibbles in tin cans – sardines, anyone? – and regular music nights (gipsy jazz bands on Mondays; electro on Thursdays and Fridays). Highly recommended.

De la Ville Café
34 bd de Bonne-Nouvelle, 10th
(01.48.24.48.09, www.delavillecafe.com).
M° Bonne Nouvelle. **Open** 11am-2am Mon-
Sat; noon-2am Sun. **Credit** MC, V.
De la Ville has brought good news to Bonne-Nouvelle. A major expansion and refurbishment (it used to be a *maison close*) have upped the ante,

bringing the in-crowd to this otherwise ignored quarter. Inside, the distressed walls and industrial-baroque feel remain, but the curvy club section at the back has become very cool. After 10pm on Fridays, Saturdays and some Thursdays, DJs splice into the night.

Dédé la Frite
135 rue Montmartre, 2nd (01.40.41.99.90). Mº Sentier or Bourse. **Open** 8am-2am daily. **Credit** MC, V.
Suits from the nearby Bourse flock here for after-work cocktails (€7) and beers (€4), before giving in to the tempting aromas emanating from the kitchen: Dédé's frites at just €3 a tray are legendary and the rest of the food, reminiscent of an American diner (burgers, fries, ketchup on the bar), is an absolute bargain too. The place looks cool as well, with distressed walls, long bar and bright colours. After hours, when the alcohol flows and the munchies have been satisfied, the music is cranked up and the party really starts.

Harry's New York Bar
5 rue Daunou, 2nd (01.42.61.71.14, www.harrys-bar.fr). Mº Opéra. **Open** 10.30am-4am daily. **Credit** AmEx, DC, MC, V.
The city's most stylish American bar is an institution beloved of expats, visitors and hard-drinking Parisians (there are over 300 whiskies). The white-coated bartenders mix some of the most sophisticated cocktails in town, from the trademark bloody mary and white lady (both invented here, so they say) to the Pétrifiant, an aptly named elixir of half a dozen spirits splashed into a beer mug. They can also whip up personalised creations that will have you swooning in the downstairs piano bar, where Gershwin composed *An American in Paris*, and where jazz concerts are held most Thursday and Friday nights.

La Jungle
56 rue d'Argout, 2nd (01.40.41.03.45, www.la-jungle.com). Mº Sentier. **Open** 10am-2am Mon-Fri; 4pm-2am Sat, Sun. **Credit** AmEx, MC, V.
Exoticism reigns at La Jungle, a former bordello that nowadays entertains the city's party animals with live afro-jazz on Wednesdays and Fridays (€2 extra on drinks), DJs on Saturdays, and jazz and blues on Sundays. Come here to enjoy exotic cocktails (€6), dishes with a Cameroonian bent and Flag beer from Senegal.

Ô Château
68 rue Jean-Jacques Rousseau, 1st (01.44.73.97.80, www.o-chateau.com). **Open** noon-midnight Mon-Wed, Sun; noon-2am Thur-Sat. **Credit** AmEx, DC, MC, V.
See p65 **Grape expectations**.

Le Tambour
41 rue Montmartre, 2nd (01.42.33.06.90). Mº Sentier. **Open** 8am-6am daily. **Credit** MC, V.
Decked out with vintage public transport paraphernalia, slatted wooden banquettes and bus stop-sign bar stools, the Tambour has a split personality: there's the daytime Tambour, frequented by pretty much everybody, and the nighttime Tambour, a well-loved nighthawk's bar where the chatty regulars give the 24-hour clock their best shot and post-partygoers pile in for *steak-frites* at 3am (food is served until 4am).

Le Truskel
12 rue Feydeau, 2nd (01.40.26.59.97, www.myspace.com/truskel_paris). Mº Bourse. **Open** 8pm-5am Mon-Fri; 6.45pm-5am Sat; 4.30pm-midnight Sun. Closed mid July-mid Aug. **Credit** MC, V.
The formula is quite simple at this pub-cum-club: an excellent selection of beers slakes your thirst, while an extensive repertoire of Britpop – sometimes live (ex-Pulp man and Paris resident Jarvis Cocker has been known to splice the night here, as have Pete Doherty and Franz Ferdinand) – assaults your ears. As a cheeky touch, a bar bell rings for no reason whatsoever, causing first-time visitors from the UK to down their drinks in one and dive for the bar.

Zenzoo
13 rue Chabanais, 2nd (01.42.96.27.28, www.zen-zoo.com). Mº Quatre-Septembre. **Open** 11am-11pm Mon-Sat. Closed Aug. **Credit** MC, V.
Between 2.30pm and 7pm, this tiny Taiwanese restaurant doubles as a 'tea bar', the only place in Paris that serves China's famous tapioca cocktails – sometimes known as 'bubble tea', they are served with an extra-wide straw to suck up the little tapioca balls at the bottom. The sensation may seem strange at first, but the tastes are great; among the flavours are mango, coconut and kumquat. Up the road at no.2, a spin-off boutique sells excellent oolong flower teas.

Champs-Elysées & western Paris

Charlie Birdy
124 rue La Boétie, 8th (01.42.25.18.06, www.charliebirdy.com). Mº Franklin D. Roosevelt. **Open** 9am-5am daily. **Credit** AmEx, V.
Take a New York loft and meld it with a colonial English gentleman's club and you're looking at Charlie Birdy – a large 'pub' with a live music programme of jazz, soul and funk that's worth listening to. If you're in a hurry, stay away – the service can be irritatingly slow. But if you take your time choosing from the 50-strong cocktail menu, sink into a comfy chesterfield and let the evening wash over you, it'll be worth it. Between 4pm and 8pm Monday to Friday, cocktails are half-price.

Le Dada
12 av des Ternes, 17th (01.43.80.60.12). Mº Ternes. **Open** 6am-2am Mon-Sat; 7am-10pm Sun. **Credit** AmEx, MC, V.
Perhaps the hippest café in this stuffy part of town, Le Dada is best known for its well-placed, sunny terrace. Inside, the wood-block carved tables and red walls provide a warm atmosphere for a crowd that tends towards the well-heeled, well-spoken and, well, loaded. That said, the atmosphere is friendly; if terracing is your thing, you could happily spend a summer's day here – just bring along your Prada shades.

L'Endroit
67 pl du Dr-Félix-Lobligeois, 17th (01.42.29.50.00). Mº La Fourche or Rome. **Open** 11am-2am Mon-Thur; 11am-4am Fri, Sat. **Credit** MC, V.
L'Endroit is one of the best spots in old Batignolles village, with great views over neo-classical Ste-Marie-des-Batignolles church, a cool thirtysomething crowd, decent wines, cocktails a go-go and excellent food that won't break the bank (€12 lunchtime menu).

Flute l'Etoile
19 rue de l'Etoile, 17th (01.45.72.10.14, www.flutebar.com). Mº Ternes. **Open** 5pm-2am Tue-Sat; 6am-10pm Sun. **Credit** AmEx, MC, V.
With a menu of some 23 different champagnes and designer decor (slick wooden panelling, blue walls and red velvet), Paris's first champagne lounge may be minuscule, but it certainly looks the part. Indeed the only indication that it's not French (it's American) is the sneaky appearance of a Californian sparkler on the champagne list. For drinkers wishing to sample different vintages without buying a whole glass (from €9), the small tasting glasses (from €5) are a thoughtful touch.

And for anyone bored by plain bubbly, cocktails such as champagne sangria and Rossini-Tini (champagne, raspberry juice, liqueur and Grey Goose vodka) make sophisticated alternatives.

Impala Lounge
2 rue de Berri, 8th (01.43.59.12.66). Mº George V. **Open** noon-2am Mon, Sun; noon-5am Tue-Sat. **Credit** AmEx, MC, V.
Dubbed the 'African Bar' by regulars, this wannabe-hip spot hams up the colonial with zebra skins, masks and a throne hewn from a tree trunk. Beer, wine, tea and standard favourites can all be had, but the best option are the cocktails, one of which claims to boost a waning libido with its mystery mix of herbs and spices. DJs rock Sunday afternoon away, and the decent snack-and-mains menu often includes ostrich.

Ladurée
75 av des Champs-Elysées, 8th (01.40.75.08.75, www.laduree.fr). Mº George V or Franklin D. Roosevelt. **Open** 7.30am-11.30pm Mon-Fri; 8.30am-12.30am Sat; 8.30am-11.30pm Sun. **Credit** AmEx, DC, MC, V.
Decadence permeates this elegant tearoom, from the 19th century-style interior and service to the labyrinthine corridors that lead to the toilets. While you bask in the warm glow of bygone wealth, indulge in tea, pastries (the pistachio pain au chocolat is heavenly) and, above all, the hot chocolate. It's a rich, bitter, velvety tar that will leave you in the requisite stupor for any lazy afternoon. The original branch at 16 rue Royale (8th, 01.42.60.21.79) is famed for its macaroons.

Libre Sens
33 rue Marbeuf, 8th (01.53.96.00.72). Mº Franklin D. Roosevelt. **Open** 11am-3am daily. **Credit** AmEx, MC, V.
Unusually for this part of town, the Libre Sens is reasonably priced and down to earth. The design is slick, with low lighting and comfortable seating; particularly attractive are the large booths that accommodate groups and couples, the electric blue bar and the fine range of cognacs. Parisians love this place for a drink after work – happy hour (between 6.30pm and 8.30pm) includes champagne and cocktails from €7.

Sir Winston
5 rue de Presbourg, 16th (01.40.67.17.37). Mº Charles de Gaulle Etoile. **Open** 9am-2am Mon, Sun; 9am-3am Tue, Wed; 9am-4am Thur-Sat. **Credit** AmEx, V.
A bit of an anomaly, this. Grand and imperial, with a bit of Baroque thrown in for good measure, and located within sight of high-end glitz, Sir Winston does a nice line in jazz and gospel brunches on a Sunday. Colonial knick-knacks, chesterfields and chandeliers make up the decor, with Winnie himself framed behind a sturdy bar counter. A battalion of whiskies stands guard beside him, and the wine list is equally *recherché*. Where this place

falters is in its somewhat sissy cocktail menu. A Sir Winston Breezer of Bacardi, melon liqueur, pineapple and banana juice? Harrumph!

Montmartre & Pigalle

Le Café Arrosé
123 rue Caulaincourt, 18th (01.42.57.14.30). Mº Lamarck Caulaincourt. **Open** 8am-2am Mon-Sat, 8am-7pm Sun. **Credit** MC, V.
On the north side of the hill, this *resto-café* doesn't feature anything hugely different from most other bistros (red banquettes, menus on blackboards, 1930s tiled floor, zinc bar and contemporary art on the walls), yet there is something inexplicably pleasant about the ambience. Perhaps it's the smiley staff, decent wine list and mouthwatering food (from €12 for a main).

Les Caves Populaires
22 rue des Dames, 17th (01.53.04.08.32). Mº Place de Clichy. **Open** 8am-2am Mon-Sat; 11am-2am Sun. Closed 2wks Aug. **Credit** MC, V.
An old soak props up the bar with his *petit rouge*, while others play chess and groups of bobos (bourgeois bohemians) revel in the cheap prices – from €2.50 for a glass of quaffable wine, €3 for a beer and €7 for a cheese or charcuterie platter. It's a charming place and vaguely reminiscent of a wooden chalet, hence its second name, Les Caves du Châlet.

La Fourmi
74 rue des Martyrs, 18th (01.42.64.70.35). Mº Pigalle. **Open** 8am-2am Mon-Thur; 8am-4am Fri, Sat; 10am-2am Sun. **Credit** MC, V.

De la Ville Café.

KARL BLACKWELL

Cafés & Bars

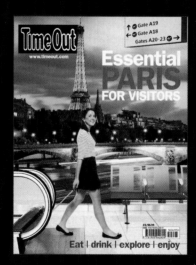

Set on the cusp of the ninth and 18th arrondissements, La Fourmi is an old bistro that has been converted for today's tastes, with picture windows lighting the spacious, roughshod interior, cool staff (and customers) and excellent music. The classic zinc bar counter is crowned by industrial lights, which helps you to see what you're reading as you rifle through the piles of flyers deciding where to go on to next; this is as good a place as any to find out what's happening in town.

Poussette Café

6 rue Pierre Sémard, 9th (01.78.10.49.00, www.lepoussettecafe.com). M° Poissonnière or Cadet. **Open** 10.30am-6.30pm Tue-Sat.

Fed up with the impracticalities of pushing her pram (*poussette*) into the local café, mother of two Laurence Constant designed her own parent- and child-friendly establishment. This upmarket *salon de thé* caters for the harassed parent (herbal teas, smoothies, quiches and salads) and demanding baby (purées, solids and cuddly toys). You can sign up for magic shows and parenting workshops via the café's website.

Au Rendez-vous des Amis

23 rue Gabrielle, 18th (01.46.06.01.60). M° Abbesses. **Open** 8.30am-2am daily. **Credit** MC, V.

Considering its proximity to the honeypot that is the Sacré-Coeur, Au Rendez-vous des Amis is still cheap, making it popular with locals and foreign students, and the odd tourist. During happy hour (8pm to 10pm), a kir or glass of wine will set you back a very reasonable €2.70. There are some cosy nooks round the back with plenty of upholstered spots to choose from.

Rouge Passion

14 rue Jean-Baptiste Pigalle, 9th (01.42.85.07.62, www.rouge-passion.fr). M° St Georges or Pigalle. **Open** noon-3pm, 7pm-midnight Mon-Fri; 7pm-midnight Sat; 11.30am-4pm Sun. **Credit** MC, V.

Two bright upstarts (Anne and Sébastien) determined to make their mark on Paris's bar scene are behind this venture – and they're going about it the right way. Offering a long list of wines (from just €3), free *assiettes apéros* (peanuts, olives and tapenades on toast) and decor that is perfect vintage chic, the formula is spot on. A small but mouthwatering selection of hot dishes, salads, cheese and *saucisson* platters (set lunch menu €20, mains from €15) help soak up the wine. Look out for the tasting classes, given by a guest sommelier.

Le Sancerre

35 rue des Abbesses, 18th (01.42.58.08.20). M° Abbesses. **Open** 7am-2am Mon-Thur; 7am-4am Fri, Sat; 9am-2am Sun. **Credit** MC, V.

This popular Montmartre rock bar is home to a frenzied mix of alcohol-fuelled transvestites, tourists, lovers and bobo locals, who all come for the cheap beer (under €4), trashy music and buzzy terrace. The decor inside is dark and scruffy, the service undeniably slow and the food (omelettes, *steak-frites*) nothing special; yet there is something irresistibly refreshing about the no-frills approach that makes this bar stand out from the multitude of try-hard cafés in the area.

Beaubourg & the Marais

Andy Whaloo

69 rue des Gravilliers, 3rd (01.42.71.20.38). M° Arts et Métiers. **Open** noon-2am Tue-Sat. **Credit** AmEx, MC, V.

Andy Whaloo, created by the people behind its neighbour 404 and London's Momo and Sketch, is Arabic for 'I have nothing'. Bijou? This place brings new meaning to the word. The formidably fashionable crowd fights for coveted 'seats' on upturned paint cans; from head to toe, it's a beautifully designed venue, crammed with Moroccan artefacts and a spice rack of colours. It's quiet early on, with a surge around 9pm, and the atmosphere heats up as the night gets longer.

L'Apparemment Café

18 rue des Coutures St-Gervais, 3rd (01.48.87.12.22). M° St-Sébastien Froissart. **Open** noon-2am Mon-Sat; 12.30pm-midnight Sun. **Credit** MC, V.

The 'Apparently' feels more like a communal living room than a café. The low lighting, cosy nooks and board games (Trivial Pursuit and Taboo, both in French) make for an excellent place to while away an afternoon. Staff even organise the occasional fortune-telling evening. The location is perfect for shoppers too, being just off the rue Vieille-du-Temple. Lunches consist of simple DIY platters of meats, cheeses and salads, but at €15 for the basic version they're a bit rudimentary for the price. Eating is obligatory during busy periods, when it's definitely advisable to book.

Le Baromètre

17 rue Charlot, 3rd (01.48.87.04.54). M° Arts et Métiers. **Open** 8am-11pm Mon-Sat. **Credit** MC, V.

This unpretentious wine bar is popular with the area's artisan types. Lunchtimes are heaving, so unless you're after the sit-down *menu du jour* (€13) served at the back, you're better off coming along for a lazy afternoon. Order a plate of cheese or the house speciality, bacon and andouillette gratin, and choose from a 20-strong list of wines by the glass, most under €3.50.

Café Livres

10 rue St-Martin, 4th (01.42.72.18.13). M° Châtelet or Hôtel de Ville. **Open** 8am-11pm Mon-Fri; 9am-11pm Sat; 9-7pm Sun. **Credit** AmEx, MC, V.

This charming café with a terrace in the shade of the Tour Saint-Jacques has lines and lines of books surrounding patrons inside. Since this is as central as can be, set just around the corner from the Hôtel de Ville, a cappuccino will set you back €6, but the atmosphere is pleasantly relaxing after a shopping marathon on rue de Rivoli. Food is served non-stop from noon to 11pm.

L'Estaminet

39 rue de Bretagne, 3rd (01.42.72.28.12). M° Temple. **Open** 9am-8pm Tue-Sat; 9am-2pm Sun. **Credit** AmEx, MC, V.

L'Estaminet is tucked away in the Marché des Enfants-Rouges, a charming neighbourhood market and one of the city's oldest. The café has a warm interior, with a grandfather clock in the corner and guests eating €13 *plats du jour* off Limoges porcelain. Wines from around €4 a glass.

L'Etoile Manquante

34 rue Vieille-du-Temple, 4th (01.42.72.48.34, www.cafeine.com). M° Hôtel de Ville or St-Paul. **Open** 9am-2am daily. **Credit** MC, V.

The hippest of Xavier Denamur's merry Marais bars. Cocktails are punchy, traditional tipples just as good, and the salads and snacks are reasonably priced and tasty – but it's the design and buzz that are the main draws. The decor is trendy but comfortable, embellished with interesting art. As in all Denamur's places, no visit is complete without a trip to the toilets: here, an electric train shuttles between cubicles, starlight beams down from the ceiling, and a hidden camera films you washing your hands. Just watch the small screen on the wall behind you.

Lizard Lounge

18 rue du Bourg-Tibourg, 4th (01.42.72.81.34, www.cheapblonde.com). M° Hôtel de Ville. **Open** noon-2am daily. **Credit** MC, V.

An anglophone favourite deep in the Marais, this loud and lively (hetero) pick-up joint provides lager in pints (€6), plus cocktails (€7) and a viewing platform for beer-goggled oglers. Bare brick and polished woodwork are offset by the occasional lizard and a housey soundtrack. Bargain boozing (cocktails €5) kicks off at 5pm; from 8pm to 10pm, there's another happy hour in the sweaty cellar bar (complete with minuscule dancefloor); on Mondays, it lasts all day. A popular weekend brunch of bacon, sausages and eggs benedict caters to the homesick.

Le Loir dans la Théière

3 rue des Rosiers, 4th (01.42.72.90.61). M° St-Paul. **Open** 11.30am-7pm Mon-Fri; 10am-7pm Sat, Sun. **Credit** V.

Le Loir dans la Théière is named after the unfortunate dormouse who gets dunked in the pot at the Mad Hatter's tea party in *Alice in Wonderland*. Its squishy sofas are the perfect complement to its comfort food: it specialises in baked goods, and the famed lemon meringue and chocolate fondant are divine. At weekends, it's packed out with tourists in search of brunch; long queues of people looking enviously at your plate, plus occasionally patchy service, can mar the experience. Come early (before noon) or be prepared to queue.

La Perle

78 rue Vieille-du-Temple, 3rd (01.42.72.69.93). M° Chemin Vert or St-Paul. **Open** 6am-2am Mon-Fri; 8am-2am Sat, Sun. **Credit** MC, V.

The Pearl achieves a rare balance between all-day and late-night venue, and has a good hetero/homo mix. In the morning, it draws early risers; lunchtime is for a business crowd; the afternoon reels in retired locals, and in the evening, screenwriters rub elbows with young dandies, keeping one eye on the mirror and an ear on the electro-rock. The menu runs from omelettes to *salade marine*. Expect a DJ later on.

Grape expectations

This has been something of a vintage year for **Ô Château**'s (*see p63*) Olivier Magny. The sommelier turned author and entrepreneur not only bagged a book deal from his satirical blog 'What Parisians Like', but has also managed to secure a bank loan with long-term business partner Nicolas to open a mammoth wine bar and tasting rooms in early 2011. In the space of eight years their company has gone from restaurant wine tastings to a 260-square metre space in Montorgeuil.

Olivier says his success is all thanks to his English-speaking clientele, many of whom have come back time and again since those first tastings. The popularity of both the wine tastings and the blog tap into the same source, his irreverent attitude to French snobbery, and the locals love it too: the French version of the book, *Dessine-moi un Parisien*, has sold 15,000 copies in a month, showing that Parisians are finally starting to appreciate the art of self-derision (the English version of the book will be published in June by Berkley Books).

When Olivier invited us to have a sneak peek at the wine bar a month before its planned opening the place was still a building site, but he seemed unphased: 'It has to open in January because... well, financially it's crazy.' Striding through the rooms, Olivier coloured in the outstanding details – a solid oak and granite horseshoe bar in the main room, mint green *tomettes* and a trapezium table in one of the vaulted tasting rooms, and comfortable leather sofas and Italian wallpaper in the private lounge bar. 'Paris wine bars tend to be small, ugly and rather cliquey. I've borrowed something from Anglo-Saxon culture in that it's open, warm and convivial.'

There will be no less than 40 wines available by the glass, including the chance to taste some very rare and expensive bottles in *soupçon*-sized quantities – thanks to new high-tech wine-saving devices, 3cl, 6cl and 12cl measures of wines like the hitherto unaffordable Château Pétrus can be experienced by mere mortals. And if you want to go further, you'll be able to take part in thrice-daily tastings in the more intimate tasting rooms.

Ô Château's loyal customers and the blog fan base will start the ball rolling, but this isn't designed to be an exclusively Anglo hangout. 'I want it to be a joyous place and an international clientele will enrich that,' says Olivier. 'But it's for people who want to learn about wine, not just drink it.'

Le Petit Fer à Cheval

30 rue Vieille-du-Temple, 4th (01.42.72.47.47, www.cafeine.com). M° St-Paul. **Open** 9am-2am daily. **Credit** MC, V.

Even a miniature Shetland pony would be pushed to squeeze his hoof into this *fer à cheval* (horseshoe) – the adorable little café, in business for more than 100 years, has one of France's smallest bars. Tucked in behind the glassy façade is a friendly dining room lined with reclaimed métro benches; if you want scenery, the tables out front overlook the bustle of rue Vieille-du-Temple. As with its sister bar L'Etoile Manquante (*see left*), the loos are worth the detour – they look as if they've been pummelled out of a defunct Dalek, with metal panels and strange knobs everywhere.

Stolly's

16 rue Cloche-Perce, 4th (01.42.76.06.76, www.cheapblonde.com). M° Hôtel de Ville or St-Paul. **Open** 4.30pm-2am daily. **Credit** MC, V.

This seen-it-all drinking den has been serving a mainly anglophone crowd for nights immemorial. The staff make the place what it is, and a summer terrace eases libation, as do the long happy hours; but don't expect anyone at Stolly's to faff about with food. There's football on TV and a plastic shark to compensate.

Wini June

16 rue Dupetit-Thouars, 3rd (01.44.61.76.41). M° Temple. **Open** 6pm-2am daily. **Credit** MC, V.

Wini June's virtual living room has become a favourite haunt of Paris fashionistas and designers, who lounge on the Empire-style or contemporary furnishings. Wine (which is served in crystal glasses) is accompanied by a selection of nibbles proffered by the attentive staff. The pint-sized terrace is an outdoor version of the interior, flanked with bamboo.

Bastille & eastern Paris

Le Baron Rouge

1 rue Théophile-Roussel, 12th (01.43.43.14.32). M° Ledru-Rollin. **Open** 10am-3pm, 5-10pm Tue-Fri; 10am-10pm Sat; 10am-4pm Sun. **Credit** AmEx, MC, V.

It sells wine, certainly – great barrels of the stuff are piled high and sold by the glass at very reasonable prices. But the Red Baron is not just a wine

Culture and cocktails

Museums are usually daytime destinations, places of discovery that welcome their guests at some civilised hour before noon and politely expel them well before dusk. However, several of Paris's museums boldly defy the convention by incorporating late-opening bars and even top-notch dining. And who are the punters? Parisians, of course, mainly the kind who frequent museums in the daylight hours, returning to savour the refined atmosphere and take advantage of some of the best views in the city. Join the *parigots* in their quest for night-time fulfilment and visit the following museum bars.

For a cultivated cocktail, head to **Le Saut du Loup** (107 rue de Rivoli, 1st, 01.42.25.49.55, www.lesautduloup.com) in the Musée des Arts Décoratifs, with its sober mix of black, white and grey reflective surfaces, a well-heeled crowd and prices to match. It's the only bar in Paris to overlook the Tuileries gardens – the perfect

spot for a consistently delicious drink at dusk.

For fun art world drinking, the bar inside the **Palais de Tokyo** fits the bill perfectly (13 av du Président-Wilson, 16th, 01.47.20.00.29, www.palaisdetokyo.com; *pictured*). The decor – all industrial concrete and bright, trendy tables and chairs – is as wacky as the drinks menu, which includes the likes of cotton candy-flavoured champagne. For culture vultures, the museum itself stays open until late.

Turning it up a notch, the Musée de l'Homme's **Café de l'Homme** (17 pl du Trocadéro, 16th, 01.44.05.30.15, www.restaurant-cafedelhomme.com) has established itself as one of the Chaillot area's best hangouts, thanks in no small part to its breathtaking terrace with views of the Palais de Chaillot's golden 1930s statues and the Eiffel Tower. Bring your dancing shoes for the DJ nights (from 11.30pm, when the restaurant closes), which last well into the small hours.

---

bar – it's more like a local chat room, where regulars congregate to yak over their *vin*, or perhaps one of the few draught beers, and maybe a snack of sausages or oysters. Despite its lack of seating (there are only four tables), it's a popular pre-dinner spot, so arrive early and don't expect too much elbow room; drinkers often spill out on to the pavement – joining the smokers.

Café Titon
34 rue Titon, 11th (09.53.17.94.10, www.cafetiton.com). Mº Faidherbe-Chaligny or Rue des Boulets. **Open** 8am-2am Mon-Sat. **Credit** MC, V.
The funky Titon is Paris's only Franco-German café – and certainly the only place in town to flog *currywurst* (German sausage in curry sauce) and chips for just €5.50. It even turns into a *biergarten* during Germany's Oktoberfest. Its Parisian side doesn't get forgotten, though, with *croques*, *tartines*, an unbeatable lunch menu (€9.80 for a main and a *café*) and scrumptious cocktails (€6.90 for a margarita).

Chez Prosper
7 av du Trône, 11th (01.43.73.08.51). Mº Nation. **Open** 8.30am-1am daily. **Credit** MC, V.
Chez Prosper welcomes punters all day long with that simplest of gestures: a smile. Yes, even when squeezing past people queuing for a spot on the sun terrace, the waiters are positively beaming. The dining/drinks area – tiled floor, large mirrors, wooden furniture – is run with military precision, and orders arrive promptly. The *steak-frites* and *croques* (served on Poilane bread) are hearty, and the naughty Nutella tiramisu is worth crossing town for.

China
50 rue de Charenton, 12th (01.43.46.08.09, www.lechina.eu). Mº Bastille or Ledru Rollin. **Open** 6pm-2am Mon-Sat; noon-2am Sun. Closed Aug. **Credit** AmEx, MC, V.
This sexy take on a 1930s Shanghai gentleman's club, with red walls, leather chesterfields and the longest bar in Paris, serves some of the finest cocktails in town (including its signature singapore sling). The Cantonese cuisine is pricey, so skip dinner and head upstairs to the cigar bar (if you're romantically inclined) or downstairs to the cellar for weekly jazz, pop and world music concerts (website has details).

Les Furieux
74 rue de la Roquette, 11th (01.47.00.78.44, www.lesfurieux.fr). Mº Bastille or Voltaire. **Open** 4pm-2am Tue-Thur; 4pm-5am Fri, Sat; 7pm-2am Sun. **Credit** MC, V.
Just when it looked like 'lounge attitude' would contaminate every bar on rue de la Roquette, Les Furieux fought back with a healthy dose of rock and metal, padded red walls, faux-leather banquettes, black paint, and rotating exhibitions of

photography on the walls. Locals flock here for the happy hour (6pm to 8pm), when cocktails with rockin' names like Grunge, Scud, and, er, Boris are half price. Diehards can pay tribute to Paris's hedonistic heyday with 12 different absinthes.

Le Houla Oups!
4 rue Basfroi, 11th (01.40.24.18.80, www.myspace.com/lehoulaoups). Mº Ledru-Rollin or Voltaire. **Open** 9am-2am Mon-Fri; 6pm-2am Sat. **Credit** MC, V.
Just off the main Roquette drag, this hip little den of rock – French rock to be precise – makes up in energy what it lacks in size. There are regular exhibitions, live concerts, film nights (usually horror or genre movies), DJs and even auction evenings. During happy hour (6pm to 8pm) beer costs just €3 a pint. To keep in the loop, send an email to houlaoups@gmail.com asking to be put on the mailing list.

Le Motel
8 passage Josset, 11th (01.58.30.88.52). Mº Ledru-Rollin. **Open** 6pm-1.45am Tue-Sun. Closed Aug. **Credit** MC, V.
Le Motel is the latest addition to the city's growing indie scene. It has a simple formula: cheap drinks and excellent music. During happy hour (6pm to 9pm) a pint of *blonde* costs €3.50 and cocktails €3. With DJs almost every night, the music ranges from cutting-edge indie to contemporary neo-folk and rock classics, with the odd Motown hit thrown in for good measure. Friendly twentysomethings cluster around faux Louis XVI armchairs or try their luck in the Sunday pop quiz.

L'Opa
9 rue Biscornet, 12th (01.46.28.12.90, www.opa-paris.com). Mº Bastille. **Open** 7.30pm-2am Wed, Thur; 8pm-6am Fri, Sat. **Credit** V.
Late opening and Eric Perier's diverse range of nightly entertainment – DJs (weekends), videos, live acts (Tuesday to Thursdays) and the odd open mic event – are the attractions here, along with free admission and fairly reasonable drinks prices. A couple of comfortable sofas take the edge off the loft-like, institutional interior, with a modest stage in one corner and an upstairs chill-out space and separate bar.

Pause Café
41 rue de Charonne, 11th (01.48.06.80.33). Mº Ledru-Rollin. **Open** 8am-2am Mon-Sat; 9am-8pm Sun. **Credit** MC, V.
Featured in Cedric Klapisch's 1996 film *Chacun Cherche son Chat*, which was shot on location in the neighbourhood, the Pause Café has managed to prolong its moment of glory thanks to its large terrace on the corner of rues Charonne and Keller. Inside, the modern salons benefit from a smattering of primary colours with ornately plastered ceilings and plenty of light. Having been immortalised on celluloid, the friendly staff occasionally let fame go to their heads: service can be excruciatingly

slow at times. The food – traditional French café fare with an Asian twist – is not bad, but you might be waiting for a while; best to order a well-mixed cocktail to pass the time.

Les Pères Populaires
46 rue de Buzenval, 20th (01.43.48.49.22, www.myspace.com/perespopulaires). Mº Buzenval. **Open** 8am-2am daily. **Credit** MC, V.
On the far side of Nation, could this funky number be the cheapest bar in Paris? Wine is a mere €2 a glass, beer is €2.40 (€4.50 for a pint) and flavoured rums cost €4. To get an idea of the look of the place, think 1970s canteen-cum-retro classroom and you'll come close. During the day, the local freelance media crowd and a handful of musicians squat the tables for the free Wi-Fi; at night DJs spin electro sounds and a party atmosphere reigns.

Le P'tit Bar
7 rue Richard Lenoir, 11th (no phone). Mº Charonne. **Open** 5pm-1am daily. **No credit cards.**
You couldn't invent this place if you tried: local soaks, immigrant South Americans, twentysomething students, Brits and retired war veterans all pop in for a taste of the most surreal experience in the 11th arrondissement, courtesy of the elderly Madame Polo, her fluffy cat and her canaries. Madame Polo is surely the last living link to a forgotten Paris and proof that in this age of excessive health and safety concerns, there are still places here that manage to slip through the net. A word of warning, though: don't drink out of the glasses – Madame Polo isn't too keen on cleaning. We recommend that you opt instead for a €3 bottle of beer.

Andy Whaloo. *See p65.*

Le Temps des Cérises

31 rue de la Cerisaie, 4th (01.42.72.08.63). M° Bastille. **Open** 7.30am-10pm Mon-Fri. **Credit** MC, V.

Not to be confused with several other cafés of the same name, this one-room *bistro à vins* has changed very little over the years. The blackboard wine list is limited but the selection is always well chosen, and food is old-fashioned and hearty (think beef stew and *blanquette de veau*). The general banter is football-centred, so get ready to rumble with the natives about the goings-on at PSG.

North-east Paris

L'Alimentation Générale

64 rue Jean-Pierre-Timbaud, 11th (01.43.55.42.50, www.alimentation-generale.net). M° Parmentier. **Open** 6pm-2am daily. **Credit** AmEx, MC, V.

The 'Grocery Store' is rue Jean-Pierre-Timbaud's answer to La Mercerie (*see right*): a big old space filled with junk. Cupboards of kitsch china and lampshades made from kitchen sponges are an inspired touch. The beer is well chosen – Flag, Sagres, Picon and Orval by the bottle – and the unusual €8 house cocktail involves basil and figs. DJs rock the joint: expect a €5 cover price for big names or live bands. Oh yes – and it has the most brazen toilet walls this side of town.

Ave Maria

1 rue Jacquard, 11th (01.47.00.61.73). M° Parmentier. **Open** 6.30pm-2am daily. **Credit** AmEx, MC, V.

Unlike some places that eschew good food for alcohol and a funky interior, colourful Ave Maria scores highly for all three. The kitsch interior is decked out in a canopy of chinoiserie parasols and a vast collection of Hindu gods. Music, a combination of reggae, funk, soul and dub, is cool but unobtrusive. Strangers sharing wooden benches devour exotic dishes from the Brazilian-inspired menu. Cocktails are equally quirky and start at just €4.50.

Bar Ourcq

68 quai de la Loire, 19th (01.42.40.12.26, http://barourcq.free.fr). M° Laumière. **Open** 3pm-midnight Wed, Thur; 3pm-2am Fri, Sat; 3-10pm Sun. **No credit cards.**

This was one of the first hip joints to hit the Canal de l'Ourcq, with an embankment broad enough to accommodate *pétanque* games (ask at the bar) and a cluster of deckchairs. It's a completely different scene from the crowded bustle along Canal St-Martin – more discerning and less self-satisfied. The cabin-like interior is cosy, and drinks are listed in a hit parade of prices, starting with €2.50 for a *demi* or glass of red. Pastas at €9, exhibitions and a regular DJ spot keep the cool clientele sated. Closed on rainy weekdays in summer.

La Bellevilloise

19 rue Boyer, 20th (01.46.36.07.07, www.labellevilloise.com). M° Gambetta. **Open** 7pm-1am Wed, Thur; 6pm-2am Fri, Sat; 11.30am-5pm Sun. **Credit** V.

The Bellevilloise is the latest incarnation of a building that once housed the capital's very first workers' co-operative. Now it competently multitasks as a bar, restaurant, club and exhibition space, hosting regular film and music festivals on the top level (where there's a fake lawn with deckchairs and a massage area). Enjoy brunch in the Halle aux Oliviers or decent views of the *quartier* from the charming terrace; downstairs the club-cum-concert venue has launched some of Paris's most exciting new bands, and on '80s nights you can hardly move for the thirtysomethings living it up like they were 20 again. There's also live jazz music with the Sunday brunch.

Café Charbon

109 rue Oberkampf, 11th (01.43.57.55.13, www.nouveaucasino.net). M° Parmentier or Ménilmontant. **Open** 9am-2am Mon-Thur, Sun; 9am-4am Fri, Sat. Closed Aug-mid Sept. **Credit** MC, V.

The bar contained within this beautifully restored belle époque building sparked the Oberkampf nightlife boom. Its booths, mirrors and adventurous music policy put trendy locals at ease, capturing the essence of café culture spanning each end of the 20th century. After more than 15 years, the formula still works – and is copied by nearby bars.

Café Chéri(e)

44 bd de la Villette, 19th (01.42.02.02.05, http://cafecherie.blogspot.com). M° Belleville. **Open** 8am-2am daily. **Credit** MC, V.

This splendid DJ bar is also an all-day café – but it doesn't compromise any of the cool that keeps it well ahead of the pack after dark. Music comes from all over, and runs from electro, rock, funk, hip hop, indie, dance and jazz to golden oldies and ghetto-inspired grooves. The interior sparkles with wit and invention – note the marvellous mural alluding to the personal sacrifices made for a life of coupledom. There's a front terrace if you need a smoke or conversational respite from the BPM. There's music from Thursdays to Saturdays after 10pm.

Le Café Noir

15 rue St-Blaise, 20th (01.40.09.75.80). M° Alexandre Dumas or Porte de Bagnolet. **Open** noon-midnight Mon-Fri; 7pm-midnight Sat. **Credit** MC, V.

In the St-Blaise district (the former village of Charonne annexed to Paris in 1860), with views on to the village church, this gorgeous high-ceilinged café, decorated with old cafetières, draws in artists, workers and an up-beat crowd of local trendies for a spot of coffee and a *verre de vin* throughout the day. At mealtimes expect inventive French cuisine, with the likes of foie gras speckled with speculoos biscuits, magret of duck with cardamom and vanilla, and pineapple and mango trifle.

Le Café des Sports

94 rue de Ménilmontant, 20th (01.46.36.48.18, www.myspace.com/lecafedessports). M° Gambetta. **Open** 10am-3am Tue-Sun. Closed Aug. **Credit** MC, V.

Le Café des Sports' fine and eclectic music programme ranges from electro (Saturdays), to pop or *chanson* (Tuesdays and Thursdays) to world dub. Beer and wine are fabulously cheap (just €2 from 6pm to 8pm) and there's even sometimes free couscous or tapas with your drink on a Monday evening. Unlike its sprawling neighbours, Le Café des Sports has just one room to call home. DJs play in the space around the back.

Chez Jeannette

47 rue du Fbg-St-Denis, 10th (01.47.70.30.89, www.chezjeannette.com). M° Strasbourg St-Denis or Château d'Eau. **Open** 8am-2am daily.

When she sold her café back in March 2007, Jeanette handed over to the young team from Chez Justine because they promised not to change a thing. The monstrous 1940s dust-coated lights, leaky loos, tobacco-stained wallpaper depicting the Moulin Rouge and PVC-covered banquettes have finally been cleaned up, and the café has become one of Paris's hippest spots for an aperitif. There's a *plat du jour* at lunch and plates of cheese and charcuterie at night; at 8pm, the fluorescent lights go off and candlelight takes over, to a cheer.

Chez Prune

36 rue Beaurepaire, 10th (01.42.41.30.47). M° Jacques Bonsergent. **Open** 8am-2am Mon-Sat; 10am-2am Sun. **Credit** AmEx, MC, V.

This supremely hip retro café, with high ceilings and low lighting, sticks to a simple formula: groups of friends crowd around the cosily ordered banquettes, picking at moderately priced cheese or meat platters. Mostly, though, they come for a few leisurely drinks or an *apéro* before heading to one of the late night venues in the area.

Le Cinquante

50 rue de Lancry, 10th (01.42.02.36.83). M° Jacques Bonsergent. **Open** *Sept-July* 5.30pm-2am daily. *Aug* 5.30pm-2am Tue-Sun. **No credit cards.**

Just down from the Canal St-Martin, the bare brick, Formica and framed '50s ads of this funky venue attract an inner circle of regulars. These days, it's established enough to produce its own T-shirts and customised bar stools. Reasonable prices – half-litre pitchers of sauvignon, Brouilly and Chablis in the €10 range – attract a mixed bag of tastes and generations. The two rooms behind the main bar are set aside for dining (affordable classics) and music (generally acoustic). Sunday is open-mic night.

La Gouttière

96 av Parmentier, 11th (01.43.55.46.42). M° Parmentier. **Open** 8am-2am Mon-Fri; 4pm-2am Sat. **Credit** V.

Far enough (five minutes) from rue Oberkampf to feel off the beaten track, the Gutter is not out-and-out libertine, but you're on the right lines. Certainly, a come-what-may approach to music, drinking and eye contact abounds in the crowded venue. Decor, assuming you can see it, consists of a few LP covers and the kind of colour scheme often put to good use in adventure playgrounds. Reasonably priced lunches (food is a French and North African mix), the occasional live band, chess and card games complete the picture.

La Maroquinerie

23 rue Boyer, 20th (01.40.33.35.05, www.lamaroquinerie.fr). M° Gambetta. **Open** 6pm-2am daily. Closed Aug. **Credit** MC, V.

La Bellevilloise.

La Maroquinerie's former life as a leather factory is little in evidence these days. It's now a bright café and bar in competition with La Bellevilloise (*see left*), with a coveted downstairs concert venue that hosts the odd literary debate and a wealth of cool music acts. The food is excellent – you can eat your way through the menu quite reasonably for around €25 – and wine sourced from across France starts at €3 a glass. The interior, with exposed brick, is cosy, and in summer chirpy locals invade the shaded terrace.

La Mercerie

98 rue Oberkampf, 11th (01.56.98.14.10). M° Parmentier. **Open** 3pm-2am daily. **Credit** MC, V.

Opposite the landmark Charbon (*see left*), the spacious Mercerie has cleaned up its act: after years of full-on grunge it has succumbed to the draw of shabby chic – or, to put it another way, a fashionable level of dishevelment. This was probably wise, as the novelty of sticky tables was beginning to wear thin, and the move has been appreciated by the party freaks who still cross town for its loud, eclectic music, live DJ programme, and cheapo happy hour (7pm to 9pm), when you can cane the house vodkas in flavours such as apricot, mango and honey. The back area, with its tea lights, provides intimacy if that's where your evening's headed.

Mon Chien Stupide

1 rue Boyer, 20th (01.46.36.25.49). M° Gambetta. **Open** 3pm-2am Tue-Sun. **Credit** MC, V.

As the action moves relentlessly eastwards from Oberkampf, the once-distant outposts of Gambetta and Bagnolet appear on the radar of the discerning bar-hopper. Colourful and humorous, My Stupid Dog is a bar for grown-ups: an undercurrent of jazzy sounds drifts along nicely, cheese platters are accompanied by a quality selection of wines, and contemporary art freckles the walls.

Au Passage

1bis passage St-Sébastien, 11th (01.43.55.07.52, www.restaurant-aupassage.com). M° St-Sébastien Froissart. **Open** 9am-10pm daily. **Credit** MC, V.

Tucked down a narrow alleyway off rue Amelot, opposite the back entrance of Pop In, you don't just happen upon Au Passage, you come because you've heard about the cheap lunchtime menus (€12.50) and the colourful local artists and wannabe *marginaux* (all almost as colourful as their teeth, stained with a glass too many of *vin rouge*). There's art on the far wall, some retro cookbooks, and a feeling that entire decades could pass without anyone really noticing.

Le Verre Volé

67 rue de Lancry, 10th (01.48.03.17.34). M° Jacques Bonsergent. **Open** 10.30am-2.30pm, 7pm-2am Tue-Sun. Closed Aug. **Credit** MC, V.

This organic-only *cave à vins* doubles up as a minuscule wine bar and restaurant. Although wine (around €4 per glass) is the focus, you're obliged to eat; a hearty sausage and mash will set you back around €15 (other mains cost up to €20). Purists who would prefer a simple snack to complement their *bon vin* should opt for a plate of charcuterie and cheese at €12. It's good to know that staff will sell you a bottle of wine (and open it) for you to drink by the canal.

The Latin Quarter & the 13th

Le Crocodile

6 rue Royer-Collard, 5th (01.43.54.32.37). RER Luxembourg. **Open** 10pm-4am Mon-Sat. Closed Aug. **Credit** MC, V.

Ignore the apparently boarded-up windows at Le Crocodile; if you're here late, then it's open. Friendly young regulars line the sides of this small, narrow bar and try to decide what to drink – not easy, given the length of the cocktail list: at last count there were 317 varieties. The generous €6-per-cocktail happy hour (Monday to Thursday before midnight) will allow you to start with a champagne *accroche-coeur*, followed up with a Goldschläger (served with gold leaf) before moving on to one of the other 316.

Le Merle Moqueur

11 rue de la Butte aux Cailles, 13th (no phone). M° Place d'Italie. **Open** 5pm-2am daily. **No credit cards.**

Amid semi-faded pseudo-tropical decor and '80s music, the Teasing Blackbird – a Butte-aux-Cailles institution – tantalises students and nostalgists with its splendid selection of rums (over 20) and a long list of cocktails. The atmosphere gets raucous after 10pm – get in early to grab one of the tables.

Le Pantalon

7 rue Royer-Collard, 5th (no phone). RER Luxembourg. **Open** 5.30pm-2am Mon-Sat. **No credit cards.**

A local café that seems familiar yet is utterly surreal. It has the standard fixtures, including the old soaks at the bar – but the regulars and staff are enough to tip the balance firmly into eccentricity. Friendly and funny French grown-ups and foreign students chat in a variety of languages; drinks are cheap enough to make you tipsy without the worry of a cash hangover.

Le Requin Chagrin

10 rue Mouffetard, 5th (01.44.07.23.24). M° Place Monge. **Open** 6pm-2am Mon-Thur, Sun; 6pm-4am Fri, Sat. **Credit** MC, V.

The 'depressed shark' hasn't lost its bite. Students and beer guzzlers of all ages still cram in for the ten *bières* on tap and the five-hour happy hour

Café Charbon. See p67.

(4-9pm), when drinks are a steal at just €2.50. You'll find all the usual Left Bank suspects: groups of friends, blokes trying to get laid and *intellos* from the nearby universities who still stimulate their brains during down time with chess and quoits.

Sputnik
14 rue de la Butte aux Cailles, 13th (01.45.65.19.82, www.sputnik.fr). M° Place d'Italie. **Open** 2pm-2am Mon-Sat; 4pm-midnight Sun. **Credit** MC, V.
A hip young crowd gathers in this rock-oriented bar, which doubles as a sports bar during important football and rugby fixtures, and trebles as an internet café at other times. Ever-changing art exhibitions add interest to the walls, and live music once a month draws an indie crowd. Fancy falling in love? Try the €8 love potion cocktail Philtre d'Amour, which is made from gin, Malibu, pineapple and strawberries.

St-Germain-des-Prés & Odéon

Le Bar Dix
10 rue de l'Odéon, 6th (01.43.26.66.83, www.le10bar.com). M° Odéon. **Open** 6pm-2am daily. **No credit cards.**
Generations of students have glugged back jugs of the celebrated home-made sangria (€3 a glass during happy hour) while squeezed into the cramped upper bar, tattily authentic with its Jacques Brel record sleeves, Yves Montand handbills and pre-war light fittings. Spelunkers and hopeless romantics negotiate the hazardous stone staircase to drink in the cellar bar, with its candle-light and century-old advertising murals. Can someone please come and slap a preservation order on the place?

Le Bar du Marché
75 rue de Seine, 6th (01.43.26.55.15). M° Mabillon or Odéon. **Open** 8am-2am daily. **No credit cards.**
The market in question is the Cours des Halles, the bar a convivial corner café opening on to the pleasing bustle of St-Germain-des-Prés. Simple dishes

like a ham omelette or a plate of herrings are in the €7 range, and muscadet is €4-€5 a glass – all proffered by waiters dressed in matching dungarees. It couldn't be anywhere else in the world.

Café de Flore
172 bd St-Germain, 6th (01.45.48.55.26, www.cafe-de-flore.com). M° St-Germain-des-Prés. **Open** 7am-2am daily. **Credit** AmEx, DC, MC, V.
Bourgeois locals crowd the terrace tables at lunch, eating club sandwiches with knives and forks as anxious waiters frown at couples with pushchairs or single diners occupying tables for four. This historic café, former HQ of the Lost Generation intelligentsia, attracts tourists and, yes, celebrities from time to time. But a *café crème* is €4.60, and the omelettes and croque-monsieurs are best eschewed in favour of the better dishes on the menu (€15-€25). There are play readings on Mondays and philosophy debates on the first Wednesday of the month, at 8pm, in English.

Chez Georges
11 rue des Canettes, 6th (01.43.26.79.15). M° Mabillon. **Open** noon-2am Tue-Sat. Closed Aug. **Credit** MC, V.
One of a dying breed of *cave-bars* in the Latin Quarter, Chez Georges is beloved of students, professionals and local eccentrics. Regulars pop in during the day to sip wine over a game of chess, and at night the *cave* fills up with people dancing to *chanson*, pop and even the odd bar mitzvah tune. The heat is mascara-melting, but it's a great way to meet new people.

Les Deux Magots
6 pl St-Germain-des-Prés, 6th (01.45.48.55.25, www.lesdeuxmagots.com). M° St-Germain-des-Prés. **Open** 7.30am-1am daily. **Credit** AmEx, DC, MC, V.
If you stand outside Les Deux Magots, you have to be prepared to photograph tourists wanting proof of their encounter with French philosophy. The former haunt of Sartre and de Beauvoir now draws a less pensive crowd that can be all too *m'as-tu vu*, particularly at weekends. The hot chocolate is still good, though, and served in generous portions. Visit on a weekday afternoon when the editors return, manuscripts in hand, to the inside tables, leaving enough elbow room to engage in some serious discussion.

Les Editeurs
4 carrefour de l'Odéon, 6th (01.43.26.67.76, www.lesediteurs.fr). M° Odéon. **Open** 8am-2am daily. **Credit** AmEx, MC, V.
It's no surprise to see row upon row of books in the bright, modern interior of Les Editeurs. A café with literary leanings, it sits on the lovely carrefour de l'Odéon, a crossroads that leads to the Luxembourg gardens. Bask in the glory of literary greats as portraits of authors and their editors look down on you. Brunch on Saturday and Sunday is good value at €25.50; in the evening, main courses come in between €17 and €26.

J'Go
Rue Clément, 6th (01.43.26.19.02, www.lejgo.com). M° Mabillon or Odéon. **Open** 11am-midnight daily. **Credit** MC, V.
As its name suggests, J'Go (pronounced gigot) is all about lamb – well, meat of various kinds, actually: a buzzing Toulouse-style wine bar in the Marché St-Germain by day, it becomes a *rôtisserie* at meal times, serving its speciality spit-roasted lamb from Quercy, black pig from Bigorre, and whole roasted chickens. The €36 set menu is well worth the splurge, offering a whole jar of pâté, a giant bowl of salad, and lamb with creamy stewed *haricots blancs*. If you'd rather stick to wine and tapas, sidle up to one of the great wooden barrels, choose your poison (blindly if necessary – at €4 a glass all wines are good) and share a plate of charcuterie or foie gras *tartines* (€10).

Moose
16 rue des Quatre Vents, 6th (01.46.33.77.00, www.mooseparis.com). M° Odéon. **Open** 4pm-2am Mon-Fri; 11am-2am Sat, Sun. **Credit** MC, V.
For those bored of overpriced cafés and unfriendly waiters, the Moose is a great alternative. This Canadian sports bar serves a vast selection of beers and even some organic Australian wines. A friendly atmosphere and delicious burgers make the Moose a great place to kick off the evening.

La Palette
43 rue de Seine, 6th (01.43.26.68.15). M° Odéon. **Open** 9am-2am Mon-Sat. Closed Aug. **Credit** MC, V.
La Palette is the café-bar of choice for the very beau Beaux-Arts students who study at the venerable institution around the corner, and young couples who steal kisses in the wonderfully preserved art deco back room decorated with illustrations. It ain't cheap – a glass of Chablis sets you back €6, a demi €4.50 – but you're paying for the prime location once frequented by such luminaries as Jim Morrison, Picasso and Ernest Hemingway. Grab a spot on the leafy terrace if you possibly can – there's formidable competition for seats.

Prescription Cocktail Club
23 rue Mazarine, 6th (01.45.08.88.09). M° Odéon. **Open** 7pm-2am Mon-Thur; 7pm-4am Fri, Sat; 7pm-midnight Sun. **Credit** MC, V.
This stylish 1930s-style speakeasy has a retro Prohibition feel but remains severely Left Bank, with crowds of well-dressed people sipping on cocktails by candlelight. It's always busy and almost impossible to navigate on weekends. But come at the start of the night for a relaxing vibe.

Le Rostand
6 pl Edmond-Rostand, 6th (01.43.54.61.58). RER Luxembourg. **Open** 8am-2am daily. **Credit** MC, V.
Le Rostand has a truly wonderful view of the Jardin du Luxembourg from its classy interior, decked out with oriental paintings, a long mahogany bar and

wall-length mirrors. It's a terribly well-behaved place. Whiskies and cocktails are pricey, as is the brasserie menu, but the snack menu serves delicious omelettes and *croques* for around €8. Perfect for a civilised drink after a stroll round the gardens.

Montparnasse

Le Café Tournesol
9 rue de la Gaîté, 14th (01.43.27.65.72). M° Gaîté. **Open** 8.30am-1.30am Mon-Sat; 9.30am-1.30am Sun. **Credit** AmEx, MC, V.
The Tournesol is young, vibrant and the best of the cafés on rue de la Gaîté. There's outdoor seating in the shadow of the Tour Montparnasse, and an exposed brick interior with a soul, funk and electro soundtrack. A croque-monsieur will set you back €6, a steak €12.50, and a *demi* of Stella €3.

L'Entrepôt
7-9 rue Francis de Pressensé, 14th (01.45.40.07.50, www.lentrepot.fr). M° Pernéty. **Open** 9am-midnight daily. **Credit** MC, V.
L'Entrepôt, housed in a former warehouse, is a wonderful multitasker and has enough to keep you keen all week. There's a café where literary readings are held, a restaurant with a terrace (a godsend in the summer), and a bar on the ground floor with live music. There's an arthouse cinema and exhibition space upstairs.

Le Select
99 bd du Montparnasse, 6th (01.45.48.38.24). M° Vavin. **Open** 7am-2am Mon-Thur, Sun; 7am-4am Fri, Sat. **Credit** MC, V.
For a decade between the wars, the junction of boulevards Raspail and du Montparnasse was where Man Ray, Cocteau and Lost Generation Americans hung out in the vast, glass-fronted cafés. Eight decades on, Le Select is the best of what have inevitably become tourist haunts. Sure, its pricey menu is big on historical detail and short on authenticity, but by and large it manages to hold on to its heyday with dignity.

The 7th & western Paris

Le Café du Marché
38 rue Cler, 7th (01.47.05.51.27). M° Ecole Militaire. **Open** 7am-1am Mon-Sat; 7am-4pm Sun. **Credit** MC, V.
This well-loved address is frequented by trendy locals, shoppers hunting down a particular type of cheese and tourists who've managed to make it this far from the Eiffel Tower. Le Café du Marché really is a hub of activity. Its *pichets* of decent house plonk always go down a treat, and mention must be made of the food – such as the huge house salad featuring lashings of foie gras and parma ham.

Café Thoumieux
4 rue de la Comète, 7th (01.45.51.50.40). M° La Tour Maubourg. **Open** noon-2am Mon-Fri; 7pm-2am Sat. Closed 3wks Aug. **Credit** AmEx, MC, V.
Café Thoumieux is a laid-back destination for cocktails, tapas and big-screen sport. Banquettes snake around the room, and spiky Aztec-pattern lamps light up the faces of the pretty young locals who have made this place their own. The flavoured vodkas are delicious.

La Palette.

OLIVIA RUTHERFORD

Shops & Services

Paris shopping has never been in better shape. Where else in the world can you find so many independent boutiques and specialist shops, right in the middle of some of the most picturesque areas of the city? Whether you're tasting cheeses for a dinner party, trying on clothes behind the velvet curtains of **Lanvin**, getting measured up for a bra or selecting hand-made gloves or a one-off piece of vintage clothing, shopping in Paris is a sensual pleasure based around quality, not quantity. Whereas we have window-shopping, they have window-licking (*lèche-vitrine*). Although chain stores have made their mark, it's still a long way removed from the grim uniformity of so many British high streets.

HOW TO SHOP

Different areas of the capital have different specialities. There are clusters of antiques shops in the seventh arrondissement, and second-hand and rare book outlets in the fifth; crystal and porcelain manufacturers still dot rue de Paradis in the tenth; furniture craftsmen as well as children's clothes shops inhabit rue du Fbg-St-Antoine; bikes and cameras are clustered on boulevard Beaumarchais; and the world's top jewellers can be found on place Vendôme. The historic covered passages in the second and ninth are also fun places in which to shop, with chic stores such as cosmetics line **By Terry** mixed in with old-style philatelists and booksellers.

Family-run food shops have thankfully not been eroded by supermarket culture, and tend to cluster in 'market streets' such as rue des Martyrs and rue Mouffetard, as well as around the many covered and open-air food markets. Here everything from a vintage bottle of armagnac to a single praline chocolate is lovingly presented, served and wrapped. Informed discussion is still very much part of the purchasing process, and beautiful, old-style shops, unchanged for decades, add to the overall pleasure.

Green, organic and ethical have also suddenly become sexy concepts to the French. Even luxury brands have embraced them, seen at the first sustainable luxury trade fair, called 1.618, at the Palais de Tokyo. The not-for-profit concept store **Merci** and the eco fashion store **House of Organic** offer guilt-free clothes shopping, and **Designpack Gallery** recycles packaging into funky and ingenious objects for the home.

Shops are generally open from 10am to 7pm Monday to Saturday, with specialist boutiques closing for an hour at lunch. Some are closed on Monday mornings. Sunday opening is found in the Marais, on the Champs-Elysées, at Bercy Village and in the Carrousel du Louvre, although this may change – President Sarkozy is currently trying to extend Sunday trading. Many shops on the Champs-Elysées stay open until midnight, and Thursday is late closing at department stores.

GENERAL

Department stores

BHV (Bazar de l'Hôtel de Ville)
52-64 rue de Rivoli, 4th (01.42.74.90.00, DIY hire 01.42.74.97.23, www.bhv.fr). Mº Hôtel de Ville. **Open** 9.30am-7.30pm Mon, Tue, Thur, Fri; 9.30am-8pm Sat; 9.30am-9pm Wed. **Credit** AmEx, MC, V.
Homeware heaven: there's even a Bricolage Café with internet access. Upper floors have a good range of men's outdoor wear, upmarket bed linen, toys, books, household appliances – and a large space devoted to every type of storage utility.

Le Bon Marché
24 rue de Sèvres, 7th (01.44.39.80.00, www.bonmarche.fr). Mº Sèvres Babylone. **Open** 10am-8pm Mon-Wed, Sat; 10am-9pm Thur, Fri. **Credit** AmEx, DC, MC, V.
The city's oldest department store, which opened in 1848, is also its most swish and user-friendly, thanks to an extensive redesign by LVMH. Luxury boutiques, Dior and Chanel among them, take pride of place on the ground floor; escalators designed by Andrée Putman take you up to the fashion floor, which has an excellent selection of global designer labels, from Lanvin to Claudie Pierlot. Designer names also abound in Balthazar, the prestigious men's section. For top-notch nibbles, try the adjoining Grande Epicerie food hall (01.44.39.81.00, www.lagrandeepicerie.fr, 8.30am-9pm Mon-Sat).

Galeries Lafayette
40 bd Haussmann, 9th (01.42.82.34.56, fashion shows 01.42.82.30.25, fashion advice 01.42.82.35.50, www.galerieslafayette.com). Mº Chaussée d'Antin/RER Auber. **Open** 9.30am-8pm Mon-Wed, Fri; 9.30am-9pm Thur. **Credit** AmEx, DC, MC, V.
The store has been undergoing a massive renovation programme of late, with the opening of Espace Luxe on the first floor, featuring luxury prêt-à-porter and accessories, and the unveiling of a vast new shoe department in the basement featuring some 150 brands. The men's fashion space on the third floor, Lafayette Homme, has natty designer corners and a 'Club' area with internet access. On the first floor, Lafayette Gourmet has exotic foods galore, plus a vast wine cellar including its own Bordeauxthèque. Now that's how to shop in style. Lafayette Maison over the road has five floors of home furnishings and design products.
Other locations Centre Commercial Montparnasse, 22 rue du Départ, 14th (01.45.38.52.87).

Printemps
64 bd Haussmann, 9th (01.42.82.50.00, www.printemps.com). Mº Havre Caumartin/RER Auber. **Open** 9.35am-8pm Mon-Wed, Fri, Sat; 9.35am-10pm Thur. **Credit** AmEx, DC, MC, V.
In the magnificently appointed Printemps you'll find everything you didn't even know you wanted and English-speaking assistants to help you find it. But fashion is where it excels; an entire floor is devoted to shoes, and the beauty department stocks more than 200 brands. In all, there are six floors of men's and women's fashion. In Printemps de la Mode, French designers sit alongside all the big international designers. The Fashion Loft offers a younger but equally stylish take on current trends. Along with furnishings, Printemps de la Maison stocks everything from tableware to design classics. For fast refuelling, Printemps has a tearoom, sushi bar and Café Be, an Alain Ducasse bakery. Or head up to Le Déli-cieux, on the ninth floor of Printemps Maison, for a drink on the terrace with wonderful views across Paris.

Tati
4 bd de Rochechouart, 18th (01.55.29.52.20, www.tati.fr). Mº Barbès Rochechouart. **Open** 10am-7pm Mon-Fri; 9.30am-7pm Sat. **Credit** MC, V.

Printemps.

Expect to find anything from T-shirts to wedding dresses, as well as bargain children's clothes and household goods at this discount heaven. It's unbeatably cheap, but don't expect high quality. **Other locations** throughout the city.

Malls

Bercy Village
Cour St Emilion, 12th (08.25.16.60.75, www.bercyvillage.com). Mº Cour St-Emilion. **Open** 11am-9pm daily. **Credit** AmEx, DC, MC, V.
This retail and leisure development housed in old wine warehouses is a relaxed place to shop. Squarely aimed at tourists and out-of-towners, the shops include Agnès b, Nature et Découvertes, Pacific Adventure, L'Occitane, Oliviers & Co and Sephora. There are also cafés, restaurants, a park and a multiplex cinema.

Drugstore Publicis
133 av des Champs-Elysées, 8th (01.44.43.79.00, www.publicisdrugstore.com). Mº Charles de Gaulle Etoile. **Open** 8am-2am Mon-Fri; 10am-2am Sat, Sun. **Credit** MC, V.
A 1960s legend, Drugstore Publicis was clad with neon swirls by architect Michele Saee following a renovation a few years ago; a glass-and-steel café stretches out on to the pavement. On the ground floor there's a newsagent, pharmacy, bookshop and upmarket deli full of quality olive oils and elegant biscuits. The basement is a macho take on Colette, keeping selected design items and lifestyle mags, and replacing high fashion with fine wines and a cigar cellar.

Forum des Halles
Rue Pierre-Lescot & rue Rambuteau, 1st (01.44.76.96.56, www.forumdeshalles.com). Mº Les Halles/RER Châtelet Les Halles. **Open** 10am-8pm Mon-Sat.
The Forum des Halles is Paris's biggest and least pleasant shopping mall, although a facelift due for completion in 2012 should improve matters considerably. Extending three levels underground, it incorporates métro stations, multiplex, gym, swimming pool and numerous restaurants, and is truly labyrinthine. High street retailers dominate the aisles: Mango, Muji, Gap, H&M, Bershka, Naf-Naf, Bodum, Habitat, Sephora, Yves Rocher, Natures et Découvertes and a flagship Fnac are all present and correct.

Critics'choice

1 **K Jacques**
Leather sandals that are the epitome of elemental chic. *See p77.*

2 **Jacques Génin**
Génin's chocolates are the stuff of dreams. *See p79.*

3 **Merci**
Still one of the hottest concept dates in the city. *See p74.*

La Galerie du Carrousel du Louvre

99 rue de Rivoli, 1st (01.43.16.47.10, www.carrouseldulouvre.com). M° Palais Royal Musée du Louvre. **Open** 10am-8pm daily. **Credit** AmEx, MC, V.

This massive underground shopping centre – open every day of the year – is home to more than 35 outlets, mostly big-name chains vying for your attention and cash. Options include the Apple Store, Virgin Megastore, Swatch Store and L'Occitane en Provence.

La Vallée Village

3 cours de la Garonne, 77700 Serris (01.60.42.35.00, www.lavalleevillage.com). Eurostar/TGV Marne La Vallée-Chessy-Parc Disneyland/RER Val d'Europe. **Open** 10am-8pm Mon-Sat; 10am-7pm Sun. **Credit** AmEx, MC, V.

La Vallée Village, located near Disneyland Paris, is discount shopping heaven. Its 90 stores feature all the usual suspects – Armani, Hilfiger and Burberry – as well as Agnès b, Zadig & Voltaire and Antik Batik.

SPECIALIST

Books & magazines

Bouquinistes

Along the quais, especially quai de Montebello & quai St-Michel, 5th. M° St-Michel. **Open** times vary from stall to stall, generally Tue-Sun. **No credit cards.**

The green, open-air boxes along the *quais* are one of the city's institutions. Most sell second-hand books – rummage through boxes packed with ancient paperbacks for something existential.

Gibert Joseph

26 bd St-Michel, 6th (01.44.41.88.88, www.gibertjoseph.com). M° St-Michel. **Open** 10am-8pm Mon-Sat. **Credit** MC, V.

Formed back in 1929, this string of bookshops is normally packed out with students. Further up bd St-Michel (nos.30, 32 & 34) are branches specialising in stationery, CDs, DVDs and art materials.

La Hune

170 bd St-Germain, 6th (01.45.48.35.85). M° St-Germain-des-Prés. **Open** 10am-11.45pm Mon-Sat; 11am-7.45pm Sun. **Credit** AmEx, MC, V.

This Left Bank institution boasts a global selection of art and design books, and a magnificent collection of French literature and theory.

English-language

Abbey Bookshop

29 rue de la Parcheminerie, 5th (01.46.33.16.24, www.alevdesign.com/abbey). M° St-Michel. **Open** 11am-7pm Mon-Sat. **No credit cards.**

Celebrating 20 years in business, the tiny Abbey Bookshop is the domain of Canadian renaissance man Brian Spence, who organises weekend hikes as well as dressing up in doublet and hose for a spot of 17th-century dancing. The tiny, narrow shop stocks old and new works, a specialised Canadian section, and highbrow subjects down the rickety staircase. Several thousand more books are tucked away in storage, and he can normally order titles for collection within two days.

Galignani

224 rue de Rivoli, 1st (01.42.60.76.07, www.galignani.com). M° Tuileries. **Open** 10am-7pm Mon-Sat. **Credit** MC, V.

Opened in 1802, this was the first English-language bookshop in mainland Europe. Today, it stocks fine art books, French and English literature, philosophical tomes and magazines.

I Love My Blender

36 rue du Temple, 3rd (01.42.77.50.32, www.ilovemyblender.fr). M° Hôtel de Ville. **Open** 10am-7.30pm Tue-Sat. **Credit** AmEx, MC, V.

Christophe Persouyre left a career in advertising to share his passion for English and American literature: all the books he stocks were originally penned in English, and here you can find their mother-tongue and translated versions.

Red Wheelbarrow

22 rue St-Paul, 4th (01.48.04.75.08, www.theredwheelbarrow.com). M° St-Paul.

La Hune.

Open 10am-6pm Mon; 10am-7pm Tue-Sat; 2-6pm Sun. **Credit** MC, V.

Penelope Fletcher Le Masson and Abigail Altman run this friendly literary bookshop in the Marais, which also has an excellent children's section.

Shakespeare & Company

37 rue de la Bûcherie, 5th (01.43.25.40.93, www.shakespeareandcompany.com). M° St-Michel. **Open** 10am-11pm Mon-Fri; 11am-11pm Sat, Sun. **Credit** MC, V.

Unequivocably the best bookshop in Paris, the historic and ramshackle Shakespeare & Company is always packed with expat and tourist book-lovers. There is a large second-hand section, antiquarian books next door, and just about anything you could ask for new.

Village Voice

6 rue Princesse, 6th (01.46.33.36.47, www.villagevoicebookshop.com). M° Mabillon. **Open** 2-7.30pm Mon; 10am-7.30pm Tue-Sat; noon-6pm Sun. **Credit** AmEx, DC, MC, V.

Village Voice stocks new fiction, non-fiction and literary magazines in English, plus literary events and poetry readings.

WH Smith

248 rue de Rivoli, 1st (01.44.77.88.99, www.whsmith.fr). M° Concorde. **Open** 9am-7pm Mon-Sat; 12.30-7pm Sun. **Credit** AmEx, MC, V.

With 70,000 English-language titles and extensive magazine shelves, this WH Smith is a home from home for Brits craving a fix of their native periodicals; the first floor has lots of books, DVDs and audiobooks.

Children

Fashion

Children's fashion is clustered on rue Bréa (6th), rue Vavin (6th) and rue du Fbg-St-Antoine (12th). **Monoprix** (www.monoprix.fr) is a good source of inexpensive children's clothes, with some branches stocking Petit Bateau basics. For chic at a snip, try the **Bonpoint** (42 rue de l'Université, 7th, 01.40.20.10.55) and **Cacharel** (114 rue d'Alésia, 14th, 01.45.42.53.04) stock shops; it may be last season's stuff, but your five-year-old is never going to know.

Bonton

82 rue de Grenelle, 7th (01.44.39.09.20, www.bonton.fr). M° Rue du Bac. **Open** 10am-7pm Mon-Sat. Closed 2wks Aug. **Credit** AmEx, DC, MC, V.

At this concept store for kids and trendy parents, T-shirts and trousers come in rainbow colours, and at pretty steep prices. Furniture and accessories are also available, as is a kids' hairdresser. **Other location** 5 Blvd des Filles du Calvaire, 3rd (01.42.72.34.69).

Finger in the Nose

17 rue Saintonge, 3rd (01.42.71.43.40, www.fingerinthenose.com). M° St-Sébastien Froissart. **Open** 11am-7pm Tue-Sat. **Credit** AmEx, MC, V.

As the name suggest, there is nothing twee about the kidswear from this Norwegian designer. In the Marais boutique blackboard walls with chalk slogans and drawings set off tough rebel urban wear for six- to 16-year-olds, including bright red Puffas, mod check jumpers, rock'n'roll T-shirts and jeans.

Jacadi

116 rue d'Alésia, 14th (01.40.44.51.87, www.jacadi.fr). M° Alésia. **Open** 11am-7pm Mon; 10am-7pm Tue-Sat. **Credit** MC, V.

Jacadi's well-made clothes for babies and children – pleated skirts, smocked dresses, dungarees and Fair Isle knits – are a hit with well-to-do parents. The rue d'Alésia store is the largest. **Other locations** throughout the city.

Papillon pour Bonton

84bis rue de Grenelle, 7th (01.42.84.42.43, www.bonton.fr). M° Rue du Bac. **Open** 10am-7pm Mon-Sat. **Credit** AmEx, MC, V.

Bonton's new venture is all about nostalgia, with hand-knits, cashmere and alpaca, dinky stripes and Liberty prints in the shades of a hand-tinted photograph (old rose, grey, aubergine, sage). Pretty buttons accompany the fine finish that Bonton is famous for, and christening robes and pyjamas complete the collection, displayed in an old perfume shop amid flowery wallpaper and hunting trophies. Pure *Bagpuss*.

Du Pareil au Même

120-122 rue du Fbg-St-Antoine, 12th (01.43.43.96.01, www.dpam.com). M° Ledru-Rollin. **Open** 10am-7pm Mon-Sat. **Credit** AmEx, MC, V.

Bright, cleverly designed basics for children aged three months to 14 years, at low prices. The Bébé branch, with fashionable accessories and clothing for kids up to two years, is a good source of gifts. **Other locations** throughout the city.

Petit Bateau

26 rue Vavin, 6th (01.55.42.02.53, www.petit-bateau.fr). M° Vavin. **Open** 10am-7pm Mon-Sat. **Credit** AmEx, MC, V.

Widely renowned in the city and beyond for its comfortable, well-made cotton T-shirts, vests and other separates, Petit Bateau carries an equally coveted teen range. **Other locations** throughout the city.

Six Pieds Trois Pouces

223 bd St-Germain, 7th (01.45.44.03.72, www.sixpiedstroispouces.com). M° Solférino. **Open** 10.30am-7pm Mon-Fri; 10am-7pm Sat. **Credit** AmEx, DC, MC, V.

The excellent array of children's and teens' shoes at Six Pieds Trois Pouces runs from Start-rite and Aster to Timberland and New Balance, alongside the shop's own brand. **Other locations** 85 rue de Longchamp, 16th (01.45.53.64.21); 78 av de Wagram, 17th (01.46.22.81.64).

Zef

15 rue Debelleyme, 3rd (01.42.76.09.65, www.zef.eu). M° St-Sébastien Froissart. **Open** 11am-7.30pm Mon-Sat. **Credit** AmEx, DC, MC, V.

Zef's designer is the daughter of fashion photographer Paolo Reversi. The trendy children's separates have a classic Italian look, in soft muted colours with adorable details like elbow patches on the jackets. Boots, sheepskin gilets and hats are part of the look. **Other locations** 32 rue de Richelieu, 1st (01.42.60.61.04); 55bis rue des Sts-Pères, 6th (01.42.22.02.93; babies and toddlers 01.42.22.45.22).

Toys & books

Traditional toyshops abound; department stores (*see p69*) go overboard at Christmas. For a selection of children's books in English, try **WH Smith** (*see left*).

Fnac Junior

19 rue Vavin, 6th (08.92.35.06.66, www.eveiletjeux.com). M° Vavin. **Open** 10am-7.30pm Mon-Sat. **Credit** AmEx, MC, V.

Fnac Junior carries books, toys, DVDs, CDs and CD-Roms for under-12s. Storytelling and other activities (Wed, Sat) take place for three-year-olds and up. **Other locations** throughout the city.

Au Nain Bleu

5 bd Malesherbes, 8th (01.42.65.20.00, www.aunainbleu.com). M° Madeleine. **Open** 10am-7pm Mon-Sat. **Credit** AmEx, MC, V.

The city's best toy shop, decorated like a circus tent, draws gasps of wonder from children. Wooden doll's houses, pirate ships and gorgeous dolls are made to last more than one generation.

Village Joué Club

3-5 bd des Italiens, 2nd (01.53.45.41.41, www.joueclub.fr). M° Richelieu Drouot. **Open** 10am-8pm Mon-Sat. **Credit** AmEx, MC, V.

Village Joué Club, the largest toy store in Paris, is spread out in and around passage des Princes.

Fashion

All the world's big-name designers have their own-label stores in Paris. In addition to international fashion juggernauts Mango, H&M and Zara, the high street has its fair share of Gallic cheapies: think **Etam**, Jennyfer and Pimkie. The highest density is in the **Forum des Halles** (see p69), on rue de Rivoli, between the métro stations of Châtelet and Louvre Rivoli, and around Galeries Lafayette and Printemps.

Designer

Azzedine Alaïa
7 rue de Moussy, 4th (01.42.72.19.19). M° Hôtel de Ville. **Open** 10am-7pm Mon-Sat. **Credit** AmEx, DC, MC, V.
Ringing the doorbell gains you entry to the factory-style showroom in the same building as Alaïa's headquarters and apartment, where the Tunisian creator continues to astound with his originality. Stunning haute couture creations are in the back room, and sexy shoes bordering on fetish are scattered among the mannequins and rails.

Balenciaga
10 av George V, 8th (01.47.20.21.11, www.balenciaga.com). M° Alma Marceau or George V. **Open** 10am-7pm Mon-Sat. **Credit** AmEx, DC, MC, V.
With Nicolas Ghesquière at the helm, the Spanish fashion house is ahead of Japanese and Belgian designers in the hip stakes. Floating fabrics contrast with dramatic cuts, producing a sophisticated urban style that the fashion *haut monde* can't wait to slip into. Bags and shoes are also available.

Balmain
44 rue François 1er, 8th (01.47.20.57.58, www.balmain.com). M° George V. **Open** 10.30am-7pm Mon-Sat. **Credit** AmEx, DC, MC, V.
A large portrait of the late Pierre Balmain surveys the scene at his eponymous shop in the middle of the Triangle d'Or. What would he have made of the clothes around him? Long gone are the afternoon dresses with perfectly positioned waists, full skirts and trapezoidal necklines. While the clothes are still astonishingly expensive and exquisitely finished, the racks are these days lined with bondage trousers, studded jackets and animal print drainpipes. There hasn't been such a good display of grungy glamour since Kensington Market closed its doors.

Carlos Miele
380 rue St-Honoré, 1st (01.42.97.53.66, www.carlosmiele.com.br). M° Concorde. **Open** 10am-7pm Mon-Sat. **Credit** AmEx, MC, V.
The Brazilian designer favoured by Sandra Bullock, Heidi Klum and J Lo brings luxury with a conscience to the rue St-Honoré. He works with several co-operatives in *favelas* and Amazonian Indians, honing traditional techniques like crochet, knotting, embroidery and featherwork.

Chanel
31 rue Cambon, 1st (01.42.86.28.00, www.chanel.com). M° Concorde or Madeleine. **Open** 10am-7pm Mon-Sat. **Credit** AmEx, DC, MC, V.
Fashion legend Chanel has managed to stay relevant, thanks to Karl Lagerfeld. Coco opened her first boutique in this street, at no.21, in 1910, and the tradition continues in this elegant interior. Lagerfeld has been designing for Chanel since 1983, and keeps on revamping the classics – the little black dress and the Chanel suit – with great success.
Other locations 42 av Montaigne, 8th (01.47.23.74.12); 25 rue Royale, 8th (01.44.51.92.93); 21 rue du Fbg-St-Honoré, 8th (01.53.05.98.95).

Comme des Garçons
54 rue du Fbg-St-Honoré, 8th (01.53.30.27.27). M° Concorde or Madeleine. **Open** 11am-7pm Mon-Sat. **Credit** AmEx, DC, MC, V.
Rei Kawakubo's design ideas and revolutionary mix of materials have influenced fashions of the past two decades, and are showcased in this fibre-glass store. Comme des Garçons Parfums (23 pl du Marché-St-Honoré, 1st, 01.47.03.15.03) provides a futuristic setting for the brand's fragrances.

Dior
26-30 av Montaigne, 8th (01.40.73.73.73, www.dior.com). M° Franklin D. Roosevelt. **Open** 10am-7pm Mon-Sat. **Credit** AmEx, DC, MC, V.

The Dior universe is here on avenue Montaigne, from the main prêt-à-porter store and jewellery, menswear and eyewear to Baby Dior.
Other locations throughout the city.

Gaspard Yurkievich
43 rue Charlot, 3rd (01.42.77.42.48, www.gaspardyurkievich.com). M° Filles du Calvaire. **Open** 11am-7pm Tue-Sat. **Credit** MC, V.
The first boutique of this native Parisian fashion missile. Hot men's and women's designs and a dangerous line of shoes are all on display.

Givenchy
28 rue du Fbg-St-Honoré, 8th (01.42.68.31.00, www.givenchy.com). M° Madeleine or Concorde. **Open** 10am-7pm Mon-Sat. **Credit** AmEx, DC, MC, V.
Givenchy's flagship store for men's and women's prêt-à-porter and accessories incorporates surreal rooms within rooms – cut-out boxes lined with white, black or mahogany panelling – providing an art gallery setting for Givenchy's cutting-edge, sculptural and monochrome designs.

Hermès
24 rue du Fbg-St-Honoré, 8th (01.40.17.47.17, www.hermes.com). M° Concorde or Madeleine. **Open** 10.30am-6.30pm Mon-Sat. **Credit** AmEx, DC, MC, V.
The fifth generation of the family now directs the Hermès empire from this 1930s building. Originally – and still – a saddler, it is no also-ran in the fashion stakes, with Jean-Paul Gaultier at the reins. Most of its clients, however, are tourists after a horsey scarf. The new Left Bank store is an absolute stunner.
Other location 17 rue de Sèvres, 6th (01.42.22.80.83).

Hervé Léger
24 rue Cambon, 1st (01.42.60.02.00, www.herveleger.com). M° Concorde. **Open** 10am-7pm Mon-Sat. **Credit** AmEx, DC, MC, V.
A couple of decades ago, Hervé Léger's silhouette-cinching bandage dresses were as evocative of the era as supermodels Linda, Christy, Naomi and Cindy. But somewhere in the mid-'90s women lost their love of Lycra, longing for the more conventional figure-flattering techniques of bias cut and tailoring. In the past few seasons, however, updated reinterpretations of Léger's style, by the likes of Christopher Kane and Marios Schwab, have been nothing short of a fashion phenomenon. Less modified versions, sold by the Léger label itself (now owned and designed by Max Azria of BCBG fame), have been less critically acclaimed, but celebrities just adore them.

Isabel Marant
16 rue de Charonne, 11th (01.49.29.71.55, www.isabelmarant.tm.fr). M° Ledru-Rollin. **Open** 10.30am-7.30pm Mon-Sat. **Credit** AmEx, MC, V.

Isabel Marant's style is easily recognisable in her ethno-babe brocades, blanket-like coats and decorated sweaters. It's a firm favourite among young trendies.
Other locations 47 rue Saintonge, 3rd (01.42.78.19.24); 1 rue Jacob, 6th (01.43.26.04.12).

Jay Ahr
2-4 rue du 29 Juillet, 1st (01.42.96.95.23, www.jayahr.com). M° Tuileries. **Open** 11am-7pm Mon-Sat. **Credit** AmEx, MC, V.
Former jewellery designer Jonathan Riss opened this shop as a fashion stylist in 2004, and struck gold with simple, figure-flaunting, '60s-inspired dresses. Think plunging necklines and Bianca Jagger in her heyday, with Ali MacGraw and Anita Pallenberg in the mix. There are no price tags on the dresses, so you have to ask; they start at around €500.

Jean-Paul Gaultier
6 rue Vivienne, 2nd (01.42.86.05.05, www.jeanpaulgaultier.com). M° Bourse. **Open** 10.30am-7pm Mon-Fri; 11am-7pm Sat. **Credit** AmEx, DC, MC, V.
Having celebrated his 30th year in the fashion business, Gaultier is still going strong. His boudoir boutique with its peach taffeta walls stocks men's and women's ready-to-wear and the reasonably priced JPG Jeans lines. The haute couture department is strictly by appointment only, and is located above the store.
Other locations 44 av George V, 8th (01.44.43.00.44).

John Galliano
384-386 rue St-Honoré, 1st (01.55.35.40.40, www.johngalliano.com). M° Concorde or Madeleine. **Open** 11am-7pm Mon-Sat.
It's hard to imagine how he manages it all, but Dior chief Galliano still has his own range and a reputation as one of the UK's most original designers. You can admire the small but diverse collection of flamboyant and feminine delights through the showcase window, or from one of the Louis XVI-style chairs inside.

Kenzo
1 rue du Pont Neuf, 1st (01.40.28.11.80, www.kenzo.com). M° Pont Neuf. **Open** 11am-7.30pm Mon-Sat. **Credit** AmEx, DC, MC, V.
Kenzo has long been a friend of Paris, having dressed the city itself in its various extravagant publicity campaigns. The flagship store has three floors of men's and women's fashion, and is crowned with the Bulle Kenzo spa and Philippe Starck-designed Kong restaurant on the fifth floor.
Other locations throughout the city.

Lanvin
22 rue du Fbg St-Honoré, 8th (01.44.71.31.73, www.lanvin.com). M° Concorde or Madeleine. **Open** 10.30am-7pm daily. **Credit** AmEx, DC, MC, V.

The couture house that began in the 1920s with Jeanne Lanvin has been reinvented by the talented and indefatigable Albert Elbaz. In October 2007, he unveiled this, the revamped showroom that set new aesthetic standards for luxury fashion retailing. Lanvin has an exhibition room devoted to her in the Musée des Arts Décoratifs, and this apartment-boutique comes close, incorporating original furniture from the Lanvin archive that has been restored. All this would be nothing, of course, if the clothes themselves were not exquisite.

Lefranc.ferrant
22 rue de l'Echaudé, 6th (01.44.07.37.96, www.lefranc-ferrant.fr). M° St-Germain-des-Prés. **Open** 11am-7pm Tue-Sat and by appointment. **Credit** AmEx, MC, V.
The opening of this boutique has been eagerly awaited by keen followers of the talented Paris duo Béatrice Ferrant and Mario Lefranc. Their trademark is a surreal approach to tailoring, as in a strapless yellow evening gown made like a pair of men's trousers – complete with flies. Prices are in the €1,000 range and they love to undertake bespoke commissions.
Other location 149 Galerie de Balois, 1st (01.58.62.20.78).

Louis Vuitton
101 av des Champs-Elysées, 8th (01.53.57.52.00, www.vuitton.com). M° George V. **Open** 10am-8pm Mon-Sat; 11am-7pm Sun. **Credit** AmEx, DC, MC, V.
The 'Promenade' flagship sets the tone for Vuitton's global image, from the 'bag bar', bookstore and new jewellery department to the women's and men's ready-to-wear. Contemporary art, videos by Tim White Sobieski and a pitch-black elevator by Olafur Eliasson complete the picture. Accessed by lift, the Espace Vuitton hosts temporary art exhibits – but the star of the show is the view over Paris.
Other locations 6 pl St-Germain-des-Prés, 6th (01.45.49.62.32); 22 av Montaigne, 8th (01.45.62.47.00).

Marc Jacobs
56 galerie de Montpensier, 1st (01.55.35.02.60, www.marcjacobs.com). M° Palais Royal Musée du Louvre. **Open** 11am-7pm Mon-Sat. **Credit** AmEx, DC, MC, V.
By choosing the Palais-Royal for his first signature boutique in Europe, Marc Jacobs brought new life – and an influx of fashionistas – to these elegant cloisters. Stocking womenswear, menswear, accessories and shoes, it has already become a place of pilgrimage for the designer's legion of admirers, who are snapping up his downtown New York style.

Martin Grant
10 rue Charlot, 3rd (01.42.71.39.49, www.martingrantparis.com). M° Temple. **Open** 10am-6pm Mon-Fri. Closed 3wks Aug. **Credit** MC, V.

FEATURED ESTABLISHMENT

Hermès, rue de Sèvres.

This high-end shop is tucked away in a second-floor Marais apartment. If you're a stickler for steady cuts, pure textiles and unfussy designs, Australian Martin Grant's interpretation of couture is for you.

Martin Margiela
23 & 25bis rue de Montpensier, 1st (womenswear 01.40.15.07.55, menswear 01.40.15.06.44, www.maisonmartinmargiela. com). Mº *Palais Royal Musée du Louvre.* **Open** 11am-7pm Mon-Sat. **Credit** AmEx, DC, MC, V.
The first Paris outlet for the JD Salinger of fashion is a pristine, white, unlabelled space. His collection for women (Line 1) has a blank label but is recognisable by external white stitching. You'll also find Line 6 (women's basics) and Line 10 (menswear), plus accessories for men and women and shoes.
Other locations 13 rue de Grenelle, 7th (01.45.49.06.68).

Miu Miu
219 rue St-Honoré, 1st (01.58.62.53.20, www.miumiu.com). Mº *Tuileries.* **Open** 11am-7pm Mon; 10am-7pm Tue-Sat. **Credit** AmEx, DC, MC, V.
Prada's younger sister has this rue St-Honoré store as its main boutique, selling its quirky women's fashions, shoes and bags.

Paul & Joe
64 rue des Sts-Pères, 7th (01.42.22.47.01, www.paulandjoe.com). Mº *Rue du Bac or St-Germain-des-Prés.* **Open** 10am-7pm Mon-Sat. **Credit** AmEx, DC, MC, V.
International fashionistas have taken a real shine to Sophie Albou's retro-styled creations. The latest collection dresses leggy young things in a superb range of winter shorts, colourful mini dresses and voluminous trousers, with their intellectual paramours in slouchy woollens, tailored jackets and chunky boots.
Other locations *Men* 56 rue Vieille-du-Temple, 3rd (01.42.72.42.06); 62 rue des Sts-Pères, 7th (01.42.22.98.98). *Women* 46 rue Etienne-Marcel, 2nd (01.40.28.03.34); 2 av Montaigne, 8th (01.47.20.57.50).

Paule Ka
223 rue St-Honoré, 1st (01.42.97.57.06, www.pauleka.com). Mº *Tuileries.* **Open** 11am-7pm Mon; 10am-7pm Tue-Sat. **Credit** AmEx, DC, MC, V.
Serge Cajfinger's '60s couture-influenced collections continue to gather a loyal following. With the opening of his rue St-Honoré boutique, he now has a foot in each of the city's fashion districts.
Other locations 20 rue Malher, 4th (01.40.29.96.03); 192 bd St-Germain, 6th (01.45.44.92.60); 45 rue François 1er, 8th (01.47.20.76.10).

Paul Smith
3 rue du Fbg-St-Honoré, 8th (01.42.68.27.10, www.paulsmith.co.uk). Mº *Concorde.* **Open** 10.30am-7pm Mon-Sat. **Credit** AmEx, DC, MC, V.
A 'so British' atmosphere is cultivated with 1940s wallpaper, antiques, old books and bric-a-brac, much of it for sale along with the colourful shirts and knitwear in which Smith excels. Collections for men, women and children, along with eyewear and accessories, are all gathered in this elegant apartment.

Prada
10 av Montaigne, 8th (01.53.23.99.40, www.prada.com). Mº *Alma Marceau.* **Open** 11am-7pm Mon; 10am-7pm Tue-Sat. **Credit** AmEx, DC, MC, V.
Miuccia Prada's elegant stores pull in fashion followers of all ages. Handbags of choice are complemented by the coveted ready-to-wear range.
Other locations 5 rue de Grenelle, 6th (01.45.48.53.14); 6 rue du Fbg-St-Honoré, 8th (01.58.18.63.30).

Rick Owens
130 galerie de Valois, 1st (01.40.20.42.52, www.owenscorp.com). Mº *Palais Royal Musée du Louvre.* **Open** 10.30am-7pm Mon; 11am-7pm Tue-Sat. **Credit** AmEx, DC, MC, V.
The LA designer and rock star favourite brings his glamour-meets-grunge style to the Palais-Royal, with hoods, zips and asymmetrical wrappings for men and women. It's not for animal lovers – the upstairs has a dedicated mink section.

Rue du Mail
5 rue du Mail, 2nd (01.42.60.19.20, www.ruedumail.com). Mº *Bourse.* **Credit** AmEx, MC, V.
Open noon-5pm Mon-Fri.
Martine Sitbon's sexy collection is a hit with Cate Blanchett, Sofia Coppola, Scarlett Johansson et al. Swooping V necklines, flirty hemlines, black satin and fruity chiffons define the look.

Sonia Rykiel
175 bd St-Germain, 6th (01.49.54.60.60, www.soniarykiel.com). Mº *St-Germain-des-Prés or Sèvres Babylone.* **Open** 10.30am-7pm Mon-Sat. **Credit** AmEx, DC, MC, V.
The queen of St-Germain celebrated the 40th birthday of her flagship store with a glamorous black and smoked glass refit perfect for narcissists: tons of mirrors reflect the flowing gowns of her current '70s throwback look. Menswear is across the street, and two newer boutiques stock the younger, more affordable Sonia by Sonia Rykiel range (61 rue des Sts-Pères, 6th, 01.49.54.61.00) and kids' togs (4 rue de Grenelle, 6th, 01.49.54.61.10). The main shop also stocks a range of designer sex toys.
Other locations throughout the city.

Stella McCartney
114-121 galerie du Valois, Jardin du Palais-Royal, 1st (01.47.03.03.80, www.stella mccartney.com). Mº *Palais Royal Musée du Louvre.* **Open** 10.30am-7pm Mon-Sat. **Credit** AmEx, DC, MC, V.
McCartney is crazy about the 'clash of history, fashion and contemporary art' at the Palais-Royal, where she has opened her sumptuous boutique overlooking the gardens. Thick carpets, maplewood and metal sculptures create a rarefied setting for women's prêt-à-porter, bags, shoes, sunglasses, lingerie, perfume and skincare.

Yohji Yamamoto
25 rue du Louvre, 1st (01.42.21.42.93, www.yohjiyamamoto.co.jp). Mº *Les Halles or Sentier.* **Open** 10.30am-7pm Mon-Sat. **Credit** AmEx, DC, MC, V.
One of the few true pioneers working in fashion today, Yamamoto is a master of cut and finish, both strongly inspired by the kimono and traditional Tibetan costume. His dexterity with form makes for unique shapes and styles, largely black. But when he does colour, it's a blast of brilliance.
Other location 4 rue Cambon, 1st (01.40.20.00.71).

Yves Saint Laurent
6 pl St-Sulpice, 6th (01.43.29.43.00, www.ysl.com). Mº *St-Sulpice.* **Open** 11am-7pm Mon; 10.30am-7pm Tue-Sat. **Credit** AmEx, DC, MC, V.
The memory of the founding designer, who died in 2008, lives on in this elegant boutique, which was splendidly refitted in red in the same year.
Other locations *Men* 32 rue du Fbg-St-Honoré, 8th (01.53.05.80.80). *Women* 38 rue du Fbg-St-Honoré, 8th (01.42.65.74.59). *Accessories* 9 rue de Grenelle, 7th (01.45.44.39.01).

Boutique & concept

AB33 and N°60
33 & 60 rue Charlot, 3rd (01.42.71.02.82, 01.44.78.91.90). Mº *Filles du Calvaire.* **Open** 11am-8pm Tue-Sun. **Credit** AmEx, MC, V.
Delicate in summer, cosy in winter, the pretty, unstructured clothes in AB33 may not make the wish list of any sultry, groomed Parisienne, but

would be perfect for her up-from-the-country Bardot-esque cousin. Owner Agathe Buchotte sells Forte, Forte, Kristina Ti and Philip Lim at this address, and in her second shop, up the road at No.60, edgier labels like McQ and Anglomania, plus a selection of slogan cotton totes.

Anikalena Skärström
16 rue du Pont aux Choux, 3rd (01.44.59.32.85, www.anikalena.com). Mº *St-Sébastien Froissart.* **Open** 11am-7pm Mon-Fri; noon-7pm Sat. Closed 2wks Aug. **Credit** MC, V.
Clean lines and streamlining are the guiding aesthetic for Anikalena's collections of sporty, sexy day and evening dresses and separates, with the occasional wow piece like the Ospoli leather jacket in 2010.

April 77
49 rue de Saintonge, 3rd (01.40.29.07.30, www.april77.fr). Mº *Filles du Calvaire.* **Open** 11am-7.30pm Mon-Sat. **Credit** MC, V.
The cult skinny jeans brand has acquired its own boutique, designed by Steven Thomas, to show off a collection inspired by the mid-'80s music scene.

Base One
47bis rue d'Orsel, 18th (01.73.75.37.10, www.baseoneshop.com). Mº *Anvers.* **Open** 11.30-8pm Tue-Fri; 11am-8pm Sat; 2.30-7pm Sun. Closed 2wks Aug. **Credit** MC, V.
Clubland duo Princesse Léa and Jean-Louis Faverole squeeze items from little-known local and international designers (Shai Wear, Li-Lei, Drolaic, OK47), plus small, established brands (Fenchurch, Motel, Consortium) into their boutique. Massive gold piggy banks from Present Time add some un-Parisian bling.

Les Belles Images
74 rue Charlot, 3rd (01.42.76.93.61, www.myspace.com/lesbellesimages). Mº *Filles du Calvaire.* **Open** 11am-7.30pm Tue-Sat. **Credit** MC, V.
A retro '60s vibe reigns at this boutique (women's and men's), where owner Sandy Bontout showcases items from current collections of obscure and big-name French and international labels, such as Ambali separates, Walk that Walk shoes and editor's picks from Veronique Leroy and Vivienne Westwood.

Colette
213 rue St-Honoré, 1st (01.55.35.33.90, www.colette.fr). Mº *Pyramides or Tuileries.* **Open** 11am-7pm Mon-Sat. **Credit** AmEx, DC, MC, V.
The renowned and much-imitated one-stop concept and lifestyle store features a highly eclectic selection of limited edition must-have accessories, fashion, sneakers, books, media, shiny new gadgets, and hair and beauty brands själ, Kiehl's and uslu airlines, all in a swanky space.

L'Eclaireur
40 rue de Sévigné, 4th (01.48.87.10.22, www.leclaireur.com). Mº *St-Paul.* **Open** 11am-7pm Mon-Sat. **Credit** AmEx, DC, MC, V.

Sophisticated, avant-garde L'Eclaireur stocks designs by Comme des Garçons, Martin Margiela, Dries van Noten, Carpe Diem and Junya Watanabe. Among its exclusive finds, check out smocks by Finnish designer Jasmin Santanen. At the secretive rue Hérold branch you have to ring the doorbell to enter. Men are catered for separately at L'Eclaireur Homme (12 rue Malher, 4th, 01.44.54.22.11).
Other locations 7 rue Hérold, 1st (01.40.41.09.89); 26 av des Champs-Elysées, 8th (01.45.62.12.32).

Galerie Simone
124 rue Vieille-du-Temple, 3rd (01.42.74.21.28). Mº *St-Sébastien Froissart.* **Open** noon-7.30pm daily. **Credit** AmEx, DC, MC, V.
Simone Gaubatz sources and cultivates talented young designers from around the world, displaying their most eye-catching creations on mannequins in this gallery-style space.

Hotel Particulier
15 rue Léopold Bellan, 2nd (01.40.39.90.00, www.hotelparticulier-paris.com). Mº *Sentier.* **Open** 11am-7.30pm Tue, Wed, Fri, Sat; 11am-9pm Thur. **Credit** AmEx, MC, V.
Paris's concept stores seduce in a way that department stores can only dream of, and new girl on the block Hotel Particulier doesn't disappoint. Positioning itself as a cosy dressing room, the boutique's small collection is as fascinating and easy to navigate as a girl's own wardrobe.

Jack Henry
25 rue Charlot, 3rd (01.42.78.93.51, www.jackhenry.fr). Mº *Filles du Calvaire.* **Open** 11am-7.30pm Tue-Sun. **Credit** AmEx, MC, V.
The work of this Paris-trained American designer has real intellectual heft to it, but you only have to touch the silky soft cotton and wool jersey from Japan to want his finely crafted, beautifully conceived tunics, skirts and jackets. Luxurious leather bags and jewellery from designers including Théodora Gabrielli, alias Dorothée, who patiently creates new pieces while serving in the shop, are also on display.

Joseph
147 bd St-Germain, 6th (01.55.42.77.55, www.joseph.co.uk). Mº *St-Germain-des-Prés.* **Open** 11am-7pm Mon, Sat; 10.30am-7pm Tue-Fri. **Credit** AmEx, DC, MC, V.
Taking a cue from its London store, Joseph opened this multi-brand shop with pieces by the likes of Balmain and Lanvin, accessories by Bijoux de Sophie and handbags by Jérôme Dreyfuss.

Kitsuné
52 rue de Richelieu, 1st (01.42.60.34.28, www.kitsune.fr). Mº *Palais Royal Musée du Louvre or Pyramides.* **Open** 11am-7.30pm Mon-Sat. **Credit** MC, V.
The London/Paris style collective's own boutique offers the entire catalogue of music compilations, as well as branded clothing that takes a back-to-basics approach using quality producers. You'll

Colette.

Ballet boutique

The **Opéra Garnier**'s formerly dowdy record shop has been transformed into a magical concept store run by Galeries Lafayette (see p80). The first part, where the old record shop used to be, hosts the world's most comprehensive collection of dance and opera books and DVDs, along with a fine collection of CDs. Among the biographies and glossy photography books, there are rarer, limited edition tomes carefully sourced from niche publishers and a large collection of dance magazines. At the back of this space big screens play the latest DVDs and you can

request to have a sneak preview of any one that takes your fancy.

Mannequins wearing Repetto tutus lure you into the second space, a long gallery theatrically lit using ceiling mirrors, which stocks an entrancing collection of toys, objets d'art and fashion for balletomanes. The children's section is a little girl's fantasy realm, with deluxe dressing-up costumes, toy theatres, and stories about the Opéra's *petits rats* and growing up to be a dancer. Adults, meanwhile, will be entranced by Sophie Mouton-Perrat's ethereal papier-mâché lights in the form of

demoiselles inspired by ballet characters. A selection of classic Paris gifts – Baccarat champagne flutes, Mariage Frères teas – have all been subtly branded for the Opéra.

Inspiration for dressing up for the gala performance is found in the form of contemporary fans by Vera Pilo and Murano glass jewellery. Finally, proving you don't have to grow up at all, there are Carrie Bradshaw-style tutus, Bompard *cache-coeurs*, Repetto shoes and a giant Tibetan goat's fleece beanbag that invites you to flump down on it wearing all of the above.

find Scottish cashmere, Japanese jeans and Italian shirts, together with items made in collaboration with Pierre Hardy and James Heeley.

Kokon To Zai
48 rue Tiquetonne, 2nd (01.42.36.92.41, www.kokontozai.co.uk). M° Etienne Marcel. **Open** 11.30am-7.30pm Mon-Sat. **Credit** AmEx, DC, MC, V.
Always a spot-on spotter of the latest creations, this tiny style emporium is sister to the Kokon To Zai in London. The neon-lit club feel of the mirrored interior matches the dark glamour of the designs. Unique pieces straight off the catwalk share space with creations by Marjan Peijoski, Noki, Raf Simons and new Norwegian designers.

LE66
66 av des Champs-Elysées, 8th (01.53.53.33.80, http://le66paris.blogspot.com). M° George V. **Open** 11am-8pm Mon-Fri; 11.30am-8.30pm Sat; 2-8pm Sun. **Credit** AmEx, DC, MC, V.
This fashion concept store is youthful and accessible, with an ever-changing selection of hip brands including Puma Black Label. Assistants, who are also the buyers and designers, make for a motivated team. The store takes the form of three transparent modules, the first a book and magazine store run by Black Book of the Palais de Tokyo, and the second two devoted to fashion. It even has its own vintage store, in collaboration with Come On Eline and Kiliwatch.

Marc by Marc Jacobs
19 pl du Marché-Saint-Honoré, 1st (01.40.20.11.30, www.marcjacobs.com). M° Tuileries. **Open** 11am-7pm Mon-Sat. **Credit** AmEx, DC, MC, V.
The new store for Jacobs' casual, punky line has fashionistas clustering like bees round a honeypot, not least for the fabulously inexpensive accessories that make great gifts. The store stocks men's and women's prêt-à-porter, plus shoes and special editions.

Margo Milin
34 rue du Bourg-Tibourg (06.61.77.14.76, www.margomilin.com). M° St-Paul. **Open** noon-7.30pm Tue-Sat; 2-6.30pm Sun. **No credit cards**.

Looking like a model herself, St Martin's graduate Marguerite Milin studied theatrical design and produces kimono-influenced wrap-around jumpers and party dresses that play with a contrast of textures and pattern versus plain. A fun, girly atmosphere is always found in the boutique.

Merci
111 bd Beaumarchais, 3rd (01.42.77.00.33, www.merci-merci.com). M° St-Sébastien Froissart. **Open** 10am-7pm Mon-Sat. **Credit** AmEx, MC, V.
See p76 **Charity shop**.

Les Prairies de Paris
23 rue Debelleyme, 3rd (01.40.20.44.12, www.lesprairiesdeparis.com). M° St-Sébastien Froissart. **Open** 10.30am-7pm Mon-Sat. **Credit** AmEx, MC, V.
Laeticia Ivanez opened this installation space/boutique in the Marais in July 2008. The whole of the ground floor is given over to art shows, gigs and happenings, with an original Peter Colombo leather chair placed centre left. Downstairs the '60s theme continues, with a cocoon-like setting in which to commune with the disco-glam separates and cute children's collection.
Other location 6 rue du Pré aux Clercs, 7th (same number).

Set Galerie
7 rue d'Uzès, 2nd (01.40.16.56.49, www.stephaneplassier.com). M° Grands Boulevards. **Open** 11am-7pm Mon-Sat. **Credit** AmEx, MC, V.
Multitalented Stéphane Plassier already has a name for himself as an interior designer, branding consultant and *metteur en scène*. Now he's opened his own concept store above the design control room of his business. Fashion lines include Dessus-Dessous (underwear), Beautiful Jacket (jackets for men) and Set in Black, a range of black dresses. The space also hosts a collection of books and objects, including a section devoted to religious kitsch.

Shine
15 rue de Poitou, 3rd (01.48.05.80.10). M° Filles du Calvaire. **Open** 11am-7.30pm Mon-Sat; 2-7pm Sun. **Credit** AmEx, MC, V.

See By Chloe, Marc by Marc Jacobs and Acne Jeans, plus Repetto shoes and Véronique Branquino, are among the goodies in this glossy showcase.

Surface 2 Air
108 rue Vieille-du-Temple, 3rd (01.44.61.76.27, www.surface2airparis.com). M° St-Sébastien Froissart. **Open** 11.30am-7.30pm Mon-Sat; noon-6pm Sun. **Credit** AmEx, MC, V.
This non-concept concept store also acts as an art gallery and graphic design agency. The cult clothing selection takes in Alice McCall's sassy frocks, Fifth Avenue Shoe Repair jeans and printed dresses by Wood Wood. For men, labels include Marios, Wendy & Jim and F-Troupe.

Womenswear

Agnès b
2, 3, 6 & 19 rue du Jour, 1st (men 01.42.33.04.13, women 01.45.08.56.56, www.agnesb.com). M° Les Halles. **Open** Oct-Apr 10am-7pm Mon-Sat. May-Sept 10.30am-7.30pm Mon-Sat. **Credit** AmEx, MC, V.
Agnès b rarely wavers from her design vision: pure lines in fine quality cotton, merino wool and silk. Best buys are shirts, pullovers and cardigans that keep their shape for years. Her mini-empire of men's, women's, children's, travel and sportswear shops is compact; see the website for details.
Other locations throughout the city.

Antoine et Lili
95 quai de Valmy, 10th (01.40.37.41.55, www.antoineetlili.com). M° Jacques Bonsergent. **Open** 11am-7pm Mon, Sun; 11am-8pm Tue-Fri; 10am-8pm Sat. **Credit** AmEx, DC, MC, V.
Antoine et Lili's fuchsia-pink, custard-yellow and apple-green shopfronts are a new raver's dream. The bobo designer's clothes, often in wraparound styles, adapt to all sizes and shapes. The Canal St-Martin 'village' comprises womenswear, a kitsch home decoration boutique and childrenswear.
Other locations throughout the city.

ba&sh
22 rue des Francs-Bourgeois, 3rd (01.42.78.55.10, www.ba-sh.com). M° Jacques

Bonsergent. **Open** 11am-7pm Mon, Sun; 11am-8pm Tue-Fri; 10am-8pm Sat. **Credit** AmEx, DC, MC, V.
This fresh, Paris-based label created by Barbara Boccara and Sharon Krief now has 350 outlets around the world, including eight Paris boutiques. You'll find dresses, skirts and blouses with ethnic touches on one side and drapey jersey on the other.
Other locations throughout the city.

COS
4 rue des Rosiers, 4th (01.44.54.37.70, www.cosstores.com). M° St-Paul. **Open** 11am-7pm Mon-Sat. **Credit** AmEx, MC, V.
H&M's upmarket brand Collection of Style (COS) now has a Paris outpost, designed by William Russell, in rue des Rosiers, causing some consternation among those who'd rather have kept this a chain-free zone.

Firmaman
200 bd Pereire, 17th (01.44.09.71.32, www.firmaman.com). M° Porte Maillot. **Open** 11am-1pm, 2-7pm Tue-Sat. **Credit** AmEx, DC, MC, V.
Realising that pregnant women have long been scouring regular boutiques for a more fashionable maternity look, Marguerite Pineau Valencienne has chosen appropriate clothes from the likes of Isabel Marant, Bash and Citizens of Humanity, displayed alongside maternity wear by Blossom, Pietro Brunelli and Virginie Castaway. The city's first maternity concept store, it also has lingerie, well-being products and gifts for new mums, dads and babies.

Iro
53 rue Vieille-du-Temple, 4th (01.42.77.25.09, www.iro.fr). M° St-Paul. **Open** 10.30am-7.30pm Mon-Sat. **Credit** AmEx, MC, V.
Fashion editors have tipped designers Laurent and Arik Bitton for stardom with what they call 'basic deluxe': skinny knits, skinny jeans, babydoll dresses and the 'perfecto' mini leather jacket. With a background in music, the brothers know how to hit just the right note for a French silhouette.
Other locations 68 rue des Sts-Pères, 7th (01.45.48.04.06).

Manoush
217 rue St Honoré, 1st (01.40.20.04.44, www.manoush.com). M° Tuileries. **Open** 10am-7pm Mon-Sat. **Credit** AmEx, DC, MC, V.
Manoush, which means 'gypsy' in French slang, has proved more than a flash-in-the-pan leftover from the boho craze of 2005 and now has four boutiques touting designer Frédérique Trou-Roy's kitsch and kooky vision.
Other locations throughout the city.

Vanessa Bruno
25 rue St-Sulpice, 6th (01.43.54.41.04, www.vanessabruno.com). M° Odéon. **Open** 10.30am-7.30pm Mon-Sat. **Credit** AmEx, DC, MC, V.
Mercerised cotton tanks, flattering trousers and feminine tops have a Zen-like quality that stems from Bruno's stay in Japan, and they somehow manage to flatter every figure type. She also makes great bags; the ample Lune was created to mark ten years in the business.
Other locations 12 rue de Castiglione, 1st (01.42.61.44.60); 100 rue Vieille-du-Temple, 3rd (01.42.77.19.41).

Zadig & Voltaire
42 rue des Francs-Bourgeois, 3rd (01.44.54.00.60, www.zadig-et-voltaire.com). M° Hôtel de Ville or St-Paul. **Open** 10.30am-7.30pm Mon-Sat; 1.30-7.30pm Sun. **Credit** AmEx, DC, MC, V.
Z&V's relaxed, urban collection is a winner. Popular separates include cotton tops, shirts and faded jeans; its winter range of cashmere jumpers is superb. The more upmarket Zadig & Voltaire De Luxe is at 18 rue François 1er (01.40.70.97.89).
Other locations throughout the city.

Menswear

Shops in **Streetwear & clubwear** (see p75) stock more casual clothes; many brands listed in **Designer** (see p71) also cater for men.

APC
38 rue Madame, 6th (01.42.22.12.77, www.apc.fr). M° St-Placide. **Open** 11am-7.30pm Mon-Sat. **Credit** AmEx, MC, V.
The look here is simple but stylish: think perfectly cut basics in muted tones. Hip without trying too hard, its jeans are a big hit with denim aficionados – the skinny version nearly caused a stampede when they came out. APC also stocks a great menswear collection.
Other locations throughout the city.

BEN ROWE

La Chemiserie

21 rue d'Uzès, 2nd (01.42.36.47.80, www.cacharel.fr). M° Grands Boulevards. **Open** 11am-7.30pm Mon-Sat. **Credit** AmEx, DC, MC, V.

Cacharel is behind this concept shirt store in a loft-style space. Cool, masculine and nonchalant, the shirts, which start at €45, have that Gallic panache for which the brand is famous, and are joined by a small selection of suits, velvet and cord blazers and cashmere scarves.

Christophe Lemaire

28 rue de Poitou, 3rd (01.44.78.00.09, www.christophelemaire.com). M° St-Sébastien Froissart. **Open** 1-7pm Mon; 12.30-7.30pm Tue-Fri; 11am-7.30pm Sat. **Credit** AmEx, DC, MC, V.

Creative director for Lacoste for seven years, Lemaire opened his own boutique in an old pharmacy. It's decorated like a fantasy apartment: the salon, in '70s gold and glitz, stocks his own-label menswear and womenswear in high-tech Japanese textiles, and leads into a soundproofed music room with a wall of old speakers where you can buy collectable Lacoste and Lemaire's own fave CDs. Next door the seductive 'Japanese salon' holds the jeans range. You can also buy the vintage lighting on display here.

Eglé Bespoke

26 rue du Mont-Thabor, 1st (01.44.15.98.31, www.eglebespoke.com). M° Concorde. **Open** 11am-7pm Mon-Sat & by appointment. **Credit** MC, V.

Two young entrepreneurs are reviving bespoke for a new generation in this tiny shop. Custom shirts start from €119 and can be delivered in a week or so; they will also make or copy shirts for women and produce made-to-order jeans for both sexes. Laser-printed buttons are perfect for stamping your beloved's shirt with a saucy message.

Jacenko

38 rue de Poitou, 3rd (01.42.71.80.38). M° St-Sébastien Froissart. **Open** 11am-7.30pm Tue-Sat; 2-7pm Sun. **Credit** MC, V.

Jacenko is a tasteful little boutique whose owner has a faultless eye for shirts, jackets, woollens and accessories that are dandy but not downright gay. McQ, Viktor & Rolf, Givenchy and John Smedley all appear.

Madelios

23 bd de la Madeleine, 1st (01.53.45.00.00, www.madelios.com). M° Madeleine. **Open** 10am-7pm Mon-Sat. **Credit** AmEx, DC, MC, V.

Madelios is a one-stop shop for men's fashion, with two floors and more than 100 labels to choose from. Suits by Kenzo, Paul Smith and Givenchy, plus shoes and accessories.

Nodus

22 rue Vieille-du-Temple, 4th (01.42.77.07.96, www.nodus.fr). M° Hôtel de Ville or St-Paul.

Open 10.45am-2pm, 3-7.30pm Mon-Sat; 1-7.30pm Sun. **Credit** AmEx, DC, MC, V.

Under the wooden beams of this cosy men's shirt specialist are displayed neat rows of striped, checked and plain dress shirts, stylish silk ties with subtle graphic designs, and silver-plated crystal cufflinks.
Other locations throughout the city.

Pull-In Underwear

8 rue Française, 2nd (01.42.36.91.06, www.pull-in.com). M° Etienne Marcel. **Open** 11am-7.30pm Mon, Wed, Fri, Sat; 11.30am-7.30pm Tue; 11.30am-2.30pm, 4-7.30pm Thur. **Credit** AmEx, MC, V.

Hailing from south-west France, Pull-In is the official underwear supplier to the French rugby team. The ultra-trendy brand makes swimwear, but its boxers in wacko patterns have now supplanted Calvin Kleins as *the* visible waistband for Gallic hip hoppers.

Purple Ice

15 rue Marie Stuart, 2nd (01.40.26.87.27, www.purpleiceboutique.com). M° Etienne Marcel. **Open** 11.30am-7.30pm Tue-Sun. **Credit** MC, V.

You'd be forgiven for assuming Romain Couapel was obsessed by Prince. He has, after all, called his shop Purple Ice, written the sign in the same '80s rock font as *Purple Rain*, and painted the walls and floor in the colour Prince called his own. But he doesn't seem that bothered by the diminutive rock guitar legend; he's more interested in the visual qualities than the back story. This attitude is mirrored in the good-looking, diverse clothes on sale: streetwear jeans by Real Real Genuine next to designer bags by JC de Castelbajac, and Vêtements de Famille's thoroughly modern take on the French Breton shirt next to Pearl Diver's retro Hawaiian shirts made in Japan.

Streetwear & clubwear

American Apparel

31 pl du Marché-St-Honoré, 1st (01.42.60.03.72, www.americanapparel.net). M° Opéra, Pyramides or Tuileries. **Open** 10am-8pm Mon-Sat; noon-7pm Sun. **Credit** AmEx, DC, MC, V.

Paris has acquired a taste for American Apparel's sweatshop-free, unisex cotton basics.
Other locations throughout the city.

Clery Brice

11 rue Pierre-Lescot, 1st (01.45.08.58.70, www.myspace.com/clerybrice). M° Les Halles/RER Châtelet Les Halles. **Open** 11am-8pm Mon-Sat; 1.30-7.30pm Sun. **Credit** MC, V.

Here you pay lofty prices to get limited editions of the coolest trainers six months before the rest of the world finds out they should be wearing them.

Ekivok

39 bd de Sébastopol, 1st (01.42.21.98.71, www.ekivok.com). M° Les Halles/RER Châtelet Les Halles. **Open** 11am-7.30pm Mon-Sat. **Credit** MC, V.

In Ekivok's graffiti-covered boutique you'll find major brands Bullrot, Carhartt, Hardcore Session and Juicy Jazz for men, and Golddigga, Punky Fish, Skunk Funk, Emilie the Strange and Hardcore Session for women, plus Eastpak accessories.

Kiliwatch

64 rue Tiquetonne, 2nd (01.42.21.17.37, http://espacekiliwatch.fr). M° Etienne Marcel. **Open** 2-7pm Mon; 11am-7.30pm Tue-Sat. **Credit** AmEx, MC, V.

The trailblazer of the rue Etienne-Marcel revival is filled to the brim with hoodies, casual shirts and washed-out jeans. Brands such as Gas, Edwin and Pepe Jeans accompany pricey second-hand garb.

Royal Cheese

24 rue Tiquetonne, 2nd (01.42.33.50.83, www.royalcheese.com). M° Etienne Marcel. **Open** 11am-1pm, 2-8pm Mon-Fri; 11am-8pm Sat. **Credit** AmEx, DC, MC, V.

Clubbers hit Royal Cheese to snaffle up hard-to-find imports: Stüssy, Cheap Monday and Lee for the boys; Insight, Sessun, Edwin and Lazy Oaf for the girls. Prices are hefty: Japanese jeans cost €200. **Other locations** 26 rue de Poitou, 3rd (01.78.56.53.56).

Y-3

47 rue Etienne-Marcel, 3rd (01.45.08.82.45, www.y-3.com). M° Bourse. **Open** 11am-7pm Mon-Sat. **Credit** AmEx, MC, V.

The first Paris boutique for this successful collaboration between Yohji Yamamoto and Adidas gives regular sportswear a kick, with high-tech fabrics, oversized pockets and elegant design.

Used & vintage

See also p81 **Antiques & flea markets.**

Adrenaline

30 rue Racine, 6th (01.44.27.09.05, www.adrenaline-vintage.com). M° Odéon. **Open** 11am-7pm Mon-Sat. **Credit** AmEx, MC, V.

This *dépôt-vente* specialises in vintage luggage and handbags. Iconic Vuitton suitcases and Kelly and Birkin bags command enormous prices, but there are some slightly more affordable pieces and a small collection of '60s couture.

La Belle Epoque

10 rue de Poitou, 3rd (06.80.77.71.32). M° St-Sébastien Froissart. **Open** 1.30-6.30pm Tue-Sat. **Credit** MC, V.

Ex-model and theatrical costumier Philippe will happily spend many hours rhapsodising about the joys of vintage. In the shop you'll find everything from the blue velours Grace Jones ensemble by Yves Saint Laurent to a selection of inexpensive '70s shirts and fake fur coats.

Come On Eileen

16-18 rue des Taillandiers, 11th (01.43.38.12.11). M° Ledru-Rollin. **Open** Sept-July 11am-8.30pm Mon-Fri; 2-8pm Sun. Aug 2-8pm Mon-Fri. **Credit** DC, MC, V.

The owners of this three-floor vintage wonderland have an excellent eye for what's funky, from cowboy gear to 1960s debutantes frocks, though prices are high.

Didier Ludot

24 galerie de Montpensier, 1st (01.42.96.06.56, www.didierludot.fr). M° Palais Royal Musée du Louvre. **Open** 10.30am-7pm Mon-Sat. **Credit** AmEx, DC, MC, V.

Didier Ludot's temples to vintage haute couture appear in Printemps, Harrods and New York's Barneys. The prices may be steep, but the pieces are truly stunning: Dior, Molyneux, Balenciaga, Pucci, Féraud and, of course, Chanel, from the 1920s onwards. Ludot also curates exhibitions, using the exclusive shop windows around the Palais-Royal as a gallery. Didier Ludot stocks his own line of vintage little black dresses, also available at La Petite Robe Noire (125 galerie de Valois, 1st, 01.40.15.01.04).

Free 'P' Star

8 rue Ste-Croix-de-la-Bretonnerie, 4th (01.42.76.03.72, www.freepstar.com). M° St-Paul. **Open** noon-10pm Mon-Sat; 2-10pm Sun. **Credit** MC, V.

L'Eclaireur. *See p73.*

DAVE BRUEL, OLIVIA RUTHERFORD

LE66.

Late-night shopping is fun at this Aladdin's cave of retro glitz, ex-army wear and glad rags that has provided fancy dress for many a Paris party.

Gabrielle Geppert
31 & 34 galerie Montpensier, 1st (01.42.61.53.52, www.gabriellegeppert.com). M° Palais Royal Musée du Louvre. **Open** 10am-7.30pm Mon-Sat. **Credit** AmEx, DC, MC, V.
If Didier Ludot is too intimidating, visit Gabrielle Geppert's shop, where much fun can be had rummaging in the back room or trying on the outrageous collection of '70s sunglasses (about €380 a pop, but they will get you into any party worth going to). A new exclusive room dedicated to accessories by the likes of Hermès and Manolo Blahnik can be opened on request, and she also carries a range of original costume jewellery by Elisabeth Ramuz.

Marie Louise de Monterey
1 rue Charles-François-Dupuis, 3rd (01.48.04.83.88, www.marielouisedemonterey.com). M° Temple. **Open** noon-7pm Tue-Sat. **Credit** MC, V.
Australian Maria Vrisakis has a wonderful eye for vintage that echoes current fashion trends, and her crisply ironed pieces are displayed in a refreshingly airy and uncluttered space. There is an adorable babywear collection and vintage Prada shoes in Cinderella sizes.

Studio W
6 rue du Pont-aux-Choux, 3rd (01.44.78.05.02). M° St-Sébastien Froissart. **Open** 2-7.30pm Tue-Sat. **Credit** MC, V.
Aesthete William Moricet's tiny shop is simply exquisite, from the vintage Courrèges and Yves Saint Laurent couture on mannequins to the glossy golden retriever who lounges among crocodile and patent leather shoes and bags.

Yukiko
97 rue Vieille-du-Temple, 3rd (01.42.71.13.41, www.yukiko-paris.com). M° St-Sébastien Froissart. **Open** 11am-1pm, 2-7.30pm Tue-Sat. **Credit** AmEx, MC, V.
Yukiko's exquisite shop is a world away from the jumble sale vibe of some second-hand clothes dens in Paris. An impressive range of vintage luxury brand accessories, her own line of simple, sexy dresses and the decor of the shop itself are all carefully colour co-ordinated, the result a harmony of burnished gold and milky pearl on salmon pink or chestnut silk against pretty pale green walls.

Charity shop Concept shopping sensation **Merci** (*see p74*) is housed in a 19th-century fabric factory. Inside, three loft-like floors heave with furniture, jewellery, stationery, fashion, household products, childrenswear and a haberdashery. That's not all. In a move that takes the trend for retailer responsibility to a new level, this most generous of general stores gives all its profits to charity.

Fashion accessories & services

Eyewear

Alain Mikli
74 rue des Sts-Pères, 7th (01.45.49.40.00, www.mikli.fr). M° Sèvres Babylone or St-Sulpice. **Open** 10am-7pm Mon-Sat. **Credit** AmEx, DC, MC, V.
Cult French designer Mikli uses cellulose acetate, a blend of wood and cotton sliced from blocks. At his flagship Starck-designed boutique, frames are laid out in a glass counter like designer sweeties.
Other locations throughout the city.

Anne et Valentin
4 rue Ste-Croix-de-la-Bretonnerie, 4th (01.40.29.93.01, www.anneetvalentin.com). M° Hôtel de Ville or St-Paul. **Open** noon-8pm Tue-Sat. Closed 12-22 Aug. **Credit** AmEx, DC, MC, V.
This modish French eyewear firm occupies a cosy three-floor Marais boutique. Anne et Valentin design chic unisex frames: light titanium models have names like Tarzan and Truman; coloured acetate frames have inventive details and fun colour combinations.

Hats & gloves

Maison Fabre
128 galerie de Valois, 1st (01.42.60.75.88, www.maisonfabre.com). M° Palais Royal Musée du Louvre. **Open** 11am-7pm Mon-Sat. **Credit** AmEx, MC, V.
This glovemaker from Millau, which was founded in 1924, has capitalised on its racy designs from the sports car eras of the 1920s and '60s. Classic gloves made from the softest leather (€100) come in 20 wild colours. Then there are the variations: crocodile, python, coyote, fur-trimmed, fingerless. But the ultimate lust object is the patent leather 'Auto' glove fastened with a massive button – between the cool of *The Avengers* and the kook of *Austin Powers*.
Other location 60 rue des Sts-Pères, 7th (01.42.22.44.86).

Maison Michel
65 rue Ste-Anne, 2nd (01.42.96.89.77, www.michel-paris.com). M° Pyramides.
Open by appointment. **Credit** MC, V.
One of the specialist businesses saved from extinction by Chanel, Maison Michel has been making hats since 1936 and supplies haute couture designers and the Paris opera. They can create the perfect panama or a flamboyant creation for the races, and also launched a prêt-à-porter range in 2006 with a range of sexy, shiny, '60s-inspired cloches and caps.

Marie Mercié
23 rue St-Sulpice, 6th (01.43.26.45.83). M° Odéon. **Open** 11am-7pm Mon-Sat. **Credit** AmEx, MC, V.
Marie Mercié's creations make you wish you lived in an era when hats were de rigueur. Step out in one shaped like curved fingers (complete with shocking-pink nail varnish and pink diamond ring) or a beret like a face with red lips and turquoise eyes. Ready-to-wear starts at €30; *sur mesure* takes ten days.

Jewellery

Dotted in and around place Vendôme, the key *joailliers* define the luxurious spirit of Paris. The Marais is home to a number of fashion and costume jewellery boutiques.

Boucheron
26 pl Vendôme, 1st (01.42.61.58.16, www.boucheron.com). M° Opéra. **Open** 10.30am-7pm Mon-Sat. **Credit** AmEx, DC, MC, V.
Boucheron was the first to set up shop on place Vendôme, attracting celebrity custom from the nearby Ritz hotel. Owned by Gucci, the grand jeweller produces stunning pieces, using traditional motifs with new accents: take, for example, its fabulous chocolate-coloured gold watch.
Other location 32 rue du Fbg-St-Honoré, 8th (01.44.51.95.20).

Cartier
13 rue de la Paix, 2nd (01.58.18.23.00, www.cartier.com). M° Opéra. **Open** 10.30am-7pm Mon-Sat. **Credit** AmEx, DC, MC, V.
This iconic French jeweller and watchmaker has impressive landmark headquarters. Downstairs, pearls, panthers and the Trinity ring jostle for attention among historic pieces commissioned by crowned heads; the upper salons house perfumer Mathilde Laurent's bespoke scents.
Other locations throughout the city.

Chanel Joaillerie
18 pl Vendôme, 1st (01.55.35.50.05, www.chanel.com). M° Opéra or Tuileries. **Open** 11am-7pm Mon-Sat. **Credit** AmEx, DC, MC, V.
Chanel launched its fine jewellery in the 1990s, reissuing the single collection – big on platinum and diamonds – that Coco herself designed some 60 years previously. The current line reinterprets the motifs – camellias, stars and comets – to create a collection of contemporary classics.

Dior Joaillerie
8 pl Vendôme, 1st (01.42.96.30.84, www.dior.com). M° Opéra or Tuileries. **Open** 11am-7pm Mon, Sat; 10.30am-7pm Tue-Fri. **Credit** AmEx, DC, MC, V.
The unabashed bling of Victoire de Castellane's designs is responsible for the fad of semi-precious coloured stones and runaway success of the 'Mimi Oui', a ring with a tiny diamond on a slim chain.
Other locations 28 av Montaigne, 8th (01.47.23.52.39).

Karry'O
62 rue des Sts-Pères, 6th (01.45.48.94.67, www.karryo.com). M° St-Germain-des-Prés.
Open 11am-7pm Mon-Sat. **Credit** MC, V.
Paris socialites come here to source their vintage jewellery, as well as modern gems by owner Karine Berrebi. Her adjacent gallery, Unique, features one-of-a-kind finds, from jewels and decorative objects to Hermès bags and the occasional Schiaparelli fur.

Marie-Hélène de Taillac
8 rue de Tournon, 6th (01.44.27.07.07, www.mariehelenedetaillac.com). M° Mabillon.
Open 11am-7pm Mon-Sat. **Credit** MC, V.
Marie-Hélène de Taillac is a fine jeweller. But unlike her colleagues across the Seine, her diamonds and emeralds in simple, unpretentious settings work well with jeans and don't make her customers look like ancestral portraits. This combination of precious stones and modern styling has made her hugely popular with the fashion elite. No doubt they also adore her Left Bank shop – a Tom Dixon-designed space in Marie-Hélène's trademark luminous pale blue and pillar box red, complete with a technicolour painting of Jaipur.

Viveka Bergström
23 rue de la Grange aux Belles, 10th (01.40.03.04.92, www.viveka-bergstrom.com). M° Colonel Fabien. **Open** 11am-7pm Mon-Sat. **Credit** AmEx, MC, V.
The daughter of Saab's aeroplane designer in the 1950s, Viveka Bergström makes tassel necklaces, oversized beaten gold rings and brooches, and conversation starters like the angel-wing bracelet and a necklace featuring a map of Paris.

Lingerie & swimwear

For swimwear, *see also p82* **Sport & fitness**.

Alice Cadolle
4 rue Cambon, 1st (01.42.60.94.22, www.cadolle.com). M° Concorde or Madeleine.
Open 10am-6.30pm Mon-Sat. Closed Aug. **Credit** AmEx, MC, V.
Five generations of lingerie-makers are behind this boutique, founded by Hermine Cadolle, who claimed to be the inventor of the bra. Great-great-granddaughter Poupie Cadolle continues the tradition in a cosy space devoted to a luxury ready-to-wear line of bras, panties and corsets. For a special treat, Cadolle Couture (255 rue St-Honoré, 1st, 01.42.60.94.94) will create indulgent bespoke lingerie (by appointment only).

Erès
2 rue Tronchet, 8th (01.47.42.28.82, www.eres.fr). M° Madeleine. **Open** 10am-7pm Mon-Sat. **Credit** AmEx, DC, MC, V.
Erès's beautifully cut swimwear has embraced a sexy '60s look complete with buttons on the low-cut briefs. To make life easier, the top and bottom can be purchased in different sizes or you can buy one piece of a bikini.
Other locations 4bis rue du Cherche-Midi, 6th (01.45.44.95.54); 40 av Montaigne, 8th (01.47.23.07.26); 6 rue Guichard, 16th (01.46.47.45.21).

Etam Lingerie
139 rue de Rennes, 6th (01.45.44.16.88, www.etam.com). M° Montparnasse-Bienvenüe.
Open 10am-8pm Mon-Sat. **Credit** AmEx, DC, MC, V.
Etam, which started out in lingerie in 1916, has now opened the largest lingerie store in Europe. It may be quantity over quality, but who can resist the 'bar à culottes' or the 'hot and spicy corner'?

Fifi Chachnil
231 rue St-Honoré, 1st (01.42.61.21.83, www.fifichachnil.com). M° Tuileries. **Open** 11am-7pm Mon-Sat. **Credit** AmEx, MC, V.
Chachnil has a new approach to frou-frou underwear in the pin-up tradition. Her chic mixes – deep red silk bras with boudoir pink bows, and pale turquoise girdles with orange trim – will have ladies and their male admirers purring in delight.
Other locations 68 rue Jean-Jacques-Rousseau, 1st (01.42.21.19.93).

Princesse Tam-Tam
52 bd St-Michel, 6th (01.40.51.72.99, www.princessetamtam.com). M° Cluny La Sorbonne. **Open** 1.30-7pm Mon; 10am-7pm Tue, Thur-Sat; 10am-1.30pm, 2-7pm Wed. **Credit** AmEx, MC, V.
This inexpensive underwear and swimwear brand, which celebrated its 25th anniversary in 2010, has traffic-stopping promotions. Bright colours and sexily transparent and sporty gear rule.
Other locations throughout the city.

Sabbia Rosa
73 rue des Sts-Pères, 6th (01.45.48.88.37). M° St-Germain-des-Prés. **Open** 10am-7pm Mon-Sat. **Credit** AmEx, MC, V.
Let Moana Moatti tempt you with feather-trimmed satin mules, or satin, silk and chiffon negligées in fine shades of tangerine, lemon, mocha or pistachio. All sizes are medium, others are made *sur mesure*; prices are just the right side of stratospheric.

Vannina Vesperini
4 rue de Tournon, 6th (01.56.24.32.72, www.vanninavesperini.com). M° Odéon. **Open** 11am-7pm Mon-Sat. **Credit** AmEx, MC, V.
Only the finest silk satin is used for this designer's underwear, camisoles and sophisticated nightwear. The boutique has a made-to-measure *atelier*.

Yoba
11 rue du Marché-St-Honoré, 1st (01.40.41.04.06, www.yobaparis.com). M° Tuileries. **Open** 11am-8pm Mon-Fri; noon-8pm Sat. **Credit** MC, V.
One for the liberated ladies, this smart boutique stocks items from wispy lingerie to sex toys.

Shoes & bags

An entire floor of footwear can be found at **Printemps** (*see p69*). Rue du Dragon, rue de Grenelle and rue du Cherche-Midi form the backbone of an area that is a must for shoe and accessory addicts.

Bruno Frisoni
34 rue de Grenelle, 7th (01.42.84.12.30, www.brunofrisoni.fr). M° Rue du Bac. **Open** 10.30am-7pm Tue-Sat. **Credit** AmEx, V.
Innovative Frisoni's shoes have a cinematic, pop edge: modern theatrics for the unconventional.

OLIVER KNIGHT

Christian Louboutin
19 rue Jean-Jacques-Rousseau, 1st (01.42.36.53.66, www.christianlouboutin.com). M° Palais Royal Musée du Louvre. **Open** 10.30am-7pm Mon-Sat. Closed 3wks Aug. **Credit** AmEx, MC, V.
Every fashionista, WAG and shoe fiend worth her salt owns or hankers after a pair of Louboutin's trademark red-soled creations. Each design is displayed to maximum advantage in an individual frame. There's a made-to-measure service. **Other locations** 38 rue de Grenelle, 7th (01.42.22.33.07); 68 rue du Fbg-St-Honoré, 8th (01.42.68.37.65).

Hervé Chapelier
1bis rue du Vieux-Colombier, 6th (01.44.07.06.50, www.hervechapelier.fr). M° St-Germain-des-Prés or St-Sulpice. **Open** 10.15am-7pm Mon-Sat. **Credit** AmEx, MC, V.
Bag yourself a classic, chic, hard-wearing, bicoloured tote at Hervé Chapelier. Sizes and prices range from a dinky purse at €22 to a weekend bag at €130.
Other locations throughout the city.

Iris
28 rue de Grenelle, 7th (01.42.22.89.81, www.irisshoes.com). M° Rue du Bac or St-Sulpice. **Open** 10.30am-7pm Mon-Sat. **Credit** AmEx, MC, V.
This white boutique stocks shoes by the likes of Marc Jacobs, John Galliano, Proenza-Schouler and Viktor & Rolf.

Jamin Puech
61 rue de Hauteville, 10th (01.40.22.08.32, www.jamin-puech.com). M° Poissonnière. **Open** 11am-7pm Mon-Fri; noon-7pm Sat. **Credit** AmEx, DC, MC, V.
The complete collection of Isabelle Puech and Benoît Jamin's dazzling handbags is displayed in a bohemian setting with antler-horn chairs.
Other locations throughout the city.

K Jacques
16 rue Pavée, 4th (01.40.27.03.57, www.kjacques.fr). M° St-Paul. **Open** 10am-6.45pm Mon-Sat; 2-6.45pm Sun. **Credit** MC, V.
Set up in Saint-Tropez in 1933 by Jacques Keklikian and his wife, the K Jacques workshop started life stitching together basic leather sandals for visitors to the Med resort. The Homère (or Homer), a Greco Roman-style sandal with five horizontal straps across the foot, was, and still is, the signature piece – Picasso loved them. Now the company offers a range of around 60 styles that subtly reflect the trends of the last 70 years, but remain, in essence, simple, hard-wearing sandals.

Moss
22 rue de Grenelle, 7th (01.42.22.01.42). M° Rue du Bac or St-Sulpice. **Open** 10.30am-7pm Mon-Sat. **Credit** AmEx, MC, V.
The three sisters who run this boutique pride themselves on sourcing cutting-edge shoes, that can be hard to find elsewhere, such as creations by former Celine stylist Avril Gau and signature designs by Laurence Dacade, Duccio del Duca and Hartian Bourdin. You'll also find scarves by Octavio Pizzaro and jewellery by Karry'O, the fourth sister.

Peggy Huyn Kinh
9-11 rue Coëtlogon, 6th (01.42.84.83.82, www.phk.fr). M° St-Sulpice. **Open** 11am-7pm Mon-Sat. **Credit** AmEx, MC, V.
Once creative director at Cartier, Peggy Huyn Kinh now makes bags of boar skin and python, as well as silver jewellery.

Pierre Hardy
156 galerie de Valois, 1st (01.42.60.59.75, www.pierrehardy.com). M° Palais Royal Musée du Louvre. **Open** 11am-7pm Mon-Sat. **Credit** AmEx, DC, MC, V.
This classy black-and-white shoebox is home to Hardy's range of superbly conceived footwear – with a price tag to match – for men and women.
Other location 9-11 pl du Palais Bourbon, 7th (01.45.55.00.67).

Repetto
22 rue de la Paix, 2nd (01.44.71.83.12, www.repetto.com). M° Opéra. **Open** 9.30am-7.30pm Mon-Sat. **Credit** AmEx, MC, V.
This ballet shoe-maker struck gold when it decided to reissue its dance shoes with pavement soles. The prowly *ballerines* and showbiz dance boots in black, metallic and spangly finishes are fun, stylish and exceptionally comfortable. They are sold alongside the full range of real balletwear; you can try out your *pointes* on a red carpet with a *barre* if you want to show off.
Other locations 51 rue du Four, 6th (01.45.44.98.65).

Rodolphe Menudier
14 rue de Castiglione, 1st (01.42.60.86.27, www.rodolphemenudier.com). M° Concorde or Tuileries. **Open** 11am-7pm Mon; 10am-7pm Tue-Sat. **Credit** AmEx, MC, V.
This boutique makes the perfect backdrop for Menudier's racy designs. Open, silver-handled drawers display his stilettos in profile, as well as outrageous thigh-high boots with Plexiglass soles; more demure customers can opt for a pair of pumps.

Roger Vivier
29 rue du Fbg-St-Honoré, 8th (01.53.43.00.85, www.rogervivier.com). M° Concorde or Madeleine. **Open** 11am-7pm Mon-Sat. **Credit** AmEx, DC, MC, V.
The fashion editors' shoeman of choice, Vivier is credited with inventing the stiletto.

Food & drink

You could spend a lifetime sampling the breads, pastries, chocolate and cheeses available in Paris. Open-air markets continue to beckon with their fresh, seasonal produce, and **Galeries Lafayette** and **Le Bon Marché** (for both, *see p69*) have luxury food halls.

Bakeries

Arnaud Delmontel
39 rue des Martyrs, 9th (01.48.78.29.33, www.arnaud-delmontel.com). M° St-Georges. **Open** 7am-8.30pm Mon, Wed-Sun. **No credit cards.**
With its crisp crust and chewy crumb shot through with irregular holes, Delmontel's Renaissance bread is one of the finest in Paris. He puts the same skill into his unsurpassable almond croissants.
Other locations 57 rue Damrémont, 18th (01.42.64.59.63).

L'Autre Boulange
43 rue de Montreuil, 11th (01.43.72.86.04, www.lautreboulange.com). M° Faidherbe Chaligny or Nation. **Open** 7.30am-1.30pm, 4-7.30pm Mon-Fri; 7.30am-1.30pm Sat. Closed Aug. **Credit** MC, V.

Christian Louboutin.

Michel Cousin bakes up to 23 different types of organic loaf in his wood-fired oven – varieties include the *flutiot* (rye bread with raisins, walnuts and hazelnuts) and a spiced cornmeal bread.

Le Boulanger de Monge
123 rue Monge, 5th (01.43.37.54.20, www.leboulangerdemonge.com). M° Censier Daubenton. **Open** 7am-8.30pm Tue-Sun. **Credit** MC, V.
Dominique Saibron uses spices to give inimitable flavour to his organic sourdough *boule*. Every day about 2,000 bread-lovers visit this boutique, which also produces one of the city's best baguettes.

Le Grenier à Pain
38 rue des Abbesses, 18th (01.46.06.41.81). M° Abbesses. **Open** 7.30am-8pm Mon, Wed-Sun. **No credit cards.**
Expect queues at this Montmartre bakery, winner in March 2010 of the 17th Grand Prix de la Baguette de Tradition Française de la Ville de Paris. As well as gaining plenty of new customers, Baker Djibril Bodian also picked up a cash prize of €4,000 and a contract to keep President Nicolas Sarkozy in bread for a year.

Moisan
5 pl d'Aligre, 12th (01.43.45.46.60, www.painmoisan.fr). M° Ledru-Rollin. **Open** 7am-8pm Tue-Sat; 7am-2pm Sun. **No credit cards.**
Moisan's organic bread, *viennoiseries* and rustic tarts are outstanding. At this branch, situated by the market, there's always a healthy queue.
Other locations throughout the city.

Du Pain et des Idées
34 rue Yves Toudic, 10th (01.42.40.44.52, www.dupainetdesidees.com). M° Jacques Bonsergent. **Open** 6.45am-8pm Mon-Fri. **No credit cards.**
Christophe Vasseur won the Gault-Millau prize for Best Bakery. Among his specialities are Le Rabelais – *pain brioché* with saffron, honey and nuts; and Le Pagnol aux Pommes, a bread studded with royal gala apple (skin on), raisins and orange flower water.

Poilâne
8 rue du Cherche-Midi, 6th (01.45.48.42.59, www.poilane.com). M° Sèvres Babylone or St-Sulpice. **Open** 7.15am-8.15pm Mon-Sat. **Credit** (€20 minimum) AmEx, DC, MC, V.
Apollonia Poilâne runs the family shop, where locals queue for country *miches*, flaky-crusted apple tarts and buttery shortbread biscuits.
Other locations 49 bld de Grenelle, 15th (01.45.79.11.49).

Cheese

The sign *maître fromager affineur* denotes merchants who buy young cheeses from farms and age them on their premises; *fromage fermier* and *fromage au lait cru* signify farm-produced and unpasteurised cheeses respectively.

Alléosse
13 rue Poncelet, 17th (01.46.22.50.45, www.fromage-alleosse.com). M° Ternes. **Open** 9am-1pm, 4-7pm Tue-Thur; 9am-1pm, 4.30-7pm Fri, Sat. **Credit** MC, V.
People cross town for these cheeses – wonderful farmhouse camemberts, delicate st-marcellins, a choice of *chèvres* and several rarities.

Fromagerie Dubois et Fils
80 rue de Tocqueville, 17th (01.42.27.11.38). M° Malesherbes or Villiers. **Open** 9am-1pm, 4-8pm Tue-Fri; 8.30am-7.45pm Sat; 9am-1pm Sun. Closed 1st 3wks Aug. **Credit** AmEx, MC, V.
Superchef darling Dubois stocks 80 types of goat's cheese, plus prized, aged st-félicien.

Fromagerie Quatrehomme
62 rue de Sèvres, 7th (01.47.34.33.45). M° Duroc or Vaneau. **Open** 8.45am-1pm, 4-7.45pm Tue-Thur; 8.45am-7.45pm Fri, Sat. **Credit** MC, V.
Marie Quatrehomme runs this *fromagerie*. Justly famous for her beaufort and st-marcellin, she also sells specialities such as goat's cheese with pesto.
Other locations 9 rue du Poteau, 18th (01.46.06.26.03).

Marie-Anne Cantin
12 rue du Champ-de-Mars, 7th (01.45.50.43.94, www.cantin.fr). M° Ecole Militaire or Latour Maubourg. **Open** 2-7.30pm Mon; 8.30am-7.30pm Tue-Sat; 8.30am-1pm Sun. **Credit** AmEx, MC, V.

1000s of things to do...

1000 Great Holiday Ideas

1000 things to do in London

1000 things to do in New York

1000 things to do in London for under £10

1000 things for kids to do in the holidays

1000 things to do in Britain

**TIME OUT GUIDES
WRITTEN BY
LOCAL EXPERTS**
Visit timeout.com/shop

Time Out
Guides

Cantin, a stout defender of unpasteurised cheese and supplier to many posh Paris restaurants, offers aged *chèvres* and amazing morbier, mont d'or and comté.

Chocolate

Cacao et Chocolat
29 rue de Buci, 6th (01.46.33.77.63, www.cacaoetchocolat.com). M° Mabillon. **Open** 10.30am-7.30pm daily. **Credit** AmEx, DC, MC, V.
This shop recalls chocolate's Aztec origins, with its choice of spicy fillings (honey and chilli, nutmeg, clove and citrus), chocolate masks and pyramids. **Other locations** 63 rue St-Louis-en-l'Ile, 4th (01.46.33.33.33); 36 rue Vieille-du-Temple, 4th (01.42.71.50.06).

Christian Constant
37 rue d'Assas, 6th (01.53.63.15.15, www.christianconstant.fr). M° Rennes or St-Placide. **Open** 9.30am-8.30pm Mon-Fri; 9am-8pm Sat, Sun. **Credit** MC, V.
A master chocolate-maker and *traiteur*, Christian Constant scours the globe for new ideas. His *ganaches* are subtly flavoured with verbena, jasmine or cardamom.

Jacques Génin
133 rue de Turenne, 3rd (01.45.77.29.01, www.jacquesgenin.com). M° Filles de Calvaire. **Open** 11am-9pm Mon-Sat. **Credit** MC, V.
Jacques Génin's creations could previously only be tasted in top restaurants. But now his impressive boutique allows you to taste *sur place* or take a bag home. The signature eclairs and tarts glisten in glass cases, and the millefeuilles are made to order for perfect freshness. The chocolate ganaches include Menthe Amante, a two-phase taste sensation that finishes with mint leaves bursting on the tongue. One part of the vast space is given over to a tearoom, and a spiral staircase leads to the *ateliers*.

Jean-Paul Hévin
3 rue Vavin, 6th (01.43.54.09.85, www.jphevin.com). M° Notre-Dame-des-Champs or Vavin. **Open** 10am-7.30pm Tue-Sat. Closed Aug. **Credit** AmEx, MC, V.
Hévin specialises in the beguiling combination of chocolate with potent cheese fillings, which loyal customers serve with wine as an aperitif. **Other locations** 231 rue St-Honoré, 1st (01.55.35.35.96); 23bis av de La Motte-Picquet, 7th (01.45.51.77.48).

La Maison du Chocolat
120 av Victor-Hugo, 16th (01.40.67.77.83, www.lamaisonduchocolat.com). M° Victor Hugo. **Open** 10am-7pm Mon-Sat; 10am-1pm Sun (closed Mon & Sun in July, Aug). **Credit** AmEx, MC, V.
Robert Linxe opened his first Paris shop in 1977, and has been inventing delicious new chocolates ever since, using Asian spices, fresh fruits and herbal infusions. **Other locations** throughout the city.

Patrick Roger
108 bd St-Germain, 6th (01.43.29.38.42, www.patrickroger.com). M° Odéon. **Open** 10.30am-7.30pm Mon-Sat. **Credit** MC, V.
Roger is shaking up the art of chocolate-making. Whereas other *chocolatiers* aim for gloss, Roger may create a brushed effect on hens so realistic you almost expect them to lay (chocolate) eggs. **Other locations** 91 rue de Rennes, 6th (01.45.44.66.13); 199 rue du Fbg-St-Honoré, 8th (01.45.61.11.46); 45 av Victor-Hugo, 16th (01.45.01.66.71).

Richart
258 bd St-Germain, 7th (01.45.55.66.00, www.richart.com). M° Solférino. **Open** 10am-7pm Mon-Sat. **Credit** AmEx, MC, V.
Each chocolate *ganache* at Richart has an intricate design, packages look like jewel boxes, and each purchase comes with a tract on how best to savour the stuff.

Drinks

Les Caves Augé
116 bd Haussmann, 8th (01.45.22.16.97, www.cavesauge.com). M° St-Augustin. **Open** 1-7.30pm Mon; 9am-7.30pm Tue-Sat. Closed Mon in Aug. **Credit** AmEx, MC, V.
Les Caves Augé is the oldest wine shop in Paris – Marcel Proust was a regular customer – and offers a serious and professional service.

Les Caves Taillevent
199 rue du Fbg-St-Honoré, 8th (01.45.61.14.09, www.taillevent.com).

Poilâne. *See p77.*

M° Charles de Gaulle Etoile or Ternes. **Open** 10am-7.30pm Tue-Sat. Closed 1st 3wks Aug. **Credit** AmEx, DC, MC, V.
Choose from nearly half a million wines to go with your meal at the nearby Taillevent restaurant (*see p52*).

Julien, Caviste
50 rue Charlot, 3rd (01.42.72.00.94). M° Filles du Calvaire. **Open** 9am-1.30pm, 3.30-7.30pm Tue-Sat; 10.30am-1.30pm Sun. Closed 3rd wk Aug. **Credit** AmEx, MC, V.
Julien promotes the small producers he has discovered, and often holds wine tastings on Saturdays.

Lavinia
3 bd de la Madeleine, 1st (01.42.97.20.20, www.lavinia.fr). M° Madeleine. **Open** 10am-8pm Mon-Sat. **Credit** AmEx, DC, MC, V.
Lavinia stocks a broad selection of French alongside many non-French wines; its glassed-in cave has everything from a 1945 Mouton-Rothschild at €22,000 to trendy and 'fragile' wines for under €10. Have fun tasting wine with the *dégustation* machines on the ground floor, which allow customers to taste a sip of up to ten different wines each week for €10.

Legrand Filles et Fils
1 rue de la Banque, 2nd (01.42.60.07.12, www.caves-legrand.com). M° Bourse. **Open** 11am-7pm Mon; 10am-7.30pm Tue-Fri; 10am-7pm Sat. Closed Mon in July & Aug. **Credit** AmEx, MC, V.
Fine wines and brandies, teas and *bonbons*, and a showroom for regular wine tastings.

Ryst Dupeyron
79 rue du Bac, 7th (01.45.48.80.93, www.vintageandco.com). M° Rue du Bac. **Open** 12.30-7.30pm Mon; 10.30am-7.30pm Tue-Sat. Closed 2wks Aug. **Credit** AmEx, MC, V.
The Dupeyrons have been selling armagnac for four generations, and still have bottles from 1868. Treasures here include 200 fine Bordeaux wines and an extensive range of vintage port.

Global

Les Délices d'Orient
52 av Emile-Zola, 15th (01.45.79.10.00). M° Charles Michels. **Open** 8.30am-9pm Tue-Sun. **Credit** MC, V.
Shelves here groan under the weight of stuffed aubergines, halva, falafel and all manner of Middle Eastern delicacies. **Other locations** 14 rue des Quatre-Frères-Peignot, 15th (01.45.77.82.93).

Izraël
30 rue François-Miron, 4th (01.42.72.66.23). M° Hôtel de Ville. **Open** 9.30am-1pm, 2.30-7pm Tue-Fri; 9.30am-7pm Sat. Closed Aug. **Credit** MC, V.
A Marais fixture, this narrow shop stocks spices and other delights from Mexico, Turkey and India.

Jabugo Ibérico & Co
11 rue Clément-Marot, 8th (01.47.20.03.13). M° Alma Marceau or Franklin D. Roosevelt. **Open** 10am-9pm Mon-Sat. **Credit** AmEx, DC, MC, V.
Spanish hams here have the Bellota-Bellota label, meaning that the pigs have been allowed to feast on acorns. Manager Philippe Poulachon compares his cured hams to the delicacy of truffles.

Markets

The city council has made markets more accessible by extending their opening hours. There are now more than 70 markets in Paris. The city council's website (www.paris.fr) has full details of each one; below is a selection of the best.

Marché Anvers
Pl d'Anvers, 9th. M° Anvers. **Open** 3-8.30pm Fri.
An afternoon market that adds to the village atmosphere of a peaceful *quartier* down the hill from Montmartre. Among its highlights are regional vegetables, hams from the Auvergne, lovingly aged cheeses and award-winning honey.

Marché Bastille
Bd Richard-Lenoir, 11th. M° Richard-Lenoir. **Open** 7am-2.30pm Thur; 7am-3pm Sun.
One of the biggest markets in Paris. A favourite of political campaigners, it's also a great source of local cheeses, farmers' chicken and excellent fish.

Marché Batignolles
Rue Lemercier, 17th. M° Brochant. **Open** 8.30am-1pm, 3.30-8pm Tue-Fri; 8.30am-8pm Sat; 8.30am-3pm Sun.
Batignolles is more down to earth than the better-known Raspail organic market, with a quirky selection of stallholders, many of whom produce what they sell. Prices are higher here than at ordinary markets, but the goods are worth it.

Marché Beauvau
Pl d'Aligre, 12th. M° Ledru-Rollin. **Open** 9am-1pm, 4-7.30pm Tue-Fri; 9am-1pm, 3.30-7.30pm Sat; 8.30am-1.30pm Sun.
This market is proudly working class. Stallholders do their utmost to out-shout each other, and price-conscious shoppers don't compromise on quality.

Marché Monge
Pl Monge, 5th. M° Place Monge. **Open** 7am-2.30pm Wed, Fri; 7am-3pm Sun.
This pretty, compact market is set on a leafy square. It has a high proportion of producers and is much less touristy than nearby rue Mouffetard.

Marché Président-Wilson
Av Président-Wilson, 16th. M° Alma-Marceau or Iéna. **Open** 7am-2.30pm Wed; 7am-3pm Sat.
A classy market attracting the city's top chefs, who snap up ancient vegetable varieties.

Saxe-Breteuil
Av de Saxe, 7th. M° Ségur. **Open** 7am-2.30pm Thur; 7am-3pm Sat.
Saxe-Breteuil has an unrivalled setting facing the Eiffel Tower, as well as the city's most chic produce. Look for farmer's goat's cheese, rare apple varieties, Armenian specialities, abundant oysters and a handful of dedicated small producers.

Pâtisseries

Arnaud Larher
53 rue Caulaincourt, 18th (01.42.57.68.08, www.arnaud-larher.com). M° Lamarck Caulaincourt. **Open** 10am-7.30pm Tue-Sat. **Credit** MC, V.
Look out for the strawberry-and-lychee flavoured *bonheur* and the chocolate-and-thyme *récif*.

Finkelsztajn
27 rue des Rosiers, 4th (01.42.72.78.91, www.laboutiquejaune.com). M° St-Paul. **Open** 10am-7pm Mon, Wed-Sun. Closed 15 July-15 Aug. **Credit** (€20 minimum) AmEx, MC, V.
This motherly, yellow-fronted shop, in business since 1946, stocks dense Jewish cakes filled with poppy seeds, apples or cream cheese.

Gérard Mulot
76 rue de Seine, 6th (01.43.26.85.77, www.gerard-mulot.com). M° Odéon. **Open** 6.45am-8pm Mon, Tue, Thur-Sun. Closed Easter & Aug. **Credit** V.
Gérard Mulot rustles up stunning pastries. Try the *mabillon*: caramel mousse with apricot marmalade. **Other locations** 93 rue de la Glacière, 13th (01.45.81.39.09).

Pierre Hermé
72 rue Bonaparte, 6th (01.43.54.47.77). M° Mabillon, St-Germain-des-Prés or St-Sulpice. **Open** 10am-7pm Tue-Fri, Sun; 10am-7.30pm Sat. Closed 1st 3wks Aug. **Credit** AmEx, DC, MC, V.
Pastry superstar Hermé attracts connoisseurs from St-Germain-des-Prés and afar with his seasonal collections. **Other locations** 4 rue Cambon, 1st (01.43.54.47.77); 185 rue de Vaugirard, 15th (01.47.83.89.96).

Treats & *traiteurs*

Da Rosa
62 rue de Seine, 6th (01.45.21.41.30, www.restaurant-da-rosa.com). M° Odéon. **Open** 10am-11pm daily. **Credit** AmEx, MC, V.
José Da Rosa used to source ingredients for top restaurants before filling his own shop with Spanish hams, Olivier Roellinger spices and Luberon truffles.

Dammann Frères
15 pl des Vosges, 4th (01.44.54.04.88, www.dammann.fr). M° St-Paul. **Open** 11am-7pm daily. **Credit** AmEx, DC, MC, V.

ELAN FLEISHER

Marché Président-Wilson. *See p79.*

Dammann Frères, fine tea importers since 1825, have opened their own boutique, a wonderful den of a place with a beamed roof and mahogany shelves displaying hundreds of exquisite black boxes. The 'orgue à thés' allows you to sniff the aromas of 160 blends. A small tin of loose tea or 24 tea bags costs €7 and they also sell traditional oriental iron teapots, all attractively gift-wrapped.

Fauchon
26 & 30 pl de la Madeleine, 8th (01.70.39.38.00, www.fauchon.com). M° Madeleine. **Open** *No.26* 8am-9pm Mon-Sat. *No.30* 9am-9pm Mon-Sat. **Credit** AmEx, MC, V.
The city's most famous food shop is worth a visit, particularly for the beautifully packaged gift items and the stunning pastries and cakes – or, as Fauchon likes to call them, '*le snacking chic*'.

Hédiard
21 pl de la Madeleine, 8th (01.43.12.88.88, www.hediard.fr). M° Madeleine. **Open** 8.30am-9pm Mon-Sat. **Credit** AmEx, DC, MC, V.
Hédiard's charming shop dates back to 1880, when they were the first to introduce exotic foods to Paris, specialising in rare teas and coffees, spices, jams and candied fruits. Pop upstairs for a cuppa in the shop's posh tearoom, La Table d'Hédiard. **Other locations** throughout the city.

Huilerie Artisanale Leblanc
6 rue Jacob, 6th (01.46.34.61.55, www.huile-leblanc.com). M° St-Germain-des-Prés. **Open** noon-7pm Tue-Fri; 10am-7pm Sat. Closed 2wks Aug. **No credit cards.**
The Leblanc family from Burgundy started making walnut oil before branching out to press pure oils from hazelnuts, almonds, pine nuts, grilled peanuts and olives. Also on offer is a selection of vinegars and mustards.

Première Pression Provence
3 rue Antoine Vollon, 12th (01.53.33.03.59, www.premiere-pression-provence.com). M° Ledru Rollin. **Open** 11am-2.30pm, 3.30-7pm Tue-Sat. **Credit** AmEx, MC, V.
Première Pression Provence is L'Occitan creator Olivier Baussan's project, where you are encouraged to taste spoonfuls of single-producer olive oil to educate your palate about the nuances of *vert*, *mûr* and *noir* (known as the '*fruités*'). Two dozen small producers send their oils direct from their Provençal olive groves to the boutiques, where they are sold in aluminium cans with colour-coded labels.
Other locations 9 rue des Martyrs, 9th (01.48.78.86.51); 37 rue du Roi de Sicile, 4th (01.49.96.55.40).

Torréfacteur Verlet
256 rue St-Honoré, 1st (01.42.60.67.39, www.cafesverlet.com). M° Palais Royal Musée du Louvre. **Open** 9.30am-6.30pm Mon-Sat. Closed Aug. **Credit** MC, V.
Eric Duchossoy roasts rare coffee beans to perfection – sip a cup here or take some home to savour.

Gifts & souvenirs

Florists

Culture(s)
46 rue de Lancry, 10th (01.48.03.58.71). M° Jacques Bonsergent or République. **Open** 11am-2pm; 3-7pm Tue-Sat. **Credit** AmEx, MC, V.
In a loft-style studio, this unusual florist combines exotic flowers, trees and garden themed items, such as floral printed rain hats. Truly original.

Au Nom de la Rose
87 rue St-Antoine, 4th (01.42.71.34.24, www.aunomdelarose.fr). M° St-Paul. **Open** *Sept-July* 10am-9pm daily. *Aug* 10am-9pm Mon-Sat. **Credit** AmEx, DC, MC, V.
Specialising in roses, Au Nom de la Rose can supply a bouquet, as well as rose-based beauty products and candles.
Other locations throughout the city.

Gifts & eccentricities

Arty Dandy
1 rue de Furstemberg, 6th (01.43.54.00.36, www.artydandy.com). M° Mabillon. **Open** 10am-7pm Mon-Sat. **Credit** AmEx, MC, V.
'Dandyism is the last spark of heroism amid decadence,' said Baudelaire. Taking this as its motto, Arty Dandy is a concept shop that embraces the surreal, the tongue-in-cheek and the poetic – an R.MUTT sticker to create your own Duchampian loo, and the 'Karl who?' bag (which KL himself has been carrying) are instant pleasers. More sublime offerings include Jaime Hayon's 'Lover' figurines and Sebastien Le Gal watercolours. There are also Alchimie anti-ageing products.

Boutique de l'Opéra National de Paris
Palais Garnier (entrance on rue Halévy), 9th (01.40.01.17.82, www.operadeparis.fr). M° Opéra. **Open** 10am-6.30pm daily (until 10.30pm on performance nights). **Credit** AmEx, MC, V.
See p74 **Ballet boutique.**

Diptyque
34 bd St-Germain, 5th (01.43.26.77.44, www.diptyqueparis.com). M° Maubert Mutualité. **Open** 10am-7pm Mon-Sat. **Credit** V.
Diptyque's divinely scented candles are the quintessential gift from Paris. They come in 48 different varieties, from wild fennel to pomander, and are probably the best you'll ever find. Prices are not cheap, but with 50 to 60 hours' burn time, they're worth every euro.

Galeries Laffitte
27 rue Laffitte, 9th (01.47.70.38.83). M° Notre-Dame-de-Lorette. **Open** 9am-7pm Mon-Fri; 10am-6.30pm Sat. **Credit** MC, V.
The basement of Galeries Laffitte houses a regular *papeterie* filled with pens and notebooks, and the ground floor has art supplies and a selection of gifts, from quality leather bags to Italian pastel-coloured diary covers.

Nature et Découvertes
61 rue de Passy, 16th (01.42.30.53.87, www.natureetdecouvertes.com). M° La Muette. **Open** 10am-7.30pm Mon-Sat. **Credit** AmEx, DC, MC, V.
This commendably ethical store stocks a great range of stuff for junior and grown-up gadgeteers, from infrared parent detectors to high-tech weather stations. It's also worth remembering that ten per cent of all the group's profits go to the Fondation Nature et Découvertes, which supports environmental causes in Europe and Africa.
Other locations throughout the city.

Sennelier
3 quai Voltaire, 7th (01.42.60.72.15, www.magasinsennelier.fr). M° St-Germain-des-Prés. **Open** 2-6.30pm Mon; 10am-12.45pm, 2-6.30pm Tue-Sat. **Credit** AmEx, DC, MC, V.
Old-fashioned colour merchant Sennelier sells oil paints, watercolours and pastels, rare pigments, primed canvases, varnishes and paper.
Other locations 4bis rue de la Grande-Chaumière, 6th (01.46.33.72.39).

Studio Harcourt
10 rue Jean Goujon, 8th (01.42.56.67.67, www.studio-harcourt.eu). M° Franklin D. Roosevelt. **Open** times vary. Reserve in advance. **Credit** AmEx, DC, MC, V.
Founded in 1934, this famous studio celebrated its 75th anniversary in 2009 and its client list reads like a celebrity Who's Who. Alain Delon, Edith Piaf and Jean Reno have all posed for a Harcourt portrait, and if you fancy joining them you can for €900 (or €1,900 for a prestige version). For that, you get to pose like a star and come away with a signed portrait for the wall back home. If your star billing doesn't run to €900, you can take a tour of the studio for €35.

Health & beauty

Cosmetics

L'Artisan Parfumeur
24 bd Raspail, 7th (01.42.22.23.32, www.artisanparfumeur.com). M° Rue du Bac. **Open** 10.30am-7.30pm Mon-Sat. **Credit** AmEx, DC, MC, V.
Among scented candles, potpourri and charms, you'll find the best vanilla perfume Paris can offer – Mûres et Musc, a bestseller for two decades.
Other locations throughout the city.

By Terry
21 & 36 passage Véro-Dodat, 1st (01.44.76.00.76, www.byterry.com). M° Palais Royal Musée du Louvre. **Open** 10.30am-7pm Mon-Sat. **Credit** AmEx, MC, V.
Terry de Gunzburg, who earned her reputation at Yves Saint Laurent, offers made-to-measure 'haute couleur' make-up by skilled chemists and colourists combining high-tech treatments and handmade precision. There's *prêt-à-porter*, too.
Other locations 30 rue de la Trémoille, 8th (01.44.43.04.04); 10 av Victor-Hugo, 16th (01.55.73.00.73).

Détaille 1905
10 rue St-Lazare, 9th (01.48.78.68.50, www.detaille.com). M° Notre-Dame-de-Lorette. **Open** 11am-2pm, 3-7pm Tue-Sat. **Credit** MC, V.
Step back in time at this shop, opened, as the name suggests, in 1905 by war artist Edouard Détaille. Six fragrances (three for men and three for women) are made from century-old recipes.

Editions de Parfums Frédéric Malle
37 rue de Grenelle, 7th (01.42.22.76.40, www.editionsdeparfums.com). M° Rue du Bac or St-Sulpice. **Open** 1-7pm Mon; 11am-7pm Tue-Sat. **Credit** AmEx, DC, MC, V.
Choose from a range of eight perfumes by Frédéric Malle, former consultant to Hermès and Lacroix. Carnal Flower by Dominique Ropion is seduction in a bottle.
Other locations 21 rue du Mont-Thabor, 1st (01.42.22.77.22); 140 av Victor-Hugo, 16th (01.45.05.39.02).

Guerlain
68 av des Champs-Elysées, 8th (01.45.62.52.57, www.guerlain.com). M° Franklin D. Roosevelt. **Open** 10.30am-8pm Mon-Sat; 3-7pm Sun. **Credit** AmEx, DC, MC, V.
The golden oldie of luxury beauty products and scents is looking as ravishing than ever. Head to the first floor to get the full measure of the history behind the house that created the mythic Samsara, Mitsouko and L'Heure Bleue.

Salons du Palais-Royal Shiseido
Jardins du Palais-Royal, 142 galerie de Valois, 1st (01.49.27.09.09, www.salons-shiseido.com). M° Palais Royal Musée du Louvre. **Open** 10am-7pm Mon-Sat. **Credit** AmEx, DC, MC, V.
Under the arcades of the Palais-Royal, Shiseido's perfumer Serge Lutens practises his aromatic arts. A former artistic director of make-up at Christian Dior, Lutens is a maestro of rare taste. Bottles of his concoctions – Tubéreuse Criminelle, Rahat Loukoum and Ambre Sultan – can be sampled by visitors. Look out for Fleurs d'Oranger, which the great man defines as the smell of happiness. Prices start at around €100.
Other locations 2 pl Vendôme, 1st (01.42.60.68.61); 29 rue de Sèvres, 6th (01.42.22.46.60); 66 bd du Montparnasse, 15th (01.43.20.95.40).

OLIVER KNIGHT

Sephora

70 av des Champs-Elysées, 8th (01.53.93.22.50, www.sephora.fr). Mº Franklin D. Roosevelt.
Open 10am-midnight Mon-Thur, Sun; 10am-1am Fri, Sat. **Credit** AmEx, DC, MC, V.
Founded in 1969, the Sephora chain has more than 750 shops around the globe. The Champs-Elysées flagship houses 12,000 brands of scent and slap.
Other locations throughout the city.

Salons & spas

Anne Sémonin

Le Bristol, 108 rue du Fbg-St-Honoré, 8th (01.42.66.24.22, www.hotel-bristol.com). Mº Champs-Elysées Clemenceau or Miromesnil.
Open 10am-8pm Mon-Sat; by appointment Sun. **Credit** AmEx, DC, MC, V.
Facials involve delicious concoctions of basil, lavender, lemongrass, ginger and plant essences. Also on offer are reflexology and a selection of massage styles, from Thai to ayurvedic. Body treatments cost from €70 to €210. Sémonin's renowned seaweed skincare products and essential oils are also on sale.
Other locations 2 rue des Petits-Champs, 2nd (01.42.60.94.66).

Appartement 217

217 rue St-Honoré, 1st (01.42.96.00.96, www.lappartement217.com). Mº Tuileries.
Open 10am-7pm Tue-Sat. **Credit** AmEx, DC, MC, V.
Opened by Stéphane Jaulin, the former beauty director of Colette, a beautiful feng-shuied Haussmannian apartment is the setting for facials using organic beauty guru Dr Hauschka's products and ayurvedic or deep tissue massages. The water has been decalcified, electrical currents are insulated, and the silky-soft kimonos are made from organic wood pulp.

Les Bains du Marais

31-33 rue des Blancs-Manteaux, 4th (01.44.61.02.02, www.lesbainsdumarais.com). Mº St-Paul. **Open** *Men* 10am-11pm Thur; 10am-8pm Fri. *Women* 11am-8pm Mon; 10am-11pm Tue; 10am-7pm Wed. *Mixed (swimwear required)* 7-11pm Wed; 10am-8pm Sat; 10am-11pm Sun. Closed Aug. **Credit** AmEx, MC, V.
This hammam and spa mixes the modern and traditional (lounging beds and mint tea). Facials, waxing and essential oil massages (€70) are also available. The hammam and standard massage are €35 each.

Hammam de la Grande Mosquée

39 rue Geoffrey St-Hilaire, 5th (01.43.31.38.20, www.la-mosquee.com). Mº Censier Daubenton. **Open** *Men* 2-9pm Tue; 10am-9pm Sun. *Women* 10am-9pm Mon, Wed, Thur, Sat; 2-9pm Fri. **Credit** MC, V.
The authentic hammam experience in this beautiful 1920s mosque has become popular with parisians, so avoid the weekends when the volume of traffic makes it less relaxing. Follow a steam session with a *gommage* (exfoliation with a rough mitt), then a massage. The hammam is €15, *gommage* €10 and massage €10 for 10mins. Swimwear is compulsory. Towel and gown hire is also available.

Hammam Med Centre

43-45 rue Petit, 19th (01.42.02.31.05, www.hammammed.com). Mº Ourcq. **Open** *Women* 11am-10pm Mon-Fri; 9am-7pm Sun. *Mixed (swimwear required)* 10am-9pm Sat. **Credit** MC, V.
This hammam is hard to beat – spotless mosaic-tiled surroundings, flowered sarongs and a relaxing pool. The exotic 'Forfait florale' option (€139) will have you enveloped in rose petals and massaged with *huile d'Argan* from Morocco, and the more simple hammam and *gommage* followed by mint tea and pastries is €39. Plan to spend a few hours here, as the soft-voiced staff take things at their own pace.

Spa Nuxe

32 rue Montorgueil, 1st (01.42.36.65.65, www.nuxe.com). Mº Les Halles. **Open** 9.30am-9pm Mon-Fri; 9.30am-7.30pm Sat. **Credit** AmEx, MC, V.
This luxurious day spa housed in stone vaults with wooden cabins and safari-style tents offers massages and skin treatments using Nuxe's gentle, plant-based products. The facials, where you undress completely, begin with a short foot, tummy and neck message for total relaxation; from €80.

House & home

Antiques & flea markets

No trip to Paris is complete without a visit to one of the city's flea markets. The enormous **Marché aux Puces de St-Ouen** has an unrivalled abundance of junk and genuine design classics; in town, traditional antiques can be found in the **Louvre des Antiquaires**, and around Carré Rive Gauche (6th), Village Suisse and rue du Fbg-St-Honoré (1st). You'll find art deco by rue de Charonne (11th). For books, look at the **bouquinistes** (*see p70*).

Louvre des Antiquaires

2 pl du Palais-Royal, 1st (01.42.97.27.27, www.louvre-antiquaires.com). Mº Palais Royal Musée du Louvre. **Open** 11am-7pm Tue-Sun. Closed Sun in July & Aug. **Credit** varies.
This upmarket antiques centre has 250 antiques dealers: perfect for Louis XV furniture, tapestries, porcelain, jewellery, model ships and tin soldiers.

Marché aux Puces d'Aligre

Pl d'Aligre, rue d'Aligre, 12th. Mº Ledru-Rollin. **Open** 7.30am-1.30pm Tue-Sun.
The only flea market in central Paris, Aligre stays true to its junk tradition with a handful of *brocanteurs* peddling books, phone cards, kitchenware and oddities at what seem to be optimistic prices.

Marché aux Puces de St-Ouen

Av de la Porte de Clignancourt, 18th. Mº Porte de Clignancourt. **Open** 11am-5pm Mon; 9am-6pm Sat; 10am-6pm Sun.

With 3,000 traders and up to 180,000 visitors each weekend, the Marché aux Puces de St-Ouen is thought to be the biggest flea market in the world. The fleas left long ago, and since 1885 what started as a rag-and-bone shantytown outside the city limits has been organised into a series of enclosed villages, some entirely covered and others with open-air streets and covered boutiques for the antiques dealers. South of this sprawls the canvas-covered part where African tat, joss sticks, fake Converse trainers and cheap batteries are perused by crowds of teenagers.

Marché aux Puces de Vanves

Av Georges-Lafenestre & av Marc-Sangnier, 14th. Mº Porte de Vanves. **Open** 7am-5pm Sat, Sun.
Vanves is the smallest of the Paris flea markets, and infinitely more tranquil than its much bigger sister at Clingancourt. It's a favourite with serious collectors, so arrive early for the pick of decent vintage clothes, dolls, costume jewellery and silverware, although not much in the way of furniture.

Le Village St-Paul

Rue St-Paul, rue Charlemagne & quai des Célestins, 4th. Mº St-Paul. **Open** 10am-7pm Mon-Sat. **No credit cards**.
This colony of antiques sellers is a source of retro furniture, kitchenware and wine gadgets.

Design & interiors

The enormous **Lafayette Maison** (*see p69*) offers a selection of design and homeware. Also great for modern furniture is biannual **Les Puces du Design** (*see p13*) every June and October.

A La Providence (Quincaillerie Leclercq)

151 rue du Fbg-St-Antoine, 11th (01.43.43.06.41). Mº Ledru-Rollin. **Open** 10am-1pm, 2.30-6pm Tue-Sat. **Credit** V.
Step into the past at this museum-piece *quincaillerie* whose 170-year-old wooden cabinets are filled with knobs, locks and other brass accoutrements for dolling up or restoring old furniture and doors. Newly crafted by artisans, the pieces look authentically antique, and there is also an expensive range of glass and crystal doorknobs. The charming couple who run it are former flight attendants.

Astier de Villatte

173 rue St-Honoré, 1st (01.42.60.74.13, www.astierdevillatte.com). Mº Palais Royal Musée du Louvre. **Open** 11am-7.30pm Mon-Sat. Closed 3wks Aug. **Credit** AmEx, MC, V.
Once home to Napoleon's silversmith, this ancient warren now houses ceramics inspired by 17th- and 18th-century designs, handmade by the Astier de Villatte siblings in their Bastille workshop.

Byzance Home

129 rue de Turenne, 3rd (01.42.77.89.42). Mº Filles du Calvaire. **Open** 11am-1pm, 2-7pm Tue-Sat. **Credit** AmEx, DC, MC, V.
In a cool loft space, interior designer Soraya Belhadia displays her *coups de cœur* for the home. Italian designers are in the majority, with Zanotta

pouffes, Lana leather chaise longue from Palomba and one-off marquetry chest by Camobio. There's lighting, smaller objects such as Byzance scented candles, and a kitchen full of covetable gadgets.

Caravane Chambre 19

19 rue St-Nicolas, 12th (01.53.02.96.96, www.caravane.fr). Mº Ledru-Rollin. **Open** 11am-7pm Tue-Sat. Closed 2wks Aug. **Credit** AmEx, MC, V.
This offshoot of Françoise Dorget's Marais shop has goodies such as exquisite hand-sewn quilts from west Bengal, crisp cotton and organdie tunics, Berber scarves, lounging sofas and daybeds.
Other locations 6 rue Pavée, 4th (01.44.61.04.20); 22 rue St-Nicolas, 12th (01.53.17.18.55).

Christian Liaigre

42 rue du Bac, 7th (01.53.63.33.66, www.christian-liaigre.fr). Mº Rue du Bac. **Open** 10am-7pm Mon-Sat. Closed 3wks Aug. **Credit** AmEx, MC, V.
This French interior decorator fitted out Marc Jacobs's boutiques. His showroom displays his elegant lighting and furniture designs.
Other locations 61 rue de Varenne, 7th (01.47.53.78.76).

Christophe Delcourt

47 rue de Babylone, 7th (01.42.71.34.84, www.christophedelcourt.com). Mº Jacques Bonsergent. **Open** 9am-noon, 1-6pm Mon-Fri. Closed Aug. **Credit** AmEx, DC, MC, V.
Christophe Delcourt's handsome art deco-influenced, geometrical lights and furniture are given a contemporary spin by their combination of stained wood and black steel.

CSAO

9 rue Elzévir, 3rd (01.42.77.66.42, www.csao.fr). Mº St-Paul. **Open** 11am-7pm Mon-Sat. **Credit** AmEx, DC, MC, V.
The CSAO (Compagnie du Sénégal et de l'Afrique de l'Ouest) boutique offers wonderful African craftwork created according to fair trade principles. The artisans often fashion their objects out of recycled materials, such as the funky furniture constructed from tins.

Designpack Gallery

24 rue de Richelieu, 1st (01.44.85.86.00, www.designpackgallery.fr). Mº Palais Royal Musée du Louvre. **Open** 10am-7pm Mon-Fri; 11am-7pm Sat. **Credit** MC, V.
Too much packaging? Not according to Fabrice Peltier who is passionate about the art of *emballage*, to the extent of opening his own boutique. Once a Tetrapak designer, he now recycles his own used packaging into desirable objects: red plastic bottles become lighting and clothes hangers, and bottle tops are melted down to become a multi-coloured armchair. African tin trinkets, Austrian vases made from cut-down bottles, and other ingenious recycling from around the world is also on sale, along with a library of books about packaging and themed exhibitions.

FR66

25 rue du Renard, 4th (01.44.54.35.36, www.fr66.com). Mº Hôtel de Ville. **Open** 10am-7pm Mon-Sat. Closed 2-3wks Aug. **Credit** AmEx, MC, V.

Fauchon.

Somewhere between a gallery and a shop, this two-level experimental space accommodates contemporary artists and designers who produce exciting and original products for the home.

Galerie Patrick Seguin
5 rue des Taillandiers, 11th (01.47.00.32.35, www.patrickseguin.com). M° Bastille or Ledru-Rollin. **Open** 10am-7pm Tue-Sat. Closed 2wks Aug. **Credit** AmEx, DC, MC, V.
Seguin specialises in French design from the 1950s: items by Jean Prouvé and Charlotte Perriand are on display in the handsome showroom. Seguin has also collaborated on some ground-breaking exhibitions around the world.

Roaring trade

In 2008, a fire swept through famous taxidermy shop **Deyrolle** (46 rue du Bac, 7th, 01.42.22.30.07, www.deyrolle.fr) and sent shockwaves across Paris. People watched in despair as the landmark store succumbed to the flames.

Opened in 1831 by Jean-Baptiste Deyrolle, a taxidermist and avid traveller, the shop had always been something of a curiosity. This haven of the exotic and eclectic at the heart of Paris was beloved of professional naturalists, amateur bug-hunters, and Surrealists such as Salvador Dalí and André Breton, who have stood in awe at the bizarre menagerie of lions, giraffes, polar bears, butterflies and bugs of all shapes and sizes, set in the confines of an authentic 19th-century *hôtel particulier*.

In response to the fire, Parisians from all walks of life came together to save the shop. At the forefront was a group of 50 artists, led by Louis-Albert de Broglie, the owner of Deyrolle since 2001, who set about raising funds by creating an art collection inspired by the remains of the original Deyrolle collection, to be auctioned at Christie's. Even famous fashion house Hermès chipped in, designing a Deyrolle scarf to raise money for the reconstruction.

The shop finally reopened in late 2009 and has amazingly lost little of its magic. It remains a great place to escape the city, buy a tiger for the living room, purchase a few creepy crawlies to scare friends and family, or simply to fire your children's imagination with the ultimate urban safari.

Sentou Galerie
26 bd Raspail, 7th (01.45.49.00.05, www.sentou.fr). M° Pont Marie. **Open** 2-7pm Mon; 10am-7pm Tue-Sat. **Credit** AmEx, MC, V.
A trend-setting shop for colourful tableware and furniture: painted Chinese flasks, vases and so on. **Other location** 29 rue François-Miron, 4th (01.42.78.50.60).

Silvera
41 rue du Fbg-St-Antoine, 11th (01.43.43.06.75, www.silvera.fr). M° Bastille or Ledru-Rollin. **Open** 10am-7pm Mon-Sat. Closed 2wks Aug. **Credit** AmEx, MC, V.
The former Le Bihan was taken over by Silvera in 2005 and is now a handsome three-floor showcase for modern design. Look out for furniture and lighting from Perriand, Pesce, Pillet, Morrison, Arad and others. **Other locations** 47 rue de l'Université, 7th (01.45.48.21.06); 58 av Kléber, 16th (01.53.65.78.78); 41 av de Wagram, 17th (01.56.68.76.00).

Talents – Création Contemporaine
1bis rue Scribe, 9th (01.40.17.98.38, www.ateliersdart.com). M° Opéra. **Open** 11am-7pm Mon-Sat. **Credit** AmEx, MC, V.
This contemporary showroom for 70 creators affiliated to the craftworkers' federation Ateliers d'Art de France is a pure white space where you'll find one-off designs in furniture, lighting, glass, ceramics and jewellery. If you want something made to measure they can put you in touch with the designers. **Other locations** 22 & 26 av Niel, 17th (01.48.88.06.58).

Kitchen & bathroom

Bains Plus
51 rue des Francs-Bourgeois, 4th (01.48.87.83.07). M° Hôtel de Ville. **Open** 2-7pm Mon, Sun; 11am-7.30pm Tue-Sat. **Credit** AmEx, MC, V.
This is the ultimate gentlemen's shaving shop: stock includes loofahs, chrome mirrors, bath oils and soaps.

E Dehillerin
18 rue Coquillière, 1st (01.42.36.53.13, www.e-dehillerin.fr). M° Les Halles. **Open** 9am-12.30pm, 2-6pm Mon; 9am-6pm Tue-Sat. **Credit** MC, V.
This no-nonsense warehouse stocks just about every kitchen utensil ever invented.

Laguiole Galerie
1 pl Ste-Opportune, 1st (01.40.06.09.75, www.forge-de-laguiole.com). M° Châtelet. **Open** 10.30am-7pm Mon-Sat. **Credit** MC, V.
Philippe Starck was behind the design for this chic boutique, a showcase for France's classic knife, the Laguiole.

Music & entertainment

Apple Store
12 rue Halévy, 9th (01.44.83.42.00, www.apple.com). M° Opéra. **Open** 9am-8pm Mon-Wed; 9am-9pm Thur-Sat. **Credit** AmEx, DC, MC, V.
Apple's second Paris store opened in summer 2010 in a stunning belle époque former bank facing the Opéra Garnier. To fit in with such hallowed surroundings, Apple strayed from its standard store model, retaining the original carved wooden staircase, wrought-iron railings, marble columns and mosaic tile floor. **Other locations** 99 rue de Rivoli, 1st (01.43.16.78.00).

Crocodisc
40-42 rue des Ecoles, 5th (01.43.54.47.95, www.crocodisc.com). M° Maubert Mutualité. **Open** 11am-7pm Tue-Sat. Closed 2wks Aug. **Credit** MC, V.
The excellent albeit expensive range includes rock, funk, African, country and classical, in the form of new and second-hand vinyl and CDs. For jazz and blues, try sister shop Crocojazz. **Other locations** Crocojazz, 64 rue de la Montagne-Ste-Geneviève, 5th (01.46.34.78.38).

Fnac Forum
Levels -1 to -3, Porte Lescot, Forum des Halles, 1st (08.25.02.00.20, ticket office 08.92.68.36.22, www.fnac.com). M° Les Halles. **Open** 10am-8pm Mon-Sat. **Credit** AmEx, MC, V.
Fnac is a supermarket of culture: books, DVDs, CDs, audio kit, computers and photographic equipment. Most branches stock everything; others specialise. All branches operate as a concert box office. **Other locations** throughout the city.

Monster Melodies
9 rue des Déchargeurs, 1st (01.40.28.09.39). M° Les Halles. **Open** noon-7pm Mon-Sat. **Credit** MC, V.
The owners are very willing to help you hunt down your treasured tracks – and with more than 10,000 second-hand CDs of every variety, that's just as well.

Sony Style
39 av George V, 8th (09.69.39.39.39, www.boutiquegeorge5.fr). M° George V. **Open** 10.30am-7.30pm Mon-Sat. **Credit** AmEx, DC, MC, V.
Sony's first European concept store brings high-tech gadgets and zen decor together in an *hôtel particulier*. Phones, cameras, computers and PlayStations are all here, and the latest innovations from Japan are beamed in on big screens to let you know what the future holds. The store also offers free IT coaching in a swanky training suite.

Virgin Megastore
52-60 av des Champs-Elysées, 8th (01.49.53.50.00, www.virginmegastore.fr). M° Franklin D. Roosevelt. **Open** 10am-midnight Mon-Sat; noon-midnight Sun. **Credit** AmEx, DC, MC, V.
The luxury of perusing CDs and DVDs till midnight makes this a choice spot, and the listening posts let you sample any CD by scanning its barcode. Tickets for concerts and sports events are available here too. **Other locations** throughout the city.

Musical instruments

Paris Accordéon
80 rue Daguerre, 14th (01.43.22.13.48, www.parisaccordeon.com). M° Denfert Rochereau or Gaîté. **Open** 10.30am-1pm, 2.30-7pm Tue-Sat. **Credit** AmEx, MC, V.
Accordions, from simple squeezeboxes to beautiful tortoiseshell models, second-hand and new.

Sport & fitness

Unless you're in the market for specialised equipment, you'll find what you want at **Go Sport** (www.go-sport.com) or the excellent **Décathlon** (www.decathlon.fr).

Citadium
50-56 rue de Caumartin, 9th (01.55.31.74.00, www.citadium.com). M° Havre Caumartin. **Open** 10am-8pm Mon-Wed, Fri, Sat; 10am-9pm Thur. **Credit** AmEx, DC, MC, V.
Cultish emporium of sporting goods, from hip watches to cross-country skis, on four themed floors. Labels include Nike, Burton and North Face.

Nauti Store
40 av de la Grande-Armée, 17th (01.43.80.28.28, www.nautistore.fr). M° Argentine. **Open** 10.30am-2pm, 3-7pm Mon-Sat. **Credit** DC, MC, V.
This shop stocks a vast range of sailing clothes and shoes from labels such as Helly Hansen, Musto and Aigle and Sebago.

René Pierre
35 rue de Maubeuge, 9th (01.44.91.91.21, www.rene-pierre.fr). M° Poissonnière. **Open** 10am-1pm, 2-6.30pm Mon-Sat. **Credit** MC, V.
France's finest table-football tables, ready for free delivery as far as Calais for UK buyers.

Tickets

The easiest way to reserve and buy tickets for concerts, plays and matches is from a **Fnac** store (*see left*). You can also reserve on www.fnac.com or by phone (08.92.68.36.22). **Virgin** (*see above*) has teamed up with Ticketnet to create an online ticket office (www.virginmega.fr). Tickets can also be purchased by phone (08.25.12.91.39) and sent to your home for a €5.50 fee.

Travel agents

Nouvelles Frontières
13 av de l'Opéra, 1st (01.42.61.02.62, www.nouvelles-frontieres.fr). M° Pyramides. **Open** 9am-7pm Mon-Sat. **Credit** V.
Agent with 16 branches in Paris. **Other locations** throughout the city.

Thomas Cook
38 av de Wagram, 8th (08.26.82.67.77, www.thomascook.fr). M° Opéra. **Open** 9am-10pm Mon-Sat. **Credit** AmEx, DC, MC, V.
Travel agent with more than 30 branches in and around Paris. **Other locations** throughout the city.

MARC DANTAN

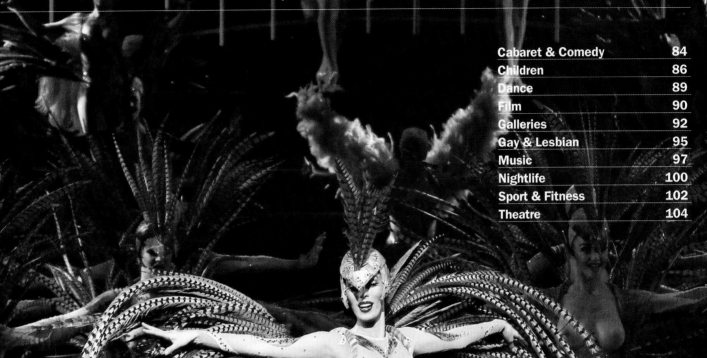

Arts & Leisure

For live arts, kids, sport and nights on the town

Photograph **Oliver Knight**

Cabaret & Comedy

True to their reputation, Paris's traditional cabarets still cater (surprisingly well) to the throngs of tourists and businessmen who come for an eyeful of boob-bouncing, posh nosh and champers. If the get-your-glitz-out-for-the-boys genre isn't your cup of tea, then a Gallic giggle is still to be had in old-fashioned *café-théâtres*, where songs and sketches accompany dinner and a bottle of plonk.

Le stand-up hit town in a big way a few years ago thanks to comedian and actor Jamel Debbouze, who opened **Le Comedy Club** – a launch pad for new French stand-up comics and a spinoff from his TV show *Le Jamel Comedy Club*, and the trend looks set to stay. If French isn't your forte, fear not: veteran Anglo venue **Laughing Matters** (105 rue du Faubourg-du-Temple, 10th, 01.53.19.98.88, www.anythingmatters.com) still provides laughs in English with comedy acts from across the Channel, the US and Australia. Circus-wise, Paris can do no wrong: the Parc de la Villette alone hosts several avant-garde extravaganzas, so whether you're looking for ringmaster-led acts, acrobatics or clowns, you'll be lapping it up big-top style throughout the year.

Cabaret & café-théâtre

The year the Eiffel Tower raised its final girders (1889), the Moulin Rouge was raising something of its own: skirts. The risqué *quadrille réaliste* (later dubbed the cancan) became such a trademark that more than 120 years later, scantily clad dancers are still slinking across the stages of Paris. These days, cabaret is an all-evening extravaganza. Male dancers and magicians complement the foxtrots, the dancing is perfectly synchronised and the whole caboodle now perfectly respectable.

Cabaret

Crazy Horse Saloon
12 av George V, 8th (01.47.23.32.32, www.crazyhorse.fr). M° Alma Marceau or George V. **Shows** 8.15pm, 10.45pm Mon-Fri, Sun; 7pm, 9.30pm, 11.45pm Sat. **Admission** *Show only* €80-€100. *Show* (incl champagne) €100-€120. **Credit** AmEx, DC, MC, V.
The Horse, whose *art du nu* was invented in 1951 by Alain Bernadin, is an ode to feminine beauty: lookalike dancers with provocative names like Flamma Rosa and Nooka Caramel, and identical body statistics (when standing, the girls' nipples and hips are all the same height) move around the stage, clad only in rainbow light and strategic strips of black tape. In their latest show, Désirs, the girls put on some tantalising numbers, with titles such as 'God Save Our Bare Skin' (a sexy take on the Changing of the Guards) and the sensual 'Vestel's Desire'.

Le Lido
116bis av des Champs-Elysées, 8th (01.40.76.56.10, www.lido.fr). M° Franklin D. Roosevelt or George V. **Lunch** 1pm. **Matinée** 3pm Tue, Sun (once a mth, dates vary). **Dinner** 7pm. **Shows** 9.30pm, 11.30pm daily. **Admission** *Matinée show* (incl champagne) €80. *Lunch & matinée show* (incl champagne) €115 Tue; €125 Sun. *9.30pm show* (incl champagne) €100. *11.30pm show* (incl champagne) €90. *Dinner & show* €140-€280. *Show & backstage tour* €110-€120. **Credit** AmEx, DC, MC, V.

This is the largest cabaret of all: high-tech touches optimise visibility, and chef Philippe Lacroix provides fabulous gourmet nosh. On stage, 60 Bluebell Girls and a set of hunky dancers slink around, shaking their bodies with sequinned panache.

Moulin Rouge
82 bd de Clichy, 18th (01.53.09.82.82, www.moulin-rouge.com). M° Blanche. **Dinner** 7pm. **Shows** 9pm, 11pm daily. **Admission** *9pm show* (incl champagne) €102. *11pm show* (incl champagne) €92. *Dinner & show* €150-€180. *Show only* 9pm €90, 11pm €80. **Credit** AmEx, DC, MC, V.
Toulouse-Lautrec posters, glittery lamp-posts and fake trees lend tacky charm to this revue. On stage, 60 Doriss dancers cavort with faultless synchronisation. Costumes are flamboyant and the *entr'acte* acts funny. The downer is the lack of space, with tables packed in like sardines. There's also an occasional matinée: lunch and show €130, show only €100.

Paradis Latin
28 rue Cardinal Lemoine, 5th (01.43.25.28.28, www.paradislatin.com). M° Cardinal Lemoine. **Dinner** 8pm daily. **Show** 9.30pm daily. **Admission** *9.30pm show* (incl champagne) €85. *Dinner & show* €123-€179. **Credit** AmEx, DC, MC, V.
This is the most authentic of the cabarets, not only because it's family-run (the men run the cabaret, the daughter does the costumes), but also because the clientele is mostly French, something which has a direct effect on the prices (this is the cheapest revue) and the cuisine, which tends to be high quality. Show-wise you can expect the usual fare: generous doses of glitter, live singing and cheesy *entr'acte* acts performed in a stunning belle époque room. There's also a twice-monthly matinée: lunch and show €95.

Café-théâtre

Les Blancs Manteaux
15 rue des Blancs-Manteaux, 4th (01.48.87.15.84, www.blancsmanteaux.fr). M° Hôtel de Ville. **Shows** from 7pm daily (phone for details). **Admission** *Show* €20; €17 students, under-25s; *2 shows* €34 (except Sat). *Dinner & 1 show* €40. **No credit cards.**
For the last 38 years, this Marais institution has been launching new talent with weekly comedy platforms. With a dinner-and-show ticket, you can dine on Thai cuisine at nearby Suan Thai.

Chez Michou
80 rue des Martyrs, 18th (01.46.06.16.04, www.michou.com). M° Pigalle. **Dinner** 8.30pm daily. **Shows** 10.30pm approx. **Admission** *Show* €35-€60. *Dinner & show* €105-€135. **Credit** MC, V.
Drag, sparkling costumes, good food and wine: Michou's show is not quite as 'blue' as his azure attire suggests. Book ahead if you want to dine.

Le Grenier
3 rue Rennequin, 17th (01.43.80.68.01, www.legrenier-dinerspectacle.com). M° Ternes. **Shows** from 7.30pm daily. **Admission** *Show* €16-€18. *Dinner & show* €27-€85. **Credit** MC, V.
If you fancy being entertained while you eat, consider the 'Loft', which still retains the allure of an old *café-théâtre* with an eclectic line-up of stand-up, *chansonniers* and magic acts all on the same bill.

Au Lapin Agile
22 rue des Saules, 18th (01.46.06.85.87, www.au-lapin-agile.com). M° Lamarck Caulaincourt. **Shows** 9pm-2am Tue-Sun. **Admission** *Show* (incl 1 drink) €24; €17 reductions (except Sat & public hols). **No credit cards.**

Feast for the senses

The promise of busty babes slinking sassily across the stage in tight knickers still attracts throngs of tourists and businessmen to Paris's glamour cabarets, turning them into some of the hottest spots on Paris's show circuit. Yet they're also some of the most expensive. A night on the glittery tiles – meal included – can easily set you back more than €200 a head. So when you're forking out, you need to know that you'll get something worthwhile, both on the stage and on your plate. The **Lido** is excellent all round: a classy, high-tech 1,000-seater art deco-style dining room, and the most contemporary of the revues, with costumes worthy of a catwalk, breathtaking fountains, and fabulous *entr'acte* acts. Chef Philippe Lacroix assures top nosh for everyone who eats, even if you can sense the machine of mass catering behind it – a reason to splurge, if you can, on the four-course Premier menu (€280), which feels lovingly prepared and includes perfect foie gras, tender lobster, an excellent steak and a gooey chocolate slice to finish. For a special treat, opt for the 'behind the scenes' tour which, before the show, takes you into the heart of the action.

Critics' choice

1 Cirque Pinder
Traditional circus, with animal antics galore. *See below.*

2 Crazy Horse Saloon
The risqué shows here are a sensual treat. *See left.*

3 Le Comedy Club
Debbouze's club is an essential stop. *See below.*

The prices have gone up and they sell their own compilation CDs, but that's all that seems to have changed since this quaint, pink bar first opened in 1860. Tourists now outnumber the locals, but the Lapin harbours an echo of old Montmartre.

Comedy & fringe

Café de la Gare
41 rue du Temple, 4th (01.42.78.52.51, www.cdlg.org). M° Hôtel de Ville. **Shows** 9pm Mon, Tue, Sun; 7pm, 8.30pm, 10pm Wed-Sat. **Admission** €20-€24; €10-€20 reductions. **Credit** MC, V.
Running since 1968, the most famous fringe theatre in Paris has 300 stage-hugging seats and hosts quality French stand-up and raucous comedies.

Le Comedy Club
42 bd de Bonne Nouvelle, 10th (08.11.94.09.40, www.lecomedyclub.fr). M° Bonne Nouvelle. **Shows** days vary. **Admission** €15-€25. **Credit** MC, V.
Jamel Debbouze, the comic known for his one-man shows and films, gives the comedy trade a helping hand with this theatre. Tuesdays and Wednesdays (7.30pm) are open mic nights. Saturdays are for the confirmed mirth merchants of Jamel's TV show.

Le Point Virgule
7 rue Ste-Croix-de-la-Bretonnerie, 4th (01.42.78.67.03, www.lepointvirgule.com). M° Hôtel de Ville. **Shows** Mon-Wed, Sat, Sun times vary. **Admission** €17; €13 reductions. *2 shows* €29, *3 shows* €36. *Children's show* €12; €10 children. **No credit cards.**
This small Marais theatre has become the ultimate launch pad for up-and-coming comedians, with shows, a *café-théâtre* school and an annual comedy festival in September.

Circus

Cirque d'Hiver Bouglione
110 rue Amelot, 11th (01.47.00.28.81, www.cirquedhiver.com). M° Filles du Calvaire. **Shows** *Late Oct-late Feb* days vary. **Admission** €25-€50. **Credit** AmEx, MC, V.
This circus now has a new façade to match its revamped interior, and crowds flock for its twice-yearly seasons which include tigers, horses and very silly clowns.

Cirque Pinder
Pelouse de Reuilly, Bois de Vincennes, 12th (01.45.90.21.25, www.cirquepinder.com). M° Porte de Charenton or Porte Dorée. **Shows** *Mid Nov-mid Jan.* **Admission** €15-€50; free under-2s. **Credit** AmEx, DC, MC, V.
Big cats are the stars of the show, but horses, elephants and monkeys also make Pinder the most traditional travelling circus in France.

Espace Chapiteaux
Parc de La Villette, 19th (01.40.03.75.75, www.villette.com). M° Porte de la Villette. **Shows** vary. **Admission** varies. **Credit** MC, V.
This big top hosts companies such as Cirque Plume, Centre National des Arts du Cirque and aerialists Les Arts Saut.

Bags packed, milk cancelled, house raised on stilts.

You've packed the suntan lotion, the snorkel set, the stay-pressed shirts. Just one more thing left to do – your bit for climate change. In some of the world's poorest countries, changing weather patterns are destroying lives.

You can help people to deal with the extreme effects of climate change. Raising houses in flood-prone regions is just one life-saving solution.

Climate change costs lives.
Give £5 and let's sort it *Here & Now*

www.oxfam.org.uk/climate-change

Be Humankind Oxfam

Children

For all its commotion and traffic-clogged boulevards, the French capital is actually a very child-friendly place to visit. Most Parisians have to raise their children in gardenless apartments, so the city powers ensure there is plenty of provision for youngsters to expend their energy outside the home: every arrondissement has spaces with playgrounds, and in the big parks like the Jardin du Luxembourg and Buttes-Chaumont, pony rides, sandpits, swings, puppet shows and boating ponds spice up the childhood of many a young Parisian.

Paris's museums and other attractions cater to children as well as adults, and also offer blissful opportunities to offload your kids on to someone else with children's workshops, held on Saturdays and Wednesdays during the school year, and daily during school holidays. If your children don't speak French, you can usually request an English speaker in advance. To find out what's coming up, contact the individual museums or check out www.paris.fr. Listings magazines like *Pariscope*, *L'Officiel des Spectacles*, *Figaroscope* (with Wednesday's *Le Figaro*) and Télérama's *Sortir* all have kids' sections too; and the free bi-monthly magazine *Paris-Mômes* is distributed with daily newspaper *Libération* in toy shops and public libraries.

Sightseeing with children can be made easier with planning. Queues at prime spots like the **Eiffel Tower** (*see p46*), **Louvre** (*see p28*) and the towers at **Notre-Dame** (*see p17*) are less disheartening in the morning. One of the most exciting ways for the family to take in the city is from a boat on the Seine; the hop-on hop-off waterborne Batobus (*see p119*) links eight prime sights, including the Eiffel Tower, the Musée d'Orsay and the Jardin des Plantes.

GETTING AROUND

One word of advice: walk whenever possible. The métro is difficult to negotiate with babies and toddlers. Two of you might manage a pushchair, but lone travellers won't and passers-by are notoriously selfish about helping out. If your babe is small enough for a baby carrier, it will save you a lot of hassle when navigating the tight turnstiles and never-ending staircases. Also try to travel between 10.30am and 5pm to

avoid the crowds. The driverless line 14 (St-Lazare to Olympiades) is a big hit with kids, who can sit at the front and peer down the tunnel as the train advances; the mostly overground lines six (Nation to Charles de Gaulle Étoile) and two (Nation to Porte Dauphine) offer attractive city views; a number of RER stations have lifts, although they are frequently broken.

Buses, on the other hand, are easier thanks to priority seats near the front for passengers with young children; many, such as nos.24, 63 and 95 (www.ratp.fr), pass numerous sights. Three- to 11-year-olds qualify for a half-price *carnet* (a book of ten tickets) for all transport, including the Montmartrobus minibus and Montmartre funicular. Taxi drivers will usually take a family of four (charging €1 to carry a pushchair and a little extra for the fourth person). If you're stuck, try G7 taxis (01.47.39.47.39), which has an English-speaking booking line.

For older kids, the recent addition of extra cycle paths across the centre (especially along the Seine, up the Canal St-Martin and along the Canal de l'Ourcq) makes a spin *en famille* an enjoyable way to get around the city while seeing the sights. Short distances are easily covered using the city's **Vélib** self-service scheme (www.velib.fr; *see p119*). For day-long fun try **Vélo et Chocolat** (75 quai Seine, 19th, 01.46.07.07.87); **Cyclo Pouce** (38 quai de Marne, 19th, 01.42.41.76.98), which provides baby seats and equipment for disabled children; or **Paris à Vélo c'est Sympa** (22 rue Alphonse Baudin, 11th, 01.48.87.60.01, www.parisvelo sympa.com). For a day out in beautiful surroundings, the Bois de Vincennes in the east and the Bois de Boulogne in the west provide woodlands, picnic areas, boating lakes and lawns.

Eating out

Affordable **Chartier** (7 rue du Fbg-Montmartre, 9th, 01.47.70.86.29, www.restaurant-chartier.com) is always a fun place to take kids, with its belle epoque dining room and waiters clad in black and white. **Tokyo Eat** at the Palais de Tokyo (13 av du Président-Wilson, 01.47.20.00.29, www.palaisdetokyo.com) is good too, with wacky decor and round, family-sized tables. For a simple snack along the lines of boiled egg and soldiers you can't beat **Coco & Co** (11 rue Bernard Palissy, 6th, 01.45.44.02.52, www.cocoandco.fr), which serves only egg dishes, in an egg-themed dining room. The restaurants on the Cour St-Emilion near Parc de Bercy are all good for traffic-free outdoor eating, and if you fancy browsing for baby clothes while

slurping on a hot coffee, the **Poussette Café** (6 rue Pierre Sémard, 9th, 01.78.10.49.00, www.lepoussettecafe.com) is a haven for stressed-out parents, with parking space for buggies and milk-warming facilities.

Babies & toddlers

Always pack a portable changing mat. A facility worth remembering is the WC chalet in the Jardin du Luxembourg, where €0.60 gives you access to loos with a padded changing table; the **Galeries Lafayette** and **Printemps** (for both, *see p69*) department stores have clean, well-equipped nappy changing facilities, as does the **Poussette Café** (*see above*). Breastfeeding in public is more common than ever, but still often frowned upon, so take a scarf for places where modesty is essential, or choose a quiet corner.

A city break with tots in tow doesn't have to mean missing out on the city's galleries and museums. Almost all of the main attractions have child-friendly activities or green spaces nearby – handy as a reward for good behaviour. There's a carefully tended garden by Notre-Dame, and the dignified **Musée Rodin** (*see p45*) has outdoor distractions such as a sandpit to dig in, a sculpture-filled garden to explore (free entry to parents with a pushchair) and a tempting ice-cream stand. And if the heady heights of the Eiffel Tower prove too daunting, more down-to-earth amusements can be found at the adjacent Champ de Mars, with its play areas and seasonal donkey rides; or there are old-style merry-go-rounds by the river.

Babysitting

Many hotels can organise babysitting (ask when you reserve). The **American Church in Paris** (65 quai d'Orsay, 7th, 01.40.62.05.00, www.acparis.org) has a noticeboard displaying ads from English-speaking babysitters and au pairs; **Baby Sitting Services** (01.46.21.33.16, www.babysittingservices.com) can organise babysitting at short notice.

Museums & sightseeing

Most museums offer children's workshops (in French) on Wednesday afternoons, at weekends and in the holidays. At the **Louvre** (*see p28*) the programme for kids varies from learning about facial expressions in paintings to Egyptian sculpture. Next door, the

Museé des Arts Décoratifs (*see p21*) offers hands-on art workshops for ages four to 14s and special tours (tailored to different age groups). The **Palais de Tokyo** (*see p25*) has inventive 'Tok Tok' story-reading for three- to five-year-olds, workshops for five- to seven-year-olds and family visits (4.30pm Sun), often led by notable contemporary artists. The **Musée Rodin** (*see p45*) runs children's clay workshops. Under-18s (and under-26s from the EU) get free admission to the national museums, including the Louvre, Musée d'Orsay, Centre Pompidou, Musée du Quai Branly and Musée Rodin.

Centre Pompidou – Galerie des Enfants
Rue St-Martin, 4th (01.44.78.12.33, www.centrepompidou.fr/enfants). M° Hôtel de Ville or Rambuteau/RER Châtelet Les Halles. **Open** *Museum* 11am-9pm Mon, Wed-Sun. *Workshops* most Wed & Sat afternoons & school hols. **Admission** *Museum* €10-€12; free under-18s (under-26s from EU countries). *Workshops* €10 (1 child & 1 adult). **Credit** MC, V.
In this ground-floor gallery, wonderfully thought out exhibitions conceived by top artists and designers introduce children to interesting aspects of modern art, design and architecture. Kids are kept enthralled with interactive elements and the opportunity to touch. There are also hands-on workshops for six- to 12-year-olds, and family workshops one Sunday afternoon a month. Audio guides for six- to 12-year-olds can also be hired for €4. Outside, look for the colourful Stravinsky fountain on the south side, designed by Niki de Saint Phalle and Jean Tinguely.

Cité de l'Architecture
Palais de Chaillot, 1 pl du Trocadéro, 16th (01.58.51.52.00, www.citechaillot.fr). M° Trocadéro. **Open** 11am-7pm Mon, Wed-Sun (until 9pm Thur). **Admission** €8; €5 reductions; free under-18s (under-26s from EU countries). **Credit** MC, V.
Over 850 life-size copies of France's architectural treasures (including portions of great cathedrals such as Chartres) make for a fascinating visit for children of all ages. To help them understand the exhibits, colourful interactive games are dotted around the permanent displays, so they can try their hand at architecture and learn the concepts of Romanesque and Gothic as they create fantastical animal heads, design stained-glass windows or build a Romanesque arch. On Saturdays at 2pm, three- to seven-year-olds can have a go at doing some building themselves with wooden blocks. Entry is €8 and you don't need to reserve (just turn up about 30 minutes beforehand).

Etoiles du Rex
1 bd Poissonnière, 2nd (01.45.08.93.58, www.legrandrex.com). M° Bonne Nouvelle. **Open** 10am-7pm Wed-Sun (tours leave every 5mins); daily during school holidays. **Admission** €9.80; €8 under-12s. **Credit** AmEx, MC, V.
The slick but cheesy 50-minute backstage tour of the glorious art deco Grand Rex cinema is a treat for any kids with acting aspirations – plus they've just dropped the prices. Be prepared to ham your heart out when, propelled by automatic doors, lifts and mystery voices, you visit the projection room, climb behind the giant screen and are thrust into a whirlwind of sound dubbing, special effects and an audition for *King Kong*.

Grévin
10 bd Montmartre, 9th (01.47.70.85.05, www.grevin.com). M° Grands Boulevards. **Open** 10am-6.30pm (last admission 5.30pm) Mon-Fri; 10am-7pm (last admission 6pm) Sat, Sun & hols. **Admission** €20; €12-€17 reductions; free under-6s. **Credit** AmEx, DC, MC, V.
This kitsch version of Madame Tussauds is a hit with kids, who can have their photo taken alongside waxworks of showbiz stars and personalities

ON THE FARM
Reserved for school classes during the week, Paris's very own farmyard, the **Ferme de Paris** (Rte du Pesage, 12th, www.paris.fr) in the Bois de Vincennes, is a real hit with kids at the weekends. Inhabitants include cows, sheep, rabbits and hens.

Critics' choice

1 **Disneyland Paris**
A slice of pure Americana in the countryside. See p88.

2 **Eiffel Tower**
The dream ticket, with stupendous views from the top. See above.

3 **Stade de France**
Football- and rugby-crazy kids will love the behind-the-scenes tours. See p87.

Children

like football star Zinédine Zidane, Brigitte Bardot, the Queen and Barack Obama. Great historical moments, such as Neil Armstrong walking on the moon, are re-enacted in the 'snapshots of the 20th century' area, a small gallery at the top of a spiral staircase near the end shows how waxworks are made, and an impressive hall of mirrors (designed by France's fetish illusionist Arturo Brachetti and with music by Manu Katche) plunges you into scenes such as an Aztec temple. On Wednesdays, Saturdays and Sundays during termtime there are special children's guided tours (French only) for seven- to 12-year-olds (€15).

Musée des Arts et Métiers

60 rue Réamur, 3rd (01.53.01.82.00, www.arts-et-metiers.net). M° Arts et Métiers. **Open** 10am-6pm Tue, Wed, Fri-Sun; 10am-9.30pm Thur. **Admission** €6.50; €4.50 reductions; free under-26s, 1st Sun of mth & after 6pm Thur. *Audio guides* €5. **Credit** V.

Abbot Grégoire founded this fascinating museum in the 18th century as 'a store for useful, new inventions'. Today, it thrills budding scientists, mechanics, astronomers, pilots or kids simply curious about the world around them with highlights that include Foucault's original pendulum, used by physician Léon Foucault in 1851 to make the rotation of the earth visible to the human eye; Clément Ader's Avion III, officially the world's first working plane (1897); and Henry Ford's 'T' model car.

Musée des Egouts

Entrance opposite 93 quai d'Orsay, by Pont de l'Alma, 7th (01.53.68.27.81). M° Alma-Marceau/RER Pont de l'Alma. **Open** *May-Sept* 11am-5pm Mon-Wed, Sat, Sun. *Oct-Apr* 11am-4pm Mon-Wed, Sat, Sun. **Admission** €4.30; €3.50 reductions; free under-6s. **Credit** MC, V.

The sewer museum retraces the history of all 2,100km (1,305 miles) of Paris's underworld through a genuinely fascinating series of films, exhibits and a trip through the tunnels. During bad weather, visiting times may change or the museum may close as sudden surges in water can make the sewers dangerous.

Musée de la Magie

11 rue St-Paul, 4th (01.42.72.13.26, www.museedelamagie.com). M° St-Paul or Sully-Morland. **Open** 2-7pm Wed, Sat, Sun (extra hours & days in school hols). **Admission** €9; €7 reductions. **No credit cards.**

Small kids love the distorting mirrors and putting their hands in the lion's mouth at this museum of magic and curiosities, housed in vaulted cellars. A short magic show is included in the visit – it's in French, but rabbits out of hats translate pretty well into any language. There's a great automated museum too, where 100 mechanical toys move into action before your kids' eyes.

Musée de la Musique

Parc de la Villette, 221 av Jean-Jaurès, 19th (01.44.84.45.00, www.cite-musique.fr). M° Porte de Pantin. **Open** noon-6pm Tue-Sat; 10am-6pm Sun. **Admission** €8; free under-26s.

This innovative music museum houses a gleamingly restored collection of instruments from the old Conservatoire, interactive computers and scale models of opera houses and concert halls. Visitors are supplied with an audio guide in a choice of languages, and the musical commentary is a joy, playing the appropriate instrument as you approach each exhibit. Once a month there are free active workshops for children over eight, who can try singing, conducting an orchestra or testing a musical instrument in the company of a musicologist (you need to reserve well in advance).

Musée National de la Marine

Palais de Chaillot, 17 pl du Trocadéro, 16th (01.53.65.69.69, www.musee-marine.fr). M° Trocadéro. **Open** 10am-6pm Mon, Wed-Sun. **Admission** €7; €5 reductions; free under-18s (under-26s from EU countries). **Credit** *Shop* MC, V.

Sail your family back in time through 400 years of French naval history. Highlights include the *Océan*, a 19th-century sailing vessel equipped with an impressive 120 cannons; a gilded barge built for Napoleon; and some extravagant, larger-than-life figureheads, from serene-faced angels to leaping seahorses. There are also dozens of model boats, dating from the 18th to the 20th century, and several old-fashioned divers' suits.

Muséum National d'Histoire Naturelle

36 rue Geoffroy-St-Hilaire, 2 rue Bouffon, 57 rue Cuvier, 5th (01.40.79.30.00, www.mnhn.fr). M° Gare d'Austerlitz or Jussieu. **Open** *Nov-Mar* 10am-5pm Mon, Wed-Sun. Grande Galerie de l'Evolution 10am-6pm Mon, Wed-Sun. *Apr-Oct* 10am-6pm Mon, Wed-Sun. *Both* Last admission 45mins before closing. **Admission** *Grande Galerie de l'Evolution* €9; €7 reductions; free under-26s. *Galeries de Paléontologie et d'Anatomie Comparée & Galerie de Minéralogie et de Géologie* €7; €5 reductions; free under-4s. *Combined 2-day ticket for all sites* €25; €20 reductions. **Credit** MC, V.

At the Natural History Museum's Grande Galerie de l'Evolution, stuffed creatures parade majestically through their various habitats. Animals of all kinds teach children about the diversity of nature and, in the endangered and vanished section (where a dodo takes pride of place), about the importance of protecting them. Also in the Jardin des Plantes complex are the small Ménagerie zoo (*see below*), separate pavilions containing hunks of meteorites and crystals in the Galerie de Minéralogie et de Géologie, and the bony remains of fish, birds, monkeys, dinosaurs and humans in the Galerie de Paléontologie et d'Anatomie Comparée.

Musée de la Poupée

Impasse Berthaud, 3rd (01.42.72.73.11, www.museedelapoupeeparis.com). M° Rambuteau. **Open** 10am-6pm Tue-Sun. **Admission** €8; €3-€5 reductions; free under-3s, under-12s Sun. **No credit cards.**

This small, private museum and doll hospital enchants little girls with its collection of some 500 dolls (mostly of French origin) and their accompanying accessories and pets, which are arranged in thematic tableaux. A few teddies and quacking ducks are thrown in for young boys, and storytelling sessions and workshops (along the lines of making doll's clothes or miniature food for dolls' houses) are held at 2pm on Wednesdays (in French, reserve in advance; €8-€13). There's even a *clinique pour poupées* if your doll is falling apart at the seams.

Stade de France

Guided visits via entrance Porte G, Stade de France, Seine St-Denis (01.55.93.00.00, tours 08.92.70.09.00, www.stadefrance.com). M° St-Denis Porte de Paris/RER Stade de France St-Denis. **Tours** *French* every 2hrs 11am-5pm daily (every hr from 10am Apr-Aug). *English* 10.30am, 2.30pm daily. **Admission** €12; €8 reductions; free under-6s. **Credit** AmEx, DC, MC, V.

After a quick scan of the museum (photos, football shirts, electric guitars from the rock stars who also play here), the tour begins by sitting in the stands and ends with a runout through the tunnel to the sound of applause. On the way, you can visit the changing and shower rooms and learn about the on-site hospital and prison cells. On match or concert days, tours are not available.

Aquariums & zoos

Cinéaqua

2 av des Nations Unies, 16th (01.40.69.23.23, www.cineaqua.com). M° Trocadéro. **Open** *Apr-Sept* 10am-7pm daily. *Oct-Mar* 10am-6pm daily. **Admission** €19.50; €12.50-€15.50 reductions; free under-3s. **Credit** MC, V.

Paris's first 'ocean entertainment centre' is a hybrid aquarium-cinema complex containing over 500 species of fish, invertebrates, sharks and coral, and several cinema screens. There are kids' clubs, with face-painting and games, from 2pm to 5pm daily, plus a touch pool offering the chance to stroke carp and sturgeon.

Ménagerie du Jardin des Plantes

57 rue Cuvier, 5th (01.40.79.37.94, www.mnhn.fr). M° Gare d'Austerlitz, Jussieu or Place Monge. **Open** 9am-6pm Mon-Sat; 9am-6.30pm Sun. **Admission** €8; €6 reductions; free under-4s. **Credit** AmEx, MC, V.

Heads rolled during the Terror, leaving many an aristocratic collection of exotic animals without a home. This *ménagerie* became the solution in 1794. Nowadays, its inhabitants include vultures, monkeys, orang-utans, ostriches, flamingos, a century-old turtle, plus another one rescued from the sewers, a lovely red panda and lots of satisfyingly scary spiders and snakes. There's a petting zoo with farm animals for small kids, and older ones can zoom in on microscopic species in the Microzoo.

Palais de la Porte Dorée Aquarium Tropical

293 av Daumesnil, 12th (01.53.59.58.60, www.aquarium-portedoree.fr). M° Porte Dorée. **Open** 10am-5.15pm Tue-Fri; 10am-7pm Sat, Sun. **Admission** €4.50-€6.50; €6-€8 1 adult with 1 or 2 children under 12; €3-€5 reductions; free under-4s. **No credit cards.**

The basement of this art deco palace, built for the Colonial Exhibition in 1931, contains the small but much-loved city aquarium and its crocodiles, brought from Dakar in 1948; other watery residents include cuttlefish, sharks, and luminous deep-water species. The Palais de la Porte Dorée is also home to the Cité Nationale de l'Histoire de l'Immigration (*see p35*).

Parc de Thoiry

78770 Thoiry-en-Yvelines (01.34.87.53.76, www.thoiry.net). 45km (28 miles) west of Paris; by car A13, A12, then N12 towards Dreux until Thoiry. **Open** times vary, see website for details. **Admission** *Safari park, park & château* €26; €19.50-€23 reductions; free under-3s. **Credit** MC, V.

As well as a beautiful château, the Parc de Thoiry houses one of Europe's first animal reserves. Follow the long safari park trail, accessible only by car, and see zebras rub their noses over your windscreen and bears amble down tracks. In the adjoining zoo, rarities include Siberian lynx and Tonkean macaques.

Performing arts & sports

When school's out on Wednesday afternoons, at weekends and during holidays, fairytales, fables and folk stories keep children entertained at the city's theatres and *café-théâtres*. The varied programme at the **Théâtre Dunois** (7 rue Louise-Weiss, 13th, 01.45.84.72.00, www.theatredunois.org) is almost entirely geared towards children. For children's theatre in an unusual setting, the **Abricadabra Péniche-Antipod** (opposite 55 quai de Seine,

Little chefs

If your nippers are showing early signs of culinary genius or, *au contraire*, don't know a spatula from their elbow, the **Ecole Ritz Escoffier** (38 rue Cambon, 1st, 01.43.16.31.50, www.ritzparis.com; *pictured*) at the Ritz has an army of master chefs ready to teach them the art of preparing and (the best bit) eating posh nosh.

Auguste Escoffier was the Ritz's first chef, famous not only for his mastery of haute cuisine but also for the recipes he left behind (especially desserts): peach melba and *poire belle-hélène* were two of his inventions, named after 19th-century Australian singer Nellie Melba and the hotel director's daughter Hélène Ellès.

In 1988, the Ritz decided to continue Escoffier's work by opening a school that 'teaches France's gastronomic traditions to professional and amateur food-lovers'. The result is a world-renowned culinary laboratory that instructs over 800 people a year, from 43 different countries. And guess what? They like them to start young. Great news for your six- to 11-year-olds, who can sign up for a two-and-a-half-hour lesson to become a Petit Marmiton du Ritz ('little Ritz kitchen hand') and learn how to cook scrumptious dishes such as handmade potato gnocchi with smoked salmon, Hallowe'en tart, cookies and brownies, and marshmallow and marzipan models. The lessons are simple, fun and easy to follow, and students get to take home their work at the end.

Although the food takes centre stage, children get a kick out of the pomp and circumstance surrounding it all. For a start, they get dressed up like real professionals, chef's hat and all, non-French speakers get their own translator, and before heading into the kitchen *atelier* they get taken past the real working kitchens. Prices begin at €95 (try to reserve as far in advance as possible), which is nothing compared to the priceless meals they'll be preparing for you when you get home.

If money is an issue or you have older children, the **Ecole Lenôtre** (Pavillon Elysée, 10 av des Champs-Elysées, 8th, 01.42.65.97.60, www.lenotre.fr) cooking school on the Champs-Elysées runs special cooking classes most Wednesdays for eight- to 17-year-olds, from €40. Younger kids' recipes stay simple (think cookies, fruit crumble and guacamole), but older children can test their skills on more complicated dishes such as herb-crusted cod with vegetable confit or tiramisu.

RITZ HOTEL PARIS

19th, 01.42.03.39.07, http://abricadabra.nerim.net) is a riverboat on the Canal de l'Ourcq with an appealing programme.

In general, children's films are dubbed into French, but you can see VO (*version originale*) screenings of the latest Hollywood hits at most venues across town. Keep a lookout for kids' showings on Wednesdays and Saturday afternoons at the Cinémathèque Française and L'Ecran des Enfants (Oct-June 2.30pm Wed) for under-13s at the **Centre Pompidou** (*see p32*). The IMAX cinema in La Villette's **Géode** (*see p90*) will keep kids enthralled too.

Each winter, France's traditional circuses come to town, complete with big cats, clowns and horses, and set up on the Pelouse de Reuilly; the **Cirque Bouglione** (*see p84*), meanwhile, occupies the gorgeous Cirque d'Hiver with its annual extravaganza. Your brood can even learn tightrope walking, juggling and numerous other circus sports between April and September on Wednesdays (daily during spring and summer holidays) at **Chapiteau d'Adrienne** (06.83.63.20.94, www.chapiteau-adrienne.fr, admission €3-€5).

Waterbabies can choose between 38 public pools (www.paris.fr), including the floating **Piscine Josephine-Baker** (*see p103*), moored on the Seine and filled with purified water pumped from the river; the art nouveau **Piscine Butte-aux-Cailles** (*see p103*), with indoor and outdoor pools fed by artesian wells; and the recently restored **Espace Sportif Pailleron** (32 rue Edouard Pailleron, 19th, 01.40.40.27.70), near Buttes-Chaumont, which has two pools and an ice rink (rollerskating in summer). At the indoor **Aquaboulevard** (*see p103*), over-threes can splash down different slides and ride the waves. Bathing caps are obligatory everywhere.

Patinoire Sonja Henie
Palais Omnisports de Paris-Bercy (01.40.02.60.60, www.bercy.fr). M° Bercy. **Open** *Sept-mid June* 3-6pm Wed; 9.30pm-12.30am Fri; 3-6pm, 9.30pm-12.30am Sat; 10am-noon, 3-6pm Sun. **Admission** €3-€6. **No credit cards**.
Bercy's Omnisports arena contains an ice rink, which is open on Wednesdays and weekends for skaters of all levels. Teenagers can also skate until late on Fridays and Saturdays, when disco lights colour the ice.

Parks & theme parks

Disneyland Paris/ Walt Disney Studios Park
Marne-la-Vallée (08.25.30.60.30, from UK 0870 503 0303, www.disneylandparis.com). 32km E of Paris. RER A or TGV Marne-la-Vallée-Chessy. By car, A4 exit 14. **Open** Times vary, see website for details. **Admission** *1 park* €53; €45 reductions; free under-3s. *1-day hopper (both parks)* €67; €57 reductions. *2-day hopper (both parks)* €118; €99 reductions; free under-7s. **Parking** €15 per day. **Credit** AmEx, MC, V.
Young ones will get a real kick out of Fantasyland, with its Alice maze, Sleeping Beauty's castle and teacup rides. Walt Disney Studios focuses on special effects and the tricks of the animation trade. Disney's newest adrenaline ride, the Twilight Zone Tower of Terror, sends daredevils plummeting down a 13-storey lift shaft.

Jardin d'Acclimatation
Bois de Boulogne, 16th (01.40.67.90.82, www.jardindacclimatation.fr). M° Les Sablons. **Open** *May-Sept* 10am-7pm daily. *Oct-Apr* 10am-6pm daily. **Admission** €2.90; €1.45 reductions; free under-3s. **Credit** (€15 minimum) MC, V.
Founded in 1860, this amusement park and garden has animals, a Normandy-style farm and an aviary, as well as boat rides, a funfair with mini rollercoasters, flying chairs, the Enchanted House for children aged two to four and two playgrounds. There's also a place to steer radio-controlled boats and mini golf. Many of the attractions cost €2.90 a go; others are free. A miniature train runs from Porte Maillot through the Bois de Boulogne to the park entrance, and has space for pushchairs (€2.70 return; €4.05-€5.40 with entry included).

Jardin du Luxembourg
Main access 2 rue Auguste Compte, 6th. M° Odéon/RER Luxembourg. **Open** *Summer* 7.30am-dusk daily. *Winter* 8am-dusk daily.
The 25-hectare park is a prized family attraction. Kids come from across the city for its pony rides, ice-cream stands, puppet shows, pedal karts, sandpits, metal swingboats and merry-go-round. The playground has an entrance fee.

Parc Astérix
60128 Plailly (08.26.30.10.40, www.parc asterix.fr). 36km N of Paris. By coach from the Louvre, the Eiffel Tower or RER Roissy-Charles de Gaulle 1 (check website for times or call 08.26.30.10.40). By car, A1 exit Parc Astérix. **Open** Times vary, see website. **Admission** €39; €29 reductions; free under-3s. **Parking** €8. **Credit** MC, V.
The park is split into Ancient Greece, the Roman Empire, the Land of the Vikings and the indomitable Gaulish Village. Thrill-seekers can defy gravity on Goudurix, Europe's largest rollercoaster, while younger kids get wet on the Grand Splatch log flume. For some serious handshaking, Astérix, Obélix and friends wander around and a jamboree of live acts pumps up the pace. The park's newest attraction is Le Défi de César, a virtual reality ride.

Parc des Buttes-Chaumont
Rue Botzaris, rue Manin, rue de Crimée, 19th. M° Buttes Chaumont. **Open** *Winter* 7am-8pm daily. *Summer* 7am-10pm daily.
This area, which was formerly mined for gypsum, was turned into a sumptuous park under Napoleon III. Spectacular in every way (including the views over Paris), it is a family magnet with Punch and Judy stands, pony rides, sandpits, waterfalls, picnic and games areas and drinks stands.

Parc de la Villette
Av Corentin-Cariou, 19th (01.40.03.75.75, www.villette.com). M° Porte de la Villette. Av Jean-Jaurès, 19th. M° Porte de Pantin.
Aside from a children's science museum, a music museum, an IMAX cinema, theatres, concert and exhibition venues, the city's former abattoir district is now made up of a succession of gardens and playgrounds. Jardin des Voltiges has climbing ropes and balancing games, and the modern Jardin des Dunes et Vents has pedal windmills, waves of bouncy tubes and giant hamster wheels. The Jardins Passagers (open after 3pm May-Sept) is a collection of gardens that teach children about flora and fauna; some even have beehives.

Stade de France. See p87.

Dance

Festival d'Automne.

Paris is home to a thriving dance scene, a rich programme of major international companies and plenty of home-grown talent. In 2011, the **Théâtre de la Ville** and **Théâtre National de Chaillot** will see a new piece by Akram Khan and a series of solo Irish dance performances by Colin Dunne. There's no shortage of ballet productions at the **Théâtre du Châtelet** and **Palais Garnier**, including Prokofiev's classic *Romeo and Juliet*. And the **Festival d'Automne** will again feature an impressive line-up of innovative dance.

There's even more of interest outside the centre of town. As the HQ for over 600 regional companies, the **Centre National de la Danse** in Pantin reaches out to its audience with a well-devised series of performances, and smaller dance 'laboratories' such as Ménagerie de Verre and Regard du Cygne showcase new work by smaller companies. Dance centres and festivals in the *banlieue* are also determined to draw audiences to their suburban locations, with a distinct mix of styles and cultures.

INFORMATION AND RESOURCES

For listings, *see Pariscope* and *L'Officiel des Spectacles*. For events coverage, look out for two monthlies: *La Terrasse* (distributed free at major dance venues) and the glossy *Danser*.

For shoes and equipment, **Sansha** (52 rue de Clichy, 9th, 01.45.26.01.38,

www.sansha.com) has a good reputation, and **Repetto** (22 rue de la Paix, 2nd, 01.44.71.83.12, www.repetto.com) supplies the Opéra with pointes and slippers; **Menkes** (12 rue Rambuteau, 3rd, 01.40.27.91.81, www.menkes.es) sells serious flamenco gear as well as outsize glam-rock boots.

Festivals

The year starts with **Faits d'Hiver** (01.42.74.46.00, www.faitsdhiver.com) and hip hop festival **Suresnes Cités Danse** (01.46.97.98.10, www.theatre-suresnes.fr) in January. May and June bring with them the **Rencontres Chorégraphiques de Seine-St-Denis** (01.55.82.08.01, www.rencontres choregraphiques.com), the **IRCAM Agora** festival (01.44.78.48.43, www.ircam.fr) and **Onze Bouge** (01.53.27.13.68, www.festivalonze.org). The **Rencontres de la Villette** (01.40.03.75.75, www.rencontresvillette. com) dishes up street dance at various suburban locations every April. You'll also find excellent smaller dance festivals at the **Maison des Arts de Créteil**, and at the **Ménagerie de Verre** in the 11th. See also pp11-13 **Calendar**.

Les Etés de la Danse

1 pl du Châtelet, 1st (01.40.28.28.40, www.chatelet-theatre.com). Mº Châtelet. **Date** 6-23 July 2011.
Founded in 2005, this festival puts the spotlight on one or two companies or choreographers, with three weeks of top-class performances. The 2011 edition focuses on the choreography of George Balanchine and Jerome Robbins, with performances by major US companies. Shows are accompanied by workshops.

Paris Quartier d'Eté

01.44.94.98.00, www.quartierdete.com. **Date** mid July-mid Aug.
This popular summer festival features eclectic programmes and free outdoor performances in Paris and the suburbs. Public rehearsals and talks give audiences the chance to meet prestigious international choreographers.

Festival d'Automne

Information: 156 rue de Rivoli, 1st (01.53.45.17.00, www.festival-automne.com). **Date** mid Sept-late Dec.
With a focus on leading French experimental companies, the festival invites big-name choreographers from around the world. Highlights in 2010 included four Merce Cunningham revivals, from *Antic Meet* (1958) to *Pond Way* (1998).

Major venues

Centre National de la Danse

1 rue Victor-Hugo, 93507 Pantin (01.41.83.27.27, box office 01.41.83.98.98, www.cnd.fr). Mº Hoche/RER Pantin. **Open** *Box office* 10am-7pm Mon-Fri. **Admission** €6-€18. **Credit** AmEx, MC, V.
This centre first opened its door in 2004, with the mission to bridge the divide between stage and spectator. It invites audiences to its quarterly 'Grandes leçons de danse', contemporary dance master classes. It also offers an expertly curated selection of performances presented in the studios, exhibitions, and a phenomenal archive of films and choreographic material.

Maison des Arts de Créteil

Pl Salvador-Allende, 94000 Créteil (01.45.13.19.19, www.maccreteil.com). Mº Créteil-Préfecture. **Open** *Box office* 1-7pm Tue-Sat. Closed mid July-Aug. **Admission** €8-€30. **Credit** MC, V.
This excellent arts centre features an eclectic programme of theatre, dance, music and digital art. Don't miss the International Exit Festival of contemporary dance, which takes place during March and in 2011 features Wayne McGregor's Random Dance and T.R.A.S.H.

Palais Garnier

Pl de l'Opéra, 9th (08.92.89.90.90, from abroad 01.71.25.24.23, www.operadeparis.fr). Mº Opéra. **Open** *Box office* 10.30am-6.30pm Mon-Sat. *Telephone bookings* 9am-6pm Mon-Fri; 9am-1pm Sat. Closed 15 July-end Aug. **Admission** €5-€180. **Credit** AmEx, MC, V.
The Ballet de l'Opéra National de Paris manages to tread successfully between classics and new productions, between the Opéra Bastille and the lavish Palais Garnier. To illustrate this, highlights in 2011 include Prokofiev's classic *Romeo and Juliet*, and Anne Teresa De Keersmaeker's 2001 *Rain*. Don't miss out on a visit to the Palais Garnier's stunning new concept store.

Théâtre du Châtelet

1 pl du Châtelet, 1st (01.40.28.28.40, www.chatelet-theatre.com). Mº Châtelet. **Open** *Box office* 11am-7pm Mon-Sat. **Admission** €10-€98. **Credit** AmEx, MC, V.
This classical music institution is strengthening its reputation in other live artistic disciplines. The theatre also plays host to the esteemed Etés de la Danse festival (*see left*).

Théâtre National de Chaillot

1 pl du Trocadéro, 16th (01.53.65.30.00, www.theatre-chaillot.fr). Mº Trocadéro. **Open** *Box office* 11am-7pm Mon-Sat. *Telephone bookings* 11am-7pm Mon-Sat. Closed 2wks Aug. **Admission** €10-€32. **Credit** MC, V.
Chaillot's three auditoriums range from cosy and experimental to a vast 2,800-seater amphitheatre. The 2011 dance programme includes a series of solo Irish dance performances by Olivier Award nominee Colin Dunne in *Out of Time*.

Théâtre de la Ville

2 pl du Châtelet, 4th (01.42.74.22.77, www.theatredelaville-paris.com). Mº Châtelet. **Open** *Box office* 11am-7pm Mon; 11am-8pm Tue-Sat. *Telephone bookings* 11am-7pm Mon-Sat. Closed July, Aug. **Admission** €13-€33. **Credit** MC, V.
This leading venue has nurtured long-standing collaborations with international choreographers. The 2011 programme includes *Vertical Road*, a new piece by Akram Khan, as well as an adaptation of Jean Genet's *Le Funambule*, choreographed and performed by Angelin Preljocaj. Some performances take place at sister venue Théâtre des Abbesses (31 rue des Abbesses, 18th).

Other venues

L'Etoile du Nord

16 rue Georgette-Agutte, 18th (01.42.26.47.47, www.etoiledunord-theatre.com). Mº Guy Môquet. **Open** *Box office* 2-6pm Mon-Fri. Closed July. **Credit** V.
This smaller venue splits its programme between theatre and contemporary multimedia dance. The Avis de Turbulences festival features a decent selection of mixed bills.

Ménagerie de Verre

12-14 rue Léchevin, 11th (01.43.38.33.44, www.menagerie-de-verre.org). Mº Parmentier. **Open** *Box office* 2-6pm Mon-Fri. Closed July, Aug. **Admission** €13; €10 reductions. **No credit cards**.
This multidisciplinary hothouse is rooted in the avant-garde, with contemporary dance and classes given by a succession of guest teachers.

Regard du Cygne

210 rue de Belleville, 20th (01.43.58.55.93, bookings 09.71.34.23.50, www.leregarducygne. com). Mº Télégraphe. **Open** *Box office* 1hr before show. Closed Aug. **Admission** free-€15. **No credit cards**.
This pared-down studio in Belleville is a great place to get a taste of the alternative dance scene. The Spectacles Sauvages nights allow unknowns to show a ten-minute piece to the public, while the Rencontres focus on the work of a particular artist and are open to all, free of charge.

Théâtre de la Bastille

76 rue de la Roquette, 11th (01.43.57.42.14, www.theatre-bastille.com). Mº Bastille or Voltaire. **Open** *Box office* 10am-6pm Mon-Fri; 2-6pm Sat. Closed July, Aug. **Admission** €22; €13-€14 reductions. **Credit** MC, V.
This small theatre showcases innovative contemporary dance and drama pieces. Worth checking out in spring 2011 is *Dominos and Butterflies* by the Busy Rocks collective.

Dance classes

Dance classes are available to suit all tastes and levels. The open-air dancing on the banks of the Seine is particularly popular in summer.

Centre de Danse du Marais

41 rue du Temple, 4th (01.42.77.58.19, www.parisdanse.com). Mº Hôtel de Ville or Rambuteau. **Open** 9am-9pm Mon-Fri; 9am-8pm Sat; 9am-7pm Sun. **Classes** €18.
There's a huge choice of classes here, with big-name teachers such as belly dance star Leila Haddad and ballet's Casati-Lazzarelli team. The five-class 'sampler' pass is a good deal at €73.

Studio Harmonic

5 passage des Taillandiers, 11th (01.48.07.13.39, www.studioharmonic.fr). Mº Bastille. **Open** 10am-6pm Mon-Fri. *Classes* 9.30am-10pm Mon-Fri; 9am-7.30pm Sat. Closed 3wks Aug. **Classes** €15-€16.
The rising star among Paris's dance schools. Studio Harmonic's claim to fame is the trademark Ragga Jam class – created by Laure Courtellemont – which combines ragga, dancehall, African dance and hip hop.

Critics' choice

1 **Festival d'Automne**
A star fixture on the arts festival circuit for more than 40 years. *See right.*

2 **Maison des Arts de Creteil**
This suburban arts centre is a vibrant hub of artistic creation. *See right.*

3 **Palais Garnier**
Matchless acoustics make this the capital's ultimate dance venue. *See right.*

IAN DOUGLAS

Dance

Film

This is where it all began, in the basement of a chic café in 1895; the Lumière brothers were from Lyon, but the city in which they chose to launch their cinematograph had to be Paris. Over a century later, filmgoing is still a central part of Paris life, with more tickets per head bought here than anywhere else in Europe; in any given week, the choice of films to watch exceeds 350 (more still, if you count the programmes of the regular festivals), and the range of screening venues is a rich mix of glitzy modern multiplexes and doughty historic *art et essai* cinemas that attract loyal and discerning audiences. What's more, cinema tickets are much cheaper in Paris than in London or New York.

MOVIEGOING IN PARIS

Happily, the rapid rise of the multiplex hasn't meant a reduction in the choice and variety of films on offer. In Paris, multiplexes regularly show films from Eastern Europe, Asia and South America, and countless independent cinemas continue to screen a hugely eclectic assortment of cult, classic and just plain obscure films. As well as retrospectives and cut-price promotions, there are often visits from directors and stars.

Local interest is strong enough to sustain several monthly movie magazines and there's a decent selection of specialist film bookshops, such as **Contacts**, in the city. Launched in 2007, the annual **Salon du Cinéma** gives film fans a chance to visit mocked-up movie sets and meet world-renowned directors and actors. Finally, French DVD labels produce some of the most expertly curated discs in the world. At **Fnac** and **Virgin Megastore** (for both, *see p82*), you're more than likely to find American and British titles otherwise unavailable in the US or UK.

CINE CITY

Construction has begun on the Cité Européenne du Cinéma in St-Denis. Backed by film director Luc Besson, the complex will house nine studios and promises to give the national film industry a massive boost when it opens in 2012.

INFORMATION AND TICKETS

New releases hit the screens on Wednesdays. Hollywood is well represented, of course, but Paris audiences have a balanced cinematic diet that satisfies their appetite for international films as well as shorts and documentaries. On top of this there are the 150-plus annual releases funded or part-funded with French money (the French film industry is still the world's third largest, after the US and India).

For venues, times and prices, consult one of the city's two main weekly listings magazines: *L'Officiel des Spectacles* and *Pariscope*. *Films nouveaux* are new releases, *Exclusivités* are the also-showing titles, and *Reprises* means rep. For non-francophone flicks, look out for two letters somewhere near the title: VO (*version originale*) means a screening in the original language with French subtitles; VF (*version française*) means that it has been dubbed into French.

Buy tickets in the usual way at the cinema – for new blockbusters, it pays to buy in advance. Online booking may entail a fee. Seats are often discounted by 20 to 30 per cent at Monday or Wednesday screenings, and the Mairie sponsors various cut-price promotions throughout the year.

If you're staying in town for a while, it might be a good idea to pick up a *carte illimité*, a season ticket that allows unlimited viewing: every multiplex chain offers one.

Cinemas

Giant screens & multiplexes

La Géode
26 av Corentin-Cariou, 19th (08.92.68.45.40, www.lageode.fr). Mº Porte de la Villette. **Admission** €10.50; €9 reductions. **Credit** MC, V.
The IMAX cinema at the Cité des Sciences occupies a shiny geodesic sphere. The vast screen lets you experience 3D plunges through natural scenery, and adventures where figures zoom out to grab you.

Le Grand Rex
1 bd Poissonnière, 2nd (08.92.68.05.96, www.legrandrex.com). Mº Bonne Nouvelle. **Admission** €7.50-€9.50; €6-€7.40 reductions. *Les Etoiles du Rex tour* €9.80; €8 reductions. **Credit** MC, V.
With its fairy-tale interior, this listed historical monument is one of the few cinemas that manages to upstage whatever it screens. Its blockbuster programming (usually in French) is suited to its vast screen. There are six smaller screens too.

Max Linder Panorama
24 bd Poissonnière, 9th (01.48.24.00.47, www.maxlinder.com). Mº Grands Boulevards. **Admission** €9; €7 reductions. **Credit** MC, V.
This state-of-the-art cinema, with THX surround sound and an 18m (60ft) screen, is named after the dapper French silent comedian who owned it between 1914 and 1925. The walls and 700 seats are all black to prevent even the tiniest twinkle of reflected light distracting the audience from

what's happening on the screen. Look for all-nighters and one-off showings of rare vintage films or piano-accompanied silents.

MK2 Bibliothèque
128-162 av de France, 13th (08.92.69.84.84, www.mk2.com). Mº Bibliothèque François Mitterrand or Quai de la Gare. **Admission** €10.50; €5-€7 reductions; €19.80 monthly pass. **Credit** MC, V.
The MK2 chain's flagship offers an all-in-one night out: 14 screens, four restaurants, a bar open until 5am at weekends and two-person 'love seats'. A paragon of imaginative programming, MK2 is growing all the time; it has added ten more venues in town. For €19.80 a month, the UGC/MK2 Illimité card offers film fans unlimited screenings at any UGC or MK2 venue, as well as some independent cinemas.

UGC Ciné Cité Bercy
2 cour St-Emilion, 12th (08.92.70.00.00, www.ugc.fr). Mº Cour St-Emilion. **Admission** €10.50; €5.90-€7 reductions; €19.80 monthly pass. **Credit** MC, V.
This ambitious 18-screen development screens art movies as well as mainstream fodder, also and hosts regular meet-the-director events. The UGC's other Ciné Cité branch, the 19-screen UGC Ciné Cité Les Halles (7 place de la Rotonde, Nouveau Forum des Halles, 1st, 08.92.70.00.00), serves the same mix of cinema and events.

Showcases

Auditorium du Louvre
Musée du Louvre, 99 rue de Rivoli, 1st (01.40.20.55.55, www.louvre.fr). Mº Palais Royal Musée du Louvre. **Admission** prices vary. **Credit** MC, V.
This 420-seat auditorium was designed by IM Pei, as part of the Mitterrand-inspired renovation of the Louvre. Film screenings are often related to the current exhibitions; silent movies with accompanying live music are regulars.

Centre Pompidou
Rue St-Martin, 4th (01.44.78.12.33, www.centrepompidou.fr). Mº Hôtel de Ville or Rambuteau. **Admission** €6; €4 reductions. **Credit** MC, V.
The varied programme at the Centre Pompidou features themed series, experimental and artists' films, and a weekly documentary session. This is also the venue for the Cinéma du Réel festival in March (www.cinereel.org).

Le Cinéma des Cinéastes
7 av de Clichy, 17th (08.92.68.97.17, www.cinema-des-cineastes.fr). Mº Place de Clichy. **Admission** €8.70; €6.90 reductions. **Credit** MC, V.
Done out to evoke the studios of old, this three-screen showcase of world cinema holds meet-the-director sessions and festivals of classic, foreign, gay and documentary films. The cinema is also big on cinema for kids, and plays host to the annual Mon Premier Festival (www.monpremier-festival.org) for three- to 15-year-olds.

La Géode.

La Cinémathèque Française
51 rue de Bercy, 12th (01.71.19.33.33, www. cinematheque.fr). M° Bercy. **Admission Films** €6.50; €3-€5 reductions. *Museum* €5; €2.50-€4 reductions; free under-6s. **Credit** MC, V.
Relocated to Frank Gehry's striking, spacious cubist building, the Cinémathèque Française now boasts four screens, a bookshop, a restaurant, exhibition space and the Musée du Cinéma, where it displays just a fraction of its huge collection of movie memorabilia.

Forum des Images
2 Grande Galerie, Porte St-Eustache, Forum des Halles, 1st (01.44.76.63.00, www.forum desimages.com). M° Les Halles. **Admission** (per day) €5; €4 under-12s. Membership available (€84-€132 per year). **Credit** AmEx, MC, V.
Partly a screening venue for old and little-known movies, and partly an archive for every kind of film featuring Paris. Today, the Forum's collection numbers over 6,500 documentaries, adverts, newsreels and films, from the work of the Lumière brothers to 21st-century reportage. They have all been digitised.

Arthouses

Accattone
20 rue Cujas, 5th (01.46.33.86.86). M° Cluny La Sorbonne/RER Luxembourg. **Admission** €7; €6 Wed, students, under-20s (except Fri nights and weekends). **No credit cards.**
Named after Pasolini's first film, this tiny Latin Quarter cinema has a clear preference for old Italian arthouse. That said, there's still plenty of room on the rolling weekly programme for the likes of Buñuel, Oshima, Roeg and Ken Russell.

Action
Action Christine *4 rue Christine, 6th (01.43.25.85.78, www.actioncinemas.com).* M° Odéon or St-Michel. **Admission** €8; €6 reductions. **No credit cards.**
Action Ecoles *23 rue des Ecoles, 5th (01.43.25.72.07).* M° Maubert Mutualité. **Admission** €8; €6 reductions. **No credit cards.**
Grand Action *5 rue des Ecoles, 5th (01.43.54.47.62, www.legrandaction.com).* M° Cardinal Lemoine. **Admission** €8.50; €6.50 reductions. **No credit cards.**
A Left Bank stalwart, the Action group is renowned for screening new prints of old movies. It's heaven for anyone who's nostalgic for Tinseltown classics and quality US independents.

Le Balzac
1 rue Balzac, 8th (08.92.68.31.23, www.cinemabalzac.com). M° George V. **Admission** €9; €5-€7 reductions. **No credit cards.**
Built in 1935 and boasting a mock ocean-liner foyer, Le Balzac scores highly for design and programming. Jean-Jacques Schpoliansky, whose grandfather opened the cinema in 1935, has been the manager for the last 35 years and is often found welcoming punters in person. The Balzac awards prizes according to audience votes.

Le Champo
51 rue des Ecoles, 5th (01.43.54.51.60, www.lechampo.com). M° Cluny La Sorbonne or Odéon. **Admission** €8; €5-€6 reductions. **No credit cards.**
The two-screen Champo has been in operation for nearly seven decades, a venerable past recognised in 2000 when it was given historic monument status. In the 1960s, it was a favourite haunt of *nouvelle vague* directors such as Claude Chabrol. Novel programming includes the occasional Nuits du Champo, a trio of films beginning at midnight and ending with breakfast (€15).

Le Cinéma du Panthéon
13 rue Victor-Cousin, 5th (01.40.46.01.21, www.whynotproductions.fr/pantheon). RER Luxembourg. **Admission** €7; €4-€5.50 reductions. **Credit** MC, V.
To celebrate its centenary in 2007, the city's oldest surviving movie house opened a tearoom with interior design by Catherine Deneuve. The Cinéma du Panthéon continues to screen new, often obscure international films and hosts meet-the-director nights and discussions.

Le Denfert
24 pl Denfert-Rochereau, 14th (01.43.21.41.01, www.allocine.fr). M° Denfert Rochereau/RER Denfert Rochereau. **Admission** €7.30; €5.30-€6.50 reductions. **No credit cards.**
This charming little cinema offers a nicely eclectic repertory selection that ranges from François

Show reel

As if film buffs weren't already spoilt for choice in Paris, they'll have another reason to get excited come 2012. The **Fondation Jérôme Seydoux-Pathé** is opening a showcase centre for its collection of film memorabilia and artefacts, including a space for exhibitions.

Established in 1896, the Société Pathé Frères was one of the founding fathers of cinema, building its reputation on savvy technical innovations and the famed pre-film Pathé newsreels. Today, the company remains one of Europe's leading distributors, producers and cinema exhibitors, and the foundation's mission is to promote the history of cinema via the Pathé story. Its collection is composed of the company's archives for everything except film reels, and includes movie posters, journals, props, cameras, and all sorts of projectionists' paraphernalia.

To house such a prestigious collection, Pathé commissioned Renzo Piano, architect of the Centre Pompidou, to design a new building on the site of a former cinema near Place d'Italie. The only stipulation was that the building's old façade

had to be conserved, as it was embellished with an elaborate sculpture by iconic artist Auguste Rodin. Piano's solution was to take visitors through the old entrance, across a short corridor, and into a brand new oval complex that will house the foundation's offices and collection. This five-storey building will be glass-fronted, with tinted panes used on certain floors to protect the archives. On the ground floor, a temporary exhibition space, including a small cinema, will host exhibitions based on the Pathé collection. Visitors will be treated to original posters, props and stills from landmark movies such as Marcel Carné's post-war classic *Les Enfants du Paradis*, as well as recent crowd-pleasers such as 2008's French box-office smash *Bienvenue chez les Ch'tis*.

The centre will also exhibit Pathé studio cameras and film projectors through the ages, while the top floor will feature a research library, accessible to the public by appointment only. Outside, visitors will be able to admire the building's audacious architecture from a small garden.

Ozon and Hayao Miyazaki to shorts and animation, as well as new-release foreign films.

L'Entrepôt
7-9 rue Francis-de-Pressensé, 14th (01.45.40.07.50, www.lentrepot.fr). M° Pernety or Plaisance. **Admission** €7; €4-€5.60 reductions. **No credit cards.**
A diverse array of documentaries, shorts, gay cinema and productions from developing nations are more common here than mainstream stuff.

Le Mac Mahon
5 av Mac-Mahon, 17th (01.43.80.24.81, www.cinemamacmahon.com). M° Charles de Gaulle Etoile. **Admission** €7; €5 reductions. **No credit cards.**
This single-screen, 1930s-era cinema has changed little since its 1960s heyday (tickets are still of the tear-off variety), when its all-American programming fostered the label '*macmahonisme*' among the buffs who haunted the place. Americana still makes up the bulk of what's on the screen.

Le Nouveau Latina
20 rue du Temple, 4th (01.42.78.47.86, www.lenouveaulatina.com). M° Hôtel de Ville. **Admission** €7; €6.50 Wed, students, under-20s. **No credit cards.**
The exciting programming at this flag-bearer for Latin cultures runs the gamut from Argentinian to Romanian films.

La Pagode
57bis rue de Babylone, 7th (01.45.55.48.48, www.allocine.fr). M° St-François-Xavier. **Admission** €8.50; €7 reductions. **No credit cards.**
This glorious edifice is not, as local legend might have it, a block-by-block import, but a 19th-century replica of a pagoda by a French architect.

Studio 28
10 rue Tholozé, 18th (01.42.54.18.11, www.cinemastudio28.com). M° Abbesses or Blanche. **Admission** €7.50; €6.30 reductions. **No credit cards.**
Studio 28 was the venue for the first screening of Buñuel's scandalous *L'Age d'Or*, and this historic cinema also features in the heartwarming *Amélie*. It offers a decent mixture of classics and recent movies, complete with Dolby sound.

Studio Galande
42 rue Galande, 5th (01.43.54.72.71, www.studiogalande.fr). M° Cluny La Sorbonne or St-Michel. **Admission** €8; €6 reductions. **No credit cards.**
Some 20 different films are screened in subtitled versions at this venerable Latin Quarter venue every week: international arthouse fare, combined with the occasional instalment from a blockbuster series. On Fridays and Saturdays, fans of *The Rocky Horror Picture Show* turn up in drag, equipped with rice and water pistols.

Festivals & events
The city plays host to a range of film festivals. *See also pp11-13* **Calendar**.

Salon du Cinéma
Parc des Expos, Porte de Versailles, 15th (www.salonducinema.com). M° Porte de Versailles. **Date** Jan.
This event features behind-the-scenes reconstructions of movie sets, allowing the public to watch the work of make-up artists, cameramen and stuntmen.

Festival International de Films de Femmes
Maison des Arts, pl Salvador-Allende, 94040 Créteil (01.49.80.38.98, www.filmsdefemmes. com). M° Créteil-Préfecture. **Date** Mar, Apr.
A selection of retrospectives and new international films by female directors.

Printemps du Cinéma
Various venues (www.printempsducinema.com). **Date** Mar.
Three days of bargain €3.50 entry films at cinemas all across Paris.

Côté Court
Ciné 104, 104 av Jean-Lolive, 93500 Pantin (01.48.91.24.91, www.cotecourt.org). M° Eglise de Pantin. **Date** June.
A great selection of new and old short films shown at Ciné 104 and a handful of neighbouring venues.

Paris Cinéma
Various venues (01.55.25.55.25, www.pariscinema.org). **Date** July.
The ninth edition of the capital's flagship festival is taking place in 2011, complete with official competitions and attendant stars.

Cinéma au Clair de Lune
Various venues (01.44.76.63.00, www.forumdesimages.net). **Date** Aug.
Night-time films on giant open-air screens in squares and public gardens around town: a party atmosphere is guaranteed.

L'Etrange Festival
Forum des Images, for listing see left (01.44.76.63.00, www.etrangefestival.com). **Date** Sept.
Explicit sex, gore and weirdness in the screenings and 'happenings' at this annual feast of all things unconventional draw large crowds.

La Master Class
Forum des Images (see left). **Date** monthly throughout the year.
Each month film critic Pascal Mérigeau interviews a well-known figure from French cinema. Recent interviewees have included Jacques Audiard and Isabelle Huppert.

Bookshops

Cinédoc
45-53 passage Jouffroy, 9th (01.48.24.71.36, www.cine-doc.fr). M° Grands Boulevards. **Open** 10am-7pm Mon-Sat. **Credit** V.
Finding what you're looking for isn't easy in this narrow bookshop. Ask the staff or take pot luck among the old photos, film magazines and books.

Ciné Reflet
14 rue Monsieur le Prince, 6th (01.40.46.02.72). M° Odéon. **Open** 1-8pm Mon-Sat; 3-7pm Sun. **Credit** MC, V.
This sprawling shop is well stocked with old photos, posters, and new and second-hand books. The English-language selection includes the *Time Out Film Guide* and magazines like *Sight & Sound*.

Contacts
14 rue St-Sulpice, 6th (01.43.59.17.71, www.la-chambre-claire.fr). M° Odéon. **Open** 2.30-6.30pm Mon; 10.30am-6.30pm Tue-Sat. **Credit** MC, V.
Truffaut's favourite *librairie* has been selling books on film for over 40 years. The stock is well organised, with a large and up-to-date selection of English-language titles. You'll also find *Film Comment* and *American Cinematographer*, plus a few videos.

Scaramouche
161 rue St-Martin, 3rd (01.48.87.78.58). M° Rambuteau. **Open** noon-1pm, 2.30-8pm Mon-Sat. **Credit** MC, V.
This shop covers cinema and *gestuelle* (mime and puppetry). The film section includes a wide range of titles in English, plus a huge collection of publicity photos and portraits.

Galleries

Galerie Lara Vincy. *See p94.*

While lamentably few French artists have broken on to the international scene – Laurent Grasso, Philippe Parreno, Sophie Calle and Mathieu Mercier are a few exceptions – and most only attain relatively modest prices that would make Russian oligarchs, YBAs and the new Chinese millionaires snigger, contemporary art is currently *à la mode* in both public and private institutions, from installations at the Louvre or Musée Bourdelle to the annual show at Galeries Lafayette or the new prize awarded by the Hôtel Meurice. Beyond the Marais powerhouses of Yvon Lambert, Chantal Crousel and Emmanuel Perrotin, brave new galleries continue to open and Paris remains a good place to discover a broad spectrum of international art.

GALLERIES IN PARIS

The commercial gallery scene is principally centred on the northern Marais. Across the river, the St-Germain-des-Prés scene has been revitalised by **Galerie Kamel Mennour** and **in situ Fabienne Leclerc**, joining a more staid modern art selection and galleries specialising in modern design. In the 13th arrondissement, the area around rue Louise-Weiss never quite fulfilled its promise of becoming Paris's Chelsea: spaces are too small and quality too varied. Even so, **Air de Paris** is usually worth a look. At the opposite end of the spectrum, the Champs-Elysées area is home to a handful of galleries presenting big names, and more classic *antiquaires*, tribal and early 20th-century art.

The **Galeries Mode d'Emploi** leaflet (also online at www.fondation-entreprise-ricard.com) provides detailed weekly listings, as does **www.paris-art.com**. At *vernissage* time, usually Saturday evenings, the city's artists, collectors, critics and curators do the rounds of what's opening. Most galleries close from mid July to late August.

Critics'choice

1 FIAC
20-23 Oct 2011.
Louvre & Grand Palais (www.fiac.com).
This prestigious fair features a decent mix of big-name French and foreign galleries.

2 Nuit Blanche
Early Oct. Various venues (www.paris.fr).
Culture by moonlight – from 7pm to 7am – as galleries and museums host after-dark installations.

3 Slick
Late Oct 2011.
Various venues (www.slick-paris.com).
Slick focuses on young galleries and emerging artists.

Beaubourg & the Marais

Art:Concept
13 rue des Arquebusiers, 3rd (01.53.60.90.30, www.galerieartconcept.com). Mº St-Sébastien Froissart. **Open** 11am-7pm Tue-Sat.
Art:Concept presents some interesting, eclectic work. Look out for constructions by Richard Fauguet, as well as installations by Michel Blazy.

FAT Galerie
1 rue Dupetit-Thouars, 3rd (01.44.54.00.84, www.fatgalerie.com). Mº Temple. **Open** 1-7pm Tue-Sat.
Making their mark in the cluster of new galleries in the Haut Marais, Aurélia Lanson and Séverine van Warsch alternate shows by emerging artists – wall drawings by Cyprien Chabert, painter Lili Phung – with unusual furniture and objects by upcoming designers.

Galerie Alain Gutharc
7 rue St-Claude, 3rd (01.47.00.32.10, www.alaingutharc.com). Mº St-Sébastien Froissart. **Open** 11am-1pm, 2-7pm Tue, Wed, Fri, Sat; 11am-1pm, 2-8pm Thur.

The last of the Bastille galleries has now moved to the Marais. Gutharc talent-spots young French artists, often giving them a first gallery show, and also presents an annual art-design crossover. Among recent discoveries, check out the dreamily surreal paintings of Marlène Mocquet.

Galerie Almine Rech
19 rue de Saintonge, 3rd (01.45.83.71.90, www.galeriealminerech.com). Mº Filles du Calvaire. **Open** 11am-7pm Tue-Sat.
Continuing the rue Louise Weiss exodus, Almine Rech has returned to the Marais. Spread over two floors, her new gallery has more of an apartment feel in which to show off big international names. Among the regulars are light installations by James Turrell, neo-minimalists John McCracken and Anselm Reyle, the eclectic clowning of Ugo Rondinone and powerful films by French artist Ange Leccia.

Galerie Anne Barrault
22 rue St-Claude, 3rd (01.44.78.91.67, www.galerieannebarrault.com). Mº St-Sébastien Froissart. **Open** 11am-7pm Tue-Sat.
After initially concentrating on photography, notably the provocative feminist stagings by Katharina Bosse, Galerie Anne Barrault now presents a wider range of media.

Galerie Anne de Villepoix
43 rue de Montmorency, 3rd (01.42.78.32.24, www.annedevillepoix.com). Mº Rambuteau. **Open** 10am-7pm Mon-Sat.
As well as pieces by such international names as Doug Aitken and Erwin Wurm, Galerie Anne de Villepoix features distinctive and varied talents on the French scene, such as the bravura monochrome paintings by Ming, witty conceptual pieces by Franck Scurti and a politically loaded take on art history by Kader Attia.

Galerie Chantal Crousel
10 rue Charlot, 3rd (01.42.77.38.87, www.crousel.com). Mº Filles du Calvaire. **Open** 11am-1pm, 2-7pm Tue-Sat.
Crousel celebrated the 25th anniversary of her gallery with a move to this space in rue Charlot's burgeoning design and fashion scene. She was the first in France to show work by Mona Hatoum and Tony Cragg. Hot younger talents include Rikrit Tiravanija and Thomas Hirschhorn, as well as Anri Sala and Melik Ohanian, two of France's most exciting video artists, and Cuban duo Jennifer Allora and Guillermo Calzadilla.

Galerie Chez Valentin
9 rue St-Gilles, 3rd (01.48.87.42.55, www.galeriechezvalentin.com). Mº Chemin Vert. **Open** 11am-1pm, 2-7pm Tue-Sat.

Chez Valentin is a gallery at the experimental cutting edge, and shows here tend to be radically conceptual but often fun: look for pseudo-documentaries by video-maker Laurent Grasso, photos by Nicolas Moulin, installations by Pierre Ardouin and projects by former Prix Duchamp winner Mathieu Mercier.

Galerie Daniel Templon
30 rue Beaubourg, 3rd (01.42.72.14.10, www.danieltemplon.com). Mº Rambuteau. **Open** 10am-7pm Mon-Sat.
A Paris institution since the 1960s and conveniently located opposite the Centre Pompidou, Galerie T mainly shows paintings – wall-friendly items for wealthy private collectors. Jean-Michel Alberola, Gérard Garouste, Philippe Cognée and Vincent Corpet all feature on the list, along with the American David Salle and German expressionist Jonathan Meese.

Galerie Dominique Fiat
16 rue des Coutures-St-Gervais, 3rd (01.40.29.98.80, www.galeriefiat.com). Mº St-Sébastien Froissart. **Open** 11am-7pm Tue-Sat.
Fiat is part of a dynamic new generation of galleries. Shows have included the word games and art world parodies by novelist and artist Thomas Lélu (who renamed the gallery Galerie Dominique Fiat Panda for the occasion) and structures by Laurent Saksik.

Galerie Emmanuel Perrotin
76 rue de Turenne & 10 impasse St-Claude, 3rd (01.42.16.79.79, www.galerieperrotin.com). Mº St-Sébastien Froissart. **Open** 11am-7pm Tue-Sat.
Now installed in an elegant Marais *hôtel particulier*, Perrotin is one of the sharpest figures in town: not content with owning a gallery in Miami and a glossy magazine, he has recently jumped on the design bandwagon with shows by Robert Stadler and Eric Benqué. As well as the quirky Japanese set of Takashi Murakami, Mariko Mori et al, and big French names such as Sophie Calle, Xavier Veilhan, Prix Marcel Duchamp winner Tatiana Trouvé and Bernard Frize, he also features the radical Austrian collective Gelatin.

Galerie Les Filles du Calvaire
17 rue des Filles du Calvaire, 3rd (01.42.74.47.05, www.fillesducalvaire.com). Mº Filles du Calvaire. **Open** 11am-6.30pm Tue-Sat.
Les Filles du Calvaire is based in spacious premises in a two-storey glass-roofed industrial building in the Marais, with an offshoot in Brussels. Shows tend to concentrate on geometrical abstraction, featuring artists such as Olivier Mosset and James Hyde, along with photography and installation.

Galleries

World Class

Perfect places to stay, eat and explore.

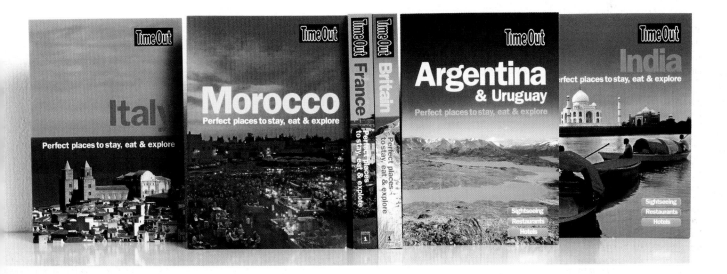

Galerie Frédéric Giroux
8 rue Charlot, 3rd (01.42.71.01.02, www.fredericgiroux.com). M° Filles du Calvaire. **Open** 11am-7pm Tue-Sat.
Worth a look for some intriguing figures on the French scene, including Delphine Kreuter, Rebecca Bournigault and the sand-covered polystyrene forms of Vincent Beurin.

Galerie Karsten Greve
5 rue du Grenier-St-Lazare, 3rd, www.galerie-karsten-greve.com). M° St-Sébastien Froissart. **Open** 11am-7pm Tue-Sat.
The Cologne gallery's smart Paris outpost is the venue for retrospective displays of top-ranking artists: think big names rather than risk taking. Jannis Kounellis, Louise Bourgeois, Pierre Soulages, John Chamberlain and Dubuffet have all featured here.

Galerie Laurent Godin
5 rue du Grenier-St-Lazare, 3rd (01.42.71.10.66, www.laurentgodin.com). M° Rambuteau. **Open** 11am-7pm Tue-Sat.
After running a public space in Lyon, Laurent Godin has quickly made a name with his Paris gallery, which features a diverse cross-generational mix, ranging from New York neo-Pop artist Haim Steinbach and waste-paper expert Wang Du to promising installations by young French artist Vincent Olinet.

Galerie Magda Danysz
78 rue Amelot, 11th (01.45.83.38.51, www.magda-gallery.com). M° Filles du Calvaire. **Open** 11am-7pm Tue-Fri; 2-7pm Sat.
Magda Danysz has moved into this three-storey space near the Cirque d'Hiver on the outer fringes of the Marais, aiming to make contemporary art accessible. She has a keen taste for artists influenced by graffiti and animation, as well as the hybrid art-design-science output of the Ultralab cooperative.

Galerie Marian Goodman
79 rue du Temple, 3rd (01.48.04.70.52, www.mariangoodman.com). M° Rambuteau. **Open** 11am-7pm Tue-Sat.
The veteran New York gallery owner can be counted on to pull out the stops with impressive shows from a roster of big international names, such as Gerhard Richter, William Kentridge and Steve McQueen.

Galerie Michel Rein
42 rue de Turenne, 3rd (01.42.72.68.13, www.michelrein.com). M° Chemin Vert. **Open** 11am-7pm Tue-Sat.
Although hampered by lack of space, Rein presents interesting multidisciplinary artists, such as Fabien Verschaere, Dora Garcia and Saadane Afif, and has recently picked up some of the talents from eastern Europe, such as Dan Perjovschi and Mark Raidpere.

Galerie de Multiples
17 rue St-Gilles, 3rd (01.48.87.21.77, www.galeriedemultiples.com). M° Chemin Vert. **Open** 2-7pm Tue-Sat.
Artist Mathieu Mercier was one of the founders of this gallery, dedicated to producing *'multiples'* (limited edition prints and artists' objects). Shows can take the form of anything from posters to soup ladles or pieces inspired by rock music.

Galerie Nathalie Obadia
3 rue du Cloître St-Merri, 4th (01.42.74.67.68, www.galerie-obadia.com). M° Hôtel de Ville. **Open** 11am-7pm Mon-Sat.
This gallery, located just around the corner from the Centre Pompidou, opened in 1993 and shows leading artsists such as Martin Barr, Lorna Simpson and Agnès Varda in a sleek, white space. A sister gallery opened in Brussels in 2008.

Galerie Nelson-Freeman
59 rue Quincampoix, 4th (01.42.71.74.56, www.galerienelsonfreeman.com). M° Hôtel de Ville or Rambuteau. **Open** 11am-1pm, 2-7pm Tue-Sat.
A tie-up with New York dealer Peter Freeman has given a more North American slant to the Nelson stable, although it continues to show big European names, such as photographer Thomas Ruff and Pedro Cabrita Reis, as well as representing late Fluxus maverick Robert Filliou.

Galerie Polaris
15 rue des Arquebusiers, 3rd (01.42.72.21.27, www.galeriepolaris.com). M° St-Sébastien Froissart. **Open** 1-7pm Tue-Fri; 11am-1pm, 2-7pm Sat.
Polaris occupies an old gym and shows artists mainly working in photo and video, such as Stéphane Couturier, known for his stunning, flattened perspective images of building sites.

Galerie Schleicher + Lange
12 rue de Picardie, 3rd (01.42.77.02.77, www.schleicherlange.com). M° Filles du Calvaire. **Open** 2-7pm Tue-Sat.
Shows put on by these two young Germans focus on artists yet to exhibit in Paris, alternating between upcoming London-based talents, such as Zoe Mendelson, and discoveries from eastern Europe. They also host Vidéo Surveillance, an occasional programme of video screenings.

Galerie Thaddaeus Ropac
7 rue Debelleyme, 3rd (01.42.72.99.00, www.ropac.net). M° Filles du Calvaire. **Open** 10am-7pm Tue-Sat.
Ropac's main base is in Salzburg, Austria, where he opened his first gallery in 1983. But he also runs this attractive Paris gallery, featuring American Pop and neo-Pop by Warhol, Tom Sachs and Alex Katz, along with European artists such as Ilya Kabakov, Sylvie Fleury and Gilbert & George.

Galerie Yvon Lambert
108 rue Vieille-du-Temple, 3rd (01.42.71.09.33, www.yvon-lambert.com). M° Filles du Calvaire. **Open** 10am-1pm, 2.30-7pm Tue-Fri; 10am-7pm Sat.
Lambert celebrated 30 years in the business in 2006, and remains a powerhouse of the French scene, with plenty of big-name stuff, a New York offshoot and a personal collection granted museum status in Avignon. The gallery includes a dedicated area for video installations, and the main space shows leading international names – American bigwigs Andres Serrano, Sol LeWitt, Nan Goldin and Jenny Holzer, plus next-generation artists Douglas Gordon and Jonathan Monk. The street-front art bookshop has a window showcase and basement gallery for younger talents.

Galerie Zürcher
56 rue Chapon, 3rd (01.42.72.82.20, www.galeriezurcher.com). M° Arts et Métiers. **Open** noon-7pm Tue-Sat.
Among the Chinese wholesalers north of Beaubourg, Zürcher shows emerging artists with a fresh take on painting and video: Marc Desgrandschamps, Camille Vivier and Elisa Sighicelli. Mathilde Rosier and Eléonore de Montesquiou are also featured.

Jousse Entreprise
6 rue St-Claude, 3rd (01.53.82.10.18, www.jousse-entreprise.com). M° St-Sébastien Froissart. **Open** 11am-7pm Tue-Sat.
Philippe Jousse presents contemporary artists – such as Matthieu Laurette, Frank Perrin and challenging video artist Clarisse Hahn – alongside 1950s avant-garde furniture by Jean Prouvé, lights by Serge Mouille and ceramics by Georges Jouve, which are also shown at the sister design gallery at 18 rue de Seine in the 6th.

Champs-Elysées & northern Paris

Galerie Jérôme de Noirmont
38 av Matignon, 8th (01.42.89.89.00, www.denoirmont.com). M° Miromesnil. **Open** 11am-7pm Mon-Sat.
In a chic space near the Elysées Palace, Jérôme de Noirmont puts on eye-catching shows featuring big names such as AR Penck, Jeff Koons, Shirin Neshat, Bettina Rheims, Fabrice Hyber, kitsch duo Pierre et Gilles, and art-world personalities Eva and Adèle.

Galerie Lelong
13 rue de Téhéran, 8th (01.45.63.13.19, www.galerie-lelong.com). M° Miromesnil. **Open** 10.30am-6pm Tue-Fri; 2-6.30pm Sat. Closed Aug.
If you hanker after Miró, Tàpies, Bacon or Kounellis, Lelong is a safe bet, with its selection of bankable, postwar international names.

Russian Tea Room
1 av Trudaine, 9th (01.45.26.04.60, www.russiantearoom.fr). M° Anvers. **Open** 2-7pm Tue-Sat.
The Russian Tea Room was set up in 2004 to promote Russian art in Europe and opened its gallery space in 2007. Exhibitions focus mainly on the young post-*perestroika* generation with an emphasis on gritty photography.

St-Germain-des-Prés

Galerie Denise René
196 bd St-Germain, 7th (01.42.22.77.57, www.deniserene.com). M° Rue du Bac or St-Germain-des-Prés. **Open** 10am-1pm, 2-7pm Tue-Sat. Closed Aug.
Denise René has remained committed to kinetic art, Op art and geometrical abstraction by Soto et al, ever since Jean Tinguely first presented his machines here in the 1950s.

Galerie G-P et N Vallois
36 rue de Seine, 6th (01.46.34.61.07, www.galerie-vallois.com). M° Mabillon or Odéon. **Open** 10.30am-1pm, 2-7pm Mon-Sat.
Interesting conceptual work in all media includes the likes of American provocateur Paul McCarthy, Turner Prize winner Keith Tyson and a clutch of French thirty- and fortysomethings, including Alain Bublex and Gilles Barbier, as well as veteran *affichiste* Jacques Villeglé.

Galerie Kamel Mennour
47 rue St-André-des-Arts, 6th (01.56.24.03.63, www.kamelmennour.fr). M° Odéon or St-Michel. **Open** 11am-7pm Tue-Sat.
After bursting on to the St-Germain art scene with shows by fashion photography crossovers David LaChapelle and Ellen von Unwerth and filmmaker Larry Clark, and introducing emerging artists Kader Attia and Adel Abdessemed, Mennour has confirmed his presence on the gallery scene with a move to these grand new premises in a *hôtel particulier*. Recent shows by an impressive cross-generational stable have included Daniel Buren, Claude Lévêque and Huang Yong-Ping.

Galerie Lara Vincy
47 rue de Seine, 6th (01.43.26.72.51, www.lara-vincy.com). M° Mabillon, Odéon or St-Germain-des-Prés. **Open** 2.30-7pm Mon; 11am-1pm, 2.30-7pm Tue-Sat.
Liliane Vincy, daughter of the founder, is one of the few characters to retain something of the old St-Germain spirit and a sense of 1970s Fluxus-style happenings. Interesting theme and solo shows include master of the epigram Ben, as well as text-, music- and performance-related pieces.

Galerie Loevenbruck
6 rue Jacques Callot, 6th (01.53.10.85.68, www.loevenbruck.com). M° Mabillon or Odéon. **Open** 11am-7pm Tue-Sat.
Galerie Loevenbruck has injected a dose of humour into St-Germain-des-Prés with artists – Virginie Barré, Bruno Peinado and Olivier Blankaert, and Philippe Mayeux – who treat conceptual concerns with a light touch and graphic talent. The gallery moved into new, larger premises at the end of 2010.

in situ Fabienne Leclerc
6 rue du Pont-de-Lodi, 6th (01.53.79.06.12, www.insituparis.fr). M° Odéon or St-Michel. **Open** 11am-7pm Tue-Sat.
Fabienne Leclerc consistently impresses with the quality of installations from a set of highly individual artists, including Mark Dion, known for his interest in zoology and classification, Indian star Subodh Gupta and video maestro Gary Hill.

13th arrondissement

Air de Paris
32 rue Louise-Weiss, 13th (01.44.23.02.77, www.airdeparis.com). M° Chevaleret. **Open** 11am-7pm Tue-Sat.
This gallery shows experimental, neo-conceptual and chaotic material. A hip international stable of artists includes Liam Gillick, Carsten Höller, Sarah Morris and Philippe Parreno.

Air de Paris.

Gay & Lesbian

Paris is home to a thriving LGBT community, visibly involved in every walk of life – right at the top of the tree sits openly gay mayor Bertrand Delanoë, who came out two years before running for office. Local gays and lesbians say they encounter very little, if any, discrimination in their day-to-day lives, and feel integrated into mainstream society. However, the annual **Gay Pride March**, held on the last Sunday in June, is a powerful reminder of what the gay rights movement has accomplished over the last 30 years, and of what is yet to be achieved.

GETTING OUT AND ABOUT

Beaubourg and the '**gay Marais**' are particularly gay-friendly. Most of the dedicated venues are to be found in the area bounded by rue des Archives, rue Vieille-du-Temple and rue Ste-Croix-de-la-Bretonnerie. A light lunch, coffee or cocktail at a neighbourhood café will provide ample opportunity to check out the talent, and a casual stroll through the nearby streets will introduce you to a seductive selection of shops. Fetishists, funky fashionistas, bohemians and bibliophiles will each find a boutique to suit their fancy. A good place to start is **Les Mots à la Bouche**, where you can peruse the gay and lesbian press or pick up a few of the free monthly magazines listing the hottest events.

In the evening, kick off the action at a café or a restaurant before moving on to the bars and clubs, which don't really get going until after midnight. Start by mixing it up at **Le Mixer** or the nearby red hot **Raidd Bar**. The **Queen** on the Champs-Elysées remains a clubbing institution, as does the smaller and more intimate **L'Insolite**. The popular **La Scène Bastille** (*see p101*) is a relatively new trendsetter; on the other side of the coin is the oldest gay club in Paris, **Le Club 18**, which is always fun and still draws a great crowd, and the always surprising **Le Tango**. Lesbians can find a few nice bars of their own on rue du Roi de Sicile, or relax at the popular and friendly **Chez Moune** near Pigalle.

INFORMATION AND RESOURCES

Magazines *Têtu* (www.tetu.com) and *Préf* (www.prefmag.com) report on goings-on in gay life and have text in English; *La Dixième Muse* (www.ladixiememuse.com) provides similar information for lesbians. There are also several free bi-weekly publications, distributed in gay bookshops, bars and clubs; the most useful are *2 X-Paris* (www.2xparis.fr), *Tribumove* (www.tribumove.com) and *AgendaQ*. And for the girls, there's *Barbi(e)turix* (www.barbieturix.com). Two excellent and informative websites provide regularly updated listings (in English) of all things gay and lesbian in the city: www.paris-gay.com and www.gayvox.com.

Centre Gai et Lesbien

63 rue Beaubourg, 3rd (01.43.57.21.47, www.centrelgbtparis.org). Mº Arts et Métiers or Rambuteau. **Open** 6-8pm Mon; 3-8pm Tue, Wed, Thur; 1-8pm Fri, Sat; 4-7pm Sun. *Library* 6.30-8pm Mon; 2-8pm Tue, Wed; 3-5pm Fri; 5-7pm Sat.

After many years on rue Keller, the Centre Gai et Lesbien has moved into more centrally located digs in the Marais. In addition to providing information on topics ranging from the sociopolitical (if you don't know what rights gays and lesbians have or don't have in France, you can find out all you need to know here) to the biomedical (the latest developments in the treatment of HIV, where to get tested for free), this multifunctional centre and library also hosts meetings for a variety of support groups and associations.

Inter-LGBT

c/o Maison des Associations du 3ème, boîte 8, 5 rue Perrée, 75003 Paris (01.72.70.39.22, www.inter-lgbt.org).
The Interassociative Lesbienne, Gaie, Bi & Trans is an umbrella group of 50 LGBT associations. It organises the Printemps des Assoces in the Espace des Blancs Manteaux (48 rue Vieille-du-Temple, 4th) every April and the annual Gay Pride March.

SOS Homophobie

01.48.06.42.41, www.sos-homophobie.org. **Open** 6-10pm Mon, Wed, Fri; 8-10pm Tue, Thur; 2-4pm Sat; 6-8pm Sun.
Victims of and witnesses to homophobic crimes and discrimination can report them to this confidential service, which offers support and publishes an annual report on homophobia.

Gay Paris

Bars & cafés

Le Bear's Den

6 rue des Lombards, 4th (01.42.71.08.20, www.bearsden.fr). Mº Châtelet or Hôtel de Ville. **Open** 4pm-2am Mon-Thur, Sun; 4pm-5am Fri, Sat. **Credit** MC, V.
The Bear's Den is a friendly local for bears, muscle bears, chubbies and their admirers. Visit the website for details on comically named theme nights such as 'Charcuterie'. Bears, wolves and men who love hairy men also gather at the nearby Wolf (*see right*).

Le Café Arena

29 rue St-Denis, 1st (01.45.08.15.16). Mº Châtelet. **Open** 9am-6am daily. **Credit** MC, V.
This bar-restaurant has a great terrace for people-watching and friendly staff; it's still the hottest rendezvous in Les Halles.

Café Cox

15 rue des Archives, 4th (01.42.72.08.00, www.cox.fr). Mº Hôtel de Ville. **Open** 1pm-2am daily. **No credit cards.**
Beefy, hairy, shaven-headed men congregate on the pavement in front of Café Cox for post-work drinks, before moving on to more intimate surroundings.

Le Duplex

25 rue Michel-le-Comte, 3rd (01.42.72.80.86, www.duplex-bar.com). Mº Hôtel de Ville or Rambuteau. **Open** 8pm-2am Mon-Thur, Sun; 8pm-4am Fri, Sat. **Credit** V.

This small bar just round the corner from the Centre Pompidou caters to a thirtysomething crowd. It's a popular meeting place for various gay associations, with friendly staff and local art on the walls.

Eagle

33bis rue des Lombards, 1st (01.42.33.41.45, www.eagleparis.com). Mº Les Halles. **Open** 6pm-4am Mon-Thur, Sun; 6pm-6am Fri, Sat. **No credit cards.**
Formerly the London, this old bar has found new life, becoming a hit with bears, daddies, leathermen and the men who admire them. Have tea and cake on the patio early on, a shot of Jack at the bar later, or penetrate deeper and enjoy the disco backroom.

Etamine Café

13 rue des Ecouffes, 4th (01.44.78.09.62, www.etamine-cafe.com). Mº St-Paul. **Open** noon-midnight Tue-Sun. **Credit** AmEx, MC, V.
This simple but delicious café is located very close to the lesbian bars of the Marais, and offers a contemporary and inventive twist on the old classics. Excellent food, affordable prices, good atmosphere.

Le Mixer

23 rue Ste-Croix-de-la-Bretonnerie, 4th (01.77.16.54.76, www.lemixerbar.fr). Mº Hôtel de Ville. **Open** 5pm-2am daily. **Credit** AmEx, MC, V.
A mixed, young and carefree crowd gathers at this watering hole for cocktails before heading off to the clubs. DJs spin techno and house to energise the crowd. Some nights are strictly for girls.

Open Café

17 rue des Archives, 4th (01.42.72.26.18, www.opencafe.fr). Mº Hôtel de Ville or Rambuteau. **Open** 11am-2am Mon-Thur, Sun; 11am-4am Fri, Sat. **Credit** MC, V.
Cruise and be cruised in the café everybody visits at some point in the evening. Pop out on to the terrace, and enjoy the people-watching.

Le Quetzal

10 rue de la Verrerie, 4th (01.48.87.99.07). Mº Hôtel de Ville. **Open** 5pm-5am daily. **Credit** MC, V.
This bar is considered to be one of the 'musts' of the Marais. You might be able to find some action in the small dark space upstairs.

Raidd Bar

23 rue du Temple, 4th (01.42.77.04.88, www.raiddbar.com). Mº Hôtel de Ville. **Open** 5pm-4am Mon-Thur; 5pm-5am Fri-Sun. **Credit** (min €10) MC, V.
The Raidd Bar is standing room only at street level, with another bar down below. The hot, herculean bartenders take turns in the wall-mounted shower for nightly shows and the dancefloor is jam-packed.

Wolf

37 rue des Lombards, 1st (01.40.28.02.52, www.wolfparis.com). Mº Les Halles. **Open** 5pm-2am daily. **No credit cards.**

Gay Pride.

Critics'choice

1 Le Quetzal
Hot men and a few drag queens keep things lively at this Marais bar. *See left.*

2 Le Bunker
This cruising club is the hottest in Paris. *See p96.*

3 Legay Choc
A deservedly popular sandwich spot with a great name in the Marais. *See p96.*

This place is popular with bears, wolves, otters and a variety of other species, mostly on the hairy side. Everyone is welcome, though, and the ambience is laid-back.

Restaurants

Le Bar à Manger (BAM)

13 rue des Lavandières-Ste-Opportune, 1st (01.42.21.01.72). Mº Les Halles. **Open** noon-3pm, 7-11pm Mon-Sat. **Credit** MC, V.
Excellent, creative cuisine in a pleasant, relaxed setting. There are *prix fixe* menus available at lunch (€18) and dinner (€32).

Le Gai Moulin

10 rue St-Merri, 4th (01.48.87.06.00, www.le-gai-moulin.com). Mº Hôtel de Ville. **Open** noon-midnight daily. **Credit** MC, V.
One of the oldest gay-run restaurants in Paris, the Gai Moulin opened its doors in 1981 and recently moved a few doors down from its original location (now a smaller café, Le Petit Canaillou, run by the same team). The owner is famously convivial, creating a lovely, friendly atmosphere. On Tuesdays, a pianist belts out French songs, and it's not uncommon for the whole room to sing along.

Le Kofi du Marais

54 rue Ste-Croix-de-la-Bretonnerie, 4th (01.48.87.48.71). Mº Hôtel de Ville. **Open** 6pm-midnight daily. **Credit** AmEx, MC, V.
Modern, simple cooking with an American twist is the speciality here. Club sandwiches, burgers and salads are menu staples. Prices are reasonable and the service is good too.

Aux Trois Petits Cochons

31 rue Tiquetonne, 2nd (01.42.33.39.69, www.auxtroispetitscochons.fr). Mº Etienne Marcel. **Open** 7.30pm-midnight daily. **Credit** MC, V.
This gay-owned, gay-run restaurant serves up traditional French cuisine with a contemporary twist. The three-course menu (€33) changes daily and is based on the freshest ingredients available. It's a very popular place, so booking is recommended.

Ze Restoo

41 rue des Blancs-Manteaux, 3rd (01.42.74.10.29). Mº Rambuteau. **Open** 7pm-1am Mon-Sat. **Credit** AmEx, MC, V.
This restaurant has become a popular place in which to eat with friends before heading out for a fun-filled evening. There's a very relaxed atmosphere, with good service and imaginative dishes.

Clubs

As well as the venues listed below, a mixed but increasingly gay crowd mingles at **Nouveau Casino** (*see p100*) and **La Scène Bastille** (*see p101*). Most gay clubs are very hetero-friendly.

Le Club 18

18 rue de Beaujolais, 1st (01.42.97.52.13, www.club18.fr). Mº Palais-Royal or Pyramides. **Open** midnight-dawn Fri-Sun. **Admission** (incl 1 drink) €10. **Credit** Bar MC, V.

Gay & Lesbian

Le Mixer. See p95.

The oldest gay club in Paris attracts a young and beautiful clientele. It is not very big, and the decor isn't all that great, but the music is fun and there's a very laid-back vibe. Everyone is here to dance and have a good time.

Le CUD Bar
12 rue des Haudriettes, 3rd (01.42.77.44.12, www.cud-paris.com). M° Rambuteau. **Open** 4pm-7am daily. **Credit** MC, V.
Upstairs is a laid-back bar, but downstairs in the old cellar is a dancefloor that can get very crowded, especially after 2am. The crowd is a mixed bunch, and it's popular with the bears.

Les Follivores & les Crazyvores
Bataclan, 50 bd Voltaire, 11th (01.43.14.00.30, www.follivores.com). M° Oberkampf. **Open** 11.30pm-dawn. **Admission** (incl 1 drink) €17. **Credit** V.
Twice a month, the Bataclan concert hall transforms itself into a club to host these two hugely popular parties. Crazyvores features music from the 1970s and '80s, and at Follivores the DJs spin gay classics from all eras mixed up with cutting-edge techno. These are big events with exuberant crowds; the drag queens put on their best ballgowns and biggest wigs, and the men sport their tightest tops. Great fun.

L'Insolite
33 rue des Petits-Champs, 1st (01.42.61.99.22, www.insolite-club.fr). M° Pyramide. **Open** 11pm-5am Mon-Thur, Sun; 11pm-7am Fri, Sat. **Admission** free Wed, Thur, Sun; €10 (incl 1 drink) Fri, Sat. **Credit** *Bar* MC, V.
Hidden away underneath an old courtyard, this small club is a fun nightspot; the music tends to major in '80s disco hits and new wave, with a few more recent club hits thrown in for good measure.

Queen
102 av des Champs-Elysées, 8th (01.53.89.08.90, www.queen.fr). M° George V. **Open** midnight-7am Mon-Thur, Sun; midnight-8am Fri, Sat. **Admission** €15 Mon-Thur, Sun; €20 Fri, Sat. **Credit** *Bar* AmEx, MC, V.
One of the oldest and largest clubs, Queen's main gay nights are Saturday@Queen and Overkitsch on Sundays in the summer months, but every night is a little gay. Big-name DJs often spin here to a crowd peppered with VIPs.

Le Tango (La Boîte à Frissons)
13 rue au Maire, 3rd (01.42.72.17.78, www.boite-a-frissons.fr). M° Arts et Métiers. **Open** 8pm-2am Thur; 10.30pm-5am Fri, Sat; 6-11pm Sun. **Admission** €8; free Thur. **Credit** V.
Wacky crowd, Madonna songs and accordion tunes. At the Friday and Saturday Bal de la Boîte à Frissons, couples dance the foxtrot, tango, madison or *guinguette* in the early part of the evening, followed after midnight by music of every variety except techno. This unusual old dance hall never fails to entertain.

Sex clubs & saunas

Le Bunker
150 rue St-Maur, 11th (01.53.36.78.87, www.bunker-cruising.com). M° Goncourt. **Open** 4pm-2am Mon-Thur; 4pm-3.30am Fri; 4pm-4.30am Sat; 4pm-1am Sun. **Admission** €7.50.
This place features all-naked and underwear-only nights during the week, and hardcore themes at the weekend. Friday is a very popular night, as is the first Saturday of the month, when Le Bunker hosts its S&M 'Red and Black Night' – not for the faint-hearted.

Le Dépot
10 rue aux Ours, 3rd (01.44.54.96.96, www.suncity.fr). M° Etienne Marcel. **Open** 2pm-8am Mon-Sat; 2-9pm Sun. **Admission** €7.50 before 9pm Mon-Sat; €10 before 2am & after 5am Mon-Sat; €13 (incl 1 drink) 2-5am Mon-Sat & after 5pm Sun; €7.50 before 5pm Sun. **Credit** MC, V.
A very busy dance club upstairs with a labyrinthine maze of cubicles, glory holes and darkrooms downstairs. The glory days of this glory hole are gone now, but it still draws a crowd, particularly on the weekends. Pickpockets work the darkrooms, so be careful.

IDM
4 rue du Fbg-Montmartre, 9th (01.45.23.10.03, www.idm-sauna.com). M° Grands Boulevards. **Open** noon-1am daily. **Admission** €21; €15 before 9.30pm & under-35s. **Credit** MC, V.
The city's best gay sauna has three levels and plenty of cabins and corridors to prowl. The wet sauna is on two levels, and the small relaxation pool and showers are always at the perfect temperature. A few times a month, there are also performances by drag queens and other singers.

Next
87 rue St-Honoré, 1st (www.lenext.fr). M° Les Halles. **Open** noon-3am Mon-Thur; non-stop Fri-Sun. **Admission** €7 before 7pm; €10 (incl 1 drink) after 7pm; €6 (incl 1 drink) under-26s. **Credit** MC, V.
This hot sex club is located in one of the chicest parts of the capital. It doesn't really get going until after many clubs have closed, and at 6am on a Sunday morning it's probably the hottest, hardest place in town. The bar upstairs is a nice place to mingle before heading downstairs to check out the sexy labyrinth.

Le QG
12 rue Simon le Franc, 4th (01.48.87.74.18, www.qgbar.fr). M° Rambuteau. **Open** 3pm-5am Mon-Thur; 3pm-7am Fri; 2pm-7am Sat; 2pm-5am Sun. **Credit** MC, V.
This bar is well known among those who enjoy the harder gay scene. Upstairs is a simple bar, but downstairs is where the real action is, with a very well equipped backroom/dungeon. It's a small place and gets crowded at weekends.

Sun City
62 bd de Sébastopol, 3rd (01.42.74.31.41, www.suncity-paris.fr). M° Etienne Marcel. **Open** noon-6am daily. **Admission** €18.50 Mon-Thur; €20 Fri-Sun; €12 after 3am; €11 under-26s. **Credit** MC, V.
Owned and operated by the Dépot team (*see above*), this Bollywood-themed venue is the largest gay sauna in Europe, with a small pool, large steam room, gym and bar. The clientele is very good looking and knows it, so there's a lot of attitude attached.

Shops & services

Boy'z Bazaar
5 rue Ste-Croix-de-la-Bretonnerie, 4th (01.42.71.67.00, www.boyzbazaar.com). M° Hôtel de Ville or St-Paul. **Open** noon-8.30pm Mon-Thur; noon-10pm Fri, Sat; 1-8pm Sun. **Credit** AmEx, MC, V.
Stocks some of the city's trendiest clothes for nightclubbers, fashionistas and urban hipsters, in the heart of the gaybourhood.
Other location 5 rue des Guillemites, 4th (01.42.71.63.86).

Les Dessous d'Apollon
15 rue du Bourg-Tibourg, 4th (01.42.71.87.37, www.lesdessousdapollon.com). M° Hôtel de Ville or St-Paul. **Open** noon-7.30pm Mon, Tue; 11am-8pm Wed-Sat; 2-8pm Sun. **Credit** AmEx, DC, MC, V.
Probably the most extensive selection of underwear – from functional to downright eccentric – that you'll ever see, plus T-shirts and accessories.

IEM
16 rue Ste-Croix-de-la-Bretonnerie, 4th (01.42.74.01.61, www.iem.fr). M° Hôtel de Ville. **Open** 1-8pm Mon-Thur; 1-9pm Fri, Sat; 2-8pm Sun. **Credit** AmEx, MC, V.
This sex hypermarket caters for those keen on the harder side of gay life. Videos, clothes and gadgets can all be found, and there are leather and rubber goods upstairs.

Legay Choc
45 rue Ste-Croix-de-la-Bretonnerie, 4th (01.48.87.56.88, www.legaychoc.fr). M° Hôtel de Ville. **Open** 8am-8pm Mon, Thur-Sun. **No credit cards.**
The pastries are delightful, and the lunch-hour sandwiches are generous, so expect lengthy queues. A satellite store, serving only sandwiches, is at 17 rue des Archives (01.48.87.24.61).

Les Mots à la Bouche
6 rue Ste-Croix-de-la-Bretonnerie, 4th (01.42.78.88.30, www.motsbouche.com). M° Hôtel de Ville or St-Paul. **Open** 11am-11pm Mon-Sat; 1-9pm Sun. **Credit** AmEx, MC, V.
An institution in the Marais, this bookshop has a large selection of gay fiction, non-fiction, magazines, and English-language books.

Nickel
48 rue des Francs-Bourgeois, 4th (01.42.77.41.10, www.nickel.fr). M° Hôtel de Ville or Rambuteau. **Open** 11am-7.30pm Mon, Tue, Fri, Sat; 11am-9pm Wed, Thur. **Credit** AmEx, MC, V.
Body and skincare treatments, strictly for men. A one-hour facial is €48-€77, a manicure €21 and an hour-long massage €48-€69. Staff are adept, friendly and knowledgeable.

Plus Que Parfait
23 rue des Blancs-Manteaux, 4th (01.42.71.09.05). M° Hôtel de Ville or St-Paul. **Open** 3-8pm Mon; noon-8pm Tue-Sat; 3-7pm Sun. *Clothes deposit* Mon-Fri. **Credit** MC, V.
This *dépôt vente*, where pristine, second-hand designer clothing is sold on commission, is a great place for men's fashion finds.

Space Hair
10 rue Rambuteau, 3rd (01.48.87.28.51, www.space-hair.com). M° Rambuteau. **Open** noon-10pm Mon; 10am-10pm Tue-Sat; 11.30am-8pm Sun. **Credit** MC, V.
Space Hair is divided into two salons, Cosmic and Classic, with a 1980s kitsch feel, late opening hours and cute stylists; it's best to book ahead.

Where to stay

Hôtel Central Marais
2 rue Ste-Croix-de-la-Bretonnerie, 4th (01.48.87.56.08, www.hotelcentralmarais.com). M° Hôtel de Ville or St-Paul. **Rates** €89 single or double; €109 triple; €7 breakfast. **Credit** MC, V.
If location and affordable rates are more important than plush surroundings, this hotel is a good bet. The barmen of the Central bar (located below the hotel) act as receptionists from 5pm until 2am, and can keep you updated on the local nightlife.

Hôtel Duo
11 rue du Temple, 4th (01.42.72.72.22, www.duoparis.com). M° Hôtel de Ville. **Rates** €200-€380 double. **Credit** AmEx, DC, MC, V.
The mixed but very gay-friendly Duo is a stylish place to rest your head. What's more, it has helpful staff at the reception – a rarity in this trendy area.

Lesbian Paris

Famous club Pulp is much missed, but the girlie scene continues to flourish, especially near the corner of rue du Roi de Sicile and rue des Ecouffes in the Marais. Most of the bars welcome men accompanied by women, but a few are women only. Some girl-only parties are staged at clubs such as **Le Tango** (*see left*); see the free monthly magazine *Barbi(e)turix* for listings.

La Champmeslé
4 rue Chabanais, 2nd (01.42.96.85.20, www.lachampmesle.com). M° Bourse or Pyramides. **Open** 4pm-4am daily. **Credit** MC, V.
This veteran girlie bar remains a popular venue for lesbian locals and visitors. Beer is the drink of choice; pull up a seat and enjoy the regular cabaret nights.

Chez Moune
54 rue Pigalle, 9th (01.45.26.64.64, www.chezmoune.com). M° Pigalle. **Open** 11pm-late Tue-Sat. **Credit** MC, V.
Probably the oldest lesbian cabaret in Paris, Chez Moune opened in 1936 and still has nightly shows. Saturdays are traditionally women only, but in the last year other phallo-friendly dance parties and cabaret shows have occasionally been held.

Le Day Off
10 rue de l'Isly, 8th (01.45.22.87.90, www.ledayoff.com). M° Gare St-Lazare. **Open** 7pm-3am Mon-Fri. **Credit** MC, V.
An apt name for this weekday-only pub – heavy drinking enjoyed by work-weary lesbians. It gets crowded in the early evening.

Dollhouse
24 rue du Roi de Sicile, 4th (09.50.74.59.74, www.dollhouse.fr). M° St-Paul. **Open** 2-8pm Mon, Sun; 1-8pm Tue-Sat; 2-8pm Sun. **Credit** MC, V.
This store specialises in lingerie and gadgets for the girls. Upstairs you'll find a selection of sophisticated and sexy underwear; head downstairs for the sexcessories.

Les Filles de Paris
57 rue Quincampoix, 4th (01.42.71.72.20). M° Rambuteau. **Open** 10pm-5am Wed-Sat. **Credit** MC, V.
The team behind Le Troisième Lieu (*see below*) are shaking up the late-night scene with this new restaurant-club. Food is served until 5am on weekends, but expect party animals to let loose and take over the tiny dancefloor from midnight onwards, when female DJs start spinning eclectic electro. Occasional burlesque shows, pole dancing classes and open-mic nights on Wednesdays add extra spice to the venue. Boys are welcome too.

Les Jacasses
5 rue des Ecouffes, 4th (01.42.71.15.51). M° St-Paul. **Open** 5pm-2am Wed-Sun. **Credit** MC, V.
This relaxed bar for women, just around the corner from the girlie bars on rue du Roi de Sicile, makes a welcome addition to the neighbourhood.

O'Kubi Caffé
219 rue St-Maur, 10th (01.42.01.35.08, www.okubicaffe.com). M° Goncourt. **Open** 6pm-2am Tue-Sat; noon-11pm Sun. **Credit** MC, V.
O'Kubi recently celebrated its third anniversary and continues to grow in popularity. It also has a bar and serves light food.

Le Rive Gauche
1 rue du Sabot, 6th (01.40.20.43.23, www.lerivegauche.com). M° St-Germain-des-Prés. **Open** 11pm-dawn Fri, Sat. **Admission** €10-€15. **No credit cards.**
This weekend women-only nightclub is one of the hottest places on the lesbian scene. The decor is '70s and the music eclectic.

Le So What!
30 rue du Roi de Sicile, 4th (no phone). M° St-Paul. **Open** 8pm-2am Thur-Sat. **Credit** MC, V.
The So What! is primarily a girlie bar, but everyone's welcome. Recent theme nights have included live rock and drag queens.

Le Troisième Lieu
62 rue Quincampoix, 4th (01.48.04.85.64). M° Rambuteau. **Open** 6pm-2am Mon-Sat. **Credit** MC, V.
Elaborate *tartines*, delicious desserts and strong drinks are the fare at this lesbian-run bar and restaurant. Despite its militant subtitle ('Cantine des Ginettes Armées'), the vibe is jovial. There are also areas devoted to music and dancing.

Unity Bar
176-178 rue St-Martin, 3rd (01.42.72.70.59, http://unity.bar.free.fr). M° Rambuteau. **Open** 4pm-2am daily. **No credit cards.**
This ladies-only bar is more butch than lipstick, with pool tables and a good beer selection.

OLIVIA RUTHERFORD

Music

While Carla Bruni may have done wonders for raising the profile of French music with her winsome folky pop, and Sarkozy's son is also in the business as a hip hop producer, there is much more to the French music scene than pure political connections. The big news in the world of classical music is the construction of the Philharmonie, a prestigious new concert venue for the city. Paris's vibrant opera scene continues to thrill, jazz is enjoying a mini revival, talented new rock bands are emerging, as are venues to accommodate them, and *chanson* is managing to reinvent itelf for a 21st-century audience. Musically speaking, this town is jumping.

Classical & Opera

After many years of argument and controversy, the construction of the much-vaunted **Philharmonie** is well under way. And architect Jean Nouvel's 2,400-seat concert hall is set to open on time in 2012. The Philharmonie will give the city a major venue for the symphonic repertoire, as well as hosting jazz and world music.

Across the city at the **Opéra de Paris**, the top job of director has passed to Nicolas Joel, who was previously in charge of the Capitole in Toulouse – a choice guaranteed to please more conservative operagoers, but frustrate modernist fans of the outgoing Gerard Mortier, whose controversial new productions infuriated and thrilled in equal measure. Those in search of the avant-garde will, however, be comforted by the ongoing success of the **Ensemble Intercontemporain**, and the important role that **IRCAM** continues to play in contemporary musical creation in Europe, forming exciting young composers such as Bruno Mantovani.

Although the Philharmonie is being built as a home for the **Orchestre de Paris** and its new musical director Paavo Järvi, it will also provide a welcome alternative to the **Maison de Radio France**, which is currently the permanent home of the estimable **Orchestre Philharmonique de Radio France** and the **Orchestre National de France**.

A success story of recent seasons has been the return to glory of the **Opéra Comique**. Under the direction of Jérôme Deschamps, the house has rediscovered a specifically French repertoire – figures like Hérold and Grétry, as well as their Baroque predecessors and contemporary successors, can now be seen in a perfect setting. At the **Châtelet**, Jean-Luc Choplin's popular programming has included a string of retro musicals recently, including *Show Boat* and *My Fair Lady* in 2010, with *Sweeney Todd* making an appearance in May 2011.

The main musical provider in summer is the **Paris Quartier d'Eté** festival (01.44.94.98.00, www.quartierdete.com), with concerts in gardens across the city. The **Festival de Saint-Denis** (01.48.13.06.07, www.festival-saint-denis.com) also offers top names in a spectacular setting.

INFORMATION AND TICKETS

For comprehensive listings, see *L'Officiel des Spectacles* or *Pariscope*. Monthly magazine *Diapason* also lists classical concerts, while *Opéra* magazine provides good coverage of all things vocal. Look out too for *Cadences* and *La Terrasse*, two free monthlies.

Orchestras & ensembles

Les Arts Florissants

01.43.87.98.88, www.arts-florissants.com.
William Christie's 'Arts Flo' remains France's leading Early Music group and his conducting of Rameau and Lully has become a benchmark of authentic performance. The group has not neglected passing on the secrets of Baroque ornamentation to the next generation, with the Jardin des Voix busy cultivating exciting young talent.

Ensemble Intercontemporain

01.44.84.44.50, www.ensembleinter.com.
Glamorous Finnish conductor Susanna Mälkki is the musical director of this bastion of contemporary music founded by, and still often conducted by, Pierre Boulez. The exacting standard of the 31 soloists is beyond reproach, and the ensemble has an enviable international reputation, making it one of the most poular on the Paris music scene.

Ensemble Orchestral de Paris

08.00.42.67.57, www.ensemble-orchestral-paris.com.
The greatly respected John Nelson has been replaced by Joseph Swensen as principal guest conductor of this chamber orchestra for the next couple of seasons. The orchestra struggles to find its specificity in a competitive field, but this season the ensemble is again heading out for mini stays in popular areas of the city in an admirable quest to try to attract new audiences.

Orchestre Colonne

01.42.33.72.89, www.orchestrecolonne.fr.
Sometimes found at the Salle Gaveau (*see p98*), this orchestra – led by composer Laurent Petitgirard – has intelligent programming, with every concert teaming a contemporary work with more popular repertoire. The excellent series of *concerts éveil* continues to provide bargain tickets for parents and children, making an ideal introduction to classical music.

Orchestre Lamoureux

01.58.39.30.30, www.orchestrelamoureux.com.
This worthy orchestra, which made the first recording of Ravel's *Boléro*, remains woefully underfunded, and its concert appearances in the capital are sparse. But musical director Yutaka Sado is a fine conductor, and his programming is uncompromising and prepared to take on the challenge of new and unusual repertoire.

Orchestre National de France

01.56.40.15.16, www.radiofrance.fr.
Daniele Gatti is now firmly in charge of France's leading orchestra, bringing along his own brand of warm Italianate theatricality, in sharp contrast to his predecessor, veteran Kurt Masur, and his more structured Germanic approach.

Orchestre de Paris

01.42.56.13.13, www.orchestredeparis.com.
Highlights for early 2011 include a Beethoven recital by Chinese piano prodigy Lang Lang and Daniel Barenboim playing Liszt.

Orchestre Pasdeloup

01.42.78.10.00, www.concertspasdeloup.com.
The Pasdeloup is the oldest orchestra in Paris, and the 2011 season celebrates its 150th anniversary with a great collection of concerts under the watchful eye of artistic director Patrice Fontanarosa.

Orchestre Philharmonique de Radio France

01.56.40.15.16, www.radiofrance.fr.
Myung-Whun Chung has now been musical director here for a decade, and the 2011 season is based around a celebration of his ten years in charge. The standard of the orchestra is considered to lag behind that of the Orchestre National.

Venues

Auditorium du Louvre

Entrance through Pyramid, Cour Napoléon, Musée du Louvre, rue de Rivoli, 1st (01.40.20.55.55, reservations 01.40.20.55.00, www.louvre.fr). M° Palais Royal Musée du Louvre. **Box office** 9am-5.30pm Mon, Wed-Fri. Closed July, Aug. **Admission** €5-€30. **Credit** MC, V.
The Auditorium du Louvre packs in a full season with chamber music, lunchtime concerts and music on film. This season is divided into themed groups, presenting young artists performing a wide range of music, including a focus on Viennese opera and string quartets from around the world in 2011.

Châtelet – Théâtre Musical de Paris

1 pl du Châtelet, 1st (01.40.28.28.40, www.chatelet-theatre.com). M° Châtelet. **Box office** 11am-7pm Mon-Sat; 1hr before performance Sun. *By phone* 10am-7pm Mon-Sat. Closed July, Aug. **Admission** €10-€141.50. **Credit** AmEx, DC, MC, V.
Jean-Luc Choplin has radically changed the programming of this bastion of Paris music-making. An attempt to rediscover the theatre's popular roots has been achieved at the expense of traditional fine music subscribers. The general impression is of programming that has been slimmed down for financial reasons, with even the previously vibrant concert programme looking threadbare. An adaptation of *The Postman* looks tempting, though.

Cité de la Musique

221 av Jean-Jaurès, 19th (01.44.84.45.00, www.cite-musique.fr). M° Porte de Pantin. **Box office** noon-6pm Tue-Sun. *By phone* 11am-7pm Mon-Sat; 10am-6pm Sun. **Admission** €9-€39. **Credit** MC, V.
The energetic programming here features a vast non-classical repertoire that includes world music and jazz. Concerts are frequently grouped into series with a pedagogic aim, tending to concentrate on the Baroque and the contemporary. The Conservatoire (209 av Jean-Jaurès, 19th, 01.40.40.45.45) hosts world-class performers and professors, and features many free concerts.

IRCAM

1 pl Igor-Stravinsky, 4th (01.44.78.48.43, www.ircam.fr). M° Hôtel de Ville.
The underground bunker next to the Centre Pompidou, set up in 1969 by the avant-garde composer Pierre Boulez to create electronic microtonal music for the new century, is looking less redundant nowadays with a full programme of courses and conferences. Not many concerts take place in the building itself, but IRCAM sponsors concerts with a modernist theme across the city. See the website for concert venues, and details of courses.

Maison de Radio France

116 av du Président-Kennedy, 16th (01.56.40.15.16, www.radiofrance.fr). M° Passy/RER Avenue du Pdt Kennedy. **Box office** 11am-6pm Mon-Sat. **Admission** €10-€85. **Credit** AmEx, DC, MC, V.
State-owned radio station France Musique broadcasts a broad range of classical concerts from this comfortless cylindrical building on the banks of the Seine. The main stage (the Salle Olivier Messiaen) may be charmless, but the quality of music-making from the Orchestre National de France and the Orchestre Philharmonique de Radio France makes up for much. The Passe Musique offers under-28s admission to four concerts for €18, or a year of concerts for €99. Watch out for free events here, as well as the enterprising Présences contemporary music festival, which welcomes Finnish conductor and composer Esa-Pekka Salonen to help celebrate its 20th anniversary in 2011.

Musée National du Moyen Age

6 pl Paul-Painlevé, 5th (01.53.73.78.16, www.musee-moyenage.fr). M° Cluny La Sorbonne. **Admission** free-€16; €13 reductions. **Credit** AmEx, MC, V.
The museum presents a worthy programme of medieval concerts in which troubadours reflect the museum's collection. There are also occasional 45- minute *heures musicales* in a similar style.

Musée d'Orsay

62 rue de Lille, 7th (01.40.49.47.57, www.musee-orsay.fr). M° Solférino/RER Musée d'Orsay. **Admission** €6-€32. **Credit** MC, V.
The museum runs a full series of lunchtime and evening concerts. The lunchtime concerts at 12.30pm concentrate on promising young artists. Evening concerts are more prestigious, with a series inspired by English poetry and literature in 2011.

Opéra National de Paris, Bastille

Pl de la Bastille, 12th (08.92.89.90.90, from abroad 01.71.25.24.23, www.operadeparis.fr). M° Bastille. **Box office** (130 rue de Lyon, 12th) 11.30am-6.30pm Mon-Sat. *By phone* 9am-6pm Mon-Fri; 9am-1pm Sat. **Admission** €5-€180. **Credit** AmEx, MC, V.
The Bastille is never going to be a beautiful building, and the unflattering acoustics and miles of corridors combine to create an atmosphere more akin to an airport than an opera house. But the standard of performance is what matters and the Bastille has some exciting evenings planned under director Nicolas Joel. The new season brings to the stage great classics such as Puccini's *Tosca*, Wagner's *Crépuscule des Dieux* and Verdi's *Otello*.

Opéra National de Paris, Palais Garnier

Pl de l'Opéra, 9th (08.92.89.90.90, from abroad 01.71.25.24.23, www.operadeparis.fr). M° Opéra. **Box office** 11.30am-6.30pm Mon-Sat. *By phone* 9am-6pm Mon-Fri; 9am-1pm Sat. **Admission** €8-€180. **Credit** AmEx, MC, V.
The Palais Garnier, with its ornate, extravagant decor and ceiling by Marc Chagall, is the jewel in the crown of Paris music-making, as well as a glistening focal point for the Right Bank. The Opéra National often favours the high-tech Bastille (*see above*) for new productions, but the matchless acoustics of the Palais Garnier are superior to the newer Bastille's, and they will surely be shaken by the Paris revival of Mozart's *Così Fan Tutte* in June 2011.

Péniche Opéra

Facing 46 quai de la Loire, 19th (01.53.35.07.77, reservations 01.53.35.07.77, www.penicheopera.com). M° Jaurès or Laumière. **Box office** 10am-7pm Mon-Fri; 2-7pm Sat. **Admission** €12-€24. **Credit** MC, V.

Critics' choice

1 Salle Pleyel
Barenboim and Haitink will be here in 2011. *See p98.*

2 Le Bus Palladium
Don't miss this legendary rock venue with a vintage house vibe. *See p98.*

3 Orchestre de Paris
One of the finest orchestras in France. *See left.*

The Péniche Opéra is an enterprising, barge-based company that produces chamber-scale shows and concerts, directed by the indefatigable Mireille Larroche. Programming ranges from Baroque rarities to contemporary creations via charming revue-style shows. This is one Paris institution that deserves to be kept afloat.

Salle Cortot

78 rue Cardinet, 17th (01.47.63.47.48, www.ecolenormalecortot.com). M° Malesherbes. **No box office. Admission** free-€25 (phone for details).

This intimate concert hall in the Ecole Normale de Musique has excellent acoustics for chamber music and master classes, which are often free.

Salle Gaveau

45 rue La Boétie, 8th (01.49.53.05.07, www.sallegaveau.com). M° Miromesnil. **Box office** 9.30am-6pm Mon-Fri; 1-9pm Sat; 1-4.30pm Sun. **Admission** €10-€100. **Credit** MC, V.

An ideal venue for chamber music, the Salle Gaveau seems to be passing through one of the least productive stages of its history. The top-quality chamber music that used to be the hall's core repertoire is a rarity. Too many variety shows and dark evenings make for sorry reading.

Salle Pleyel

252 rue du Fbg-St-Honoré, 8th (01.42.56.13.13, www.sallepleyel.fr). M° Ternes. **Box office** noon-7pm Mon-Sat; 2hrs before show Sun. *By phone* 11am-7pm Mon-Sat; 11am-5pm Sun. **Admission** €10-€190. **Credit** MC, V.

Home to the Orchestre de Paris, the restored concert hall looks splendid. If the improved acoustics are only partially successful, the venue has nevertheless regained its status as the capital's leading concert hall for large-scale symphonic concerts, and should keep it until the completion of the city's new concert hall in 2012.

La Sorbonne

Amphitheatre Richelieu, 17 rue de la Sorbonne, 5th (01.42.62.71.71, www.musiqueen sorbonne.fr). M° Cluny La Sorbonne or Odéon. **Box office** by phone or at the door. **Admission** €18-€40. **Credit** MC, V.

The lecture theatre of the university continues with a series of ambitious concerts featuring the orchestra and chorus of the Sorbonne. Standards waver but the setting is impressive.

Théâtre des Bouffes du Nord

37bis bd de la Chapelle, 10th (01.46.07.34.50, www.bouffesdunord.com). M° La Chapelle. **Box office** 11am-6pm Mon-Sat. **Admission** €10-€28. **Credit** MC, V.

This elegant theatre directed by Micheline Rozan and Peter Brook boasts one of the most imaginative programmes of chamber music in the capital. Adventurous programming this year includes the return of veteran harpsichordist Gustav Leonhardt.

Théâtre des Champs-Elysées

15 av Montaigne, 8th (01.49.52.50.50, www.theatrechampselysees.fr). M° Alma Marceau. **Box office** noon-7pm Mon-Sat; 2hrs before show Sun. *By phone* 11am-6pm Mon-Fri; 2-6pm Sat. **Admission** €5-€160. **Credit** AmEx, MC, V.

This beautiful art nouveau theatre, with bas-reliefs by Bourdelle, hosted the scandalous première of Stravinsky's *Le Sacre du Printemps* in 1913. Michel Franck took over as director in 2010. It remains the favourite venue for visiting foreign orchestras, and the prestigious line-up of visiting maestros includes Lorin Maazel, Riccardo Muti and Christian Thielemann, as well as Covent Garden's musical director Antonio Pappano. Staged performances include a new production of Mozart's opera *Idomeneo*, as well as Verdi's *Il Trovatore* and Handel's *Ariodante*.

Théâtre National de l'Opéra Comique

Pl Boieldieu, 2nd (01.42.44.45.40, tickets 08.25.01.01.23, www.opera-comique.com). M° Richelieu Drouot. **Box office** 11am-7pm Mon-Sat; 11am-5pm Sun. *By phone* 11am-7pm Mon-Sat; 11am-5pm Sun **Admission** €6-€115. **Credit** AmEx, DC, MC, V.

Its promotion to national theatre status has brought this jewel box of a theatre back to life and the opening seasons have been welcomed with enthusiasm by press and public alike. The 2011 season includes Offenbach's *Les Brigands* and Prokofiev's *Les Fiançailles au Couvent*.

Théâtre du Tambour-Royal

94 rue du Fbg-du-Temple, 11th (01.48.06.72.34, www.tambourroyal.jimdo. com). M° Belleville or Goncourt. **Box office** 6.30-8pm Tue-Fri; 3-8pm Sat, Sun. *By phone* 10am-8pm Mon-Sat. **Admission** €16-€21. **Credit** MC, V.

This charming venue is where Maurice Chevalier launched his career. Its programming includes occasional concerts of light repertoire and revue-style shows, including the popular Best of Mozart, but expectations should not be raised too high.

Théâtre de la Ville

2 pl du Châtelet, 4th (01.42.74.22.77, www.theatredelaville-paris.com). M° Châtelet. **Box office** 11am-7pm Mon; 11am-8pm Tue-Sat. *By phone* 11am-7pm Mon-Sat. **Admission** €13-€18. **Credit** MC, V.

Programming in this vertiginous concrete amphitheatre, hidden behind a classical façade, features hip chamber music outfits such as the Kronos and Takács Quartets and Early Music pioneer Fabio Biondi. The season here spills over to performances at Les Abbesses (31 rue des Abbesses, 18th), which shares the same phone number and box office hours, but is closed on Mondays.

Rock, Roots & Jazz

The capital is overflowing with authentic concert venues, from monster stadiums to intimate bars and jazz clubs, and venues like **Nouveau Casino** and **L'International** give precious stage space to those on the way up the musical ladder.

Chanson française is still going strong, helped by the revival of **Les Trois Baudets**, a government-subsidised *chanson* hall in the heart of Pigalle – French law dictates that 40 per cent of music broadcast in France must be in the French language.

Jazz is having a mini revival too: after the disappearance of old flames like Le Slow Club (once one of the most famous jazz joints in Europe), Le Bilboquet and Les 7 Lézards, a handful of new joints have opened up, while flagship clubs **Au Duc des Lombards**, **New Morning** and **Le Sunset/Le Sunside** continue to book top-notch acts.

Paris is also a European leader for world music, particularly African and Arab acts. And don't forget that every 21 June, the whole city turns into one giant music venue for the **Fête de la Musique** (*see p11-13*), when a party in the street is guaranteed.

FESTIVAL FEVER

Paris is home to some big festivals. **Rock en Seine** (www.rockenseine.com) takes place 27-29 Aug 2011 and hosted bands such as Massive Attack and Arcade Fire in 2010.

INFORMATION AND RESOURCES

Website www.gogoparis.com selects regular concert highlights and also features a decent gig list for the coming months, with all information provided in English and French; www.infoconcert.com is also worth a look. The weekly magazine *Les Inrockuptibles* is a valuable resource. Alternatively, try bi-monthly gig bible *Lylo*, free in bars and branches of Fnac. The **Fnac** and **Virgin Megastore** ticket offices (for both, *see p82*) also display details of up-and-coming concerts. For reduced tickets try www.billetreduc.com.

Rock & pop

Stadium venues

Palais des Congrès

Porte Maillot, 17th (www.viparis.com). M° Porte Maillot. **Open** times vary. **Credit** MC, V.

The sound and the views are good wherever you sit in this state-of-the-art amphitheatre. The likes of Tori Amos, Cliff Richard and 'Sex Bomb' Tom Jones have all recently graced the stage.

Palais Omnisports de Paris-Bercy

8 bd de Bercy, 12th (08.92.39.01.00, www.bercy.fr). M° Bercy. **Box office** 11am-6pm Mon-Sat. **Credit** AmEx, DC, MC, V.

The traditional venue for rock and pop behemoths: Supertramp and Lady Gaga were among the big draws last year, and Kylie Minogue and Usher are calling in here in 2011.

Zénith

211 av Jean-Jaurès, 19th (www.zenith-paris.com). M° Porte de Pantin. **Open** times vary. **Credit** MC, V.

State-of-the-art sound and credible bands make this the large venue of choice. Amy Macdonald and Deep Purple played here last year.

Bar & club venues

Le Bataclan

50 bd Voltaire, 11th (01.43.14.00.30, www. le-bataclan.com). M° Oberkampf. **Open** times vary. **Credit** MC, V.

This distinctive venue, fashioned like a Chinese pagoda with a distinctive multi-coloured façade, first opened in 1864 and remains admirably discerning in its booking of rock, world, jazz and hip hop acts.

Batofar

Opposite 11 quai François-Mauriac, 13th (09.71.25.50.61, www.batofar.org). M° Bibliothèque François-Mitterrand or Quai de la Gare. **Open** 9pm-late Wed-Sat. **Admission** €5-€20. **Credit** MC, V.

This enduringly hip party boat lays on DJs, rappers and assorted underground noise-merchants for the benefit of an up-for-it crowd. It comes into its own in the summer, when the terrace opens at 7pm.

Le Bus Palladium

6 rue Fontaine, 9th (01.45.26.80.35, www.lebuspalladium.com). M° St-Georges, Pigalle or Blanche. **Open** *Concerts* times vary. *Club* 10.30pm-5am Tue, Fri, Sat. **Admission** free-€25. **Credit** AmEx, MC, V.

Graced by the likes of Mick Jagger and The Beatles in its heyday, this rock venue is back on the map. While the new generation gets wild in the pit, former regulars are trying to catch their breath at the restaurant upstairs (8pm-5am Tue-Sat). Check the programme for concerts. Club nights on Tuesdays, Fridays and Saturdays are a guaranteed riot, and diners get in for free.

La Cigale/La Boule Noire

120 bd de Rochechouart, 18th (01.49.25.81.75, www.lacigale.fr, www.laboule-noire.fr). M° Anvers or Pigalle. **Open** times vary. **Credit** MC, V.

Easily one of Paris's finest venues, the lovely, horseshoe-shaped theatre La Cigale is linked to more cosy venue La Boule Noire, good for catching cult-ish visiting indie and rock acts (many from the UK).

Les Disquaires

6 rue des Taillandiers, 11th (01.40.21.94.60, www.lesdisquaires.com). M° Bastille. **Open** 7pm-late daily. **Admission** free. **Credit** MC, V.

This party bar provides live pop, rock, DJs and electro to a hip crowd of thirtysomethings bent on partying like they were 20 again. It's a fine spot for discovering underground Paris sounds.

Elysée Montmartre

72 bd de Rochechouart, 18th (01.44.92.45.36, www.elyseemontmartre.com). M° Anvers. **Open** *Bar* 11am-midnight daily. *Concerts* times vary. **Credit** *Bar* MC, V.

The Elysée Montmartre still hosts enduring party night Le Bal (*see p100*), but mostly reserves its stage for mid-sized alternative rock and electronic acts, plus a handful of disco old-timers and the occasional headliner.

La Flèche d'Or

102bis rue de Bagnolet, 20th (01.44.64.01.02, www.flechedor.fr). M° Alexandre Dumas. **Open** 8pm-2am Wed-Sat. *Concerts* times vary. **Admission** free. **Credit** MC, V.

This much-loved indie and electro venue, which reopened in November 2009 after a six-month shutdown, is a great place for music, with three or four bands playing a night. It also gives monthly residencies to local groups and DJs.

L'International

5-7 rue Moret, 11th (01.49.29.76.45, www.linternational.fr). M° Ménilmontant. **Open** 2pm-2am Tue-Sat; 6pm-midnight Sun. **Concerts** 8pm, 10pm daily. **Admission** free. **Credit** MC, V.

This concert-bar is a breath of fresh air, with free entry and a string of on-the-up bands playing to hip indie crowds every night of the week. Once a month there's an after-party until 4am.

Mains d'Oeuvres

1 rue Charles-Garnier, 93400 St-Ouen (01.40.11.25.25, www.mainsdoeuvres.org). M° Garibaldi or Porte de Clignancourt. **Open** *Bar* 9.30am-midnight daily. *Concerts* 8.30pm, days vary. **Admission** free-€20. **Credit** *Bar* MC, V.

A hub for fringe musical and performance activity just outside Paris, the Mains d'Oeuvres is a huge former leisure centre for car factory workers that specialises in leftfield electro, rock mavericks and multimedia artists. It frequently hosts the Festival des Attitudes Indé for up-and-coming bands.

La Maroquinerie

23 rue Boyer, 20th (01.40.33.35.05, www.lamaroquinerie.fr). M° Gambetta. **Open** *Box office* (in person only) 2.30-6.30pm Mon-Fri. **Concerts** 8pm Mon-Fri. Closed Aug. **Credit** MC, V.

Literary discussion and rock 'n' roll coexist at this happening locale. It's home to the Inrocks Indie Club nights, featuring up-and-coming rock acts, but there are still traces of its world music roots.

La Mécanique Ondulatoire

8 passage Thière, 11th (01.43.55.16.74, www.myspace.com/lamecanique). M° Bastille or Ledru Rollin. **Open** 6pm-2am Mon-Sat. **Concerts** from 8pm Tue-Sat. **Admission** €4-€7. **Credit** MC, V.

Cementing Bastille's status as Paris's prime hangout for rockers, this exciting venue has three levels and alternates eclectic DJs with live acts in the cellar, plus there's jazz on Tuesday nights.

Le Motel

8 passage Josset, 11th (01.58.30.88.52, www.myspace.com/lemotel). M° Ledru Rollin. **Open** 6pm-1.45am Tue-Sun. Closed Aug. **Credit** MC, V.

This most Anglophile of Paris bars, with Stone Roses and Smiths posters adorning the walls, manages to fit plenty of live bands, including some of the best new local talent, on to its tiny stage.

Nouveau Casino

109 rue Oberkampf, 11th (01.43.57.57.40, www.nouveaucasino.net). M° Ménilmontant, Parmentier or St-Maur. **Open** *Concerts* times vary. **Credit** *Bar* MC, V.

A bankable and loveable, albeit rather commercial, venue run by the adjacent Café Charbon, with fab gigs and club nights featuring rock, dub and garage, plus reasonable drinks prices.

Olympia

28 bd des Capucines, 9th (08.92.68.33.68, www.olympiahall.com). M° Opéra. **Open** *Box office* 10am-9pm Mon-Sat; 10am-7pm Sun. *Concerts* times vary. **Credit** AmEx, DC, MC, V.

The Beatles, Frank Sinatra, Jimi Hendrix and Edith Piaf have all performed here, as did Jacques Brel. Now it's mainly home to nostalgia and *variété*, with a smattering of contemporary sounds.

O'Sullivans by the Mill

92 bd de Clichy, 18th (01.53.09.08.49, www.osullivans-pubs.com). M° Blanche. **Open** noon-5am Mon-Thur; noon-6am Fri-Sun. **Concerts** times vary. **Credit** MC, V.

This Irish chain bar is all about late, late nights, with grizzly rock gigs, DJs and open mic nights the first Wednesday of the month. Thursday's Funked Up (11pm-3am) night is always wild.

Point Ephémère

200 quai de Valmy, 10th (01.40.34.02.48, www.pointephemere.org). M° Jaurès or Louis Blanc. **Open** noon-2am daily. *Concerts* 8.30pm daily. **Credit** AmEx, DC, MC, V.

This converted warehouse is a classy affair, bringing together up-and-coming local rock, jazz and world gigs with a decent restaurant, dance and recording studios and exhibitions.

Le Reservoir

16 rue de la Forge-Royale, 11th (01.43.56.39.60, www.reservoirclub.com). M° Faidherbe Chaligny or Ledru-Rollin.

Chanson revival

While 1930s Britain was revelling in Hollywood exports, France was whooping it up with its own answer to American culture: Le Music Hall. This form of cabaret (leagues away from the glitzy boob-wobbling of today) saw the rise of stars Charles Trenet, Edith Piaf and Maurice Chevalier, followed after World War II by Jacques Brel, Georges Brassens and Serge Gainsbourg, whose poetry and humour became the emblem of *chanson française*.

While *chanson* artists performed across the city, one small theatre, **Les Trois Baudets** (*see below*), launched more musical careers between 1947 and 1966 than anywhere else – Gainsbourg, Brel, Hénri Salvador and Brigitte Fontaine all performed there. But in 1967 the unthinkable occurred. The Trois Baudets closed, becoming an erotic cabaret, then a crumbling concert venue, before falling into disrepair in 1996. In 2001, after much lobbying (notably by Charles Aznavour) and the rise of the 'new' *chanson française* in the charts thanks to next-generation songwriters like Bénabar, Anaïs and Vincent Delerm, it was decided that Paris lacked a theatre devoted to francophone music, and that Les Trois Baudets – the cradle of *chanson* – should be brought back to life.

Ten years on the makeover is spectacular. Done up in black and red, with a theatre named after founder Jacques Canetti, it offers enough musical genres (rock, electro, folk and slam) to appeal to a wide range of fans. And for the artists themselves, getting such high-profile stage space is a rare treat indeed.

Open 8pm-5am Tue-Sat; 11.30pm-4.30pm Sun. **Admission** free-€12. **Credit** AmEx, DC, MC, V.
This classy, Anglo-inspired venue hosts regular club nights and live indie acts, as well as low-key performances from larger acts. It also serves a decent 'jazz brunch' on Sundays.

La Scène Bastille
2bis rue des Taillandiers, 11th (01.48.06.50.70, www.la-scene.com). M° Bastille. **Open** midnight-6am Wed-Sun. *Concerts* 7.30-10.45pm Mon-Fri. Closed Aug. **Admission** free-€20. **Credit** MC, V.
This beautifully designed bar offers you the option of chilling out in alcoves or joining the kids to groove to hip hop, funk and jazz.

Le Trabendo
211 av Jean-Jaurès, 19th (01.49.25.89.99, www.trabendo.fr). M° Porte de Pantin. **Open** times vary. **Credit** MC, V.
This quirky spot in the 19th has carved out a niche in all things alternative, from post-rock to drum 'n' bass, avant-garde hip hop to modern jazz.

Le Who's Bar
13 rue du Petit Pont, 5th (01.43.54.80.71, www.myspace.com/whosbar). M° St-Michel. **Open** 6.30pm-5.30am daily. **Admission** free. **Credit** MC, V.
With Picasso-style frescoes on the walls and a nightly programme of live pop and rock, Le Who's is St-Michel's hippest music bar. Expect live acoustics on weekdays and harder all-round rock at weekends.

Chanson

La Bellevilloise
19-21 rue Boyer, 20th (01.46.36.07.07, www.labellevilloise.com). M° Gambetta or Ménilmontant. **Open** 5.30pm-2am Wed-Fri; 11am-2am Sat, Sun. **Admission** free. **Credit** MC, V.
Is there anything that Paris's former co-operative doesn't do? There's food, drinks, DJs and live music – lashings of it, not only in the downstairs concert hall but in the Oliviers restaurant and upstairs bar too. The music selection is eclectic, but there's a folky, world bent.

FEATURED ESTABLISHMENT

Chez Adel
10 rue de la Grange-aux-Belles, 10th (01.42.08.24.61). M° Jacques Bonsergent. **Open** noon-midnight Tue-Sun. *Concerts* 5pm Tue-Sun. **Admission** free. **Credit** MC, V.
Patron Adel is probably the most renowned *chanson* café owner in Paris, and this fine den of kitsch attracts countless devotees with its repertoire of *chanson* and Eastern European sounds.

Le Limonaire
18 Cité Bergère, 9th (01.45.23.33.33, http://limonaire.free.fr). M° Grands Boulevards. **Open** 7pm-2am Mon; 6pm-2am Fri-Sun. *Concerts* 10pm Tue-Sat; 7pm Sun. Closed Mon, Sun in July & Aug. **Credit** MC, V.
Serious *chanson* takes the limelight and performances vary from piano-led *chansonniers* to cabaret. Arrive at 8pm if you want to eat.

Au Magique
42 rue de Gergovie, 14th (01.45.42.26.10, www.aumagique.com). M° Pernety. **Open** 8pm-2am Wed-Sun. *Concerts* 9.30pm Wed, Thur; 10pm Fri, Sat. **No credit cards.**
Artiste-in-residence Marc Havet serenades punters with politically incorrect *chanson* at weekends; you can also expect poetry events and exhibitions of photos and paintings.

Sentier des Halles
50 rue d'Aboukir, 2nd (01.42.61.89.90, www.lesentierdeshalles.fr). M° Sentier. **Open** 7pm-midnight Tue-Sat. *Concerts* 8-10pm Tue-Sat. Closed Aug. **No credit cards.**
Le Sentier has developed beyond its traditional *chanson* base to embrace a variety of modern styles plus the occasional stand-up act.

Les Trois Baudets
64 bd de Clichy, 18th (01.42.62.33.33, www.lestroisbaudets.com). M° Pigalle. **Open** 6pm-1.30am Tue-Sat. Closed Aug. **Admission** €5-€20. **Credit** MC, V.
All dolled up in black and red, with a 250-seater theatre, an enviable sound system, two bars and a restaurant, this concert hall encourages *chanson française* and other musical genres (rock, electro, folk and slam) – as long as they're in French.

Le Vieux Belleville
12 rue des Envierges, 20th (01.44.62.92.66, www.le-vieux-belleville.com). M° Pyrénées. **Open** *Concerts* 9pm Thur-Sat. Closed mid Aug. **Credit** MC, V.
If you're looking for an authentic Belleville rendezvous, there's no better location than this old-style café with terrace, where the traditions of accordion music and croaky *chanson* endure.

World & traditional

Cité de la Musique
221 av Jean-Jaurès, 19th (01.44.84.44.84, www.cite-musique.fr). M° Porte de Pantin. **Open** noon-6pm Tue-Sat; 10am-6pm Sun. *Concerts* Tue-Sat (times vary). **Admission** €18-€40. **Credit** MC, V.
This museum/concert complex welcomes big names from all over the globe, and also does a fine line in contemporary classical, avant-jazz and electronica.

Institut du Monde Arabe
1 rue des Fossés-St-Bernard, 5th (01.40.51.38.38, www.imarabe.org). M° Jussieu. **Open** 10am-6pm Tue-Sun. *Tickets* 10am-5pm Tue-Sun; 90mins before show. *Concerts* usually 8.30pm Fri, Sat. **Admission** €8-€26. **Credit** MC, V.
This huge, plush auditorium attracts some of the biggest names in the world of Arab music.

Le Kibélé
12 rue de l'Echiquier, 10th (01.48.24.57.74, www.kibele.fr). M° Bonne Nouvelle. **Open** noon-2pm, 7pm-midnight Mon-Sat. *Concerts* 9.30pm Mon-Sat. **Admission** free-€5. **Credit** AmEx, MC, V.
Music from across the Mediterranean and beyond in an intimate vaulted cellar, with a decent Turkish restaurant overhead. Before the concerts, other acts such as one-man shows take to the stage from 7.30pm.

Musée Guimet
6 pl d'Iéna, 16th (01.56.52.53.00, auditorium 01.40.73.88.18, www.guimet.fr). M° Iéna. **Open** 10am-6pm Wed-Mon. *Concerts* 8.30pm some Thur, Fri & Sat. **Admission** €17; €12 reductions. **Credit** MC, V.
Indian and Asian music by visiting troupes, as well as dance and theatre, takes pride of place in the auditorium of the Musée Guimet.

Satellit' Café
44 rue de la Folie-Méricourt, 11th (01.47.00.48.87, www.satellit-cafe.com). M° Oberkampf, Parmentier or St-Ambroise. **Open** *Bar* 8pm-1am Tue, Wed; 8pm-3am or 5am Thur; 10pm-6am Fri, Sat; 6pm-2am Sun. *Club* 11pm-6am Thur-Sat. *Concerts* 9pm Tue-Thur. **Admission** €10 concerts; €12 club (incl 2 drinks); €8 reductions. **Credit** *Bar* MC, V.
This bar lends its sound system to all things global, but the focus is on traditional African music mixed in with the occasional bit of Bollywood.

Théatre de la Ville
2 pl du Châtelet, 4th (01.42.74.22.77, www.theatredelaville-paris.com). M° Châtelet. **Open** *Box office* 11am-7pm Mon-Sat. *Concerts* 8.30pm Mon-Fri; 5pm Sun. **Admission** €13-€18. **Credit** MC, V.
Music and dance of the highest order can be found here, with jazz and music from just about anywhere you can think of (Iraq, Japan, Thailand, Brittany) amid the classical recitals.

Jazz & blues

Ateliers de Charonne
21 rue de Charonne, 11th (01.40.21.83.35, www.ateliercharonne.com). M° Charonne or Ledru-Rollin. **Open** 7pm-1am Tue-Sat. **Admission** free. *Dinner & concert* €35. **Credit** MC, V.
This spanking new jazz club is the place to see the rising stars of gypsy jazz (*jazz manouche*). If you want to grab a good spot near the front of the stage, reserve for dinner and the show.

Autour de Midi-Minuit
11 rue Lepic, 18th (01.55.79.16.48, www.autourdemidi.fr). M° Blanche. **Open** noon-2.30pm, 7pm-late Tue-Sun. *Concerts* 9.30pm Tue, Wed; 10pm Thur-Sat; 7pm Sun. **Admission** free-€5. **Credit** MC, V.
The Tuesday night *boeuf* (jam session) is always free, as are many other concerts – some by big names like Laurent Epstein, Yoni Zelnik and Bruno Casties. The upstairs restaurant serves reasonably priced French classic cuisine.

Le Baiser Salé
58 rue des Lombards, 1st (01.42.33.37.71, www.lebaisersale.com). M° Châtelet. **Open** *Concerts* daily (times vary). **Admission** *Chanson* €13; €8 in advance. *Jazz* €12-€25. **Credit** AmEx, DC, MC, V.
The 'Salty Kiss' divides its time between passing *chanson* merchants, world artists and jazzmen of every stripe, from trad to fusion.

Caveau de la Huchette
5 rue de la Huchette, 5th (01.43.26.65.05, www.caveaudelahuchette.fr). M° St-Michel. **Open** *Concerts* 10.15pm-2.30am Mon-Wed, Sun; 10.15pm-6am Thur-Sat. **Admission** €12 Mon-Thur, Sun; €14 Fri, Sat; €10 reductions. **Credit** MC, V.
This medieval cellar has been a Paris mainstay for more than 60 years. Jazz shows are followed by early-hours performances in a swing, rock, soul or disco vein.

Caveau des Oubliettes
52 rue Galande, 5th (01.46.34.23.09, www.caveaudesoubliettes.fr). M° St-Michel. **Open** 5pm-4am daily. *Concerts* 10pm daily. **Admission** free. **Credit** MC, V.
A foot-tapping frenzy echoes in this medieval dungeon, complete with instruments of torture, a guillotine and underground passages. Mondays are Pop Rock Jam nights with the JB Manis Trio, Tuesdays are Jazz Jam Boogaloo nights with Jeff Hoffman, and there are various other jam sessions during the rest of the week.

Au Duc des Lombards
42 rue des Lombards, 1st (01.42.33.22.88, www.ducdeslombards.com). M° Châtelet. **Open** *Concerts* 8pm Mon-Sat. Closed mid Aug. **Admission** €18-€25; free after midnight Fri, Sat. **Credit** MC, V.
This venerable jazz spot goes from strength to strength, attracting a high class of performer and a savvy crowd. Check out the '*bon plans*' section of the website, which offers reduced-price tickets.

Lionel Hampton Jazz Club
Hôtel Méridien Etoile, 81 bd Gouvion-St-Cyr, 17th (01.40.68.30.42, www.jazzclub-paris.com). M° Porte Maillot. **Open** *Concerts* 10pm-2am Mon-Sat; 12.30pm Sun. **Admission** (incl 1 drink) €26. **Credit** MC, V.
This hotel venue has a strong US bias, with lots of R&B and gospel, but native acts get a look in as well. It's not particularly progressive, but classy nonetheless (and the cocktails are great).

New Morning
7-9 rue des Petites-Ecuries, 10th (01.45.23.51.41, www.newmorning.com). **Open** 8pm daily. *Concerts* 9pm daily. **Admission** €15-€25. **Credit** MC, V.
One of the best places to see the latest cutting-edge jazz exponents on show, with a policy that also embraces *chanson*, blues, world music and sophisticated pop.

Le Petit Journal Montparnasse
113 rue du Commandant René-Mouchotte, 14th (01.43.21.56.70, www.petitjournal montparnasse.com). M° Gaîté or Montparnasse-Bienvenüe. **Open** 8pm-2am daily. *Concerts* 10pm Mon-Sat. **Admission** (incl 1 drink) €25; €15 reductions; €60 dinner. **Credit** MC, V.
A two-level jazz brasserie with New Orleans sound, big bands, Latin and soul-gospel.

Le Sunset/Le Sunside
60 rue des Lombards, 1st (01.40.26.46.60, www.sunset-sunside.com). M° Châtelet. **Open** *Concerts* 8pm, 9pm, 10pm daily. **Admission** free-€30. **Credit** MC, V.
A split-personality venue, with Sunset dealing in electric groups and Sunside hosting acoustic performances. Their renown pulls in big jazz names.

Le Swan Bar
165 bd de Montparnasse, 6th (01.44.27.05.84, www.swanbar.fr). M° Raspail or Vavin. **Concerts** 7.30pm & 9.30pm Tue-Sat. **Admission** varies. **Credit** MC, V.
A modern, American-style jazz bar perfect for traditional jazz, torch songs and jamming. Occasional classical and tango concerts are thrown in for good measure.

Théâtre du Châtelet
1 pl du Châtelet (01.40.28.28.40, www.chatelet-theatre.com). M° Châtelet. **Open** times vary. **Admission** €25-€150. **Credit** AmEx, DC, MC, V.
This venerable theatre and classic music hall has another life as a jazz and *chanson* venue, with performances by top-notch international musicians.

Nightlife

Ritzy places such as the **VIP Room** and **Le Baron** are still the talk of the town, but more low-key indie venues such as **Panic Room** are pulling in a diverse crowd – with the emphasis more about having fun than posing.

Another new nightlife twist is the recent wave of designer-led hotel cocktail bars, which are attracting some big-name DJs. **Mama Shelter** (*see p113*), which created a huge buzz when it opened, may be famous for its great design by Philippe Starck, but it's also picking up style points for its music selection; the **Hôtel Ritz** (*see p108*) boasts some of the finest resident DJs in the bar on weekends; the **Murano Urban Resort** (*see p112*) hosts Lucky Star on Thursday nights, when a famous French actor and/or singer takes over the decks; and the **Kube Hotel** (*see p112*) has daily DJ sets. For listings, check www.parisbouge.com, www.novaplanet.com, www.radiofg.com and www.lemonsound.com. Radio stations FG (98.2FM) and Nova (101.5FM) also provide details on what's happening.

Club bars

Andy Whaloo
69 rue des Gravilliers, 3rd (01.42.71.20.38, www.myspace.com/andywhaloo). Mᵒ Arts et Métiers. **Open** 6pm-2am Tue-Sun. **Admission** free. **Drinks** €5-€14. **Credit** AmEx, MC, V.
Owned by the people behind Momo and Sketch in London, Andy Whaloo serves sumptuous snack food and is tastefully decorated with Moroccan artefacts. The seating is made from upturned paint cans, and the DJs play an eclectic mix, featuring everything from hip hop to techno and stepping up the volume as the night progresses.

Baxo
21 rue Juliette Dodu, 10th (01.42.02.99.71, www.baxo.fr). Mᵒ Colonel Fabien. **Open** 9am-3pm, 5pm-2am Mon-Fri; 5pm-2am Sat, Sun. **Admission** free. **Drinks** €3-€10. **Credit** MC, V.
A spanking new hybrid venue that triples as a restaurant, bar and DJ lounge for an übercool, bobo clientele. Friday nights are for resident DJs, and Saturdays bring live bands and guest splicers.

Café Chéri(e)
44 bd de la Villette, 19th (01.42.02.02.05). Mᵒ Belleville. **Open** 8am-2am daily. **Admission** free. **Drinks** €2.80-€7. **Credit** MC, V.
A popular DJ bar, especially during the summer, when fashionistas flock to the terrace. Live music is played from Thursdays to Saturdays after 10pm. Expect anything from DJ Jet Boy's electro punk to rock, funk, hip hop, rare groove, indie, dance, jazz and '80s classics.

Critics' choice

1 **New Morning**
Hip, no-frills jazz joint with consistently excellent live music on tap. *See p101.*

2 **Le Magnifique**
Named after a 1970s film, this snazzy cocktail bar is a retro treat. *See p101.*

3 **Le Montana**
This exclusive club even manages to out-hype Le Baron. *See p101.*

Chacha Club
47 rue Berger, 1st (01.40.13.12.12, www.chachaclub.fr). Mᵒ Châtelet. **Open** 8pm-5am Mon-Sat. **Admission** varies. **Drinks** €4-€12. **Credit** MC, V.
The Chacha Club was the first high-profile establishment to open a fumoir, and it forms just one of the sexy attributes of this hot haunt near Les Halles that is attracting a spectacularly good-looking clientele through its doors. In the style of a private club, but with no membership requirement (only a trio of exacting 'physionomists' stand at the door), it combines restaurant, bar and club in a suite of intimate rooms with subdued lighting and seductive, 1930s-inspired decor.

La Fourmi
74 rue des Martyrs, 18th (01.42.64.70.35). Mᵒ Pigalle. **Open** 8.30am-2am Mon-Thur, Sun; 8am-4am Fri, Sat. **Admission** free. **Drinks** €1.60-€8. **Credit** MC, V.
La Fourmi was a precursor to the industrial-design, informal, music-led bars that have sprung up around Paris – and it's still very much a style leader, attracting everyone from in-the-know tourists to fashionable Parisians. Great throughout the day for coffees or a beer, it has a small seating area outside and an always busy bar with DJ decks. You can stay into the early hours at weekends, but it's also a handy pre-club rendezvous and flyer supplier.

Lizard Lounge
18 rue du Bourg-Tibourg, 4th (01.42.72.81.34, www.cheapblonde.com). Mᵒ Hôtel de Ville or St-Paul. **Open** noon-2am daily. **Admission** free. **Drinks** €5.50-€8.50. **Credit** AmEx, MC, V.
This three-level, trendy Marais hangout has a boozer upstairs serving beer in pint glasses, a mezzanine for crowd voyeurs, and a more full-on DJ bar in the booth-filled basement – often full, due to its modest proportions. Local DJs play a variety of contemporary styles.

La Mezzanine de l'Alcazar
62 rue Mazarine, 6th (01.53.10.19.99, www.alcazar.fr). Mᵒ Odéon. **Open** 7pm-2am Wed-Sat. **Admission** free. **Drinks** €9-€13. **Credit** AmEx, DC, MC, V.
The stylish, Conran-owned Mezzanine is the upstairs posher sister of the Wagg, which is intended to be a clubbier venue. Naturally, both have become well-heeled hangouts, but the Mezzanine remains the venue of choice for the suited and booted.

Panic Room
101 rue Amelot, 11th (01.58.30.93.43). Mᵒ St-Sébastien Froissart. **Open** 6pm-2am Tue-Sat. Closed 2wks Aug. **Admission** free. **Drinks** €5-€8. **Credit** MC, V.
This newcomer has quickly carved out a niche on the rock scene, and it's not nearly as daunting as its name suggests. The excellent Goldrush collective has live acts and DJs blasting the sound system in the basement, while upstairs friendly barmen serve affordable cocktails behind a concrete counter. The indie crowd and occasional media celebs are loving it.

Le Troisième Lieu
62 rue Quincampoix, 4th (01.48.04.85.64, www.myspace.com/letroisiemelieu). Mᵒ Rambuteau. **Open** 6pm-5am Thur-Sat. **Admission** free. **Drinks** €2.50-€6. **Credit** MC, V.
Opened by Les Ginettes Armées, organisers of renowned Sunday lesbian and mixed events, the Troisième Lieu tends towards electro and house. The ground floor hosts DJs mixing eclectic sounds for chatting and relaxing to, whereas the basement is more dancefloor-oriented.

Le Wax
15 rue Daval, 11th (01.40.21.16.16, www.lewax.fr). Mᵒ Bastille. **Open** 5pm-2am Wed, Thur; 5pm-5am Fri-Sun. **Admission** free. **Drinks** €4.50-€10. **Credit** MC, V.
During the week, the Wax – clad in 1970s psychedelic orange – is a funky bar where DJs play groove until 2am. But at weekends it becomes a (tiny) nightclub that keeps a youthful crowd awake until 5am with house and electro.

Chacha Club.

Le Zèbre de Belleville
63 bd de Belleville, 20th (01.43.55.55.55, www.lezebre.com). Mᵒ Belleville. **Open** times vary. **Admission** €6-€15. **Drinks** €5-€10. **No credit cards**.
This stylish cabaret/theatre bar is used by Dan Ghenacia and the Freak 'n' Chic posse for buzzy after-parties on Sundays. It's usually a circus and cabaret venue; check flyers for event information.

Cool clubs

Bateau Concorde Atlantique
Port de Solférino, 23 quai Anatole-France, 7th (01.47.05.71.03, www.bateauconcorde atlantique.com). Mᵒ Assemblée Nationale/RER Musée d'Orsay. **Open** 11pm-5am Mon-Fri; 5pm-5am Sat; 6pm-5am Sun. Closed mid Sept-mid June. **Admission** free-€10. **Drinks** €5-€8. **Credit** MC, V.
With its terrace and voluminous dancefloor, this two-level boat is a clubbing paradise in the summer. The celebrated Respect crew held a fondly remembered Wednesday night here, and are still involved in putting on parties at the venue, alongside other cool crews like Ed Banger.

Batofar
Opposite 11 quai François-Mauriac, 13th (09.71.25.50.61, www.batofar.org). Mᵒ Quai de la Gare. **Open** 11pm-6am Mon-Sat; 6am-noon 1st Sun of mth. **Admission** free-€12. **Drinks** €3.50-€8. **Credit** MC, V.
In recent years, the Batofar has gone through a rapid succession of management teams, with varying levels of success. The current managers have helped revive the venue's tradition of playing cutting-edge music, including electro, dub step, techno and dancehall nights.

Le Divan du Monde
75 rue des Martyrs, 18th (01.40.05.06.99, www.divandumonde.com). Mᵒ Abbesses or Pigalle. **Open** 8pm-2am Tue-Thur; 7.30pm-5am Fri, Sat. **Admission** €5-€30. **Drinks** €3.50-€8. **Credit** AmEx, MC, V.
After a drink in the seriously cool Fourmi opposite, pop over to the Divan for one-off parties and regular events. The upstairs specialises in VJ events, and downstairs holds dub, reggae, funk and world music club nights.

Elysée Montmartre
72 bd de Rochechouart, 18th (01.44.92.45.36, www.elyseemontmartre.com). Mᵒ Anvers. **Open** midnight-6am Fri, Sat. **Admission** €10-€20. **Drinks** €4-€10. **Credit** Bar MC, V.
A gig venue and club, the Elysée hosts big nights by outside promoters, such as NME Club and We Are the 90's, for young clubbers.

Le Folie's Pigalle
11 pl Pigalle, 9th (01.48.78.55.25, www.lefoliespigalle.com). Mᵒ Pigalle. **Open** midnight-dawn Mon-Thur; midnight-noon Fri, Sat; 6pm-midnight Sun. **Admission** €20 (incl 1 drink); €7 Sun eve. **Drinks** €10. **Credit** AmEx, MC, V.
The racy Folie's Pigalle's programme has everything from dancehall and hip hop to techno and electro, go-go dancers, striptease shows and Paris's only transsexual spectacle on Sunday evenings.

Le Gibus
18 rue du Fbg-du-Temple, 11th (01.47.00.78.88, www.gibus.fr). Mᵒ République or Temple. **Open** midnight-6am Fri, Sat. **Concerts** 8-11.30pm Fri. **Admission** €5-€20. **Drinks** €3-€8. **Credit** Bar MC, V.
A famous 1980s punk venue, Le Gibus has gone through plenty of style changes during its life. Today, it takes in R&B, reggae, '80s pop and hip hop, plus the occasional striptease mixte.

Nouveau Casino
109 rue Oberkampf, 11th (01.43.57.57.40, www.nouveaucasino.net). Mᵒ Parmentier. **Open** midnight-5am Wed-Sat. **Admission** €5 before 1am, €10 after. **Drinks** €5-€10. **Credit** Bar MC, V.
Conveniently surrounded by the numerous bars of rue Oberkampf and tucked behind the legendary Café Charbon, Nouveau Casino is a concert venue that also hosts some of the city's liveliest club nights. Local collectives, international names and record labels, such as Versatile, host nights here; it's worth checking the website for one-offs and after-parties.

Point Ephémère
200 quai de Valmy, 10th (01.40.34.02.48, www.pointephemere.org). Mᵒ Jaurès or Louis Blanc. **Open** 10am-2am daily. **Admission** varies. **Drinks** €3-€7. **Credit** AmEx, DC, MC, V.
This hunk of Berlin in Paris was only ever meant to be temporary, but thankfully it's still around. An uncompromising programming policy delivers some of the best electronic music in town; there's also a restaurant and bar with decks and a gallery, and terrace space by the canal in summer.

Red Light
34 rue du Départ, 15th (01.42.79.94.53, www.leredlight.com). Mᵒ Edgar Quinet or Montparnasse Bienvenüe. **Open** midnight-11am Fri, Sat. **Admission** (incl 1 drink) €20-€25. **Drinks** from €10. **Credit** MC, V.
The former Enfer ('Hell') may have changed names, but it remains a trance, techno and house dynamo with DJs spinning tunes to a young, up-for-it, often gay, well-groomed crowd. Expect a mixture of local and international guest DJs.

Le Régine
49 rue de Ponthieu, 8th (01.40.39.07.07, www.leregine.com). Mᵒ St-Philippe-du-Roule. **Open** 7pm-5am Thur; midnight-6am Fri, Sat. **Admission** €10-€15. **Drinks** €5-€10. **Credit** MC, V.
Régine was once a key figure on the Paris nightlife scene, and the club she created is experiencing a rejuvenation. Her portrait still sits by the entrance for a touch of '70s nostalgia, but the revamped venue has shifted from disco to sophisticated electro, inviting the cream of international

Nightlife

OLIVER KNIGHT

DJs to the decks. The after-work La French, followed by the insane Pan-Pan Cul-Cul night (where guys get in for free if they're dressed as girls), makes a safe bet for a wild Thursday.

La Scène Bastille

2bis rue des Taillandiers, 11th (01.48.06.50.70, www.la-scene.com). M° Bastille. **Open** 7.30pm-midnight Mon-Thur; 7.30pm-6am Fri-Sun. Closed Aug. **Admission** €10-€12. **Drinks** €4-€9. **Credit** *Bar* MC, V.

This tastefully decorated club-bar-restaurant holds rock concerts, as well as club events most Thursdays to Saturdays. The programming here changes constantly, so check what's on.

Le Scopitone

5 av de l'Opéra, 8th (01.42.60.64.45, www.scopitoneclub.com). M° Pyramides. **Open** from 7pm Tue-Sat; *Club* midnight-5am Thur-Sat. **Admission** free. **Drinks** €5-€15.

Don't let the picture of Beethoven fool you: this small club is all about electro-rock, with black-painted walls and live acts taking to the stage at weekends. Gigs aren't free, but DJ sets by the likes of MGMT and 'music label battles' are interesting alternatives on other nights. The crowd is young and dressed to impress, but the Scopitone is easier to get into than it ever was when it was Paris Paris.

Le Social Club

142 rue Montmartre, 2nd (01.40.28.05.55, www.parissocialclub.com). M° Bourse or Grands Boulevards. **Open** 11.30pm-3am Wed; 11pm-6am Thur-Sat. **Admission** free-€12. **Drinks** €4-€10. **Credit** AmEx, MC, V.

Set right in the hub of the city's club activity around Grands Boulevards, this electro venue has some of the hippest acts from the French and international scene, thanks to its owner's multidisciplinary career as a producer and founder of the record label Uncivilized World.

Wagg

62 rue Mazarine, 6th (01.55.42.22.01, www.wagg.fr). M° Odéon. **Open** 11.30pm-6am Fri, Sat; 3.30pm-2am Sun. **Admission** €12 Fri, Sat; €12 Sun (incl drink). **Drinks** €7-€10. **Credit** AmEx, DC, MC, V.

Refurbished as part of the Conran makeover of the Mezzanine upstairs, Wagg went through a period of attracting big-name DJs, but has settled down as home to a well-to-do Left Bank crowd. Expect funk, house and disco, plus salsa lessons on Sundays.

Glitzy clubs

Le Baron

6 av Marceau, 8th (01.47.20.04.01, www.clublebaron.com). M° Alma Marceau. **Open** 11pm-6am daily. **Admission** free. **Drinks** from €10. **Credit** MC, V.

This small but supremely exclusive hangout for the international jet set used to be an upmarket brothel, and has the decor to prove it. It only holds 150, most of whom are regulars you'll need to befriend in order to get past the door. But if you manage to get in, you'll be rubbing shoulders with celebrities and super-glossy people.

Le Cab

2 pl du Palais-Royal, 1st (01.58.62.56.25, www.cabaret.fr). M° Palais Royal Musée du Louvre. **Open** 11.30pm-5am Wed-Sat. *Restaurant* 8-11.30pm Tue-Sat. **Admission** free Tue, Wed; €20 Thur-Sat. **Drinks** €13. **Credit** AmEx, MC, V.

Le Cab is owned by the management behind Club Mix and Queen, and R&B and commercial house dominate the playlist. The doormen are tough, and if they don't like you, you won't get in (unless you've booked for dinner).

MadaM

128 rue La Boétie, 8th (01.53.76.02.11). M° Franklin D. Roosevelt or George V. **Open** 7pm-2am Thur; midnight-6am Fri, Sat; 10.30pm-4am Sun. **Admission** free. **Drinks** €20. **Credit** AmEx, DC, MC, V.

MadaM's late-night sessions (kicking in at 4am at weekends) are renowned for the young, moneyed crowd they attract. The music on offer is mainly electro and house (French), with several up to date international tunes thrown into the mix for good measure.

Le Magnifique

25 rue de Richelieu, 1st (01.42.60.70.80, www.lemagnifique.fr). M° Palais Royal-Musée du Louvre. **Open** 8pm-5am daily. **Admission** free. **Drinks** €14-€35. **Credit** AmEx, DC, MC, V.

The decor, dominated by wood, dark leather and animal furs, is elegant, with a hint of porno chic that leaves you picturing Warhol and his posse partying in a corner. The place comes to life after midnight, when the bar turns into a club with a soundtrack of dancefloor-fillers from the past three decades. The fantastic cocktail menu, a selection of sushi (€8-€30) and the separate fumoir add to the appeal.

Le Montana

28 rue St-Benoît, 6th (no phone). M° St-Germain-des-Prés. **Open** 11pm-5am daily. **Admission** free. **Drinks** €10-€15. **Credit** AmEx, DC, MC, V.

Revamped by über-cool graphic artist André (*see right* **Night vision**), Le Montana is a VIP magnet – Lenny Kravitz, Vanessa Bruno and Kate Moss have all hit the floor here since the relaunch. The biggest challenge is getting through the door.

VIP Room

188 rue de Rivoli, 1st (01.58.36.46.00, www.viproom.fr). M° Palais-Royal or Tuileries. **Open** midnight-5am Thur-Sat. **Admission** free. **Drinks** €20. **Credit** AmEx, DC, MC, V.

The VIP has moved from its Champs-Elysées address into the former Scala nightclub, but other than that, nothing has changed. It's still a hit with the people who also enjoy the VIP's sister venues in Cannes and St Tropez during the summer, and the music is still dance-oriented.

Mainstream clubs

La Machine du Moulin Rouge

90 bd de Clichy, 18th (01.53.41.88.89, www.lamachinedumoulinrouge.com). M° Blanche. **Open** 9pm-6am Wed-Sat. *Terrace* 3pm-6am Wed-Sat **Admission** free until 11pm, then €10-€20. **Drinks** €3-€7. **Credit** MC, V.

So long La Loco, enter La Machine. This three-floor bar/club/live venue has had a substantial makeover and is now reborn with a dash of decadence. The main dancefloor, La Chaufferie, used to be the Moulin Rouge's boiler room and the old pipes remain, but the new *Alice in Wonderland*-style decor is a breath of fresh air. If you can't take the heat, head for the new terrace or switch to the bouncing Central, a concert hall showcasing new and established talent.

Mix Club

24 rue de l'Arrivée, 15th (01.56.80.37.37, www.mixclub.fr). M° Montparnasse Bienvenüe. **Open** 11pm-6am Thur-Sat. **Admission** free-€20. **Drinks** €8. **Credit** MC, V.

The Mix has one of the city's biggest dancefloors. Regular visitors include Erick Morillo's Subliminal and Ministry of Sound parties, and in-house events include David Guetta's 'Fuck Me I'm Famous', 'Hipnotic' and 'One Night With Paulette', plus just about everyone else who's big in France – or anywhere else in the world, for that matter.

Queen

102 av des Champs-Elysées, 8th (01.53.89.08.90, www.queen.fr). M° George V. **Open** midnight-7am Mon-Thur, Sun; midnight-8am Fri, Sat. **Admission** €15 Mon-Thur, Sun; €20 Fri, Sat. **Drinks** €10. **Credit** *Bar* AmEx, MC, V.

Once the city's most fêted gay club and the only venue that could hold a torch to the Rex, with a roster of top local DJs holding court, Queen's star faded a little in the early noughties but is now starting to shine more brightly again. Last year, it introduced more themed nights.

Rex

5 bd Poissonnière, 2nd (01.42.36.10.96, www.rexclub.com). M° Bonne Nouvelle. **Open** 11.30pm-6am Wed-Sat. **Admission** free-€15. **Drinks** €5-€15. **Credit** *Bar* MC, V.

The Rex's new sound system puts over 40 different sound configurations at the DJ's fingertips, and has proved to be a magnet for top turntable stars. Once associated with iconic techno pioneer Laurent Garnier, the Rex has stayed at the top of the Paris techno scene, and occupies an unassailable position as the city's serious club music venue.

Showcase

Below Pont Alexandre III, 8th (01.45.61.25.43, www.showcase.fr). M° Champs-Elysées Clemenceau. **Open** 10pm-dawn Fri, Sat; 11am-3pm Sun. **Admission** free-€30. **Drinks** €3.50-€8. **Credit** MC, V.

This vast venue, in converted boat hangars below Pont Alexandre III, is where music-crazed insomniacs come on weekends to discover up-and-coming bands and dance until daybreak. The club has lost some of its hype over the last couple of years, but high-profile guest DJs have been setting the bar higher lately: Carol Cox, will.i.am and Calvin Harris have all made appearances in the past year.

World, jazz & rock 'n' roll

Le Cabaret Sauvage

59 bd Macdonald, 19th (01.42.09.03.09, www.cabaretsauvage.com). M° Porte de la Villette. **Open** 11pm-dawn, days vary. **Admission** €10-€20. **Drinks** €4-€8. **Credit** AmEx, MC, V.

A stylish venue that's taken over by outside promoters for occasional club nights. There often used to be a world music element, but recently electronic and drum 'n' bass nights have begun to be held here, and, since the demise of Pulp, techno label Kill the DJ has started using the venue. Check the website for details.

La Chapelle des Lombards

19 rue de Lappe, 11th (01.43.57.24.24, www.la-chapelle-des-lombards.com). M° Bastille. **Open** 11.30pm-6am Tue-Sun. **Admission** free Mon-Thur, Sun; €20 Fri, Sat (free for women Tue-Thur & before midnight Fri). **Drinks** €6-€12. **Credit** MC, V.

With Afrojazz and Latino bands and DJs providing the music, Latinos and Africans lead the dancefloor in this popular world music venue. Smart dress only.

Favela Chic

18 rue du Fbg-du-Temple, 11th (01.40.21.38.14, www.favelachic.com). M° République. **Open** 8pm-2am Tue-Thur; 8pm-4am Fri, Sat. **Admission** free Tue-Thur; €10 (incl 1 drink) Fri, Sat. **Drinks** €6-€19. **Credit** MC, V.

The Brazilian-themed Favela Chic attracts an up-for-it, international and dressy crowd for some serious samba and other Latin dancing. There are decent DJs, live acts, and Brazilian food and drinks too.

La Java

105 rue du Fbg-du-Temple, 10th (01.42.02.20.52, www.la-java.fr). M° Belleville or Goncourt. **Open** 9pm-3am Wed, Thur; 11pm-6am Fri, Sat; 2pm-2am Sun. **Admission** €5-€10. **Drinks** €3-€7. **Credit** MC, V.

Tucked inside the crumbling, disused Belleville market, La Java plays rock, salsa and world music, with live bands every weekend.

New Morning

7-9 rue des Petites-Ecuries, 10th (01.45.23.51.41, www.newmorning.com). M° Château d'Eau. **Open** times vary. **Admission** approx €10. **Drinks** €3-€7. **Credit** MC, V.

Low key it may be but it's still worth looking out for the occasional A-lister – Spike Lee and Prince have been known to grace New Morning.

Night vision

The streets of Paris are buzzing with the name of André. In queues outside tiny clubs people refer to him as the man who saved Parisian nightlife; wherever you go, he is the talk of the town. But if you dare to ask 'André who?', you'll be met with a patronising look. It's André, period.

Dressed in dark shades and black leather jacket, the youthful 38-year-old is elusive, but his name is a gateway to excitement. Having gone from underground street artist to head of a multi-national brand, he has single-handedly redefined the meaning of cool in under a decade.

Last year was all about L'Appartement, an ephemeral project launched by André (Sareiva, if you must know) and Lionel Bensemoun, aka La Clique. The duo are at the helm of a string of venues, each one more exclusive than the last, with André decorating the place and Lionel taking care of finance. Hidden away in a Left Bank *hôtel particulier*, invite-only L'Appartement allowed the chosen few to party in a 3,000 sq ft flat, with everything arranged to make them feel at home: you could pour your own drink, tuck into an all-you-can-eat gourmet buffet and rifle through the collection of old vinyl. The only rule was to keep the address a secret and let the rumour spread.

L'Appartement is just the latest episode in André's string of nightlife ventures, which began in the early noughties with the relaunch of Paris Paris. This soon became the place to see and be seen, and people were queueing up to bust a move on the tiny dancefloor. The pattern was repeated with **Le Baron** (*see left*), an old escort bar taken over in 2003, and more recently **Le Montana** (*see left*), an even smaller venue around the corner from Café de Flore, revamped by La Clique in 2009 and preferred by those who now deem the Baron too passé.

Unsurprisingly, André's empire is spreading beyond the capital. Pop-up Barons have opened in Cannes and Miami, with a permanent branch in Tokyo and another on the cards for New York. He is also behind the **Hôtel Amour** (*see p109*), as well as the hugely successful **La Fidélité** (www.lafidelite.com; *pictured*).

In 2011, André is opening a new bar-restaurant, Phantom, in the once drab Gare de l'Est area. In the meantime, he's focusing on breaking into cinema with his first script: a tragic love story about two teenagers in which the hero is a young street artist – think Romeo and Juliet with spray paint and Ray-Bans making out to a Blondie soundtrack, and you'll start to get the idea.

FEATURED ESTABLISHMENT

Sport & Fitness

Every year, Paris hosts some 600 sports events, including 170 at national or international level. Its 366 sports complexes include 32 stadiums, 38 swimming pools and 43 tennis centres. These municipal facilities are doted with generously subsidised tariffs, while world-class professional venues enjoy heavy investment. Current projects include an extensive revamp for Stade Roland Garros, home to the French tennis open, a major expansion of rugby's Stade Jean-Bouin, and the reopening of the legendary art deco swimming pool, the Piscine Molitor.

Spectator sports

The national stadium is the 80,000-capacity **Stade de France** (see p87), served by stations on the RER B (La Plaine Stade de France) and RER D (Stade de France St-Denis) lines just one stop from the Gare du Nord. As well as top football matches, it hosts home legs for rugby's Six Nations and athletics.

Indoor events, including judo, basketball, handball and tennis, take place at the **Palais Omnisports de Paris-Bercy** (8 bd de Bercy, 12th, 08.92.39.01.00, www.popb.fr, M° Bercy). The **Stade Roland Garros** (Porte des Mousquetaires, 2 av Gordon-Bennett, 16th, 01.47.43.48.00, www.fft.fr/roland garros, M° Porte d'Auteuil) stages the French tennis open; the **Parc des Princes**, home of Paris St-Germain football club, also hosts rugby and other sporting events.

Tickets for many sports are sold online at www.ticketnet.fr, and at branches of **Fnac** and **Virgin Megastore** (for both, see p82). For football and rugby internationals at the Stade de France, contact the respective national associations (www.fff.fr, www.ffr.fr). Influential daily newspaper *L'Equipe* offers excellent press coverage (in French) of all major sports events.

Basketball

Paris-Levallois Basket
Stade Coubertin, 82 av Georges-Lafont, 16th (01.45.27.79.12, www.parislevallois.com). M° Porte de St-Cloud. **Tickets** from €8. **Credit** MC, V. *Palais des Sports Marcel-Cerdan, 141 rue Danton, 92300 Levallois (01.46.17.06.30, www.parislevallois). M° Pont de Levallois.* **Tickets** from €8. **Credit** MC, V.
PL was born in 2007 following the merger of the region's two biggest clubs, Paris Basket Racing and Levallois Sporting Club Basket. Games are played at the Paris and Levallois sites.

Football

Paris St-Germain
Stadium *Parc des Princes, 24 rue du Commandant-Guilbaud, 16th (01.47.43.71.71, tickets & information 32.75, www.psg.fr). M° Porte de St-Cloud.* **Tickets** €25-€100. **Credit** MC, V.
Shops *27 av des Champs-Elysées, 8th (01.56.69.22.22). M° Franklin D. Roosevelt.* **Open** 10am-10pm Mon-Sat; 10am-8pm Sun. **Credit** AmEx, MC, V. *Parc des Princes (01.47.43.72.91).* **Open** 10am-7pm Mon-Sat & 2hrs after game on match days. **Credit** AmEx, MC, V.
A group of donors set up PSG by amalgamating local clubs in 1970. During the 1980s and '90s, the club won silverware aplenty, but its star has since faded. In 2010, the team finished 13th in Ligue 1. For tickets, book online and pick them up from any branch of Fnac (see p82).

Horse racing

The full racing schedule, the *Calendrier des Courses*, is published by *France Galop* (www.france-galop.com).

Hippodrome d'Auteuil
Route des Lacs, 16th (01.40.71.47.47). M° Porte d'Auteuil.
Steeplechasing in the Bois de Boulogne. The big event is the Gras Savoye Grand Steeplechase de Paris on the last Sunday in May.

Hippodrome de Chantilly
16 av du Général-Leclerc, 60500 Chantilly (03.44.62.44.00). Train from Gare du Nord.
Flat racing 40km (25 miles) from Paris. The fashion parade turns out in force for the Prix de Diane in June; the full length of the course is used for the Prix du Jockey Club the weekend before.

Hippodrome d'Enghien
Pl André-Foulon, 95230 Soissy-sous-Montmorency (01.34.17.87.00). Train from Gare du Nord.
Steeplechasing and floodlit trotting at this course 18km (11 miles) north of Paris.

Hippodrome de Longchamp
Rte des Tribunes, 16th (01.44.30.75.00). M° Porte d'Auteuil then free bus.
Flat racing in the Bois de Boulogne. This course hosts the racing season's most fashionable social event, the Prix de l'Arc de Triomphe Lucien Barrière. Women in wild hats get in for free.

Hippodrome de Maisons-Laffitte
1 av de la Pelouse, 78602 Maisons-Laffitte (01.39.12.81.70). RER Maisons-Laffitte then bus.
Flat racing.

Hippodrome de Paris-Vincennes
2 route de la Ferme, 12th (01.49.77.14.70). M° Château de Vincennes/RER Joinville-le-Pont then free bus.
Trotting in the Bois de Vincennes. Floodlights on winter evenings add to the atmosphere.

Hippodrome de St-Cloud
1 rue du Camp Canadien, 92210 St-Cloud (01.47.71.69.26). RER Rueil-Malmaison.
Flat racing.

Rugby

Stade Français Paris
Stade Jean-Bouin, 26 av du Général-Sarrail, 16th (01.40.71.71.00, www.stade.fr). M° Porte d'Auteuil. **Tickets** €5-€65. **Credit** AmEx, MC, V.
Stade Français are one of the top teams in France. Home matches tend to take place on Saturday evenings. Note that the stadium is undergoing major work in 2011, and home matches will be played at alternative venues.

Activities & team sports

Some venues require proof of health insurance, ID and passport-sized photos for membership. Note that joining a club or taking part in a competitive event (even a fun run) usually requires a medical certificate from a doctor.

All-round sports clubs

The **Standard Athletic Club** (route Forestière du Pavé de Meudon, 92360 Meudon-la-Forêt, 01.46.26.16.09, www.standac.com) is a private sports club that welcomes English speakers. Full membership costs €860 per year. There are tennis and squash courts, an outdoor pool and workout facilities.

Local multi-sports clubs include **Lagardère Paris Racing** (01.45.67.55.86, www.lagardereparisracing.com), **ASPTT de Paris** (01.58.14.21,80, www.aspttparis.com), **Paris Université Club** (01.44.16.62.62, www.puc.asso.fr) and **Stade Français** (01.40.71.33.45, www.stadefrancais.com).

Athletics & running

Paris has plenty of municipal tracks, open to individual runners for a modest monthly subscription; for details pick up the *Guide du Sport* (www.sport.paris.fr). Joggers use the banks of the Seine and the parks (Jardin du Luxembourg, Tuileries and Parc de la Villette), as well as the expansive Bois de Boulogne and Bois de Vincennes. The Paris Marathon takes place in April (see pp11-13 Calendar), and other classic road races include the Paris half-marathon in March and the Paris-Versailles in September (www.parisversailles.com).

Boules, pool & bowling

Boules or *pétanque* pitches are scattered all over Paris. Contact the **Fédération Française de Pétanque** (04.91.14.05.80, www.petanque.fr). Some pool venues require ID or a passport.

Bowling Mouffetard
73 rue Mouffetard, 5th (01.43.31.09.35, www.bowlingmouffetard.fr). M° Place Monge. **Open** 3pm-2am Mon-Fri; 10am-2am Sat, Sun. **Admission** €3.30-€6 per set. Shoe hire €2. **Credit** MC, V.
Central venue with eight lanes and pool tables.

Cercle Clichy Montmartre
84 rue de Clichy, 9th (01.48.78.32.85, www.cerclecm.com). M° Place de Clichy. **Open** 1pm-6am daily. **Admission** Pool from €12/hr. Billiards from €12/hr. **Credit** (€25 min) MC, V.
Historic venue with tables aplenty. No under-18s.

Climbing

To use any municipal climbing wall, you will need to obtain a personal ID card. Take a photo, your passport, proof of valid insurance and the fee (€4 per month) to the centre you want to use. For the real thing, try the superb boulder formations in the Forêt de Fontainebleau; **Grimporama** (www.grimporama.com) has full details, including maps, on its website. The **Club Alpin du pays de Fontainebleau** (01.64.22.67.18, caf77.free.fr) organises group climbs and weekend outings.

Centre Sportif Poissonnier
2 rue Jean-Cocteau, 18th (01.42.51.24.68). M° Porte de Clignancourt. **Open** 6am-8pm Mon-Fri; 8am-9.30pm Sat; 8am-5pm Sun. **Admission** free. **No credit cards.**
The largest of the six municipal walls in Paris.

MurMur
55 rue Cartier-Bresson, 93500 Pantin (01.48.46.11.00, www.murmur.fr). M° Aubervilliers–Pantin Quatre Chemins. **Open** 9.30am-11pm Mon-Fri; 9.30am-6.30pm Sat, Sun.
Admission €8-€15; €4-€7.50 reductions. Joining fee €15. **Credit** AmEx, MC, V.
One of Europe's best climbing walls, with 1,550sq m (16,000sq ft) of wall. MurMur also has a wall at Issy-les-Moulineaux (see website for details).

Cycling

City cycling is growing in popularity, thanks to Mayor Delanoë's expansion of bike lanes and the Vélib initiative. The **Fédération Française de Cyclisme** (01.49.35.69.00, www.ffc.fr) has details of the many local cycle clubs. The **Stade Vélodrome Jacques-Anquetil** (Bois de Vincennes, 12th, 01.43.68.01.27) is regularly open to amateur cyclists, and the circuits by the Hippodromes at **Vincennes** and **Longchamp** (see left) attract large groups of road cyclists. **Mieux se Déplacer à Bicyclette** (01.43.20.26.02, www.mdb-idf.org) organises free rides for members (€30 per year).

Mountain biking (VTT, or *vélo tout terrain*) is popular in the many forests on the outskirts of Paris, including the Forêt de Montmorency in the north and the Fôret de Meudon in the south.

Buzibi
67 rue de Croulebarbe, 13th (01.47.07.16.75, www.buzibi.fr). M° Corvisart. **Open** 10am-7.30pm Tue-Sun. **Credit** MC, V.
A specialist electric bike shop. Buy, rent, get repairs.

Gepetto & Vélos
59 rue du Cardinal-Lemoine, 5th (01.43.54.19.95, www.gepetto-velos.com). M° Cardinal Lemoine. **Open** 9am-7.30pm Tue-Sun. **Credit** MC, V.
Rents, sells and repairs all types of bicycles.

Vélo Bastille
22 rue Alphonse Baudin, 11th (01.48.87.60.01, www.parisvelosympa.com). M° Richard Lenoir. **Open** 9.30am-1pm, 2-6pm Mon, Wed-Fri; 9am-7pm Sat, Sun. **No credit cards.**
Vélo Bastille offers repairs, rentals and guided cycling tours of the city.

Fitness clubs

Club Med (www.clubmedgym.fr) dominates the health club scene, with 22 branches in Paris and the western suburbs, including five Waou Clubs with spa facilities. Single visits cost €26, and annual memberships start at €840. Other leading fitness centres include **Vit'Halles** (see p103) and **Forest Hill** (www.forest-hill.com).

Critics' choice

1 Piscine Josephine-Baker
This glass-roofed pool uses filtered water from the Seine. See p103.

2 Stade de France
Watch Europe's rugby elite scrum down and battle it out. See left.

3 Hippodrome de Longchamp
Home to the Prix de l'Arc de Triomphe, Europe's richest race. See left.

Playing the blues

One story dominated the back pages of the French press in the latter part of 2010 – France's disastrous South Africa World Cup campaign, which was marred by infighting and inept displays on the field. Heroes when they lifted the biggest footballing prize of all in 1998 on home soil, the team's performance (or lack of it) in the 2010 World Cup was a grisly tale of self-destruction, which resulted in a humiliating exit both on and off the pitch – the team managed just one draw and two defeats and finished bottom of their group, while Raymond Domenech's (*pictured*) reign as coach ended in acrimony when he refused to shake hands with South Africa boss Carlos Alberto Parreira at the end of France's 2-1 defeat by the hosts in Bloemfontein. Striker Nicolas Anelka was sent home after refusing to apologise for verbally abusing Domenech, prompting the rest of the squad to boycott a training session in protest.

The various controversies forced French Football Federation president

Jean-Pierre Escalettes to resign, while head of state Nicolas Sarkozy pledged to personally lead an investigation into the affair.

Domenech's replacement in the hot seat is the former World Cup winner Laurent Blanc, nicknamed Le Président, who played 97 times for his country and scored 16 goals. Blanc's first move as manager was to suspend all 23 players from the 2010 World Cup squad for his opening game, as collective punishment for their conduct in South Africa. France lost that game 2-1 to Norway in Oslo, and they also lost their first Euro 2012 qualifier to Belarus, but victory a few days later against Bosnia & Herzegovina restored a little pride to the battered Bleus. The resurgence has since continued with victories against Romania, Luxembourg and England, and the PR machine is now back in top gear, with the announcement that an estimated £2.5 million of World Cup player bonuses will be dished out to amateur clubs instead.

The non-profit **La Gym Suédoise** (01.45.00.18.22, www.gymsuedoise.com) holds one-hour gym sessions in ten locations across Paris. Membership is €75-€125 per term, or €10 per session. Unlike most gyms, it runs free trials at specified locations.

Club Quartier Latin
19 rue de Pontoise, 5th (01.55.42.77.88, www.clubquartierlatin.com). M° Maubert Mutualité. **Open** 9am-midnight Mon-Fri; 9am-7pm Sat, Sun. **Admission** *Pool* from €4.20. *Gym* from €20; from €16 reductions. **Credit** MC, V.
Home to the Pontoise pool (*see right*), this venerable centre houses no-frills fitness facilities, and has a room for step, aerobics, stretching and yoga classes. There's a sauna too.

Espace Vit'Halles
48 rue Rambuteau, 3rd (01.42.77.21.71, www.vithalles.fr). M° Rambuteau. **Open** 8am-10.30pm Mon-Fri; 9am-7pm Sat; 10am-7pm Sun. **Admission** €25/day. **Credit** AmEx, MC, V.
This sunken-level health club has Technogym fitness machines, a sauna and some of the best classes in the city, particularly for step and spinning; the classes cost extra.

Football & jorkyball

For information on the local amateur leagues, contact the **Ligue Ile-de-France de Football** (01.42.44.12.12, paris-idf.fff.fr). To join a weekend kickabout, try the Bois de Boulogne near Bagatelle, the Bois de Vincennes or the Champ de Mars.

Jorkyball 92
51 blvd de la Liberté, 92320 Chatillon (01.40.84.01.01, www.jorkyball92.com). M° Châtillon-Montrouge. **Open** 10am-midnight Mon-Fri; 10am-8pm Sat, Sun. **Admission** €40/hr for a court. **Credit** MC, V.
Invented in France, Jorkyball is a form of two-on-two football heavily influenced by squash. It's played on artificial turf and this centre on the southern outskirts of Paris boasts eight courts.

Ice skating

The most popular open-air skating rink is the free one in front of the Hôtel de Ville, which is open from December to February. Smaller wintertime rinks are also erected at other locations. *See also pp11-13* **Calendar**.

Patinoire de Boulogne
1 rue Victor-Griffuelhes, 92100 Boulogne-Billancourt (01.46.08.00.88, www.patinoire boulogne.com). M° Marcel Sembat. **Open** 3-6pm Wed; 10.30am-1pm, 3-6pm, 9pm-midnight Sat; 10am-1pm, 3-6pm Sun (open daily during school hols). **Admission** €5.50; €4.60 reductions. **No credit cards.**
Year-round indoor rink with free skate rental.

Patinoire Pailleron
32 rue Edouard-Pailleron, 19th (01.40.40.27.70, www.pailleron19.com). M° Bolivar. **Open** noon-1.30pm, 4-10pm Mon, Tue, Thur; noon-10pm Wed; noon-1.30pm, 4pm-midnight Fri; noon-midnight Sat; 10am-6pm Sun. **Admission** €4-€6; €3-€4 reductions. **No credit cards.**
Reopened in 2006, this rink is part of a renovated art deco sports complex. Skaters can sign up for hockey and dance lessons on the ice.

Patinoire Sonja Henie
Palais Omnisports de Paris-Bercy (01.40.02.60.60, www.bercy.fr). M° Bercy. **Open** Sept-mid June 3-6pm Wed; 9.30pm-12.30am Fri; 3-6pm, 9.30pm-12.30am Sat; 10am-noon, 3-6pm Sun. **Admission** €3-€6. **No credit cards.**
Protection, helmets and skates for hire (€3).

In-line skating

You can hire skates from **Nomades** (37 bd Bourdin, 4th, 01.44.54.07.44, www.nomadeshop.com). For lessons for all ages, try the **Roller Squad Institute** (01.56.61.99.61, www.rsi.asso.fr). And for impressive in-line skating and skateboard acrobatics, head for the **Espace Glisse de Paris** (*see right*).

Rowing & watersports

Paris residents can row, canoe and kayak for free on Saturdays at the **Base Nautique de la Villette** (41bis quai de la Loire, 19th, 01.42.40.29.90). Reserve a week in advance and bring along proof of residence, two photos and a swimming certificate (obtainable at any pool). You can go waterskiing and wakeboarding at the **Club Nautique du 19ème** (Bassin de Vitesse de St-Cloud, 92100 Boulogne-Billancourt, 01.42.03.25.24, www.cn19.fr). Serious rowers can join the annual Traversée de Paris. Contact the **Ligue**

Ile-de-France d'Aviron (94736 Nogent-sur-Marne, 01.48.75.79.10). For a leisurely paddle, hire a boat at Lac Daumesnil or Lac des Minimes in the Bois de Vincennes, or at Lac Supérieur in the Bois de Boulogne.

Rugby

For a good standard of play, try the **Athletic Club de Boulogne** (Stade du Saut du Loup, av de la Butte-Mortemart, 16th, 01.41.10.25.30, www.acbb.fr), which fields two teams. The **British Rugby Club of Paris** (58-60 av de la Grande Armée, 17th, www.brfcparis.com) fields two teams in the corporate league.

Skateboarding

Espace Glisse de Paris
Stade des Fillettes, 54bis bd Ney, 18th (01.40.05.62.00). M° Porte de la Chapelle. **Open** daily. **Admission** free.
This covered complex provides urban sports fans with a vast space. There are bowls and street furniture, plus a funbox and beginners area. Different time slots are allocated for skaters, bladers and BMXers, so check ahead. Equipment can be hired.

Squash

No membership is necessary to play squash at the **Club Quartier Latin** (*see left*), which charges €20-€30 per 40-minute match (racket rental from €3). The **Standard Athletic Club** (*see p102*) rents squash courts to members or on payment of a €275 seasonal fee.

Squash Montmartre
14 rue Achille-Martinet, 18th (01.42.55.38.30, www.squash-montmartre.fr). M° Lamarck Caulaincourt. **Open** 10am-11pm Mon-Fri; 10am-8pm Sat, Sun. **Admission** from €16. **Credit** MC, V.
Period memberships are available at this club, as well as equipment hire.

Swimming

Pools are plentiful and cheap. Most require a swimming cap and ban bermudas, and many are open late. Swimming to music is integral to **Nuit Blanche** in October (*see pp11-13*).

4 rue Louis-Armand, 15th (01.40.60.10.00, www.aquaboulevard.com). M° Balard. **Open** 9am-11pm Mon-Thur; 9am-midnight Fri; 8am-midnight Sat; 8am-11pm Sun. **Admission** *6hrs* €20-€25; €12 reductions. **Credit** AmEx, MC, V.
With year-round summer temperatures, this water park is great fun for kids. An extra charge gets you a steam bath and three saunas.

Piscine Butte-aux-Cailles
5 pl Paul-Verlaine, 13th (01.45.89.60.05). M° Place d'Italie. **Open** 7-8.30am, 11.30am-1.30pm, 4.30-9pm Tue; 7am-7pm Wed; 7-8.30am, 11.30am-6.30pm Thur, Fri; 7-8.30am, 10am-6.30pm Sat; 8am-6pm Sun. **Admission** €3; €1.70 reductions. **Credit** AmEx, MC, V.
This listed complex, built in the 1920s, has one main indoor pool and two outdoor pools (open in the summer). The water is a temptingly warm 28°C, thanks to the natural sulphurous spring.

Piscine Georges-Vallerey
148 av Gambetta, 20th (01.40.31.15.20). M° Porte des Lilas. **Open** 11.45am-1.30pm Mon; 11.45am-1.30pm, 5.15pm-10pm Tue, Thur; 10am-1pm, 2-7pm Wed; 9am-5pm Sat, Sun. **Admission** €3; €1.70 reductions. **Credit** (€15 minimum) MC, V.
Built for the 1924 Olympics, this complex features a retractable Plexiglas roof, a 50m pool (often split into two 25m pools) and one for kids.

Piscine Josephine-Baker
Quai François-Mauriac, 13th (01.56.61.96.50). M° Quai de la Gare. **Open** 7-8.30am, 1-9pm Mon; 1-11pm Tue, Thur; 7-8.30am, 1-9pm Wed, Fri; 11am-8pm Sat; 10am-8pm Sun. **Admission** €3; €1.70 reductions. **Credit** MC, V.
Moored on the Seine by the Bibliothèque Nationale, the pool-in-a-boat is back to shipshape, apparently cured of the technical problems that plagued it since opening a few years ago. The complex boasts a 25m main pool (with sliding glass roof), a paddling pool and café, and a schedule of exercise classes.

Piscine Keller
14 rue de l'Ingénieur Keller, 15th (01.45.71.81.00). M° Charles Michels. **Open** noon-10pm Mon; 7-8.30am, noon-10pm Tue, Thur; 7am-2pm Wed; noon-10pm Fri; 9am-9pm Sat; 9am-7pm Sun. **Admission** €3; €1.70 reductions. **Credit** V.
Fully renovated in 2008, this 50m pool features a retractable roof and uses an innovative, chlorine-free water treatment method. Lane-swimming is prioritised, and there's a 15m pool for kids.

Piscine Pontoise Quartier Latin
18 rue de Pontoise, 5th (01.55.42.77.88, www.clubquartierlatin.com). M° Maubert Mutualité. **Open** 7-8.30am, 12.15-1.30pm, 4.30-8pm Mon, Fri; 7-8.30am, 12.15-1.30pm, 4.30-7pm Tue, Thur; 7-8.30am, 11.30am-7.30pm Wed; 10am-7pm Sat; 8am-7pm Sun. *Night swimming* 8.15-11.45pm Mon-Fri. **Admission** €4.20; €2.40 reductions; €10 for all 8.15-11.45pm. **No credit cards.**
A beautiful art deco pool with two mezzanine levels. It has private locker rooms, plus night swimming to underwater music. Small fee for lockers.

Piscine Suzanne-Berlioux
Forum des Halles, 10 pl de la Rotonde, 1st (01.42.36.98.44). M° Les Halles. **Open** 11.30am-11pm Mon; 11.30am-10pm Tue; 7-8.15am, 10am-11pm Wed; 11.30am-10pm Thur, Fri; 9am-7pm Sat, Sun. **Admission** €3.80; €3 reductions. **Credit** (€8 minimum) MC, V.
Although usually pretty busy, this 50m pool with its own tropical greenhouse is good for lane swimming. There are no lockers, so you need to check in belongings with the attendants. It reopened in 2010 after renovation.

Tennis & table tennis

The six tennis courts at the **Jardin du Luxembourg** (01.43.25.79.18) are convenient, but there's a better selection at the **Centre Sportif La Faluère** (113 route de la Pyramide, 12th, 01.43.74.40.93) in the Bois de Vincennes.

To find public table tennis in parks around town, consult the *Guide du Sport* (*see p102*).

Centre Sportif Suzanne-Lenglen
2 rue Louis-Armand, 15th (01.44.26.26.50). M° Balard. **Open** 8am-10pm Mon-Sat; 8am-6pm Sun. **Admission** from €7.50. **No credit cards.**
Fourteen courts, two of which are covered.

Sport & Fitness

Theatre

Paris's stages continue to go global. British-born Peter Brook is the stalwart English-language provider at the **Théâtre des Bouffes du Nord**, although he does tremendous credit to the French classical repertoire too. Villette's **Le Tarmac** theatre (Parc de la Villette, behind the Grand Halle, 19th, 01.40.03.93.90, http://letarmac.fr) houses the TILF (Théâtre International de Langue Française), the only theatre in France dedicated to the Francophone world, welcoming visiting troupes from Africa, Asia and Canada; and on the other side of the *Périph*, the **MC93 Bobigny** hosts international companies performing in their own tongues.

After the huge success of Tennessee Williams's *Baby Doll* at the **Théâtre de l'Atelier** (1 place Charles-Dullin, 18th, 01.46.06.49.24, www.theatre-atelier.com), translations of English and American plays remain firmly in vogue. Several theatres have hopped on the bandwagon, with Hitchcock's *Les 39 Marches* (The 39 Steps) enjoying an extended run at the **Théâtre de la Bruyère** (5 rue de la Bruyère, 9th, 01.48.74.76.99, www.theatrelabruyere.com). Last year saw another Tennessee Williams classic, *A Streetcar Named Desire*, starring silver-screen beauty Isabelle Huppert, at the **Odéon, Théâtre de l'Europe** (also known for its multitude of European-language plays). Meanwhile, Shakespeare's *Cymbeline* got an airing at the MC93 Bobigny.

Aside from Huppert at the Odéon, recent celebrity draws have included Audrey Tautou in Henrick Ibsen's *Maison de Poupée* (A Doll's House) and Julie Depardieu in Sacha Guitry's *Nono* at the **Théâtre de la Madeleine**.

On the musicals front, the **Théâtre du Châtelet** is pioneering the art form. After *My Fair Lady* in early 2011 comes Sondheim's *Sweeney Todd* in May.

If singing and dancing are too light-hearted for you, get serious at the **Comédie Française** on the Right Bank, which continues to uphold the classics with flair. The **Théâtre National de Chaillot**, **Théâtre du Rond Point**, **Théâtre de la Ville** and **Théâtre de la Bastille** (76 rue de la Roquette, 11th, 01.43.57.42.14, www.theatre-bastille.com) all offer relentlessly new and exciting spectacles that frequently combine off-the-wall theatre with dance or music too.

Critics' choice

1 Comédie Française
The gilded mother of French theatres has a great line-up for 2011. *See right.*

2 Lavoir Moderne Parisien
Bastion of alternative theatre in a converted washhouse. *www.rueleon.net.*

3 Théâtre du Châtelet
This is the best bet in the capital for quality musical theatre. *See right.*

Odéon, Théâtre de l'Europe.

And in the Bois de Vincennes, a special theatre bus takes you out to the **Cartoucherie**, a factory remade as a theatre commune that's home to five innovative companies, including Ariane Mnouchkine's award-winning **Théâtre du Soleil**.

SHOWS IN ENGLISH

Despite first appearances, catching a play in English in Paris is easy – when you know where to look. Aside from the Théâtre de l'Odéon, which programmes productions in English, German, Spanish and Italian, Peter Brook's Théâtre des Bouffes du Nord offers regular plays in English, and the **Centre Pompidou** (pl Georges-Pompidou, 4th, 01.44.78.12.33, www.cnac-gp.com) often follows suit.

Several companies offer a range of English-language shows and English translations of French works. Local improv troupe the **Improfessionals** (www.improfessionals.com) has been treading the boards of central Paris for the last seven years, offering off-the-cuff stuff; the **Théâtre en Anglais** group (4bis rue de Strasbourg, 92600 Asnières, 01.55.02.37.87, http://theatre.anglais.free.fr) travels around France, but usually stages a well-crafted interpretation of Shakespeare's *Romeo and Juliet* at the Bataclan (50 bd Voltaire, 11th, 01.43.14.00.30, www.le-bataclan.com) for its Paris stint.

Shakespeare is also performed in English every June at the Bois de Boulogne's Théâtre de Verdure du Jardin Shakespeare (01.40.19.95.33, www.jardinshakespeare.fr) by the **Tower Theatre Company** (+44 207 353 5700, www.towertheatre.org.uk).

TICKETS AND INFORMATION

For weekly listings check out *L'Officiel des Spectacles* and *Pariscope* (available from news kiosks). Tickets can be bought at the theatres, from **Fnac** or **Virgin Megastore** (for both, *see p82*) or online at www.theatreonline.com. Check out www.theatresprives.com for half-price tickets to performances during the first week of a new show.

Right Bank

Cartoucherie de Vincennes
Route du Champ de Manoeuvre, Bois de Vincennes, 12th. Mº Château de Vincennes, then shuttle bus.

Théâtre de l'Aquarium *(01.43.74.72.74, www.theatredelaquarium.com).*
Théâtre du Chaudron *(01.43.28.97.04, www.theatreduchaudron.fr).*
Théâtre de l'Epée de Bois *(01.48.08.39.74, www.epeedebois.com).*
Théâtre du Soleil *(01.43.74.87.63, www.theatre-du-soleil.fr).*
Théâtre de la Tempête *(01.43.28.36.36, www.la-tempete.fr).*
Past the Château de Vincennes in the middle of the woods, five independent theatres offer up a first-class selection of politically committed fare. This drama-lover's heaven is housed in ex-army munitions warehouses.

Comédie Française
All *www.comedie-francaise.fr.*
Salle Richelieu *2 rue Richelieu, 1st* (08.25.10.16.80). *Mº Palais Royal Musée du Louvre.* **Box office** 11am-6pm daily. **Admission** €12-€39. *1hr before show* €5 for cheapest seats only. **Credit** AmEx, MC, V.
Studio-Théâtre *Galerie du Carrousel du Louvre, 99 rue de Rivoli, 1st* (01.44.58.98.58). *Mº Palais Royal Musée du Louvre.* **Box office** 2-5pm on performance day. **Admission** €9-€18. **Credit** MC, V.
Théâtre du Vieux Colombier *21 rue du Vieux Colombier, 6th* (01.44.39.87.00). *Mº St-Sulpice.* **Box office** 11am-6pm daily. **Admission** €12-€29. **Credit** MC, V.
The Comédie Française turns out season after season of classics, as well as lofty new productions. The red velvet and gold-flecked Salle Richelieu is located right by the Palais-Royal; under the same management are the Studio-Théâtre, a black box inside the Carrousel du Louvre, and the Théâtre du Vieux Colombier.

Théâtre des Bouffes du Nord
37bis bd de la Chapelle, 10th (01.46.07.34.50, *www.bouffesdunord.com). Mº La Chapelle.* **Box office** 11am-6pm Mon-Sat. **Admission** €18-€28; €14-€25 reductions. **Credit** MC, V.
Peter Brook's playground for more than 30 years, the Bouffes du Nord treats us to an adaptation of Shakespeare's *The Comedy of Errors* in 2011. The Bouffes du Nord also has one of the best chamber music programmes in the capital.

Théâtre du Châtelet
1 pl du Châtelet, 1st (01.40.28.28.40, *www.chatelet-theatre.com). Mº Châtelet.* **Box office** 10am-7pm Mon-Sat. **Admission** €20-€111.50. **Credit** AmEx, DC, MC, V.
The Châtelet is fast becoming Paris's main venue for musicals from Broadway and the West End – such as *My Fair Lady* – usually performed in the original language by visiting companies.

Théâtre de la Madeleine
19 rue de Surène, 8th (01.42.65.07.09, *www.theatremadeleine.com). Mº Madeleine.* **Box office** 11am-7pm daily. **Admission** €15-€42. **Credit** MC, V.
The theatre where Sacha Guitry composed 24 of his plays, between 1932 and 1940, continues to contribute to France's repertoire with top-notch creations by emerging and established artists. After *Nono*, starring Julie Depardieu in 2010, *Diplomatie* by Cyril Gely takes to the stage in 2011.

Théâtre Marigny
Av de Marigny, 8th (01.53.96.70.30, *www.theatremarigny.fr). Mº Champs-Elysées Clemenceau or Franklin D. Roosevelt.* **Box office** 11am-6.30pm Mon-Sat; 11am-3pm Sun. **Admission** €25-€52. **Credit** MC, V.
Théâtre Marigny is one of the most expensive nights out for theatregoers in Paris. But then not many other theatres can boast a location off the Champs-Elysées; a deluxe interior conceived by Charles Garnier (of Opéra fame); high-profile casts and an illustrious pedigree stretching back 150 years. Productions in 2010 included the French adaptation of Pinter's *The Lover*.

Théâtre National de Chaillot
1 pl du Trocadéro, 16th (01.53.65.30.00, *www.theatre-chaillot.fr). Mº Trocadéro.* **Box office** 11am-7pm Mon-Sat. **Admission** €21.50-€32; €11-€24 reductions. **Credit** MC, V.
Get here early, grab a cocktail and gaze in awe at the Eiffel Tower through the lobby window. Chaillot's three auditoriums range from cosy and experimental to a 2,800-seater amphitheatre. In 2011, the season is well endowed in the dance department, including Irish dance phenomenon Colin Dunne's *Out of Time* in June.

Théâtre du Rond Point
2bis av Franklin D. Roosevelt, 8th (01.44.95.98.21, *www.theatredurondpoint.fr). Mº Champs-Elysées Clemenceau or Franklin D. Roosevelt.* **Box office** noon-7pm Tue-Sat; noon-4pm Sun. **Admission** €27-€34; €14 under-30s; €25 over-60s. **Credit** MC, V.
More than just a theatre, this historic venue multitasks as a bookshop, tearoom and restaurant. So once you've fed your mind on contemporary, avant-garde and sometimes politically slanted theatre, make a night of it and opt for dinner as well.

Théâtre de la Ville & Théâtre des Abbesses
01.42.74.22.77, www.theatredelaville-paris.com. **Box office** 11am-7pm Mon; 11am-8pm Tue-Sat. **Admission** €16-€33; €10-€24 reductions. **Credit** MC, V.
Théâtre de la Ville *2 pl du Châtelet, 4th. Mº Châtelet.*
Théâtre des Abbesses *31 rue des Abbesses, 18th. Mº Abbesses.*
At its two sites, the 'City Theatre' turns out consistently innovative programming. Instead of running a standard rep company, the house imports music, dance and theatre productions. Highlights for 2011 include Shakespeare's *The Winter's Tale* directed by Lilo Baur at Théâtre des Abbesses.

Left Bank

Le Lucernaire
53 rue Notre-Dame-des-Champs, 6th (01.45.44.57.34, *www.lucernaire.fr). Mº Notre-Dame-des-Champs or Vavin.* **Box office** 10am-7pm daily. **Admission** €20-€30; €10-€20 reductions. **Credit** MC, V.
Three theatres, three cinemas, a restaurant and a bar make up this versatile cultural centre. Theatre-wise, Molière and other classic playwrights get a good thrashing, but so do up-and-coming authors.

Odéon, Théâtre de L'Europe
Pl de l'Odéon, 6th (01.44.85.40.00, bookings 01.44.85.40.40, *www.theatre-odeon.fr). Mº Odéon.* **Box office** 11am-6.30pm Mon-Sat. **Admission** €10-€32; €6-€20 reductions. **Credit** MC, V.
Highlights for 2011 include the *Aeschylus Trilogy*, directed by Oliver Py, and Victor Hugo's *Mille Francs de Récompense*, plus the Impatience festival for young theatre companies (9-18 June).

Théâtre de la Huchette
23 rue de la Huchette, 5th (01.43.26.38.99, *www.theatrehuchette.com). Mº Cluny La Sorbonne or St-Michel.* **Box office** 3.30-9pm Mon; 5-10.30pm Tue-Fri; 2.45-10.30pm Sat. **Admission** €22; €15 reductions. *Double bill ticket* €32; €23 reductions. **Credit** MC, V.
Ionesco's absurdist classic *La Cantatrice Chauve* (The Bald Soprano) has been playing here for more than 50 years, on a double bill with his *La Leçon*.

Hotels

The best beds: budget, boutique and blowout

Photograph **Shangri La**

Hotels

Paris remains one of the most visited cities in the world, and despite a drop in hotel bookings in 2009, the French capital is upbeat about the future. Tourism figures may have suffered during the global financial crisis but it didn't put the brakes on a host of new hotels that have flourished all over the city. Whether they are part of the new trend for boutique hotels from the high-end chains, or independently owned, their defining mark is fabulous design and attention to detail. This year you can luxuriate in very fine surroundings without having to pay top dollar, and increasingly these 20- to 40-room boutiques have their own spas and bars, making well-being and conviviality part of the chic experience.

STAYING IN PARIS

Paris's luxury palaces continue to offer the ultimate dream hotel experience: at the **Crillon**, the **Bristol**, the **George V**, the **Plaza Athénée** and the **Ritz** uniformed flunkeys whisk you through revolving doors to an otherworldly domain of tinkling china, thick carpets and concierges for whom your wish is their desire, for a generous tip. And 2011 is set to bring even more competition to the luxury sector with the completion of the new **Shangri-La** in the 16th and the complete makeover of the **Royal Monceau** on avenue Hoche by Philippe Starck.

Better value for money can be found at Paris's increasingly luxurious boutique hotels. For several hundred euros less a night than a palace, you can be soothed by fine linen, marble baths and a dreamy pool and hammam at **Le Metropolitan**, walk through silk taffeta curtains to your own terrace at **Le Petit Paris**, fall into a deep sleep at the pure white technological marvel that is the **Hôtel Gabriel**, and fraternise at the trendy cava bar of the Spanish-owned **Banke**. For those who like a bit more glitz, the sparkly **Diamond Opéra** and unabashedly sexy **Sublim Eiffel** use fibre optics to create your own starry galaxy. All of these hotels have made the smooth move of abandoning petty pay-per-hour Wi-Fi in favour of providing it free, and Nespresso machines and iPod docks are making an appearance in bedrooms too.

Further down the scale, there is now a wide choice of moderately priced and even budget design hotels, especially in the trendy east and north-east of the city, such as the Starck-designed **Mama Shelter**, **Standard Design Hotel**, **Le Quartier Bastille** and **20 Prieuré**. And shoestring travellers should definitely check into the new **St Christopher's Inn** on the Canal d'Ourcq, whose façade is lit up like an art installation at night. But if Paris wouldn't be Paris for you without chintzy wallpaper, springy beds and a bathroom on the landing never fear: faithful stalwarts the **Esmeralda** and **Henri IV** are still going strong.

Hotels are graded according to an official star rating system designed to sort the deluxe from the dumps – but we haven't followed it in this guide, as the ratings merely reflect room size and amenities such as lifts or bars, rather than other important factors such as decor, staff or atmosphere. Instead, we've divided the hotels by area, then listed them in four categories, according to the standard prices (not including seasonal offers or discounts) for one night in a double room with en suite shower/bath. For **Deluxe** hotels, you can expect to pay more than €350; for properties in the **Expensive** bracket, €220-€350; for **Moderate** properties, allow €130-€219; while **Budget** rooms go for less than €130. For **gay hotels**, *see p96*.

Note that all hotels in France charge a room tax (*taxe de séjour*) of around €1 per person per night, although this is sometimes included in the rate. Children under 12 often stay for free when sharing a room with parents (check when booking), and small pets usually cost between €10 and €20 extra per night. Hotels are often booked solid and cost more during the major trade fairs (January, May, September), and it's hard to find a good room during Fashion Weeks (January, March, July and October). At quieter times, hotels can often offer special deals at short notice; phone ahead or check their websites.

Hôtel des Deux-Iles.

The Islands

Expensive

Hôtel du Jeu de Paume
54 rue St-Louis-en-l'Ile, 4th (01.43.26.14.18, www.jeudepaumehotel.com). M° Pont Marie. **Rates** €285-€360 double. **Credit** AmEx, DC, MC, V.
With a discreet courtyard entrance, 17th-century beams, private garden and a unique timbered breakfast room that was once a real tennis court built under Louis XIII, this is a charming and romantic hotel. These days, it is filled with an attractive array of modern and classical art, and has a coveted billiards table. A dramatic glass lift and catwalks lead to the guestrooms as well as two self-catering apartments, which are simple and tasteful, the walls hung with beautiful Pierre Frey fabric.

Paris Yacht
Quai de la Tournelle, between Pont de Sully & Pont de la Tournelle, 5th (06.88.70.26.36, www.paris-yacht.com). M° Maubert Mutualité. **Rates** (incl breakfast) €300 double. **No credit cards**.
Paris Yacht has to be the city's quirkiest place to sleep – as long as you don't get seasick. Bobbing peacefully on the Left Bank opposite the Ile St-Louis and five minutes' walk from Notre-Dame, this two-cabin houseboat was built in 1933, and has been in service everywhere from Bastia to the Canal de Bourgogne. Now converted to accommodate up to four guests (welcomed with a bottle of champagne from the owners), the boat is equipped with everything from central heating to high-speed internet. During the summer, the terrace on the upper deck provides the perfect Seine-side setting for dinner.

Moderate

Hôtel des Deux-Iles
59 rue St-Louis-en-l'Ile, 4th (01.43.26.13.35, www.deuxiles-paris-hotel.com). M° Pont Marie. **Rates** €195 double. **Credit** AmEx, MC, V.
This peaceful 17th-century townhouse offers 17 air-conditioned rooms kitted out in toned down stripes, *toile de Jouy* fabrics and neo colonial-style furniture. Its star features are a tiny courtyard off the lobby and a vaulted stone breakfast area. All the rooms and bathrooms were freshened up in 2007 (fortunately saving the lovely tiles on the bathroom walls).

Budget

Hospitel Hôtel Dieu
1 pl du Parvis-Notre-Dame, 4th (01.44.32.01.00, www.hotel-hospitel.com). M° Cité or Hôtel de Ville. **Rates** €131 double. **Credit** MC, V.
If the thought of sleeping in a working hospital doesn't put you off (half the rooms here are used by families of the Hôtel Dieu hospital's in-patients and staff), you can stay in one of 14 recently renovated, spotless rooms with colourful contemporary decor, right in the middle of Ile de la Cité in

Critics' choice

1 Royal Monceau
Raffles' new offering is perfect for luxury lounging. *See p110.*

2 Hôtel Amour
Love is the theme at this boutique beauty. *See p109.*

3 Mama Shelter
Designer looks and decent prices in the 20th. *See p113.*

THE BEST ADDRESSES IN PARIS, THE BEST HOTELS IN EUROPE
PARISMARAIS.COM

DISCOVER LE MARAIS, PARIS' FAVORITE DISTRICT AND 1000 CHARMING HÔTELS IN EUROPE.

Paris is the gateway to Europe. After a week in the City of Light, you may want to spend a few nights in Le Marais most exclusive boutique hotels, and then extend your stay by visiting the prestigious resorts we have selected for you in Europe. Some top destinations are the Loire Valley, the French Riviera and Monaco. Other prestigious cities include Rome, Venice, Vienna, Salzburg, Barcelonna, Madrid, Prague, Dubrovnik, Budapest, Geneva, Lausanne, Montreux, Brussels, Bruges, London, Bath, Brighton, Athens, Copenhagen… Throughout Europe, these cities are the very fabric of local culture and are famous for their history. All of these exquisite places are now at your fingertips, and at preferential prices. We have chosen the best of the best in the three, four and five star categories to make your stay in Europe your most memorable ever. When booking with us, you can be sure to get the best rooms in the best hotels.

PARISMARAIS.COM
THE BEST ADDRESSES IN LE MARAIS
THE BEST HOTELS IN EUROPE

PARISMARAIS is a member of PARIS TOURISM OFFICE and IGLTA © Photos PARISMARAIS.COM / Montgomery Conseil - RCS Paris 450774219.

Paradise in Paris

Credit crunch? What credit crunch? In 2010, Paris welcomed no less than two new palace hotels – the Royal Monceau and the **Shangri-La Paris** (for both, *see p110*). When two more Asian big-hitters, Mandarin Oriental and Peninsula, open between 2011 and 2012, Paris's palace offerings will be up from nine to 11. That's a lot of extra luxury, and a sure sign that there's plenty of life left in the five-star market.

While the Royal Monceau has opted for Philippe Starck's signature bold decor, Pierre-Yves Rochon's design at the Shangri-La is an ode to French Imperialism, with lavish colonial-style paintings, knick-knacks and light fittings, artfully mixed with century-old marble floors, stained-glass windows and thick velveteen fabrics. Half of the 81 rooms and suites look out on to Eiffel's filigree tower, and the top-floor Suite Panoramique provides what could easily be Paris's best panorama over the Left Bank, stretching from the city's western suburbs all the way across the centre, past the Eiffel Tower to beyond Notre-Dame.

Shangri-La may be a Chinese company, but it has gone out of its way to ensure that the building's 'French' architectural heritage remains intact: The mansion, built in 1896 by botanist Roland Bonaparte (Napoleon Bonaparte's great-nephew), drips in Napoleonic carvings and gilding; and there's a Louis XIV-style salon whose splendour rivals Versailles. All of these touches have been painstakingly preserved – especially the €18,000-per-night Imperial Suite, where you can live like the Bonaparte family amid period furniture, original panelling, marble fireplaces and a walk-in dressing room bigger than the average Paris studio flat.

Dining-wise, expect the best of France and Asia, including Shang Palace, Paris's first ever gourmet Cantonese restaurant; L'Abeille, a gastronomic affair overlooking the interior garden; and La Bauhinia Brasserie (named after the iconic flower on Hong Kong's flag), set beneath a 1930s Eiffel-style cupola and serving excellent Chinese and French dishes.

front of Notre-Dame. A medical smell is present but not strong, bathrooms are quite large, and you couldn't ask for a better sightseeing base.

Hôtel Henri IV
25 pl Dauphine, 1st (01.43.54.44.53, www.henri4hotel.fr). M° Pont Neuf. **Rates** €59-€81 double (incl breakfast). **Credit** MC, V.
On tree-lined, triangular Place Dauphine, surrounded by some of Paris's most expensive real estate on Ile de la Cité and a stone's throw from Notre-Dame, the Henri IV remains Paris's best value budget hotel. You therefore need to book well ahead to get a room. The rooms are simple and unadorned, but clean, and the three paupers' penthouses with balconies and rooftop views go first. Eleven of the 15 rooms have en suite bathrooms; the others offer very, very cheap rates.

The Louvre & Palais-Royal

Deluxe

Hôtel Costes
239 rue St-Honoré, 1st (01.42.44.50.00, www.hotelcostes.com). M° Concorde or Tuileries. **Credit** AmEx, DC, MC, V.
Attitude definitely counts in this temple of notoriety – a place so trendy its website only contains contact details and an online boutique of its own *ultra-branché* products, and where innumerable A-listers still gravitate to the low-lit bar after all these years. The Costes boasts one of the best pools in Paris, a sybaritic, Eastern-inspired affair with an underwater music system. Rooms are a modern take on Napoleon III, designed by Jacques Garcia. The same management is responsible for the sleek Hôtel Costes K (81 av Kléber, 16th, 01.44.05.75.75), which has a fabulous spa.

Hôtel de Crillon
10 pl de la Concorde, 8th (01.44.71.15.00, www.crillon.com). M° Concorde. **Rates** €680-€860 double. **Credit** AmEx, DC, MC, V.
The Crillon lives up to its *palais* reputation with decor strong on marble, mirrors and gold leaf. Les Ambassadeurs restaurant has an acclaimed chef and a kitchen with a glassed-in private dining area for groups of no more than six who wish to dine amid the bustle of the 80-strong kitchen staff. If you have euros to spare, opt for the Presidential Suite (the only one with a view over the American Embassy). The Winter Garden tearoom is a must.

Hôtel Ritz
15 pl Vendôme, 1st (01.43.16.30.30, www.ritzparis.com). M° Concorde or Opéra. **Rates** €550-€870 double. **Credit** AmEx, DC, MC, V.
Chic hasn't lost its cool at the grande dame of Paris hotels, where each of the 162 bedrooms (of which 56 are suites), from the romantic Frédéric Chopin to the glitzy Impérial, ooze sumptuousness. But then what else can one expect from a hotel that has proffered hospitality to Coco Chanel, the Duke of Windsor, Proust, and Dodi and Di? There are plenty of corners in which to strike a pose or quench a thirst, from Hemingway's elegant cigar bar to the Ancient Greece-themed poolside hangout.

Hôtel Sofitel le Faubourg
15 rue Boissy-d'Anglas, 8th (01.44.94.14.14, www.sofitel.com). M° Concorde or Madeleine. **Rates** €305-€485 double. **Credit** AmEx, DC, MC, V.
This hotel is close to all the major couture boutiques, which is no surprise, as it used to house the *Marie Claire* offices. The rooms have Louis XVI armchairs, large balconies, walk-in wardrobes and Roger & Gallet goodies in the bathrooms; for shopping widowers, there's a small gym and a hammam. It's quiet too: the street has been closed to traffic since 2001 because the American embassy is on the corner.
Other locations Sofitel Arc de Triomphe, 14 rue Beaujon, 8th (01.53.89.50.50); Hôtel Scribe, 1 rue Scribe, 9th (01.44.71.24.24).

Le Meurice
228 rue de Rivoli, 1st (01.44.58.10.10, www.lemeurice.com). M° Tuileries. **Rates** €665-€920 double. **Credit** AmEx, DC, MC, V.
With its extravagant Louis XVI decor, mosaic tiled floors and modish restyling by Philippe Starck, Le Meurice is looking grander than ever. All 160 rooms (kitted out with iPod-ready radio alarms) are done up in distinct historical styles; the Belle Etoile suite on the seventh floor provides panoramic views of Paris from its terrace. You can relax in the Winter Garden to the strains of regular

jazz performances; for more intensive intervention, head over to the lavishly appointed spa with treatments by Valmont. Don't miss dinner at the hotel's three Michelin-starred restaurant, which has chef Yannick Alléno at the helm.

Le Westin
3 rue de Castiglione, 1st (01.44.77.11.11, www.westin.com/paris). M° Tuileries. **Rates** (incl breakfast) €400-€580 double. **Credit** AmEx, DC, MC, V.
In the heart of shopping HQ, the Westin mixes belle époque features with pale limestone walls, beautiful vintage-style furniture (inspired by the 1930s and '40s), a neoclassical fountain and patio. Its sleek modern bedrooms, decked out with top-end gadgets and the award-winning Heavenly Bed, sport balcony views over the Tuileries gardens. The bathrooms are sumptuous, and some have their own balconies. There's an excellent restaurant, Le First, with a sleek, deep purple and pearly grey, boudoir-like interior designed by Jacques Garcia.

Expensive

Hôtel Brighton
218 rue de Rivoli, 1st (01.47.03.61.61, www.esprit-de-france.com). M° Tuileries. **Rates** €229-€304 double. **Credit** AmEx, DC, MC, V.
With several rooms overlooking the handsome Tuileries gardens, the Brighton is great value, so book well ahead for a room with a view. Recently restored, it has a classical atmosphere, from the high ceilings in the rooms to the faux-marble and mosaic downstairs.

Moderate

Hôtel Mansart
5 rue des Capucines, 1st (01.42.61.50.28, www.esprit-de-france.com). M° Madeleine or Opéra. **Rates** €160-€310 double. **Credit** AmEx, DC, MC, V.
This spacious hotel has real style, with a light, roomy lobby decorated with murals inspired by formal gardens. The 57 bedrooms feature pleasant fabrics, antiques and paintings; five of the rooms have an excellent view of place Vendôme.

Hôtel des Tuileries
10 rue St-Hyacinthe, 1st (01.42.61.04.17, www.hotel-des-tuileries.com). M° Tuileries. **Rates** €202-€272 double. **Credit** AmEx, DC, MC, V.
The fashion pack just adores this 18th-century hotel (the staircase is listed), located in prime shopping territory. Done out with ethnic rugs, a smattering of animal prints, bright art and antique furniture, the 26 comfy bedrooms feel like they belong more in an eccentric family home than a central Paris hotel.

Le Relais du Louvre
19 rue des Prêtres St-Germain-l'Auxerrois, 1st (01.40.41.96.42, www.relaisdulouvre.com). M° Pont Neuf or Louvre-Rivoli. **Rates** €170-€215 double. **Credit** AmEx, MC, V.
The cellar of this characterful hotel, with its antiques and wooden beams, was once used by revolutionaries to print anti-royalist literature. It also inspired Puccini's Café Momus in *La Bohème*. The rooms are decorated in floral fabrics, and the front ones look out on to St-Germain-l'Auxerrois church. There's also a top-floor apartment for up to five people.

Budget

Hotel du Lion d'Or
5 rue de la Sourdière, 1st (01.42.60.79.04, www.hotel-louvre-paris.com). M° Tuileries. **Rates** €95-€135 double. **Credit** MC, V.
Simple, brightly coloured rooms and fully furnished studios (with kitchenettes) that can sleep up to five make the Golden Lion a popular choice for families and groups of friends.

Opéra to Les Halles

Deluxe

Hôtel Westminster
13 rue de la Paix, 2nd (01.42.61.57.46, www.warwickwestminsteropera.com). M° Opéra/RER Auber. **Rates** €350-€630 double. **Credit** AmEx, DC, MC, V.

Hotels

Hôtel Fouquet's Barrière. *See p110.*

This luxury hotel near place Vendôme has more than a touch of British warmth about it, no doubt owing to the influence of its favourite 19th-century guest, the Duke of Westminster (after whom the hotel was named; the current Duke reportedly still stays here). The hotel fitness centre has a top-floor location, with a beautiful tiled steam room and views over the city, and the cosy bar features deep leather chairs, a fireplace and live jazz at weekends.

InterContinental Paris Le Grand
2 rue Scribe, 9th (01.40.07.32.32, www.paris.intercontinental.com). Mº Opéra. **Rates** €285-€685 double. **Credit** AmEx, DC, MC, V.
This 1862 hotel is the chain's European flagship – but, given its size, perhaps 'mother ship' would be more appropriate: this landmark establishment occupies the entire block (three wings, almost 500 rooms) next to the opera house; some 80 of the honey-coloured rooms overlook the Palais Garnier. The space under the vast *verrière* is one of the best oases in town, and the hotel's restaurant and coffeehouse, the Café de la Paix, poached its chef, Laurent Delarbre, from the Ritz. For a relaxing daytime break, head to the I-Spa for one of its seawater treatments.

Expensive

Hôtel Ambassador
16 bd Haussmann, 9th (01.44.83.40.40, www.hotelambassador-paris.com). Mº Chaussée d'Antin or Richelieu Drouot. **Rates** €260-€360 double. **Credit** AmEx, DC, MC, V.
If you're looking for some vintage style but can't face another gilded Louis XIV interior, check into this historic, Haussmann-era hotel, which sets traditional furniture against contemporary decor in each of the 294 bedrooms. The low-lit Lindbergh Bar is named after the pilot who dropped in for a celebratory drink and cigar after his solo transatlantic flight in 1927. The hotel is ideally situated for shopping at the *grands magasins*.

Hôtel Concorde Opéra Paris
108 rue St-Lazare, 8th (01.40.08.44.44, www.concorde-hotels.com). Mº St-Lazare. **Rates** €220-€330 double. **Credit** AmEx, DC, MC, V.
Guests here are cocooned in soundproofed luxury. The 19th-century Eiffel-inspired lobby with jewel-encrusted pink granite columns is a historic landmark: the high ceilings, walls and sculptures look much as they have for over a century. Rooms are spacious, with double entrance doors and exclusive Annick Goutal toiletries; the belle époque brasserie, Café Terminus, and sexy Golden Black Bar were designed by Sonia Rykiel. Guests have access to a nearby fitness centre.

Moderate

Hôtel Amour
8 rue Navarin, 9th (01.48.78.31.80, www.hotelamourparis.fr). Mº St-Georges. **Rates** €150-€280 double. **Credit** AmEx, MC, V.
Opened back in 2006, this boutique hotel is a real hit with the in crowd. Each of the 20 rooms is unique, decorated on the theme of love or eroticism by a coterie of contemporary artists and designers such as Marc Newson, M&M, Stak, Pierre Le Tan and Sophie Calle. Seven of the rooms contain artists' installations, and two others have their own private bar and a large terrace on which to hold your own party. The late-night brasserie has a coveted outdoor garden, and the crowd is young and beautiful and loves to entertain.

Hôtel Arvor Saint Georges
8 rue Laferrière, 9th (01.48.78.60.92, www.arvor-hotel-paris.com). Mº St-Georges. **Rates** €142-€172 double. **Credit** AmEx, DC, MC, V.
Don't be put off by the slightly austere façade; the owner intended it this way to contrast with the homely atmosphere that reigns inside. Although you're right in the middle of the city, the hotel has the feel of a quiet country house. The decor is delicate and uncluttered, and most of the 30 spacious rooms, including six suites, overlook the rooftops (no.503 has the best view of the Eiffel Tower). The small terrace is the ideal spot to take a break from the Paris buzz.

Hôtel Britannique
20 av Victoria, 1st (01.42.33.74.59, www.hotel-britannique.fr). Mº Châtelet/RER Châtelet les Halles. **Rates** €190-€221 double. **Credit** AmEx, MC, V.
Smiling staff in stripy waistcoats welcome you to this adorable hotel, where guest areas and rooms are cocooned in thick drapes, luscious carpets and a mishmash of British colonial-style furniture that make you feel like you've stepped into an English country cottage. Enjoy deeply delicious pastries in the warm, rustic breakfast room, or book a top floor *chambre* and eat them on your plant-filled balcony – a rare oasis of greenery for such a central and reasonably priced hotel.

Hôtel Langlois
63 rue St-Lazare, 9th (01.48.74.78.24, www.hotel-langlois.com). Mº Trinité. **Rates** €140-€150 double. **Credit** MC, V.
Built as a bank in 1870, this belle époque building became the Hôtel des Croisés in 1896. In 2001, after featuring in the Jonathan Demme film *Charade*, it changed its name to Hôtel Langlois in honour of the founder of the Cinémathèque Française. Its 27

spacious, air-conditioned bedrooms are decorated in art nouveau style; the larger ones have delightful hidden bathrooms.

Résidence Hôtel des Trois Poussins
15 rue Clauzel, 9th (01.53.32.81.81, www.les3poussins.com). Mº St-Georges. **Rates** €190-€215 double. **Credit** AmEx, DC, MC, V.
Just off the beaten track in a pleasant *quartier*, and within walking distance (uphill) of Montmartre, the Résidence offers hotel accommodation in the traditional manner, and also has some rare self-catering studios for people who'd rather cook than eat out. Now completely redone, the decor is pleasantly traditional, with a preference for yellow.

Budget

Hôtel Chopin
10 bd Montmartre or 46 passage Jouffroy, 9th (01.47.70.58.10, www.hotel-chopin.com). Mº Grands Boulevards. **Rates** €92-€106 double. **Credit** MC, V.
Handsomely set in a historic, glass-roofed arcade next door to the Grévin museum, the Chopin's original 1846 façade adds to its old-fashioned appeal. The 36 rooms are quiet and functional, done out in either salmon and green or blue.

Hôtel du Cygne
3 rue du Cygne, 1st (01.42.60.14.16, www.hotelducygne.fr). Mº Etienne Marcel/RER Châtelet Les Halles. **Rates** €107-€132 double. **Credit** MC, V.
This traditional hotel in a 17th-century building has 20 compact, cosy and simple rooms embellished with touches such as antiques and homemade furnishings. It's on a pedestrianised street in the bustling Les Halles district, so light sleepers might prefer the rooms overlooking the courtyard.

Hôtel Madeleine Opéra
12 rue Greffulhe, 8th (01.47.42.26.26, www.hotel-madeleine-opera.com). Mº Havre-Caumartin or Madeleine. **Rates** €95-€110 double. **Credit** MC, V.
This bargain hotel is located just north of the Eglise de la Madeleine, in the heart of the city's theatre and *grands magasins* districts. Its sunny lobby sits behind a 200-year-old façade that was once a shopfront. The 23 rooms are a touch basic, but still nice enough, and breakfast is brought to your room every morning.

Champs-Elysées & western Paris

Deluxe

Four Seasons George V
31 av George V, 8th (01.49.52.70.00, www.fourseasons.com/paris). Mº Alma Marceau or George V. **Rates** €750-€1,095 double. **Credit** AmEx, DC, MC, V.
There's no denying that the George V is serious about luxury: chandeliers, marble and tapestries; glorious flower arrangements; divine bathrooms; and ludicrously comfortable beds in some of the largest rooms in all of Paris. The Versailles-inspired spa includes whirlpools, saunas and a menu of treatments for an unabashedly metrosexual clientele; non-guests can now reserve appointments. It's worth every euro.

Hôtel le A
4 rue d'Artois, 8th (01.42.56.99.99, www.paris-hotel-a.com). Mº Franklin D. Roosevelt or St-Philippe-du-Roule. **Rates** €365-€444 double. **Credit** AmEx, DC, MC, V.
The black-and-white decor of this designer boutique hotel provides a fine backdrop for the models, artists and media types hanging out in the lounge bar area; the only splashes of colour come from the graffiti-like artworks by conceptual artist Fabrice Hybert. The 26 rooms all have granite bathrooms, and the starched white furniture slip covers, changed after each guest, make the smallish spaces seem larger than they are. The dimmer switches are a nice touch – as are the lift lights changing colour at each floor.

Hôtel le Bristol
112 rue du Fbg-St-Honoré, 8th (01.53.43.43.00, www.hotel-bristol.com). Mº Champs-Elysées Clémenceau. **Rates** €770-€980 double. **Credit** AmEx, DC, MC, V.
The award-winning Bristol, set plum on rue du Faubourg St-Honoré, already boasts a loyal following of fashionistas and millionaires. But a 2009 extension, which added 26 bedrooms and suites to

the 161 existing rooms, makes for an impressive sight, even to the most jaded celebrity. Spread across seven floors of a Hausmann-inspired building, the new wing is all about space and light, with high ceilings, vast floor space and bathrooms made from pink Portuguese marble. The new wing has also brought with it a hip new restaurant, Le 114 Faubourg, headed up by young chef Eric Desbordes. If 114 Faubourg sounds a little too trendy, then indulge yourself instead at Eric Frechon's renowned gastronomic restaurant in the older part of the hotel, which leads out on to the hotel's famous garden (one of the largest hotel gardens in Paris) and boasts three Michelin stars.

Hôtel Daniel

8 rue Frédéric-Bastiat, 8th (01.42.56.17.00, www.hoteldanielparis.com). M° Franklin D. Roosevelt or St-Philippe-du-Roule. **Rates** €420-€490 double. **Credit** AmEx, DC, MC, V.
A romantic hideaway close to the monoliths of the Champs-Elysées, the city's new Relais & Châteaux property is decorated in chinoiserie and a palette of rich colours, with 26 rooms cosily appointed in *toile de Jouy* and an intricately hand-painted restaurant that feels like a courtyard. With meals at around €50 a head, the gastronomic restaurant Le Lounge is a pretty good deal for this neighbourhood; the bar menu is served at all hours.

Hôtel Fouquet's Barrière

46 av George V, 8th (01.40.69.60.00, www.fouquets-barriere.com). M° George V. **Rates** €730-€950 double. **Credit** AmEx, DC, MC, V.
This grandiose five-star hotel is built around the famous fin-de-siècle brasserie Le Fouquet's. Five buildings form the hotel complex, housing 107 rooms (including 40 suites), upmarket restaurant Le Diane, the Sparis spa, an indoor swimming pool and a rooftop terrace for hire. Jacques Garcia, of Hôtel Costes and Westin fame, was responsible for the interior design, which retains the Empire style of the exterior while incorporating luxurious modern touches inside – flat-screen TVs and mist-free mirrors as standard in the marble bathrooms. And, of course, it's unbeatable in terms of location – right at the junction of avenue George V and the Champs-Elysées.

Hôtel Plaza Athénée

25 av Montaigne, 8th (01.53.67.66.65, www.plaza-athenee-paris.com). M° Alma Marceau. **Rates** €830-€935 double. **Credit** AmEx, DC, MC, V.
This palace is ideally placed for power shopping at Chanel, Louis Vuitton, Dior and other avenue Montaigne boutiques. Material girls and boys will enjoy the high-tech room amenities such as remote-controlled air con, internet and video-game access on the TV via infrared keyboard, and mini hi-fi. Make time for a drink in the Bar du Plaza, a cocktail bunny's most outré fantasy, with flattering lighting, high chairs for great leg-crossing opportunities and ridiculous drinks.

Hôtel de Sers

41 av Pierre-1er-de-Serbie, 8th (01.53.23.75.75, www.hoteldesers.com). M° Alma Marceau or George V. **Rates** €450-€680 double. **Credit** AmEx, DC, MC, V.
Behind its stately 19th-century façade, the Hôtel de Sers calls itself a baby palace, displaying an ambitious mix of minimalist contemporary furnishings, with a few pop art touches. Original architectural details, such as the grand staircase and reception, complete the picture. The large top floor apartment affords dreamy views over Paris's rooftops.

Hôtel Square

3 rue de Boulainvilliers, 16th (01.44.14.91.90, www.hotelsquare.com). M° Passy/RER Avenue du Pdt Kennedy. **Rates** €380-€580 double. **Credit** AmEx, DC, MC, V.
Located in the upmarket 16th, this courageously modern hotel has a dramatic yet welcoming interior, and attentive service that comes from having to look after only 22 rooms. They're decorated in amber, brick or slate colours, with exotic woods, quality fabrics and bathrooms seemingly cut from one huge chunk of Carrara marble. View the exhibitions in the atrium gallery or mingle with the media types at the hip Zebra Square restaurant and DJ bar.

Hôtel de la Trémoille

14 rue de la Trémoille, 8th (01.56.52.14.00, www.hotel-tremoille.com). M° Alma-Marceau. **Rates** €495-€660 double. **Credit** AmEx, DC, MC, V.
Manager Olivier Lordonnois has pushed the Trémoille to another level. The recent opening of a new restaurant-bar-lounge and improved spa and

Pretty in pink Behind a sober frontage, the 33-room **Jardins de la Villa** (*see right*) is an unexpectedly playful affair, with a couture theme and a penchant for fuchsia pink. It's dotted with surreal touches – not least the high heel-shaped couch in reception. Beautifully appointed rooms pair modern luxuries (Nespresso machines, free Wi-Fi, sleek flatscreen TVs) with old-fashioned attention to detail (proper soundproofing and thick, light-blocking curtains), while suites come with extra floor space and flourishes. The location is off the tourist trail, though close to the métro; not one to pick if you like being in the thick of things, perhaps, but perfect for a little peace and quiet.

fitness facilities have made it a serious competitor to the other palaces nearby. The 93 rooms are decorated to evoke no fewer than 31 different 'atmospheres', and the bathrooms are filled with Molton Brown products. A unique feature is the 'hatch', which enables room service to deliver your meal without disturbing you.

Hôtel de Vigny

9-11 rue Balzac, 8th (01.42.99.80.80, www.hoteldevigny.com). M° George V. **Rates** €440-€520 double. **Credit** AmEx, DC, MC, V.
One of only two Relais & Châteaux in the city, this hotel has the feel of a private, plush townhouse. Although it's just off the Champs-Elysées, the Vigny pulls in a discerning, low-key clientele. Its 37 bedrooms and suites are decorated in tasteful stripes or florals, with marble bathrooms. Enjoy dinner in the art deco Baretto restaurant, or have a cup of tea in the library.

Jays Paris

6 rue Copernic, 16th (01.47.04.16.16, www.jays-paris.com). M° Kléber or Victor Hugo. **Rates** €420-€690 suite. **Credit** MC, V.
Introducing a new concept on the Paris hotel scene, Jays is a luxurious *boutique-apart* hotel that trades on a clever blend of antique furniture, modern design and high-tech equipment. The marble staircase, lit entirely by natural light filtered through the glass atrium overhead, gives an instant feeling of grandeur, and leads to five suites, each with a fully equipped kitchenette. A cosy salon is available to welcome in-house guests and their visitors.

Opéra Diamond

4 rue de la Pépinière, 8th (01.44.70.02.00, www.paris-hotel-diamond.com). M° St-Lazare. **Rates** €450-€510 double. **Credit** AmEx, DC, MC, V.
This sparkling newcomer to the Opéra/St-Lazare district lives up to its name with a night-sky decor made up of black granite resin punctuated with crystals and LEDs. The 30 rooms are equally splendid with Swarovski crystal touches to the furniture, black bathrooms and satin curtains that close to become a huge photomontage of a female nude crossed with architectural imagery. The Executive rooms on the fifth floor have iPod stations, Nespresso machines, and speakers in the bathrooms. A grassy courtyard with a fountain adds to the appeal. Unashamedly bling, but rather magical when night falls. Check the website as rates are often heavily discounted.

Pershing Hall

49 rue Pierre-Charron, 8th (01.58.36.58.00, www.pershinghall.com). M° George V. **Rates** €470-€560 double. **Credit** AmEx, DC, MC, V.
The refreshing mix of 19th-century grandeur and contemporary comfort makes Pershing Hall feel quite large, but this luxury establishment is really a cleverly disguised boutique hotel with just 26 rooms. Fashionable locals frequent the stylish bar and restaurant terrace. Designed by Andrée Putman, the neat bedrooms emphasise natural materials, with stained grey oak floors and fine mosaic-tiled bathrooms with geometric styling and copious towels.

Royal Monceau

37 Avenue Hoche, 8th (01.42.99.88.00, www.leroyalmonceau.com). M° Charles de Gaulle Etoile. **Rates** €730-€930 double. **Credit** AmEx, DC, MC, V.
This new Starck-designed incarnation of the legendary old grande dame opened to the public (or at least those who could afford it) in October 2010, offering everything from cosy studio rooms to the 190 sq m Royal Monceau suite. With no fewer than three restaurants, desserts from star pastry chef Pierre Hermé and an indoor pool and spa, the Royal Monceau is firmly back in the big league. *See also p3* **Raffles at the Royal**.

Le Sezz

6 av Frémiet, 16th (01.56.75.26.26, www.hotelsezz.com). M° Passy. **Rates** €335-€470 double. **Credit** AmEx, DC, MC, V.
Le Sezz opened its doors in 2005 with 27 deluxe rooms and suites – the work of acclaimed French furniture designer Christophe Pillet. The understated decor represents a refreshingly modern take on luxury, with black parquet flooring, rough-hewn stone walls and bathrooms partitioned off with sweeping glass façades. The bar and public areas are equally chic.

Shangri-La Paris

10 av d'Iéna, 16th (01.53.67.19.98, www.shangri-la.com). M° Iéna. **Rates** €750-€1,265 double. **Credit** AmEx, DC, MC, V.
See p108 **Paradise in Paris**.

Expensive

Hôtel Keppler

10 rue Keppler, 16th (01.47.20.65.05, www.keppler.fr). M° George V or Charles de Gaulle Etoile. **Rates** €300-€490 double. **Credit** AmEx, DC, MC, V.
This newly renovated boutique hotel is a family-run treasure, decorated with striped wallpaper, funky mirrors, animal prints and various knick-knacks. None of the 39 rooms is huge, but all are cleverly thought through, so that lack of space is never an issue and the whole experience is pleasantly cosy. The top floor suites have their own (large) balcony – perfect for an alfresco breakfast – and views over Paris's rooftops towards the Eiffel Tower.

Hôtel Pergolèse

3 rue Pergolèse, 16th (01.53.64.04.04, www.pergolese.com). M° Argentine. **Rates** €260-€290 double. **Credit** AmEx, DC, MC, V.
The Pergolèse was one of the first designer boutique hotels in town, but still looks contemporary a decade or so after being kitted out by Rena Dumas-Hermès with art deco-style furniture by Philippe Starck and rugs by Hilton McConnico. Rooms feature pale wood details and cool, white-tiled bathrooms.

Hôtel Regent's Garden

6 rue Pierre-Demours, 17th (01.45.74.07.30, www.hotel-paris-garden.com). M° Charles de Gaulle Etoile or Ternes. **Rates** €290-€440 double. **Credit** AmEx, DC, MC, V.
This elegant hotel – built for Napoleon III's physician – features appropriately Second Empire high ceilings and plush upholstery, and a lounge overlooking a lovely walled patio. There are 39 large bedrooms, some with gilt mirrors and fireplaces. It's an oasis of calm just ten minutes from the Champs-Elysées, and the first hotel in Paris to receive an Ecolabel, for its recycling and energy- and water-saving efforts.

Les Jardins de la Villa

5 rue Bélidor, 17th (01.53.81.01.10, www.jardinsdelavilla.com). M° Porte Maillot. **Rates** €280-€420 double. **Credit** AmEx, DC, MC, V.
See left **Pretty in pink**.

Le Metropolitan

10 pl de Mexico, 16th (01.56.90.40.04, www.radissonblu.com). M° Trocadero. **Rates** €270-€410 double. **Credit** AmEx, DC, MC, V.
This new 40-room offering from Radisson Blu is supremely sleek. The discreet entrance is only a few metres wide, but once inside the triangular structure opens out into surprising volumes, with a monumental art deco-style fireplace, and cream leather and black granite reminiscent of New York in the 1930s. The first floor contains a swank insiders' cocktail bar, but the biggest surprise of all is the breathtaking view of the Eiffel Tower from the front façade, best enjoyed through the huge oval window while lying on the four-poster bed of the sixth floor suite. All rooms exude *luxe, calme et volonté* with solid oak floors, linen curtains and baths or showers carved from black or cream marble. And below ground is a sublime pool and hammam reserved for guests.

Renaissance Paris Arc de Triomphe

39 av de Wagram, 17th (01.55.37.55.37, www.marriott.com). M° Ternes. **Rates** €319-€389 double. **Credit** AmEx, DC, MC, V.
You can't miss it. This six-storey undulating glass façade on avenue de Wagram is like no other part of the neighbourhood. All rooms are stylishly done out in pale greys, charcoals and dark wood, with Eames-style furniture. Nice high-tech touches include an iPod dock on the bedside radio and a large flat-screen TV with Wi-Fi keyboard. Bathrooms are a glory of polished metal, tasteful tiles and gleaming glass. The Makassar restaurant serves delicate and delicious Franco-Asian fusion food.

Moderate

Hôtel Elysées Ceramic

34 av de Wagram, 8th (01.42.27.20.30, www.elysees-ceramic.com). M° Charles de Gaulle Etoile. **Rates** €220 double. **Credit** AmEx, DC, MC, V.
Situated between the Arc de Triomphe and place des Ternes, this comfortable hotel has one of Paris's finest art nouveau ceramic façades dating from 1904; inside, the theme continues with a ceramic cornice around the reception. All 57 rooms have been renovated in sophisticated chocolate or pewter tones with modern, art nouveau-inspired wallpaper and light fixtures. Outside is a terrace garden perfect for taking afternoon tea or evening cocktails.

Montmartre & Pigalle

Deluxe

Hôtel Particulier Montmartre

23 av Junot, 18th (01.53.41.81.40, www.hotel-particulier-montmartre.com). M° Lamarck Caulaincourt. **Rates** €390-€590 suite. **Credit** MC, V.

CHRISTOPHE BIELSA

Kube Hotel.

Visitors lucky (and wealthy) enough to manage to book a suite at the Hôtel Particulier Montmartre will find themselves in one of the city's hidden gems. Nestled in a quiet passage off rue Lepic, in the heart of Montmartre and opposite a mysterious rock known as the *Rocher de la Sorcière* (witch's rock), this sumptuous *Directoire*-style house is dedicated to art, with each of the five luxurious suites personalised by an avant-garde artist. The private garden conceived by Louis Bénech (famous for the Tuileries renovation) adds the finishing touch to this charming hideaway.

Expensive

Hôtel Banke
20 rue La Fayette, 9th (01.55.33.22.22, www.derbyhotels.com). M° Le Peletier. **Rates** €210-€315 double. **Credit** AmEx, MC, V.
This swish establishment occupies the former HQ of the CCF bank, a magnificent early 20th-century building. The Banke is owned by the Spanish Derby Hotels chain, and Catalan flair comes through in a just-this-side-of-kitsch approach to dressing up the splendid lobby, with gold leather chesterfields and Swarovski-studded armchairs by Bretz, as well as Starck Perspex bar stools and transparent tables in the circular Lolabar. Some of the executive rooms seem rather small for the price tag, but all is quality here, with parquet flooring, green Bizazza mosaics in the bathroom and luxurious burgundy taffeta on the bed. The Josefin restaurant serves fine Catalan food with a small choice of excellent Spanish wines. Food, design and location are all pretty much spot on, but the ultimate treat here is the sleep you'll have.

Kube Hotel
1-5 passage Ruelle, 18th (01.42.05.20.00, www.kubehotel.com). M° La Chapelle. **Rates** €300-€400 double. **Credit** AmEx, DC, MC, V.
The younger sister of the Murano Urban Resort (*see right*), Kube is an edgier and more affordable hotel. Like the Murano, it sits behind an unremarkable façade in an unlikely neighbourhood – in this case, the ethnically diverse Goutte d'Or. The Ice Kube bar by Grey Goose serves up vodka glasses that, like the bar itself, are carved from ice; drinkers pay €38 to down four vodka cocktails in 30 minutes. Also on the menu, 'aperifood' and 'snackubes' by culinary designer Nicolas Guillard. The art brunch on

Sundays introduces a different artist each month, with DJs and a buffet. To top off the futuristic style, access to the 41 rooms is by fingerprint technology.

Moderate

Hôtel des Arts
5 rue Tholozé, 18th (01.46.06.30.52, www.arts-hotel-paris.com). M° Abbesses or Blanche. **Rates** €140-€165 double. **Credit** MC, V.
The wagging tail of Caramel the black labrador welcomes guests to this Montmartre gem, pleasantly decorated in oriental rugs, wooden bookcases and Provençal-style furniture. The rooms here are simple but inviting, some affording pleasant views of the hidden roof gardens and windmills of the *Butte*. Art by local artists is displayed in the basement breakfast room.

Hôtel Royal Fromentin
11 rue Fromentin, 9th (01.48.74.85.93, www.hotelroyalfromentin.com). M° Blanche or Pigalle. **Rates** €179 double. **Credit** AmEx, DC, MC, V.
Wood panelling, art deco windows and a vintage glass lift echo the hotel's origins as a 1930s cabaret hall; its theatrical feel attracted Blondie and Nirvana. It's just down the road from the Moulin Rouge, and many of its 47 rooms overlook Sacré-Coeur. Rooms have been renovated in French style, with bright fabrics and an old-fashioned feel.

Terrass Hotel
12-14 rue Joseph-de-Maistre, 18th (01.46.06.72.85, www.terrass-hotel.com). M° Place de Clichy. **Rates** €200-€270 double. **Credit** AmEx, DC, MC, V.
There's nothing spectacular about this classic hotel, but for people willing to pay top euro for the best views in town, it fits the bill. Ask for room 704 and you can lie in the bath and look at the Eiffel Tower. Julien Rocheteau, trained by Ducasse, is at the helm of gastronomic restaurant Diapason; in fine weather, opt for a table on the seventh-floor terrace, open from June to September.

Timhotel Montmartre
11 rue Ravignan, 18th (01.42.55.74.79, www.timhotel.fr). M° Abbesses or Pigalle. **Rates** €150-€180 double. **Credit** AmEx, DC, MC, V.

The location adjacent to picturesque place Emile-Goudeau makes this one of the most popular hotels in the Timhotel chain. It has 59 rooms, comfortable without being plush; try to bag one on the fourth or fifth floor for stunning views over Montmartre. Special offers are often available at quieter times of the year; ring for details.

Budget

Hôtel Eldorado
18 rue des Dames, 17th (01.45.22.35.21, www.eldoradohotel.fr). M° Place de Clichy. **Rates** €73-€82 double. **Credit** AmEx, DC, MC, V.
This eccentric hotel is decorated with flea market finds. The Eldorado's winning features include a wine bar, one of the best garden patios in town and a loyal fashionista following. The cheapest rooms have shared bathrooms and toilets.

Hôtel Ermitage
24 rue Lamarck, 18th (01.42.64.79.22, www.ermitagesacrecoeur.fr). M° Lamarck Caulaincourt. **Rates** (incl breakfast) €96-€100 double. **No credit cards.**
This 12-room townhouse hotel stands on the calm, non-touristy north side of Montmartre, only five minutes from Sacré-Coeur. The bedrooms are large and endearingly overdecorated, with bold floral wallpaper; those higher up have fine views.

Beaubourg & the Marais

Deluxe

Murano Urban Resort
13 bd du Temple, 3rd (01.42.71.20.00, www.muranoresort.com). M° Filles du Calvaire or Oberkampf. **Rates** €440-€650 double. **Credit** AmEx, DC, MC, V.
Behind this unremarkable façade is a super cool and supremely luxurious hotel, popular with the fashion set for its slick lounge-style design, excellent restaurant and high-tech flourishes – including coloured light co-ordinators that enable you to

change the mood of your room at the touch of a button. The handsome bar has a mind-boggling 140 varieties of vodka to sample, which can bring the op art fabrics in the lift to life and make the fingerprint access to the hotel's 43 rooms and nine suites (two of which feature private pools) a late-night godsend.

Expensive

Hôtel Bourg Tibourg
19 rue du Bourg-Tibourg, 4th (01.42.78.47.39, www.hotelbourgtibourg.com). M° Hôtel de Ville. **Rates** €230-€260 double. **Credit** AmEx, DC, MC, V.
The Bourg Tibourg has the same owners as Hôtel Costes (*see p108*) and the same interior decorator – but don't expect this jewellery box of a boutique hotel to look like a miniature replica. Aside from its enviable location in the heart of the Marais and its fashion-pack fans, here it's all about Jacques Garcia's neo-Gothic-cum-Byzantine decor – impressive and imaginative. Scented candles, mosaic-tiled bathrooms and luxurious fabrics in rich colours create the perfect escape. There's no restaurant or lounge – posing is done in the neighbourhood bars.

Hôtel du Petit Moulin
29-31 rue de Poitou, 3rd (01.42.74.10.10, www.hoteldupetitmoulin.com). M° St-Sébastien Froissart. **Rates** €190-€350 suite. **Credit** AmEx, DC, MC, V.
Within striking distance of the hip shops around rue Charlot, this turn-of-the-century façade masks what was once the oldest *boulangerie* in Paris, lovingly restored as a boutique hotel by Nadia Murano and Denis Nourry. The couple recruited no lesser figure than Christian Lacroix for the decor, and the result is a riot of colour, trompe l'oeil effects and a savvy mix of old and new. Each of its 17 exquisitely appointed rooms is unique, and the walls in rooms 202, 204 and 205 feature drawings and scribbles taken from Lacroix's sketchbook.

Les Jardins du Marais
74 rue Amelot, 11th (01.40.21.20.00, www.lesjardinsdumarais.com). M° Bastille. **Rates** €222-€382 double. **Credit** AmEx, DC, MC, V.

Hotels

The centrepiece of this ultra-swish hotel is a vast courtyard, filled with tables, potted plants and lampposts that wouldn't look out of place in Narnia. Inside, it's smart and modern; the lobby looks tastefully trendy in its steely black and white marble, with purple furnishings and Philippe Starck chairs. The rooms were all renovated in 2009. The in-house restaurant is a favourite with the local media crowd.

Moderate

Hôtel de la Bretonnerie
22 rue Ste-Croix-de-la-Bretonnerie, 4th (01.48.87.77.63, www.bretonnerie.com). M° Hôtel de Ville. **Rates** €135-€165 double. **Credit** MC, V.
With wrought ironwork, exposed stone and wooden beams, the labyrinth of corridors in this 17th-century *hôtel particulier* is full of atmosphere. Tapestries, rich colours and the occasional four-poster bed give the 29 rooms individuality. Location is convenient too.

Hôtel Duo
11 rue du Temple, 4th (01.42.72.72.22, www.duoparis.com). M° Hôtel de Ville. **Rates** €200-€380 double. **Credit** AmEx, DC, MC, V.
An unbeatable location, designer decor, a gym with sauna and a convivial cocktail bar make this a popular choice for laptop-wielding young professionals. Its Jean-Philippe Nuel decor is so striking that passers-by sometimes enquire about the price of the outsize lampshades and mustard-coloured armchairs in the huge lounge lobby, which also has a bamboo courtyard garden. Based on a palette of brown with contrasting turquoise, mustard, lime green, pink or blue, each room is different and you can request a balcony, beams, wallpaper, a bath, separate loo, and road or courtyard preference. The suite, which sleeps four, even has its own little courtyard off the bedroom.

Hôtel St-Louis Marais
1 rue Charles V, 4th (01.48.87.87.04, www.saintlouismarais.com). M° Bastille or Sully Morland. **Rates** €115-€140 double. **Credit** AmEx, DC, MC, V.
Built as part of a 17th-century Célestin convent, this peaceful hotel had its bathrooms redone and Wi-Fi access installed a few years ago. Rooms are compact and cosy, with wooden beams, tiled floors and simple, traditional decor.
Other locations Hôtel St-Louis Bastille, 114 bd Richard Lenoir, 11th (01.43.38.29.29); Hôtel St-Louis Opéra, 51 rue de la Victoire, 9th (01.48.74.71.13).

Hôtel St-Merry
78 rue de la Verrerie, 4th (01.42.78.14.15, www.hotelmarais.com). M° Châtelet or Hôtel de Ville. **Rates** €160-€230 double. **Credit** AmEx, MC, V.
The Gothic decor of this former presbytery attached to the Eglise St-Merry is ideal for a Dracula set, with wooden beams, stone walls and plenty of iron; behind the door of room nine, an imposing flying buttress straddles the carved antique bed. On the down side, the building has no lift, and only thesuite has a TV.
Other locations Hôtel Saintonge Marais, 16 rue de Saintonge, 3rd (01.42.77.91.13).

Budget

Grand Hôtel Jeanne d'Arc
3 rue de Jarente, 4th (01.48.87.62.11, www.hoteljeannedarc.com). M° Chemin Vert or St-Paul. **Rates** €90-€116 double. **Credit** MC, V.
The Jeanne d'Arc's strong point is its location on a quiet road close to pretty place du Marché-Ste-Catherine. A recent refurbishment has made the reception area striking, with a huge mirror adding the illusion of space. The bedrooms are colourful and comfortable.

Hôtel Paris France
72 rue de Turbigo, 3rd (01.42.78.00.04, www.paris-france-hotel.com). M° Temple. **Rates** €109-€132 double. **Credit** AmEx, DC, MC, V.
A great central location, sweet lift, spruce staff and clean, pleasant rooms are on offer here. The attic has views of Montmartre and (if you lean out far enough) the Eiffel Tower.

Hôtel du Septième Art
20 rue St-Paul, 4th (01.44.54.85.00, www.paris-hotel-7art.com). M° Pont Marie or St-Paul. **Rates** €95-€150 double. **Credit** AmEx, DC, MC, V.
Ideally located in a lively part of the Marais, the quaint façade hides a treasure trove of movie

FEATURED ESTABLISHMENT

memorabilia, which takes up most of the reception space. Exposed brick walls and devoted staff make for a friendly, cosy atmosphere. The decor in the bedrooms isn't exactly groundbreaking, but everything is clean and well equipped. Beware, there's no lift.

Bastille & eastern Paris

Deluxe

Hôtel Marceau Bastille
13 rue Jules César, 12th (01.43.43.11.65, www.hotelmarceaubastille.com). M° Bastille. **Rates** €350-€450 double. **Credit** AmEx, DC, MC, V.
This slick boutique hotel has 55 rooms divided into two different styles: urban or *écolo* (eco-friendly), some with a balcony. The bar-lounge, overlooking a pleasant, bamboo-planted patio, is surrounded by a gallery that exhibits works of contemporary artists.

Moderate

Le Pavillon Bastille
65 rue de Lyon, 12th (01.43.43.65.65, www.pavillonbastille.com). M° Bastille. **Rates** €195-€215 double. **Credit** AmEx, DC, MC, V.
The best thing about this hotel is its location between the Bastille opera and the Gare de Lyon. The 25 rooms may be small, but you're a stone's

throw from the Viaduc des Arts, where an elevated garden has replaced the railroad's tracks and arty boutiques now occupy the arches.

Le Quartier Bastille, Le Faubourg
9 rue de Reuilly, 12th (01.43.70.04.04, www.lequartierhotelbf.com). M° Faidherbe Chaligny or Reuilly-Diderot. **Rates** €133-€148 double. **Credit** AmEx, DC, MC, V.
Close to the Bastille and the hip 11th arrondissement, the Quartier Bastille (a branch of Franck Altruie's chain of budget design hotels) flashes funky, neo-1970s furniture and just the right amount of colour. Rooms are minimalist.

Standard Design Hotel
29 rue Taillandiers, 11th (01.48.05.30.97, www.standard-hotel.com). M° Ledru Rollin. **Rates** €180-€250 double. **Credit** AmEx, DC, MC, V.
The Standard's black and white interior, with the occasional splash of colour, is satisfyingly generic and a winner with visitors looking for a break from the sometimes heavy atmosphere of older, more traditional hotels. The rooms have all mod cons, the breakfast room awakens the senses with bold stripes, and you can roll into bed after a night out in Bastille's cool bars and restaurants.

Budget

Mama Shelter
109 rue de Bagnolet, 20th (01.43.48.48.48, www.mamashelter.com). M° Alexandre Dumas, Maraîchers or Porte de Bagnolet. **Rates** €89-€199 double. **Credit** AmEx, DC, MC, V.

Room with a view

You can't miss it. The six-storey undulating glass façade on avenue Wagram is like no other part of the neighbourhood; at night, when it's all lit up, this very 21st-century building looks like a frozen waterfall.

Welcome to one of the city's most striking hotels, the **Renaissance Paris Arc de Triomphe** (*see p110*). It stands on the site of the Théâtre de l'Empire, a former theatre and TV studio that was severely damaged in a gas explosion in 2005, and had to be demolished – thus creating a rare construction opportunity within sight of the Arc de Triomphe. The design of the hotel was entrusted to star French architect Christian de Portzamparc, but the massively thick, curving pieces of his glass façade were beyond the manufacturing capability of France, and had to be made in Germany.

Bedrooms at the front of the hotel are flooded with natural light, of course; and exhibitionists can, by drawing back the ceiling-to-floor

gauze curtains and positioning themselves in the right part of the window's curve, undress and canoodle in full view not just of the street below and the buildings opposite, but also of their next door neighbours. All rooms are stylishly done out in pale greys, charcoals and dark wood, with Eames-style furniture and magenta cushions.

Nice high-tech touches include an iPod dock on the bedside radio, glass-topped bedside surfaces that are illuminated from below, a wardrobe whose light switches on automatically as you approach, and a large flat-screen TV with Wi-Fi keyboard. The drinks cabinet includes a coffee machine.

Bathrooms are a glory of polished metal, tasteful tiles and gleaming glass and ceramics, with gourmet toiletries that include lemongrass soap. Nor does the gourmet experience stop in the shower: the Makassar restaurant serves delicate Franco-Asian fusion food.

Philippe Starck's latest design commission is set a stone's throw east of Père Lachaise, and its decor appeals to the young-at-heart with Batman and Incredible Hulk light fittings, dark walls, polished wood and splashes of bright fabrics. Every room comes equipped with an iMac computer, TV, free internet access and a CD and DVD player; and when hunger strikes, there's a brasserie with a romantic terrace.

Le Quartier Bercy Square
33 bd de Reuilly, 12th (01.44.87.09.09, www.lequartierhotelbs.com). M° Daumesnil or Dugommier. **Rates** €123-€143 double. **Credit** AmEx, DC, MC, V.
You'd never think that lime green and brown stripes would match bold silver and white replica 19th-century wallpaper, but it does at the boutique Quartier Bercy Square (another of Franck Altruie's addresses) in the trendy 12th arrondissement. Rooms are small but inviting, often using coloured light to create atmosphere.

North-east Paris

Expensive

Hôtel Gabriel
25 rue du Grand Prieuré, 11th (01.47.00.13.38, www.gabrielparismarais.com). M° République. **Rates** €240-€280 double. **Credit** AmEx, DC, MC, V.
Paris's first 'detox hotel' is a shrine to quality kip and healthy living. The air-conditioned, pure white rooms are not short on techno wizardry: there's an iPod station for which you can borrow an iPod pre-programmed with anything from Goldfrapp to Shirley Bassey; free Wi-Fi, of course; and the sine qua non of sleep aids, the NightCove device. This white box is easily programmed to emit sounds and light that stimulate melatonin: choose between sleep, nap or wake-up programmes such as the sound of rain or tropical birdsong. If you're still feeling rundown, then take yourself downstairs for a detox massage. A partner gym, suggested jogging routes and green taxis complete the healthy vibe.

Moderate

Le Général Hôtel
5-7 rue Rampon, 11th (01.47.00.41.57, www.legeneralhotel.com). M° République. **Rates** €190-€220 double. **Credit** AmEx, DC, MC, V.
A fashionable find near the nightlife action of the 11th, Le Général was one of Paris's first boutique bargains when it opened back in 2003. It is still notable for its remarkably moderate rates and sleek, neutral-toned interior.

Budget

Le 20 Prieuré Hôtel
20 rue du Grand Prieuré, 11th (01.47.00.74.14, www.hotel20prieure.com). M° République. **Rates** €95-€172 double. **Credit** AmEx, MC, V.
This young, funky and affordable place benefits from particularly welcoming staff. Each bedroom features a blow-up of a Paris landmark covering the entire wall behind the bed, giving you the illusion that you are sleeping halfway up the Eiffel Tower. Bathrooms are mundane in comparison, but things brighten up again in the light-flooded breakfast room.

Hôtel Beaumarchais
3 rue Oberkampf, 11th (01.53.36.86.86, www.hotelbeaumarchais.com). M° Filles du Calvaire or Oberkampf. **Rates** €110-€130 double. **Credit** AmEx, MC, V.
This contemporary hotel is located in the heart of the Oberkampf area, not far from the Marais and Bastille. Its 31 rooms are brightly decorated with colourful walls, bathroom mosaics and wavy headboards; breakfast is served on the tiny garden patio or in your room.

The Latin Quarter & the 13th

Expensive

Hôtel Résidence Henri IV
50 rue des Bernardins, 5th (01.44.41.31.81, www.residencehenri4.com). M° Cardinal Lemoine. **Rates** €250-€310 double. **Credit** AmEx, DC, MC, V.

Hotels

Book for bedtime

Juliette Récamier was the great society beauty of the Napoleonic era. Married at the age of 15 to a man that was probably her father, Juliette had a stack of lovers and was seemingly irresistible to everyone but Bonaparte himself, who had her banished. She returned to run her influential literary salon for 30 years at the Abbaye-aux-Bois, a few hundred metres from **Hôtel La Belle Juliette** (*see p115*), which counted Châteaubriand, Madame de Stael, Augustus of Prussia and the Duchess of Devonshire among its clique.

The fascinating Juliette is the inspiration for this new four-star hotel in St-Germain-des-Prés which pays more than lip service to the lady. Alain Bisotti, general manager of the Hôtels Paris Rive Gauche group, which also includes the Hôtel du Panthéon, Hôtel des Grands Hommes and Hôtel Design Sorbonne, has collected an archive of rare books, a play, a pianola roll, miniatures, illustrations and portraits of Juliette, which guests can consult on the iMac computers in their rooms. Other antique books and engravings are scattered around the hotel.

Interior designer Anne Gelbard, famous for fusing metal leaf to fabric, paper and feather for haute couture fashion designers, has filled the 34 rooms with the distinctive colours of the Napoleonic era and of Juliette's famous portrait by Gérard – pale yellow, eau-de-nil, duck-egg blue, slate and Augustan red. It's classical without being constricting, as there is also contemporary furniture and lighting, high-tech communications and luxury bathrooms. Each floor reflects a different episode in Juliette's eventful life.

The Talma bar is named after a romantic actor of the time and offers organic breakfasts, lunches by Une Fête à Paris (who cater at Cathérine Deneuve's café above the Cinéma du Panthéon) and Italian tapas at night inspired by Juliette's exile in Italy.

As Juliette was a beauty, there had to be a beauty salon, and it features natural facelifts using gold acupuncture needles and Sentara facial products, as well as a range of relaxing massages.

Juliette's world of loose morals and exquisite taste, smells and images makes this an outstanding place for a romantic break.

This belle époque-style hotel has a mere eight rooms and five apartments, so guests are assured of the staff's full attention. Peacefully situated next to square Paul-Langevin, it's just a few minutes' walk from Notre-Dame. The four-person apartments come with a mini-kitchen featuring a hob, fridge and microwave – although you may be reduced to eating on the beds in the smaller ones.

Le Petit Paris
214 rue St-Jacques, 5th (01.53.10.29.29, www.hotelpetitparis.com). M° Maubert Mutualité/RER Luxembourg. **Rates** €240-€320 double. **Credit** AmEx, MC, V.
This brand new Latin Quarter venture is a dynamic exercise in taste and colour. The 20 rooms, designed by Sybille de Margerie, are arranged by era, running from the puce and purple of the medieval rooms to the wildly decadent orange, yellow and pink of the swinging '60s rooms, replete with specially commissioned sensual photographs of Paris monuments. Luxury abounds with finest silks, velvets and taffetas. Some of the rooms have small terraces, and those with baths have a TV you can watch while soaking. An honesty bar in the lounge and ultramodern jukebox encourage conviviality.

Moderate

Five Hôtel
3 rue Flatters, 5th (01.43.31.74.21, www.thefivehotel.com). M° Les Gobelins or Port Royal. **Rates** €202-€342 double. **Credit** AmEx, MC, V.
The rooms in this stunning boutique hotel may be small, but they're all exquisitely designed, with Chinese lacquer and velvety fabrics. Fibre optics built into the walls create the illusion of sleeping under a starry sky, and you can choose from four different fragrances to subtly perfume your room (the hotel is entirely non-smoking). Guests staying in the suite have access to a private garden with a jacuzzi.

Hôtel la Demeure
51 bd St-Marcel, 13th (01.43.37.81.25, www.hotel-paris-lademeure.com). M° Les Gobelins. **Rates** €170-€210 double. **Credit** AmEx, DC, MC, V.
This comfortable, modern hotel on the edge of the Latin Quarter is run by a friendly father and son. It has 43 air-conditioned rooms with internet access, plus suites with sliding doors to separate sleeping and living space. The wrap-around balconies of the corner rooms offer lovely views of the city, and bathrooms feature either luxurious tubs or shower heads with elaborate massage possibilities.

Hôtel Design de la Sorbonne
6 rue Victor-Cousin, 5th (01.43.54.58.08, www.hotelsorbonne.com). M° Cluny La Sorbonne/RER Luxembourg. **Rates** €100-€350 double. **Credit** AmEx, DC, MC, V.
It's out with the old at this charming, freshly renovated design hotel, with bold, designer wallpapers, floral prints, lush fabrics and quotes from French literature woven into the carpets. Bedrooms are all equipped with iMac computers and there's a revamped breakfast room as well.

Select Hôtel
1 pl de la Sorbonne, 5th (01.46.34.14.80, www.selecthotel.fr). M° Cluny La Sorbonne. **Rates** (incl breakfast) €164-€225 double. **Credit** AmEx, DC, MC, V.
Located at the foot of the Sorbonne, this 68-room hotel delivers pure, understated chic with its clever blend of modern art deco features, traditional stone walls and wooden beams. The winter garden and airy common areas have recently been redone in a sleek, contemporary style.

Budget

Familia Hôtel
11 rue des Ecoles, 5th (01.43.54.55.27, www.hotel-paris-familia.com). M° Cardinal Lemoine or Jussieu. **Rates** (incl breakfast) €107-€137 double. **Credit** AmEx, DC, MC, V.
This old-fashioned Latin Quarter hotel has balconies hung with tumbling plants and walls draped with replica French tapestries. Owner Eric Gaucheron extends a warm welcome, and the 30 rooms have personalised touches such as sepia murals, cherry-wood furniture and stone walls. The Gaucherons also own the Hôtel Minerve next door – book in advance for both.
Other locations Hôtel Minerve, 13 rue des Ecoles, 5th (01.43.26.81.89).

Hôtel les Degrés de Notre-Dame
10 rue des Grands-Degrés, 5th (01.55.42.88.88, www.lesdegreshotel.com). M° Maubert-Mutualité or St-Michel. **Rates** (incl breakfast) €115-€170 double. **Credit** MC, V.
On a tiny street across the river from Notre-Dame, this vintage hotel is an absolute gem. Its ten rooms are full of character, with original paintings, antique furniture and exposed wooden beams (nos.47 and 501 have views of the cathedral). It has an adorable restaurant and, a few streets away, two studio apartments that the owner rents out to preferred customers only.

Hôtel du Panthéon
19 pl du Panthéon, 5th (01.43.54.32.95, www.hoteldupantheon.com). M° Cluny La Sorbonne or Maubert Mutualité/RER Luxembourg. **Rates** €100-€310 double. **Credit** AmEx, DC, MC, V.
The 36 rooms of this elegant hotel are beautifully decorated with classic French *toile de Jouy* fabrics, antique furniture and painted woodwork. Some enjoy impressive views of the Panthéon; others squint out on to a hardly less romantic courtyard, complete with chestnut tree.

Hôtel Résidence Gobelins
9 rue des Gobelins, 13th (01.47.07.26.90, www.hotelgobelins.com). M° Les Gobelins. **Rates** €79-€98 double. **Credit** AmEx, MC, V.
A tiny lift leads to colourful rooms, all equipped with satellite TV and telephone. The breakfast room overlooks a private garden, and there's free internet use available at the reception. The hotel is entirely non-smoking.

St-Germain-des-Prés & Odéon

Deluxe

L'Hôtel
13 rue des Beaux-Arts, 6th (01.44.41.99.00, www.l-hotel.com). M° Mabillon or St-Germain-des-Prés. **Rates** €250-€640 double. **Credit** AmEx, DC, MC, V.
Guests at the sumptuously decorated L'Hôtel these days are more likely to be models and film stars than the starving writers who frequented the place during Oscar Wilde's last days (the playwright died on the ground floor here in November 1900). Under Jacques Garcia's careful restoration, each room has its own special theme:

Artus Hotel.

Hotels

Mistinguett's *chambre* retains its art deco mirror bed, while Oscar's tribute room is appropriately clad in green peacock murals. Don't miss out on dinner in the fabulously decadent restaurant, run by talented chef Philippe Bélisse.

Hôtel La Belle Juliette
92 rue du Cherche-Midi, 6th (01.42.22.97.40, www.hotel-belle-juliette-paris.com). Mº Vaneau. **Rates** €300-€450. **Credit** AmEx, DC, MC, V. *See p114* **Book for bedtime**.

Hôtel Lutetia
45 bd Raspail, 6th (01.49.54.46.46, www.lutetia-paris.com). Mº Sèvres Babylone. **Rates** €240-€590 double. **Credit** AmEx, DC, MC, V.
This historic Left Bank hotel is a masterpiece of art nouveau and early art deco architecture that dates from 1910. It has a plush jazz bar and lively brasserie. Its 250 rooms, revamped in purple, gold and pearl grey, maintain a 1930s feel. Big-name guests in years gone by have included Picasso, Josephine Baker and de Gaulle. It was also the Abwehr (German military intelligence) HQ during the Nazi occupation.

Villa d'Estrées
17 rue Gît-le-Coeur, 6th (01.55.42.71.11, www.villa destrees.com). Mº St-Michel. **Rates** €365-€405 double. **Credit** AmEx, DC, MC, V.
Jewel colours, sumptuous fabrics, stripes and patterns are the hallmarks of this polished boutique hotel; there's nothing at all minimalist about Villa d'Estrées, which was designed by Jacques Garcia. Each of the ten rooms and suites is individually decorated, all with a nod to Empire style and a crisp, slightly masculine feel.

Expensive

Artus Hotel
34 rue de Buci, 6th (01.43.29.07.20, www.artushotel.com). Mº Mabillon. **Rates** €250-€310 double (incl breakfast). **Credit** AmEx, DC, MC, V.
The recently renovated Artus Hotel is the ideal spot for a classic taste of Paris – you couldn't be any closer to the heart of the Left Bank action if you tried. Inside the look is chic boutique, with 27 individually designed rooms and suites, ranging from cosy to capacious. Staff are eager to help and full of local tips.

Hôtel de l'Abbaye Saint-Germain
10 rue Cassette, 6th (01.45.44.38.11, www.hotelabbayeparis.com). Mº Rennes or St-Sulpice. **Rates** (incl breakfast) €260-€380 double. **Credit** AmEx, DC, MC, V.
A monumental entrance opens the way through a courtyard into this tranquil hotel, originally part of a convent. Wood panelling, well-stuffed sofas and an open fireplace in the drawing room make for a relaxed atmosphere, but, best of all, there's a surprisingly large garden. The 43 rooms and duplex apartment are tasteful and luxurious.

Le Placide
6 rue St-Placide, 6th (01.42.84.34.60, www.leplacidehotel.com). Mº Sèvres-Babylone, St-Placide or Vaneau. **Rates** €220-€370 double. **Credit** AmEx, DC, MC, V.
With only ten rooms, the Placide is just about as bijou as it gets. White, chrome and neutral tones reign throughout (as does bark- or bamboo-inspired wallpaper), broken only by the occasional funky cushion. Rooms are spacious: all have large bathrooms as well as their own sitting area. The stylish ground-floor duplex has been designed for disabled guests.

Relais Saint-Germain
9 carrefour de l'Odéon, 6th (01.44.27.07.97, www.hotel-paris-relais-saint-germain.com). Mº Odéon. **Rates** (incl breakfast) €285-€370 double. **Credit** AmEx, DC, MC, V.
The rustic, wood-beamed ceilings remain intact at the Relais Saint-Germain, a 17th-century hotel bought and renovated by much-acclaimed chef Yves Camdeborde (originator of the *bistronomique* dining trend) and his wife Claudine. Each of the 22 rooms has a different take on eclectic Provençal charm, and the marble bathrooms are positively huge by Paris standards. Guests get first dibs on a sought-after seat in the 15-table Le Comptoir restaurant next door.

La Villa
29 rue Jacob, 6th (01.43.26.60.00, www.villa-saintgermain.com). Mº St-Germain-des-Prés. **Rates** €280-€370 double. **Credit** AmEx, DC, MC, V.
Refreshingly modern and stylish, the charismatic La Villa features cool faux crocodile skin on the bedheads and crinkly taffeta over the taupe-

coloured walls. Wonderfully, your room number is projected on to the floor outside your door; very useful for any drunken homecomings.

Moderate

Le Clos Médicis
56 rue Monsieur-le-Prince, 6th (01.43.29.10.80, www.closmedicis.com). Mº Odéon/RER Luxembourg. **Rates** €215-€270 double. **Credit** AmEx, DC, MC, V.
Looking more like a stylish, private townhouse than a hotel, Le Clos Médicis is located by the Luxembourg gardens. Decor is refreshingly modern, with bedrooms done out with taffeta curtains and chenille bedcovers, and antique floor tiles in the bathrooms. The cosy lounge has a working fireplace.

Grand Hôtel de l'Univers
6 rue Grégoire-de-Tours, 6th (01.43.29.37.00, www.hotel-paris-univers.com). Mº Odéon. **Rates** €185-€280 double. **Credit** AmEx, DC, MC, V.
Making the most of its 15th-century origins, this hotel features exposed wooden beams, high ceilings, antique furnishings and toile-covered walls. Manuel Canovas fabrics lend a posh touch, but there are also useful services such as a laptop for hire. The same team runs the Hôtel St-Germain-des-Prés (36 rue Bonaparte, 6th, 01.43.26.00.19), which has a medieval-themed room and the sweetest attic in Paris.

Hôtel du Globe
15 rue des Quatre-Vents, 6th (01.43.26.35.50, www.hotel-du-globe.fr). Mº Odéon. **Rates** €170 double. **Credit** MC, V.
The Hôtel du Globe has managed to retain much of its 17th-century character – and very pleasant it is too. Gothic wrought-iron doors open into the florid corridors, and an unexplained suit of armour supervises guests from the tiny salon. The rooms with baths are somewhat larger than those with showers, and if you're an early booker you might even get the room with the four-poster bed (ask when reserving).

Hôtel des Saints-Pères
65 rue des Sts-Pères, 6th (01.45.44.50.00, www.espritfrance.com). Mº St-Germain-des-Prés. **Rates** €160-€220 double. **Credit** AmEx, MC, V.
Built in 1658 by one of Louis XIV's architects, this hotel has an enviable location near St-Germain-des-Prés' designer boutiques. It boasts a charming garden and a sophisticated, if small, bar. The most coveted room is no.100, with its fine 17th-century ceiling by painters from the Versailles School; it also has an open bathroom, so you can gaze at scenes from the myth of Leda and the Swan while you scrub.

Hôtel Villa Madame
44 rue Madame, 6th (01.45.48.02.81, www.hotelvillamadameparis.com). Mº St-Sulpice. **Rates** €189-€285 double. **Credit** AmEx, MC, V.
This revamped hotel (formerly called the Regents), located in a quiet street, is a lovely surprise, with its courtyard garden used for breakfast in the summer months. Honey- and chocolate-coloured woods mix with warm-toned velvets to make the rooms (which all feature plasma screens) feel cosy and inviting; some even have small balconies with loungers.

Budget

Hôtel de Nesle
7 rue de Nesle, 6th (01.43.54.62.41, www.hoteldenesleparis.com). Mº Odéon. **Rates** €75-€100 double. **Credit** MC, V.
Only nine of the 20 rooms are en suite, but all are decorated with colourful murals, and many overlook a charming garden courtyard.

Montparnasse

Expensive

Hôtel des Académies et des Arts
15 rue de la Grande Chaumière, 6th (01.43.26.66.44, www.hotel-des-academies.com). Mº Notre-Dame des Champs, Raspail or Vavin. **Rates** €189-€314 double. **Credit** AmEx, DC, MC, V.
Reopened in early 2007 after a full refurbishment, this small boutique hotel scores highly on style. There are cosy salons, fireplaces and an extensive

Hôtel de l'Abbaye Saint-Germain.

collection of art books. The 20 immaculate rooms are individually designed around four themes (Paris, Actor, Man Ray or Rulhmann), and offer wonderful views over the rooftops or down on to the spectacular Jérôme Mesnager mural which graces the courtyard.

Hôtel Aviatic

105 rue de Vaugirard, 6th (01.53.63.25.50, www.aviatic.fr). M° Duroc, Montparnasse Bienvenüe or St-Placide. **Rates** €235-€285 double. **Credit** AmEx, DC, MC, V.

This historic hotel has masses of character, from the Empire-style lounge and garden atrium to the bistro-style breakfast room and polished marble floor in the lobby. New decoration throughout, in beautiful steely greys, warm reds, elegant, striped velvets and *toile de Jouy* fabrics, lends an impressive touch of glamour, and the service is consistently with a smile. For lunch on the hop, staff will pack up a picnic so you can eat in the nearby Luxembourg gardens.

Moderate

Hôtel Delambre

35 rue Delambre, 14th (01.43.20.66.31, www.delambre-paris-hotel.com). M° Edgar Quinet or Vavin. **Rates** €140-€160 double. **Credit** AmEx, MC, V.

Occupying a narrow slot in a small street between Montparnasse and St-Germain, this hotel was home to surrealist André Breton in the 1920s. Today it's modern and friendly, with cast-iron details in the 13 rooms and newly installed air-conditioning. The mini suite in the attic, comprising two separate rooms, is particularly pleasant and sleeps up to four.

Hôtel Istria Saint-Germain

29 rue Campagne-Première, 14th (01.43.20.91.82, www.hotel-istria-paris.com). M° Raspail. **Rates** €190 double. **Credit** AmEx, DC, MC, V.

Behind this unassuming façade is the place where the artistic royalty of Montparnasse's heyday – the likes of Man Ray, Marcel Duchamp and Louis Aragon – once lived. The Istria Saint-Germain has been modernised since then, but it still has plenty of charm, with 26 bright, simply furnished rooms, a cosy breakfast room and a comfortable communal area. Film fans take note: the artists' studios next door featured in Godard's *A Bout de Souffle*.

Budget

Solarhôtel

22 rue Boulard, 14th (01.43.21.08.20, www.solarhotel.fr). M° Denfert Rochereau. **Rates** €59 double.

See below **Sustainable sleep**.

The 7th & western Paris

Deluxe

Le Bellechasse

8 rue de Bellechasse, 7th (01.45.50.22.31, www.lebellechasse.com). M° Assemblée Nationale or Solférino/RER Musée d'Orsay. **Rates** (incl breakfast) €340-€390 double. **Credit** AmEx, MC, V.

A former *hôtel particulier*, the Bellechasse fell into the hands of Christian Lacroix, already responsible for the makeover of the Hôtel du Petit Moulin (*see p112*). It reopened in July 2007, duly transformed into a trendy boutique hotel. Only a few steps away from the Musée d'Orsay, it offers 34 splendid – though rather small – rooms.

Le Montalembert

3 rue Montalembert, 7th (01.45.49.68.68, www.montalembert.com). M° Rue du Bac. **Rates** €240-€500 double. **Credit** AmEx, DC, MC, V.

Grace Leo-Andrieu's impeccable boutique hotel is a benchmark of quality. It has everything that *mode* maniacs (who flock here for Fashion Week) could want: bathrooms stuffed with Molton Brown toiletries, a set of digital scales and plenty of mirrors with which to keep an eye on their figure. Clattery stairwell lifts are a nice nod to old-fashioned ways in a hotel that is otherwise *tout moderne*.

Expensive

Hôtel Duc de Saint-Simon

14 rue de St-Simon, 7th (01.44.39.20.20, www.hotelducdesaintsimon.com). M° Rue du Bac. **Rates** €250-€285 double. **Credit** AmEx, DC, MC, V.

A lovely courtyard leads the way into this popular hotel situated on the edge of St-Germain-des-Prés. Of the 34 romantic bedrooms, four have terraces over a closed-off, leafy garden. It's perfect for lovers, though if you can do without a four-poster bed there are more spacious rooms than the Honeymoon Suite.

Moderate

Hôtel La Bourdonnais

111-113 av de La Bourdonnais, 7th (01.47.05.45.42, www.hotellabourdonnais.com). M° Ecole Militaire. **Rates** €185-€230 double. **Credit** AmEx, DC, MC, V.

The Bourdonnais feels more like a traditional French bourgeois townhouse than a hotel, with 56 bedrooms decorated in rich colours, antiques and Persian rugs. The lobby opens on to a winter garden and patio.

Hôtel Lenox

9 rue de l'Université, 7th (01.42.96.10.95, www.lenoxsaintgermain.com). M° St-Germain-des-Prés. **Rates** €150-€240 double. **Credit** AmEx, DC, MC, V.

This venerable literary and artistic haunt is unmistakably part of St-Germain-des-Prés. The art deco-style Lenox Club Bar, open to the public, features comfortable leather club chairs and jazz instruments on the walls. Bedrooms, reached by an astonishing glass lift, have more traditional decor and city views.

Sublim Eiffel

94 bd Garibaldi, 15th (01.40.65.95.95, www.sublimeiffel.com). M° Sèvres-Lecourbe. **Rates** €159-€179 double. **Credit** AmEx, MC, V.

Some Barry White on your iPod is essential for this luuurve hotel not far from the Eiffel Tower. Carpets printed with paving stones and manhole covers lead to the rooms, where everything has been put in place for steamy nights. It's all to do with the lighting effects, which include a starry Eiffel Tower or street-scene lights above the bed and sparkling LEDs in the showers, filtered by coloured glass doors. Lovers should head for the suite, with its jacuzzi, huge shower, bathrobes and DVDs, and book the Romance package (rose petals on the bed and champagne). All guests get the use of the mini-gym and hammam, and there is a massage room too. The bar adds a bit of jazz to a neighbourhood in need of some action.

Budget

Hôtel Eiffel Rive Gauche

6 rue du Gros-Caillou, 7th (01.45.51.51.51, www.hotel-eiffel.com). M° Ecole Militaire. **Rates** €105-€155 double. **Credit** MC, V.

The Provençal decor and warm welcome make this a nice retreat. For the quintessential Paris view at a bargain price, ask to stay on one of the upper floors: you can see the Eiffel Tower from nine of the 29 rooms. All feature Empire-style bedheads and modern bathrooms. Outside, there's a tiny, tiled courtyard with a bridge. If this is fully booked, try sister hotel Eiffel Villa Garibaldi (48 bd Garibaldi, 15th, 01.56.58.56.58).

Youth accommodation

Auberge Internationale des Jeunes

10 rue Trousseau, 11th (01.47.00.62.00, www.aijparis.com). M° Ledru-Rollin. **Rates** (incl breakfast, per person) €19-€21. **Credit** AmEx, MC, V.

Cleanliness is a high priority at this large, 120-bed hostel close to Bastille and within easy distance of the Marais. Rooms accommodate between two and four people, and the larger ones have their own shower and toilet. With the lowest hostel rates in central Paris, the place does tend to fill up fast in summer, but advance reservations can be made. Although the hostel is open all hours without any late-night curfew, the rooms are closed for cleaning every day between 10am and 3pm. Under-35s only.

Auberge Jules-Ferry

8 bd Jules-Ferry, 11th (01.43.57.55.60, www.hihostels.com). M° République. **Rates** (incl breakfast & linens, per person) €23. **Credit** MC, V.

This friendly IYHF hostel has 100 beds in rooms for two to six. There's no need – indeed, no way – to make advance bookings. There's no curfew, though rooms are closed between 10am and 2pm.

BVJ Paris/Quartier Latin

44 rue des Bernardins, 5th (01.43.29.34.80, www.bvjhotel.com). M° Maubert Mutualité. **Rates** (incl breakfast, per person) €29 dorm; €35 double. **No credit cards.**

The BVJ hostel has 121 beds with homely tartan quilts in clean but bare modern dorms (accommodating up to ten), and rooms with showers. There's also a TV lounge and a work room in which to write up your journal.

Other locations BVJ Paris/Louvre, 20 rue Jean-Jacques-Rousseau, 1st (01.53.00.90.90).

MIJE

6 rue de Fourcy, 4th (01.42.74.23.45, www.mije.com). M° St-Paul. **Rates** (incl breakfast, per person; €2.50 obligatory membership) €30 dorm (18-30s); €36 double. **No credit cards.**

MIJE runs three 17th-century Marais residences – one is a former convent – that provide the most attractive hostel sleeps in Paris. Its plain, clean rooms have snow-white sheets and sleep up to eight people; all have a shower and basin. The Fourcy address has its own restaurant on site (evenings only). The curfew is at 1am unless you arrange otherwise.

Other locations (same phone) 12 rue des Barres, 4th; 11 rue du Fauconnier, 4th.

St Christopher's Inn

159 rue de Crimée, 19th (01.40.34.34.40, www.st-christophers.co.uk/paris-hostels). M° Crimée, Jaurès, Laumière or Stanlingrad. **Rates** per person €28-€35 dorm; €42-€47 double. **Credit** AmEx, MC, V.

If you don't mind bunking up with others, you could try this branch of the English youth hostel chain in a former boat hangar on the Canal de l'Ourcq. The decor in the bedrooms has a sailor's cabin feel, with round mirrors, bubble-pattern wallpaper and 1950s-inspired cabin furniture. The hostel really comes into its own in its bar Belushi's, where the usual backpack brigade are joined by Parisians bent on taking advantage of the canal setting, satellite sports, lunchtime brasserie and some of the cheapest drinks in the city.

Bed & breakfast

Alcove & Agapes

Le Bed & Breakfast à Paris, 8bis rue Coysevox, 18th (01.44.85.06.05, www.bed-and-breakfast-in-paris.com).

This B&B booking service offers over 100 *chambres d'hôtes* (€80-€320 for a double, including breakfast; three-, four- and five-bed rooms available too) with hosts who range from artists to grannies. Extras can include anything from dinner to cooking classes.

Good Morning Paris

43 rue Lacépède, 5th (01.47.07.28.29, www.goodmorningparis.fr).

This company has 100 rooms in the city. Prices range from €69 to €109 for doubles, and €106 for an apartment that sleeps two to four people. There's a minimum stay of two nights.

Apart-hotels & flat rental

A deposit is usually payable on arrival. Small ads for private short-term lets run in the fortnightly anglophone mag *FUSAC* (01.56.53.54.54, www.fusac.fr); or check out www.frenchconnections.co.uk, which has a selection of furnished apartments for four or more people, and www.apartmentservice.com.

Citadines Apart'hotel

Central reservations 01.41.05.79.05, www.citadines.com. **Rates** €110-€615. **Credit** AmEx, DC, MC, V.

The 16 modern Citadines complexes across Paris tend to attract a mainly business clientele. Room sizes vary from slightly cramped studios to quite spacious two-bedroom apartments.

Paris Address

Central reservations 01.43.20.91.57, www.parisaddress.com. **Rates** €80-€400. **Credit** AmEx, DC, MC, V.

Paris Address has over 280 apartments for rent in the heart of Paris and offers a friendly reception service – a great alternative to staying in a hotel.

Paris Appartements Services

20 rue Bachaumont, 2nd (01.40.28.01.28, www.paris-apts.com). M° Sentier. **Open** 9am-6pm Mon-Fri. *Key pick-up* 24hrs. **Rates** (min 5 nights) €100-€214. **Credit** AmEx, MC, V.

This organisation specialises in short-term rentals, offering furnished studios and one-bedroom flats in the first to fourth arrondissements.

Swell Apartments

11 rue Duhesme, 18th (+44 (0)7725 056 421, www.swell-apartments.co.uk). M° Lamarck Caulincourt. **Rates** €113-€131 (min 3 nights). **Credit** MC, V.

Don't be put off by the tatty entrance; this one-bedroom flat on the north side of Montmartre (sleeping two) is lovely inside. The bedroom, with blue and white walls, has a crystal chandelier and marble fireplace. The cosy lounge has elegant furniture.

Sustainable sleep

If you want green accommodation in Paris but don't want to spend more than €60 a night, you could always try Camping du Bois de Boulogne (www.campingduboisdeboulogne.fr), where a guilt-free sleep in a tent with your own solar-fuelled pocket torch costs less than €20. But for a proper stay in a centrally heated room with ensuite bathroom, things get trickier.

The average cost for a night in a Paris hotel is €184.20, and more often than not that bill comes with a substantial CO_2 tag. But one hotel in the 14th, the **Solarhôtel** (*see above*) has managed to strike a great balance between price and sustainability.

It's not an attractive building, with beige stucco cladding and electric-blue window frames, but three solar panels (which create enough energy to illuminate the façade at night) are an outward sign of the ecological efforts being made inside. The simple ensuite bedrooms are all equipped with low-energy lamps, and the corridors are fitted with low-consumption, sensor-operated lights that switch on and off when you move. It may not sound like much, but if all 25,000 of France's hotels did the same, it is estimated that the country would require one less nuclear reactor. Then there's the water supply: taps and toilets are all fitted with water-saving devices, and three huge barrels collect natural rainwater for use in the hotel's garden and basement toilets. Clients and staff are encouraged to recycle, with separate bins for plastics, paper, glass and batteries, and biodegradable waste from the organic breakfast gets turned into compost in a barrel in the garden.

So what about the cost of all these measures? Manager Franck Laval believes that making these changes saves money in the long run – hence the Solarhôtel's low prices. Staying in a double room costs just €59 a night. It's a first on Paris's budget hotel scene and one that will hopefully catch on.

Essentials

Everything you need to know

Photograph **Olivia Rutherford**

Getting Around

Arriving & leaving

By air

Roissy-Charles-de-Gaulle airport
01.70.36.39.50, www.adp.fr.
Most international flights use Roissy-Charles-de-Gaulle airport, 30km (19 miles) north-east of Paris. Its three main terminals are some way apart, so check which one you need for your return flight. The terminals are linked by the free CDGVAL driverless train.

The **RER B** (RATP helpline, 08.91.36.20.20, www.transilien.com) is the quickest way to central Paris (about 40mins to Gare du Nord; 45mins to RER Châtelet-Les Halles; €8.70 single). RER trains run every 10-15mins, 4.58am-11.58pm daily from the airport to Paris.

Air France buses (08.92.35.08.20, www.cars-airfrance.com; €15 single, €24 return, €7.50 under-11s, free under-2s) leave every 30mins, 5.45am-11pm daily, from both terminals, and stop at porte Maillot and place Charles-de-Gaulle (35-50min trip). Air France buses also run to Gare Montparnasse and Gare de Lyon (€16.50 single, €27 return, €8 under-11s, free under-2s) every 30mins (45-60min trip), 7am-9pm daily; there's a shuttle bus between Roissy and Orly (€19 (no return), €9.50 under-11s, free under-2s) every 30mins, 5.55am-10.30pm daily from Roissy; 6.30am-10.30pm Mon-Fri, 7am-10.30pm Sat, Sun from Orly. The **RATP Roissybus** (08.92.69.32.46, www.ratp.fr; €9.10) runs every 15-20mins, 5.45am-11pm daily, between the airport and the corner of rue Scribe/rue Auber (at least 45mins); buy tickets on the bus. **Paris Airports Service** is a door-to-door minibus service between airports and hotels, 24/7. The more passengers on board, the less each one pays. Roissy prices go from €26 for one person to €99 for eight people, 6am-8pm (minimum €41, 4-6am, 8-10pm); book on 01.55.98.10.80, www.parisairportservice.com. **Airport Connection** (01.43.65.55.55, www.airport-connection.com; booking 7am-11pm) runs a similar service. Prices for Roissy are €20 for one person to €89 for five or more. A **taxi** to central Paris can take 30-60mins depending on traffic. Expect to pay €30-€50, plus €1 per luggage item.

Orly airport
01.70.36.39.50, www.adp.fr.
Domestic and international flights use Orly airport, 18km (11 miles) south of the city. It has two terminals: Orly-Sud (mainly international) and Orly-Ouest (mainly domestic).

Air France buses (08.92.35.08.20, www.cars-airfrance.com; €11.50 single, €18.50 return, €5.50 under-11s, free under-2s) leave both terminals every 30mins, 6.15am-11.15pm daily, and stop at Invalides and Montparnasse

(30-45mins). The **RATP Orlybus** (08.92.69.32.46, www.ratp.fr; €6.40) runs between the airport and Denfert-Rochereau every 15mins, 5.35am-11.30pm (30min trip); buy tickets on the bus. The high-speed **Orlyval** (www.orlyval.fr) shuttle train runs every 4-7mins (6am-11pm daily) to RER B station Antony (€10.25 to Châtelet-les-Halles); getting to central Paris takes about 35mins. You could also catch the **Paris par le train bus** (€6.20) to Pont de Rungis, where you can take the RER C into central Paris. Buses run every 20mins, 4.34am-11.14pm daily from Orly-Sud; 35min trip. Orly prices for **Paris Airports Service** and **Airport Connection** door-to-door facility (*see above*) are €25 for one person and €5-€12 each for extra passengers depending on numbers. A **taxi** into town takes 20-40mins and costs €16-€26, plus €1 per luggage item.

Paris Beauvais airport
08.92.68.20.66, www.aeroportbeauvais.com.
Beauvais, 70km (44 miles) from Paris, is served by budget airlines such as **Ryanair** (08.92.78.02.10, www.ryanair.com). Buses (€15) leave for Porte Maillot 15-30mins after each arrival; buses the other way leave 3hrs 15mins before each departure. Get tickets from the arrivals lounge or on the bus.

Major airlines
Aer Lingus *08.21.23.02.67, www.aerlingus.com.*
Air France *36.54, www.airfrance.fr.*
American Airlines *08.26.46.09.50, www.americanairlines.fr.*
bmibaby *0044.8458.101.100, www.bmibaby.com.*
British Airways *08.25.82.54.00, www.britishairways.fr.*
British Midland *0044.1332.648.181, www.flybmi.com.*
Continental *01.71.23.03.35, www.continental.com.*
Easyjet *08.99.65.00.11, www.easyjet.com.*
KLM & NorthWest *08.92.70.26.08, www.klm.com.*
United *08.10.72.72.72, www.united.fr.*

By car
Options for crossing the Channel with a car include: **Eurotunnel** (08.10.63.03.04, www.eurotunnel.com); **Brittany Ferries** (08.25.82.88.28, www.brittanyferries.com); **P&O Ferries** (08.25.12.01.56, www.poferries.com); and **SeaFrance** (0044.8454.580.666, www.seafrance.com).

Shared journeys
Allô-Stop *30 rue Pierre Sémard, 9th (01.53.20.42.42, www.allostop.net). Mº Poissonnière.* **Open** 10am-1pm, 2-6pm Mon-Fri; 10am-1pm, 2-4pm Sat. **Credit** MC, V.

Call several days ahead to be put in touch with drivers. There's a fee (€5 under 250km, 155 miles; €8 over 250km), plus a contribution towards the petrol expenses, paid to the driver (from €5 under 100km, 62 miles, up to €90 for over 2,000km, 1,243 miles).

By coach
International coach services arrive at the Gare Routière Internationale Paris-Gallieni at Porte de Bagnolet, 20th. For reservations (in English), call **Eurolines** on 08.92.89.90.91 (€0.34 per min) or 01.41.86.24.21 from abroad, or visit the website, www.eurolines.fr. Fares start from €19 for a single journey from London to Paris.

By rail
From London, **Eurostar** services (UK: 0044.8432.186186, www.eurostar.com) to Paris depart from the dedicated terminal at St Pancras International. Thanks to the new high-speed track, the journey from London to Paris now takes 2hrs 15mins direct, slightly longer for trains stopping at Ashford and Lille. Eurostar services from the new terminal at Ebbsfleet International, near junction 2 of the M25, take 2hrs 5mins direct. Fares start at £69/€88 for a London-Paris return ticket. Passengers must check in at least 30mins before departure time. Trains arrive at Gare du Nord (08.92.35.35.35, www.sncf.fr), with easy access to public transport and taxi ranks.

Cycles can be taken as hand luggage if they are dismantled and carried in a bike bag. You can also check them in at the EuroDespatch depot at St Pancras (Esprit Parcel Service, 0844 822 5822) or Sernam depot at Gare du Nord (01.48.74.14.80). Check-in should be done 24hrs ahead; a Eurostar ticket must be shown. The service costs £20/€25.

Maps
Free maps of the métro, bus and RER systems are available at airports and métro stations. Other brochures from métro stations are *Paris Visite – Le Guide*, with details of transport tickets and a small map, and *Plan de Paris*, a fold-out one showing *Noctambus* night bus lines. A Paris street map (*Plan de Paris*) can be bought from newsagents. The blue *Paris Pratique* is clear and compact.

Public transport
Almost all of the Paris public transport system is run by the **RATP** (Régie Autonome des Transports Parisiens; 32.46, www.ratp.fr): the bus, métro (underground) and suburban tram routes, as well as lines A and B of the RER (Réseau Express Régional) suburban express railway, which connects with the métro within the city centre. National rail operator **SNCF** (36.35, www.sncf.fr) runs RER lines C, D and E, and serves the Paris suburbs (*Banlieue*), as well as the French regions and international destinations (*Grandes Lignes*).

Fares & tickets
Paris and suburbs are divided into six travel zones; zones 1 and 2 cover the city centre. RATP tickets and passes are valid on the métro, bus and RER. Tickets and *carnets* can be bought at métro stations, tourist offices and *tabacs* (tobacconists); single tickets can also be bought on buses (€1.80). Hold on to your ticket in case of spot checks; you'll also need it to exit from RER stations.

● A single ticket *T+* costs €1.70, but it's more economical to buy a *carnet* of ten for €12.

● A one-day *Mobilis* pass costs from €5.90 for zones 1 and 2 to €16.70 for zones 1-6 (not including airports).
● A one-day *Paris Visite* pass for zones 1-3 is €9; a five-day pass is €28.30, with discounts on some attractions.
● One-week or one-month *Carte Orange* passes (passport photo needed) offer unlimited travel in the relevant zones; if bought in zones 1 or 2, each is delivered as a Navigo swipe card. A *forfait mensuel* (monthly *Carte Orange* valid from the first day of the month) for zones 1 and 2 costs €60.40; a weekly *forfait hebdomadaire* (weekly *Carte Orange* valid Mon-Sun inclusive) for zones 1 and 2 costs €18.35 and is better value than *Paris Visite* passes.

Métro & RER
The Paris **métro** is the fastest and cheapest way of getting around the city. Trains run 5.30am-12.40am Mon-Thur, 5.30am-1.30am Fri-Sun. Individual lines are numbered, with each direction named after the last stop. Follow the orange *Correspondance* to change lines. Be prepared for the fact that some interchanges, such as Châtelet-Les-Halles, Montparnasse-Bienvenüe and République, involve long walks. The exit (*Sortie*) is indicated in blue. The driverless line 14 runs from Gare St-Lazare to Olympiades. Pickpockets and bag-snatchers are rife – pay special attention as the doors are closing.

The five **RER** lines (A, B, C, D and E) run 5.30am-1am daily through Paris and out into the suburbs. Within Paris, the RER is useful for faster journeys – Châtelet-Les-Halles to Gare du Nord is one stop on the RER, and six on the métro. Métro tickets are valid for RER journeys within zones 1 and 2.

Buses
Buses run 6.30am-8.30pm, with some routes continuing until 12.30am, Mon-Sat; limited services operate on Sunday and public holidays. You can use a métro ticket, a ticket bought from the driver (€1.80) or a travel pass to travel on the buses. Tickets should be punched in the machine next to the driver; passes should be shown to the driver. When you want to get off, press the red request button.

Night buses
After the métro and normal buses stop running, the only public transport – apart from taxis – are the 47 **Noctilien** lines, running between place du Châtelet and the suburbs (hourly 12.30am-5.30am Mon-Thur; half-hourly 1am-5.35am Fri, Sat); look out for the Noctilien logo on bus stops or the N in front of the route number. A ticket costs €1.70 (€1.80 from the driver); travel passes are valid.

River transport
Batobus
(08.25.05.01.01, www.batobus.com).
River buses stop every 15-30mins at: Eiffel Tower, Musée d'Orsay, St-Germain-des-Prés (quai Malaquais), Notre-Dame, Jardin des Plantes, Hôtel de Ville, Louvre, Champs-Elysées (Pont Alexandre III). They run Nov, Dec, Feb-mid Mar 10.30am-4.30pm; mid Mar-May & Sept, Oct 10am-7pm; June-Aug 10am-9.30pm. A one-day pass is €13 (€7, €9 reductions); two-day pass €17 (€9, €12 reductions); five-day pass €20 (€10, €14 reductions); season-ticket €60 (€38 reductions). Tickets can be bought at Batobus stops, online at www.batobus.com, RATP ticket offices and the Office de Tourisme (*see p120*).

Trams
Two modern tram lines operate in the suburbs, running from La Défense to Issy-Val de Seine and from Bobigny Pablo Picasso to St-Denis;

Travel advice

For current information on travel to a specific country – including the latest news on health issues, safety and security, local laws and customs – contact your home country's government department of foreign affairs. Most have websites with useful advice for would-be travellers. For information on travelling to France from within the European Union, including details of visa regulations and healthcare provision, see the EU's travel website: http://europa.eu/travel.

Australia
www.smartraveller.gov.au

Canada
www.voyage.gc.ca

New Zealand
www.safetravel.govt.nz

Republic of Ireland
foreignaffairs.gov.ie

UK
www.fco.gov.uk/travel

USA
www.state.gov/travel

Paris by boat

Cruising along the River Seine is a delightful way to see Paris. The companies below all run a variety of tours. Most boats depart from the quays in the 7th and 8th, and proceed on a circuit around the islands. Check online for full tour details and times: many companies operate more than one type of tour, though the basic tour usually runs every 20-60mins in summer. Rates are for one day only, though other tickets may be available.

Batobus Tour Eiffel
Various stops (08.25.05.01.01, www.batobus.com). **Tickets** €12; €6 reductions.

Bateaux-Mouches
Pont de l'Alma, 8th (01.42.25.96.10, www.bateaux-mouches.fr). Mº Alma-Marceau. **Tickets** €10; €5 reductions; free under-4s.

Bateaux Parisiens
Port de la Boudonnais, 7th (01.76.64.14.45, www.bateaux parisiens.com). RER Champ de Mars. **Tickets** €11; €5 reductions; free under-3s.

Vedettes de Paris
Port de Suffren, 7th (01.44.18.19.50, www.vedettes deparis.com). Mº Bir-Hakeim. **Tickets** €11; €5 reductions; free under-4s.

Vedettes du Pont-Neuf
Sq du Vert-Galant, 1st (01.46.33.98.38, www.vedettes dupontneuf.com). Mº Pont-Neuf. **Tickets** €12; €6 under-12s; free under-4s.

a third runs between the Garigliano Bridge in the west of the city to Porte d'Ivry in the south-east. They connect with the métro and RER; fares are the same as for buses.

Rail travel

Suburban destinations are served by the RER. Other locations farther from the city are served by the SNCF railway; the TGV high-speed train has slashed journey times. There are few long-distance bus services. Tickets can be bought at any SNCF station (not just the one from which you'll travel), SNCF shops and travel agents. If you reserve online or by phone, you can pay and pick up your tickets from the station or have them sent to your home. SNCF automatic machines (*billeterie automatique*) only work with French credit/debit cards. Regular trains have full-rate White (peak) and cheaper Blue (off-peak) periods. You can save on TGV fares by buying special cards. The *Carte 12/25* gives under-26s a 25-50 per cent reduction; even without it, under-26s are entitled to 25 per cent off. Buy tickets in advance to secure the cheaper fare. Before you board any train, stamp your ticket in the orange *composteur* machines located on the platforms, or you might have to pay a hefty fine. *See also p120* **Lost Property**.

SNCF reservations & tickets
National reservations & information 36.35 (€0.34 per min), www.sncf.com. **Open** 7am-10pm daily.

Mainline stations

Gare d'Austerlitz Central and south-west France and Spain.
Gare de l'Est Alsace, Champagne and southern Germany.
Gare de Lyon Burgundy, the Alps, Provence and Italy.
Gare Montparnasse West France, Brittany, Bordeaux, the south-west.

Gare du Nord Eurostar, Channel ports, north-east France, Belgium and Holland.
Gare St-Lazare Normandy.

Taxis

Paris taxi drivers are not known for their flawless knowledge of the Paris street map; if you have a preferred route, say so. Taxis can also be hard to find, especially at rush hour or early in the morning. Your best bet is to find a taxi rank (*station de taxis*, marked with a blue sign) on major roads, crossroads and at stations. A white light on a taxi's roof indicates the car is free; an orange light means the cab is busy. There is a service charge of €2.20. The rates are then based on zone and time of day: **A** (10am-5pm Mon-Sat central Paris, €0.89 per km); **B** (5pm-10am Mon-Sat, 7am-midnight Sun central Paris; 7am-7pm Mon-Sat inner suburbs and airports, €1.14 per km); **C** (midnight-7am Sun central Paris; 7pm-7am Mon-Sat, all day Sun inner suburbs and airports; all times outer suburbs, €1.38 per km). Most journeys in central Paris cost €6-€12; there's a minimum charge of €6, plus €1 for each piece of luggage over 5kg or bulky objects, and a €0.70 surcharge from mainline stations. Most drivers will not take more than three people, but they should take a couple and two children. There is a charge of €2.95 for a fourth adult passenger.

Don't feel obliged to tip, although rounding up to the nearest euro is polite. Taxis are not allowed to refuse rides if they deem them too short and can only refuse to take you in a certain direction during their last half-hour of service (both rules are often ignored). Complaints should be made to the **Bureau des Taxis et des Transports Publics**, 36 rue des Morillons, 75732 Paris Cedex 15 (01.55.76.20.05). *See also p120* **Lost Property**.

Phone cabs

These firms take phone bookings 24/7; you also pay for the time it takes your taxi to reach you.

If you wish to pay by credit card, mention this when you order.

Alpha *01.45.85.85.85, www.alphataxis.fr.*
G7 *01.47.39.47.39, www.taxis-g7.fr.*
Taxis Bleus *08.91.70.10.10, www.taxis-bleus.com.*

Driving

If you bring your car to France, you must bring its registration and insurance documents.

As you come into Paris, you will meet the Périphérique, the giant ring road that carries traffic into, out of and around the city. Intersections, leading on to other main roads, are called *portes* (gates). Driving on the Périphérique is not as hair-raising as it might look, though it's often congested. Some hotels have parking spaces that can be paid for by the hour, day or by types of season tickets.

In peak holiday periods, the organisation Bison Futé hands out brochures at motorway *péages* (toll gates), suggesting less crowded routes. French roads are categorised as *Autoroutes* (motorways, with an 'A' in front of the number), *Routes Nationales* (national 'N' roads), *Routes Départementales* (local, 'D' roads) and rural *Routes Communales* ('C' roads). *Autoroutes* are toll roads; some sections, including most of the area around Paris, are free.

Infotrafic *08.92.70.77.66 (€0.34 per minute), www.infotrafic.fr.*
Bison Futé *08.00.10.02.00, www.bison-fute.equipement.gouv.fr*
Traffic information for Ile-de-France *08.26.02.20.22, www.securiteroutiere.gouv.fr.*

Breakdown services

The AA and RAC do not have reciprocal arrangements with an equivalent organisation in France, so it's advisable to take out additional breakdown insurance cover, for example with a company like **Europ Assistance** (0844 338 5533, www.europ-assistance.co.uk). If you don't have insurance, you can still use its service (08.10.00.50.50, available 24/7), but it will charge you the full cost. Other 24-hour breakdown services in Paris include: **Dan Dépann Auto** (08.00.25.10.00, www.dandepann.fr).

Driving tips

● At junctions where no signposts indicate right of way, the car coming from the right has priority. Many roundabouts now give priority to those on the roundabout. If this is not indicated (by road markings or a sign with the message *Vous n'avez pas la priorité*), priority is for those coming from the right.
● Drivers and all passengers must wear seat belts.
● Under-tens are not allowed to travel in the front of a car, except in baby seats facing backwards.
● You should not stop on an open road; you must pull off to the side.
● When drivers are flashing their lights at you, this often means they will not slow down and are warning you to keep out of the way.

Parking

There are still a few free on-street parking areas in Paris, but they're often full. If you park illegally, you risk getting your car clamped or towed away (*see below*). It's forbidden to park in zones marked for deliveries (*livraisons*) or taxis. Parking meters have now been replaced by *horodateurs*, pay-and-display machines, which take a special card (*carte de stationnement* at €15 or €40, available from *tabacs*). Parking is often free at weekends, after 7pm and in August.

Car hire

To hire a car, you must be 25 or over and have held a licence for at least a year. Some agencies accept drivers aged 21-24, but a supplement of €20-€25 per day is usual. Take your licence and passport with you. Bargain firms may have an extremely high charge for damage: read the small print.

Hire companies

Hire companies

Ada *01.48.06.58.13, 08.25.16.91.69, www.ada.fr.*
Avis *08.21.23.07.60, 08.20.05.05.05, www.avis.fr.*
Budget *08.25.00.35.64, www.budget.fr.*
EasyCar *08.26.10.73.23, www.easycar.com.*
Europcar *08.25.35.83.58, www.europcar.fr.*
Hertz *01.55.31.93.21, www.hertz.fr.*
Rent-a-Car *08.91.70.02.00, www.rentacar.fr.*

Chauffeur-driven cars

Chauffeur Services Paris *(01.80.40.00.86, www.csparis.com).* **Open** 24hrs daily. **Prices** from €125 airport transfer; €240 for 4 hours. **Credit** AmEx, DC, MC, V.

Cycling

In 2007, the mayor launched a municipal bike hire scheme – **Vélib** (www.velib.paris.fr). There are now over 20,000 bicycles available 24 hours a day, at nearly 1,500 'stations' across the city. Just swipe your travel card to release the bikes from their stands. The *mairie* actively promotes cycling in the city and the Vélib scheme is complemented by 400km (250 miles) of bike lanes snaking their way around Paris.

The Itinéraires Paris-Piétons-Vélos-Rollers – scenic strips of the city that are closed to cars on Sundays and holidays – continue to multiply; www.paris.fr can provide an up-to-date list of routes and a downloadable map of cycle lanes. A free *Paris à Vélo* map can be picked up at any mairie or from bike shops. Cycle lanes (*pistes cyclables*) run mostly N-S and E-W. N-S routes include rue de Rennes, av d'Italie, bd Sébastopol and av Marceau. E-W routes take in the rue de Rivoli, bd St-Germain, bd St-Jacques and av Daumesnil. You could be fined (€22) if you don't use them. Cyclists are also entitled to use certain bus lanes (especially the new ones, set off by a strip of kerb stones); look out for traffic signs with a bike symbol.

Cycles & scooters for hire

Bike insurance may not cover theft.
Freescoot *63 quai de la Tournelle, 5th (01.44.07.06.72, www.freescoot.fr). Mº Maubert Mutualité or St-Michel.* **Open** 9am-1pm, 2-9pm daily; closed Sun Oct-mid Apr. **Credit** AmEx, MC, V. Bicycles & scooters.
Left Bank Scooters *(06.82.70.13.82, www.leftbankscooters.com).* This company hires out vintage-style Vespas (from €90 per day), with delivery and collection from your apartment or hotel. Various tours also available.

Tours

Bus tours

The following companies offer hop-on, hop-off bus tours of the city with commentary. Prices are for one day.

Les Cars Rouges *01.53.95.39.53, www.carsrouges.com.* **Tickets** €24; €12 4-11s.
Cityrama *01.42.66.56.56, www.pariscityrama.com.* **Tickets** €29; €15 4-11s.
Paris Vision *01.42.60.30.01, http://fr.parisvision.com.* **Tickets** €22.

Bike tours

Fat Tire Bike Tours *01.56.58.10.54, http://fattirebiketours.com/paris.* **Tickets** €28; €26 reductions. Bike tours of the city, with the main tour starting at the south leg of the Eiffel Tower. Tours run daily at 11am, with a 3pm tour added in summer. Check online for full details.

Walking tours

Paris Walking Tours *01.48.09.21.40, www.paris-walks.com.* **Tickets** €12; €8-€10 reductions. Led by long-term resident expats, these daily walking tours (times vary by season) explore various city locales.

Getting Around

Resources

Addresses

Paris arrondissements are indicated by the last two digits of the postal code: 75002 denotes the second, 75015 the 15th, and so on. The 16th arrondissement is divided into two sectors, 75016 and 75116. Some business addresses have a more detailed postcode, followed by a Cedex number, which indicates the arrondissement; *bis* or *ter* is the equivalent of 'b' or 'c' after a building number.

Age restrictions

For heterosexuals and homosexuals, the age of consent is 15. You must be 18 to drive, and to consume alcohol in a public place. You must be 16 to buy cigarettes.

Customs

Custom declarations are not usually necessary if you arrive from another EU country and are carrying legal goods for personal use. The amounts given below are guidelines only:
● 800 cigarettes, 400 small cigars, 200 cigars or 1kg loose tobacco.
● 10 litres of spirits (more than 22% alcohol), 90 litres of wine (less than 22% alcohol) or 110 litres of beer.

Coming from a non-EU country, you can bring:
● 200 cigarettes, 100 small cigars, 50 cigars or 250g tobacco.
● 1 litre of spirits (more than 22% alcohol) or 2 litres of wine or beer (more than 22% alcohol).
● 50g (1.76oz) of perfume.

Tax refunds

Non-EU residents can claim a refund or *détaxe* (around 12 per cent) on VAT if they spend over €175 in any one day in one shop and if they live outside the EU for more than six months in the year. At the shop concerned ask for a *bordereau de vente à l'exportation*, and when you leave France have it stamped by customs. Then send the stamped form back to the shop. *Détaxe* does not cover food, drink, antiques, services or works of art.

Disabled

General information (in French) is available on the Secrétaire d'Etat aux Personnes Handicapées website: www.handicap.gouv.fr. The métro and buses are not wheelchair-accessible, with the exception of métro line 14 (Météor), stations Barbès-Rochechouard (line 2) and Esplanade de la Défense (line 1), and bus lines 20, 21, 24, 26, 27, 29, 30, 31, 38, 39, 43, 53, 54, 60, 62, 63, 64, 80, 81, 88, 91, 92, 94, 95, 96 and PC (Petite Ceinture) 1, 2 and 3. Forward seats on buses are intended for people with poor mobility. RER lines A, B, C, D and some SNCF trains are wheelchair-accessible in parts. For a full list of wheelchair-accessible stations: 08.10.64.64.64, www.infomobi.com. Paris taxis are obliged by law to take passengers in wheelchairs.
Aihrop *3 av Paul-Doumer, 92508 Rueil-Malmaison Cedex (01.41.29.01.29)*. **Open** 9.30am-12.30pm, 1.30-5.30pm Mon-Fri. Closed Aug.
Transport for the disabled, anywhere in Paris and Ile-de-France; book 48 hours in advance.

Embassies & consulates

For a full list of embassies and consulates, see the Pages Jaunes (www.pagesjaunes.fr) under 'Ambassades et Consulats'. Consular services (passports, etc) are for use by citizens of that country only.
Australian Embassy *4 rue Jean-Rey, 15th (01.40.59.33.00, www.france.embassy.gov.au)*. *M° Bir-Hakeim.* **Open** *Consular services* 9.15am-noon, 2-4.30pm Mon-Fri; *Visas* 10am-noon Mon-Fri.
British Embassy *35 rue du Fbg-St-Honoré, 8th (01.44.51.31.00, www.ukinfrance.fco. gov.uk). M° Concorde. Consular services: 18bis rue d'Anjou, 8th. M° Concorde.* **Open** 9.30am-12.30pm, 2.30-4.30pm Mon-Fri.
Visas: 16 rue d'Anjou, 8th (01.44.51.31.01). **Open** 9.30am-noon by phone; 2.30-4.30pm. British citizens wanting consular services (new passports, etc) should ignore the long queue along rue d'Anjou for the visa department, and instead walk straight in at no.18bis.
Canadian Embassy *35 av Montaigne, 8th (01.44.43.29.00, www.amb-canada.fr). M° Franklin D. Roosevelt.* **Open** 9am-noon, 2-5pm Mon-Fri.
Consular services: 01.44.43.29.02. **Open** 9am-noon Mon-Fri.
Visas: 37 av Montaigne, 8th (01.44.43.29.16). **Open** 8.30-11am Mon-Fri.
Irish Embassy *12 av Foch, 16th. Consulate 4 rue Rude, 16th (01.44.17.67.00, www.embassy ofireland.fr). M° Charles de Gaulle Etoile.* **Open** *Consular/visas* 9.30am-noon Mon-Fri; by phone 9.30am-1pm, 2.30-5.30pm Mon-Fri.
New Zealand Embassy *7ter rue Léonard-de-Vinci, 16th (01.45.01.43.43, www.nzembassy. com/france). M° Victor Hugo.* **Open** 9am-1pm, 2-5.30pm Mon-Fri (closes 4pm Fri). *July, Aug* 9am-1pm, 2-4.30pm Mon-Thur; 9am-2pm Fri. *Visas* 9am-12.30pm Mon-Fri.
Visas for travel to New Zealand can be applied for on the website www.immigration.govt.nz.
South African Embassy *59 quai d'Orsay, 7th (01.53.59.23.23, www.afriquesud.net). M° Invalides.* **Open** 8.30am-5.15pm Mon-Fri. *Consulate & visas* 8.30am-noon Mon-Fri.
US Embassy *2 av Gabriel, 8th (01.43.12.22.22, http://france.usembassy.gov). M° Concorde.
Consulate & visas: 4 av Gabriel, 8th (08.10.26.46.26). M° Concorde.* **Open** *Consular services* 9am-12.30pm, 1-3pm Mon-Fri. *Visas* 08.92.23.84.72 or check website for non-immigration visas.

Internet access

Many hotels offer internet access – and an increasing number of public spaces are setting themselves up as Wi-Fi hotspots.
Milk *31 bd de Sébastopol, 1st (01.40.13.06.51, www.milklub.com). M° Châtelet or Rambuteau/ RER Châtelet Les Halles.* **Open** 24hrs daily. This is the biggest internet café in Paris.
Other locations throughout the city.

Left luggage

Gare du Nord

There are self-locking luggage lockers (6.15am-11.15pm daily) situated on Level -1 under the main station concourse: small (€3.50), medium (€7) and large (€9.50) for 48 hours.

Roissy-Charles-de-Gaulle airport

Bagages du Monde *(01.34.38.58.90, www.bagagesdumonde.com).* **Terminal 1** *Niveau Départ, Porte 14 (01.34.38.58.82).* **Open** 8am-8pm daily. **Terminal 2A** *Niveau Départ, Porte 3-4 (01.34.38.58.80).* **Open** 8am-8pm daily. **Terminal 2F** *Niveau Arrivée, Porte 4-5 (0134.38.58.81).* **Open** 7am-7pm daily. Company with counters in Roissy-Charles-de-Gaulle and an office in Paris (102 rue de Chemin-Vert, 11th, 01.34.38.58.97, open 9am-noon, 2-6pm Mon-Fri; 10am-5pm Sat). Can ship baggage worldwide, or store luggage.

Lost property

Bureau des Objets Trouvés

36 rue des Morillons, 15th (08.21.00.25.25, www.prefecture-police-paris.interieur.gouv.fr). M° Convention. **Open** 8.30am-5pm Mon-Thur; 8.30am-4.30pm Fri.
Visit in person to fill in a form specifying details of the loss. This may have been the first lost property office in the world, but it is far from the most efficient. Huge delays in processing claims mean that if your trip to Paris is short, you may need to nominate a proxy to collect found objects after you leave, although small items can be posted. If your passport was among the items lost, you'll need to go to your consulate to get a single-entry temporary passport in order to leave the country.

Money

Withdrawals in euros can be made from bank and post office automatic cash machines. The specific cards accepted are marked on each machine, and most can give instructions in English. Credit card companies charge a fee for cash advances, but rates are often better than banks.

Banks

French banks usually open 9am-5pm Monday to Friday (some close at lunch); some banks also open on Saturday. All are closed on public holidays, and from noon on the previous day. Note that not all banks have foreign exchange counters. The commission rates vary between banks; the state-owned Banque de France usually offers good rates. Most banks accept travellers' cheques, but may be reluctant to accept personal cheques even with the Eurocheque guarantee card, which is not widely used in France.

Bureaux de change

If you happen to be arriving in Paris early in the morning or late at night, you will be able to change money at the **American Express** bureaux de change in terminals 1 (01.48.16.13.26), 2A, 2B, 2C and 2D (01.48.16.48.40) and 2E (01.48.16.63.81) at Roissy, and at Orly Sud (01.49.75.77.37); all open 6.30am-11pm daily. **Travelex** has bureaux de change at the following mainline train stations:
Gare Montparnasse *01.42.79.03.88.* **Open** 8am-6.30pm daily.
Gare du Nord *01.42.80.11.50.* **Open** 6.30am-10pm daily.

Postal services

Post offices (*bureaux de poste*) are open 8am-7pm Mon-Fri; 8am-noon Sat, apart from the 24-hour post office listed below. Details of all branches are included in the phone book: under 'Administration des PTT' in the *Pages Jaunes*; under 'Poste' in the *Pages Blanches*. Most post offices contain automatic machines (in French and English) that weigh your letter, print out a stamp and give change, saving you from wasting time in an enormous queue. You can also usually buy stamps and sometimes envelopes at a tobacconist (*tabac*). For more information refer to www.laposte.fr.
Main Post Office *52 rue du Louvre, 75001 Paris, 1st (36.31). M° Les Halles or Louvre Rivoli.* **Open** 24hrs daily for poste restante, telephones, stamps, faxes, photocopying and a modest amount of banking operations.

Telephones

All French phone numbers have ten digits. Paris and Ile-de-France numbers begin with 01; the rest of France is divided into four zones (02-05). Mobile phone numbers start with 06. If you are calling France from abroad, leave off the 0 at the start of the ten-digit number. The country code is 33. To call abroad from Paris dial 00, then the country code, then the number. France Télécom has a useful website with information on rates and contracts: www.agence.francetelecom.com.
France Télécom English-Speaking Customer Service *(08.00.36.47.75, from abroad +33 1.55.78.60.56).* **Open** 9am-5.30pm Mon-Fri. Freephone information line in English on phone services, bills, payment, internet.

Public phones

Most public phones in Paris, almost all of which are maintained by France Télécom, use *télécartes* (phonecards). Sold at post offices, *tabacs*, airports and train and métro stations, they cost €7.50 for 50 units and €15 for 120 units. For cheap international calls, you can also buy a *télécarte à puce* (card with a microchip) or a *télécarte pré-payée*, which features a numerical code you dial before making a call.

Time

France is one hour ahead of Greenwich Mean Time (GMT). France uses the 24hr system (for example, 18h means 6pm).

Tipping

A service charge of ten to 15 per cent is legally included in your bill at all restaurants, cafés and bars. However, it is polite to leave a cash tip of €1-€2 or more for a meal.

Tourist offices

Office de Tourisme et des Congrès de Paris *25 rue des Pyramides, 1st (08.92.68.30.00 recorded information available in English & French, www.parisinfo.com). M° Pyramides.* **Open** 9am-7pm daily. Information on Paris and the suburbs, shop, bureau de change, hotel reservations, phone cards, museum cards, travel passes and tickets. Multilingual staff.
Other locations throughout the city.

Weights & measures

France uses only the metric system; remember that all speed limits are in kilometres per hour. One kilometre is equivalent to 0.62 miles (1 mile = 1.6km). Petrol, like other liquids, is measured in litres (one UK gallon = 4.54 litres; 1 US gallon = 3.79 litres).

Women

Though Paris is not an especially threatening city for women, the precautions you would take in any major metropolis apply here: be careful at night in certain areas, including Pigalle, the rue St-Denis, Stalingrad, La Chapelle, Château Rouge, Gare de l'Est, Gare du Nord, the Bois de Boulogne and Bois de Vincennes. If you receive unwanted attention, a politely scathing *N'insistez pas!* (Don't push it!) will make your feelings abundantly clear. If things get too heavy, go into the nearest shop or café.

Resources

Emergencies

Crime

If you're assaulted or robbed, report the incident as soon as possible. You'll need to make a statement (*procès verbal*) at the *point d'accueil* closest to the site of the crime. To find the nearest, call the Préfecture Centrale (08.91.01.22.22) or go to www.prefecture-police-paris.interieur.gouv.fr.

Credit card theft

In case of credit card loss or theft, call one of the following 24hr services which have English-speaking staff:

American Express
08.00.83.28.20.
Diners Club
08.20.82.05.36.
MasterCard
08.00.90.13.87.
Visa
08.00.90.11.79.

Police

The French equivalent of 999 or 911 is **17** (**112** from a mobile), but don't expect a speedy response. That said, the Préfecture de Police has no fewer than 94 outposts in the city.

Health care

Nationals of non-EU countries should take out insurance before leaving home. EU nationals staying in France can use the French Social Security system, which refunds up to 70 per cent of medical expenses. UK residents travelling in Europe require a European National Health Insurance Card (EHIC). This allows them to benefit from free or reduced-cost medical care when travelling in a country belonging to the European Economic Area (EEA) or Switzerland. For further information, refer to www.dh.gov.uk/travellers.

If you're staying for longer than three months, or working in France but you are still making National Insurance contributions in Britain, you will need form E128 filled in by your employer and stamped by the NI contributions office in order to get a French medical number. Consultations and prescriptions have to be paid for in full on the spot, and are reimbursed on receipt of a completed *fiche*. If you undergo treatment, the doctor will give you a prescription and a *feuille de soins* (bill of treatment). Stick the small stickers from the medication boxes on to the *feuille de soins*. Send this, together with the prescription and details of your EHIC card, to the local **Caisse Primaire d'Assurance Maladie** for a refund. For those resident in France, more and more doctors now accept the **Carte Vitale**, which lets them produce a virtual *feuille de soins* and you to pay only the non-reimbursable part of the bill. Information on health insurance can be found at www.ameli.fr. Track refunds with Allosecu (08.11.90.09.07).

Accident & emergency

Hospitals specialise in one type of emergency or illness – refer to the Assistance Publique's website (www.aphp.fr). In a medical emergency, call the Sapeurs-Pompiers or SAMU. The following (in order of district) have 24hr accident and emergency services:

Adults

Hôpital Hôtel-Dieu *1 pl du Parvis Notre-Dame, 4th* (01.42.34.82.34).
Hôpital St-Louis *1 av Claude-Vellefaux, 10th* (01.42.49.49.49).
Hôpital St-Antoine *184 rue du Fbg-St-Antoine, 12th* (01.49.28.20.00).
Hôpital de la Pitié-Salpêtrière *47-83 bd de l'Hôpital, 13th* (01.42.16.00.00).
Hôpital Cochin *27 rue du Fbg-St-Jacques, 14th* (01.58.41.41.41).
Hôpital Européen Georges Pompidou *20 rue Leblanc, 15th* (01.56.09.20.00).
Hôpital Bichat-Claude Bernard *46 rue Henri-Huchard, 18th* (01.40.25.80.80).
Hôpital Tenon *4 rue de la Chine, 20th* (01.56.01.70.00).

Children

Hôpital Armand Trousseau *26 av du Dr Arnold-Netter, 12th* (01.44.73.74.75).
Hôpital St-Vincent de Paul *74-82 av Denfert-Rochereau, 14th* (01.58.41.41.41).
Hôpital Necker *149 rue de Sèvres, 15th* (01.44.49.40.00).
Hôpital Robert Debré *48 bd Sérurier, 19th* (01.40.03.20.00).

Private hospitals

American Hospital in Paris *63 bd Victor-Hugo, 92200 Neuilly* (01.46.41.25.25, www.american-hospital.org). M° Porte Maillot, then bus 82. **Open** 24hrs daily.
English-speaking hospital. French Social Security refunds only a small percentage of treatment costs.
Hertford British Hospital (Hôpital Franco-Britannique) *3 rue Barbès, 92300 Levallois-Perret* (01.46.39.22.22, www.british-hospital.org). M° Anatole-France. **Open** 24/7.
Most staff here speak English.

Contraception & abortion

To get the pill (*la pilule*) or coil (*stérilet*), you need a prescription, available on appointment from the two places listed below, from a *médecin généraliste* (GP) or from a gynaecologist. The morning-after pill (*la pilule du lendemain*) can be had from pharmacies without prescription but is not reimbursed. Condoms (*préservatifs*) and spermicides are sold in pharmacies and supermarkets, and there are condom machines in most métro stations, club lavatories and on some street corners.
Centre de Planification et d'Education Familiales *27 rue Curnonsky, 17th* (01.48.88.07.28). M° Porte de Champerret. **Open** 9am-5pm Mon-Fri.
Free consultations on family planning and abortion.
MFPF (Mouvement Français pour le Planning Familial) *4 square Ste Irenée, 11th* (01.48.07.87.07, www.planning-familial.org). M° St Ambroise. **Open** 10am-1pm, 2-6pm Mon-Fri.
Phone for an appointment for prescriptions and contraception advice. For abortion advice, turn up at the centre at one of the designated time slots.

Dentists

Dentists are found in the *Pages Jaunes* under *Dentistes*. For emergencies, contact:
Hôpital de la Pitié-Salpêtrière (*see above*) also offers 24hr emergency dental care.
SOS Dentaire *87 bd Port-Royal, 13th* (01.43.37.51.00). M° Les Gobelins/RER Port-Royal. **Open** by phone 9am-midnight.
A telephone service for emergency dental care.

Doctors

You'll find a list of GPs in the *Pages Jaunes* under *Médecins: Médecine générale*. For a social security refund, choose a doctor or dentist who is *conventionné* (state registered).

Centre Médical Europe *44 rue d'Amsterdam, 9th* (01.42.81.93.33). M° St-Lazare. **Open** 8am-7pm Mon-Fri; 8am-6pm Sat.
Practitioners in all fields; modest fees.
SOS Médecins *36.24, www.sosmedecins.com.*
House calls cost €35 before 7pm; from €50 after and on holidays; prices are higher if you don't have French social security.
Urgences Médicales de Paris *01.53.94.94.94.* Doctors make house calls for €35 during the day (€60 if you don't have French social security); €50/€80 until midnight; €63.50/€90 after midnight. Some speak English.

Helplines

Alcoholics Anonymous in English
01.46.34.59.65, www.aaparis.org.
A 24hr recorded message gives details of Alcoholics Anonymous meetings at the American Cathedral or American Church.

Allô Service Public
39.39, www.service-public.fr. **Open** 8am-7pm Mon-Fri; 9am-2pm Sat.
A source of information for all aspects of tax, work and administration matters. They even claim to be able to help if you have problems with neighbours. The catch: you can only dial from inside France, and operators speak only French.

Counseling Center
01.47.23.61.13.
English-language counselling service, based at the American Cathedral.

Drogues Alcool Tabac Info Service
08.00.23.13.13, www.drogues.gouv.fr.
Phone service, in French, for help with drug, alcohol and tobacco problems.

Narcotics Anonymous
08.00.88.12.88, www.narcotiquesanonymes.org.
The helpline is open daily 6-8pm. Meetings in English are held three times a week.

SOS Dépression
01.40.47.95.95, http://sos.depression.free.fr. **Open** 24hrs daily.
People listen and/or give advice to those suffering from depression. Can send round a counsellor or psychiatrist in case of a crisis.

SOS Help
01.46.21.46.46, www.soshelpline.org. **Open** 3-11pm daily.
English-language helpline.

Opticians

Branches of **Alain Afflelou** (www.alain afflelou.com) and **Lissac** (www.lissac.com) stock hundreds of frames and can make prescription glasses within the hour. For an eye test, you'll need to go to an *ophtalmologiste*. Contact lenses can be bought over the counter if you have your prescription details with you.
Hôpital des Quinze-Vingts *28 rue de Charenton, 12th* (01.40.02.15.20).
Specialist eye hospital offers on-the-spot consultations for eye problems.
SOS Optique *01.48.07.22.00, www.sosoptique.com.*
24hr repair service for glasses.

Pharmacies

French *pharmacies* sport a green neon cross. A rota of *pharmacies de garde* operate at night and on Sundays. If closed, a pharmacy will have a sign indicating the nearest one open. Staff can provide basic medical services like bandaging wounds (for a small fee) and will indicate the nearest doctor on duty. *Parapharmacies* sell almost everything pharmacies do but cannot dispense prescription medication.

Night pharmacies

Grande Pharmacie de la Nation *13 pl de la Nation, 11th* (01.43.73.24.03). M° Nation. **Open** 8am-11pm daily.
Matignon *2 rue Jean-Mermoz, 8th* (01.43.59.86.55). M° Franklin D. Roosevelt. **Open** 8.30am-2am daily.
Pharmacie des Champs-Elysées *84 av des Champs-Elysées, 8th* (01.45.62.02.41). M° George V. **Open** 24hrs daily.
Pharmacie Européene de la Place de Clichy *6 pl de Clichy, 9th* (01.48.74.65.18). M° Place de Clichy. **Open** 24hrs daily.
Pharmacie des Halles *10 bd de Sébastopol, 4th* (01.42.72.03.23). M° Châtelet. **Open** 9am-midnight Mon-Sat; 9am-10pm Sun.
Pharmacie d'Italie *61 av d'Italie, 13th* (01.44.24.19.72). M° Tolbiac. **Open** 8am-2am daily.
Pharma Presto *01.61.04.04.04, www.pharma-presto.com.* **Open** 24hrs daily. Delivery (€40 8am-6pm; €55 6pm-8am & weekends) of medication.

STDs, HIV & AIDS

Cabinet Médical (Mairie de Paris) *2 rue Figuier, 4th* (01.49.96.62.70). M° Pont-Marie. **Open** 9am-12.30pm, 1.30-6.30pm Mon-Fri; 9.30-noon Sat.
Free, anonymous tests (*dépistages*) for HIV, hepatitis B and C and syphilis (wait one week for results). Good counselling service, too.
Le Kiosque Infos Sida-Toxicomanie *36 rue Geoffroy-l'Asnier, 4th* (01.44.78.00.00). M° St-Paul. **Open** 10am-7pm Mon-Thur; 1-7pm Fri; 11am-2pm, 3-7pm Sat.
Youth association offering information and counselling on AIDS, sexuality and drugs
SIDA Info Service *08.00.84.08.00, www.sida-info-service.org.* **Open** 24hrs daily.
Confidential AIDS information in French. English-speakers available 2-7pm Mon, Wed, Fri.

Emergency numbers

Most of the following emergency services operate a round-the-clock schedule. If you find yourself in a medical emergency, such as a road traffic accident, phone the Sapeurs-Pompiers, who have trained paramedics.

Ambulance (SAMU) 15
Police 17
Fire (Sapeurs-Pompiers) 18
Emergency (from a mobile phone) 112
Centre anti-poison 01.40.05.48.48

Vocabulary

In French, the second person singular (you) has two forms. Phrases here are given in the more polite *vous* form. The *tu* form is used with family, friends, children and pets; you should be careful not to use it with people you do not know sufficiently well. Courtesies such as *monsieur, madame* and *mademoiselle* are generally used more than their English equivalents.

General

● **good morning/afternoon, hello** bonjour; **good evening** bonsoir; **goodbye** au revoir
● **OK** d'accord; **yes** oui; **no** non; **how are you?** comment allez vous?/vous allez bien?; **how's it going?** comment ça va?/ça va? (familiar)
● **sir/Mr** monsieur (M.); **madam/Mrs** madame (Mme); **miss** mademoiselle (Mlle)
● **please** s'il vous plaît; **thank you** merci; **sorry** pardon; **excuse me** excusez-moi; **I am going to pay** je vais payer
● **do you speak English?** parlez-vous anglais?; **I don't speak French** je ne parle pas français; **I don't understand** je ne comprends pas; **speak more slowly, please** parlez plus lentement, s'il vous plaît
● **it is** c'est; **it isn't** ce n'est pas; **good** bon/bonne; **bad** mauvais/mauvaise; **small** petit/petite; **big** grand/grande; **beautiful** beau/belle; **well** bien; **badly** mal; **a bit** un peu; **a lot** beaucoup; **very** très
● **with** avec; **without** sans; **and** et; **or** ou; **because** parce que
● **who?** qui?; **when?** quand?; **what?** quoi?; **which?** quel?; **where?** où?; **why?** pourquoi?; **how?** comment?; **at what time/when?** à quelle heure?
● **forbidden** interdit/défendu; **out of order** hors service (HS)/en panne; **daily** tous les jours (tlj)

On the phone

● **hello** allô; **who's calling?** c'est de la part de qui?/qui est à l'appareil?; **this is... speaking** c'est... à l'appareil; **I'd like to speak to...** j'aurais voulu parler à...; **hold the line** ne quittez pas; **please call back later** rappelez plus tard s'il vous plaît; **you must have the wrong number** vous avez dû composer un mauvais numéro

Getting around

● **where is the (nearest) métro?** où est le métro (le plus proche)?; **when is the next train for...?** c'est quand le prochain train pour...?; **ticket** un billet; **station** la gare; **platform** le quai; **entrance** entrée; **exit** sortie
● **left** gauche; **right** droite; **straight on** tout droit; **far** loin; **near** pas loin/près d'ici; **street map** un plan; **road map** une carte

Sightseeing

● **museum** un musée; **church** une église; **exhibition** une exposition; **ticket** (*museum*) un billet; (*theatre, concert*) une place
● **open** ouvert; **closed** fermé; **free** gratuit; **reduced price** un tarif réduit

Accommodation

● **do you have a room (for this evening/for two people)?** avez-vous une chambre (pour ce soir/pour deux personnes)?; **full** complet; **room** une chambre; **bed** un lit;
double bed un grand lit; (a room with) **twin beds** (une chambre à) deux lits; **with bath(room)/shower** avec (salle de bain/douche); **breakfast** le petit déjeuner; **included** compris

At the café or restaurant

● **I'd like to book a table (for three/at 8pm)** je voudrais réserver une table (pour trois personnes/à vingt heures); **lunch** le déjeuner; **dinner** le dîner
● **coffee** (espresso) un café; **tea** un thé; **wine** le vin; **beer** une bière; **mineral water** eau minérale; **tap water** eau du robinet/une carafe d'eau; **the bill, please** l'addition, s'il vous plaît

Shopping

● **cheap** pas cher; **expensive** cher; **how much?/how many?** combien?; **have you got change?** avez-vous de la monnaie?; **I'll take it** je le prends
● **I would like...** je voudrais...; **may I try this on?** est-ce que je pourrais essayer cet article?; **do you have a smaller/larger size?** auriez-vous la taille en-dessous/au dessus?; **I'm a size 38** je fais du 38

Staying alive

● **be cool** restez calme; **I don't want any trouble** je ne veux pas d'ennuis; **I only do safe sex** je ne pratique que le safe sex

Numbers

● **0** zéro; **1** un, une; **2** deux; **3** trois; **4** quatre; **5** cinq; **6** six; **7** sept; **8** huit; **9** neuf; **10** dix; **11** onze; **12** douze; **13** treize; **14** quatorze; **15** quinze; **16** seize; **17** dix-sept; **18** dix-huit; **19** dix-neuf; **20** vingt; **21** vingt-et-un; **22** vingt-deux; **30** trente; **40** quarante; **50** cinquante; **60** soixante; **70** soixante-dix; **80** quatre-vingts; **90** quatre-vingt-dix; **100** cent; **1000** mille; **10,000** dix mille; **1,000,000** un million

Days, months & seasons

● **Monday** lundi; **Tuesday** mardi; **Wednesday** mercredi; **Thursday** jeudi; **Friday** vendredi; **Saturday** samedi; **Sunday** dimanche
● **January** janvier; **February** février; **March** mars; **April** avril; **May** mai; **June** juin; **July** juillet; **August** août; **September** septembre; **October** octobre; **November** novembre; **December** décembre
● **spring** le printemps; **summer** l'été; **autumn** l'automne; **winter** l'hiver

Books

Non-fiction

Robert Baldick *The Siege of Paris* A gripping account of the Paris Commune of 1871.
Antony Beevor & Artemis Cooper *Paris after the Liberation* Rationing, freedom, Existentialism.
NT Binh *Paris au cinéma* Attractively illustrated hardback round-up of Paris sights on film.
Henri Cartier-Bresson *A propos de Paris* Classic black-and-white shots by a giant among snappers.
Vincent Cronin *Napoleon* A fine biography of the emperor.
Léon-Paul Fargue *Le Piéton de Paris* The city anatomised, just before World War II.
Jean-Marie Gourio *Brèves de comptoir* An anthology of wisdom and weirdness overheard at café counters. A French classic.
Alastair Horne *The Fall of Paris* Detailed chronicle of the Siege and Commune 1870-71.
Douglas Johnson & Madeleine Johnson *Age of Illusion: Art & Politics in France 1918-1940* French culture in a Paris at the forefront of modernity.
J-K Huysmans *Croquis Parisiens* The world that Toulouse-Lautrec painted.
Ian Littlewood *Paris: Architecture, History, Art* Paris's history and its treasures.
Henri Michel *Paris Allemand; Paris Résistant* Detailed, two-volume account of life in Paris during the Occupation.
Noel Riley Fitch *Literary Cafés of Paris* Who drank what, where.
Virginia Rounding *Les Grandes Horizontales* Entertaining lives of four 19th-century courtesans.
Simon Schama *Citizens* Epic, readable account of the Revolution.
Thibaut Vandorselaer *Paris BD* A lovely series of walking trails around the city, illustrated entirely with 'BD' (cartoon) frames.

Fiction & poetry

Louis Aragon *Le Paysan de Paris* A great Surrealist view of the city.
Honoré de Balzac *Illusions perdues; La Peau de chagrin; Le Père Goriot; Splendeurs et misères des courtisanes* Much of the 'Comédie Humaine' cycle of novels is set in Paris.
Charles Baudelaire *Le Spleen de Paris* Prose poems, Paris settings.
Louis-Ferdinand Céline *Mort à crédit* Vivid, splenetic account of an impoverished Paris childhood.
Victor Hugo *Notre Dame de Paris* Romantic vision of medieval Paris. Quasimodo! Esmeralda! The bells!
W Somerset Maugham *Christmas Holiday* Young, middle-class Brit spends Christmas with a prostitute in Paris.
Gérard de Nerval *Les Nuits d'octobre* Late-night Les Halles and environs, mid 19th century.
Georges Perec *La Vie, mode d'emploi* Cheek-by-jowl life in a Haussmannian apartment building.
Raymond Queneau *Zazie dans le Métro* Paris in the 1950s: bright and very *nouvelle vague*.
Nicolas Restif de la Bretonne *Les Nuits de Paris* The sexual underworld of Louis XV's Paris.
Georges Simenon *Rue Pigalle; Maigret et les braves gens,* etc. Many of the famous Maigret books are set in Paris.
Emile Zola *L'Assommoir, Nana; Le Ventre de Paris* Accounts of the underside of the Second Empire from the master Realist.

The ex-pat angle

Janet Flanner *Paris Journal* Three volumes of reports on postwar Paris arts and politics, written for the *New Yorker.*
Adam Gopnik *From Paris to the Moon* A New Yorker raises a family in this alien city.
Henry Miller *Tropic of Cancer* Love and low life: lusty and funny.
George Orwell *Down and Out in Paris and London* Work in a Paris restaurant, hunger in a Paris hovel, suffering in a Paris hospital.

Film

Olivier Assayas *Irma Vep* Jean-Pierre Léaud and Maggie Cheung try to remake Feuillade's vampire classic in 1990s Paris. And fail.
Luc Besson *Subway* Christophe Lambert goes underground.
Marcel Carné *Hôtel du Nord* Arletty stars in this poetic slice of life by the Canal St-Martin.
René Clair *Paris qui dort* Clair's surrealist silent comedy is one of the best Paris films ever made.
Louis Feuillade *Fantômas* Supervillain Fantomas repeatedly outwits Paris law enforcers in Feuillade's masterful silent serials.
Jean-Luc Godard *A Bout de Souffle* Belmondo, Seberg, Godard, the Champs-Elysées, the attitude, the famous ending. Essential viewing.
Jean-Luc Godard *Une Femme est une femme* Belmondo and Karina, and Godard's first feature in colour – the Grands Boulevards, the attitude, the music.
Edouard Molinaro *Un Témoin dans la ville* Lino Ventura on the run in 1950s nocturnal Paris. Superb *noir.*
François Truffaut *Les 400 Coups* The first of the Antoine Doinel cycle.
Agnès Varda *Cléo de 5 à 7* The *nouvelle vague* heroine spends an anxious afternoon in the city.
Claude Zidi *Les Ripoux (Le Cop)* Cops Philippe Noiret and Thierry Lhermitte scam the whole of the Goutte d'Or.

Music

Air *Moon Safari* Relaxing, ambient beeps and sonics from that rara avis, a credible French pop group.
Miles Davis *Ascenseur pour l'échafaud* The soundtrack to Louis Malle's film is superb after-dark jazz.
Fréhel *1930-1939* The immortal Fréhel sings of love, drugs and debauchery in true *chanson réaliste* style.
Naive New Beaters *Wallace* Great pop from a hot Paris band.
Pink Martini *Sympathique* 'Je ne veux pas travailler' and other dinner-party starters by some French-singing Americans.
Serge Gainsbourg *Le Poinçonneur des Lilas* Classic early Gainsbourg.

Websites

www.culture.fr Cultural events in Paris and other big French cities.
www.edible-paris.com Customised gastronomic itineraries in Paris by the editor of Time Out's *Eating & Drinking in Paris* guide.
www.meteo.fr Weather forecasts and stats from the state meteorology office.
www.pagesjaunes.fr The Paris yellow pages, with maps and photos of every address in the city.
www.parissi.com Films, concerts and a strong clubbing calendar.
www.parisinfo.com Official site of the Office de Tourisme et des Congrès de Paris.
www.pidf.com Official site of the Paris regional tourist board; a gold mine of information on museums, events, transport, shopping, etc.
www.ratp.com Everything you'll need to know about using the buses, métro, RER and trams.
www.timeout.com/paris A pick of the best current events and good hotels, restaurants and shops.
www.velib.paris.fr All you need to know about using Velib'.

iPhone apps

Escargo (£1.19) Translates more than 1,800 food/cooking terms from French to English.
Patrimap (free) Pinpoints nearby monuments along with potted descriptions, and also features a series of itineraries.
RATP Lite (free) Access a wide range of Paris transport maps.
Vélib' (free) Tells you where bikes are available around the city, plus there's a calorie counter and short-term weather forecast.
Musée du Louvre (free) The ideal accompaniment for a trip round the world's largest museum.

Index

Advertisers' Index

Index

Discover the city from your back pocket

Essential for your weekend break, over 30 top cities available.

POCKET SIZED *from* £6.99/ $11.95

**TIME OUT GUIDES
WRITTEN BY
LOCAL EXPERTS**
Visit timeout.com/shop

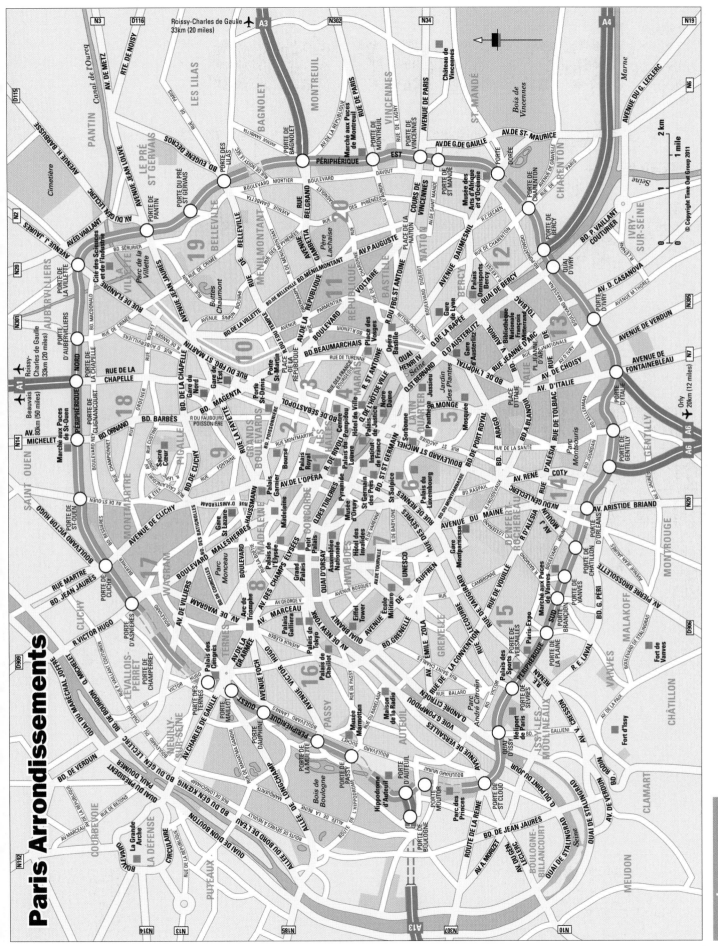

Paris Arrondissements

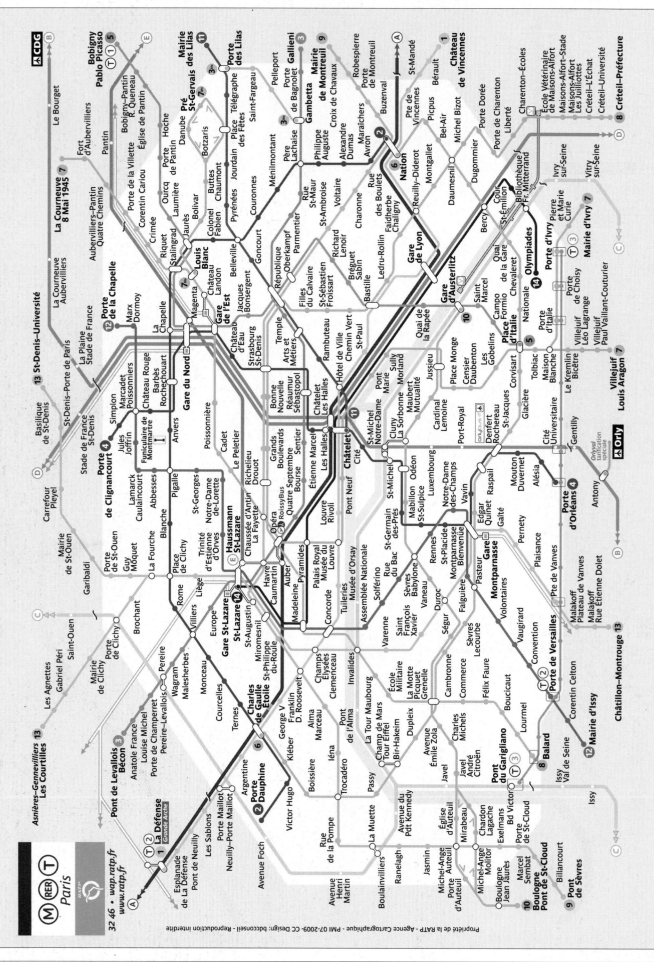